The Dutch Language in Japan (1600–1900)

Brill's Studies in Language, Cognition and Culture

Series Editors

Alexandra Y. Aikhenvald (*Cairns Institute, James Cook University*)
R.M.W. Dixon (*Cairns Institute, James Cook University*)
N.J. Enfield (*University of Sydney*)

VOLUME 24

The titles published in this series are listed at *brill.com/bslc*

The Dutch Language in Japan (1600–1900)

A Cultural and Sociolinguistic Study of Dutch as a Contact Language in Tokugawa and Meiji Japan

By

Christopher Joby

BRILL

LEIDEN | BOSTON

Cover illustration: *Bridge in the Rain (after Hiroshige)* by Vincent van Gogh (1853–1890), Paris, October–November 1887. Oil on canvas, 73.3 cm × 53.8 cm. s0114V1962. F0372. Van Gogh Museum, Amsterdam (Vincent van Gogh Foundation).

Library of Congress Cataloging-in-Publication Data

Names: Joby, Christopher, author.
Title: The Dutch language in Japan (1600-1900) : a cultural and
  sociolinguistic study of Dutch as a contact language in Tokugawa and
  Meiji Japan / by Christopher Joby.
Description: Leiden ; Boston : Brill, [2021] | Series: Brill's studies in
  language, cognition and culture, 1879-5412 ; volume 24 | Includes
  bibliographical references and index.
Identifiers: LCCN 2020036027 (print) | LCCN 2020036028 (ebook) | ISBN
  9789004436442 (hardback) | ISBN 9789004438651 (ebook)
Subjects: LCSH: Dutch language—Japan—History. | Dutch language—Influence
  on Japanese. | Japanese language--Foreign elements—Dutch. | Languages
  in contact—Japan—History. | Language and culture—Japan. |
  Japan—Civilization—Dutch influences.
Classification: LCC PF913.J3 J63 2021 (print) | LCC PF913.J3 (ebook) |
  DDC 439.310952—dc23
LC record available at https://lccn.loc.gov/2020036027
LC ebook record available at https://lccn.loc.gov/2020036028

Typeface for the Latin, Greek, and Cyrillic scripts: "Brill". See and download: brill.com/brill-typeface.

ISSN 1879-5412
ISBN 978-90-04-43644-2 (hardback)
ISBN 978-90-04-43865-1 (e-book)

To Wim Boot
Sine quo non

∵

Contents

Acknowledgements

When I first had the idea for this book in 2014, I realized that I would need the help of others to write it. I have been fortunate that many people have been able to assist me in different ways, allowing me to reach my goal, which on occasion seemed unobtainable. I have no doubt that without the help of Professor Wim Boot, Emeritus Professor of Japanese at Leiden University, I would not have been able to write this book. Since January 2015, when I first met Professor Boot, he has always been just an email away. He has pointed me to valuable sources, sensitively corrected my errors and reviewed two of the chapters in this book, always with a dose of *bonhomie*. So, it is to Professor Boot that I dedicate this book.

Another scholar, whose help and encouragement have been invaluable to me, is Professor Nicoline van der Sijs. Her vision of the story of the Dutch language as one that goes far beyond the boundaries of the Low Countries is one that I share and her many books and articles on this subject have inspired me to pursue my own interest in it. Professor Van der Sijs was also kind enough to review an earlier version of a chapter in this book and I am extremely grateful to her for that.

A chance meeting at a Dutch Studies conference in 2018 brought me into contact with Professor Shimizu Makoto, Professor in Germanic Studies at Hokkaido University in Japan. He was kind enough to review two of my chapters and has been extremely generous with his time in answering queries about some of the more challenging aspects of this subject. I am also grateful to Natsue Heyward, who has been working as a research assistant for me in the final stages of this project. One feature of this book is that the personal names and Japanese primary sources are written in Roman script and Japanese script. Natsue's remarkable diligence and thoroughness have been invaluable to me as I have prepared the manuscript for publication.

I was fortunate enough to be awarded an Isaac Alfred Ailion Fellowship in 2019, which allowed me to do research as a guest of the Scaliger Institute at Leiden University Library from October 2019 to January 2020. I am very grateful to the Ailion Foundation for the grant associated with this fellowship and to members of the selection committee, above all Dr. Kasper van Ommen, who acted as my host during the fellowship. I am also grateful to the late Professor Harm Beukers and Nadia Kreeft for their support.

I was able to take this research leave by permission of the Dean of the Faculty of English at Adam Mickiewicz University, Poznań, Professor Joanna Pawelczyk, her predecessor, Professor Katarzyna Dziubalska-Kołaczyk, and the head of the department of Dutch and S. African studies, Professor Jerzy Koch. I am grateful to all of them for this period of leave and to colleagues who took classes in my absence. Other scholars have given me their time, advice and encouragement as I have written this book. They include Peter Austin, Olivier Bailblé, Anna Bogdan, Rebekah Clements, Elia da Corso, Ton Harmsen, Reinier Hesselink, Simon Kaner, Jill Kraye, Koos Kuiper, Radu Leca, Matsuda Kiyoshi, Wolfgang Michel, Jan Pekelder, Olf Praamstra, Martine Robbeets, Timon Screech, Anastasia Stefanaki, Ulrich Tiedau, Hans vande Velde, Aafke van Ewijk, Marc van Oostendorp, Joop van der Horst, Cynthia Viallé, Boudewijn Walraven and Guita Winkel.

I am also grateful to the many staff in libraries and archives whose help and advice I have relied on in writing this book. While in Leiden, I made constant use of the Special Collections as well as the general library collection and am grateful for the assistance provided by staff at the library. In Japan, I made several visits to the National Diet Library, Tokyo, the library of the Matsūra Historical Museum, Hirado, and Takeo City library, and am grateful to staff there for their help. Other libraries and archives whose staff I wish to thank include the British Library in London, the University of East Anglia Library and the Lisa Sainsbury Library in Norwich, and the Nationaal Archief in The Hague. Furthermore, thanks are due to Mr. Tadashi Koike at Waseda University Library, Tokyo for assisting me in gaining the necessary permissions for the many illustrations in this book from the Waseda collection.

A book is nothing without its publisher and I was delighted that Brill agreed to publish this book. The editor, Elisa Perotti, has been particularly helpful in guiding me through the publication process in a friendly and clear manner, and it has been invaluable to have Elisa's support.

Finally, a word of thanks to family members. My sister Lyn has supported me in many ways during my academic career and I am grateful to her for this. My late father and mother, Richard and Christine, were also very supportive. It was on family holidays to the Low Countries that I first fell in love with the Dutch language. Both were geography teachers who gave me a love of maps and of travel and I am grateful to both of them for giving me the *Wanderlust* which has allowed me to write this book.

Professor Christopher Joby
Poznań, 2020

Illustrations

Abbreviations and Glossary of Japanese Terms

Abbreviations

BL	British Library
cMJ	contemporary Modern Japanese
J.	'native' Japanese word
LUB	*Leiden Universiteitsbibliotheek*
LUL	Leiden University Library
LWC	Language of wider communication
MTL	Modern Taiwanese Language (orthography)
NA	*Nationaal Archief*, The Hague
NDL	National Diet Library, Tokyo
NKD	*Nihon kokugo daijiten*
R.O.C.	Republic of China (Taiwan)
S.-J.	Sino-Japanese word
Ser.	Serrurier
SK	*Seimi kaisō* (1837–1849)
VOC	*Vereenigde Oost-Indische Compagnie* ('Dutch East India Company')
WNT	*Woordenboek der Nederlandsche Taal* ('Dictionary of the Dutch language')
WUL	Waseda University Library, Tokyo

Glossary of Japanese Terms

ateji 当て字	lit. 'assigned characters', primarily refers to *kanji* used phonetically
bakufu 幕府	Shogunal administration
Bansho shirabesho 蕃書調所	'Office for the Investigation of Barbarian books'
Bansho wage goyō 蕃書和解御用	'Office for the Translation of Barbarian books'
Betsudan fūsetsugaki 別段風説書	'Special [Dutch] Book of Rumours'
bugyō 奉行	Governor of Nagasaki
daikan 代官	(Nagasaki) magistrates
daimyō 大名	'feudal lord'
furigana 振り仮名	*kana* to aid pronunciation
gairaigo 外来語	'pure' loanwords
goshuinsen 御朱印船	trading ship authorized by the shogun
han 藩	feudal domain

honzōgaku 本草学	pharmacognosy
kana 仮名	Japanese syllabaries including *katakana* (angular) and *hiragana* (cursive)
kanbun 漢文	modified literary Sinitic used in Japan
kango 漢語	Sino-Japanese (S.-J.) word.
keikotsūji 稽古通詞	'apprentice interpreter'
kotsūji 小通詞	'junior interpreter'
kundoku 訓読	the reading or interpreting of Chinese texts by Japanese using a system of glosses and marks
kun'yaku 訓訳	interpretative translation into Japanese with the addition of glosses
kun'yomi 訓読み	'native' Japanese reading of *kanji* (*kun*-reading)
machidoshiyori 町年寄	Nagasaki city elders
meisho-chō 銘書帳	'Title ledgers'
metsuke 目付	censors or inspectors
Nagasaki kaisho 長崎会所	the office that regulated commercial activity in Nagasaki
naitsūji 内通詞	'private interpreters'
ōmetsuke 大目付	senior censor/inspector-general
on'yomi 音読み	Chinese-derived reading of *kanji* (*on*-reading)
Oranda fūsetsugaki 和蘭風説書	'Dutch Book of Rumours'
Orandayuki 阿蘭陀行	lit. 'women who go to the Dutch'
otona 乙名	heads of wards in Nagasaki, some of whom had oversight of Deshima
ōtsūji 大通詞	'senior interpreter'
ranga 蘭画	Dutch-style art
rangaku 蘭学	Dutch studies
rangakusha 蘭学者	Student or disciple of Dutch studies
ranpeki-daimyō 蘭癖 (らんぺき) 大名	*daimyō* 'crazy' about all things Dutch
ranpō 蘭方	Dutch/Western medicine
ransho 蘭書	Dutch books
rōmaji 羅馬字	Roman script used to write Japanese
ryū 流	School of thought
sakoku 鎖国	The period during which access to Japan was restricted
shijuku 私塾	Private academies
Tenmondai 天文台	Astronomical observatory or 'Bureau of Astronomy' in Edo
Tenmonkata 天文方	'Astronomy officers'

tōtsūji 唐通詞	Chinese interpreters in Nagasaki
tsūji nakama 通詞仲間	'Interpreters' Guild'
wago 和語 or *Yamato kotoba* 大和言葉	a 'native' Japanese word (J.).
yōgaku 洋学	Western studies
Yōsho shirabesho 洋書調所	'Office for the Investigation of Western Books'
yottsu no kuchi 四つの口	'four gates'

Prologue

1   Introduction

In early 1954 in the Ueno Library (上野図書館) in Tokyo, a significant discovery was made. 3630 'discarded' books were found which had clearly not been looked at for many years.[1] On further inspection, it turned out that many of these books dated from prior to 1854, a period during which Japan had been more or less isolated from Western countries with one exception, the Netherlands. It was therefore natural that most of these books were written in Dutch. Indeed, the books found in the Ueno Library were just some of the many thousands of books in Dutch that had been imported into Japan in the seventeenth, eighteenth and nineteenth centuries on subjects as varied as medicine, astronomy and classical verse. The study, and in more than one thousand cases the translation, of these books was to have a profound effect on Japanese society. However, by 1954 it seems that this influence on Japanese cultural, social and intellectual life had to a large extent been forgotten. Exactly one hundred years earlier, in 1854, Japan had signed the Convention of Kanagawa with the United States, essentially forcing it to do business with Western countries other than the Netherlands, which had been its sole Western trading partner since 1639. Other Western countries such as Britain, France and Prussia quickly followed, establishing political, commercial and social relations with Japan. Only six years later, in 1860, the Dutch closed their trading post at Deshima in Nagasaki Bay as the larger Western countries competed for business and encouraged Japan to adopt modern Western technology and practices.

In 1877 the fear was already being expressed that the Dutch contribution to Japan would quickly be forgotten. On 14 February, Mr. K. Mitsukuri, a member of a family that had long been interested in the knowledge mediated by Dutch, gave an address to the Asiatic Society of Japan in Yokohama, in which he emphasized the importance of Dutch studies or *rangaku* (蘭学) to the history of Japan.[2] 'The good that came out of it is incalculable', he told his audience, which

---

1   During the Meiji era, these books were transferred from the Education Ministry to the Imperial Library. However, by this time the Japanese had shifted to studying Western knowledge via English and German, and so these books written in Dutch fell into disuse and were forgotten. They were discovered in 1954 in the warehouse of the Ueno Library and were recognized as valuable materials on how Dutch learning was acquired during the Edo period.

2   The first name of K. Mitsukuri is not given. One possibility is Kakichi Mitsukuri (1857–1909), who studied in the United States in the 1870s. He would later become a noted author and translator. Further investigation may reveal if he was in Tokyo in 1877 to give this speech.

to judge by the membership list was largely British and American. 'Above all', he continued, 'if this had not somewhat prepared the public mind, we should not now be taking advantage of facilities which free intercourse with other countries has opened to us' (Mitsukuri 1877: 216). In other words, Mitsukuri was arguing that it was the study and translation of Dutch books during Japan's period of isolation, which meant that it was better prepared than other countries in East Asia to engage with and benefit from the innovations that were introduced after 1854. One could, however, read Mitsukuri's assertions as a recognition that already by 1877, there was a risk that this would be forgotten. In the subsequent years, it does seem that Mitsukuri's words were in some sense prophetic, as scholarship on Dutch studies was only sporadic.[3] However, if the Ueno find did not necessarily serve to re-ignite an interest in Dutch studies on its own, it was at least a symbol of the recovery of a chapter in Japanese history that had largely receded into the background. The books in the Ueno collection were put on display in the year that they were discovered, which helped to revive distant memories of the influence of Dutch studies on Japan.[4]

2   Literature Review

In the period since 1954 and above all in the last thirty or forty years, much academic work has been done on the presence of the Dutch in Japan and their influence on Japanese cultural, social and intellectual life. Books by Timon Screech and exhibition catalogues such as those for Kobe City Museum and Takeo City Museum illustrate the various ways in which the Dutch exerted influence directly and indirectly on Japanese cultural life.[5] Scholars such as Wim Boot, Grant Goodman and Terrence Jackson have focussed on the influence of Dutch studies on the intellectual life of Japan, with Jackson paying particular attention to the networks and discursive spaces formed by those who engaged in Dutch studies.[6]

---

3   'Dutch studies' is typically used to translate the Japanese term *rangaku* (蘭学). This is an important term in the present book and is analysed more fully in Chapter 2.

4   *List of foreign books collected under the Shogunate regime*, Preface. See also Miyasita (1975: 9). Many of the books dating from prior to the 1850's had previously been owned by the *Yōsho shirabesho* (洋書調所 'Institute for the Investigation of Western Books'), the office of the shogunate responsible for screening foreign books. This had previously been called the *Bansho shirabesho* (蕃書調所 'Institute for the Investigation of Barbarian Books').

5   See, for example, Screech (2012). The exhibition catalogues are Shirahara (2007), and Michel *et al.* (2014).

6   See, for example, Boot (2008), Goodman (2013), and Jackson (2016).

As for the Dutch language in Japan, work has been published in Japanese by scholars such as Ishiwata Toshio, Katagiri Kazuo, Koga Jūjirō, Saitō Shizuka, Sugimoto Tsutomu and Yoshizawa Norio.[7] Several of these authors focus on Dutch loanwords in Japanese, with Koga having produced a vast lexicon of loanwords from Dutch and other European languages in the Nagasaki dialect.[8] The present volume will bring some of this work to a new audience.

This book complements and adds to existing literature in several ways. An important book on the history of language in Japan is 'The Languages of Japan' (Cambridge, 1990) by Shibatani Masayoshi. This book, however, focusses on the two 'indigenous' languages in Japan, Japanese and Ainu, and so has relatively little to say on other languages that have been used in the country. The present book in some sense complements Shibatani's work by analysing the history of Dutch in Japan, which, it is to be hoped, will contribute to our understanding of the linguistic landscape of Japan in the Tokugawa period (1603–1868). As for general studies of the history of Dutch, these tend to treat Dutch in Japan in a very summary manner and often contain fundamental errors. For example, C.G.N. de Vooys, 'Geschiedenis van de Nederlandse taal' (Groningen, 1970), Marijke van der Wal and Cor van Bree, 'Geschiedenis van het Nederlands' (Utrecht, 1992) and Jelle Stegeman, 'Handbuch Niederländisch: Sprache und Sprachkultur von den Anfängen bis 1800' (Darmstadt, 2014) write nothing on this subject. Bruce Donaldson, 'Linguistic History of Holland and Belgium' (Leiden, 1983), writes very little. One statement by Donaldson is perhaps indicative of his view on the subject as well as that of others in the field of Dutch studies (p. 109):

> The [Dutch] settlements in South America, West Africa, India, Taiwan and Japan were in most cases little more than trading posts, or factories as they were called. Thus the influence of the Dutch language in these areas was minimal and is difficult or impossible to trace nowadays.

In 'Dutch: Biography of a Language' (Oxford, 2013), Roland Willemyns writes a few paragraphs about Dutch in Japan, but these contain several factual errors. For example, Willemyns (2013: 211–212) suggests that there were only Dutch at the trading post on Deshima. However, as this book makes clear there were other Europeans as well as non-Europeans on Deshima. Herman Vekeman and

---

7   De Groot (2005: 5–6) discusses the scope of some of these studies and raises questions about the accuracy of the knowledge of Dutch of authors such as Katagiri in *Oranda tsūji no kenkyū*.

8   See for example the five-volume Sugimoto (1976–1982). Volume five includes a summary in English (pp. 905–918). See also Yoshizawa and Ishiwata (1979) and Koga (2000).

Andreas Ecke, 'Geschichte der niederländischen Sprache' (Bern, 1992), write a few lines on Dutch in Japan (p. 115). While what they write is factually correct, they make no mention of the grammatical influence of Dutch on Japanese or of the scale and influence of translations from Dutch into Japanese. I would suggest that one reason for this state of affairs in Dutch studies is that such works tend to give priority to the history of Dutch in the Dutch language area.

Several works in English focus on one aspect of Dutch in Japan. Frits Vos has written articles on Dutch loanwords in Japanese (e.g., Vos 1963, 2014), while Fumiko Earns has written on the influence of Dutch on Japanese syntax (e.g., Earns 1993 and 1996). Henk de Groot (2005), on the other hand, focussed on the learning of Dutch by Japanese in an unpublished Ph.D. thesis. He provides extensive analysis of the materials used by Japanese for learning Dutch, which provides much valuable information for Chapter 2 of this book. In her study of translation in early modern Japan, Rebekah Clements (2015) devotes a chapter to the translation of Dutch texts into Japanese. Translation from Dutch to Japanese is the subject of Chapter 6.

3   Dutch as a Contact Language in Japan

To date, however, there has been no monograph in a Western language which provides a comprehensive analysis of the knowledge and use of the Dutch language in Tokugawa Japan. It is the aim of this book to provide such an analysis. To put the book in terms more familiar to linguists, the focus of the book is language contact. This has been defined as 'the situation in which languages, or rather, instantiations of language systems through their speakers, influence each other synchronically in shared socio-semiotic contexts' (Steiner 2008: 319). An interesting question that the book attempts to answer is 'what happened when Dutch came into contact with other languages in Tokugawa Japan?' In doing so, it engages with literature on language contact such as Thomason and Kaufman (1988) and more recently Lim and Ansaldo (2015). Thomason and Kaufman (1988: 73–76) propose a model for language contact, in cases where a close typological fit between contact languages is absent. This makes a correlation between intensity of contact and changes effected in the borrowing language. The present book will analyse the extent to which the contact between Dutch and other languages in Japan, above all varieties of Japanese, led to interference in these languages on a lexical, syntactic and graphic level.

However, this book is by no means limited to the study of internal changes resulting from language contact. In their book on language contact, Lim and Ansaldo (2015: 3) argue that 'the most powerful approach to language contact is a sociolinguistic one'. As such, they suggest that language contact 'is the study of human societies, their histories, cultures and ideologies, and how these impact on human behaviour' (Lim and Ansaldo 2015: 2). The present author concurs recognizing that a study of language contact must necessarily take account of the social and historical context in which this contact and its results occurred. This is particularly important in the case of Dutch as a contact language in Japan for the consequences of this contact went far beyond the linguistic, not least because of the impact on Japanese social and intellectual life resulting from the many translations made from Dutch to Japanese during the Tokugawa period. In fact, as Peter Burke (2005: 7) argues, internal and external factors are complementary rather than being mutually exclusive. For example, as discussed in Chapter 7, contact with Dutch led to the coining of many new scientific terms, extending the meaning of existing words, employing morphemes that continue to be productive, forming new hybrid words, and in at least one case a new *kanji* or character, in Japanese. These additions to and extensions of the Japanese lexis went hand-in-hand with changes in the intellectual culture in Japan resulting from the reading and translating of Dutch scientific texts. Therefore, the present book adopts an interdisciplinary approach employing the resources not only of the discipline of linguistics, and sub-disciplines such as contact linguistics, phonetics, syntactics and morphology, but also those of social and cultural history and translation studies, as well as Dutch studies and Japanology.

In truth, although most of the story told in this book takes place during the rule of the Tokugawa shoguns, it begins and ends a little before and after this period. The first Dutch ship to reach Japan, the *Liefde* ('Love'), was shipwrecked on the shores of eastern Kyushu in 1600. Although at least one Dutchman, Dirk Gerritsz. Pomp (1544–c. 1608), had already visited Japan aboard Portuguese ships before this date, it is in 1600 that our story begins.[9] It concludes in 1900 during the Meiji period (1868–1912). By this time Japan had opened its ports to other Europeans and to the Americans, and their languages had largely replaced Dutch as the dominant European language in Japan, although the latter did not give up without a fight.

The story unfolds in two principal *dramatis loci*. The first is western Kyushu, where the Dutch had two trading posts, first at Hirado (1609–1641) and then

---

9 Pomp provided information about Japan that Jan Huygen van Linschoten used in his book *Itinerario* (1596).

on Deshima, an artificial island in Nagasaki Bay (1641–1860). The second is Edo, the capital of Tokugawa Japan, subsequently renamed Tokyo. As interest in imported Dutch books increased, scholars in Edo engaged with and translated these books. However, the censors of the shogunal administration, the *bakufu*, became concerned about the potential dangers of the import of foreign ideas and established offices to control the circulation and translation of Dutch books. Over time, other *loci* emerged. Interest in Dutch medicine led to the establishment of medical schools elsewhere in Japan, such as the *Tekijuku* in nineteenth-century Osaka and the *Igakkan* in Sendai to the north of Edo. Japanese who studied Dutch medicine practised it across Japan, giving rise to *zaison no rangaku*, or "the study of Dutch or Western learning in the countryside" (Nakamura 2005: 2).

4   Issues Concerning the Japanese Language

Several choices have had to be made concerning how Japanese is rendered in this book. First, the principal audience for this book is scholars who are not fully conversant with Japanese. However, it is to be hoped that the book will be of interest to Japanologists and Japanese scholars in a range of disciplines. Therefore, in the main text, the personal names of Japanese are given in Roman script. The rendering in Roman script is based on the version of the name given in the *hiragana* syllabary in the database of the National Institute of Japanese Literature (henceforth NIJL). One complication here is that Japanese often assumed names in addition to those they were given at birth. One consequence of this is that secondary sources often refer to the same individual by different names. Where possible, I give the *tōitsu chosha mei* 統一著者名, sometimes translated as the 'uniform (author) name', in the NIJL database, but also other given names frequently used in secondary sources. I give the personal names in Roman and Japanese script in an index. As for the names of works written in Japanese, in the main text these are written in Roman script, again based on the *hiragana* renderings in the NIJL database.[10] They are supplemented by a translation in English. The titles are presented in the Index of Japanese Primary Sources by Title in Roman script, Japanese script and English translation. Where possible, I have added the unique NIJL database ID and the

---

10   Dating is another problem. Japanese sources such as the NIJL database give dates based on lunar years in Japanese eras. These often begin and end in the middle of solar years. Therefore, I have used the Western solar calendar year which corresponds most closely to the Japanese era year.

relevant numbers in the Kerlen and Serrurier catalogues of Japanese books in the Netherlands and the Leiden University Library collection respectively. I also give the call number of the title at Waseda University Library (WUL). This will allow the reader to consult scans of the relevant work on the Waseda Kotenseki Sogo database of Japanese and Chinese classics.

Second, the order in which Japanese personal names are presented requires a brief explanation. Here, I follow standard practice. In all cases, the first instance of the name is given by family or clan name followed by the first name. However, for names from the Tokugawa period, in the second and subsequent instances the first or pen name is given. For example, in the first instance I name Mukai Genshō (向井元升) and thereafter refer to him as Genshō (元升). For names from the Meiji period (1868–1912) and thereafter, in the second and subsequent instances, only the family name is given. This includes Japanese authors of the secondary sources cited in this book. For example, in the first instance I give the name of the Japanologist Matsuda Kiyoshi and thereafter Matsuda. In the bibliography, family names are given in capital letters.

Third, the Japanese sound system is based on *morae*. In Roman script, using the modified Hepburn system, syllables consisting of two *morae* are often identified with a stroke over the vowel (a macron), e.g., Ōsaka, where the first syllable consists of two *morae*. To facilitate reading, this book only uses *morae* by exception for place names. So, although one could use *morae* for place names such as Osaka and Tokyo, forms without *morae* are typically used as these are the forms with which many readers will be more familiar. Finally, the front matter includes a glossary of important Japanese terms used in this book.

5 Terminology and Periodization

Before providing a chapter summary, a brief word is in order about the Dutch language and the term 'Dutch'. First, what was to become standard Dutch was very much in its infancy in the early years of the Dutch presence in Japan. For example, an important work in what Roland Willemyns refers to as the 'corpus planning' or 'language planning' of Dutch, the States Bible (*Statenbijbel*), was first published in 1637, by which time some 200 Dutch ships had reached Japan.[11] Second, as a consequence of this a wide variety of Germanic dialects were spoken in the Low Countries, which broadly fall under the umbrella of

---

11 For the *Statenbijbel*, see Willemyns (2013: 93). For the terms 'corpus planning' and 'language planning', see pp. 81 and 93. For an excellent account of the rise of standard Dutch, see Van der Sijs (2004).

Nederduytsch (lit. 'Low German'), the last part of which gives us the English word 'Dutch'.[12] People in Japan whose first language was a variety of Dutch came from different parts of the Low Countries. While most of them came from the northern Netherlands, some came from the south. Furthermore, other Europeans in Japan, above all Germans and Scandinavians, also used Dutch, and this is not to mention the Japanese who did so. Therefore, it would perhaps be better to talk along with Peter Burke of 'Dutches' rather than one homogeneous 'Dutch' (Burke 2005: 5). Finally in this regard, the word 'Dutch' is also typically used in histories of European expansion to describe the people who spoke varieties of Dutch as a first language. This is problematic as it includes people from the southern Netherlands, i.e., modern-day Belgium. Furthermore, other Europeans such as German and Swedish physicians are often included under this term without further explanation. Where clarification is necessary, it will be provided (Joby 2015: 15).

A brief word is also in order about periodization. In broad terms, the shift from Late Middle Dutch to Early Modern or New Dutch (*Nieuwnederlands*) took place in the sixteenth century. The subsequent shift to Late Modern or New Dutch can be situated in the nineteenth century (Willemyns 2013: 80). Therefore, our story of Dutch in Japan takes place in the period of Modern Dutch, although there were changes within this period, above all the moves towards standardization described above.

6   Chapter Summaries

The remainder of this prologue provides a summary of the contents of each chapter. The first chapter provides a broadly chronological account of the Dutch and other Europeans in Tokugawa Japan. It pays specific attention to the Dutch, who played a role in the spread of the language in Japan, as well as to other Europeans, often posing as Dutchmen, such as German physicians, who knew Dutch. In subsequent chapters language process is the primary analytical tool. Therefore, they focus on the processes that arose as a result of contact between Dutch and other languages in Japan. These include the learning of Dutch (Chapter 2), the various ways in the knowledge of Dutch was operationalized (Chapter 3), contact and competition with other languages (Chapter 4), interference in Dutch texts (Chapter 5), translation from Dutch to Japanese (Chapter 6), lexical, syntactic and graphic interference in Japanese (Chapter 7), and language shift and recession (Chapter 8). It is to be hoped

---

12   For the origins of the word 'Dutch' see Willemyns (2013: 4–6).

that these chapters contribute to the broader corpus of secondary literature on these language processes. For example, to date relatively little academic attention has been paid to the motivations for code switching (lexical interference) in historical contexts. Finally, the epilogue draws together the main themes discussed in the book, reflects on the extent to which the central research questions have been answered, and suggests further research that might usefully be carried out.

Chapter 1   Those Who Already Knew Dutch in Japan

This chapter has two aims. First, it analyses which non-Japanese knew Dutch before arriving in Japan. Second, it provides details of the activities of the Dutch and fellow Europeans in Japan, which will provide the reader with a historical framework with which to navigate and interpret the material presented in the subsequent chapters. It attempts to fulfil these aims by providing a broadly chronological account of the evidence for a knowledge of Dutch among non-Japanese in Japan. Apart from native speakers from the Low Countries, this includes other Europeans who acquired Dutch before arriving in Japan and various non-Europeans, who had picked up a partial knowledge of the language. It begins by analysing what the sources tell us about the knowledge of Dutch among surviving crewmembers of the *Liefde* including the Englishman, Will Adams. Between 1609 and 1641, the Dutch, now under the aegis of the Dutch East India Company (*Vereenigde Oost-Indische Compagnie* henceforth VOC), operated a trading post (*factorij*) on Hirado, a small island off western Kyushu. Here, primary and secondary sources including records of communications with Japanese and other Europeans will be analysed for evidence of the knowledge of Dutch among non-Japanese. In 1641, the Dutch were forced by the Japanese authorities to move to Deshima, a small artificial island in Nagasaki Bay. They continued to trade with the Japanese from this base until the middle of the nineteenth century, when the Americans forced Japan to open its ports to other Western countries. This chapter charts the gradual decline in the volume of Dutch trade with Japan as well as the increased interest among Japanese in Western technical instruments such as telescopes and in Dutch books, many of which they would translate. It also analyses important instances of cultural exchange including the regular visits by the Dutch to Edo (Tokyo) to pay homage to the shogun, and the role that the Dutch played in informing the *bakufu* about developments outside Japan, in particular through the special reports (*Betsudan fūsetsugaki*) they compiled. Furthermore, this chapter introduces Europeans whose knowledge of Dutch allowed them to make a significant contribution to the history of contact between Dutch and other languages in Tokugawa Japan. Among native speakers, directors or *opperhoofden* of the Dutch trading posts such as Isaac Titsingh, Hendrick Doeff and Jan Cock Blomhoff each played important roles in this story. Non-Dutch Europeans, who made valuable contributions to Dutch as a contact language in Japan, include the German physicians Engelbert Kaempfer and Philipp Franz von Siebold, and the Swedish physician and botanist, Carl Peter Thunberg. Finally, evidence is presented for the knowledge of Dutch amongst non-Europeans from outside Japanese, such as servants and slaves. Much of this evidence is in the form of metalinguistic comment.

Chapter 2   *Learning Dutch in Tokugawa Japan*

Whereas Chapter 1 introduces those who already knew Dutch when they arrived in Japan, Chapter 2 focuses on how Japanese learnt Dutch in the Tokugawa period in a broadly chronological order. During the Hirado period (1609–1641) and the first decades of the Dutch presence in Nagasaki, there is limited evidence for the learning of Dutch. Nevertheless, although much of the communication between the Dutch and Japanese took place via Portuguese, the sources do indicate that some Japanese interpreters were able to speak Dutch. In the early 1670s, several decades after the Portuguese had been expelled from Japan and with the Dutch having established themselves in Nagasaki, junior interpreters were sent to Deshima to receive instruction from native speakers. We have details about how Japanese learnt Dutch and the quality of the Dutch they spoke. While some Japanese attained a decent level of Dutch, European comments on their command of the language were typically not positive.

Over time, in order to improve the level of Dutch spoken by the Japanese, learning aids were developed including lexicons, learners and grammars, which were often based on books imported from Europe. Copies of many of these still survive and provide us with valuable information about how Japanese learnt Dutch. As interest in the knowledge mediated by Dutch books spread, first in Nagasaki then to Edo and subsequently to other towns in Japan, private academies (*shijuku*) dedicated to Dutch studies (*rangaku*) such as Ogata Kōan's *Tekijuku* in Osaka were opened. Students of *rangaku* (*rangakusha* 蘭学者) learnt not only about the science contained in Dutch books but also the language that mediated this science. By the nineteenth century we can talk in terms of thousands of Japanese students of the Dutch language and *rangaku*. They would write essays in Dutch and read and translate Dutch scientific books into Japanese.

Chapter 3   *The Many Uses of Dutch in Japan*

This chapter analyses the various ways in which the knowledge of Dutch was operationalized by Japanese and non-Japanese in Tokugawa Japan. Dutch was both spoken and written. Where evidence for the speaking of Dutch is available, often in the form of metalinguistic comment, it will be presented. However, given the historical nature of this study, most of the evidence necessarily concerns the written use of the language. While some uses of Dutch such as record-keeping and letter-writing are perhaps somewhat mundane and predictable, other uses are less so. Artists from Edo and Nagasaki added Dutch inscriptions to their works and signed their names in Roman script. Possible reasons for this include a desire to conjure up the 'exotic' and to engage with the 'other'. World maps were imported, and Japanese began to make their own maps of other parts of the world. Japanese cartographers often used Dutch toponyms clothed in *katakana* script. However, they also employed a range of strategies to coin Japanese names for geographical features such as seas and rivers based on Dutch source material. Dutch could also be found in the material culture in Japan, on objects as diverse as sake bottles and gravestones. Other uses of Dutch include giving Dutch nicknames to Japanese and switching into Dutch in Japanese texts. In short, this chapter aims to illustrate the multifarious ways in which Dutch was used in Japan.

Chapter 4   Language Contact

Dutch came into contact not only with varieties of Japanese but also with several other European and East Asian languages in Tokugawa Japan. In some cases, Dutch merely 'rubbed shoulders' with other languages in a shared socio-semiotic context with little or no evidence of influence. In other cases, there is evidence of influence and of language competition, defined by Peter Burke (2004: 70) as 'the struggle for the centre [involving] attempts to marginalize rivals'. This chapter analyses the nature of the relationship between Dutch and contact languages during the period under review.

In the seventeenth century, Dutch faced competition from Portuguese. Possible reasons are presented for the persistence of Portuguese long after the native speakers had been expelled from Japan in 1639. By the early eighteenth century, however, the knowledge and use of Portuguese had all but disappeared. In the field of learning in which Dutch became increasingly important, it faced competition from Sinitic varieties. These included *wényán* (文言, Classical Chinese), often referred to as literary Sinitic, knowledge of which was a *sine qua non* for educated Japanese during this period, and *kanbun* (漢文), a form of literary Sinitic used in Japan (Clements 2015: 99–100; Steininger 2017: 12).[13] However, Japanese who could read literary Sinitic were

---

13 Terminology in this regard is not uniform. While some scholars accept the term 'literary Sinitic', others prefer to use alternative terms (Steininger 2017: 12–13). Proponents of the

able to apply the techniques for translating or interpreting texts written in that Sinitic mode to translating texts written in Dutch. In the late eighteenth and early nineteenth centuries, as foreign vessels became an increasingly common sight off the Japanese coast, Japanese interpreters were ordered to learn English, French and Russian. English, French and German would in due course supersede Dutch as Languages of Wider Communication (LWC) in Japan. Other languages with which Dutch shared a socio-semiotic context and where we can talk of influence and indeed competition to a greater or lesser extent were Latin, Malay and Manchu. Finally, there is limited evidence for Dutch functioning in a shared socio-semiotic context with Korean and Ainu. However, there is no sense in which we can talk here of influence or competition.

Chapter 5   Interference in Dutch Texts

This chapter analyses the interference in Dutch texts that resulted from contact between Dutch and other languages in Japan. There is no evidence of structural interference in Dutch as a result of this contact. Therefore, the focus is on lexical interference. While a few words can be classed as loanword borrowings, most lexical interference involves code switching, i.e., the insertion of words or phrases from one language into a text primarily written in another, although the chapter does not make a sharp distinction between loanword borrowing and code switching. Some of this lexical interference involved inserting words from Latin, Portuguese, Sinitic varieties and Malay. However, most of it involved the insertion of Japanese words and phrases in Roman script. In some cases, the interference is motivated by the author's discourse strategy, while in other cases the motivation is 'gap-filling', i.e., where an appropriate term in Dutch did not exist, although again the distinction is not absolute. In the former category we can place switching at the beginning and end of texts including for the purpose of dating a text; and switching for quoting speech, providing information, and giving a proverb. Switching for the purpose of

---

term suggest that it has two advantages. One is that it attempts to separate this form of writing from exclusive association with China and to place it in a broader Sinophone context in East Asia (although of course 'Sinitic' derives from the late Latin word for 'China'). The other is that it emphasizes a contrast between written and spoken Sinitic modes. I use the term in this book, although recognize that it is problematic and not universally accepted. On occasion, for the sake of simplicity I use the term 'Chinese'. *Kanbun* literally means '(Classical) Chinese (or Han) writing' (cf. *hanmun* for 'Chinese writing' in Korean). The distinction between *wényán* and *kanbun* is one of degree rather than kind (Steininger 2017: 12). Furthermore, different varieties of Sinitic styles of writing were used in Japan (Clements 2015: 30). Finally, Japanese developed a system of marks which allowed the Japanese reader to adapt Chinese syntactic order to Japanese. Reading Chinese texts with the help of these marks is called *kundoku* (訓読). See also Ch. 4, n. 57.

gap-filling is analysed by twelve themes including coinage, clothing and food and drink. Particular attention is paid to differences between Japanese and Dutch phonology and how these differences influenced the graphic realization of Japanese words and phrases in Dutch texts. Finally, there is an analysis of the morphological integration of Japanese words into Dutch texts.

Chapter 6   Translation from Dutch

More than 1,000 translations were made from Dutch sources in Tokugawa Japan. Drawing on many primary sources and work by authors such as Wolfgang Michel and Rebekah Clements, this chapter analyses the history of translating from Dutch into Japanese, and on occasion *kanbun*, using as a framework questions posed by Peter Burke in analysing translation in early modern Europe (Burke 2007: 7–38): Who translates? What? For whom? In what manner? and with what consequences? The focus of this chapter is on Japanese translations of Dutch books on scientific disciplines such as medicine and astronomy. It charts the development of this process from the recording and translation of oral instructions by Dutch and German physicians in manuscript in the mid-seventeenth century, through to the publication of multi-volume works in the first half of the nineteenth century such as Udagawa Yōan's *Seimi kaisō* ('Principles of Chemistry', 1837–1849), a foundational text in the study of chemistry in Japan. One result that emerges from this investigation is that the translations under review often do not fit the contemporary understanding of translation, which Theo Hermans (1985: 9) describes as 'a transcendental and utopian conception of translation [in which] the original, the whole original, and nothing but the original [is reproduced]'. In many cases, translation was understood rather as a means by which to extract information from a source text and language and to produce a new text incorporating that information in the target language. This information was sometimes gathered from a variety of sources, both oral and written, and rather than translate an entire source text, Japanese translators would often only translate sections of the source text they found useful.

The chapter also analyses other translations such as letters to and from Japanese officials and Dutch reports on events outside Japan, known as *Oranda fūsetsugaki* and the *Betsudan fūsetsugaki*, mentioned above. The latter were special reports compiled by the Dutch for the Japanese in the nineteenth century as European powers became more dominant in East Asia. Particular attention is paid throughout to the effect of translations from Dutch on Japanese society and culture. For example, the knowledge of Dutch medicine mediated by these translations would present a serious challenge to Japanese medicine, which was essentially based on traditional Chinese medicine. What the

Japanese translated tells us something about what they found interesting and useful in other cultures.

Chapter 7   Lexical, Syntactic and Graphic Interference by Dutch in Japanese

This chapter analyses three types of interference in Japanese resulting from contact with Dutch. One consequence was the emergence of many contact-induced words in Japanese. These often tell us what was lacking in Japan and the areas of Dutch activity of interest to Japanese. Using the typology for lexical contact phenomena proposed by Winford (2003), this chapter provides an extensive list of contact-induced words by type and theme. Some words ('pure' loanwords or *gairaigo*) were simply adopted by Japanese with little modification of the Dutch. Authors such as Vos (2014) state that over 300 Dutch such contact-induced words have entered Japanese. Many words for food and drink, nautical terms and the names of chemical elements and plants fall into this category. Other contact-induced words, particularly those in the natural sciences, are classified as loan translations. These have been translated into Japanese on a morpheme-by-morpheme basis. The chapter argues that this was facilitated by the high 'morphosemantic transparency' of Dutch scientific terms. Japanese have also created many hybrid words in which one part is Dutch and the other Japanese or Sino-Japanese. Furthermore, some contact-induced words are only used in dialects rather than in standard Japanese. The chapter argues that taking all these types of lexical contact phenomena into account the total number of words in Japanese resulting from contact with Dutch may well exceed 1,000. Furthermore, some of these words have in turn been borrowed by languages that have come into contact with Japanese, in particular Sinitic varieties and Korean.

Another consequence of contact between Dutch and Japanese, above all as a result of translating from the former to the latter, is that Japanese syntax has been modified in several ways. Therefore, this chapter presents and analyses the secondary literature on this subject. Finally, contact with Dutch led some authors to write Japanese in Roman script, *rōmaji* (羅馬字). While some Japanese advocated a wider adoption of this script, others viewed it as a barbarism to be resisted.

Chapter 8   Language Shift and Recession

This chapter charts the final stages of the story of Dutch as the dominant European language in Japan. It identifies three stages in the process of language shift away from Dutch as an L2 or L3 in Japan. First, in the early nineteenth century, Japanese began to learn other European languages, in part as a result of fears about a possible foreign invasion. Second, in the period between 1854 and the end of the Tokugawa period in 1868, the evidence points two ways. On the one hand, there was an increased use of Dutch. It was used as an LWC between Japanese and Europeans and Americans, and furthermore, Japanese often used Dutch as an intermediate language with which to learn other European languages, above all English, French and German. However, the increased use of these other European languages also signalled a gradual retreat from Dutch. This accelerated in the third and final phase after the Meiji Restoration in 1868 as the Japanese, realizing that there were now greater powers in the world than the Dutch, quickly shifted to these other European languages. Tellingly, a dictionary of physics published in Japan in 1888 included terms in Japanese and these three languages, but not in Dutch. By 1900, when our story ends, there is little evidence for the use of Dutch in Japan.

Epilogue
Here, I draw together the main themes discussed in the book and reflect on the extent to which one of the central research questions has been answered, 'what happened when Dutch came into contact with other languages in Tokugawa Japan?' The epilogue answers this by analysing the various roles that Dutch performed in Japan. These include its role as a 'metalect', i.e., a language which conveys information (in this case Western learning), a 'thuralect' (from the Ancient Greek θύρα 'door'), a language through which other languages could be learnt, and an 'emporiolect', a language of trade. Furthermore, the epilogue suggests further research that might usefully be carried out to advance this field of enquiry.

Let us now return to the year 1600, when the subject of our story, the Dutch language, first made landfall in Japan....

Those Who Already Knew Dutch in Japan

1   Introduction

The aim of the first two chapters of this book is to analyse who knew Dutch in Japan. The next chapter investigates which Japanese learnt Dutch in Tokugawa Japan and how they learnt it.[1] This chapter examines which non-Japanese knew Dutch before arriving in Japan. Together these two chapters will provide the basis for the subsequent analysis of the use of Dutch by both Japanese and non-Japanese. Furthermore, this chapter provides details of the activities of the Dutch and fellow Europeans in Japan, which arms the reader, particularly the reader unfamiliar with this story, with a historical framework within which to place the material presented in the subsequent chapters.

The non-Japanese can be divided into three groups: people from the Low Countries whose first language was a variety of Dutch, people from elsewhere in Europe, and those who were neither Japanese nor European. Between 1600 and 1860 some 800 Dutch ships arrived in Japan at the two Dutch trading posts in western Kyushu, Hirado and Deshima, most of them under the flag of the Dutch East India Company (*Vereenigde Oost-Indische Compagnie* henceforth VOC), which functioned between 1602 and 1799.[2] Precise figures are difficult to obtain. However, we can reckon that each ship had around 100 men on board, about one half of whom came from the Dutch language area in the Low Countries. This gives us a total of some 40,000 people, almost all men, who came to Japan in this period and whose first language was a variety of Dutch. The chapter provides a broadly chronological account of those whose first language was Dutch. Furthermore, it introduces some of the important figures in this story, such as Isaac Titsingh (1745–1812), and Hendrick Doeff (1777–1835), who were both *opperhoofden*, or chiefs, of the Dutch trading post (*factorij*) on the island of Deshima in Nagasaki Bay. Titsingh corresponded with several Japanese in Dutch. This correspondence provides us with a valuable window onto the use of Dutch by Japanese. Doeff, on the other hand, compiled an

---

1   The Tokugawa shogunate ruled Japan from 1603 to 1868. The first Tokugawa shogun, Ieyasu, came to power in 1600, but the date at which the shogunate was officially established at Edo was 1603 (Vos 1989: 358).

2   For a history of the VOC, see Gaastra (2003). It was, though, reckoned that one in five of the ships that sailed for Japan did not make it. For a list of some of these, see Screech (2005: 75).

© CHRISTOPHER JOBY, 2021 | DOI:10.1163/9789004438651_003

extensive Dutch-Japanese lexicon and wrote a memoir of his time in Japan, which provides useful insights into how Japanese learnt and used Dutch.

The chapter then analyses other Europeans who knew Dutch, again in broadly chronological order. What is striking in this regard is the number of Germans who went to Deshima, often having to pose as Dutchmen. Many of these Germans were physicians. Two of these who both contributed to the development of the Dutch language in Japan are Engelbert Kaempfer (1651–1716) and Philipp Franz von Siebold (1796–1866). Kaempfer, who was in Japan from 1690 to 1692, taught Dutch grammar to his Japanese assistant. Von Siebold, who arrived in Japan in 1823, established a medical school near Nagasaki, where the medium of instruction was Dutch. Swedes also worked as physicians in Japan. One of these who knew and used Dutch was Carl Peter Thunberg (1743–1828), a botanist who had studied under the famous Swedish botanist Carl Linnaeus (1707–78).

Finally, there is an analysis of the evidence for the knowledge of Dutch among non-Japanese and non-Europeans. These are primarily servants and slaves who worked for the Dutch in Japan and crewmembers of Dutch ships. Most of these individuals came from South and East Asia.

2 The Dutch in Japan

This section provides a chronological account of the people in Tokugawa Japan whose first language was Dutch or more properly a variety of Dutch.

2.1 *The First Dutchman in Japan*

The first Dutch ship reached Japan in 1600. However, the first Dutchman to reach the country was Dirk Gerritsz. Pomp (1544–1604) from Enkhuizen. He made two visits to Japan aboard Portuguese ships. The first of these was in 1573, when he travelled from Goa to Japan via China. Little else is known about this visit (De Vries 2002: 9). In 1584, Pomp again set sail from Goa on a Portuguese ship. He arrived in Nagasaki on 31 July 1585 and remained in Japan for eight months. Pomp's experiences of Japan formed the basis of the report about the country in the *Itinerario* of Jan Huygen van Linschoten (1563–1611) published in 1596 (1979: 65–69).[3] Van Linschoten's report that the Portuguese were not popular in East Asia encouraged the Dutch to focus trading activities in this area (Meilink-Roelofsz 1962: 130–131).

---

3 See also Corr (1995: 27, 31) and IJzerman (1915: 13–24).

In what follows, there is an analysis of the Dutch in Japan after Pomp; first, the crew of the *Liefde*, then the Dutch at their two trading posts in western Kyushu, Hirado (1609–41) and Deshima (1641–1860). Where appropriate, evidence for the presence of Dutch elsewhere in Japan, such as the capital of Tokugawa Japan, Edo (江戸, modern-day Tokyo), will be analysed.

2.2   *The Crew of the* Liefde

The Dutch language crashed onto the shores of Japan in April 1600 in the form of sailors who were shipwrecked on the *Liefde* ('Love').[4] This ship had set sail from Goeree in Holland in June 1598 with a crew of one hundred and ten, but only twenty-four arrived in Japan, six of whom died shortly afterwards (Clulow 2014: 39–40; De Lange 2006: 153; Bruijn *et al.* 1979: 6–7).[5] Some of those who survived were referred to as Flemings by the English, who operated a trading post at Hirado between 1613 and 1623 (Clulow 2013). For example, the Englishman John Saris (c. 1580–1643) described the ship's clerk, Melchior van Santvoort, as 'one Melser van Jonford, a Fleming'. He referred to another crewmember Jan Joosten van Lodensteyn (1556?–1623) as 'John Yozen the Fleming', although he was born in Delft, in the province of Holland.[6] This is another example of the problems arising from the terminology for the people and language varieties of the Low Countries discussed in the prologue. In fact, it is likely that most of the surviving members of the crew of the *Liefde* came from the Dutch Republic in the northern Netherlands, although they probably spoke different varieties of Dutch. One survivor who did not come from the Low Countries was the ship's pilot, the Englishman William (Will) Adams (1564–1620), who was born in Gillingham, Kent.

The *Liefde* was later destroyed and so the survivors settled as best they could in Japan. The Japanese clearly felt that some of the surviving crewmembers could be of use to them. Indeed, soon after their arrival, the captain of the

---

4   It ran aground on the coast of Usuki in Bungo Province (now Usuki City, Ōita Prefecture) on the eastern coast of Kyushu (Viallé and Cryns 2018: 15).

5   There is a report in Japanese sources of a Dutch ship, under the command of Hector Kars, arriving in Hirado in 1597. If they are true, this would have been the first Dutch ship to come to Japan (Mulder 1985: 20–23). However, there is no evidence for this in Dutch sources. It is possible, though again there is no evidence to confirm it, that Kars skippered a Portuguese or Spanish ship.

6   Writing in 1613, Saris remarks that Van Santvoort was 'very stayde and understanding, boath in the language as also in the traficke' (Satow 1900: 102–103, quoted in De Lange (2006: 240)). This suggests that Van Santvoort had by now become competent in Japanese. For more on Jan Joosten van Lodensteyn, see Iwao (1959). The head of the English trading post, Richard Cocks (c. 1565–1624), in a letter to the East India Company in 1613 refers to 'Flemynges' (Cocks 1978: II:257–258).

Liefde, Jacob (Jaap) Quaeckernaeck, Van Lodensteyn and Adams were summoned to Osaka on the orders of Tokugawa Ieyasu (1542–1616), who consulted them for their knowledge. It fell to the Englishman, Will Adams, to speak on behalf of the ship's crew. At first, Ieyasu questioned Adams not by language but by signs. This, Adams later decided, was to allow Ieyasu to form an impression of him, for presently a Portuguese interpreter was introduced, through whom he was interrogated (Murakami and Murakawa 1900: 23–24; De Lange 2006: 170). At this time, Portuguese was a Language of Wider Communication (LWC) between Europeans and East Asians.

In due course, some of the surviving crewmembers moved to different parts of Japan. Van Lodensteyn worked as a merchant. In Osaka in 1609, he and Pieter Jansz. welcomed the Dutch embassy passing through on the way to Edo (De Lange 2006: 211). Van Lodensteyn married a Japanese Christian woman and eventually settled in Edo, where as well as trading he became a confidant of the shogun on foreign and military affairs and contributed to the development of relations between the Dutch Republic and Japan (De Lange 2006: 178–179).[7] His name, Jan Joosten, survives in several toponyms in central Tokyo, analysed in Chapter 7.

In 1609, Pieter Blanckert and Thomas Cornelisz. met the VOC Embassy to Tokugawa Ieyasu in Fuchū (府中) near Edo.[8] Melchior van Santvoort accompanied a Dutch mission to Nagasaki to gain information about local trading conditions (Viallé and Cryns 2018: 13–14). Some of the other surviving crew members had settled at Uraga (浦賀), on Edo (now Tokyo) Bay, taken Japanese wives and learnt the language. Jan Cousynen, who had been the boatswain of the *Liefde*, gained a good command of Japanese and so would be employed as the first Dutch-Japanese interpreter for twenty guilders a month (De Lange 2006: 211, 215).[9] In his memoirs published in 1833, Hendrick Doeff, the head of the Dutch factory at Deshima (*opperhoofd*) from 1803 to 1817, reported that in 1629, when the Governor of Nagasaki (*bugyō* 奉行) imposed restrictions on the practice of Christianity, there were two surviving members of the crew of the *Liefde*, Melchior van Santvoort and Vincent Romeyn. They were living as private individuals in Nagasaki, with Van Santvoort establishing himself as an independent merchant (Doeff 1833: 48; Clulow 2014: 40). Romeyn was one of the Dutchmen who piloted local trading ships authorized by the shogun

---

7　Clulow (2014: 40) asserts that Van Lodensteyn and Adams were not as influential as they would later claim.

8　Pieter Blanckert, Thomas Cornelisz., Michiel Physz., Jan Tol and Jan Roos were chosen to operate the *Liefde*'s guns in a campaign against the warlord, Uesugi Kagekatsu (1556–1623) (De Lange 2006: 178).

9　See also Viallé and Cryns (2018: 14), who give his name as Cousynsen.

(*goshuinsen* 御朱印船). In Nagasaki harbour in 1630 there was a Japanese junk piloted by Romeyn, and a Siamese junk piloted by another Dutchman, Pieter Jansz. Quick (Boxer 1950: 4).[10] Romeyn's name appears in the Hirado *dagregister* as late as 1637 (*Diaries kept by the heads of the Dutch Factory in Japan* 1974– (henceforth *Diaries*): II:279).

2.3 The Dutch at Hirado

After the arrival of the *Liefde* in 1600, it would be nine years before more sailors, whose first language was Dutch, reached Japan. They arrived in July 1609 on two VOC ships, the *Griffioen* ('Griffin') and the *Rode Leeuw met Pylen* ('Red Lion with Arrows') at Hirado (平戸), on the northwest coast of the island of Kyushu, in the far west of the Japanese archipelago.[11] This had long been an entry point for ships arriving in Japan (De Lange 2006: 243).[12] Importantly, the ships brought with them a letter from the stadholder, Prince Maurits. Two of the merchants were chosen as ambassadors to take the letter to Tokugawa Ieyasu, the *de facto* ruler of the country, whom they met at Sunpu (駿府) near Edo. Within ten days they received permission to conduct 'free trade' and establish a trading post (Clulow 2014: 46–55; Viallé and Cryns 2018: 13–14). One of the VOC representatives, Nicolaes Puyck (d. 1664), kept a diary of the journey to Sunpu, which is one of the first records we have written by a Dutchman in Japan.[13] After gaining this permission, the Dutch established a trading post at Hirado with the help of Will Adams, and began to trade with the Japanese.[14]

Hirado was a busy port. As well as the Dutch and English, and indeed Portuguese and Spanish, Japanese came to the port in the first part of the seventeenth century to participate in piratical expeditions supported by the Matsūra clan, which exercised some degree of independent control over Hirado.[15] The port was also the base for Chinese sea-lord organizations such as that of Li

---

10 Boxer suggests that Quick and other pilots may well have been using Dutch maps for navigation. See also Shapinsky (2006: 18). While Boxer refers to Pieter Jansz. Quick, De Lange refers to Pieter Jansz. Given the names of the other survivors, this would appear to be the same individual.

11 The two ships had set sail from the Dutch Republic in December 1607 (Viallé and Cryns 2018: 11).

12 http://www.vocsite.nl/schepen/detail.html?id=10386 and http://www.vocsite.nl/schepen/detail.html?id=10593. Consulted 1 April 2020.

13 For Puyck's journal, see Van Opstall (1972: II:345–355) and Clulow (2014: 49–55).

14 The trade permit (*handelspas*) that the Dutch obtained is MS. The Hague, *Nationaal Archief*, 1.04.21–1A1.

15 For the Dutch and English at Hirado and references to the Spanish and Portuguese there, see Gunn (2018: Ch. 4).

Dan (d. 1625), which was inherited and expanded by Zheng Zhilong (1604–61). It would be his son, Zheng Chenggong (1624–62), who would bring the Dutch occupation of Taiwan to an end in 1662 (Clulow 2010).[16]

The Dutch factory at Hirado, and indeed its successor at Deshima, was managed by an *opperhoofd*. The first *opperhoofd* at Hirado was Jacques Specx (1589–1652), who had arrived there on board the *Griffioen*, just shy of his twentieth birthday (Viallé and Cryns 2018: 11; De Lange 2006: 214–215).[17] The VOC based a small staff of merchants permanently in Hirado from 1609 to 1641. Including the two ships that arrived in 1609, between 1609 and 1640, 221 Dutch vessels arrived at Hirado under the flag of the VOC (De Lange 2006: 244).[18] Each ship had around 100 men on board, about one half of whom would have had Dutch as their first language. So over 10,000 men (it was almost always men), whose first language was Dutch, came to Hirado during this period. Including Specx, seven men served as *opperhoofd* at Hirado.[19] Specx served as *opperhoofd* from 1609 to 1621, being replaced for a short time by Hendrick Brouwer (Feb. 1613–Aug. 1614) (Viallé and Cryns 2018: 15). Specx was succeeded in turn by Leonardt Camps (1621–23 (d. 1623)), Cornelis van Nijenroode (1623–32), Pieter van Santen (1633), Nicolaes Couckebakker (1633–39), who began the practice of keeping a regular factory journal or *dagregister* in earnest in 1633, and finally, François Caron (1639–41).[20]

Caron is an interesting figure and an example of how working for the VOC offered an opportunity of career progression for ambitious men. He was born in Brussels in 1600 to a French Huguenot family. However, the family moved to the Dutch Republic whilst he was still an infant. In 1619 Caron arrived in Japan as a cook's mate. He worked at the Hirado factory for over two decades, from 1619 to 1641, and learnt Japanese, which would allow him to act as an interpreter for the Dutch. Caron became the last *opperhoofd* at Hirado in 1639 (Boxer 1935: xv–xvi).[21] Later, in 1662 Caron would publish a detailed account of Japan, *Rechte beschryvinge van het machtigh koninghrijck van Iappan* ('A True

---

16   See also Clulow (2012) and Shapinsky (2014: 254).

17   Specx was a junior merchant. He was assisted by three merchants and an errand boy. Melchior van Santvoort was appointed as the VOC's agent at Sakai, near Osaka. The term *opperhoofd* literally means 'supreme head' but was more akin to the English concept of 'factor'.

18   See also Bruijn *et al.* (1979).

19   http://wolfgangmichel.web.fc2.com/serv/histmed/dejimasurgeons.html. Consulted 1 April 2020.

20   Willem Jansen acted as *opperhoofd* at the beginning of January 1633 (*Diaries*: I:xi). Van Nijenroode's daughter, Cornelia, by his Japanese concubine would become a wealthy merchant in Batavia (Shapinsky 2006: 9 n. 31).

21   For more on Caron, see also Commelin (1969: IV:134–175).

Description of the Mighty Kingdom of Japan') in The Hague. An English translation was published in London in the following year (Boxer 1935).[22]

Caron acted as an interpreter in the 'Nuyts affair'. This concerned Pieter Nuyts (1598–1655), a Dutchman who arrived at Hirado by a rather circuitous route. Nuyts was the VOC Governor of Taiwan (then called Formosa). In April 1628, two Japanese junks commanded by Hamada Yahyōe, arrived in Tayouan Bay, where the Dutch had operated a trading post since 1624. Fearing that this was the start of an invasion, Nuyts ordered the vessels to be searched and stripped of their weapons. Yahyōe was detained but after two months he lost his patience and using a ruse managed to take Nuyts hostage. Having negotiated compensation, Yahyōe returned to Japan. However, he brought these events to the attention of the shogun and the Japanese suspended trading with the VOC. Eventually, in order to be allowed to begin trading again with Japan, the VOC took the extraordinary step of handing Nuyts over to the Japanese authorities. He was incarcerated, spending four years in prison at Hirado.[23] However, he put his time in prison to good use. He possessed many books by classical and Renaissance authors such as Erasmus, Petrarch, Plautus, Machiavelli and Seneca and used these as sources for two works that he wrote in Dutch, *Lof des Elephants* ('In Praise of the Elephant') and *Beschrijvinge vande Riviere Nylus in Aegipten* ('Description of the River Nile in Egypt').[24] He also learnt Japanese (Kennedy 1963: 103). Apart from the odd exception such as Nuyts, the Dutch lived in relative freedom on Hirado; some of them intermingled with the native population and got married.[25]

Due to Portuguese trading activities including those in Japan between 1549 and 1639, the Portuguese language had become the LWC between Europeans and Asians in the seas of East Asia, alongside Malay (Clulow 2014: 275 n. 68). Some Japanese interpreters in Hirado could speak Dutch and so using their services as well as those of one or two Dutch who spoke Japanese, such as Jan Cousynen and François Caron, it was sometimes possible to go directly from Dutch to Japanese (and back). In other cases, though, it was necessary to go via Portuguese, as some interpreters employed by the VOC were more familiar with this language than Dutch (*Diaries*: II:229; Katagiri 1985: 7, quoted in

---

22   On leaving Hirado, Caron went first to Batavia and then back to Europe. He would later become a French citizen and Director-General of the French East India Company.

23   For a detailed account of the Nuyts affair, see Clulow (2014: 227–247). See also Blussé (2000, 2003).

24   Isaac Titsingh owned a copy of Nuyts's *Lof des Elephants* (Lequin 2003: 201).

25   The extent to which the Dutch mixed with local women led Pieter Nuyts to declare in 1627 that Hirado would soon have 'as many Dutch mestizos as thorough Japanese for inhabitants, an intolerable and ignominious matter' (Massarella 1990: 234).

Kornicki 2018: 93). Furthermore, VOC documents often had to pass through Portuguese on their way from Dutch to Japanese.

As well as trading with Japan, Portuguese as well as other Europeans had been engaged in missionary activity there since the middle of the sixteenth century. However, the Japanese authorities objected to their proselytizing activities and in the wake of the Shimabara Rebellion (*Shimabara no Ran*) of 1637/8, which was in part inspired by the Christian faith, in 1639 all Portuguese were expelled from Japan (De Lange 2006: 221; De Groot 2005: 2 n. 5).[26] The Dutch were more cautious than the Portuguese and other Catholics about displaying their Christian identity in Japan. Nevertheless, it seems that they attached dates in the Christian era to their buildings. In November 1640, the powerful government official, Inoue Masashige (1585–1661), visited the Dutch trading post at Hirado and subsequently informed the Dutch that such an explicit display of their Christian faith would not be tolerated and that they would have to dismantle all their buildings at Hirado (*Diaries*: IV:298–299).[27] This included a new warehouse, the Christian date on which seems to have drawn particular ire from Masashige.[28] The Dutch were ordered to remove to Nagasaki Bay, about eighty kilometres to the south of Hirado, where an artificial island had been built for the Portuguese four years earlier. On 10 February 1641 the Dutch ship *Castricum* left Hirado, marking the end of the Dutch presence there (De Lange 2006: 221).

The island in Nagasaki Bay to which the Dutch removed was originally known as *Tsukishima* (築島, lit. 'Constructed island'), but was subsequently

---

26   An edict by the Council of Regency dated 5 July 1639 stated that no Portuguese could enter Japanese ports. This was presented to Captain-Major Vasco Palha de Almeida, who put into Nagasaki, but was not allowed ashore. He was given a copy of the edict and told to sail to Macau to hand it to the Portuguese authorities there. In 1640, a ship carrying four dignitaries from Macau returned, but they and the crew were incarcerated. Because they refused to renounce their Christianity, they were executed.

27   In the *dagregister* it was recorded that Masashige had told the Dutch 'ghij schrijft den datum van Christj geboorte boven op den top ende gevels uwer huisen in 't gesicht ende oogen onses heele lants natie'. Trans: 'you write the date of Christ's birth above on the top and gables of your houses in full view of all the people of our country' (*Diaries*: IV:299). Given that Hirado was far away from most of the Japanese population (and in numerals few would understand), this was something of an exaggeration. It may be that the Japanese objection to displaying this date was merely an excuse to take Dutch trade away from Hirado, where local rulers were thought to be too powerful.

28   The date was in forged iron over the door of the new warehouse. There is disagreement on the date on the warehouse. The Swedish physician Thunberg gave the date 1638 (Screech 2005: 236). The building of the new warehouse commenced in December 1638 (*Diaries*: III:337). Boxer (1935: lxii) gives the date 1637, which seems unlikely, whilst De Lange (2006: 221) gives the date of completion, 1640.

FIGURE 1   Nagasaki Harbour (workshop of) Kawahara Keiga (c. 1833–c. 1836)
             RIJKSMUSEUM, AMSTERDAM

called *Deshima* (出島, lit. 'Island sticking out [into Nagasaki Bay]').[29] Nagasaki
was not completely new territory for the Dutch for during the Hirado period,
they had a permanent representative there and VOC-employees at Hirado visited Nagasaki regularly (Boxer 1935: xxvii, xl). The Dutch continued to trade
with the Japanese at Deshima, although their movements beyond the island
were strictly controlled.[30] It was here that the Dutch would have their factory
in Japan until it closed in 1860.

<hr />

29   The island was constructed by the partial destruction of the site of the Jesuit compound
      in Nagasaki that had occupied a tongue of land, which, between December 1634 and
      July 1636, was razed to the ground. The soil on this land was then used for the reclamation
      of the island in the bay in order to intern the Portuguese. One reason that the Dutch were
      forced to move to Deshima was that investors in the island were concerned about losing
      their money as a result of the ejection of the Portuguese. The Dutch paid 55 *kanme* or bars
      of silver. I thank Reinier Hesselink for this information.
30   The island was connected to the mainland by one stone bridge with a gate.

2.4 The Dutch at Deshima

It is often thought that after 1640 Japan closed itself off to the outside world, following a policy that was subsequently described as *sakoku* (鎖国).[31] However, this is not the case. Rather, after 1640 Japanese contact with foreigners was closely regulated. Recent scholarship describes Japanese foreign relations during the Tokugawa period (1603–1868) as a system mediated by 'four gates' (四つの口 *yottsu no kuchi*): through the Satsuma domain to the Ryūkyū kingdom, through the Tsushima domain to Korea, through the Matsumae domain to the Ainu in Ezochi (now Hokkaido), and through Nagasaki to Chinese and Dutch traders (Matsukata 2011: 101). Our focus will be on the last of these gates.

One difference between the conditions for the Dutch at Hirado and those that pertained at Deshima was that at Hirado both the voc and the Japanese authorities employed interpreters. After the move to Deshima, however, the Governor of Nagasaki (*bugyō*) refused to grant permits to interpreters employed by the voc. The *bugyō* carried out the administration of justice and was directly answerable to the shogun in Edo.[32] Therefore from this time on, the only interpreters working with the Dutch were those selected and employed by the *bugyō* (De Groot 2005: 23). At Hirado and in the first decades of the Dutch stay at Deshima, although some of the interpreters did speak Dutch, communication between Dutch and Japanese was still conducted via Portuguese. The Dutch were not permitted to learn Japanese (although some did so); they of course used their native tongue amongst themselves and for their record-keeping. As I have already suggested, it is probable that different varieties of Dutch could be heard at Deshima. Furthermore, in the written records at least there was significant lexical interference in the Dutch used in Japan from contact languages such as varieties of Japanese and Portuguese. Examples of this lexical interference are analysed in Chapter 5.

Some ninety Dutchmen would be *opperhoofd* at the trading post in Japan. Several of these such as Isaac Titsingh, who was *opperhoofd* intermittently between 1779 and 1784, and Hendrick Doeff, who was *opperhoofd* between 1803 and 1817, played an important role in the story of Dutch in Japan. More details about them and other prominent Europeans at Deshima are given in section 2.5 of this chapter. Apart from *opperhoofd*, other positions at the Dutch factory on Deshima typically occupied by Dutchmen included those

---

31   For a nuanced account of *sakoku*, see Tjoa (1990).

32   There were three to four *bugyō*, who were responsible for the administration of justice (Verwayen 1998: 344; Blussé *et al.* 1992: xviii). The fact that the *bugyō* were directly answerable to the shogun also helps to explain why the Dutch were forced to move to Nagasaki.

FIGURE 2   View of Deshima (workshop of) Kawahara Keiga (c. 1833–c. 1836)
RIJKSMUSEUM, AMSTERDAM

of secretary (*schrijver* or *scriba*), warehouse manager (*pakhuismeester*), and bookkeeper (*boekhouder*).[33]

The numbers on Deshima at any one time varied, but a figure of between fifteen to twenty VOC employees was normal. Most of these were Dutch, although several physicians were German and Swedish, and several other positions were occasionally given to non-Dutch (Blussé *et al.* 2000: 48). Their numbers were swelled by the arrival of about six ships a year, a state of affairs that continued into the early eighteenth century. If we assume, as with Hirado, that about half of the crew of about 100 were Dutch, then we can reckon that some 30,000 Dutch arrived in Nagasaki Bay, although only a few of these would have disembarked and entered Deshima.[34] Even though the Dutch could

33   For these and other positions see https://wolfgangmichel.web.fc2.com/serv/histmed/dejimasurgeons.html. Accessed 1 April 2020.

34   This may be something of an overestimate for by the second half of the eighteenth century the VOC employed an increasing number of Asian crewmembers (Van Rossum 2014a: 143). In 1851, Cornelis Assendelft de Coningh (1856: 27) estimated that two-thirds of the crew on board his ship were not Dutch, although he does not give a figure for non-Europeans.

only leave Deshima by a guarded gate, entries in the factory journal or *dagregister* make it clear that some of the Dutch were permitted to visit Nagasaki when necessary.[35]

As well as the Dutch who arrived at Deshima on what one might call 'scheduled' voc ships, other Dutch arrived in more straitened circumstances. In 1662, when Zheng Chenggong captured Taiwan, many Dutch women and children fled to Japan, where they were granted entry at Deshima (Doeff 1833: 249). They would though have to leave Deshima as only Dutch men were permitted to stay in Japan. In 1666 the Dutchman Hendrik Hamel (1630–92) arrived at Deshima. He had been shipwrecked on the island of Jeju in 1653 sailing on the *Sperwer* ('Sparrow Hawk') from Taiwan to Japan. He had subsequently been held against his will in Joseon Korea for some thirteen years but had managed to escape and reach Japan. After a short while at Deshima, Hamel was taken by an interpreter to the *bugyō* who interrogated him about Joseon Korea. Hamel kept a journal in Japan which included a detailed account of questions asked him by the Governor (Savenije 2003: 119–133). As with other Dutch authors, he rendered the name Nagasaki as *Nangazackij*, and referred to the shogun as *Keijser*, although the actual Emperor lived in Kyoto.[36]

While most of the Dutch who went to Japan remained in Hirado or Deshima, others passed through or stayed in other parts of the country. Survivors from the *Liefde* in Osaka and Edo have already been mentioned. The voc could only trade with Japan by the grace of the shogun, who resided in Edo. Beginning in 1633, every year voc representatives would make the journey (*hofreis* in Dutch, *Edo sanpu* 江戸参府 in Japanese) from western Kyushu to Edo to have an audience with and pay homage to the shogun. The journey would last some three months, taking them past the island of Shikoku and through cities such as Osaka, and thence along the *Tōkaidō* (東海道) to Edo. This was annual until 1790, although in a few years there was no *hofreis*.[37] Thereafter it took place once every four years until 1858. It was on this route that the Dutch language made its way to Edo. Over time, it was picked up by prominent Japanese who lived along the route and in Edo by leading Japanese scholars and administrators. There would be 167 *hofreizen* in total (Katagiri 1985: 208–226).

Sometimes on the *hofreis*, the Dutch would be required to write Dutch words for Japanese. In 1745/6 at the court in Edo, Jan Louis de Win (*opperhoofd*

---

35   See for example, Vermeulen *et al.* (1986–: 1:23).
36   In the form 'Nangazackij' the 'ng' reflects the prenasalization of 'g'. This is analysed in more detail in Chapter 5.
37   For a full list of the *hofreizen*, beginning in 1633, see Katagiri (1985: 208–226). Katagiri provides details of both the Japanese interpreters and the Dutch on each *hofreis*.

1745–46, 1747–48), was required to write down Dutch words on Japanese paper for the amusement and edification of the shogunal family. Some of those who went on the *hofreis* kept private journals. The one kept by the *opperhoofd* Isaac Titsingh in 1780 provides much valuable information about the Dutch experience in Japan as well as the knowledge and use of the Dutch language there (Lequin 2011: 61–134). The *hofreis* party was accompanied by the senior physician at Deshima, and in one case at least he was required to treat one of the shogun's officials (Michel 1999: 117). Again, in the early part of our story, in Edo and elsewhere beyond western Kyushu, Portuguese was used alongside Dutch for communication between the Dutch and Japanese, but over time its role as an LWC in Japan diminished and eventually disappeared.

In 1643, the VOC ship *Breskens* was sent from the VOC headquarters in East Asia, Batavia (now Jakarta), to explore Japan and surrounding islands. The crew went ashore at several locations such as Yamada (山田) in northern Japan.[38] At Nambu (南部), ten crewmembers went ashore, but were captured and taken to Edo, suspected of being Jesuits (Hesselink 2002: 1). Eventually, the *opperhoofd* at Deshima, Jan van Elseracq, arrived in Edo, accompanied by the Japanese interpreter, Hideshima Tōzaemon, who had been employed by the VOC in Hirado and who spoke Dutch (Hesselink 2002: 88). Van Elseracq confirmed that the captives were Dutch and so they were released (Vermeulen *et al.* 1986–: XI:117; Doeff 1833: 49–50). One VOC vessel that was heading for Deshima but did not make it was the *Peperbaal* ('Pepper Sack'). On 26 August 1663 it was shipwrecked on the Mishima Islands to the south of Kyushu. It had 107 crew and 41 soldiers on board (Bruijn *et al.* 1979: 140–141).

As for its trading activities, the VOC imported and exported a range of goods through Deshima. It exported Japanese silver on the intra-Asian trade circuit. This would be used to purchase cotton textiles, which would either be exported to Europe, or brought back to Japan. In addition, VOC ships imported Chinese silk into Japan. Between 1624 and 1662 the VOC exchanged the silk for silver at its trading post at Fort Zeelandia on Taiwan (Shimada 2006: 132–133).[39] Apart from silver, another chief export was Japanese copper, both to Europe and as part of the intra-Asian trade. However, from 1715 onwards the Tokugawa shogunate restricted exports, in part as a result of the reduction in the amount of Japanese copper mined, but also because of an increased demand for copper cash (Shimada 2006: 3–4). After this date the number of VOC ships arriving at Deshima was reduced from six to two per year, although in some years this

---

38   For a full account of this episode, see Hesselink (2002).

39   For more on the Dutch in Taiwan including the use of the Dutch language, see for example Heylen (2001) and Chiu Hsin-hui (2008).

number was exceeded (Shimada 2006: 160).[40] In 1790 the permitted number of VOC ships was further reduced to one per year (Shimada 2006: 163–164).

Besides these bulk trade products, the VOC imported scientific instruments such as telescopes that were being developed in Europe. In addition, books were imported, most although not all of which were written in Dutch. These were often traded on a private basis by VOC crewmembers. The books, which typically dealt with scientific matters such as medicine and astronomy, fuelled the intellectual movement of Dutch Studies (*rangaku* 蘭学), which will be discussed frequently in this book.

2.5 *Prominent* opperhoofden

Whereas some *opperhoofden* came and went within 12 months, others stayed for longer and play an important role in our story. Two to mention here are Isaac Titsingh and Hendrick Doeff.

While many of the *opperhoofden* were well-educated merchants, Isaac Titsingh, who was *opperhoofd* intermittently between 1779 and 1784, stands out from most of the others. His father was an Amsterdam surgeon. He himself matriculated aged 19 in December 1764 at Leiden University to study law. Fellow students came to Leiden from all over Europe. Within a few weeks of Titsingh, other students from Silesia, the Polish-Lithuanian commonwealth, Scotland, England, Ireland and France as well as different parts of the Dutch Republic matriculated at Leiden (Du Rieu 1875: col. 1084). Such diversity may have helped the young Titsingh prepare for a life where he would frequently engage with other cultures and languages. After his time in Japan, Titsingh worked for the VOC in Bengal and China, before returning to Europe, where he made the acquaintance of leading intellectuals and patrons. In 1797, he was elected to membership of the Royal Society of London.[41] He later removed to Paris where he died in 1812. Titsingh is important for our purposes as he wrote extensively in Dutch during his time in Japan. Apart from the private journal on the 1780 *hofreis*, he wrote other works such as a philosophical discourse for a Japanese associate, which remained in manuscript (Lequin 2011: 15–60). However, perhaps his greatest contribution in relation to the present study is his work with Japanese, some of whom were Nagasaki interpreters, some students or scholars of *rangaku* (*rangakusha* 蘭学者), and some who were both.

---

40   In August 1751, for example, three VOC ships arrived at Deshima (Shimada 2006: 156).

41   Titsingh's published correspondence from Deshima provides us with interesting insights into the nature of the contact between the Dutch and the Japanese at this time (Lequin 1990). Of particular interest is his correspondence in Dutch with the *rangakusha*, Kutsuki Masatsuna, between 1785 and 1807 (Lequin 1992). This is analysed in Chapter 3.

He helped Japanese to improve their Dutch. Among other things this involved correcting dialogues that they had penned in order to practise their spoken Dutch. Titsingh also corresponded with several Japanese both during his time in Japan and after he had left the country. Touchingly, some of them would ask him to correct their Dutch and return their revised letters. Furthermore, he provided his Japanese friends and associates with Dutch books, often in return for presents such as Japanese coins. He was an accomplished multi-lingual. Besides Dutch and Latin, he wrote in French and English and often inserted Japanese apophthegms and short verses in Roman script (*rōmaji*) in his correspondence. Back in Europe he published several works on Japan and left an extensive range of manuscripts which were dispersed after his death (Lequin 2003). In short, he was an Enlightenment polymath.

Hendrick Doeff (1764–1837) was cut from different cloth, but made his own distinctive contribution to Dutch in Japan. He was born in Amsterdam and joined the VOC as a clerk. The glory days of the company itself were now far in the past and for several reasons including the Fourth Anglo-Dutch War (1781–84) and internal corruption, it ceased trading in 1799. Its assets and activities were taken over by the Dutch state. In 1803, after working for several years as a clerk at Deshima, Doeff was appointed as *opperhoofd*. In Europe, the Napoleonic Wars were at their height. The Dutch Republic had come to an end in 1795. In the wake of the French Revolution, this was replaced by the Batavian Republic (1795–1806), which in turn was replaced by the Napoleonic Kingdom of Holland (1806–10), after which the Low Countries were fully annexed by France. As Napoleon began to use Dutch resources against the British, the latter took retaliatory measures, capturing Batavia and other Dutch colonies. For several years, no Dutch ships reached Deshima. After 1815 with the end of the Napoleonic Wars, the Dutch again sent ships to Deshima and Doeff was finally able to leave in 1817.

For our purposes Doeff's time in Japan is notable for two reasons. First, in 1808, a British frigate, the *Phaeton*, entered Nagasaki Bay in order to ambush Dutch ships. This incursion led the Japanese to realize that their coastal defences were weak. Furthermore, fearing more such incursions, interpreters were ordered to learn English, French and indeed Russian, for Russian ships had started to reach the shores of Japan. The introduction of these languages was an early sign that Dutch would eventually be superseded in Japan by other European languages. Doeff was called on to teach French to the Japanese (Irwin 2011: 48). Second, Doeff used his time in Japan to learn Japanese and to compile, along with Nagasaki interpreters, a Dutch-Japanese dictionary based on a French-Dutch lexicon compiled by François Halma (Vande Walle 2001b: 129). Although the lexicon remained incomplete by the time of

Doeff's departure, it would eventually become known as the *Nagasaki* or *Zūfu* (or sometimes *Dūfu* (Doeff)) *Haruma*. The main aim of the dictionary was to help improve the Dutch of the Nagasaki interpreters with whom Doeff worked.

It was left to Doeff's successor, Jan Cock Blomhoff (1779–1853), to complete the lexicon project. He was *opperhoofd* for six years from 1817 to 1823. He had brought his family to Deshima, including his wife, Titia Bergsma, and their son, Johannes, and a Dutch wet-nurse, Petronella Muns. Unfortunately, they were not allowed to stay, but the women caused quite a stir as the first Western women in Japan for over 150 years. Artists made many pictures of them (Bersma 2002; Hemmes 2017). Some of these included Dutch inscriptions. They are analysed in Chapter 3.

By this time, the Japanese still only permitted one Dutch ship a year to enter Nagasaki Bay. With the odd exception this state of affairs continued until 1853 (Matsukata 2007: 300–302).[42] There was little profit in this for the Dutch, but it provided the Netherlands with a special place amongst European nations. For the Japanese, it provided a useful source of news from abroad. Since 1641, the Dutch had provided the shogunal authorities or *bakufu* (幕府) with an annual report of events outside Japan. This was translated into Japanese and given the name *Oranda fūsetsugaki* ('Dutch Book of Rumours'). As incursions by foreign ships increased and news of the First Opium War in China (1839–42) reached Japan, the Dutch were required to produce an additional report, focussing on the consequences of the war for the surrounding area. This was translated into Japanese and given the title *Betsudan fūsetsugaki* ('Special [Dutch] Book of Rumours'). While some Japanese opposed the influence that *rangaku* was having on Japanese society, others saw Dutch books on matters such as artillery and fortifications as a means by which Japan could defend itself against possible foreign invasion.

A seminal moment for Japan and indeed for the Dutch and the Dutch language in Japan came in 1853 when an American naval fleet under the command of Commodore Matthew Perry reached Uraga at the mouth of Edo Bay. Perry delivered a letter demanding that American ships be allowed to stop off in Japanese ports, apart from Nagasaki, and that Japan should open commercial relations with the United States. He indicated that he would return the following year to receive an answer from the Japanese. When he did so, the Japanese, aware of the naval power at Perry's disposal, acquiesced to his demands and in 1854 the Convention of Kanagawa was concluded between the United States and Japan, a key step in the opening of Japan to other Western countries. Other European nations soon followed and within the space of five

---

42   Two ships arrived in 1842 and 1844.

or six years the Dutch went from being the only European, indeed Western, nation permitted to trade with Japan to being only one of several such nations. Between 1854 and May 1859, 37 ships arrived at Deshima as Japan began to open its ports to other Western countries (Matsukata 2007: 302–303). In 1860, the last *opperhoofd*, Janus Henricus Donker Curtius (1813–79), who had been in post since 1852, formally closed the Dutch trading post at Deshima. After this, the Dutch trading post was replaced by a vice-consulate at Nagasaki (De Groot 2005: 2). Like some of his predecessors, Donker Curtius learnt something of the Japanese language. In 1857 he published a small Japanese grammar, *Proeve eener Japansche spraakkunst* ('Model of Japanese grammar') (Leiden: A.W. Sythoff), which was added to and improved by Johann Joseph Hoffmann (born in Würzburg in 1805), Professor of Japanese and Chinese at Leiden University.

Although the winds of change were now blowing through Japan, this is not quite the end of the story, for Dutch was often used for negotiations between the Japanese and foreign powers until 1870. Furthermore, Dutchmen were involved in helping Japan make the transition into the modern world. For example, the Dutch helped to establish the Japanese navy. With the assistance of the *opperhoofd* at Deshima, a Dutch gunboat from the East Indies naval squadron was presented to the Japanese in the 1850s. This was the first boat in the Japanese navy. The instruction of Japanese naval cadets by Dutch naval personnel in Nagasaki from 1855 to 1857 was given in Dutch and translated into Japanese by interpreters (Huyssen van Kattendyke 1860: 201). Dutch books on naval and military science were translated into Japanese. The Dutch naval engineer, Hendrick Hardes, took charge of constructing a naval repair yard at Nagasaki, and another Dutchman, J.L.C. Pompe van Meerdervoort (born in Brugge in 1829), a naval medical officer, oversaw the construction of the first military hospital in Japan (Burke-Gaffney 2009: 15; Blussé *et al.* 2000: 183). The Dutchman A.J.C. Geerts (1843–83) taught various scientific subjects at the school attached to the Nagasaki hospital (Beukers 2018: 98–101). He gave instruction in Dutch which translated into Japanese.

The Japanese, however, realized that there were more powerful nations in the world, such as the United States, Britain, Germany and France, with which they needed to engage, and it was only a matter of time before the Dutch language would lose its privileged position in Japanese society. The last Dutch language book published in Japan in the nineteenth century was a Dutch translation of the Japanese fairy tale, *Shitakiri suzume* (舌切雀). The naval engineer, Pieter Gerard van Schermbeek (1848–1901), spent time in Japan and published his translation as *De musch met de geknipte tong* ('The Sparrow with the Cut Tongue') in Tokyo in 1886 with illustrations by Kobayashi Eitaku (also Sensai

Eitaku) (1843–90). Two years later, in 1888 a dictionary of physics published in Japan in 1888 included terms in Japanese, English, French and German, but not in Dutch (Montgomery 2000: 222). The shift and recession of Dutch in Japan is analysed in more detail in Chapter 8.

3 Non-Dutch Europeans

Let us now retrace our steps somewhat and discuss some of the many non-Dutch Europeans working in Tokugawa Japan. In some cases, there is direct evidence not only for a knowledge of Dutch but also the use of the language. In other cases, we have to rely on metalinguistic comment, or simply recognize, as in the case of Germans who worked with the Dutch, that it is likely, although by no means certain, that they had at least a passive knowledge if not an active one of Dutch.

Before providing a broadly chronological account of non-Europeans at Hirado and Deshima, a brief word is in order about VOC crewmembers. As noted above, most of those who went to Japan did not disembark, although towards the end of the Tokugawa period, some did come ashore. The VOC was very much a multinational organization. Many European nationalities were represented amongst VOC crewmembers including Germans, Austrians, Scandinavians, Swiss, English, Scots, Irish and Poles (Boxer 1988: 81, 89–90; Gaastra 1991: 88–91; 2003).[43] In the account of his journey to Japan, the Swede Carl Peter Thunberg noted that amongst the crew on his VOC ship as well as Dutchmen there were men from several other European nations including Danes, Germans, Portuguese, Spaniards and Swedes.[44] It is likely that at least some of these nationalities were represented in the crews that reached Japan. One Frenchman who arrived at Deshima in the 1690s was Salomon Melon, a cooper from Rochelle (Vermeulen *et al.* 1986–: II:179). By the eighteenth century, as many as one in five physicians on VOC ships were German (Bruijn 2009: 157). Cornelis Assendelft de Coningh (1856: 27) wrote that in 1851 a Finn and an Italian were on board the ship that brought him to Deshima. He tells us that their Dutch was painfully bad (*het Hollandsch zoo deerlijk radbraakte*). He observes that (even!) a Japanese was able to spot this, and the Dutch tried to explain this away by saying they were 'Berg-Hollanders' ('Mountain Dutch'). Generally, however, there is very little data about which language(s)

---

43   See also Van Rossum (2014a: 143) for a detailed analysis of the origin of VOC crew members.
44   Most of the non-Dutch Europeans in the employ of the VOC were Germans and Scandinavians (Boxer 1988: 81; Gaastra 1991).

crewmembers spoke on board the VOC ships. In fact, it is likely that the use of gesture played an important role in communication between those who did not share a common first language.

The first non-Dutch European to reach Japan onboard a Dutch ship was the English pilot of the *Liefde*, Will Adams in 1600. By the time that the first VOC ships arrived at Hirado in 1609, Adams could speak Japanese fluently and had a reasonable command of Portuguese. As for Dutch, we have one letter written by Adams in Dutch from Edo in 1616. A Dutch commentator writes that given the imperfect (*gebrekkig*) quality of the Dutch it is likely that Adams himself composed the letter (Wieder 1923–25: 76–78). We do not know, however, what language he used to speak with the Dutch (De Lange 2006: 165). It may have been Dutch or Portuguese, or perhaps a mixture of the two, but our current state of knowledge does not allow us to say anything more definitive.[45]

In the first half of the seventeenth century, several Germans arrived at the Dutch trading posts in western Kyushu. One who reached Hirado in late 1638 or early 1639 was the German gunner Hans Wolfgang Braun from Ulm in Bavaria (Weber 2004: 29).[46] A German surgeon who worked at Hirado from 1639 to 1641 was Hans Pauts from Oschersleben in Saxony-Anhalt.[47] Jürgen or Juriaen Henselingh was a barber surgeon from Marburg. He worked first as junior surgeon at Hirado then as senior surgeon at Deshima from 1639 to 1644. He had been ordered to stay longer in Japan by the *bakufu* and Nagasaki *bugyō* in order to teacher surgery to Japanese (Mishima 2004: 179; *Diaries*: V:195; VI:38). There is no direct record of him speaking Dutch, although there are entries in the *dagregister* indicating that he communicated with Dutchmen in Japan (e.g., *Diaries*: VII:189). Given that he was working with Dutchmen for five years and spoke a closely-related language, it is most probable that he knew some of the language. The senior surgeon at Deshima from 1645 to 1646 was the German Karl Kempf from Landsberg in Pfalz, while Boxer records that another German, Jacob Merklein, worked for a short time as a surgeon at Deshima during the 1640s (Boxer 1935: xxxii, xxxiii).[48]

---

45   Corr (1995: 112–114) writes that the Dutch considered Adams to be a Dutchman. He refers to a letter written in 1608 in Pattani by Victor Sprinckel, which refers to Adams's love for the 'fatherland', i.e., the Dutch Republic.

46   Braun cast mortars at Hirado and inscribed one of these in Latin: *Hans Wolfgang Braun von Ulm me fecit Firando 1639* ('H.W.B. from Ulm made me, Hirado 1639'). See also Boxer (1935: xlix).

47   https://wolfgangmichel.web.fc2.com/serv/histmed/dejimasurgeons.html. Accessed 2 April 2020. A note to the *dagregisters* (*Diaries*: VI:180) records that Pauts was born at Oss in Noord-Brabant. However, the first name Hans is at least suggestive of a German.

48   See Merklein (1663). Merklein does not appear in Wolfgang Michel's list of VOC employees at Hirado and Deshima. https://wolfgangmichel.web.fc2.com/serv/histmed/

The German Caspar Schamberger (1623–1706) from Leipzig worked as senior surgeon in Japan for two years (1649–51) and visited Edo on the *hofreis* in 1650 (De Groot 2005: 13, 26). He was required to spend an extended period in Edo due to the poor health of the shogun, Tokugawa Iemitsu (1604–51). It would be Schamberger's success in treating a member of Iemitsu's court that was one of the first indications for the Japanese that there was some value in Western medicine and learning more generally. This learning, mediated orally and through imported Dutch books, would eventually have a significant impact on Japanese society (Michel 1999: 117). Schamberger spent ten months at Edo instructing the court physicians in Dutch medicine and inspired the *Kasuparuryū* ('the school of Caspar'), a school or style of medicine that continued until the end of the Tokugawa period in 1868 (Michel 1993b: 288: Vos 1963: 343).[49] The Japanese interpreters working with Schamberger provided students with words in both Dutch and Portuguese (De Groot 2005: 26).[50] This reflects the fact that Portuguese continued to compete with Dutch in communication between the Japanese and Europeans long after the Portuguese themselves had been expelled from Japan. Schamberger also taught surveying to Higuchi Gon'emon (1601–84) of Nagasaki (also known as Kobayashi Yoshinobu), although we have no details of the language in which he did this. Some of Gon'emon's own students subsequently founded schools of surveying (Boxer 1950: 13). Other Europeans who made the *hofreis* to Edo were the Swedes, Juriaen Schedel and Olof Eriksson Willman (c. 1620–73). Schedel was an army corporal and was required to give instruction in mortar shooting to Japanese in Edo. He is described as a *vuurwerker* (maker of munitions) in the *dagregister* (*Diaries*: XII:31). Willman mentions Schedel in the journal of his travels to the East Indies and Japan.[51]

In 1650, another German, Caspar Schmalkalden (1616–73), arrived in Japan. He had spent two years working as a surveyor for the VOC in Taiwan, where he probably acquired at least some Dutch. The case of Frederick Coyett (c. 1620–87) is somewhat different. He was born in Stockholm of Dutch heritage. He

---

dejimasurgeons.html. Accessed 2 April 2020. This is an extremely useful list, although it is not complete.

49 See also Michel (1999). Michel refers to the notion of *kasuparu-ryūgeka* or 'the Caspar school surgery'. 'School' is used here in the sense of school of thought, rather than a physical location. It signals an approach to medicine, in which knowledge was recorded and circulated in manuscripts and, later, books.

50 De Groot notes that this vocabulary was written in *katakana*, the simplified syllable writing system, which did not adequately represent the sounds of Dutch or Portuguese.

51 For Willman's journal, see Willman (2013). This was published in Swedish in 1667 as *Een kort Beskriffningh På een Reesa till Ostindien och förbeskreffne Japan Then een Swänsk Mann och SkepsCapiteen Oloff Erichsson Willman benembdh giordt hafwer*. Visingsborg.

was twice *opperhoofd* at Deshima (1647–48 and 1652–53). Subsequently, he became the last VOC Governor of Taiwan. Several Germans worked at Deshima in the second half of the seventeenth century. One German physician was Johannes Winsch from Erfurt. He became the senior surgeon at the Dutch factory in 1651 (Vermeulen *et al.* 1986–: XII:33). However, no direct evidence that he knew Dutch has yet emerged. Another was Hans Jürgen or Juriaen Hancke from Breslau, who was senior surgeon at Deshima from 1655 to 1657. Oral instructions on surgery from Hancke formed the basis of one of the first Japanese manuscripts on Dutch or German medicine (Michel 1995). Although we lack direct evidence for Hancke's knowledge of Dutch, given that he had worked for the VOC at Batavia since 1647 and given the closeness of German to Dutch he was probably quite comfortable with the latter.

Germans who worked on Deshima in the 1670s include the pharmacists Godefried Haeck and Frans Braun and the junior surgeons Mathaeus Hans Otter from Dresden and Heinrich Muche (1649–c. 1696) from Breslau, who was also an accomplished artist. One *opperhoofd* from Germany was Andreas Cleyer (c. 1634–c. 1698). He was born in Kassel and trained as a physician. In 1665 he arrived in Batavia as a soldier. He married a Dutch woman and changed his Christian name to Andries. He served as *opperhoofd* in 1682–83 and 1685–86, during which time he made journal entries and wrote letters in Dutch (Vos 1989: 55; Cleyer 1985: 8). Cleyer employed a fellow German, Georg Meister, privately at Deshima.

Engelbert Kaempfer (1651–1716) came from Lemgo in Northern Germany. He worked at Deshima as a physician, making two *hofreizen* to Edo, but he was also a botanist. Although he was mostly restricted to Deshima, he was permitted to venture into Nagasaki and the surrounding area with his Japanese assistant Imamura Gen'emon (also Eisei 1671–1736) to study the local botany. This would form the basis of his later work, *Flora Japonica* (Werger-Klein 1993: 56).[52] Kaempfer was one of several intellectuals who worked at Deshima. He knew several classical and vernacular languages including Dutch. He taught Gen'emon to read and write Dutch as well as Dutch grammar (Vande Walle 2001b: 131; Werger-Klein 1993: 56).

A brief word is in order about Kaempfer's study of Japanese, which is all the more interesting given that foreigners were forbidden from learning the language.[53] Kaempfer undertook a detailed study of Japanese pronunciation and

---

52   This was first published in Kaempfer's *Amœnitatum exoticarum politico-physico-medicarum fasiculi v* (Lemgo, 1712).

53   Later, Johannes van Overmeer Fisscher (1833: 91–92) wrote that learning Japanese was forbidden and those who did so had to do it in the greatest secrecy, 'in geen geval kunnen

made serious attempts to develop a transliteration system accurately reflecting that pronunciation. In *Amœnitatum Exoticarum politico-physico-medicarum fasiculi v* ('Five fascicles of Exotic Political-Physical-Medical Delights', Lemgo, 1712), a book on observations he made during his travels in Asia, he gives the reader guidance on how to pronounce the transliterations, e.g., 'g' should be pronounced like 'gu' in French. In a later publication, *The History of Japan* (London, 1727), he discusses the letter 'l' and the difficulties Japanese have with certain individual consonants and consonant sequences (p. 382). He writes 'it must be observ'd that the Japanese, not being able rightly to pronounce the letter *l*, write and pronounce *Horanda*, instead of *Holanda*. *Fanrei Borowara* is the name of the Ambassador *Henry Brouwer*, spelt after the Japanese manner'.[54] The second feature mentioned here is a function of the fact that the canonical syllable structure of Old Japanese phonotactics was (Consonant) Vowel ((c)v) (Shibatani 1990: 121–122). It explains why Japanese inserts vowels in consonant clusters in Dutch loanwords, something analysed in more detail in Chapter 7. Regarding the additional syllable-final 'n' that Japanese some-times insert, Kaempfer writes in *The History of Japan* (p. 414), 'it [is] not incon-sistent with the beauty of the Japanese language to [...] add to some syllables the letter *n*, which they do frequently for the sake of an easier and more agree-able pronunciation. Thus, sometimes [the Japanese] write [...] *Firangawa* for *Firakawa*, *Nangasaki* for *Nagasaki* and so on'. He concludes 'I thought it nec-essary once for all to make this observation, and to entreat the reader, not to take it amiss if he meets with the same names differently written in different places' (Michel 2012: 113). The phenomenon that Kaempfer is describing here is prenasalization. This often prompted authors of Dutch texts to add an 'extra' 'n' to Japanese words. Further examples are analysed in Chapter 5.

Two *opperhoofden* in the eighteenth century were born in Germany, Joan Aouwer (*opperhoofd* 1716–17, 1718–20) from Nürnberg and Johannes Thedens (*opperhoofd* 1723–25). Thedens (1680–1748) was born in Friedrichstadt, which was a largely Dutch settlement in the German state of Schleswig, so he may

---

de Hollanders verpligt worden, het Japansch te verstaan, integendeel is het aanleeren dier taal eigenlijk verboden en al hetgene, hetwelk wij van die kennis verzamelen, moet onder de grootste geheimhouding en in vertrouwen behandeld worden'. One wonders, though, whether exceptions were made, or a blind eye was turned to certain individuals, such as Von Siebold. Overmeer Fisscher himself, who spent most of the 1820s in Japan, clearly learnt some Japanese, although he did not have a 'full command' of the language (Effert 2008: 102–103).

54   I assume that Kaempfer is referring here to Hendrick Brouwer, the second *opperhoofd* at Hirado (1613–14).

have had Dutch heritage. In the first half of the eighteenth century, three surgeons at Deshima were born in Germany. However, the rendering of one name, Carel Frederik, from Aachen (junior surgeon 1729–30) may suggest he was of Dutch heritage or had assumed a Dutch name (although it may simply be that his name was rendered in a Dutch manner by a Dutch clerk). The two other German-born surgeons were Christian Berwig/Berbigh from Saxony (junior surgeon 1733–39) and Andreas Köhler from Stralsund (senior surgeon 1748–49). In the second half of the eighteenth century, more than half of the senior surgeons at Deshima were born in Germany or Scandinavia.[55] Among those born in Germany, most if not all seem to have been of German heritage, such as Rudolf Bauer from Breslau (by now in the Kingdom of Prussia), senior surgeon 1759–62. Among the Scandinavians are the Swedes, Carl Peter Thunberg from Jönköping (senior surgeon 1775–76), of whom more shortly, and Johan Arnold Stützer (1763–1821) from Stockholm (senior surgeon 1777–78). Several Germans filled other positions at Deshima. Herman Köhler was a bookkeeper and storeman for many years, while Ernst Rudolph Christian von Beckstein from Hessenkassel was a bookkeeper, as was Fredrik Willem Schindeler from Dannenberg in Northern Germany (Winkel 2004: 49).

As for the question of whether these individuals knew Dutch, in some cases the evidence is somewhat circumstantial. German and Dutch are closely related and furthermore many of those mentioned would have been the only non-Dutch Europeans at Deshima, so it is reasonable to assume that they had at least serviceable Dutch. In other cases, the evidence is more direct. The *opperhoofden* Aouwer and Thedens kept the company diary (*dagregister*) in Dutch at Deshima.[56]

Like some of the Germans who resided on Deshima, the Swede Carl Peter Thunberg was a botanist who paid his way in Japan as a surgeon.[57] In December 1771 he left Holland as a ship's surgeon, and having spent three years in the Cape Colony in order to learn the Dutch language (as well as

---

55   The increase in non-Dutch surgeons, and the predominance of Germans among them, is part of a pattern, which as noted above, emerged in the VOC more generally. By the last quarter of the eighteenth century, 80% of non-Dutch surgeons were German, or 31% of the total of Dutch and non-Dutch surgeons (Bruijn 2009: 157–159).

56   It is possible that a Dutch clerk wrote the *dagregister* entries, dictated by Aouwer and Thedens in Dutch. I would suggest that an alternative scenario where Aouwer or Thedens dictated the text in German, which the clerk subsequently translated and wrote down is unlikely.

57   Thunberg has been described as an apostle of his fellow Swede, Carl Linnaeus, who lived and worked in the Netherlands for many years. He was commissioned by Johannes Burman and his son Nicolaas to visit the Dutch colonies and Japan to collect specimens for Dutch botanical gardens.

undertaking some botanical study), he was able to pass himself off as a Dutchman (Screech 2005: 7). In August 1775 he arrived at Deshima and was appointed head surgeon of the trading post. Severe restrictions were placed on the movements of those on the island. Thunberg was, however, one of the few to be allowed to conduct some botanical research ashore. He would later publish his account of Japan's plant-life, *Flora Japonica*, in Latin in Leipzig in 1784. Here, Thunberg records collecting plant species with two Japanese physicians. They would tell him the Japanese names for the plants and he, in return, would tell them the Latin and Dutch names (*latina et belgica* [*nomina*]) (Thunberg 1784: xviii). Furthermore, Thunberg corresponded with several Japanese in Dutch.

In the nineteenth century, the most famous German to work at Deshima was the physician, Philipp Franz von Siebold (1796–1866). He knew and used Dutch extensively. It seems he tried to pass himself off as a Dutchman. However, some of the Japanese did realize that there was something different about Von Siebold's Dutch. He was described in Japanese as a *yama orandajin*. This may be because, as with other non-Dutch, he was referred to as a 'Berg-Hollander', i.e., a 'mountain Dutchman'. However, another version of this story is that *yama orandajin* translates 'High German' (*Hoogduitser*) (as opposed to a 'Low German' *Nederduitser*, i.e., Dutchman) (Kouwenhoven 2000: 19; Vos 1989: 360–361). Von Siebold established a medical school, the *Narutakijuku* (鳴滝塾) at Narutaki, close to Nagasaki, which had around fifty students (Sansom 1973: 260). There, he gave lectures in Dutch once a week and required students to submit dissertations written in Dutch. Two other German medical experts who worked at Deshima in the first half of the nineteenth century were the pharmacist Dr. Heinrich Bürger (1804–58) from Hameln and Dr. Otto Gottlieb Johann Mohnike (1814–87) from Stralsund.[58] Bürger and Von Siebold were in Japan at the same time. Further research may tell us whether they spoke German or Dutch or perhaps both to each other.

Here, a word is in order about several of the assertions that Roland Willemyns makes about those who went to Japan in his book on the history of the Dutch language (2013). One assertion he makes is that Deshima was 'populated exclusively by Dutchmen'. From the foregoing this is clearly not the case. Furthermore, several groups of Japanese visited Deshima regularly. Among these were the Dutch interpreters and the *Orandayuki* (阿蘭陀行), literally the 'women who go to the Dutch', i.e., the Japanese women who were the girlfriends or concubines of the Dutch. In fact, a set of regulations introduced

---

58 http://wolfgangmichel.web.fc2.com/serv/histmed/dejimasurgeons.html. Accessed 2 April 2020.

in the middle of the seventeenth century stipulated that they were the only women who could visit Deshima (Vos 1971: 615). The Japanese officials responsible for keeping an eye on Deshima were the *otona* (乙名). They had their own room on the island (Moeshart 2001: 32). Willemyns (2013: 212) also writes that 'the Dutch were the only foreigners admitted [to Japan]'. Willemyns' reference to 'foreigners' is problematic, for Asians such as the Chinese and Koreans were permitted to trade with the Japanese. 'Europeans', or later 'Westerners', would be a more appropriate term. The non-Dutch Europeans were able to enter Japan by not giving their place of birth (Screech 2005: 72, 76).

Another point to make in relation to Willemyns' account concerns the number of Dutch, including those who passed themselves off as Dutch, admitted to Deshima. Willemyns (2013: 212) writes that their number never exceeded ten. Other commentators disagree. Whilst the number of Dutch on Deshima was sometimes as low as two or three, it sometimes exceeded ten.[59] One commentator states that a figure of between fifteen and twenty VOC employees on the island was normal (Blussé *et al.* 2000: 48). In 1670 François de Haese (*opperhoofd* 1669–70) recorded that 'according to custom' twenty-one to twenty-three Dutch could be on Deshima at any one time (Vermeulen *et al.* 1986–: XIII:366). Whilst it may seem on the one hand that the difference is small, over a period of more than two centuries this would amount to a significant number of people.

4   Non-Europeans (Excluding Japanese)

The third group of non-Japanese who had some knowledge of Dutch were non-Europeans. There is very little direct evidence for knowledge of Dutch in this group, so in large part we must rely on metalinguistic comment. The group can be divided into two sub-groups: VOC crewmembers and servants and slaves of Europeans.

Many of the crew members of VOC ships came from different parts of Asia.[60] Here it is important to distinguish between ships on the intercontinental routes and those on intra-Asian routes. Those that arrived at Deshima generally fell into the latter category. In the seventeenth and eighteenth centuries, the VOC typically employed largely European crews on the intercontinental shipping routes, although by the second half of the eighteenth century it employed an increasing number of Asian crewmembers. On the intra-Asian

---

59   I thank Reinier Hesselink for this observation.
60   There are also reports of 'Moors' aboard VOC ships arriving in Japan. One assumes they came from North Africa (Vermeulen *et al.* 1986–: x:96).

ships, the VOC employed South Asian, Javanese and Chinese crewmembers as well as Europeans. Although in the seventeenth century the intra-Asian fleet was four to five times larger than the intercontinental fleet, by the eighteenth century this difference lessened. We know little about the languages spoken by the Asian crewmembers beyond what might reasonably be deduced from their origins.

Given that many crewmembers nevertheless spoke Dutch as a first language, it is possible that other non-European VOC crewmembers acquired some knowledge of the language on the long voyages in East Asia, but currently we can say nothing more concrete. It is likely that Low Portuguese or Malay was used by some crewmembers. It may also be that hybrid languages evolved with words from several languages, possibly including Dutch, and, as noted above, it is also likely that the use of gestures played an important role in communication between men with different first languages (Shapinsky 2006: 21–22). Occasionally, the records do indicate that a crewmember knew Dutch. For example, one non-European VOC crewmember who knew Dutch is discussed at length in the Deshima *dagregister* for 1641. He was born in Tartary and had made contact with a Dutch merchant in Muscovy. That merchant had taken him to Holland where he learnt Dutch. He subsequently sailed to Batavia and thence to Japan (Vermeulen *et al.* 1986: XI:133–135).

The Dutch employed servants at Deshima, some of whom were of Javanese origin (Vos 1963: 341). They may have known some words of Dutch, although Low or creolized Portuguese was often used as an LWC among indigenous people from the Dutch East Indies. In 1646, Willem Verstegen (*opperhoofd* 1646–47) records that a servant knew Dutch. He gives no further details, but the servant was most probably not Japanese (*Diaries*: x:28–29). There were also Asian slaves at Deshima (Winkel 1999: 54).[61] Some of these probably spoke Malay and Low Portuguese (Van der Velde 1995: 46).[62] In one year, 1687/88, there were

---

61 These slaves are often referred to as *kurobō*. In *Saiyū nikki*, Shiba Kōkan (1927: 101) refers to *kuronbo* 黒んぼ.

62 In the *dagregister* for January 1684, reference is made to a black servant, who was required to travel on the *hofreis* to Edo as he could speak some Japanese (Vermeulen *et al.* 1986–: 1:30). The presence of servants and slaves at the Dutch trading post again contradicts Willemyns' assertion that it was populated exclusively by Dutchmen. Earlier, in October 1628, in a journal kept by Pieter Jansz. Muijser, a list of the names of those who would go on the *hofreis* includes those of three black men, viz. ('Swarten') Diogenes uijt Sijlon (from Ceylon), Pedro Cock vande Cust and Domingo Wassen vande Cust (from the coast) (MS. The Hague, *Nationaal Archief*, 1.04.21, nr. 270). Further evidence comes from paintings of life on Deshima, typically from after the period under discussion here. These show the Dutch playing a type of billiards or cards in their leisure time, often accompanied by black servants. In the account of his voyage to Deshima, Thunberg records that there were 34 slaves on board, along with a crew of about 110 (Screech 2005: 72, 76).

ten servants and slaves at Deshima (Gaastra 1991: 94).[63] The *dagregister* records that some slaves had no command of Dutch, although it does provide one clear example of a slave who did speak Dutch.[64] In March 1792 the *opperhoofd* Petrus Chassé recorded that he had to offer one of his slaves in part payment for the expenses of the *hofreis* to Edo. The slave was said to be 'somewhat conversant in Dutch' (Vermeulen *et al.* 1986–: X:21).

One other group to mention here are the captains of Chinese junks. Some of these also traded with Taiwan when the VOC was active there and may have picked up some Dutch. One concrete example is a captain of a junk from Nanjing (*Nankijns joncxken*) in Nagasaki in 1647 who knew 'weynigh Duyts', i.e., little Dutch, but nevertheless some (*Diaries*: I:153).

5 Conclusion

The aim of this initial chapter has been twofold. First, it has provided a chronological overview of the Dutch presence in Tokugawa and early Meiji Japan. This will give readers a useful historical framework within which to place the material presented in subsequent chapters. Second, it has provided details of which non-Japanese knew Dutch in Japan. This will be complemented by material in the next chapter on the Japanese who learnt Dutch. In this chapter, non-Japanese who knew Dutch have been divided into three groups: the Dutch, itself a somewhat problematic term; non-Dutch Europeans; and non-Japanese non-Europeans. The picture that has emerged is that alongside the Dutch at the trading posts in Hirado and Nagasaki, there were many non-Dutch. This illustrates that statements such as Deshima was 'populated exclusively by Dutchmen' made by Willemyns (2013: 212) are incorrect.

Furthermore, this chapter has introduced figures who play an important role in the story of Dutch in Japan. While some of these were Dutch, such as Isaac Titsingh and Hendrick Doeff, others were not Dutch. The German physicians,

---

There were certainly some slaves in Batavia who learnt Dutch; they could only wear a hat or cap if they had a fair command of the language. Others may have spoken creolized Portuguese (Groeneboer 1998: 28, 3).

63   Gaastra presents a table (14) giving figures for 'inheems personeel en slaven op de "Indische Comptoiren" van de VOC, 1687/1688'. He gives the figure of 10 for 'inheems personeel' in Japan. I take this to mean people from South-East and South Asia, rather than 'native' Japanese.

64   For further details on slaves at Deshima, see http://wolfgangmichel.web.fc2.com/serv/histmed/dejima surgeons.html. Accessed 2 April 2020.

Engelbert Kaempfer and Philipp Franz von Siebold, both used Dutch and promoted its use amongst Japanese. The same can be said of the Swedish botanist and physician, Carl Peter Thunberg.

As well as indicating who knew Dutch in Tokugawa Japan, this chapter has introduced themes that will be analysed in more detail later in this book. It will already be clear that Dutch faced competition from other European languages in Japan. In the seventeenth century, Portuguese continued to function as an LWC in Japan long after the expulsion of the Portuguese in 1639. In the nineteenth century, as the number of foreign ships entering Japanese waters increased, the *bakufu* ordered interpreters to learn Russian, English and French in order to deal with any possible invasions. The theme of language competition will be analysed in detail in Chapter 4.

Another theme that has been touched on several times is individual multilingualism. German and Swedish physicians knew Dutch. Isaac Titsingh knew at least four European languages and learnt some Japanese. Other Europeans became more proficient in Japanese. Educated Japanese could read and write literary Sinitic. This multilingualism was the key to the language processes such as code switching and translation which are analysed in Chapters 5 and 6 of this book. It was also key to the process of Japanese learning Dutch. Two examples presented in this chapter are those of the German Engelbert Kaempfer teaching Dutch to his Japanese assistant Imamura Gen'emon and Hendrick Doeff learning Japanese, which allowed him to compile a lexicon which helped Japanese to learn Dutch. Many more examples of Japanese learning Dutch are analysed in the next chapter in this story of what happened after the arrival of the Dutch language in Japan in 1600.

Learning Dutch in Tokugawa Japan

1 Introduction

This chapter focuses on the learning of Dutch in Japan. It takes a broadly chronological approach to analysing the evidence for Japanese learning the Dutch language. During the Hirado period (1609–41) and the first decades of the Dutch presence in Nagasaki, there is limited evidence for the learning of Dutch. Much of the communication between the Dutch and Japanese took place via Portuguese, although in some cases this intermediate language was not required.

In the early 1670s, several decades after the Portuguese had been expelled from Japan and with the Dutch having established themselves in Nagasaki, the first official moves were made to send junior interpreters to the Dutch for instruction. We have details about the nature of this education and the quality of the Dutch spoken by the Japanese. Although some Japanese attained a decent level of Dutch, European comments on Japanese command of the language were typically not flattering.

Over time, to improve the level of Dutch spoken, and written, by Japanese, learning aids were developed including lexicons, learners and grammars, which were often based on books imported from Europe. Copies of many of these still survive and provide us with valuable information about how Japanese learnt Dutch. As interest in the knowledge mediated by Dutch books spread, first in Nagasaki then to Edo and subsequently to other towns and regions in Japan, schools were established which were devoted to *rangaku*.[1] Students or scholars of *rangaku* (*rangakusha*) learnt not only about the science contained in Dutch

---

1 *Rangaku* is typically translated as 'Dutch studies'. The first syllable of the term *rangaku* derives from the second syllable of the Portuguese word for 'Holland', *Oranda*, whilst *gaku* means 'study' or 'learning' in Japanese. It is in fact a broad term that covers the study in Japan not only of books written in Dutch but also of translations into Dutch and translations of them into literary Sinitic. De Bary *et al.* (2005: 362) observe that the word *rangaku* emerged in the 1770s to differentiate from the Nagasaki interpreters those with an interest in the scholarship of Holland and the West more broadly. In the late nineteenth century, the term was to some extent replaced by *yōgaku* (洋学, 'Western learning'). Mervart (2015: 15 n. 15) describes *rangaku* as a brand name used to distinguish itself in the 'intellectual marketplace' in the later Edo period. In this regard it can be contrasted with *kangaku* (漢学, 'Chinese studies', literally 'Han studies') and indeed *wagaku* 和学 or *kokugaku* 国学, learning based on classical Japanese texts (Clements 2015: 96; Boot 2013: 190).

© CHRISTOPHER JOBY, 2021 | DOI:10.1163/9789004438651_004

books but also the language that mediated this science. By the nineteenth century we can talk in terms of thousands of Japanese students of the Dutch language and *rangaku*. Although the study of the language and the knowledge it mediated often went together, the focus in this chapter is on the learning of the Dutch language.

2 Status Quaestionis

Much detailed work on the learning of Dutch by Japanese and the materials that facilitated this process has been done by De Groot (2005). Unfortunately, this remains unpublished, but is an invaluable source for this subject and the present chapter makes frequent reference to it. De Groot has, however, published several articles and book chapters on specific aspects of this subject, to which the present chapter refers (e.g., De Groot 2004, 2016). Additionally, De Groot (2005) provides a useful literature review (pp. 12–22), and again this chapter refers to several of the works mentioned there. One part of this story to which De Groot pays less attention is the very beginning of Japanese attempts to learn Dutch. Another author who has published books and articles on the first steps taken by the Japanese to learn Dutch and the learning materials developed to support this process is Wolfgang Michel. He focusses on the role played by physicians at Deshima which was two-fold. First, they showed the Japanese that they had something to learn from the Dutch, i.e., medical knowledge, and second, with the assistance of interpreters, they provided rudimentary wordlists, which allowed the Japanese to begin to engage with the Dutch language. Michel (1999) takes as its subject the German physician, Caspar Schamberger, while Michel (1993b) analyses the role of another German physician, Engelbert Kaempfer, in transmitting knowledge of Dutch to his Japanese assistant. Other authors, too, have described Kaempfer's work in teaching Dutch such as Paul van der Velde (1993, 1995). The *opperhoofd* Isaac Titsingh did much to promote Dutch among his Japanese associates. He gave tuition in Dutch, corresponded with Japanese in Dutch, developed learning materials and provided Japanese friends with learners and lexicons. Frank Lequin's books (e.g., 1990, 2003) are invaluable sources on this aspect of Titsingh's work.

Several authors focus less on individuals and more on the networks and institutions that facilitated the learning of Dutch. Terrence Jackson (2016) analyses the social and intellectual networks that mediated the spread of Dutch as well as of Western learning. His work on discursive spaces, where information and ideas were exchanged about the Dutch language and learning, complements work on learning materials and individual Japanese by authors such as

De Groot. Richard Rubinger (1982) and Ellen Gardner Nakamura (2005) both
analyse *loci* for learning Dutch. While Rubinger investigates the private academies established during the Tokugawa period, where the Dutch language and
rangaku were taught, Nakamura explores the spread of Dutch and *rangaku*
outside the established centres of learning such as Nagasaki and Edo. This was
often facilitated by physicians returning to their *han* after studying in one of
these towns.

Editions of the accounts of learning Dutch by *rangakusha* add to our knowledge of this subject. Two to mention here are Sugita Genpaku (1969) and
Fukuzawa Yukichi (2007), both of whom record the challenges they faced
in trying to master a language so different from their own. Japanese authors
have published primary sources, which contribute to our understanding of
this subject. Numata Jirō (1976) has published work in Dutch by the Japanese
scholar Aoki Kon'yō, while Katagiri Kazuo (1985) provides extensive details
of the Dutch interpreters at Deshima. Matsuda Kiyoshi (1998) gives details of
Dutch books and learning materials owned by Dutch and Japanese. These help
us to understand the circulation of learning materials such as Dutch lexicons
and grammars. This chapter brings much of this material to those who do not
read Japanese for the first time. Furthermore, it makes extensive reference to
Dutch primary sources such as the Deshima *dagregister* (factory journal) and
to the learning materials themselves. Copies of many of these are preserved in
the Special Collections at Leiden University Library. Extensive bibliographical
details are provided in the Index of Japanese Primary Sources by Title. These
include references to these materials in the Serrurier (1896) and Kerlen (1996)
catalogues and the ID numbers from the online NIJL database.

3   Learning Dutch up to 1670

Most of the information that we have about the learning of Dutch in the Hirado
period and the first decades of the Nagasaki period comes from the *dagregisters*, typically in the form of metalinguistic comment. Occasionally, we have
other sources such as wordlists that include Dutch. Katagiri (1985: 7, quoted in
Kornicki 2018: 93) suggests that there were already Japanese interpreters with
a command of Dutch active on Kyushu in the 1630s, working either for the
VOC or for Nagasaki officials, who, one assumes, had dealings with the Dutch.
Unfortunately, there is little information about how they learnt the language. It
may well have been from the Dutch, as there seem to have been fewer restrictions on contact between the Dutch and Japanese at Hirado than there would

be at Nagasaki. Over time, interpreters, who were often hereditary, would learn some of the language within their families (Kornicki 2018: 93).

In August 1641, at the start of the Dutch period at Deshima, the VOC employed just two Japanese interpreters along with a clerk, two cooks and two valets (Vermeulen *et al.* 1986–: XI:22–23). It had been compelled by the Nagasaki *bugyō* to dismiss others whom it employed. In time, the VOC was in fact no longer allowed to employ interpreters. Instead, the Dutch were required to make use of the services of interpreters selected and employed by the *bugyō*'s office (De Groot 2005: 23).[2]

While some interpreters knew only Portuguese, others had acquired some Dutch (De Groot 2005: 24). The *dagregister* for 1641 records that the interpreter Hideshima Tōzaemon was proficient in Portuguese and quite competent (*redelijck ervaren*) in Dutch (*Diaries*: V:136). However, we are not told how he acquired his knowledge of Dutch. Tōzaemon appears again in the *dagregister* in 1643, when he is said to be proficient (*wel ervaeren*) in Dutch. We are also told that he had come from Hirado and had been a servant and interpreter for the VOC there. It may well be that extended contact with the Dutch at Hirado had allowed him to gain a knowledge of the Dutch language (Vermeulen *et al.* 1986–: XI:117; *Diaries*: VII:136). An entry in 1645 tells us that Tōzaemon spoke Dutch quite well. However, it also tells us that he had slit his belly, i.e., committed *seppuku*, although the reason is not given (Vermeulen *et al.* 1986–: XI:204).

Two years earlier, in 1643, a knowledge of Dutch among four interpreters is hinted at. They were required to provide a verbatim translation of a proclamation from the shogun into Dutch. Jan van Elseracq (*opperhoofd* 1641–42; 1643–44) records that the translation was made. Van Elseracq was subsequently questioned to ensure that he had understood the contents of the proclamation. If, as seems likely, one or more of these interpreters did know Dutch, we are not, unfortunately, told how they acquired their knowledge of the language (Vermeulen *et al.* 1986–: XI:152).[3] At this time, as Willem Verstegen (*opperhoofd* 1646–47) noted, Portuguese interpreters were still employed to

---

2 Kornicki (2018: 93) observes that this was much to the dissatisfaction of the Dutch, who no longer trusted the interpreters, seeing them as something akin to spies for the Nagasaki *bugyō* and his overlord, the Tokugawa shogun. For the Dutch view that the interpreters also acted as spies see Vos (1980: 11).

3 The interpreters were Koffioye (spelt in the *dagregister* as Kohyōe), Ishibashi Shōsuke, Nishi Kichibyōe and Namura Hachizaemon. Nishi Kichibyōe was one of long line of interpreters from the Nishi family. One possibility is that some of them had worked for the Dutch at Hirado. This seems to have been the case for Namura Hachizaemon at least (Vermeulen *et al.* 1986–: XI:2).

facilitate communication between Dutch and Japanese (Vermeulen *et al.* 1986–: XI:249).[4] In 1650 a VOC delegation visited Edo on the annual *hofreis*. One member of the delegation, the Swede Juriaen Schedel, gave lessons in ballistics to the Japanese during an extended stay in Edo (Vos 1980: 4). Unfortunately, no details survive of the language in which the tuition was given. One possibility is Dutch, but another is Portuguese. Another member of the Dutch delegation was the German-born physician, Caspar Schamberger. One of the shogun's counsellors, Inaba Masanori (1623–96), *daimyō* (大名, 'feudal lord') of Odawara, was suffering from gout. The physicians trained in Chinese medicine were not able to cure him, but Schamberger was able to do so (Michel 1999: 117). From this point on, the shogun and his courtiers realized that the Dutch, including the German Schamberger, had something to offer them in terms of medicine and so they asked Schamberger to stay in Edo in order to give instruction in Western medicine. He remained in Edo for ten months and in the course of time, a medical school or approach to medicine based on his instruction, called the *Kasuparuryū* (カスパル流, 'the school of Caspar'), emerged (De Groot 2005: 26).

Some interpreters made progress in Dutch. In 1651, Shizuki Magobē was said to speak good Dutch (*die goet Duyts spreeckt*) (*Diaries*: XII:224). One interpreter whose knowledge of Dutch was limited was the junior interpreter, Motoki Ryōi (1628–97). In 1664/65, he was appointed interpreter for the *hofreis* to Edo. However, as he knew little of the court etiquette and furthermore little Dutch, Jacob Gruijs (*opperhoofd* 1664–65), sought a replacement for him (Vermeulen *et al.* 1986–: XIII:139). One other Japanese to mention here is Nishi Genpo (also Kichibei ?–1684). He worked as an interpreter at Nagasaki and knew both Dutch and Portuguese. He took instruction in Western medicine from the Dutch physician, Willem ten Rhijne (1647–1700), who was at Deshima from 1674 to 1676.[5] Genpo would eventually become the shogun's chief physician. In 1668 he received a diploma signed by Constantin Ranst (*opperhoofd* 1667–68) (Michel 2001: 416; Goodman 2013: 38; Iwao 1961: 173–174).[6]

---

4   For the dates of the *opperhoofden*, visit http://wolfgangmichel.web.fc2.com/serv/histmed/dejimasurgeons.html. Accessed 5 April 2020.

5   Ten Rhijne was one of the first, if not the first, Dutch physicians in Japan, who had received a thorough medical training. He studied at Franeker and Leiden (Vos 1980: 4).

6   Iwao provides an English translation of the diploma. Although the original language of the diploma is not stated it is likely to have been Dutch.

4 Learning Dutch after 1670

Initially, there were three ranks of interpreter: *ōtsūji* (大通詞, 'senior interpreter'), *kotsūji* (小通詞, 'junior interpreter'), and *keikotsūji* (稽古通詞, 'apprentice interpreter').[7] In order to keep an eye on the Japanese interpreters and the Dutch, officials known as *metsuke* (目付) were appointed by the *bakufu* in Edo. In addition to the 'core' interpreters there was a large group of interpreters, called the *naitsūji* (内通詞), who only became active for two to three months each year when Dutch ships were in Nagasaki Bay.[8] Precise figures for the number of active interpreters are difficult to establish, although when Dutch ships were in port their number may have been as high as one hundred and fifty despite the fact that there were usually only about twenty Europeans at Deshima (De Groot 2005: 24–25).[9]

In the seventeenth century, Dutch classes for junior interpreters were held in the chambers of the *tsūji nakama* (通詞仲間, 'Interpreters' Guild') in Edo-machi Street just outside Deshima.[10] Here, they were drilled by their Japanese seniors, without the input of the Dutch. This would not necessarily be a disadvantage, but the evidence available leads to the conclusion that the interpreters' command of Dutch was lacking in certain respects. During the seventeenth century, the Japanese who studied Dutch focussed mainly on the spoken language and had a limited vocabulary (Vande Walle 2001b: 129).

No doubt aware of this, in November 1673, the Nagasaki *bugyō* ordered young boys aged 10 to 12 to go to Deshima to receive daily instruction in speaking, reading and writing Dutch directly from the VOC employees on the island.[11] In 1684–85 and in subsequent years there are further references in the

---

7 Other ranks emerged, such as for example *kuchi keiko* (口稽古, 'student'), a grade below *keikotsūji*. This was the rank at which Motoki Yoshinaga began his career as interpreter (at the age of 13). He would rise to become an *ōtsūji* (Harada 2000: 122).

8 *Naitsūji* could be translated as 'informal or private interpreters'.

9 For an extensive list of interpreters in a broadly chronological order, see Katagiri (1985: 208–226).

10 The translation 'Interpreters' Guild' is given by De Groot (2005: 3 n. 10), reflecting the monopoly that these interpreters enjoyed. In Dutch documents written at Deshima this body is usually referred to as the *tolkencollege* ('College of interpreters'); see for example, Lequin (2011: 155). In note 157, Lequin provides a summary of the constituency and function of the *tsūji nakama*.

11 The *dagregister* entry for 9 November 1673 reads, *9en Comen de tolcken ons bekent maecken dat den Gouverneur [...] geordonneert hadde, seeckere Japanse jongen van omtrent 10 a 12 Jaeren out, dagelijcx hier op het eijlandt te laeten comen om door een van 't Compt. dienaeren in de Nederlantse taal, mitsgaders int lesen en schrijven deselve onderwesen te worden.* [9th. The interpreters came to inform us that the Governor ... had ordered certain Japanese boys of about 10 to 12 years old to come here daily to the island to be instructed

dagregister to junior interpreters learning Dutch, but also on occasion Portuguese (Boxer 1950: 60). By the late 1680s it was clearly expected that some of the interpreters would have a serviceable knowledge of Dutch. The interpreter Namura Hachizaemon was said to speak the language well (Van der Velde 1995: 49).[12] Baba Ichirōbē was one of the best *keikotsūji*. However, he was passed over for promotion due to his rudeness (Vermeulen *et al.* 1986–: II:167–168, Blussé *et al.* 1992: 525).[13] Some, though, simply fell short in their command of Dutch. Another *keikotsūji*, Nakayama Kizaemon, was said to understand only a little Dutch (Blussé *et al.* 1992: 542).[14] The *bugyō* were angry with one interpreter, Sinnemon, who, it was thought, pretended to read Dutch (Vermeulen *et al.* 1986–: II:64).[15] There were clearly concerns about his knowledge of the language, as Hendrik van Buijtenhem (*opperhoofd* intermittently 1684–93) was required to find out who had taught him Dutch (Vermeulen *et al.* 1986–: I:65).[16]

In 1690, the German-born physician Engelbert Kaempfer (1651–1716) arrived at Deshima. He recorded that there were four senior and four junior interpreters. However, the modern Japanese scholar Itazawa Takeo mentions seven senior interpreters and up to thirty-two junior interpreters (Itazawa 1933: 17, quoted in De Groot 2005: 24). The reason for this difference is not clear. There were also the seasonal *naitsūji* discussed above (De Groot 2005: 25). Kaempfer was provided with a Japanese assistant, Imamura Gen'emon, who procured Japanese books and other materials for him (Michel 1993b: 248; Van der Velde 2000b: 25). Kaempfer taught his assistant, whom he referred to as a 'clever fellow', to read and write Dutch as well as grammar (Vande Walle 2001b: 131; Werger-Klein 1993: 56). This meant, as Kaempfer himself noted, that Gen'emon could write and speak the language much better than any Japanese interpreter

---

by one of the Company's employees in the Dutch language, in both reading and writing of the same] (quoted in De Groot (2005: 24 n. 3)). Boxer (1950: 60) also gives the date 9 November 1673. Sugimoto (1976–82: V: 907) asserts that an entry in the *dagregister* for 15 December 1670, states that it was on this date that the *bugyō* sent young persons of between ten and twelve to Deshima on daily basis to learn to read and write Dutch. Torii (2000: 117), on the other hand, places the order from the Nagasaki Governor in 1671. This may be because his office began to keep a register in that year.

12 The Dutch refer to him with various versions of his name including Nammera Gompats (Blussé *et al.* 1992: 543).

13 Ichirōbē was often drunk; he was eventually banished.

14 He was referred to as Nackajamma Diuna by the Dutch (Vermeulen *et al.* 1986–: II:180).

15 There were *bugyō* in Nagasaki and in Edo (for surety). Before the government changed hands, the *bugyō* would go to Nagasaki to inspect the Dutch ships (Blussé and Remmelink 2004: 806).

16 For Sinnemon (*Sjinemon*), see also Blussé *et al.* (1992: 549).

before him (De Groot 2005: 39). Gen'emon's Dutch would later be praised by Hendrik Dijkman (*opperhoofd* intermittently 1694–1701) (Van der Velde 1995: 48). After Kaempfer left Japan in 1692, Gen'emon continued to study and use Dutch. In September 1695, he took an examination along with two other interpreters in both Dutch and Portuguese in the presence of Dijkman and the physician Matthijs Racquet (Van der Velde 1993: 177).

Although by now young interpreters did go to the Dutch for tuition, they also continued to learn at the *tsūji nakama*. While some interpreters seem to have become quite proficient in Dutch, others were less successful. In truth they faced several obstacles. First, the interpreters would have had problems with the pronunciation of Dutch. One factor that contributed to this was that Dutch was typically recorded in the *katakana* syllabary, which does not adequately represent the wider range of syllables in Dutch, including, for example, several diphthongs (De Groot 2005: 28–29).[17] Differences between the phonology of Dutch and Japanese are analysed in detail in Chapter 5.

Second, as already noted, the position of interpreter was often hereditary, passed down from one generation to the next. There were several hereditary interpreter families whose names appear frequently in the records. These include Motoki, Yoshio, Shizuki, Kobayashi, Narabayashi and Nishi (Boxer 1950: 61).[18] Again, this is not necessarily a problem, but it did mean that interpreters were employed on the basis of the family they belonged to rather than their skills as interpreters, and furthermore, that they probably began learning Dutch from family members rather than the Dutch on Deshima. On the other hand, there were cases of men with the necessary skills being adopted into interpreter families. To some extent this alleviated the problem of natural sons who lacked language skills.

Third, the manner in which the interpreters learnt Dutch is likely to have contributed to the poor level of Dutch that some of them attained. In 1785/86 the Edo scholar, Ōtsuki Gentaku (also Bansui 1757–1827), who spent several months taking lessons from the Nagasaki interpreters, commented that their method was based largely on the rote learning of phrases, with no attention paid to the structural features of the language (De Groot 2005: 26–28, 29). This is likely to have been exacerbated by their learning the language from other Japanese rather than native speakers.

---

17   We gain an insight into how the Japanese perceived the sound of Dutch from a comment made by a Japanese who encountered members of the *hofreis* in Nagoya in 1712: 'They pronounced their language with lips and tongue and this caused a hissing sound' (Krieger 1940: 8).

18   Some of the interpreters from these families would become *rangakusha*, such as Yoshio Kōgyū (also called Kōsaku), Motoki Yoshinaga and Shizuki Tadao.

Three other points are in order. First, most of the Dutch who came to Deshima were merchants. They were considered socially inferior and it may be that there was an aversion amongst the Japanese to learning a language associated primarily with merchants. This suggestion requires further investigation (De Groot 2005: 26–27).[19] Second, one possible reason for the slow spread of Dutch in Japan, including amongst Japanese scholars, is that the interpreters who acquired a knowledge of the language were reluctant to share this with other Japanese. De Groot (2005: 25–27) posits that this is because the members of the Interpreters' Guild at Nagasaki were sworn in writing to protect 'national secrets'. We can assume, he goes on, that the Dutch language was one such secret. If this is so, then we could see Dutch in terms of a 'cryptolect' at this time, i.e., a language which was the preserve of a few, chosen individuals, who, moreover, often belonged to a small number of families.[20] Third, the persistence of Portuguese long after the expulsion of native speakers is striking. Possible reasons for this are discussed in Chapter 4.

In the eighteenth century, Nagasaki interpreters continued to learn Dutch, with the intermittent help of native speakers on Deshima. However, an important shift during this period was that scholars in Edo also began to learn Dutch. A critical figure in this regard was the eighth Tokugawa shogun Yoshimune (ruled 1716–45). He was interested in the sciences and came to recognize the value of Dutch as a *metalect*, or language that mediated knowledge about sciences such as anatomy, astronomy and botany (Nakamura 2005: 7).[21] In relation to botany, he was particularly keen on developing methods for import substitution. Therefore, he ordered several Edo scholars, Aoki Kon'yō (also Bunzō 1698–1769, it was common to have more than one name at this time), Noro Genjō (1693–1761) and Kitajima Kenshin (*fl.* 1719–38) to learn Dutch and

---

19   Olof Eriksson Willman makes the same point in his account of Japan, stating that as the Japanese considered the Dutch to be merchants, they were held in very low esteem (Willman 2013: 64, 120 n. 234). The *bushi* (武士) were at the top of the social order, and under them came the farmers, artisans and the merchants in that order.

20   Despite these concerns, the interpreters clearly played a vital role in the Dutch commercial enterprise on Deshima and had their own room on the island (Vermeulen *et al.* 1986–: 1:35). Their importance to this project is underlined by frequent reference to them in the *Generale Missiven* ('General Reports') sent by the Governors General of the Dutch East Indies to the *Heren XVII* of the VOC. However, there is little reference in these reports to the language they used. This silence may suggest that it was Dutch, although this is not certain (Coolhaas 1960–64).

21   Yoshimune realized the importance of studying European science by seeing the illustrations to Johannes Jonston's book on quadrupeds. This was originally written in Latin, but a Dutch translation of it was brought to Japan. Yoshimune requested the Dutch to translate the animals' names for him (Screech 2012: 319–320).

what he called the 'horizontal script' from the Nagasaki interpreters who visited Edo on the *hofreis* in the 1730s and 1740s.[22] Kon'yō, who would write an
account of the Dutch monetary system and some treatises on the Dutch language, received help in reading the Western writing system from the Nagasaki
interpreters (Vos 1963: 343). Among those he met were Yoshio Kōgyū (1724–
1800, also Kōsaku) and Nishi Zenzaburō (1715–68) (De Groot 2005: 101–102;
Keene 1969: 14; Goodman 2013: 148).[23] Zenzaburō, along with another interpreter, Moriyama Kinzaemon (1721–67), was praised for his knowledge of Dutch
and described in the *dagregister* as one of the pillars of the *tsūji nakama*.[24]

Kon'yō was tutored with a Dutch book that he received from one of the
interpreters. This was probably Barend Hakvoord's *Oprecht Onderwijs der
Letter-konst* ('True Instruction in Grammar', 1727) (Sugimoto 1976–82: V:912;
De Groot 2005: 106). In fact, Kon'yō adds to our understanding of how the
Japanese acquired a knowledge of Dutch, and more specifically how they were
able to both understand and internalize more complex Dutch sentences, using
a method that owed something to the manner in which texts written in literary Sinitic were translated into Japanese. He would put a Japanese gloss over
the Dutch text, give a phonetic version of the Dutch in Japanese *katakana*,
provide a consecutive Chinese translation of the Dutch and finally re-arrange
the Japanese words into a Japanese sentence (Nishikawa-van Eester 2017:
246–247). Kon'yō compiled rudimentary wordlists in which he gave *katakana*
and *kanji* equivalents. He also practised writing Roman letters in various scripts
such as Gothic (which he referred to as *drukletter* ('print letter')) and cursive
(*trekletter*, 'decorative letter'). Furthermore, he wrote out syllables in Roman
script and added *katakana* equivalents. This is of interest as he often gave two
katakana equivalents, one for a short vowel, the other for a long vowel, e.g.,
for 'ha', he gives both ハ /ha/ and ハア /haa/. This is an important distinction
in Dutch and demonstrates a good grasp of its phonology (Numata *et al.* 1976:
11–68; De Groot 2005: 101–108). Kon'yō would pass his knowledge of Dutch and
indeed texts written in Dutch onto other *rangakusha*. One of these was Maeno

---

22   Noro Genjō was a *honzōgakusha* 本草学者, i.e., someone who studied pharmacognosy
      (*honzōgaku* 本草学). This recommended him to shogun Yoshimune, who had an interest
      in the subject, and who appointed Genjō as the official responsible for Dutch pharmacog-
      nosy. He would write a work on Dutch plants, *Oranda honzō wage* ('Dutch *materia medica*
      translated into Japanese') (Shirahata 2001: 267, NIJL ID 2132856). See also De Groot (2005:
      44) and Vos (1963: 343).

23   Feenstra Kuiper (1921: 253), observes that Kon'yō found the quality of the Dutch spoken by
      the interpreters inadequate and so turned to the Dutch in order to make progress in the
      language.

24   Moriyama Kinzaemon was the adopted son of Moriyama Tokudayū; see Blussé and
      Remmelink (2004: 241, 854).

Ryōtaku (1723–1803). He acquired an excellent knowledge of Dutch and experimented with writing Roman letters in many different forms. He wrote the alphabet in Gothic script, with *katakana* approximations underneath, on occasion writing capital letters, or *hōfutorēteru* (Dutch: *hoofdletter*) as he described them (Numata *et al.* 1976: 69–183, esp. 76). Furthermore, he wrote the Roman numerals with *katakana* equivalents, e.g., エル ('eru') for L (50) and セ ('se') for C (100). In addition, he made a table of syllables, giving two-letter syllables in Roman script with *katakana* equivalents underneath, e.g., AM アム (pronounced 'amu'). Ryōtaku wrote *katakana* equivalents for things such as the Dutch numbers (1 *een*, 2 *teuee*, etc.), and the points of the compass (e.g., *Ōsuto* (*Oost* = East) and *Nōrudo* (*Noord* = North)) (Numata *et al.* 1976: 84, 88, 98). In short, he filled many pages with his attempts at writing Dutch and transcribing and translating it into Japanese. These attempts can perhaps be described as *probationes linguae*.

Ryōtaku would, in turn, use his knowledge of Dutch to assist the Edo scholar Sugita Genpaku (1733–1817) in his translation into Japanese of the Dutch translation (*Ontleedkundige Tafelen* ('Anatomical Tables' 1734)) of a Latin edition of a work by Johann Adam Kulmus. The project to translate this book took almost three and a half years to complete and was eventually published in 1774 as *Kaitai shinsho* (lit. 'New Treatise on Anatomy'). In 1815, Genpaku completed *Rangaku kotohajime* ('The Beginnings of Dutch Learning', first published 1869), in which he describes the trials and tribulations of translating from Dutch to Japanese. In it, he notes that the Nagasaki interpreter, Nishi Zenzaburō, mentioned above, had discouraged him from learning Dutch, arguing that it was too difficult (De Groot 2005: 25; Sugita 1969: 14–15). Zenzaburō was not alone among Japanese in expressing how difficult he found it to learn Dutch.[25] Despite initially being dissuaded, Genpaku would nevertheless persist with learning the language. In fact, in *Rangaku kotohajime* he made an interesting contrast between Chinese and Dutch. He observed that while Chinese was, as he saw it, primarily a rhetorical language, Dutch expressed facts and was easier to learn (De Bary *et al.* 2005: 370). He observes that the articles *de* and *het*, which are lacking in Japanese, left him and his fellow translators at sea and even a word such as *zinnen* (Dutch 'senses') was beyond their comprehension

---

25   For example, Fukuda Sōtei, a pupil of Takano Chōei, expressed it in a Dutch proverb that he wrote in his diary in 1836: 'Drops of water make a stone hollow, not by their force, but because they fall so many times upon it' (Nakamura 2005: 87). Nakamura refers to Kanai Kōsaku, 'Fukuda Kōsai no rangaku no michi to Agatsuma rangaku' 1985, p. 38, as her source. I have been unable to consult this. However, it is likely that the original Dutch expression is 'De gestage druppel holt de steen' ('The constant drip hollows out the stone'). I thank Wim Boot for providing me with this information.

(Sugita 1969). Despite these difficulties, many words that Genpaku and his colleagues coined in order to render the Dutch anatomical terms are still in use in contemporary Modern Japanese (cMJ). Other Japanese took advantage of the Dutch visit to Edo on the *hofreis*. The interpreter Imamura Kinzō (also Sanbei 1722–78) asked for a copy of the Dutch alphabet in longhand and print on behalf of the Nagasaki *bugyō* in Edo, Kuze Hirotami, *Tango-no-kami* (1737–1800) (Blussé and Remmelink 2004: 395).

In Nagasaki, the interpreters were periodically required to take exams. For example, they took exams held by the *opperhoofd* on the orders of the *bugyō* in 1768 and 1778 (Boxer 1950: 63; Blussé and Remmelink 2004: 327). In 1777, apprentice interpreters in Nagasaki were sent to Deshima for a couple of days per month to learn Dutch from native speakers. An initial condition was that they would be taught not in the houses of the Dutch, but in those of the *otona* (乙名, the local officials responsible for managing and maintaining Deshima). But, in November 1777 the *dagregister* records that the Dutch were planning to petition the Nagasaki *bugyō* to teach the apprentices in their own homes so that they could show them Dutch objects. This would, we are told, give the interpreters more opportunities to ask questions; i.e., questions that they might not ask in the presence of their Japanese seniors (Vermeulen *et al.* 1986–: VIII:167). Nevertheless, this attempt was not successful, so the VOC assistants agreed to teach Dutch to the interpreters in the house of the *otona*. An entry for 7 December 1777 tells us that one of the assistants gave lessons to junior interpreters at the house of the *otona* on Deshima. Thereafter, there are intermittent records in the *dagregister* of the Dutch assistants giving language instruction to the apprentice interpreters, as it was recognized that this would be of use to the VOC. In April 1778, the assistant Michiel Adriaan van Groenenberg gave them instruction, while in January and February 1779 the assistants Fredrik Willem Schindeler and Harmanus Meijer gave instruction in the house of the *otona*. However, at the end of February it was agreed that during the quiet period, perhaps somewhat counterintuitively, lessons would be suspended (Vermeulen *et al.* 1986–: VIII:167, 173, 179–180). Nevertheless, the arrangement clearly worked well for in July 1779 the Japanese asked if the instruction could be increased to eight times per month. Arend Willem Feith (*opperhoofd* intermittently 1771–81) gave permission for this (Vermeulen *et al.* 1986–: VIII:181).

Isaac Titsingh, whom we met in Chapter 1, was one of the most learned Deshima *opperhoofden*. He took it upon himself to try and improve the quality of the interpreters' Dutch. He encouraged the interpreters to write dialogues in Dutch, which he would then correct and return to the interpreters who would then translate them into Japanese. This, Titsingh reckoned, would help the interpreters' Dutch as well as his own Japanese. The characters in the dialogues varied. One was between someone from Osaka and a local person from Nagasaki, while another was between friends who had not seen each other for a long time (Lequin 2003: 81). Indeed, one Japanese, Hori Dennojō, produced a Dutch-Japanese phrase book dated to around 1780. This remained in manuscript with Titsingh's corrections (Lequin 2003: 84).[26]

In the 1780s there are further *dagregister* entries indicating that the Dutch gave instruction in their language to trainee interpreters. On 29 January 1784, Hendrik Romberg (1744–93, *opperhoofd* intermittently 1783–90) recorded that the *bugyō* was going to grant permission for 'the provisional junior interpreters and apprentices' to visit Deshima fifteen days a month for language instruction from the Dutch. They had to seal this in blood! A few days later, on 2 February, he records that they came for their first lesson (Vermeulen *et al.* 1986–: IX:51, 52). Shortly afterwards, Romberg departed for Edo on the *hofreis*. On 6 February his deputy Albertus François Domburg recorded that the apprentice interpreters came for Dutch lessons and would continue to do so every other day (Vermeulen *et al.* 1986–: IX:55). While some interpreters made progress, others were less successful. In 1786, Johan Fredrik Baron van Rheede tot de Parkeler (1757–1802, *opperhoofd* intermittently 1785–89) recorded that the Dutch did not trust the senior interpreter Narabayashi Shinbei (or Eizaemon 1722–87) to translate his words and compliments on a public occasion, because of his 'scant knowledge of the Dutch language' (Vermeulen *et al.* 1986–: IX:99; Blussé and Remmelink 2004: 858).

In 1786/7 Romberg recorded that he was continuing to give instruction to interpreters and that they would even come to his room to learn. He also wrote that the junior interpreter Narabayashi Jūbei (1750?–1801) had told him that several great nobles were applying themselves to learning the Dutch language, and indeed manners, and that they had great hopes for the future (Blussé and Remmelink 2004: 857). A few weeks later, Romberg records that he himself was giving instruction to the children of several nobles including the son of the Lord of Tanba, who was learning to read Dutch.[27] He goes on, 'Thus, I am spending my time here as a schoolteacher, which I don't find enjoyable' (Vermeulen *et al.* 1986–: IX:128–129).

As knowledge of Dutch and the learning it mediated spread, *daimyō* often gave financial support for *rangakusha* to pursue their studies. This was no mere altruism on their part but resulted from a desire to improve agricultural

---

26   Hori Dennojō's name is spelt variously including Dennozio (Blussé and Remmelink 2004: 846).

27   At this time, the Lord of Tanba was the *daimyō* and close friend of Isaac Titsingh, Kutsuki Masatsuna.

yields and exploit natural resources in their domain. They clearly considered that it would be useful to invest in these students to help them achieve this. Some *daimyō* went a step further and learnt some Dutch themselves. One was Shimazu Shigehide, Lord of Satsuma (1745–1833), an early supporter of *rangaku*. The *dagregister* for 1787 records an encounter just outside Edo between Shigehide and the Dutch on the *hofreis*. He addressed Romberg in 'broken Dutch' saying 'Romberg, I have not seen you for a long time'.[28]

Although the interpreters were appointed by the Nagasaki *bugyō*, the *bugyō* themselves do not, in general, seem to have taken much interest in the Dutch language. However, an entry in the *dagregister* in March 1796 indicates that the *bugyō* at that time was an 'amateur of the Dutch language' who to the great concern of the interpreters was making progress in learning Dutch and so, they feared, might be able to gauge their own competence in the language. Whilst some of the interpreters had a good knowledge of the language, this was by no means the case for all of them. Gijsbert Hemmij (*opperhoofd* 1792–98) reports that the *bugyō* himself tested the interpreters on parts of Rembert Dodoens's herbal *Cruydt-boeck* that they had been set three months earlier, although he does not tell us what the results of the examination were (Vermeulen *et al.* 1986–: x:84; Blussé and Remmelink 2004: 700). Apart from the interpreters, Buddhist priests, local Japanese officials and Japanese merchants also visited Deshima. Our current state of knowledge does not allow us to answer the question as whether any of those belonging to the first two groups knew any Dutch; in most, if not all, cases, they will probably have relied on the interpreters to communicate with the Dutch.[29] As for merchants, at least in the late Tokugawa period, some did know Dutch (Assendelft de Coningh 1879: II:19).

In concluding this section, many thousands of Japanese learnt Dutch, primarily at Nagasaki and Edo, but also elsewhere in Japan.[30] Those at Nagasaki

---

28 Dutch: 'Romberg, ik heb je in lang niet gezien' (Hesselink 2005: 521; Vermeulen *et al.* 1986–: IX:127). In Late Modern Dutch this would be 'Ik heb je al lang niet gezien'. Jonathan Israel (2011: 580) notes that Shimazu Shigehide spoke Dutch fluently, although this seems to be somewhat of an overstatement. On his second *hofreis* to Edo in 1782, Isaac Titsingh received a visit from Shigehide as well as the Shogunal Astronomer. However, Titsingh did not record the language(s) in which they communicated (Lequin 2011: 66).

29 One other group who may have learnt some Dutch were the *Orandayuki*. Vos (1971: 631) observes that they mixed Dutch and Malay words in their conversation. Hesselink (1995: 200) asserts that some of them spoke Dutch quite well, citing Vos (1971). He does not, however, give a page number, and I cannot find such a statement in Vos's article. It may well be that some of the *Orandayuki* did speak decent Dutch given the amount of time they spent with Dutchmen. However, more research needs to be done before such a conclusion can be justified.

30 For numbers of those who studied Dutch at Nagasaki, see Hiramatsu (1999: 409–412).

were above all the interpreters. However, there were often complaints about the quality of their Dutch. In the 1690s, Engelbert Kaempfer complained about the general standard of Dutch amongst the Nagasaki interpreters.[31] In April 1751, Hendrick van Homoet (*opperhoofd* intermittently 1749–54) noted that the interpreters could only express themselves in 'faulty Dutch' (Blussé and Remmelink 2004: 163). In November 1768, Jan Crans (*opperhoofd* intermittently 1763–69) recorded that he found it extremely difficult to communicate with some of the interpreters (Blussé and Remmelink 2004: 327).[32] Similarly, in April 1780, Isaac Titsingh reports that on the *hofreis* seven shogunal physicians visited the Dutch. They asked Titsingh some questions. However, he was concerned that the incompetence of the interpreters might mean that his answers would be a hindrance rather than a help to the physicians (Blussé and Remmelink 2004: 431).

5   The Formalization of Studying Dutch and *rangaku*

Towards the end of the eighteenth century, concerted efforts were made to improve the quality of education in Dutch at Nagasaki and elsewhere with the compilation of learning materials such as grammars, dictionaries and learners to assist Japanese in gaining a functional knowledge of the language. Examples of these are considered in the next section. Already in the seventeenth century, Japanese were developing intellectual traditions or schools of thought, *ryū* (流), based on Dutch medical texts and oral instructions. In the eighteenth century, the houses of leading *rangakusha* formed nodes for the exchange of information and ideas on *rangaku*, and by the end of this century, the first private schools dedicated to *rangaku* were being established. As interest in Dutch sources developed, so did a desire to learn the Dutch language.

5.1   *Schools of Thought* ryū (流)

Mention has already been made of the *Kasuparuryū*, or 'Caspar-style of medicine' which studied the teachings of the German physician, Caspar Schamberger. It continued to function until the end of the Tokugawa period (1603–1868).[33] Early examples of manuscripts written by adherents of

---

31   He described one group of ten interpreters as 'spies' who hardly understood a word of Dutch between them (Van der Velde 1995: 45). See also Nagazumi (1993: 33–34).

32   Crans expressed the wish that the examinations would be devolved to the Dutch as it was extremely difficult to communicate with some of the less-experienced interpreters.

33   Michel also refers to the Japanese notion of *kasuparu-ryūgeka* or 'the Caspar school surgery' (Vos 1963: 343; Michel 1993b: 288).

the 'Caspar-style' are analysed in Chapter 6. The interpreter, Narabayashi Chinzan (1649–1711), began as a *kotsūji* in Nagasaki and subsequently became an *ōtsūji* (Clements 2015: 157). In this capacity, he worked closely with the physicians Willem Hoffman, Willem ten Rhijne and indeed Engelbert Kaempfer. In 1691 he was appointed as *baku-i* (幕医) or medical official for the *bakufu*. He would go on to establish the *Narabayashiryū* (楢林流). Further investigation would be required to establish whether and to what extent adherents to this intellectual tradition used Dutch (Ianello 2012: 110; Michel 1993b: 286).

At the end of this century and in the early years of the eighteenth century, other schools or intellectual traditions, emerged, which although giving priority to Chinese medicine, certainly engaged with Western medicine. Among these is the *Yoshidaryū* (吉田流, Yoshida-style). This was founded by Yoshida Jian (1644–1713) who had studied at Nagasaki and who wrote two treatises on medicine (Goodman 2013: 40–41).

5.2 Loci *for Intellectual Exchange*

Dutch was taught at the *tsūji nakama*, and so this can be considered a *locus* for learning Dutch. As we have seen, the efforts of senior interpreters in instructing their junior counterparts in the language had mixed results. But we should also note, as in the case of Narabayashi Chinzan, that it fostered an early interest in Dutch learning (*rangaku*), particularly in the field of medicine. As interest in the content of Dutch books amongst the interpreters increased, they began to assemble a small library in their chambers just outside Deshima. This work started towards the end of the seventeenth century (De Groot 2005: 3).

Terrence Jackson makes the important point that in the second half of the eighteenth century regular meetings in private houses, sometimes referred to as 'salons', were often the 'primary generative nexus' for the learning of Dutch and the texts it mediated in cities such as Edo (Jackson 2009: 46–99).[34] In Edo, the meetings, known as *Oranda zashiki* (和蘭座敷), held by the physician Katsuragawa Hosan (also Kuninori, 1728–83), which began in the late 1750s, were probably the most famous.[35] They were convened at his home near Nihonbashi, close to the Nagasakiya. These were discursive spaces, where guests would drink *sake* and discuss what they had learned about Dutch medicine and science. Participants included Maeno Ryōtaku and other *rangakusha*, such

---

34 See also Jackson (2016: 41–76).
35 *Zashiki* (座敷) are mat rooms where these meetings or 'salons' were held. The *Oranda zashiki* were sometimes referred to as *Oranda beya* ('Dutch room').

as Hosan's son, Katsuragawa Hoshū (1751–1809) (Jackson 2016: 62). As well as functioning as *loci* for knowledge exchange, *Oranda zashiki* were spaces where wealthy participants could offer capital to participants with the necessary knowledge for projects such as translations.[36] One very knowledgeable participant was the *rangakusha* Ōtsuki Gentaku, mentioned above.[37] He came from Ichinoseki domain in northern Honshu. From there he had been sent to Edo to be tutored by Sugita Genpaku. However, it was Genpaku's fellow Edo scholar, Maeno Ryōtaku, who would instruct Gentaku in the fundamentals of the Dutch language, and in a short while he became 'thoroughly versed in the essentials of Dutch learning'. He was then sent to Nagasaki to learn more Dutch from the interpreters, particularly Motoki Yoshinaga (also Einoshin, 1735–94), and was partly funded by Kutsuki Masatsuna (1750–1802), *daimyō* of Fukuchiyama domain in Tanba (De Bary *et al.* 2005: 371; Rubinger 1982: 107). Masatsuna was a *ranpeki-daimyō*, one of the *daimyō* who were 'crazy' about all things Dutch. Yoshinaga had clearly devoted much time to studying Dutch, closely analysing Dutch pronunciation and the writing system (Vande Walle 2001b: 137–138). In Nagasaki, meetings were convened on the upper floor of the Dutch-style house of the interpreter, Yoshio Kōgyū, mentioned above. This came to be known as the *Kōmō zashiki* ('the Dutch (lit. 'red-haired') mat-room') and became famous amongst scholars throughout Japan (Clements 2015: 157).[38]

Returning to Gentaku, we get a flavour of the results of his study of Dutch in *Seihin taigo* ('Conversations with Western Visitors', c. 1800).[39] Here, he recorded Dutch words, phrases and proverbs that he learnt from native speakers, written in Roman script with *katakana* pronunciation guides and *kanji* translation. Sometimes the Roman script is not quite right. He writes *versnaapling* where it should be *versnapering*, meaning a tasty snack.[40] The name of the *opperhoofd* Mr. Gijsbert Hemmij is rendered in *katakana* as *Mēsuteru Geisuberuto Hemumii*, reflecting the classic Consonant-Vowel pattern of Japanese phonotactics, but also hinting at how the Japanese pronounced Hemmij's name. Gentaku quotes Dutch proverbs such as *Het geld dat stom is, maakt regt dat krom is* (lit. 'Money which is dumb, can make bent things straight', i.e., money

---

36 Boot (2008: 90–91) gives the example of Matsūra Seizan acquiring from Yoshio Kōgyū a copy of the Dutch translation of Kaempfer's 'Description of Japan', an appendix of which Shizuki Tadao would translate.

37 See Jackson (2016: 64) for Gentaku's attendance at the Katsuragawa *Oranda zashiki*.

38 Furukawa Koshōken refers to the *Kōmō zashiki* in his journal *Saiyū zakki* ('Miscellaneous Records of Travels to the West', 1783). Quoted in Yonemoto (2003: 87).

39 The NIJL database (ID 3184347) gives a terminus *post quem* of Kansei 6, i.e., 1794. It was published in facsimile in 1978.

40 In the seventeenth century, the variant *versnapeling* is recorded (WNT).

allows people to do what is not right (either by buying other off, or bribing them)). Furthermore, he inserts the occasional words of English, French and Latin with *katakana* added for pronunciation. Gentaku also lists the names of Dutch medical books about which the Dutch physicians informed him and fellow *rangakusha*. In short, the work is a treasure trove of information about the European material with which Japanese engaged in the mid- to late-Tokugawa period.

5.3 *Private Schools or* shijuku (私塾) *for the Study of Dutch and* rangaku

Having returned to Edo, Gentaku established the *Shirandō* (芝蘭堂), the first *shijuku* or private academy for the study of Dutch, in Kyōbashi, Edo in 1786 (Clements 2015: 164; Vos 1963: 346).[41] Although its location changed several times, it was always situated close to the Nagasakiya (Hesselink 1995: 204). It was, though, a relatively modest institution compared to those that would emerge in the nineteenth century. It is reckoned that between 1789 and 1826, only 94 students enrolled, i.e., about 2.5 per year (Rubinger 1982: 109; Horiuchi 2003: 12).

Yoshio Kōgyū, just mentioned, taught *rangaku* to Sugita Genpaku and opened a medical school dedicated to *rangaku* in the final decades of the eighteenth century. It enrolled some six hundred students or about 34 per year (Screech 1996: 15). In some sense the establishment of these schools marked a formalization and institutionalization of the study of the Dutch language and learning, which continued into the nineteenth century. In the first half of the century, two forms of institution emerged for the study of Dutch. One was the *Bansho wage goyō* ('Office for the Translation of Barbarian Books'), which could be seen as a national research institute for *rangaku* and which made many translations from Dutch to Japanese.[42] I will have more to say on this in Chapter 6. The other type of institution is the *shijuku*, of which the *Shirandō* was an early example. Further *shijuku* were opened that specialized in *rangaku* and the language that mediated it. Two of note are the *Narutakijuku* (鳴滝塾) near Nagasaki and the *Tekijuku* (適塾) in Osaka. Let us take a closer look at these and other *shijuku*.

The *Narutakijuku* medical school at Narutaki, close to Nagasaki, was established by the German physician, Philipp Franz von Siebold (1796–1866)

---

41   At least in the early days, the study of Dutch was mainly if not completely done by process of translation (Harada 2000: 124).

42   This institution had various other names including *Bansho Shomēru* (Chomel) *wage no goyō* (Clements 2015: 185).

in 1824/5. It had around fifty to sixty students from some twenty provinces, something which contributed to the spread of Dutch medicine across Japan (Goodman 2013: 265 n. 20). In terms of numbers it seems to have been the second most popular academy in early-modern Nagasaki (Boot 2013: 200; Sansom 1973: 260; Rubinger 1982: 116). Von Siebold gave lectures in Dutch once a week as well as carrying out various medical duties in Nagasaki. The collection at Narutaki, which is now a museum, includes prescriptions in Dutch and a medical licence in Dutch conferred on one student, Kō Ryōsai (1799–1846), by Von Siebold in 1829. Students were required to write essays in Dutch. The Narutaki collection includes a student thesis (*montei ronbun* 門 弟論文) in Dutch by Ryōsai entitled *Nihon shippei-shi* ('Record of Diseases in Japan').[43] Often the themes were not related to medicine (Rubinger 1982: 116). One essay in Dutch was on comma-shaped beads (*magatama* 曲玉) by another *Narutakijuku* student, Itō Keisuke (1803–1901). He would become an important figure in the field of biology in Japan.[44] These essays in Dutch are likely to have formed part of the students' assessment there and were used by Von Siebold for his own research (Clements 2015: 162).[45] So, just as works on *rangaku* in Japanese are often the fruit of exchanges between several Japanese and Europeans, so too Western works on Japan, which are often ascribed to one author, are the result of work by both Westerners and Japanese. The fact that such intellectual exchange took place for the most part in Dutch underlines its role as a *metalect* in Tokugawa Japan.

Another student at Von Siebold's school was Takano Chōei (1804–50). He supported himself in his studies by doing paid translation work for Von Siebold. Of the forty-two extant essays written by students at the *Narutakijuku*, eleven are by Chōei (Clements 2015: 162). His Dutch-language skills were highly regarded. He would later write *Seisetsu igen sūyō* ('Fundamentals of Western Medicine', 1832), based in part on Dutch translations of medical works originally written in German and French. In 1830 Chōei himself established a school for teaching Western medicine, the *Daikandō* in Edo (Nakamura 2005: 32–37).

---

43   This is likely to be the essay listed by Goodman (2013: 265 n. 21) as *Beschrijving van eenige op Japan voorkomende merkwaardige ziekten* ('Description of some noteworthy illnesses in Japan').

44   Goodman (2013: 265 n. 21), gives the title as *Beschrijving van de 'magatama', of buigende juweel* ('Description of the 'magatama' or comma-shaped (lit. 'bowing') jewel'). At p. 265 n. 21, Goodman gives a list of the essays or dissertations, including Itō Keisuke's essay, which were incorporated into Von Siebold's *Nippon*. Of the eleven essays mentioned, five were by one student, Takano Chōei. Goodman also gives the title and author of twelve other dissertations.

45   See also Goodman (2013: 184–185) on the *Narutakijuku*.

Other students at the *Narutakijuku* would return home to their *han* or domain, contributing to the spread of Western medicine across Japan.

Other schools were opened at around this time. In 1829 in the Fukugawa district of Edo, Tsuboi Shindō (1795–1848) opened the *Nisshūdō* (日習堂), where several hundred students enrolled, and in 1833 another school devoted to *rangaku*, the *Shōsendō* (象先堂) was opened by the *rangakusha*, Itō Genboku (1801–71). This was one of the most popular schools for *rangaku*, with more than 400 students enrolling until it closed in 1870 (Goodman 2013: 177–180; Rubinger 1982: 118–119). It clearly took Dutch studies seriously with the rules of the school stating that students were forbidden to read books other than Dutch books or translations of Dutch books (Rubinger 1982: 120).

So far, the focus of our analysis of schools where Dutch was taught has been Nagasaki and Edo, which reflects the fact that many such schools were established in or close to these towns. However, this is by no means the whole story, for in the first half of the nineteenth century new nodes for learning Dutch and *rangaku* emerged. In 1822, the *Igakkan* (医学館) was established in Sendai *han*, to the north of Edo, for the study of Dutch medicine. One of the *rangakusha* in its service, Sasaki Chūtaku (1790–1846), would translate several Dutch works into Japanese (Goodman 2013: 160). In 1838, a Japanese physician, Ogata Kōan (1810–63), established a *shijuku*, the *Tekijuku*, at Kawaramachi, Osaka.[46] He had been a pupil of Tsuboi Shindō, and studied *rangaku* in Osaka, Edo and Nagasaki before returning to Osaka to set up the *Tekijuku* for the study of the Dutch language and medicine. The number of books at the *Tekijuku* is a matter of some dispute. According to one contemporary account there were only about ten books, while a later source, Kōan's great-grandson, Professor Ogata Tomio, argues that the number was much larger.[47] One Japanese translation of a Dutch book at the *Tekijuku* was *Zōshi* ('Description of the Organs', 1759) by Yamawaki Tōyō (1705–62). This was the first work on dissection-based anatomy inspired by Western medicine to be published in Japan (Clements 2015: 148 n. 33).[48] There were also Dutch books on medicine, some of which were translations of books written in other European languages including German, French and Latin; for example, we find the medical books of Georg Wilhelm Consbruch,

---

46   For an extensive account of the *Tekijuku*, see Rubinger (1982: 126–151).

47   The contemporary source is the student, Fukuzawa Yukichi. It may be that he was referring only to printed books for general use, whereas it is suggested that students had access to many more books including handwritten copies (Fukuzawa 2007: 344–346).

48   Murata (1999) provides details of how Kōan obtained some of the books for the *Tekijuku*. The article is in Japanese. It states that Kōan obtained some books from former students including Fukuzawa Yukichi, whom he asked to obtain a Dutch lexicon. Sugita Genpaku (1969: 26–27) records that he was familiar with Tōyō's book.

Handboek der Algemeene Ziektekunde ('Manual of General Pathology'), translated into Dutch from German (Amsterdam, 1817); Anthelme Richerand, *Nieuwe Grondbeginselen der Natuurkunde van den Mensch* ('New First Principles of Human Physiology'), translated from French (1st ed. Amsterdam, 1821); and *Grondbeginselen der Scheikunde* ('First Principles of Chemistry') (Amsterdam, 1803), a Dutch translation of a Latin work on chemistry by Joseph Jacob von Plenck. Students were required to spend much time copying these books for their own study. They were, though, able to make use of a set of volumes of the Dutch-Japanese lexicon, the *Zūfu Haruma* (1833) of which more below, and copies of grammars such as Matthijs Siegenbeek's *Grammatica of Nederduitsche Spraakkunst, 2nd ed.* (Leiden, 1822), and a Japanese edition of Siegenbeek's *Syntaxis of Woordvoeging der Nederduitsche Taal* (1st ed. Leiden, 1810).[49]

Both these learning aids became popular among students of Dutch in Japan. They were published by the Dutch *Maatschappij tot nut van 't algemeen* ('Society for Public Welfare'), which was dedicated to making learning accessible, and became known collectively as the 'Maatschappij grammar manuals'.[50] Other learning materials at the *Tekijuku* included Pieter Weiland's grammar, *Nederduitsche Spraakkunst* ('Dutch grammar') (Dordrecht, 1846) and his Dutch spelling guide, *Handwoordenboek voor de Spelling der Hollandsche Taal* ('Concise Dictionary for the Spelling of the Dutch language') (The Hague, 1812), and a lexicon by the Amsterdam physician, Lodewijk Meijer (1629–81), *Woordenschat, bevattende in drie deelen, de verklaring der basterdwoorden, kunstwoorden en verouderde woorden* (12th ed. Dordrecht, 1805) (Fukuzawa 2007: 344–345). The students at the *Tekijuku* compiled a lexicon of compound words for use at the school.[51]

Kōan translated Dutch medical books into Japanese. He would become personal physician to the shogun and his family in 1861 and died a year later in 1862. Amongst the students at the *Tekijuku* was Fukuzawa Yukichi (1835–1901). He was born in Nakatsu in north-east Kyushu to a low-ranking samurai family. In 1854, a few months after the return of Commodore Perry and the black ships, he set out for Nagasaki in order to study gunnery and Dutch, for he realized that anyone who wanted to study the subject would need to understand the

---

49 The *Grammatica* was also published in Deventer and Groningen.
50 See also Goodman (2013: 180–184) on the *Tekijuku*.
51 This remains in the collection at the *Tekijuku*. It was given the title in Roman script 'Diqugozen in Tekiduk verzamelae'. This mixture of transcribed Japanese and Dutch should more properly be rendered *Jukugosen in Tekijuku verzameld*, i.e., 'strips of paper with compound words collected in the Tekijuku'. I thank Wim Boot for providing this explanation.

language.[52] In his autobiography, entitled *Fukuō jiden* ('A Self-Chronicle of Old Man Fuku[zawa]', 1899), he records that his first teacher was a medical student, Matsuzaki Teiho, who had been sent to Nagasaki by the *daimyō* of Satsuma (Fukuzawa 2007: 37). He began by studying simple ABC's and notes that it took him three days to learn the twenty-six letters of the alphabet (Fukuzawa 2007: 22). He goes on to record that he often went to the 'interpreter's house' and to a house of physicians who practiced Dutch or Western medicine. He reckoned, somewhat imprecisely, that it took him fifty or a hundred days to understand something of the Dutch language. He studied Dutch for about a year in Nagasaki, which gave him a considerable advantage when he began studying at the *Tekijuku* in 1857 (Fukuzawa 2007: 25, 37). In his autobiography, he provides a short account of how learning and using Dutch took place there. There were, he records, two phases. The first involved junior students reading aloud from Siegenbeek's *Grammatica* and *Syntaxis* in the presence of their seniors. The second stage involved reading in groups (*kaidoku* 会読). Here, the students would be subject to the criticism and evaluation of more advanced students. Once they had passed this stage, students could function independently and read Dutch texts on their own. They would make use of the copy of the *Zūfu Haruma*, which was kept in a special three-mat (*tatami*) room, the 'Doeff Room', at the *Tekijuku*. If they could not find a word in it, they could consult a monolingual Dutch lexicon. Six times a month, the advanced students would read texts in a group, which were in effect tests to evaluate their progress (Horiuchi 2003: 12–13). Fukuzawa would become a *jukuchō* (塾長) or senior student monitor at the school, as he later recorded in his autobiography. This meant that he would preside over students reading the most difficult texts (Fukuzawa 2007: 56–57, 343).

In his autobiography, Fukuzawa writes that he was saddened when he reached Yokohama and discovered that no-one understood Dutch. He thus determined to learn English and was relieved to discover that he could apply his knowledge of Dutch directly to English, including its 'sideways writing' (Fukuzawa 2007: x). In 1858 Fukuzawa himself established a private *rangaku* school in Edo, which was the predecessor of Keiō University (*Keiō Gijuku Daigaku* 慶應義塾大学), founded in 1868. Likewise, the *Tekijuku* was the forerunner of Osaka University.

---

52   In an exchange with his brother he tells him that he would have to study *gensho* (原書). This refers to any books in their original language, although he describes them as books printed in the Netherlands 'with letters printed sideways' (Fukuzawa 2007: 21–22).

It is estimated that some 3,000 men studied at the *Tekijuku* (Fukuzawa 2007: 342).[53] Taking Japan as a whole, we can in fact talk in terms of many thousands of students of Western medicine and the Dutch language there in the late eighteenth and nineteenth centuries. Aoki Toshiyuki has studied the origins of over 5,000 students on the rolls of 12 famous schools of Western medicine or *ranpō* (蘭方).[54] He found that only one of Japan's 69 historical provinces, the island of Iki, had no students at these schools. This illustrates that knowledge of the Dutch language and the learning it mediated spread far beyond western Kyushu and the capital, Edo (Nakamura 2005: 100).

The desire of medical practitioners in Japan to understand Western medicine was one of the most significant reasons for Japanese wanting to gain a knowledge of Dutch. It was not only in schools such as those just discussed that students of medicine would engage with Dutch. Medical apprentices across Japan would live and work with their teachers for some seven to ten years. As part of their training in the late eighteenth and early nineteenth centuries, they would study the Dutch language (Nakamura 2005: 46). In addition to running a school, Takano Chōei taught Dutch alongside Western medicine to several physicians and would-be physicians *in situ*, as it were. Amongst these were the physicians Fukuda Sōtei (1791–1840), Yanagida Teizō and Takahashi Keisaku who lived in villages around Nakanojō in Gunma Prefecture in central Honshu. In return for his *rangaku* scholarship, they provided him with financial patronage (Nakamura 2005: 85–95). Chōei's work with these and other physicians outside the main nodes of the study of Dutch such as Nagasaki, Edo and Osaka, is part of what Nakamura (2005: 2) refers to as the 'burgeoning field of history in Japan: *zaison no rangaku* 在村の蘭学 or "study of Western learning or 'Dutch Studies' in the countryside"'. So, the study of the Dutch language and the learning it mediated did not merely take place in schools, but in complex networks, where *rangakusha* moved from place to place to further their knowledge and to transfer it and the texts that mediated Dutch learning in what Jackson refers to as a 'virtual library' system. This allowed those who could not buy these texts to have access to them (Jackson 2009: 141–227). Furthermore, in many *han* in the late eighteenth and nineteenth century, *rangaku*, including the learning of the Dutch language, was stimulated by a local *daimyō* (Goodman 2013: 147).

A useful insight into the study of Dutch and *rangaku* is provided by Hiramatsu Kanji (1999: 409–412). He analysed the details of more than 1,000

---

53   Horiuchi (2003: 12) gives a much lower figure of 612 students between 1844 and 1862.
54   This is as opposed to *kanpō* (漢方), or 'Chinese style' medicine. In reality, though, *ranpō* was a blend of Chinese and Western medicine.

people who studied at Nagasaki during the Tokugawa period. It should, however, be noted that this is not an exhaustive list and, furthermore, does not include students of several prominent schools where Dutch and *rangaku* were taught, such as Von Siebold's *Narutakijuku*, nor does it include students who only stayed for a short while. Therefore, its results are indicative. Nevertheless, they provide a useful picture of who was studying in Nagasaki, where they came from and what they studied (Boot 2013: 200). In one analysis the place of origin of 1,052 students is given by region. Here, the largest group of students, 262 or 24.9%, came from Kyushu, the island on which Nagasaki is situated, 204 (19.4%) came from Chūgoku, the part of Honshu nearest to Kyushu, 121 (11.5%) students came from Tōhoku in the north of Honshu and one student even came from Hokkaido (Hiramatsu 1999: 409). This illustrates that students came from all over Japan to study in Nagasaki. Second, Hiramatsu provides an analysis of 1433 students in Nagasaki by subject. The most popular subject by far was medicine (560 students). The second most popular subject was *rangaku* (132), followed by gunnery (128). These figures are further analysed by the region from which students came. Of the 132 students who studied *rangaku*, the largest group came from Kyushu (36), while the second largest group came from the smallest of the four main islands, Shikoku. Sixteen students came from distant Tōhoku, and one from Hokkaido. This analysis also indicates that many different subjects were studied at Nagasaki. Apart from those just mentioned, we find subjects as diverse as the Chinese language, religion and astronomy (Hiramatsu 1999: 410). Given that students came from all over Japan and studied such a range of subjects, Nagasaki must have been quite a place for people to meet and exchange ideas during the late Tokugawa period. Finally, Boot makes the important point that the Japanese were under no obligation to study Western learning. The fact they did so suggests that they, or their sponsors, found something useful in it which led them to devote time and money and travel great distances in order to engage with it, in what was clearly a crowded marketplace for study (Boot 2013: 201).

6   Materials for Learning Dutch

Just as the *loci* for learning Dutch increased and in some sense became more sophisticated from the seventeenth to the mid-nineteenth century, so too did the materials with which Japanese learnt Dutch. In the seventeenth and early eighteenth centuries, rudimentary wordlists were the principal form of learning material. Towards the end of the eighteenth century as interest in *rangaku* increased and *shijuku* for *rangaku* opened, the first Japanese-Dutch lexicons were compiled as well as primers for the Dutch language. In the first half of the nineteenth century, further such books and Dutch grammars were compiled although they often remained in manuscript, while other Dutch learning material was imported.

6.1   Wordlists in the Seventeenth Century

The wordlists in Portuguese and Dutch given to the students of Caspar Schamberger in Edo in the early 1650s were if not the first, then some of the first wordlists compiled to assist students in learning Dutch (De Groot 2005: 26). Further wordlists were compiled by those who studied and practised his style of surgery. In the *Tōryū Denki Yōsatsu Nukigaki* (1681), and the list of medical terms (*Orandakō wage*) in the *Oranda gekasho* ('Dutch Surgery Book', 1696), inspired by Caspar-style surgery, most of the terms are still Portuguese, and there are words in Dutch as well as Latin.[55] Kaiser (1996: 22) makes the point that while the Dutch and Latin terms are identified as such, the Portuguese are not, suggesting that this was still the established layer of technical terms in this area.[56]

Given his background it is not surprising that during his time in Japan (1690–92), the physician Engelbert Kaempfer produced a Japanese-German glossary (Michel 1993a: 206). Although it was officially forbidden, he clearly did learn some Japanese. While by this time early attempts were being made to translate Dutch texts into Japanese, it seems that prior to the last decade of seventeenth century there is no evidence for the existence of purely Japanese-Dutch wordlists. One person who attempted to rectify this situation was Kaempfer's protégé, Imamura Gen'emon, mentioned above. De Groot records that he compiled a manuscript entitled *Oranda shōi* ('Dutch words and their meanings'), probably in the late 1690s, several years after Kaempfer's departure from Japan in 1692. This lists in Dutch and Japanese several of the functions performed at Deshima, such as 'senior merchant' and 'accountant', as well as ranks held by Japanese in Nagasaki. It is not simply a wordlist, but also provides descriptions of European terms and names such as the Dutch *keizer* ('emperor') and, perhaps surprisingly, provides detailed information about Christianity. De Groot is probably right in concluding that the vocabulary and these descriptions are the fruit of discussions between Kaempfer and Gen'emon (De Groot 2010: 204–205; 2005: 39).

---

55   In the NIJL database, the author is given as Nishi Genpo: Book ID 2130805. He died, however, in 1684, i.e., twelve years before the date given by Kaiser. Further investigation may reveal the reason for this apparent discrepancy.

56   For the *Oranda gekasho*, see also Michel (2005: 178).

6.2 Materials Produced by Arai Hakuseki and Aoki Kon'yō

In 1708 the Italian priest, Giovanni Battista Sidotti (1668–1714), was arrested after entering Japan illegally and initially detained in Nagasaki. Gen'emon would accompany Sidotti to Edo, where he made the acquaintance of the neo-Confucian scholar, Arai Hakuseki (1657–1725). It is most likely that Gen'emon and Hakuseki worked together on word lists which formed part of Hakuseki's *Gaikoku no jichōsho* ('A Record of Foreign Matters'), a series of seven manuscripts that he produced between 1712 and 1716. Hakuseki would write Japanese words and phrases and Gen'emon would add Dutch equivalents beneath them. Their encounter in Edo was the first extensive contact between a Japanese intellectual and a Nagasaki interpreter (Van der Velde 1993: 188; De Groot 2005: 45; 2010: 207–208). Further contact between the groups they represented would be vital in the development of *rangaku*. In this regard, the early stages of *rangaku* can be understood as the result of the transfer of knowledge and culture both internationally from Europeans to the Nagasaki interpreters and nationally from the interpreters to Edo scholars. During the second half of the seventeenth century and the early eighteenth century, Japanese and Dutch (in *katakana*) or Japanese, Dutch and Portuguese wordlists in the so-called *kuchi* group were compiled. Seventeen of these have so far been identified. One, *Orandakuchi*, is dated 1710 and preserved in the collection of the department of medicine at Kyoto University. Another wordlist, *Oranda wagoshū iroha yori* ('A Collection of Dutch and Japanese Words in *Iroha* Sequence'), includes the name of Kawaguchi Ryōan (1629–87), an adherent of the school of medicine initiated by Caspar Schamberger, mentioned above (Michel 2010c: n. 7).[57] One other *kuchi*, the *Orandakuchi iroha wake* ('Part of a Dutch Wordlist in *Iroha* Sequence') is dated as late as 1802 (De Groot 2005: 49–51).[58] *Iroha* in the title refers to the specific way of ordering words based on their initial *kana*, which takes its name from the first three *kana* (いろは (*i-ro-ha*)) of the poem entitled *i-ro-ha uta*, in which all syllables of the *kana* syllabary appear only once; hence, it was used as the equivalent of the Western ABC.

One person who invested time in developing material for himself and others to learn Dutch was the Edo scholar, Aoki Kon'yō who, as noted above, was ordered by Tokugawa Yoshimune to learn Dutch from the Nagasaki interpreters in Edo. In 1740 Kon'yō produced a manuscript *Oranda moji ōtsūji tōsho*

---

57 Michel (2005: 175) refers to Ryōan as 'the most outstanding adherent of Schamberger's surgery'. He carried Schamberger's teaching from Nagasaki to other parts of Japan including Kyoto and even to Shikoku within less than twenty years.

58 *Kuchi* usually means 'mouth', but here means 'word' or 'language'. This is not in the NIJL database.

('Answers from the senior interpreters regarding the Dutch script').[59] This includes general words written in Roman script such as those for the seasons, natural features and numbers. In 1742 Kon'yō wrote *Oranda moji ryakukō* ('Some brief thoughts on Dutch script').[60] This includes a guide to the pronunciation of letters in Roman and Gothic script with (approximate) equivalents in *katakana* to assist in pronunciation, and a list of some 700 Dutch words with translations and approximate *katakana* transcriptions. One difference from *Oranda moji ōtsūji tosho* is that *Oranda moji ryakukō* includes words relating to commerce, anatomy and medicine. De Groot argues that the Edo scholar Kon'yō used a Nagasaki source for this, a view supported by the fact that in the second and third part of the list, there are words from the Nagasaki dialect. It is likely that the material was copied from an interpreter's glossary (De Groot 2005: 102–104).

Two further small works in manuscript produced by Kon'yō contain complete Dutch sentences with a *katakana* pronunciation guide and translations into Japanese. These are *Oranda wayaku* ('Translations from Dutch', 1743), which contains five sentences, and *Oranda wayaku kōshū* ('Translations from Dutch, later collection', 1744) (four sentences). One of these sentences *Voor 't gedaen geschenk bedank u* (lit.: 'for the given present (I) thank you'), has a feature that is typical of the Dutch produced by the interpreters; it lacks a subject pronoun, a common aspect of Japanese sentences, in which the pronoun has to be deduced from the context.

Annually between 1749 and 1758 Kon'yō produced manuscripts with the name *Oranda bun'yaku* ('Translations of Dutch sentences'). Together they contain some 800 Dutch words with Japanese translations and *katakana* transcriptions. They are largely based on Hakvoord's *Oprecht Onderwijs der Letter-konst*, mentioned above, which was written for use as a textbook in Dutch primary schools (De Groot 2005: 106–107; Harada 2000: 123).

None of Kon'yō's work was published, but he was the first scholar in Edo to engage seriously with Dutch and he provided useful material for subsequent Edo scholars to learn to read and write Dutch, which would be vital to the emergence of *rangaku*. For example, Maeno Ryōtaku, who would become a pioneer Edo scholar in *rangaku*, wrote that he had read Kon'yō's *Oranda wayaku* and learnt a little of the language from that, prior to being ordered, in 1769, to

---

59   *Oranda moji ōtsūji tosho* is listed as *Oranda moji daitsūji tosho* in the NIJL database (ID 753286).

60   *Oranda moji ryakukō* is on the NIJL database, ID 753311. *Ryakukō* is also transcribed as *ryakkō*. The original was destroyed by fire, so Kon'yō re-wrote it in 1746 (De Groot 2005: 101–102).

go to Nagasaki, where he studied the Dutch language and Western medicine (De Groot 2005: 108).

6.3 Imported Learning Materials

Dutch books were imported into Japan from the seventeenth century onwards.[61] In 1754, the Deshima *dagregister* records that books imported into Japan from Java were presented to the *tsūji nakama* in Nagasaki. These were two copies of François Halma's Dutch-French dictionary, *Woordenboek der Nederduitsche en Fransche Taalen* (Amsterdam, 1708), one of Pierre/Pieter Marin's Dutch-French *Groot Nederduitsch en Fransch Woordenboek* and a Latin-Dutch lexicon, the *Nieuw woordenboek der Nederlandsche en Latijnsche taal* (1st ed. 1704) by David van Hoogstraten (De Groot 2005: 85; Boot 2013: 197).

Another lexicon that was imported was Lodewijk Meijer's *Woordenschat* (1st ed. Amsterdam 1650), mentioned above.[62] However, the first attempt to use this and other dictionaries to compile Dutch-Japanese lexicons would not begin until the 1760s. The *dagregister* for 1766/67 records that the senior interpreter 'Sensabro' was compiling a Dutch-Japanese dictionary (Blussé and Remmelink 2004: 314). This is Nishi Zenzaburō. He compiled an early Dutch-Japanese but by his death in 1768, he had only reached the letter 'B'. This was based on Marin's Dutch-French lexicon (Goodman 2013: 69).[63]

In about 1765, what has been described as the first popular book on Dutch culture and science, *Oranda banashi* ('Dutch Tales'), was published by the botanist Gotō Mitsuo (also Rishun, 1696–1771). It included a table with Dutch letters in Gothic, Roman and Italic script, with approximate *katakana* equivalents

---

61   For the process by which books were imported and checked by the Inspectorate of Books in Nagasaki, see Ōba (2012: 69–72).

62   Feenstra Kuiper (1921: 253). De Groot (2005: 86 n. 52) observes that the reason that early Dutch-Japanese lexicons were based on bilingual as opposed to monolingual Dutch dictionaries is that the latter 'did not exist' until the publication of volumes of Weiland's *Nederduitsch Taalkundig woordenboek* between 1799 and 1811. However, this is not strictly speaking the case, for the first edition of the monolingual *Woordenschat* was printed in 1650 (the first edition printed by Meijer was the 5th edition in 1669) (Michel 2018: 62). It should be admitted that Meijer's lexicon focussed on Dutch words derived from Romance languages, principally French and Latin, but it was monolingual and it was used as the basis for Dutch-Japanese lexicons. As noted in the text, Katsuragawa Hoshū received a copy of it from Isaac Titsingh in 1785. Nakagawa Jun'an also received a copy from Titsingh via Hendrik Romberg. He describes it as 'Boek in de Woordenschat' (Lequin 1990: 1:15).

63   Zenzaburō compiled his dictionary in secret, pretending to be too ill to turn up for work. De Groot (2004: 162) records that Zenzaburō reached the letter 'D', although he was unable to complete it. Blussé and Remmelink (2004: 859) record that Zenzaburō 'never got any further than the first three letters'. One problem that the secondary sources face is that no copy of the work has survived.

beneath each letter. In fact, it seems, as Sugita Genpaku reported in *Rangaku kotohajime*, that the very presence of this table in the book, which perhaps provoked fears of 'barbarian' influences among *bakufu* officials, led to it being confiscated and destroyed, although thankfully some copies clearly survived (Jackson 2016: 62).

Japanese who befriended the Dutch would often place orders for books with them. In a letter dated 1785, the *rangakusha* Kutsuki Masatsuna informed his friend Isaac Titsingh, now in Chinsura, Bengal, that he had recently received several books from him, delivered by two Dutch at Deshima.[64] These included two grammars or learners: a copy of Pieter Marin's 'Nieuwe franse en Nederd[uytsche] Spraakkonst', Moonen's 'Nederduitsche Spraakkonst', and a lexicon: 'Buys woorde boek van de letter A tot Z'.[65]

Dutch was not the only European language of interest to Masatsuna. He also requested a Latin dictionary from Titsingh and a French learner 'Corneille, beknopte Leerwyse der franse taal' (Lequin 1992: 2–3). This refers to Louis Cornelle's *Beknopte en klaare leerwyze der Fransche taale* (Rotterdam, 1783) (Lequin 2003: 206). In exchange, Masatsuna sent his friend Japanese coins, as both men were interested in numismatics. Another recipient of books from Titsingh was the physician Katsuragawa Hoshū (1751–1809). In a letter to Titsingh in 1785 Hoshū thanked him for several books. Most of these were on medicine, but he also received 'Myers woorde schat', i.e., Lodewijk Meijer's *Woordenschat*.[66] Although Hoshū's Dutch is comprehensible, it nevertheless leaves something to be desired. For example, there are several grammatical and orthographical errors in the phrase 'ik had UWE: sou send de sommige mineraaren', where it seems he wants to tell Titsingh that he would have sent him some minerals in exchange for the books, but his house and two warehouses had burnt down the previous year (Lequin 1990: II:547). Indeed, the Swede Carl Peter Thunberg once commented that Hoshū, whom he met on the *hofreis* at Edo, spoke 'tolerable Dutch' (Screech 1996: 18).[67] Nevertheless,

---

64   Henrik Andries Ulps and Hendrik Godfried Duurkoop.

65   Lequin (2003: 206) identifies these as Pieter Marin, *Nieuwe Fransche en Nederduitsche spraakwyze* [...] (Amsterdam, 1752) (1st ed. 1694); Arnold Moonen, *Nederduitsche spraek-kunst, ten dienste van in- en uitheemschen* [...] (Amsterdam, 1706); and Egbert Buys, *Nieuw en volkomen woordenboek van konsten en weetenschappen* [...] (Amsterdam, 1769–1778).

66   There is a book in the Johannes a Lasco Bibliothek in Emden (shelfmark Ri 1349/1350 R), described as *Woordenschat* and attributed to Meijer. One problem is that the date of publication is given as 1620 (Amsterdam: Hendrick Boom), while Meijer was not born until 1629. Further investigation may reveal whether this is indeed an earlier, perhaps the first, edition of *Woordenschat*.

67   Thunberg also commented that Nakagawa Jun'an spoke Dutch 'tolerably well', better indeed than Katsuragawa Hoshū (Screech 2005: 153).

Hoshū, who became private physician to the shogun in 1783, was to be become an important *rangakusha* in Edo. Titsingh also sent a copy of the Meijer lexicon to Hoshū's friend and fellow *rangakusha*, Nakagawa Jun'an (1739–86), and the fourth edition of a lexicon compiled by Pieter Marin (1667–1718) to Imamura Kinsaburō (also Kinbei) (Lequin 2003: 208–209).[68]

At some point in the 1770s a handbook of Dutch expressions in *katakana*, *Verscheijde Spreek Wijzen* ('Various Expressions'), likened by De Groot to a Berlitz phrasebook, was probably compiled by a Nagasaki interpreter. It was apparently intended for the host of an inn in Kyoto, where the Dutch would stay on their *hofreis*. Although the Dutch of some simpler phrases is correct, that of more complex phrases is less precise. One example of an incorrect phrase is *Nog wat u blijf* rendered in *katakana* as (ノウ・ワット・ユー・ブレイフ *nou watto yuu bureifu*). The phrase should be *Blijft u nog wat* ('Stay a little longer') (De Groot 2005: 30–32). This and other incorrect Dutch phrases sheds light on the problems faced by the Dutch in communicating with Japanese via some interpreters.

6.4 Materials Developed by Ōtsuki Gentaku, Maeno Ryōtaku and Morishima Chūryō

By the end of the eighteenth century, however, some more successful projects aimed at providing Dutch learning aids for Japanese were being undertaken. One of these was a primer entitled *Rangaku kaitei* ('Guide to Dutch Learning'), which includes a Dutch vocabulary and a concise Dutch grammar (Sansom 1973: 204). This was published in 1788 by Ōtsuki Gentaku, after he had returned to Edo from Nagasaki. It had circulated in manuscript for five years before appearing in print (Clements 2015: 163–164). The *kaitei* in the title can be understood as 'steps', for Gentaku viewed learning Dutch as a series of progressive didactic steps. He wrote that if one wants to learn *rangaku*, it is necessary to act like a child of five or six years old who begins with the characters 'one', 'two' and 'three': the child needs to learn their shape, how to read them and write them (Horiuchi 2003: 3).

As many of his readers may not previously have encountered a language written in Latin script, Gentaku devotes a section of his work to describing how letters in the alphabet are joined to form phonetic units. He provides a table of syllables in the Latin alphabet and their *katakana* equivalents to assist the reader. He also describes the manner, in which the Nagasaki interpreters learnt Dutch, which informed his own approach to studying the language. They begin by reading and writing (Dutch) letters. They then move on to composing and

---

68   The Marin lexicon is probably his Dutch-French dictionary.

reading the syllables, after which they commit daily to memory conversations which they find in a work called *Samenspraak* ('dialogues'). Once they have mastered this stage, they study phrases from a work called *Opstellen* ('compositions'), regarding which they interrogate their seniors, friends, and even the Dutch. He concludes that when they have mastered the principles of this, they are ready to translate whatever they want (Horiuchi 2003: 4–5).

Before we leave Gentaku, a final word is in order. In *Rangaku kaitei*, he observes that Dutch books were often written in a colloquial style. Likewise, in an early English learner for Japanese, *Angeria Kōgaku Shōsen* ('First Steps in the Study of English', 1811), Motoki Shōei (also Shōzaemon 1767–1822) noted the similarities between written and spoken English. Twine (1991: 27–28) suggests that this would eventually lead in the late Tokugawa period to several dictionaries and grammars for *rangakusha*, which gave Japanese equivalents in their colloquial rather than literary forms. Furthermore, an early Japanese-Dutch dictionary, *Rango yakusen* ('A Selection of Dutch Words Translated', 1810), rejected 'esoteric vocabulary choices in favour of the common' and its grammar was that of the spoken language. Likewise, the Japanese chosen for the *Zūfu Haruma* was colloquial 'in order not to obscure the meaning of the Dutch' (Twine 1991: 78). Indeed, as the primary aim of the lexicon was to improve the Dutch of the Nagasaki interpreters, as Hendrick Doeff notes in the introduction, the Japanese entries were written 'in de platte Nangasakijsche stijl', i.e., in the everyday Nagasaki style, so that the interpreters young and old could understand them. Later grammars also used examples from conversational Japanese rather than formal written Japanese. These included Ōba Sessai's (1805–73) *Yaku Oranda bungo* ('Dutch Grammar in Translation', 1855–57) and Tōda Shōan's (d. 1865) *Oranda bunten yakugosen* ('A Short Dutch Grammar (in translation)', 1856) (Twine 1991: 79).[69]

When, in the early 1770s, Sugita Genpaku and fellow Edo scholars were translating *Heelkundige Onderwijzingen* ('Lessons in Surgery'), a Dutch translation of a German surgical textbook by Lorenz Heister, their efforts were hindered by the lack of a suitable Dutch-Japanese dictionary. They did have a small dictionary, most probably a Dutch monolingual lexicon, that Maeno Ryōtaku had procured in Nagasaki, but they found it difficult to work out suitable Japanese equivalents for the terms they looked up in it (Sugita 1969: 34–35). Ryōtaku himself seems to have had plans to produce a dictionary similar to the Qing Chinese Kangxi dictionary, compiled at the command of the Kangxi Emperor (ruled 1662–1722), which contained more than 40,000 words. It is not known, however, if anything came of Ryōtaku's plans (Sugita 1969: 40).

---

69   Twine refers to *Oranda Bunten Yakugosen Shohen*.

In 1798 the Edo scholar Morishima Chūryō (1756–1810), originally called Katsuragawa Hosan, published the *Bangosen* ('Lexicon of Barbarian Words') (De Groot 2016: 65–74; 2005: 55). Timon Screech (2012: 325) refers to this as 'first Japanese-Dutch conversational dictionary'.[70] However, De Groot asserts that it is more of a wordlist consisting of (mainly) Dutch words. On each page there are two rows of words with the Japanese given in characters above and the non-Japanese or 'barbarian' words (Dutch along with a few Portuguese and Latin words) in *katakana* below. The fact that the non-Japanese words were written in *katakana* meant that Japanese pronunciation deviated somewhat from the Dutch (De Groot 2016: 64). For example, 'square' is given above as 方 and beneath this the Dutch *vierkant*, rendered in *katakana* as *hīrukanto*, and 'fish' 魚 (Dutch *visch*) as *hisu*. The words in the *Bangosen* are grouped by category according to the traditional manner of Chinese lexicons, with words concerning the sky/heaven coming first, followed by those relating to earth and then to mankind. So, the first four of more than twenty categories were 1. astrological and meteorological words, 2. words relating to earth such as stone, water and ice, 3. words relating to time such as months and adverbs of time (a category that had not yet emerged in Japanese) and 4. words relating to humans such as relations, occupations and friends (Feenstra Kuiper 1921: 256–259). This lexicon includes the earliest known mention of several Dutch loanwords in Japanese, such as *mesu* メス (< Dutch *mes*), a general word for 'knife' in Dutch, which has come to mean 'scalpel' in Japanese (see Chapter 7). It is described in Japanese as a *kokatana* (削刀), where *ko* means to scrape or sharpen and *katana* 'knife' or dagger (see fig. 3).

6.5 *The Halma Lexicons*

A significant step forward in the provision of learning material was made with the compilation of the *Edo Haruma* ('Edo Halma', also *Haruma wage* 'Halma Translated (into Japanese)'), a Dutch-Japanese lexicon based on the Dutch-French lexicon of François Halma, which marked a shift away from Dutch-Japanese wordlists towards alphabetical lexicons (see fig. 4). This was compiled by a group of scholars in Edo and a former interpreter, Ishii Shōsuke (1743–?). The team was led by Inamura Sanpaku (1759–1811), a physician from Inaba province in Western Honshu. He had studied under Ōtsuki Gentaku at the *Shirandō* and had learnt Dutch at Nagasaki (Hesselink 1995: 206–207).[71] His

---

70   Screech has the date 1788.

71   Hesselink (1995: 204 n. 53) notes that the Sinitic characters used for *Shirandō* (芝蘭堂) have a variety of associations. He prefers to translate it as 'Herb and Orchid Hall', while Fukuoka (2012: 42) asserts that the name means 'Hall of Holland in Shiba', the district of Edo where it was established. These interpretations are not mutually exclusive.

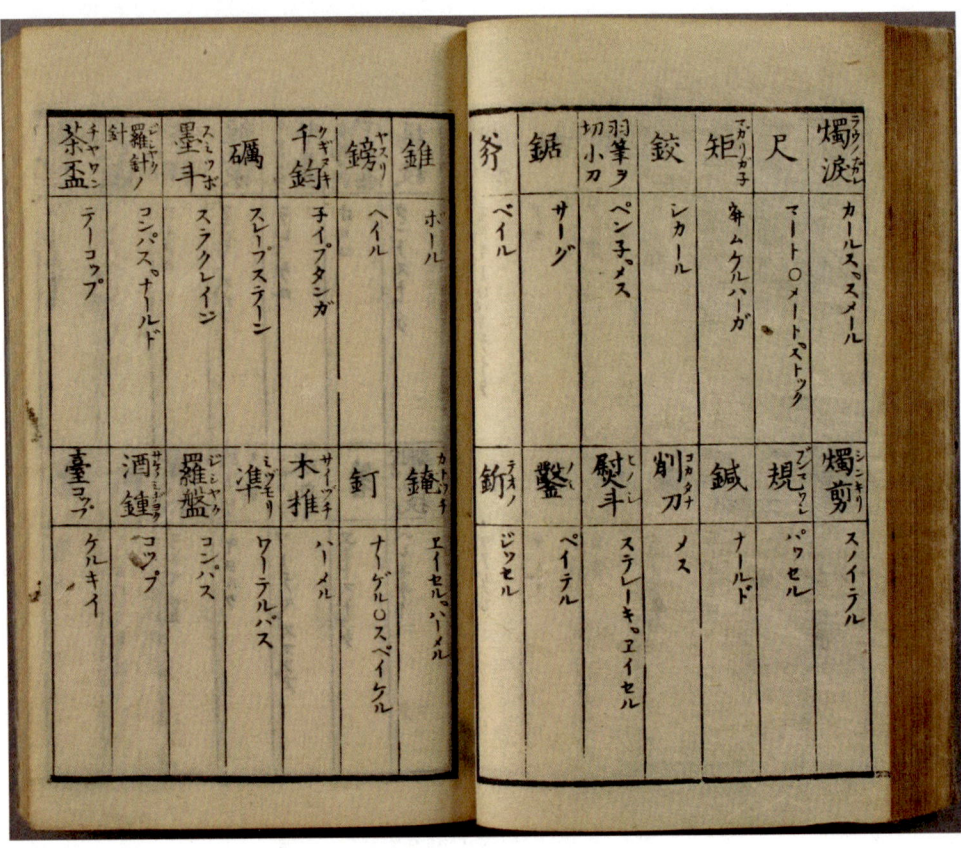

FIGURE 3   A page from *Bangosen* including *mesu* in *katakana* (メス)
WUL 文庫 08 C0514

time in Edo and Nagasaki had convinced him of the need for a Dutch-Japanese lexicon. The lexicon included some 80,000 words, divided into 30 parts. It was completed in 1796. It is arranged by Dutch alphabetical order, rather than by category (as in, for example, *Bangosen*), with Dutch words on the left of the page and Japanese equivalents in Japanese script on the right. Furthermore, there is often an indication of the grammatical function of the Dutch words, e.g., w.w. (*werkwoord*) is placed next to verbs and z. (*zelfstandig naamwoord*) next to nouns with the appropriate grammatical gender. Only thirty copies of the lexicon were printed using wood-carved movable type letters. These copies only contained the Dutch entries and so Japanese translations had to be added by hand (De Groot 2016: 162–163). The short print run meant that only a limited number of people had access to it (Clements 2015: 155–156). Boxer observes that Sanpaku distributed or possibly sold parts to fellow *rangakusha*.

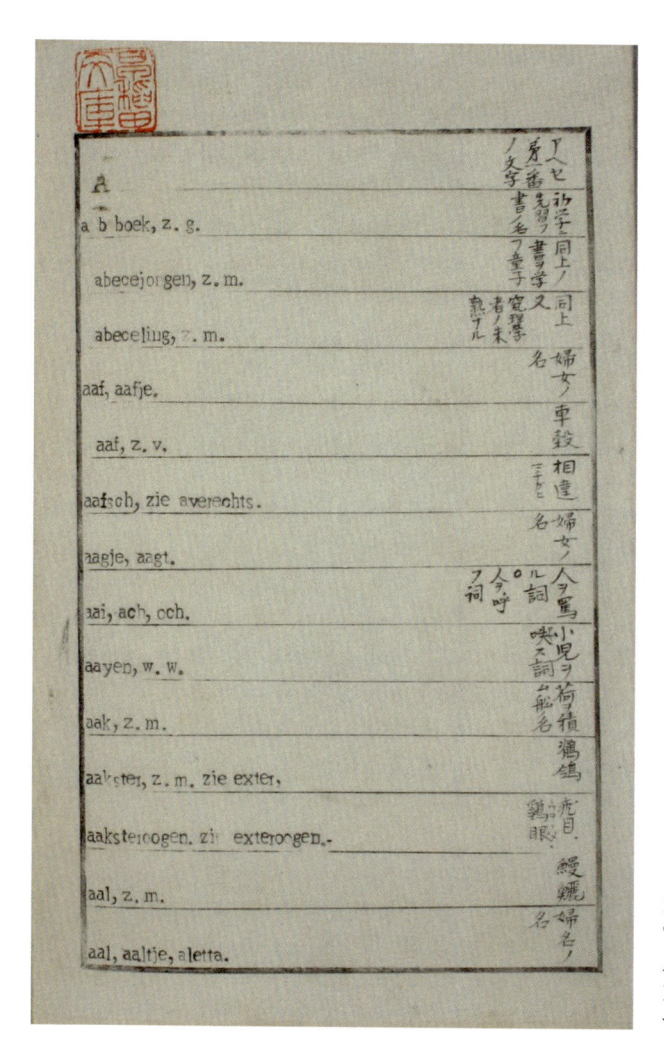

Unfortunately, only a few parts survive (Boxer 1950: 65–66). In 1810, a physician and former student of Sanpaku, Fujibayashi Fuzan (1781–1836), produced an abridged version of the *Edo Haruma* called *Yakken* ('Key (or Keys) to Translation') in octavo, together with a grammatical treatise similar to that of *Rangaku kaitei* (Boxer 1950: 66). The title is well chosen for the purpose of such a lexicon was to 'unlock' the door to Dutch texts in order to allow translators to access them and render them in Japanese.[72]

Between 1811 and 1817, Hendrick Doeff (*opperhoofd* 1803–17) compiled another Japanese-Dutch dictionary based on the Halma lexicon. This became

---

72   *Yakken* also includes many botanical terms from Latin.

known as the *Nagasaki* or *Zūfu* (or sometimes *Dūfu*) *Haruma*. In the preface, Doeff tells the reader that he had worked with eleven Nagasaki interpreters selected by the Governor of Nagasaki, including Yoshio Kōgyū's son Joen (also Gonnosuke; Yoshioka 1965: 53–54). As noted above, it was aimed at improving the Dutch of the Nagasaki interpreters which Doeff referred to disparagingly as *Japansch-Hollandsch* ('Japanese Dutch') (Doeff 1833: 244; De Groot 2005: 34; Goodman 2013: 141; Effert 2012). Like its Edo predecessor, this lexicon was arranged alphabetically. However, the involvement of a native speaker meant that it could provide more information about the Dutch entries and in some cases sample sentences. For example, next to the entry for 'eel', Dutch *aal*, we find 'z.m zekere vis', i.e., it is a masculine noun (*zelfstandig naamwoord, man-nelijk*) and it is defined as a certain type of fish. On the next line we read *een aal bij den staart houden. Spreek w[oord]*. This means 'to hold an eel by its tail, proverb', but can be taken to mean 'to deal with something that might get out of hand' (see fig. 5).[73] Doeff had plenty of time on his hands, as no ships arrived at Deshima for many years, largely a function of the Napoleonic Wars. By the time of his departure, in 1817, Doeff had completed the first draft of the dictionary. Doeff's work was continued in the following few years by interpreters with the help of his successor as *opperhoofd*, Jan Cock Blomhoff. Further corrections and additions were made, and the work was finally completed in 1833. Copies were presented to the shogun and the Nagasaki *bugyō*. The entire work comprised over 100,000 entries (De Groot 2004: 163–165).[74]

6.6   *Other Lexicons Developed in the Nineteenth Century*

In 1810, Okudaira Masataka (1781–1855) *daimyō* of Nakatsu published a six-volume woodblock-print Dutch-Japanese lexicon, comprising over 7,000 words. It had the twin-title *Rango yakusen*, mentioned above, and *Nieuw Verzameld Japans en Hollandsch Woordenboek* (Katagiri 1985: 392). Although Masataka's name appears on the title page, most of the work on the lexicon was done by the up-and-coming Nagasaki interpreter and *rangakusha*, Baba Teiyū (also Sajūrō 1787–1822) and several other *rangakusha* (De Groot 2005: 188–189; Tanaka 2017: 33–34).[75] Here, as with the earlier wordlists, words were grouped in *iroha* sequence and sub-divided by category. For example,

---

73   The final word in Dutch is nowadays usually *hebben* 'to have'.
74   De Groot also writes that a copy was presented to the *Bansho shirabesho* in Edo. This was only founded in 1856. So, it is not clear whether the presentation was made in or after 1856 or to one of the predecessor organizations of the *Bansho shirabesho*.
75   For the title page, see Van Gulik (2000: 19).

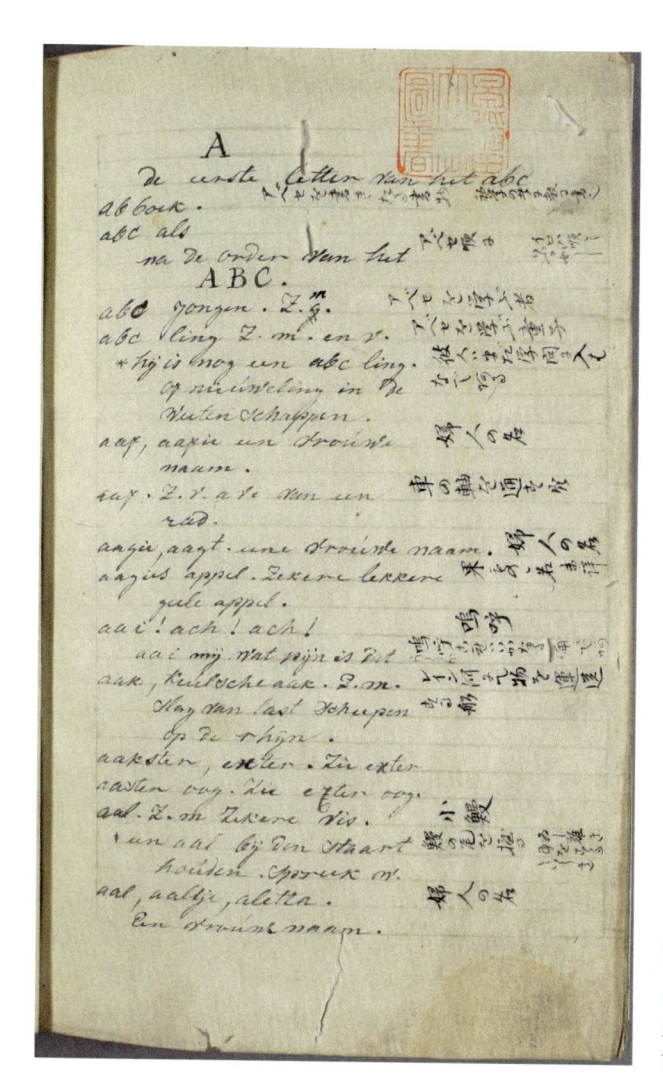

FIGURE 5
The first entries in
the *Nagasaki* or *Zūfu
Haruma*. Part 1
WUL 朩 10 01749

under the first letter, the *katakana* イ ('i'), words in the subcategory of *tenmon* (天文) (written and read r-to-l 文天) (meteorology or more properly astronomy) include the 'setting sun' *ondergaande zon* and 'lightning' *blexem* (Late Modern Dutch, *bliksem*), which begin with this letter in Japanese. Japanese words in *kanji* and *furigana* are on the right of the page, and the Dutch equivalents in Roman script are on the left (Sugimoto 1999: 168; Goodman 2013: 160). The *kanji* and *furigana* are written vertically, to be read top to bottom and right to left, while the Dutch words are written horizontally, to be read left to right (see fig. 6). While such an arrangement is in some sense to be expected, it illustrates well the complexity of both producing and reading such lexicons.

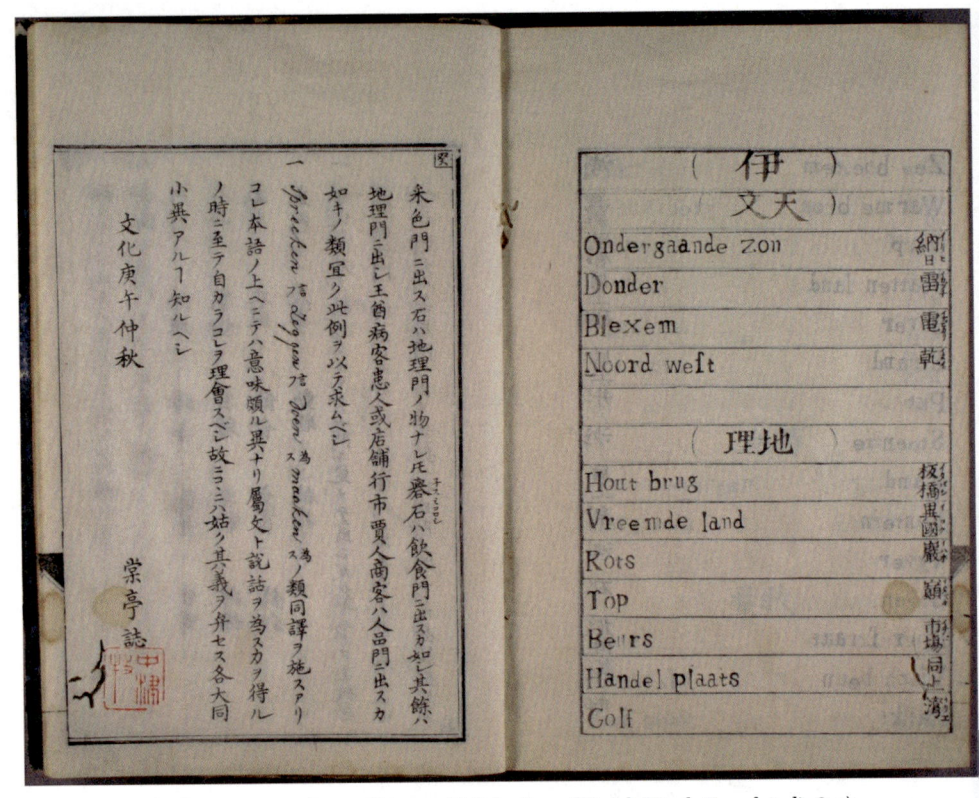

FIGURE 6   The first entries in *Rango Yakusen* ('A Selection of Dutch Words Translated', 1810)
WUL 文庫 08 A0210

In Edo in 1822, Masataka published a Dutch-Japanese dictionary based on the first part of the twelfth edition (Dordrecht, 1805) of Lodewijk Meijer's *Woordenschat*. Reference in the full title to *basterdtwoorden* ('Bastard or impure words') points to Dutch words borrowed from other languages, above all French. The Dutch-Japanese lexicon was compiled by Masataka's personal physician, Ōe Shuntō (1787–1844), rendered as *Ooye Suntoo* on the title page. It had the twin titles *Nieuwe-Gedruct Bastaardt Woorden-Boek* and *Basutādo jibiki* ('Bastard Dictionary'). The lexicon is in some sense a compromise between Western and Japanese writing systems and lexicography. It has some 7,000 entries arranged in order according to the Latin alphabet.[76] Within each letter, however, there are subheadings for the first two letters of the Dutch words which points to the importance of syllables in Japanese phonology and morphology. Each entry

---

76   This lexicon is also referred to as *Basutādo jisho* (De Groot 2005: 93–94).

from left to right has a Dutch word and one or more Japanese equivalents. The Dutch lemmas are taken from Meijer's lexicon and are the 'bastard' words for which he had given words derived from Germanic roots (for example, in Meijer's lexicon *abandonneren* (sic) (French root) has the synonyms *verlaten* and *opgeeven* (sic) (Germanic roots)). In the *Basutādo jibiki* the Japanese equivalents are written from right to left. There is a foreword in Dutch by Masataka, although the quality of the Dutch leaves something to be desired.[77]

At first sight it is perhaps somewhat surprising that Meijer's dictionary was used as the source for the Dutch-Japanese dictionary. Meijer's lexicon and similar ones were part of a 'purist' language movement in the seventeenth century, whose supporters felt that there were too many 'foreign' words, above all ones of French and Latin origin, in Dutch. They wished to show that such words could be replaced by synonyms with Germanic roots, and to encourage the use of these synonyms (Van Oostendorp and Van der Sijs 2018: 17–18). Therefore, there is a certain irony in basing a dictionary on words which the original author, Meijer, had wanted his readers to avoid using. There are, for example, thirty-eight words beginning with the Latinate prefix *circum-*. However, there were relatively few monolingual Dutch dictionaries in print at this time and it may simply be that this was one of the few monolingual Dutch lexicons in Japan, if not in fact the only one.

Other lexicons were compiled, such as the *Oranda bunten jirui, zenpen* ('Dutch grammar and vocabulary, front part', 1856) by Iizumi Shijō. It begins with a glossary of grammatical terms in Dutch and Japanese. It adopts the Japanese grammatical terms developed by the leading Edo *rangakusha* Mitsukuri Genpo (1799–1863), such as *daimeishi* (代名詞) for 'pronoun' and *dōshi* (動詞) for 'verb', of which more below. It then provides a lexicon with Dutch terms on the left and Japanese equivalents on the right. The Dutch terms are listed in syllabic order, again probably because of the importance of syllables to Japanese phonology and morphology.

However, none of these other lexicons had the impact of the two lexicons based on Halma's dictionary. One other lexicon to mention is that compiled by the German physician, Philipp Franz von Siebold with the help of the Japanese 'Totoroki Buhitsiro, Oka Kenkai, Tsiusiro and Gonosuke', which remained unpublished.[78] This consists of eighty-four sheets, eighty-two of which contain

---

77 This is reproduced in Michel (2007: 67). See also Michel (2018) for parallel texts of Meijer's lexicon and the Dutch-Japanese lexicon.

78 Serrurier 64, Kerlen 1207. These are the names as given by Serrurier. Oka Kenkai (1799–1839) was the first *jukuchō* of the *Narutakijuku*. Tsiusiro may be Yoshio Chūjirō (1787–1833),

entries in the Japanese *iroha* sequence (from イ (i) to ス (su)), with sub-groups based on number of syllables. Each page has two columns of entries. For each entry, on the left the Japanese word is given in *katakana* and *kanji*. The Dutch equivalent is given on the right with further notes in German and in some cases examples of usage in Japanese. This lexicon was clearly intended for Von Siebold's personal use. It is dated 1828, the year before his expulsion from Japan. It is not known whether he planned to add to the lexicon (De Groot 2004: 171). This lexicon is another example of the collaborative nature of works produced at the interface between Dutch and Japanese.

Finally, let us return to the *Zūfu Haruma*, as this formed the basis of two subsequent lexicons. One was the *Oranda jii* ('Dutch vocabulary'). This lexicon eventually appeared in print in four volumes from 1855 to 1857. This was shortly after the arrival of Commander Perry, when the need for Dutch learning materials suddenly increased, as Dutch was initially the LWC between Japanese and Europeans. The other was the *Rango tsū* ('Understanding the Dutch Language'). It was primarily compiled by the *rangakusha* Maki Tenboku (also Bokuchū, 1809–63), who had been a student of Mitsukuri Genpo.[79] It was published in 1858, again in the wake of Perry's arrival (De Groot 2004: 167–168).

6.7   *Dutch Grammars in Japan*

As for Dutch grammars and their role in the learning of the language in Japan, an early example is Willem/William Sewel's *Nederduytsche Spraakkonst* ('Dutch grammar', Amsterdam, 1708). The Nagasaki interpreter and *rangakusha* Shizuki Tadao (1760–1806) was one of the, if not the, first Japanese to get to grips with Dutch grammar. He taught Dutch to other Japanese. Furthermore, he produced several grammars in manuscript and was clearly influenced by Sewel's grammar (De Groot 2000: 119). We see this in his later works, such as *Oranda shihinkō* ('A Study of the Dutch Parts of Speech'), in which he applies European linguistic principles to Japanese grammar. His work was not published but was used for the instruction of other interpreters, such as Baba Teiyū (Vos 2000a: 102). In his 1814 *Oranda bunpan tekiyō* ('An Outline of Dutch Grammar'), Teiyū records that Tadao had spoken to him of Sewel's book and how it had transformed his understanding of grammar (De

---

a member of the Yoshio interpreter family, possibly Yoshio Kōgyū's grandson. Gonosuke is Yoshio Gonnosuke (also Joen 1785–1831), the son of Yoshio Kōgyū. Totoroki Buhitsiro was the name of a samurai scholar from Hizen province who compiled the initial list of Japanese words for Von Siebold.

79   Kerlen (no. 1314) gives a later date of passing, 1894.

Groot 2005: 156–157). Teiyū, who would himself teach Dutch at the *Tenmondai* (天文台, 'Bureau of Astronomy'), produced a revised version of Tadao's *Oranda shihinkō*, which had a limited circulation under the title *Teisei rango kyūhinshū* ('Revised collection of the nine parts of speech of the Dutch language', 1814) (Vos 2000a: 102; Clements 2015: 156). Another early Japanese work on Dutch grammar was *Orandago hōkai* ('Interpretation of Dutch grammar'). This was compiled by Fujibayashi Fuzan, mentioned above, and printed in 1811 (Clements 2015: 26).[80] In 1812 in Kyoto, Fuzan published a version of his grammar specifically for physicians, *Imonsuchi Orandago hōkai* ('What every doctor most know: Dutch grammar explained'), although much of the language is of a general nature.[81] This grammar has a preface (*Voorrede*) of nearly 500 words written in Dutch by 'Ba. Sazuro', i.e., Baba Sajūrō (Teiyū) in very serviceable Dutch, which though not error-free, illustrates that he had become quite an advanced user of the language. Teiyū asserts that a knowledge of Dutch allows Japanese not only to translate Dutch medical books, but also to treat sick people better (*men verkrijgt door* [*het Nederlands leren*] *ook de bekwaamheid om de zieken behoorlijk te behandelen*). He observes that for about 100 years Japanese had been forbidden from writing Dutch letters, and so had only been able to learn it orally. It is not clear what prohibition Teiyū might be referring to, but he gives this as a reason for Japanese not making as much progress in Dutch as might have been expected over this period. He sees a book such as this as a 'torch' (*fakkel*) for those who want to learn Dutch. In the text itself, Fuzan grapples with Dutch grammatical terms, such as *lidwoorden* ('articles'), which he renders as *rittouōruden* (リ, リ) (Japanese lacks grammatical articles). Finally, Shizuki Tadao's student Ōtsuki Banri (also Genkan, 1785–1837) was the author of an early work on Dutch conjunctions *Oranda setsuzokushi kō* ('A Study of Dutch Conjunctions', 1826) (Vos 1980: 13).

In 1833, Tsurumine Shigenobu (1788–1859) published *Gogaku shinsho* ('New book on the study of language') (Vos 2000a: 103). This was a grammar of Japanese, rather than of Dutch, but importantly for us, Shigenobu introduced Japanese grammatical terms based on Dutch terms. Although these would later be replaced, it contributed to a process whereby Japanese grammar was understood within the framework of the Western grammatical tradition.

---

80 Mention should also be made of *Ran'yaku benmō* ('Dutch grammar', 1793) by Udagawa Genzui (1755–97), which Vande Walle (2001b: 143) describes as 'a kind of grammar' (Sugimoto 1979: 85). This was one of the first descriptions, if not the first, of Dutch grammar written in Japanese. Udagawa Genzui also wrote *Seiyō igen*, a Dutch-Japanese glossary of medical terms.

81 The date given in the Dutch preface is 1815. The NIJL database has Bunka 9 (1812).

A seminal moment in the development of the Japanese understanding of Dutch grammar was the arrival in Japan of the second edition of Siegenbeek's *Grammatica of Nederduitsche Spraakkunst* (1822). Several volumes based on the *Grammatica* were produced in Japanese, typically under the title *Oranda bunten* (和蘭文典, 'Dutch Grammar'). Perhaps the most successful of these was the *Oranda bunten zenpen* ('Dutch Grammar, First/Front Part') published by Mitsukuri Genpo in 1842 (De Groot 2016: 74).[82] Importantly, like Shigenobu, Genpo provided Japanese equivalents, or translation loanwords, for Dutch grammatical terms. However, his were often less cumbersome than those coined by Shigenobu and some of them are still current in Japanese today (Vos 2000a: 103). For example, Genpo coined the word *fuku-shi* (副詞) for 'adverb' based on the Dutch *bijwoord*, which is still the standard Japanese term. Further examples are given in Chapter 7. This was not only a question of coining new words, but of thinking differently about language and how words could be categorized, i.e., by syntactic function rather than meaning.

In 1847, Genpo compiled *Kaisei zōho bangosen* ('Revised and Enlarged Lexicon of Foreign Words'). This was a development of and significant improvement on the *Bangosen* produced almost fifty years earlier by Morishima Chūryō (De Groot 2016: 74). In this new edition, Dutch words were written in both Roman script and *katakana* (in *Bangosen* only *katakana*), there were twice as many entries as in the earlier version and it included new categories to reflect Japan's changing circumstances, such as a group of words under the heading 'firearms' (*kaki* 火器). Despite this, its importance in the development of *rangaku* should not be overemphasized, particularly in comparison with the two *Haruma* lexicons. Its value, like that of its predecessor, lay primarily in assisting Japanese with the learning of vocabulary and committing dialogues to memory.

As we have seen, copies of other Dutch grammars such as Pieter Weiland's *Nederduitsche Spraakkunst* were also imported into Japan as interest in the Dutch language grew.[83] Indeed, such was the demand for these books, that some such as Siegenbeek's 1822 *Grammatica* were re-printed in Japan.[84] One final point is that both the Weiland and Siegenbeek grammars were quite normative and prescriptive. They were heavily influenced by Latin grammars

---

82   Another Japanese translation of the *Grammatica* was *Sōyaku Garamachika* published in Edo in 1856.

83   There is a copy of the Weiland grammar with the seal of the Nagasaki Censor's Office in Leiden University Library Special Collections, LUB shelf mark 1074 H 11.

84   There is a copy of a Japanese re-print (Edo, 1857) in Leiden University Library Special Collections, that was owned by Mitsukuri Genpo, LUB shelf mark 1371 C 18: 1.

rather than being based on everyday speech (Willemyns and Van der Sijs 2009: 306). This would mean that the Dutch that Japanese would have learnt from them would be somewhat stilted and antiquated rather than contemporary, although still useful for reading and translating texts.

6.8   *Guides to Dutch Pronunciation*

Finally, the Dutch concern about the pronunciation of their language was clearly shared by some Japanese. One work that attempted to provide guidance on Dutch pronunciation was *Seion hatsubi* ('A Detailed Study of Western Sounds', Edo, 1826), a two-part work compiled by Ōtsuki Genkan. In the second part, Genkan provides detailed guides to pronouncing Dutch letters and open and closed syllables. He also gives Arabic numerals with Dutch renderings

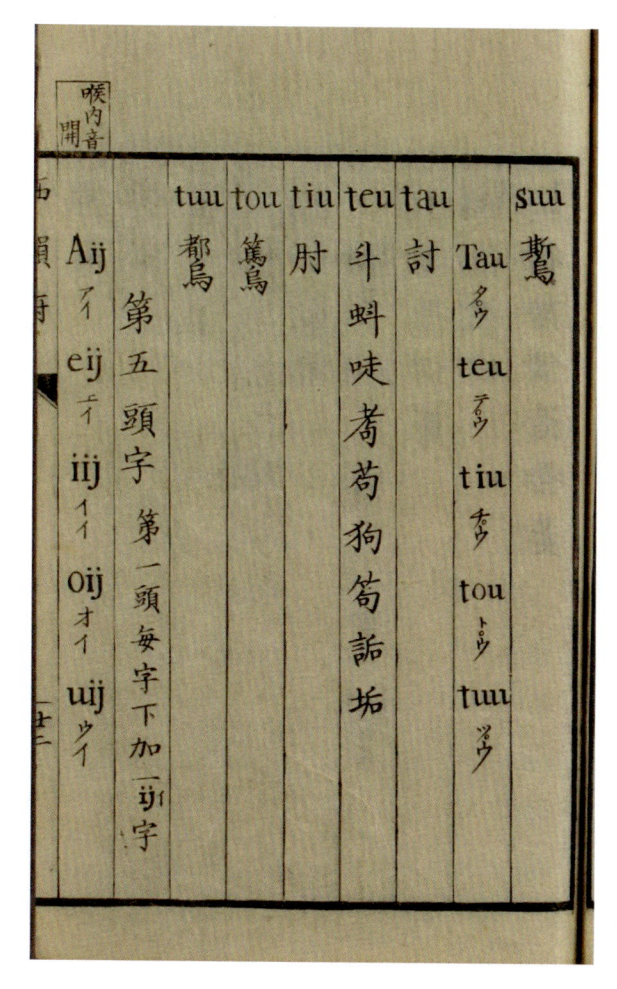

FIGURE 7
Dutch triphthongs in
Seiinpu ('Storehouse of
Western sounds', 1833).
WUL 文庫 08 C0011

and Roman numerals with Latin renderings, both in *katakana* (Part II, p. 32). Furthermore, Genkan provides an account of the origins of writing in Dutch (Part II, pp. 1–6). In Edo in 1833 Genkan published *Seiinpu* ('Storehouse of Western sounds'). This second work is smaller than the first although it does also provide detailed guides to pronouncing Dutch letters and open and closed syllables. One minor difference is that whereas the former uses the grapheme ⟨y⟩, which is not native to Dutch, the latter uses the digraph ⟨ij⟩. It presents series of Dutch phonemes such as *aij, eij, iij, oij* and *uij* (p. 22), which are likely to have been pronounced as triphthongs. However, the *katakana* renderings only have two vowels, in effect making them diphthongs, *ai, ei*, etc. The diphthong /ɛi/, rendered graphically with the digraph ⟨ij⟩, is represented with the *kana* イ 'i' (see fig. 7).

7   Conclusion

There is more to say on learning Dutch in Tokugawa Japan. However, what this chapter has attempted to do is give a sense of which Japanese learnt the language, and why, where, and how they learnt it. The picture that has emerged is that the process of learning Dutch developed in a series of steps, like the *kaitei* to which Ōtsuki Gentaku's book refers. It began as a means to an end for assisting communication between VOC employees and Japanese in Western Kyushu, first at Hirado, but then to a much greater extent at Nagasaki. Contact between Nagasaki interpreters and Edo scholars, including that which was initiated by Shogun Yoshimune, led to the latter becoming increasingly interested in Dutch learning and the language or *metalect* that mediated it. As the Japanese became aware of the value of this learning, particularly but by no means exclusively in the field of medicine, other nodes of learning emerged in Osaka, Sendai and elsewhere. In the process, the *loci* of learning developed and became more formalized, as did the learning materials.

In the early Tokugawa period, learning took place in the *tsūji nakama* in Nagasaki, along with the family homes of interpreters, and buildings on Deshima. As interest in the Dutch language and learning spread, other *loci* emerged, such as the *Oranda zashiki* of Katsuragawa Hosan in Edo and the *Kōmō zashiki* of Yoshio Kōgyū in Nagasaki. These functioned as discursive spaces for the exchange of information about the Dutch language and the learning it mediated. Eventually, towards the end of the eighteenth century, *shijuku* such as the *Shirandō* were established. They began on a small scale, but in the course of the first half of the nineteenth century, their number and size increased, with a school such as the *Tekijuku* in Osaka reckoned to have had some 3,000 students on its register. A parallel process was the increased sophistication and westernization of learning materials. Early wordlists, where Dutch words were mixed with Portuguese and Latin and in which words were presented in the Japanese *iroha* sequence, gave way by the turn of the nineteenth century to alphabetical lexicons based on Western models such as the two *Haruma* dictionaries. The *Zūfu Haruma* and the Dutch-Japanese dictionary compiled by Von Siebold and several Japanese are just two examples of how learning materials were often the result of collaborative projects between Dutch and Japanese, rather than the product of one person's work as the notion of authorship sometimes suggests. Likewise, learners and grammars were compiled during the nineteenth century to meet the increasing demand for Dutch learning materials. In the case of grammars, the work of Mitsukuri Genpo not only assisted others in learning Dutch, but also provided a set of Japanese grammatical terms based on Dutch terms, which are still used in Japanese today. This in some sense placed Japanese within a Dutch or Indo-European grammatical framework.

The process just described was not a linear one and there were *kaitei* backwards, or sideways, as well as forwards. While some of those who learnt Dutch, such as Fukuzawa Yukichi, reached a high level of knowledge of the language which allowed them to translate Dutch books into Japanese and produce learning materials to assist others in learning Dutch, other students of the language such as some of the Nagasaki interpreters made little progress. Even in the nineteenth century, Hendrick Doeff still referred disparagingly to the *Japansch-Hollandsch* of some of the interpreters (De Groot 2005: 34). For many, though, such as Fukuzawa Yukichi, it was not merely an anodyne, pragmatic exercise in language acquisition, but a journey to the West and the opportunity to engage with a language and culture that was both exotic and useful (Horiuchi 2003: 2).

It is important that we do not overstate the knowledge of Dutch in Tokugawa Japan. With reference to the work of Itazawa Takeo, Kornicki (2001: 272) records that in the nineteenth century at any one time there were several hundred Japanese who were literate in Dutch. However, given what has been written in this chapter about the number Japanese studying *rangaku*, this seems a somewhat conservative estimate. Taking interpreters and students in Nagasaki together with *rangakusha* in Edo, and the many students of *ranpō* in Osaka along with the practitioners of *zaison no rangaku*, I would put the figure in the low thousands. More work, however, needs to be done before precise figures can be provided. Perhaps what we could agree on is that those who did know the language were able to break the code of Dutch and thus gain access to the riches of Western science. As a result, above all from the middle of the eighteenth century onwards, they were able to exert significant cultural and social influence in Tokugawa Japan. The following chapters explore how those Japanese who knew Dutch and the non-Japanese discussed in Chapter 1 put their knowledge of the language into practice in Tokugawa Japan.

CHAPTER 3

The Many Uses of Dutch in Japan

1 Introduction

The first two chapters analysed who already knew Dutch, and who learnt the language in Japan and how they did so. The rest of this book analyses how those who knew Dutch applied their knowledge. The present chapter starts this process by exploring the different ways in which Dutch was used in Tokugawa Japan. It does so by analysing in turn the spoken and written use of the language. Apart from native speakers, Dutch was spoken by other Europeans and Japanese; in some cases between members of the same group, and in other cases between members of different groups. Metalinguistic comments provide interesting examples of these cases. Furthermore, such comments give us insights into how the Dutch viewed Japanese efforts to speak Dutch. Dutch was used in everyday conversation; as a medium for teaching the language to Japanese; and as a language of instruction to teach Japanese about the scientific knowledge mediated by imported books.

As for written Dutch, a factory journal, the *dagregister*, was kept by the Dutch from the 1620s onwards. This in some sense functioned as the memory of the factory. Regular reports were written in Dutch and translated for the Japanese authorities, and some Dutch, such as Isaac Titsingh, kept private journals. These sources contain examples of code switching, which are analysed in Chapter 5. Many letters were written in Dutch. Of interest in this regard is the correspondence between Titsingh and Japanese interpreters and scholars. This chapter analyses several letters from this correspondence. Towards the end of the period under review, Dutch books were printed in Japan. These included Dutch learning materials to meet the demand for Dutch in the years after 1854 and Dutch books on subjects of interest and use to the Japanese such as those on military and naval matters.

It was common for works of art in Japan, such as *ukiyo-e* prints, to include both images and text. The sense of the exotic conjured up for the Japanese by Dutch writing, particularly in the late eighteenth century, led to a plethora of art works, some original, some copied, which included Dutch writing. World maps and maps of different parts of the world were imported into Japan. Japanese mapmakers would produce their own versions of these maps, often using Dutch toponyms clothed in the *katakana* syllabary or *ateji* (phonetic *kanji*) with *furigana*. Furthermore, Dutch writing was added to material objects, ranging from the gravestones at the Dutch cemetery near Nagasaki to ceramic bottles of sake, for both informational and decorative purposes. Japanese associates of the Dutch were sometimes given Dutch nicknames. Various Japanese from the shogun down asked the Dutch to write some words of their language. These are examples of *Spielerei*. Finally, by no means all the books written in Dutch that came into the hands of Japanese were translated. For some Japanese, it seems that the purpose of acquiring books was simply to read them, while in other cases, the purpose may simply have been to adorn the shelves of their substantial libraries with exotic titles.

Given that this is a historical survey and that, as several commentators have noted, what remains is often the result of historical accident, what follows is primarily a qualitative analysis of the use of Dutch in Tokugawa Japan, although quantitative data is provided where this is available.[1] Nevertheless, it aims to add to our knowledge of the manifold consequences of the contact between Dutch and other languages, above all Japanese, in this period.

2   Spoken Dutch

It is not possible to identify all the situations in which Dutch was spoken in Tokugawa Japan, and much of our evidence comes in the form of metalinguistic comment. It is likely that Dutch spoke their first language to one another at Hirado and Deshima, although there will have been a certain amount of variation, particularly in the early seventeenth century when the standard variety of the language was only beginning to emerge (Van der Sijs 2004: 29–53). In Chapter 1, it was stated that some 800 Dutch ships reached Kyushu and that about half of the crew of a hundred or so men would have spoken Dutch. This allows us to conclude that around 40,000 Dutch-speaking crewmembers who reached Japan spoke Dutch, although only some of them would have come ashore. As well as using Dutch amongst themselves in their daily activities, those who spoke Dutch as a first language used it to communicate with the interpreters at Hirado and Deshima.

Those who wrote Dutch often needed to incorporate words from other languages such as Japanese, Sinitic varieties, Malay and Portuguese.[2] Wordlists from the seventeenth century contain both Dutch and Portuguese words.

---

1   For example, Labov (1982: 20) wrote that what we have are 'fragments ... that ... are the result of historical accidents beyond the control of the investigator'.
2   See Lohanda (2018) for non-Dutch words which formed part of the VOC vocabulary.

Furthermore, official reports contain examples of switching into Portuguese with words such as *novos* ('news'). This may suggest that there was switching between Dutch and Portuguese in speech during the seventeenth century, but currently we can say nothing more concrete.

Intermittently, the Dutch, and indeed non-Dutch Europeans, were required to teach the Dutch language to apprentice interpreters. One of the more successful enterprises in this regard was the instruction given by the German physician Engelbert Kaempfer to his assistant Imamura Gen'emon (Michel 1993b: 248; Van der Velde 1995; and 2000b: 25). Kaempfer realized that the approach for teaching Dutch to the interpreters was not very productive and so he decided to teach Gen'emon Dutch grammar (Vande Walle 2001b: 131; Werger-Klein 1993: 56; Doeff 1833: 5). This clearly paid dividends for Gen'emon repeatedly received praise for his language skills from the Dutch authors of the *dagregister* (De Groot 2005: 35, 38).

Towards the end of the Tokugawa period, Dutch and non-Dutch Europeans gave instruction in Dutch in specialized fields. One famous example is Philipp Franz von Siebold, who taught medicine in Dutch at his medical school, the *Narutakijuku*. In the late 1850s, the Dutch naval medical officer Johannes (J.L.C.) Pompe van Meerdervoort taught medicine in Nagasaki. The procedure by which he did so was protracted, though effective. He lectured in Dutch, a Nagasaki interpreter would translate into Japanese and then his assistant Matsumoto Jun (also Ryōjun 1832–1907) copied the translation, which was subsequently distributed to the students. This procedure continued for the first two and a half years of Pompe van Meerdervoort's time in Japan. In his account of his time in Japan he notes that his students said they had studied Dutch, but only the grammar, so they were unable to communicate with him in the language. This explains why what Pompe van Meerdervoort taught them needed to be translated. The situation was gradually mitigated as a teacher at the naval school who was part of the detachment and who had taught in the Netherlands began to give instruction in Dutch.[3] Pompe van Meerdervoort himself set about learning Japanese and after a few months could make himself understood, though in the Nagasaki dialect rather than the Edo-based variety which would form the basis of Modern Japanese (Pompe van Meerdervoort 1970: 85; Frellesvig 2010: 378–379).[4]

---

3 Pompe van Meerdervoort also oversaw the construction of the first military hospital in Japan (Blussé *et al.* 2000: 183).

4 Broadly speaking, Modern Japanese is based on the variety that emerged in Edo in the Edo period, but is heavily influenced by the Kyoto-based variety that was dominant prior to

On a different note, plays were performed in Dutch at Deshima. In 1820, to mark the departure of the *bugyō*, Tsutsui Masanori (1778–1859), the drama group at Deshima, *Ars Longa, Vita Brevis*, performed two farces in Dutch, both translations from French, *Twee Jaagers en het Melkmeisje* ('The Two Hunters and the Milkmaid') and *De Ongeduldige* ('The Impatient Person').[5] They were so well received that the Dutch had to perform them again (Scholten 1990: 190, 195).

The group of Japanese with whom the Dutch spoke their first language most frequently was the Nagasaki interpreters. On the one hand, it may be useful to think of the interpreters as a membrane between speakers of Dutch and Japanese, filtering each language as it passed through them. On the other hand, some Dutch seemed to have viewed them as something closer to a wall, preventing or inhibiting effective communication with Japanese. They would often pass comment on the quality of the Dutch spoken by the interpreters. While the quality of Dutch spoken by Engelbert Kaempfer's assistant Gen'emon won praise, the German physician complained about the general standard of Dutch amongst the Nagasaki interpreters (Vande Walle 2001b: 130–131). Apart from interpreting, they were a source of local gossip and news for the Dutch (Vermeulen *et al.* 1986–: IX:128).

The record of a visit to the *bugyō*'s house in 1745 by Jacob van der Waeijen (*opperhoofd* intermittently 1740–45) and several interpreters gives an interesting insight into how the Dutch worked with the interpreters, as well as telling us something about the Dutch they spoke. The day before the visit, the interpreter Suenaga Tokuzaemon (1678–1749) had asked Van der Waeijen to keep what he said as brief as possible. This, Van der Waeijen concluded, was so that Tokuzaemon would not be embarrassed by only saying a few words in Japanese when the Dutch were saying much more. Van der Waeijen was clearly concerned that Tokuzaemon would miss out important things that he said, so at one point he switched briefly to Japanese. This was in order to ensure that the *bugyō* heard mention of 15,000 chests of copper (Blussé and Remmelink

---

the Edo period (Frellesvig 2010: 378–379). Frellesvig (2010: 1) dates Modern Japanese from 1600 onwards, i.e., the period during which Edo emerged as the dominant political and economic centre in Japan. Japanese dialects are divided into three groups in Misao Tōjō's classification, Eastern, Western and Kyushu. The Nagasaki dialect is one of the Kyushu dialects (Shimoji 2018: 89).

5   *De twee Jaagers en het Melkmeisje* was written by Philip Fredrik Lijnslager in 1778 and *De Ongeduldige* by Pieter Gerard (P.G.) Witsen Geijsbeek in 1795.

2004: 69).[6] This episode illustrates several things. First, there was little trust between the two parties; second, the level of Tokuzaemon's Dutch was questionable; and, third, Van der Waeijen had learnt at least a little Japanese, perhaps in order to overcome as far as possible the challenges in using interpreters whose knowledge of Dutch was far from perfect.

Towards the end of the eighteenth century, Isaac Titsingh was at first not impressed by the interpreters. On 19 February 1780 he wrote that they were 'het uijtvaagsel van alle Japanders', i.e., 'the dregs of all Japanese'. Lequin (2011: 70) notes, though, that Titsingh's opinion changed as he got to know some of the interpreters at Deshima such as Motoki Yoshinaga and Yoshio Kōgyū, with whom he tried to work on scientific projects. Titsingh's successor, Van Rheede tot de Parkeler, expressed opinions on several of the interpreters, although these often concerned their character, rather than their ability as interpreters. He regarded Namura Motojirō (1729?–88) as 'the best, the most obliging and the most capable', who spoke 'very good Dutch'. He endearingly referred to Yoshio Kōgyū as 'an old rogue [...] but an oracle of the Guild of Interpreters', while he averred that Hori Monjūrō (or Toyosaburō, 1753?–1804) spoke good Dutch (Screech 2006: 21–23). Van Rheede tot de Parkeler observed that another interpreter, Namura Shinpachi (1720?–88) was good at Dutch expletives, although otherwise incompetent (Screech 2006: 23; Lequin 2003: 35).

In the late eighteenth century, the Swedish physician, Carl Peter Thunberg, who had learned his Dutch in Cape Colony, decried the lack of interest in Dutch shown by the Japanese (Vos 1980: 14). In the nineteenth century, Hendrick Doeff referred disparagingly to the language the interpreters spoke and wrote as *Japansch-Hollandsch* ('Japanese Dutch') (De Groot 2005: 28–29; 33). The fact that the interpreters often learned Dutch using pronunciation guides in *katakana*, which does not adequately represent the wider range of syllables in Dutch, is likely to have been one of the reasons for such comments. In his journal from 1861, the merchant Cornelis Theodoor van Assendelft de Coningh (2012: 20) records that the interpreter 'Saknozio', i.e., Yoshio Sakunojō, who had worked on the translation of Chomel's *Dictionnaire oeconomique*. spoke in 'halting, stumbling Dutch'. A little earlier, however, he records that a Japanese servant had spoken to him 'in fairly good Dutch' (*vrij goed Hollandsch*) (Assendelft de Coningh 2012: 14). Other comments were also more positive. In his account of Japan, published in 1833, Johannes (J.F.) van Overmeer Fisscher

---

6 Van der Waeijen recorded his own Japanese as *ietsman gosin fake agekami*, which is literally 15,000 chests of copper. In cMJ, these words would be transcribed as 'ichi man gosen hako akagane'.

(1800–48) (1833: 307–308) wrote that most of the 'servants of the *opperhoofd*' (*opperhoofds-dienaren*), who were in the main 'private interpreters' (*onderhandsche tolken*) by which he probably means *naitsūji*, all understood Dutch ('die allen Hollandsch verstonden').[7] This comment perhaps also points to a more general truth that the Dutch of the *naitsūji* was often better than that of other interpreters.

The Dutch spoken by *rangakusha* did not escape comment. The physician Katsuragawa Hoshū spoke 'tolerable Dutch' at Edo with Thunberg, who was there on the *hofreis* (Screech 1996: 18). Overmeer Fisscher (1833: 306) states that several *rangakusha* such as Ōtsuki Gentaku and Udagawa Yōan (he calls them *Gentak* and *Woedagawa*) 'all understood Dutch' ('allen Hollandsch verstonden') and would daily come to ask the Dutch questions, while they were in Edo. Apart from telling us about the quality of the Dutch spoken by Japanese interpreters and scholars, it almost goes without saying that these comments tell us that Japanese were speaking Dutch.

On one or two occasions the records provide quotations of Japanese speaking Dutch. Several *daimyō* knew Dutch. In Chapter 2, the example was given of the *opperhoofd* Hendrik Romberg quoting Shimazu Shigehide, Lord of Satsuma. Overmeer Fisscher records that on the *hofreis* he encountered two sons of the *daimyō* of 'Nagatz' (*Nakatsu han*). He quotes the older son saying in *Hollandsche woorden* 'Eerstemaal gezien'. This means 'first time seen'. Overmeer Fisscher (1833: 317) explains that the equivalent in Japanese is used when people meet each other for the first time.

In other cases, there is no direct reference to the language that is spoken, but other evidence may suggest that Dutch was spoken. For example, in his private journal of the 1780 *hofreis*, Isaac Titsingh records that the VOC delegation stayed at the *Nagasakiya* (Dutch Inn) in Nihonbashi, Edo and that among the Japanese he met in Edo were the *daimyō* of Fukuchiyama domain in Tanba, Kutsuki Masatsuna, and the physicians Nakagawa Jun'an and Katsuragawa Hoshū.[8] All three men corresponded with Titsingh in Dutch, so it is reasonable to assume that they exchanged at least some words in Dutch when they met, although the assistance of interpreters cannot be ruled out.

So, Dutch was spoken in Japan for different purposes, in variable quality, and by different groups of people. Dutch and non-Dutch Europeans as well

---

7   For a detailed account of Overmeer Fisscher's career and the background to his 1833 publication, see Effert (2008: 88–117).

8   The party also went to the 'Comedie' at Osaka and Kyoto and to the copper refinery at Sakai (Lequin 2011: 62).

as Japanese spoke the language. While the Dutch would often pass (less than favourable) comment on the Dutch spoken by Japanese, one may also wonder whether the Dutch spoken by less well-educated *moedertaalsprekers* (lit. 'mother tongue speakers') was always of a good quality. Not surprisingly, there is no comment on this in the Dutch records, but this, too, may have contributed to the communication problems between Dutch and Japanese.

3   *Rangaku*

A word is in order about the use of Dutch within the context of the movement that became known as *rangaku* (蘭学). There are two principal ways in which a knowledge of Dutch was applied within this context. The first to mention is the learning of Dutch. As we saw in the last chapter, thousands of Japanese studied the Dutch language and the texts it mediated, primarily but not exclusively at schools established for this purpose such as the *Shirandō shijuku*. They were helped in this enterprise by the publication of learning aids such as Ōtsuki Gentaku's primer *Rangaku kaitei* ('Guide to Dutch Learning') and dictionaries such as the two *Haruma* lexicons.

The second way in which a knowledge of Dutch was applied within the context of *rangaku* was in the reading and translation of imported Dutch texts. It is reckoned that more than 1,000 books on a range of subjects including medicine, astronomy and geography were translated from Dutch to Japanese during the Tokugawa period. These translations, which would have a profound effect on Japanese intellectual life and society more generally, are the subject of Chapter 6 in this book. As will become clear, the books that were translated from Dutch to Japanese were themselves often translations of works originally written in other European languages, such as German, French, English and Latin, something of which, as Timon Screech argues, the Japanese were aware by the late eighteenth century. Indeed, given this, Screech suggests that *rangaku* should more properly be rendered as 'European studies' although this loses the vital role that Dutch nevertheless played in this movement (Screech 2012: 318).[9] In the later nineteenth century the term was replaced by *yōgaku* (洋学, 'Western learning').

---

9 Furthermore, Screech notes that the importance of the pictures in the Western books in Japan cannot be underestimated.

4   Record-Keeping

An important source for our understanding not only of Dutch activities but
also of the use of the Dutch language in Japan is the factory journal or *dagregister*. This was typically added to every day by the *opperhoofd* of the Dutch
factory, or in his absence, for example when he was on the *hofreis*, by another
employee at the factory, often dictating it to one or more clerks (*scriba*).[10]
Even if 'nothing happened', an entry would be made to that effect (Blussé and
Remmelink 2004: 441). In the early years of the Dutch trading post at Hirado
no factory journal was maintained. A journal was maintained from 2 August
1620 onwards. However, the two books in which this was kept, the first from
2 August 1620 to 12 January 1624, and the second from 12 January 1624 to
28 February 1626 have not survived.[11] From 17 October 1625 to 29 January
1626 the VOC representatives Pieter Jansz. Muijser and Isaacq M. Bogaert
kept a journal on the *hofreis* (*Journael vande Reijse*) from Hirado (*Firando*) to
Edo.[12] Muijser and Pieter Nuyts kept a much more extensive journal for their
hofreis, which departed from Hirado on 15 August 1627 and which took the form
of a special embassy to the shogun (Clulow 2014: 78).[13] We also have an extract from the *dagregister* kept by Muijser for the period 29 June to 31 October
1628. At the end of this extract Muijser records in detail the start of a new
hofreis.[14] Between 1631 and 1633 Willem Jansz. Amersfoort kept a *dagregister*,
again at Edo, not the Dutch factory.[15] The reason for this was that he was having to deal with the Japanese response to the so-called 'Nuyts affair' described
in Chapter 1. The opening scenes in this sorry tale took place shortly after
Pieter Nuyts's arrival in Taiwan following the special embassy to Edo. It would
conclude with Nuyts's incarceration for several years in Japan (Clulow 2014:
225–238).

From 1633 onwards, there was a concerted effort to keep a regular journal at the Dutch factory with the first entry in the journal being made on

---

10   Clerks of the factory were required to make two additional copies of the diary. These
      were forwarded to Batavia every year, and one would be sent on to the directors of the
      Company (*Heeren Zeventien*) in Amsterdam (Hesselink 2005: 515).

11   These journals or *Grootboucken* were sent from Japan to Taiwan by order of the *ōmetsuke*
      Inoue Masashige and the Governor of Nagasaki when the Dutch transferred their trad-
      ing post from Hirado to Nagasaki. MS. The Hague *Nationaal Archief*, VOC (1.04.02), 1134,
      fol. 467r.

12   MS. The Hague, *Nationaal Archief*, VOC (1.04.02), 1092, fols. 340–344.

13   MS. The Hague, *Nationaal Archief*, VOC (1.04.02), 1095, fols. 449–509.

14   MS. The Hague, *Nationaal Archief*, 1.04.21, nr. 270. This was during the Pieter Nuyts affair
      described in Ch. 1 (Clulow 2014: 226–228).

15   MS. The Hague, *Nationaal Archief*, 1.04.21, nr. 271–274.

6 September 1633 by Nicolaes Couckebakker (*opperhoofd* 1633–39). As senior staff at the factory came and went at regular intervals, the *dagregister* formed an invaluable resource as the memory of the factory in cases where the Japanese wanted to discuss events that had happened before the arrival of the current *opperhoofd*, some of whom were only in post for a year. While some pages no longer survive, we have a reasonably complete set of *dagregister* manuscripts until 1 December 1833. The manuscripts include some of the journals of the *hofreis* to Edo between 1647 and 1830.[16] We also have fairly complete records of the *dagregisters* for 1843 to 1860, the year in which the trading post at Deshima was closed, although manuscripts for a few years are missing.[17] Today, these manuscripts are preserved in the Dutch national archive (*Nationaal Archief*) in The Hague. Transcriptions of the *dagregister* until 1651 have been published as have annotated English translations from the beginning of the Deshima period until 1800.[18] In addition to the 'regular' *dagregister*, the Dutch also kept, from time to time, a secret *dagregister*, which they clearly did not want Japanese eyes to see. One example is the 'secret journal' that the *opperhoofd*, Isaac Titsingh, kept during his time in Japan in the 1780s.[19] This was primarily a record of his dealings with the Nagasaki *bugyō*, which he kept in order to send to Batavia (Screech 2006: 185–206). Later, 'secret journals' included accounts of the unexpected arrival of Russian and American ships at Deshima prior to 1853.[20] Other records such as accounts were also kept at Deshima, where a bookkeeper was employed.

From 1641 to 1859, the Dutch compiled an annual report, the *Oranda fūsetsugaki* ('Dutch Book of Rumours'), for the Japanese authorities on events outside Japan. In the early years, at least, this was compiled by the Dutch in Japan based on oral reports of those arriving on board voc ships, and subsequently translated by the Nagasaki interpreters (Iwao 1976–79: II:25–26).[21]

---

16   For the *dagregisters* kept at the factory, MS. The Hague, *Nationaal Archief*, 1.04.21, nrs. 53–249, for those kept on the *hofreis*, nrs. 260–269.

17   MS. The Hague, *Nationaal Archief*, 1.04.21, nrs. 1613–1624.

18   For the transcriptions, see *Diaries* (1974–). For the translations, see Vermeulen *et al.* (1986–); Blussé *et al.* (1992); and Blussé and Remmelink (2004).

19   Titsingh was the *opperhoofd* on three occasions: 1779–1780, 1781–1783, and in 1784.

20   MS. The Hague, *Nationaal Archief*, 1.04.21, nr. 250–259.

21   Matsukata (2011: 102) describes the process of compiling the *fūsetsugaki* slightly differently. He observes that when a Dutch ship arrived in Nagasaki harbour, interpreters interviewed the *opperhoofd* (who, one assumes, had spoken to voc crewmembers) about news concerning the outside world. This news was conveyed to the Nagasaki magistrate (*bugyō*) and then to *bakufu* authorities in Edo. See also Matsukata (2007). In March 1669, François de Haese (*opperhoofd* 1669–70) recorded in the *dagregister* that while in Edo an interpreter had visited him and written down news about Europe and the Dutch East

The *opperhoofd* would then sign the translation (trusting that the Japanese translation was accurate). He would also make a record of the information that had been provided to the Japanese, sometimes in the *dagregister*, sometimes elsewhere. For example, on 8 August 1678, Albert Brevinck (*opperhoofd* intermittently 1677–80), recorded that he had given the interpreters the news that the Prince of Orange had married the daughter of the King of England, i.e., the future William III of England had married the future Mary II (in fact daughter of James II, then Duke of York). Here, Brevinck refers to the Prince of Orange, who was a *stadholder* and not a king of the United Provinces, as *syn Conincklycke Hoogheyt*, i.e., 'his Royal Highness', perpetuating the myth that the Dutch had told the Japanese, that their ruler was not simply a prince, but a king (Iwao 1976–79: II:314).[22]

As well as these more official documents, Dutchmen kept personal journals in Japan. Isaac Titsingh kept a personal journal of the *hofreis* to Edo in 1780. This is far more detailed than the more official accounts of the *hofreis*, with Lequin, who published the journal, asserting that it is the most extensive such document made during the period of the Dutch presence in Japan. For example, Titsingh gives some 170 Japanese names of the places through which the *hofreis* train passed. Titsingh was perhaps the most intellectual and cosmopolitan *opperhoofd* and provides many valuable observations on life in Japan (Lequin 2011: 61–134). In the seventeenth century, three VOC employees who kept personal records of their experiences in Japan were the merchant Nicolaes Puyck on the journey to Edo in 1609 to gain trading rights for the Dutch, the Swede Olof Eriksson Willman (1651–52) and Hendrick Indijck (*opperhoofd* 1660–61; 1662–63) on the *hofreis* to Edo in 1663.[23] In the eighteenth century, Jan van der Cruijsse (c. 1700–1738, *opperhoofd* 1736–37) wrote a journal at a time when *rangaku* was starting to take root and in the nineteenth century, on the *hofreis* of 1818, Jan Cock Blomhoff made a private journal which he sent to his wife, Titia, in Holland.[24] Others who kept personal records of

---

Indies. He also noted that his version accorded with that told by a Dutch colleague to the Governor of Nagasaki (Vermeulen *et al.* 1986–: XIII:332).

22   For the origins of this myth, see Clulow (2014: 41–43).

23   For Puyck's journal, see Van Opstall (1972: II:345–355); and Clulow (2014: 49–55). For Willman's journal, see Willman (2013) As this was written in Swedish, probably soon after his return to Sweden (p. 18), there will be no detailed linguistic study of it here. For Indijck's journal, see Vermeulen *et al.* (1986–: XIII:371–374).

24   For Van der Cruijsse, see Van der Velde (2000a). For Cock Blomhoff, see Blomhoff (2000a). MS. LUB, BPL 3651 is Cock Blomhoff's official report of the 1818 *hofreis*, entitled *Aantekeningen op de Reize Na-en-Van Jedo in Japan.*

their experiences in Japan include Engelbert Kaempfer (in Japan 1690–92), and Hendrick Doeff, Philipp Franz von Siebold and Overmeer Fisscher, who were all there in the nineteenth century. Each of them published works based on their experiences in Japan on their return to Europe.

A word is in order about François Caron's *Rechte beschryvinge van het machtigh koninghrijck van Iappan* ('A True Description of the Mighty Kingdom of Japan'), an unauthorized edition of which appeared as early as 1648 in Amsterdam. Caron was a merchant at Hirado prior to 1639 and then *opperhoofd* from 1639 to 1641. The work began life in 1636 as Caron's responses to a series of questions from the newly-appointed Directeur-Generaal at Batavia, Philips Lucasz.[25] It went through ten editions in the United Provinces and was translated into English, German, French and Latin. It would provide the most comprehensive account of Japan in Europe until the publication of Kaempfer's 'History of Japan' in 1727–28 (Boxer 1935: cxxviii–cxxix).

One other work to mention, again by Titsingh, is an essay entitled *Discours philosophique* ('Philosophical Discourse') that he wrote in Dutch at Deshima in December 1779 for his friend Gotō Sōzaemon (1725–80), a *bakufu* official in Nagasaki. This was based on Volume I of the best-selling Dutch work *Katechismus der Natuur* ('Catechism of Nature' Amsterdam, 1777–79) by Johannes Martinet (1729–95). Screech goes so far as to say that this essay 'marks an important moment in the transmission of Enlightenment thought to Japan' (Lequin 2011: 15–60; 2003: 203; Screech 2006: 34–36 and Chs. 9–10).[26]

Finally, the Japanese who knew Dutch would often sign their names on official documents in *rōmaji*, next to which they placed their seal. One manuscript compiled by Motoki Yoshinaga (also Einoshin) includes eight signatures by Japanese who knew Dutch. Einoshin signed his name *Motogi Enosin*, while Namura Katsuemon (also Shinpachi) signed himself *Namoera Katsemon*, with the digraph ⟨oe⟩ pointing to a Dutch orthographical influence (Screech 2006: 22).

---

25   MS. LUB, D H 213, *Verklaringh op verscheyden Vragen 't Japance Rijk concernerende door den Edele Heer Philips Luijcasz, Directeur-Generaal wegens den nederlanschen Stand in India voorgestelt ende door den Edele President François Caron beantwoord*. The first authorized edition was published in 1661 (Boxer 1935: cxxviii).

26   Titsingh knew Martinet. Screech (2006: 207) asserts that Titsingh gave a copy of his book to Kutsuki Masasuna. A Japanese book influenced by Martinet's *Katechismus der Natuur* was Doi Toshitsura's (1789–1848) *Sekka zusetsu* ('A Pictorial Explanation of Snowflakes', 1832).

5   Correspondence

Correspondence, both official and unofficial, provides another extensive resource for the study of Dutch in Japan. An early example is a letter written in
Dutch by the first *opperhoofd* Jacques Specx (1609–12; 1614–21) to one of the
survivors from the *Liefde*, Melchior van Santvoort in 1615 (Wieder 1923–25:
98–99).[27] In 1616 the Englishman, Will Adams, wrote a letter in Dutch from
Edo to Specx, peppered with occasional hints of his English mother tongue
(Wieder 1923–25: 76–78). In January 1617, Specx wrote in Dutch from Hirado
to John Jourdain, the President of the English at Bantam (Murakami and
Murakawa 1900: 199). We also have letters (in Dutch) from other survivors from
the *Liefde*, such as Jan Joosten van Lodensteyn, as well as other Dutch at Hirado
including the second *opperhoofd*, Hendrick Brouwer (1613–14) (Wieder 1923–
25: 87–119). In fact, thousands of letters written as early as 1623 into the nineteenth century from the Dutch factories to the Governor-General in Batavia,
other Dutch factories in South and East Asia and the Japanese authorities
are preserved at the Dutch National Archive in The Hague.[28] The archive also
holds many letters written in Dutch to the factories in Japan.[29]

Engelbert Kaempfer, Carl Peter Thunberg, Philipp von Siebold and Isaac
Titsingh wrote private letters. Kaempfer wrote letters not only in Dutch, but
also in German and Latin, to correspondents in Batavia and Europe (Meier-
Lemgo 1965). In 1776, after departing from Edo on the *hofreis*, Thunberg began to
correspond in Dutch with two *rangakusha*, Nakagawa Jun'an and Katsuragawa
Hoshū, to both of whom he had taught medicine and whom he described as
his 'beloved pupils' (Screech 2005: 165). Before taking his leave of them in Edo,
he had presented them with certificates, indicating what they had been taught,
which he explicitly states were written in Dutch. These, Thunberg observes,
made the two Japanese very happy and proud (Screech 2005: 165). Von Siebold
wrote letters in Dutch in Japan to among others the Japanese explorer and cartographer, Mamiya Rinzō (1775–1844) and, on his return to Japan, his daughter

---

27   For details of other letters written in Dutch to and from Hirado, see Viallé and Cryns (2018:
      32–33).

28   MS. The Hague, *Nationaal Archief,* 1.04.21, nr. 482–591. The *opperhoofd* at Nagasaki re-
      ported to the Products and Civilian Stores (*Lands Producten en Civiel Magazijnen*) within
      the larger colonial government on Batavia, but at times he sent letters directly to the
      Governor-General, the senior administrator in Asia (Matsukata 2011: 102).

29   MS. The Hague, *Nationaal Archief,* 1.04.21, nr. 276–349.

Ine, who was the first female physician in Japan. These are on display in the *Naratakijuku* collection.[30]

Perhaps the best preserved and arguably most interesting private correspondence from a linguistic perspective is that of Isaac Titsingh. He wrote letters in Dutch, but with a significant amount of code switching into other languages. He corresponded not only with fellow Dutch VOC-employees such as Hendrik Duurkoop (1736–78) and Petrus Chassé, but also with a range of Japanese, mostly after he had left Japan. The correspondence is testimony to the fact that Titsingh 'stood in the centre of a web of open-minded savant *Rangakusha*' (Lequin 2003: 33). Rather touchingly, the Japanese who wrote to Titsingh would sometimes ask him to correct their Dutch and return their letters with corrections. Some of his correspondents such as Narabayashi Jūbei (1750?–1801) and Nishi Kichirōbei (also Kichibei 1747?–1818) were Nagasaki interpreters, while others occupied more prominent positions in Japanese society, such as the *daimyō* Kutsuki Masatsuna (Lequin 1990). The written Dutch of Narabayashi Jūbei and Nishi Kichirōbei is far from perfect. If one is looking for positive aspects, they have a decent lexical range and use very respectful forms of address to Titsingh, which perhaps appealed to the Japanese sense of social rank. In his letter to Titsingh from Deshima on 26 November 1785 Jūbei wrote 'Ik ben ... dank ... over de vriendschap ... van UWelEdele Grootachtbaar[heid]', which can be translated as 'I am thankful for the friendship of Your (Noble) Great-worshipful[ness]'. Likewise, Kichirōbei wrote to Titsingh two days earlier addressing him as 'WelEdele Agtbaare Heer Titsingh' ('Most Noble and Worshipful Mr. Titsingh') (Lequin 1990: 1:10–12).[31] Titsingh's correspondence with Kutsuki Masatsuna continued for over twenty years from 1785, when Masatsuna wrote from Edo to his friend, now at Chinsura in Bengal. It lasted until 1807 when Titsingh wrote to Masatsuna from Amsterdam, not aware that he had passed away five years earlier (Lequin 1992).

An early letter in the correspondence written by Masatsuna to Titsingh in 1787 illustrates that he had not yet mastered the language (Lequin 1992: 16):

Aan de WelEdele Heer Titsingh, Directeur van Bengale ... UwEdele misive, uit handen van den Heer Romberg door bestelling de Heer Ulps met

---

30 There is also a letter from Von Siebold to his Japanese wife, Taki, in Japanese in the *Narutakijuku* collection. It is not clear if he composed this himself, or with the help of a Japanese.

31 It must be admitted that the *opperhoofd* Van Rheede tot de Parkeler also uses this form of address to Titsingh, but perhaps it at least shows that these Japanese were attuned to forms of address appropriate to their addressee.

> hem brief laat ontfangen, en het mijn beantwoord voor het afschrift van uE: brief van aan den Tolken ...

Although the Dutch of Japanese such as Masatsuna was by no means perfect, one should remember that at this time, there were no Dutch-Japanese lexicons or Dutch grammars for Japanese. I should add that Masatsuna's handwriting in Dutch was wonderfully ornate.[32] He had clearly mastered 'the horizontal script'.

In November 1785, the interpreter Hori Monjūrō wrote a letter to Titsingh. This includes an extensive range of Dutch words and is for the most part comprehensible (Lequin 1990: 1:13–15). This accords with Van Rheede tot de Parkeler's comment that he spoke 'good Dutch' (Screech 2006: 21–22). In some cases, one can see the possible influence of Japanese. For example, Monjūrō refers to *twee boek* rather than *twee boeken* ('two books'), possibly influenced by the fact that Japanese does not add a plural suffix to non-animate nouns, but instead uses count words.[33] However, he clearly had some grasp of Dutch syntax. For example, in the main clause *Tot hier toe heb ik op Collegie geschreven* ('Upto here I have written at the interpreters' guild'), he observes the Dutch rule of subject-verb inversion. In subordinate clauses, he follows the rule that verbs are clause-final, e.g., *Een woord* [...] *is net overeengekomen* [...] *dat wij dit Jaar een goede opperhoofd krijgen zou* ('We have just received word that we shall get a good *opperhoofd* this year').[34] This is not to say that he always does this, and he may have got some help from a native speaker at Deshima, but it certainly challenges the notion that the Japanese were not competent users of Dutch. Furthermore, one should remember that many Dutch wrote in a manner that deviated from the norms set by the cultural elite at this time.

The *opperhoofd* Jan Cock Blomhoff corresponded with Japanese in Dutch. One letter that he received from an interpreter begins by asking Blomhoff to give the person who showed him the letter a bit of sugar: *WelEdel Heer Bromhof* (sic) *ik verzoek UwEd. zeer vriendelijk om een weinigie Zuijker aan thoonder dezes af te geven*.[35] The interpreter uses ⟨r⟩ instead of ⟨l⟩ for Blomhof's name, reflecting the fact that Japanese only has one liquid phoneme /r/ usually realized

---

32 For an example, see Lequin (2003: 34, fig. 11).

33 Interestingly, he does give plural forms to animate objects such as *twee heeren* ('two gentlemen') and *de burgemeesters* ('two mayors'), something which is found in Japanese accidence.

34 The final verb should be *zouden*. Japanese does not have verb suffixes indicating person and number so again the lack of distinction between singular and plural may be influenced by the author's first language.

35 I thank Guita Winkel for this information provided to me in an email dated 14 June 2017.

as [ɾ] (Labrune 2012: 92).[36] Sometimes, letters had to be written quickly. On 4 October 1808, the British frigate the *Phaeton* arrived in Nagasaki Bay. The next day, the *opperhoofd* Hendrick Doeff wrote a letter in Dutch to the *bugyō* warning him of the dangers that the *Phaeton* posed.[37] One assumes that a translation into Japanese was made with equal haste. Above, it was noted that Udagawa Yōan 'understood Dutch'. He could also write very serviceable Dutch, as evidenced by a letter that he wrote to Willem de Sturler (*opperhoofd* 1823–26) in the eighth year of the *Bunsei* (文政) era (1825–26), seeking to learn more about the Linnaean classification of the natural world. He renders *Bunsei* as *Boenzij* and signs himself *WOEDAGAWA JOOAN*. The ⟨oe⟩, ⟨ij⟩ and ⟨j⟩ reflect the influence of Dutch orthography (Hoffmann and Serrurier 1882: 117–118).

Occasionally, Japanese wrote to each other in Dutch. One example is a very ornate valedictory letter from Katsuragawa Hoan (1797–1844) to Ōtsuki Bankei (1801–78) (see fig. 8). Hoan wishes Bankei well on his journey from Edo to Nagasaki to pursue Dutch studies. Hoan gives the letter a title, *Op het vertrek van den Heer Ootsoeki Heijziro*. Heijirō was one of Bankei's pen names. The Dutch is of very high quality. Hoan knows to split separable verbs viz. *op te helderen* (to clarify), to invert subject and object after an adverb viz. *en teffens verzoek ik u*; and to place the verb at the end of a subordinate clause. The letter is dated *den 16 Sanguats 10 Boenzeij*, i.e., the 16th of the third month in the 10th year of the *Bunsei* era (1827). Two letters by Japanese, Ono Ranzan (1729–1810) and Kimata Takihito, addressed at the turn of the nineteenth century to another Japanese, Yūnoki Tokiwa, were also written in good Dutch. They relate to a work by Tokiwa on *Fungi clavati*, which were believed to be the origin of insects.[38] Ranzan, who signs himself 'Ono Lanzan', was an important figure in the development of botany in Japan and was called the 'Japanese Linnaeus'

---

36   Other Japanese do this as well. For example, Kutsuki Masatsuna wrote to Isaac Titsingh in 1786 'heb ik firiciteert' instead of 'heb ik [ge]feliciteerd' ('I have congratulated') (Lequin 1992: 9). Such errors are by no means constant. Another of Titsingh's Japanese correspondents Hori Monjūrō writes *filisiteerdende* ('congratulating') (Lequin 1990: 1:13). *Zuiker* is typically written with and pronounced with a word-initial /s/. However, according to the *Woordenboek der Nederlandsche Taal* (WNT) the word does have a word-initial /z/ in a few varieties of Dutch and there are instances when it starts with the grapheme ⟨z⟩.

37   The letter is preserved in the *Nationaal Archief* in The Hague. I thank Noboru Oi for bringing it to my attention.

38   The letters were attached to a copy of Tokiwa's *Natsukusa fuyumushi no zu* (1801) in Leiden University Library (Ser. 1023, Kerlen 1117). Kerlen reproduces the letters (Plate 18). The authors give the month (both December), but not the year in which they wrote their letters.

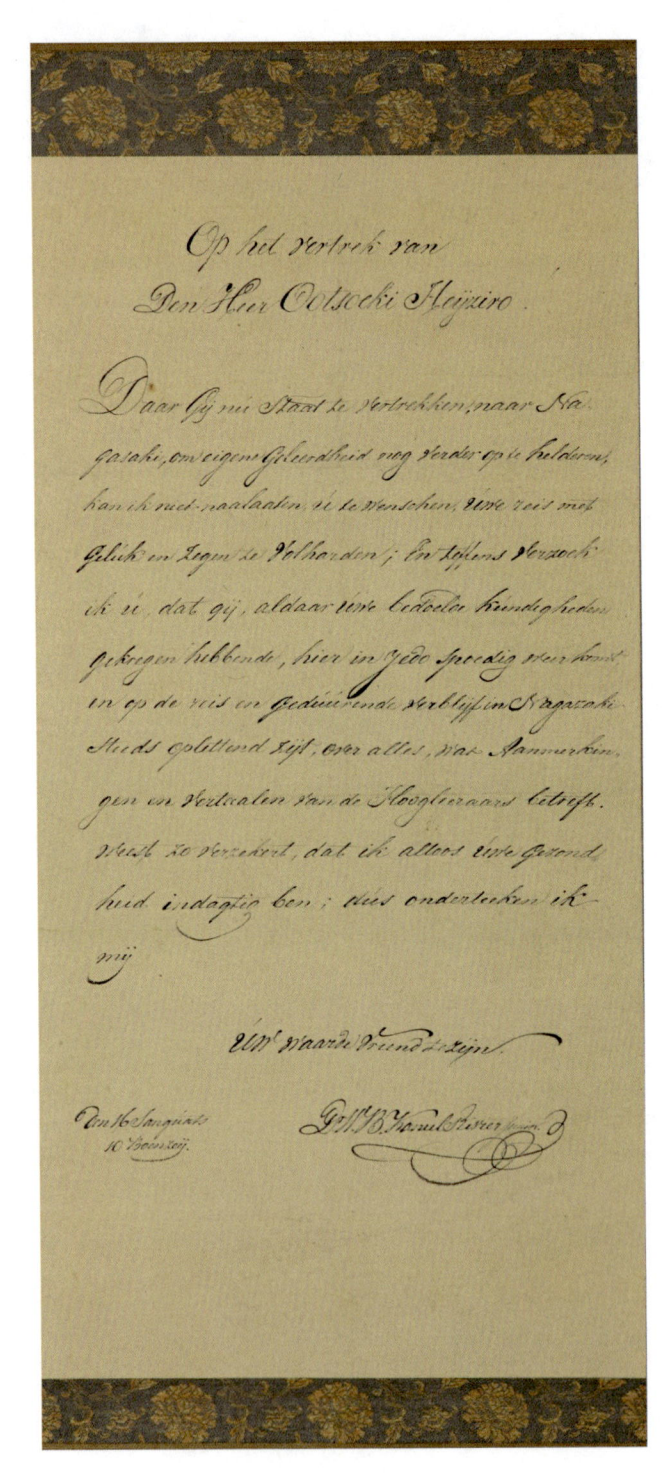

FIGURE 8
A letter from
Katsuragawa Hoan to
Ōtsuki Bankei (1827)
WUL 文庫 08 B0183

by Von Siebold. Further research may establish to what extent Dutch was the language of correspondence between *rangakusha*.

On a different note, short messages, too, were written in Dutch. The Dutch merchant, Van Assendelft de Coningh, stayed in Yokohama during his visit to Japan from 1859 to 1861. In the record of his time in Japan he reproduces some of the messages that he received from Japanese associates, which he had kept as 'curiosities' (*curiositeiten*), reproducing them in part to illustrate the poor quality of the Dutch. One request from a Japanese asks the Dutchman to come to the customs office to deal with a matter: *Aan den Heer Coningh Gelieve U kom, tot de Tolkantoor, om eenige zaak te behandelen, Tolkantoor Officier.* Another message asks him for eau de Cologne: *Aan den Heer Coningh, Ik verzoek dat, als u niet spijt, gelieve een kist oud kloinie (eau de Cologne) te geven* (Assendelft de Coningh 1879: II:102–104). In each case, the Dutch is understandable, but not without error.[39]

6 Printing of Dutch Books

After the opening of Japan in 1854, there was a sudden increase in demand for books in Dutch, for in the first years Dutch was used as the LWC between Japanese and Europeans. To meet this demand, Dutch books were printed in Japan. Many of these books were printed in Nagasaki, while some give the place of printing specifically as Deshima. Pompe van Meerdervoort (1970: 86) refers to a printing shop on the island and a list of employees on Deshima in 1861 gives 'G. Indermaur' as the printer.[40] An early example is a multi-volume military book *Reglement op de exercitien en manoeuvres der infanterie* ('Code for infantry drills and manoeuvres'), (re-)printed (*nagedrukt*) in Nagasaki in the second half of the 1850s, of which there are six copies in the Ueno collection. The printing of Van der Pijl's learner *Gemeenzame Leerwijs, voor degenen, die de Engelsche taal beginnen te leeren* ('General Learner for those who want to begin to learn the English language') in Nagasaki in 1857 tells us a couple of things. First, that already by 1857 the demand for learning English was such that it could not be met by simply importing books, and second, that English was being learnt via Dutch. Another book in the Ueno collection printed in Nagasaki in 1858 is an everyman's guide to physics, *Volks-natuurkunde* (Ueno catalogue no. 3161). At Deshima in 1858, the last *opperhoofd* at the Dutch

---

39 Assendelft de Coningh (2012: 86–87) was clearly not impressed by the Dutch of the Japanese with whom he had contact, observing that it was often incomprehensible.
40 *Nederlandsche en Japansche Almanak voor het Jaar 1861.*

trading post, Jan Hendrik [Janus Henricus] Donker Curtius (*opperhoofd* 1852–60), published a treaty ('Traktaat') between the Dutch government and the *bakufu*, which set out the nature of the new relationship between the Dutch and the Japanese. In 1861, on his return to Japan after his banishment, Von Siebold published a series of letters in Dutch *Open brieven uit Japan* ('Open letters from Japan') at Deshima (Ueno no. 3635). In the same year, a Dutch-Japanese almanac with the title *Nederlandsche en Japansche Almanak voor het Jaar 1861* was printed at 'Desima. Ter Nederlandsche drukkery', i.e., on the Dutch press at Deshima (Kerlen 1120). In some cases, the publishing details of Dutch books reprinted in Japan are not given. One example is a book on military matters, *Voorschrift omtrent de wapens* ('Instructions concerning weapons'), originally printed in The Hague in 1852 (Ueno no. 645).

7 Dutch Names

The Dutch gave Dutch names to Japanese. Many of these were recorded by the *opperhoofd* Willem de Sturler in a manuscript, which was later published (Hoffmann and Serrurier 1882: 111–113). Let us add some detail to this. An early example is Brasman, the name given to the Nagasaki interpreter Yokoyama Yozaemon (1602–92) (Cleyer 1985: 49). This probably derives from the Dutch verb *brassen*, to be gluttonous, so it means 'glutton'.[41] Above, reference was made to an encounter between the Dutch on the *hofreis* and the two sons of the *daimyō* of Nakatsu. Overmeer Fisscher wrote that the younger son, who was clearly showing an interest in things Dutch, had the Dutch sobriquet (*den Hollandschen bijnaam*) *Maurits*, possibly after the *stadholder* and Prince of Orange of the same name (Overmeer Fisscher 1833: 317). This was, in fact, Okudaira Masanobu (b. 1809), the son of Okudaira Masataka, both of whom were enthusiasts for *rangaku*. Masataka was given the name of another *stadholder*, Frederik Hendrik, by Hendrick Doeff in 1806 (Goodman 1986: 160). In 1826 the Sanobu family of Shimonoseki, a port on the route of the *hofreis* in the far west of Honshu, took the name Van Dalen ('of the valleys'), while earlier in 1716 the Ito family also of Shimonoseki had taken the Dutch surname Van den Berg ('of the mountain') (Goodman 2013: 263 n. 21). In 1858 the Dutch undertook their final *hofreis* to Edo. In the party was Jonkheer Dirk de Graeff van Polsbroek (1833–1916), who kept a journal on the journey. At Shimonoseki, the Dutch encountered an official whom Van Polsbroek refers to as 'den tweeden burgemeester'. He learns that this official had been given the name Hendrik

---

41 *WNT*. Kraft (Cleyer 1985: 170) suggests it means Schwaetzer, German for 'chatterbox'.

van den Berg by Hendrick Doeff many years earlier.[42] The fact that the Dutch name of one leading family in Shimonoseki was 'of the valleys' while that of the other was 'of the mountain' gave rise to a verse that Van Polsbroek found hanging outside the Van den Berg house, where the Dutch were staying: 'Bergen en Daalen ontmoeten elkander nooyt maar menschen wel' ('Mountains and Valleys never meet each other, but people (i.e., the Van den Bergs and Van Dalens) do [meet each other]'). This had been written by Doeff in 1814 on an ink drawing of a landscape with Mt. Fuji in the background, by the Dutch physician Jan Frederik Feilke (Kobe City Museum 1998: 63). Another verse that hung outside the Van den Berg house was written by Okudaira Masataka, a.k.a. Frederik Hendrik. It is of no great literary merit, but underlines the enthusiasm for the Dutch that he and other family members had:

> *Op het verzoek van den Hospes van het Hollandsche logement te*
> *Simenisiko,*
> *Hendrik van den Berg is een van de menschen*
> *Die het bloeijen van het Hollandsch handel wenschen.*
> *Hij is als wij een van de liefhebbers van de Hollandsche Waaren.*
> *Zoo moet hij hoopen de schepen jaarlijks naar Japan vaaren.*

> [At the request of the host of the Dutch lodgings at Shimonoseki,
> Hendrik van den Berg is one of the people
> Who wish for the flowering of Dutch trade,
> He is, like us, one of the lovers of Dutch wares,
> And so he must hope that the ships sail to Japan each year]

Under the verse is written *Geschreven door den vorst en kasteel eigenaar van Nakats in 't landschap Boezen, Frederik Hendrik* ('Written by the Prince and Castle-owner of Nakatsu in the county of Buzen, FH'). In 1822 the *opperhoofd* Jan Cock Blomhoff wrote a laudatory verse to Frederik Hendrik (Kobe City Museum 1998: 47).[43] Other Dutch verses written by Doeff and Cock Blomhoff also hung outside the house (De Graeff van Polsbroek 1987: 36–37). One other Japanese who wrote Dutch verse was the *rangakusha* Tsuji Norinobu (Ranshitsu) (1756–1835). Goodman (2013: 144–145) observes that he had a great interest in languages, studying Malay, Greek, Korean and Pali alongside Dutch.

---

42 This would appear to be the keeper of the Dutch hostel at Shimonoseki, Itō Mokunojō.
43 See Waseda University Library Call no. 文庫 08 B0155 for another example of Masataka signing himself as Frederik Hendrik.

The Dutch gave Imamura Gen'emon the affective sobriquet 'Vadertje Ginnemon' ('Father Gen'emon') (Van der Velde 2000b: 25).[44] Hendrick Doeff gave another *rangakusha* Baba Teiyū the name 'Abraham' (did his family name sound like Abra(ham)?) (Goodman 2013: 128). The Japanese family name Katsuragawa means 'cinnamon river' (the *kanji* 桂 *katsura* refers to the cinnamon tree, *Cercidiphyllum japonicum*), so several generations of the family used the Dutch equivalent of this, 'Kaneelrivier' (Hoffmann and Serrurier 1882: 105–107). For example, Katsuragawa Hoan signed the letter to Ōtsuki Bankei *Dr. W.B. Kaneel Rivier Junior*. W.B. refers to Wilhelmus Botanicus, a Latin sobriquet, of which more in the next chapter.

Other Japanese, too, were given Dutch names in the first half of the nineteenth century. Some were jocular. Four Japanese physicians were given the names Pieter Gezond (Peter Healthy), Willem Beterschap (William Get Better), Kornelis Hersteld (Cornelius Got Better) and Flip Genezen (Philip Cured), while the Dutch were perhaps wary of Gerrit Pasop (Gerrit Watch out!). A few women received Dutch names, too. The wife of Hendrik van den Berg was called Carolina Vrolijk (Carolina Jolly), whilst the wife of Frederik Hendrik was called Charlotta (Lotje) Blom (Charlotte Bloom) (Hoffmann and Serrurier 1882: 112–114).

On a slightly different note, the Dutch gave names to places in Japan, in some sense decontextualizing and recontextualizing them as Dutch places. One example is a mountain overlooking Nagasaki Bay. It was said that during the persecution of Catholic Christians in Japan, missionaries were forced to jump to their death from the mountain. The Dutch thus gave it the name *Papenberg* ('Papist mountain'). Overmeer Fisscher (1833: 271–272) refers to this name in his book on Japan published in 1833. Another example of a Dutch toponym for a Japanese geographical feature is *Straate Specx* or Specx Strait. This was named after Jacques Specx and used to indicate the strait between the island of Hirado and Kyushu. It appears on a Dutch map printed in 1860, based on information provided by Von Siebold (Huyssen van Kattendyke 1860: after p. 236). In his journal from the final years of the Tokugawa era, Dirk de Graeff van Polsbroek refers to the Strait of Shimonoseki (or Kanmon Straits (関門海峡)) between Honshu and Kyushu as *De Straat van de Capellen* ('Chapel Straights') (De Graeff van Polsbroek 1987: 35).

One final example of a Dutch name being given to something Japanese concerns a boardgame. On the 1776 *hofreis*, Thunberg observed that the interpreters gave the game *sōbutsu* (lit. win or lose) (more properly *e-sugoroku* 絵双六 'picture-sugoroku'), which was similar to snakes and ladders, the Dutch name

---

44   -*tje* is a diminutive suffix which can be used in an affective sense.

Ganse-speel (Screech 2005: 128, 282 n. 73). This was probably inspired by the Dutch game *Ganzenbord(spel)* ('Goose board (game)').

8 Code Switching

Chapter 5 analyses code switching into other languages in Dutch texts. Here, a word is in order about Japanese authors switching into Dutch. One motivation for this was to describe the Dutch and the Low Countries. One salient example is Morishima Chūryō's *Kōmō zatsuwa* ('Red-haired miscellany'. 1787). This work, which to some extent stands in the Japanese tradition of *ehon* (絵本, 'picture book') combining picture and narrative, was aimed at a general audience. In it, Chūryō provides extensive details of daily life in the Low Countries. In one section he discusses prostitutes, rendering the Dutch word *hoer* ('whore') as *ūru*. In discussing the price for the services of prostitutes, he introduces the *rijksdaalder* (*rekisutātoru*) and says that it is often *matorosu* ('sailors', Dutch *matroos*), who go with the prostitutes (Vos 1971: 628; Winkel 2004: 49). A variant of this, *madorosu*, has become embedded in Japanese. The insertion of the first 'o' and addition of a final 'u' may be explained by the fact that the canonical syllable structure of classical Japanese was (Consonant) Vowel ((c)v) (Shibatani 1990: 121–122). Other words for which he provides *katakana* equivalents are as varied as 'lion' (*rēū*, Dutch *leeuw*), 'Japan' (*yapan*, Dutch *Japan*) and 'God' (*hotto*, Dutch *God* [xɔt]) (Winkel 2004: 61, 63). He also describes the sea route from Europe to Japan switching to render European toponyms in *katakana* such as *amusuterudamu, rondon, gorōto buritaniya* and even perhaps unwittingly incorporating some Latin from his source referring to the *Oseānusu Okeddentārisu* ('Oceanus Occidentalis'), i.e., the Western Ocean or Atlantic (Morishima Chūryō and Ōtsuki Gentaku 1972: 51–52).

In *Ransetsu benwaku* ('A clarification of misunderstandings in theories [about] the Dutch', 1799), Ōtsuki Gentaku switches to render Dutch terms. In Japanese *kana*, he renders 'beer' as *bīru* (now a Dutch loanword in Japanese < Dutch *bier*), 'glass' *garasu* (again a Dutch loanword in Japanese (< Dutch *glas*)) and jar as *furesu* (< Dutch *fles*) (Morishima Chūryō and Ōtsuki Gentaku 1972: 152, 159). The Edo artist Shiba Kōkan (1747–1818) switched into Dutch in his journal on his visit to Nagasaki in 1788. This went through several reprints and editions, being published in 1815 as *Saiyū nikki* ('Diary of a Western Journey'). Like Chūryō, he uses the Dutch word for 'sailor' transcribing it as *matarosu*.[45]

---

45 For an English summary of *Saiyū nikki*, see Plutschow (2006: 199–223), although some of the transcriptions, such as those for *lekker*, are incorrect. Kōkan (1927: 101) notes that

He also used the Portuguese loanword *kapitan* (in *hiragana*) for the *opperhoofd* and the Dutch loanword *koppu* (in *katakana*), both of which had by now become embedded in Japanese texts (Shiba Kōkan 1927: 107, 101, 106). In describing a visit to the Dutch-style house of the interpreter Yoshio Kōgyū, he refers to a small boy in Kōgyū's house who spoke some Dutch. Kōkan switched to report that the boy called horses '*pārudo*' (Dutch *paard*) and beef *kūpaisu* (*koevlees*— 'cow meat'). When he gave the boy a sweet potato, he said '*rekkeru, rekkeru*' and ate it. Kōkan explains that this means 'delicious'. In fact, it is a rendering of the Dutch *lekker* (Shiba Kōkan 1927: 112). The small boy was most probably Yoshio Joen (also Gonnosuke 1785–1831), the son of Kōgyū and his concubine, who would himself become an interpreter and assist Hendrick Doeff in the compilation of his Dutch-Japanese lexicon (De Groot 2000: 120). A few days later, Kōkan reports that he painted what is now a well-known ink wash portrait of Kōgyū with two angels floating above him. He switches into Dutch to refer to one of the angels, who was blowing a trumpet, as *engeru rūfu*, probably a rendering in *katakana* of the Dutch *engel roeper* ('angel trumpeter') (Shiba Kōkan 1927: 113; French 1974: 67).[46] In the picture, he added Kōgyū's name in *rōmaji*. On a visit to Deshima to meet the Dutch, he reports that one word he heard was *teikenen, teikenen*. This was probably *tekening* ('drawing') as he was then shown a map that he wanted to study. He later refers to the *aneisu uein*, i.e., 'aniseed (Late Modern Dutch *anijs*) wine' (possibly absinthe) that the Dutch drink (Shiba Kōkan 1927: 100, 106). Kōkan was clearly somewhat enraptured by the artistic potential of perspectival art in the Western tradition, going so far as to proclaim the 'brilliance and superiority of Western [painting methods]' (Takeuchi 2004: 6).[47] He had a copy of Gerard de Lairesse's *Groot Schilderboek* ('Great Painter's Book'), first published in Amsterdam in 1707 (French 1974: 80). He rendered this in *katakana* as *konsuto shikirudobūku*, the first word being *kunst* (or the variant *konst*), the Dutch for 'art' and the second his version of *Schilderboek*. This, incidentally, is thought to be the first use of *kunst* by a Japanese (Takeuchi 2004: 6). Kōkan's interest in Western art led him to write *Seiyō gadan* ('Discussion

---

the black servant he encountered on Deshima spoke 'an Indian language' (*tenjikugo* 天竺語—*tenjiku* is an old term for India) which the Dutch did not understand. This may be Malay, as he was said to come from Java (*yaha*) (French 1974: 64, 67).

46   The form *rūfu* is slightly problematic. *Rūpuru* and *rūfuru* from the Dutch *roeper* appear in Japanese texts from c. 1750, but more in the sense of loudspeaker. However, Japanese also uses *rappa* for trumpet or bugle from the Chinese 喇叭 *lǎba*. It is probable, though not beyond doubt, that Kōkan's version is inspired by the Dutch word.

47   In a similar vein, he wrote 'It is like seeing the actual thing, or walking through the real place' (Screech 2012: 323).

of Western Painting', 1799) (Takeuchi 2004: 6; French 1974: 81). We return to Kōkan below.

Other Japanese went to Nagasaki and kept journals of their experiences there, including their encounters with the Dutch. In *Saiyū zakki* ('Miscellaneous Records of Travels to the West', 1783), the scholar and physician Furukawa Koshōken (1726–1807) switches to give the ranks of the Dutch at Deshima. However, perhaps the most interesting insight he gives is that women would stand on the bridge at Deshima and shout in Dutch 'I love you' (Plutschow 2006: 99).

A final example of switching into Dutch in Japanese texts concerns translators at the *Bansho shirabesho* in Edo, a successor to the official *Bansho wage goyō*, who translated the *Javasche Courant*, an official newspaper published in Batavia, into Japanese. The National Diet Library in Tokyo holds copies of the Japanese translations made in 1862.[48] As one might expect there were quite a few non-Japanese names in the source documents which were typically transliterated into *katakana*, supplemented by *kanji* where necessary. In the first edition there is reference to place names such as Batavia, rendered as *Batahiya* (バタヒヤ) ('v' is not a native sound in Japanese) and *neuyoruku* (New York), and to people such as the Italian revolutionary Giuseppe Garibaldi (1807–82). His surname is rendered as *garibaruji* (ガリバルヂ).[49] There is no phoneme /di/ in the native Japanese sound system, so the final syllable is rendered [ji] or more accurately [zi] (Labrune 2012: 63). The non-Japanese names have lines next to them to indicate that they are foreign terms. More work needs to be done on this interesting subject to supplement this introductory review.

9   *Spielerei*

Japanese rulers required the Dutch to amuse them with samples of their mother tongue. In Edo in 1746, Jan Louis de Win (*opperhoofd* 1745–46, 1747–48) and the senior surgeon Philip Pieter Musculus had an audience with the former shogun (Yoshimune) and the crown prince. De Win was given three pieces of paper on which he wrote 'CRAANVOGEL' ('crane', Late Modern Dutch *kraanvogel*), 'SPARREBOOM' ('Spruce fir') and 'SCHILDPAD' ('Tortoise'). This reflects Yoshimune's interest in the study of nature, but perhaps more importantly, these are all symbols of long life in Japanese culture. Musculus

---

48   *Kanpan Batahiya shinbun* ('Official Batavian newspaper'). ed. and tr. by *Bansho shirabesho*. Toto: Rokyukan, 1862. 23 vols. <Call no. WB43-82>. See also http://www.ndl.go.jp/nichiran/e/s1/s1_4.html (accessed 8 April 2020).

49   http://dl.ndl.go.jp/info:ndljp/pid/9366500, pp. 1 and 13, Yr. 1862. Accessed 6 April 2020.

was given two sheets of paper on which he wrote 'BERG' ('mountain') and 'BAMBOES' ('bamboo'). Musculus was then given 12 sheets of paper on which to write Dutch words for the crown prince (Blussé and Remmelink 2004: 94). Something similar happened in Nagasaki. In 1748, Jacob Balde records that the Lord of Hizen visited Deshima and at his request some Dutch words were written on a sheet of paper (Blussé and Remmelink 2004: 123). In Kyoto (Miyako) in 1780 on a stopover on the *hofreis* Isaac Titsingh recorded that the clerk (*scriba*) was asked to write some Dutch letters (*Hollandsche letteren*) on pieces of paper. The Dutch also did this for some women standing outside the window of their lodgings (Lequin 2011: 82–83).

10   Image and Text

It was common in Tokugawa Japan for text and image to appear together in the same pictorial space, in part a reflection of relatively high rates of literacy. This was the case in a variety of media from *ukiyo-e* woodblock prints to painted silk hanging scrolls (*kakejiku* 掛け軸). Several Japanese artists adorned their work with Dutch writing. It clearly conjured up a sense of the 'exotic' or 'other'. In some cases, it seems to have been used largely for decoration while in other cases it was used primarily to convey information. The two nodes for this were Edo and Nagasaki. Several Edo artists and printmakers, such as Shiba Kōkan, mentioned above, Katsushika Hokusai (1760–1849) and Ishikawa Tairō (1765–1817), incorporated Dutch in their work, as did the Nagasaki artists Kawahara Keiga (1786–c. 1860) and Ishizaki Yūshi (1768–1846). Furthermore, several Dutchmen produced illustrations furnished with Dutch texts, which require our attention.

10.1   *Shiba Kōkan*

In about 1788 Shiba Kōkan produced a hand-coloured etching of a view of Edo's main bridge, the *Ryōkoku bashi* (lit. 'Bridge of two countries'), which is a good example of *ranga* (蘭画) or 'Dutch-style art'. He gave it the Dutch title *Tweelandbruk* (lit. 'Two country bridge'), for 'horizontal writing' (*yoko moji* 横文字) was becoming popular and seemed exotic to visitors to Edo. Furthermore, Kōkan wrote the Dutch in mirror writing, so that the picture could be viewed and read correctly in a device consisting of a mirror and lens.[50]

---

50   In 1654/5 an artist, probably the well-known Kanō Tan'yū (1602–74) of the famous Kanō school (狩野派, *Kanō-ha*) of Japanese art, visited the Dutch at Edo to look at what was probably a more complex viewing device or peep box (Screech 2012: 313–314).

These pictures were referred to as *megane-e* (眼鏡絵, 'spectacles picture'), and the device sometimes as *Oranda megane* (和蘭眼鏡, lit. 'Dutch glasses'). In another view he included a temple to the goddess Benten, which he translated into Dutch as *Temper Ienoshima* (Screech 2012: 330–331).[51] *Temper* should be rendered *tempel* ('temple').[52]

Another type of artwork that was popular was the hanging scroll. This would typically be displayed for a short time, perhaps when someone was visiting, and then rolled up and stored away. In around 1790 Kōkan produced a hanging scroll of two Dutch ambassadors walking by the walls of Edo Castle. Above them is an inscription in Dutch which reflects the prevailing frugality of the shogunal regime: *Men moet eeten om te leeven, maar niet leeven om te eeten* ('One must eat to live, and not live to eat') (Screech 2000: 90, 92). On a hanging scroll depicting Shichirigahama beach near Edo dated to the late Kansei era (寛政, 1789–1801), Kōkan signed his name in *kanji* and added Dutch words and his name in *rōmaji* (Clark 2017: 76, 77).[53] On a two-panel folding screen depicting the same view of Shichirigahama beach dated 1796 in the right-hand margin Kōkan gives his name in *kanji* and below this in *rōmaji* as *S:a Kookan*.

In one work, *Ikoku kōjō zu* (異国工場図, 'Scene in a Foreign Factory'), Kōkan adds the legend in Dutch *De tinnegieter, Zoekt in u Zelfs den Schat, Van 't allerschoonste Vat* ('The tin smith. Seek in yourself the treasure of the most beautiful container'). This is based on the emblem book, *Spiegel van het menselyk bedryf* ('Mirror of Trades') by Jan and Kaspar Luyken (1st ed. Amsterdam 1694), which has the same apophthegm (p. 26) (Tsukahara 2007a: 125; French 1974:

---

51   A hanging scroll by Kōkan, dated to the 1780s, has the title *Kensu oshō zu* ('Illustration of the (Chinese) Buddhist monk Xianzi' (Kensu is the Japanese rendering of Xianzi)). In fact, despite claiming to be a picture of the Chinese Buddhist monk Xianzi (蜆子), the monk depicted looks decidedly Western and Kōkan's picture is probably based on one brought to Japan by Jesuit missionaries. It includes a couple of words in Roman script, one of which is *paap*. This is the Dutch word for 'papist'. The other word appears to be *Siens*, which is probably a rendering of the Dutch *Chinees*, i.e., Chinese. This is problematic for a couple of reasons. First, the title does not match the picture, although the title may simply be a (not very successful) attempt to hide the picture's origin. Second, it is not clear if Kōkan himself added the Dutch words. It is certainly possible, for there is also a version of Kōkan's name (*Kookangoschiba*, i.e. *Kōkan gō* (pen name) *Shiba*) in *rōmaji*. If not, then given that they are in Dutch, it is at least reasonable to conclude that the words were added during the Tokugawa period. See also Narusawa (2007b: 66, Plate 37).

52   The rendering *temper* is a consequence of the fact that Japanese has only one liquid phoneme.

53   The Dutch is not clear—possibly *bijzonder* (special) or *eerste zonder/zender*. This is followed by *in Japan Siba*. One suggestion is that it means 'Shiba the first unique person in Japan'. This requires further investigation. See (Shiba Kōkan 1927: 96) for another example of Kōkan signing his name in *rōmaji*.

95–96).[54] A woodblock print depicting a basketmaker includes the Dutch word for this occupation, *Mandmaaker* (French 1974: 98).

As noted above, Kōkan visited Nagasaki in 1788. His main objective was to try to improve his skills in Western painting techniques. He had met the Dutch party in Edo on the *hofreis*, which included the senior surgeon Johan Arnold Stützer. In order to gain a pass to Deshima, he disguised himself as a merchant. Once on the island he encountered Stützer again. In his diary Kōkan refers to Stützer as Dutch; he was in fact Swedish but may have needed to tell Kōkan he was Dutch. So, we have an encounter between a Japanese artist disguised as a merchant meeting a Swede trying to pass himself off as a Dutchman. Kōkan recorded words that he heard Stützer say, or at least, words he thought the surgeon said: *Minēru komu kāmoru. Minēru* (*meneer*), he remembered, meant 'you' (it is a polite form of address to a man < *mijn heer*), *kom* 'come' and *kāmoru* (*kamer*) 'room', so he followed Stützer upstairs (Shiba Kōkan 1927: 100). In his diary, Shiba made a sketch of his encounter with Stützer accompanied by dialogue in *kanji* and *katakana* (French 1974: 62–64). This would later appear as a woodblock print in his published travelogue *Saiyū nikki* (Traganou 2004: 99). Next to Stützer in the illustration are the *kanji* for 'Dutchman' (蘭人, *orandajin*), a *katakana* rendering of Stützer's name, *sutottsuru*, and a phrase in *katakana* representing the garbled Dutch *iki kāmoru komu iki kāmoru komu* (イキ カーモル コム) (roughly: I come to [the] room'), with a gloss in *kanji* (Shiba Kōkan 1927: 102–103; French 1974: 64).[55] In another picture Kōkan adds the words クロ坊スワルトヨング (*kurobō suwarutoyongu*). *Kurobō* is a rendering of the Japanese for black boy or slave. *Suwarutoyongu* equates to the Dutch *zwarte jonge(n)*, lit. 'black boy'. This refers to a black slave on Deshima, whom, Kōkan tells us in the text, he was asked to draw by the interpreter Matsujūrō. In the bottom left-hand corner of the picture, Kōkan adds a key to explain what *suwaruto* and *yongu* mean to the Japanese reader (Shiba Kōkan 1927: 105, 101; Plutschow 2006: 214). Kōkan also made sketch of Hendrik Duurkoop's grave, which he visited during his stay in Nagasaki. He published this in a book of

---

54   French (1974: 88–89) suggests that Kōkan's source is *Iets voor Allen* ('Something for Everyone'). This was first published in German in 1699 by Father Abraham von St. Clara (1644–1709) as *Etwas fuer Alle*, and subsequently translated into Dutch by Isaac le Long (1683–1772). The same print (in reverse) does indeed appear in *Iets voor Allen* (2nd part, p. 184). French notes that Kōkan had access to a Dutch edition and may even have owned a copy.

55   Each word is glossed with a *kanji* equivalent. I interpret the line after *komu* as duplicating this phrase.

woodblock prints *Saiyū ryodan* ('Western journey') in 1790 (Screech 2012: 337). In the portrait of Yoshio Kōgyū on a hanging scroll (1788), mentioned above, Kōkan includes a *rōmaji* rendering of another name for Kōgyū, Yoshio Kōsaku, above two angelic figures. The name Yoshio begins with the grapheme ⟨j⟩, reflecting the fact that Dutch uses ⟨j⟩ to graphically realize /j/ (Screech 1996: 15). This is but one example of how during the Edo period forms of romanization for Japanese based on Dutch orthography became dominant (previously, the main influence had been Portuguese orthography) (Seeley 2000: 135). One other illustration by Kōkan is that of a dirigible balloon on a blue and white ceramic plate. This is dated 1797, only a few years after the first crossing of the English Channel in such a craft. Under the balloon is the Dutch *luchtschip*, literally 'Air Ship' (French 1974: 138–139).

10.2 Image and Text in Works by Other Edo Artists

The Edo *ukiyo-e* artist Keisai Eisen (1791–1848) specialized in painting pictures of beautiful women. Several have Dutch inscriptions. One has the words *Kojorukki een meid uit Tamaja spelende kokju* ('Koyorukki a girl from Tamaya playing the *kokyū*' (胡弓, a Japanese stringed instrument)). Another depicts a beautiful Japanese woman under a blossoming plum tree with the words in *rōmaji, Baikwa bizien Pruim bloem schoon mensch*. The first two words are transliterations of Japanese words for plum blossom (*baikwa*) and beautiful person (*bizien*), while the next four words are the Dutch equivalent. Plum blossom symbolizes beauty (Nagasaki Shiritsu Hakubutsukan 2000: 46).

The 'Sino-Japanese-Dutch Miscellany' (*Sangoku wakanran zatsuwa* 'Three-country Japanese-Chinese-Dutch Chit-Chat'), published in Edo in 1803 by Kanwatei Onitake (1760–1818) included illustrations by Katsushika Hokusai, better known for his 'Thirty-Six Views of Mount Fuji', which included 'The Great Wave off Kanagawa' (Roberts 1976: 48).[56] The illustration on the opening page depicts a Chinese, a Japanese woman and a Dutchman. Above the Dutchman is a Japanese description in *rōmaji* with *katakana* equivalents in subscript. The first sentence tells us that this is the Dutch merchant 'Snpipyt'.[57] 'Dutch' is rendered in *rōmaji* as *HOLRAN[D]O* with a *furigana* gloss, while 'merchant' (商人) is rendered in *rōmaji* as *AQOED[O]*. This is normally rendered phonetically

---

56   This is recorded as *Wakaran monogatari* (和漢蘭雑話, ID 542983) in the NIJL database.
57   Screech (1996: 36) observes that in the accompanying story Snpipyt becomes Sunperupei, which to the Japanese ear sounds like Thunberg plus the Japanese for 'fart' *he*.

as *akiudo*, as it is in the *katakana* subscript by Hokusai.[58] The digraph ⟨oe⟩ (in
AQOED[O]) renders the phoneme /u/ in Dutch (Screech 1996: 35).[59]

Another Edo artist who inscribed Dutch on his works was the high-ranking
samurai Ishikawa Tairō. He adopted the Dutch name *Tafel Berg* (lit. 'Table
mountain'), and signed works, such as a hanging scroll painting of a generic
Dutch woman, with this name in beautifully-crafted handwriting (Nagasaki
Shiritsu Hakubutsukan 2000: 82; Katsumori 2007: 106; Screech 1996: 161). A picture of the Hamada brothers taking Pieter Nuyts prisoner in Taiwan in 1628 is
also ascribed to Tairō. It is annotated in Japanese and Dutch and exploits a fundamental difference between their scripts: the Japanese is written vertically in
the left-hand margin and the Dutch horizontally beneath the picture (Nagasaki
Shiritsu Hakubutsukan 2000: 83). In the late eighteenth and early nineteenth
century, there was a certain craze for Hippocrates, the 'Father' of Western medicine. Tairō produced a hanging scroll of ink on silk depicting Hippocrates for
the *rangakusha* Yoshikawa Sōgen in 1799. Underneath the portrait, which is
derived from a Dutch work, is *HIPPOCRATES COÜS in Griekenland*, a Dutch
inscription meaning Hippocrates of Kos in Greece. In the early nineteenth
century, Tairō produced another hanging scroll depicting Hippocrates based
on Gilles Demarteau's copper engraving of François Bucher's 'Head of a Man'.
To the left of Hippocrates' head, Tairō indicated in Japanese that he had copied
the work. Above, there is a Dutch inscription *Afbeelding van den vermaarden ge-
neesheer, Hippokrates* ('Representation of the famous physician, Hippocrates').
Below is a date *den 15en sioguats* (i.e., the first month, *shōgatsu*) *Anno 1825*, the
place, *Decima*, and the name 'Dr. von Siebold', suggesting the German physician added the Dutch years later (Nagasaki Shiritsu Hakubutsukan 2000: 81;
Katsumori 2007: 106–107). The Edo Rinpa-school artist and *haiku* poet, Sakai
Hōitsu (1761–1829), also produced a hanging scroll depicting Hippocrates,
Hipokuratesu zō ('Portrait of Hippocrates').[60] At the top of the scroll is a Dutch
aphorism 'Hippocrates says, sickness is healed not by eloquence but by medicine' (Katsumori 2007: 108).[61] Underneath is the place, *Jedo* (Edo), and the

---

58   Jan Cock Blomhoff commissioned Hokusai to paint European-influenced paintings in
      1822. On the next *hofreis* in 1826, Von Siebold and the new *opperhoofd* Willem de Sturler
      collected them and subsequently took them out of Japan. A Dutch influence can be seen
      in the Dutch paper Hokusai used and the deep perspective in some of the paintings. Five
      of the paintings can be seen in Clark (2017: 82–89). However, none of them includes any
      Dutch writing.

59   Later in the inscription /j/ is rendered with the grapheme ⟨j⟩.

60   *Rinpa* (琳派, lit. 'school of Kōrin') takes its name from Ogata Kōrin (尾形光琳, 1658–
      1716), one of the most celebrated artists during the Edo period.

61   Dutch: *Hippocrates zegt, dat de ziektens niet geneezen worden door welsprekenheit maar
      door Geneesmiddelen.* Katsumori asserts that the Dutch contains two errors, which

signature of the *opperhoofd*, Hendrick Doeff. He did not necessarily write the aphorism but may have suggested it to Hōitsu during the *hofreis*.

The German physician, Lorenz Heister (1683–1758), whose books were translated into Japanese, was certainly revered if not quite venerated in the manner of Hippocrates. A Dutch translation of his *Chirurgie* ('Surgery', 1718) was critical to the development of anatomical study in Japan. A portrait of Heister made in around 1820 has much writing in Dutch above and below (Screech 2005: 55–56, 59). It is signed *Caneel Rivier Junior* ('Cinnamon River Junior'). This indicates that it was painted by a member of the Katsuragawa family, probably Hoan (Winkel 2004: 81). We have a Dutch proverb transcribed in a beautiful cursive script on a piece of paper which is signed *Caneel Rivier Junior* (Nagasaki Shiritsu Hakubutsukan 2000: 92).[62] Other artists also signed their work with a penname in *rōmaji*. Satake Yoshiatsu (1748–85), *daimyō* of Akita in northern Honshu, founded an art school called *Akita ranga* (秋田 蘭画) (lit. 'Akita Dutch art'). This resulted from contact with the *rangakusha* and polymath Hiraga Gen'nai (1728–80).[63] Yoshiatsu used his sobriquet, *Shozan* (曙山), to sign his paintings. He signed one work 'Siozan schildereij' (roughly 'a painting by Shozan'). and another 'Siozan Sinynet'. The second word should be *signet*—Dutch for 'seal' (Nara *et al.* 1965: fig. 29). He also signed works with the words *Segutter vol Beminnen* (roughly 'Sea-god(s) full of love'), rendered in the form of a seal (Screech 1996: 53; 2000: 76; 2005: 43).[64] The Edo-born artist Kitayama Kangan (1767–1801) was given the Dutch name Van Dyck, rendered in *katakana* as *handeiki*. This was because his work was said to remind some of the Dutch of the Flemish grandmaster Anthony van Dyck (French 1974: 184; Roberts 1976: 68). Kangan produced a copy of a bust of Lorenz Heister including Heister's name.

---

suggests that the person who wrote it was not Dutch. It is certainly true that one might expect *ziektes* instead of *ziektens* and *welspreekenheit/d* instead of *welsprekendheit*, but these should be seen as deviations from the norm, rather than errors *sensu stricto*, and so I think it is going too far to say that it is necessarily so that the person who wrote these words was not Dutch.

62 The proverb runs *Het leeren werd niet ingedrongen. De Lust moet weesen in de jongen* ('Learning cannot be drummed in. There must be a desire (to learn) in the youth').

63 Gen'nai had been invited to try and help improve copper production in Akita. He did not succeed, but Yoshiatsu was enthused about things Dutch by Gen'nai (Screech 2005: 42).

64 *Segutter* in fact seems to owe more to High German than Dutch (*Seegötter* as opposed to *Zeegoden*). Furthermore, the grapheme ⟨u⟩ could be read as ⟨ö⟩. So, this could be a mixture of German and Dutch, or simply bad Dutch.

10.3   *Image and Text in Works by Morishima Chūryō, Ōtsuki Gentaku and Motoki Shōei*

A word is in order about the use of Dutch alongside illustrations in books that emerged from the *rangaku* movement. Morishima Chūryō's *Kōmō zatsuwa* includes illustrations of new inventions and novelties from Europe. One of these depicts an airship. Here, the Dutch *luchtsloep* ('air sloop') is rendered in *katakana* as *ryukutosurōpu* (Screech 2006: 54).[65] Other illustrations are furnished with renderings in *katakana* including *raketto* for badminton racket (a game introduced to the Japanese by the Dutch), *rūpuru* for a loud hailer (Dutch: *roeper*), *mikorasukōbyun* for a microscope, and *konsutofontein* for a fountain (Dutch: *kunstfontein*).[66] The work also includes a picture of a 'flying dragon' with the *katakana* inscription *darāka*, from the Dutch *draakje* ('little dragon').[67] This was derived from a preserved lizard given to the Katsuragawa family by Carl Peter Thunberg (Winkel 2004: 44; Screech 2005: 41–42). Illustrations of items of clothing furnished with Dutch descriptions in *katakana* include a hat *ūdo* (Dutch: *hoed*), trousers *buruku* (Dutch: *broek*), underpants *ondoruburuku* (Dutch: *onderbroek*), stockings *kōsu* (Dutch: *kous*), and a shirt *hemuto* (Dutch: *hemd*) (Morishima Chūryō and Ōtsuki Gentaku 1972: 115–118). Just as Westerners are curious about kimonos and samurai attire, so here Japanese were curious about Dutch clothing.

One year after Morishima Chūryō's *Kōmō zatsuwa* appeared, in 1788 work started on a similar book, *Ransetsu benwaku* ('A clarification of misunderstandings in theories about the Dutch'). This was based on responses by the Edo *rangakusha* Ōtsuki Gentaku to questions by his students. This was eventually published in 1799 with the title *Bansui yawa* ('Evening Tales of Bansui' (Bansui

---

65   Chūryō copied the picture of the balloon from a print owned by Kutsuki Masatsuna (Winkel 2004: 54). The name of the inventors of the hot air balloon, the Montgolfier brothers, is rendered as *Montogoruhīru*.

66   The *dakuten* ˚ (which indicates a 'b') and the *handakuten* ˚ (which indicates a 'p') may be interchangeable. For *rūpuru* see also Winkel (2004: 69–70). The microscope is accompanied by illustrations of insects by Shiba Kōkan based on illustrations in Jan Swammerdam's *Biblia Natura* (Leiden, 1737–38) (Winkel 2004: 54). See also Screech (1996: 143 (dragon), 195 (microscope)) for these illustrations.

67   The same lizard is depicted separately by Satake Yoshiatsu. He also refers to it as a *darāka* (Nara 1965: fig. 18). Titsingh had brought the lizard from southern Africa. Screech (2005: 42) writes that Yoshiatsu names Africa as *rimia*. However, the *furigana* reading of the same *ateji* in Chūryō's *Bangosen* is *ribia*. This, I would suggest, is derived from the toponym Libya. Yoshiatsu does not give *furigana* for 未. This has two *on*-readings, *mi* (which Screech applies) and *bi*, the one that Chūryō gives.

was one of Gentaku's pennames)) (Goodman 2000: 124; Winkel 2004: 65–67).[68] One interesting difference is that whereas Chūryō's book uses *katakana* for non-Japanese objects Gentaku's work uses *hiragana*. *Hiragana* often indicate a more light-hearted discourse register, although this case may simply be a function of the fact that at this time there were no 'rules' for how to render foreign terms in Japanese. One example in Gentaku's work is an illustration of eating utensils including a knife, fork and spoon. These are rendered in *hiragana* as *mesu, horuko* and *reiperu* (Dutch: *mes, vork* and *lepel*) (Morishima Chūryō and Ōtsuki Gentaku 1972: 164) (*mesu* would become a loanword referring only to 'scalpel' in Japanese). Gentaku also presents illustrations of animals and plants such as the ostrich *sutoruisu.hofugeru* (Dutch *struisvogel*) and the olive tree *oreifubōmu* (Dutch *olijfboom*) (Morishima Chūryō and Ōtsuki Gentaku 1972: 170, 182). New instruments were illustrated, such as the camera obscura *donkurukāmuru* (Dutch *donkerkamer*) and the thermometer *terumomeitoru*, and a small world map is included with names which seem to owe more to Romance languages than Dutch (e.g., *igirisu* for England from Portuguese and *furansu* (France)) (Morishima Chūryō and Ōtsuki Gentaku 1972: 198–199; 208–209). As elsewhere, the distance between the Dutch and Japanese renderings can in part be explained by the canonical syllable structure of Old Japanese ((Consonant) Vowel ((c)v)), the fact that Japanese only has one liquid consonant, and in the case of *vork* and *struisvogel*, the lack of 'v' in the native Japanese sound system (Shibatani 1990: 121–122).

Another extensive work by Gentaku was based on written responses to questions about Western science from his students. The fruits of these exchanges were first circulated in manuscript and later published in a series of books from 1819 onwards under the title *Ran'en tekiho*.[69] The volumes include many annotated illustrations. They are mainly written in modified literary Sinitic (*kanbun*), which is occasionally glossed with *katakana*. In vol. 1 p. 7, there is a picture of aloe, with the word *aroe* in *ateji* and *furigana*. This was a recent Dutch loanword in Japanese. In vol. 3 p. 28 there is a picture of a (chained) orang-utan with a Japanese rendering *oranūtan* in *ateji* and *furigana*. This was a loanword via Dutch from Malay. A page from a manuscript under this title which annotates an illustration of a date palm tree and frond merits close

---

68 Some sources have a publication date of 1797. The NIJL database has the year Kansei 11, i.e., 1799.

69 It is not easy to translate this title into English (or indeed Dutch). A literal translation of the title would be 'Picking flowers in the Dutch garden'. A more fluent translation is 'A handbook of Dutch medicinal plants', although some authors translate it more loosely as 'Selections Translated from Dutch Books'. 'Selection of Dutch curiosities' is another possible translation. I thank Wim Boot for this information.

attention. On the left of the annotation is the Latin name *Palma Dactifera* (sic, it should be *dactylifera*) and a Dutch equivalent *Dadel draagende Dadelboom* ('Date-bearing date palm'). In the right-hand margin, the Dutch and the Latin are rendered in *katakana* with *kanji* below indicating which is which, viz. 蘭 (*ran*) referring to 'Dutch' (*rango* or *orandago*) and 羅 (*ra*) to Latin (*ratengo*) (Kobe City Museum 1998: 97, item 145). Above the *katakana* is a series of *kanji*: first, 物乙忙 (with a *furigana* pronunciation guide ウェイマン), which refers to Wei(n)man(n), the German author of the source of Gentaku's picture; second, 草木 (plants and trees, so 'botany'); third 図譜 'illustration'; and fourth 所蔵 'to be found in' (i.e., this is to be found in (Johann Wilhelm) Weinmann's illustration of botany).[70]

On one level, the Dutch and Latin words and *katakana* equivalents simply annotate the images. However, in this case something deeper is possibly going on, too. In 'The Order of Things' Michel Foucault (1994: 132) writes that the discourse of natural history in Europe is 'nothing more than the nomination of the visible' ('L'histoire naturelle ce n'est rien d'autre que la nomination du visible' *Les Mots et Les Choses* (1966)). In other words, natural history emerged in the space of possibility between naming and seeing. In this space, things and words exist *as* and *within* representation, i.e., they both constitute and are intrinsic to the representation (Fukuoka 2012: 55). By giving the name of the plant in various linguistic modes Gentaku is trying to construct a representation that marries picture and text, things and words. Furthermore, by providing the species name in Latin (along with its Dutch equivalent) in Roman script, and both Latin and Dutch names in *katakana*, glossed with *kanji*, he is simultaneously pointing to the exoticity of his source and attempting to domesticate or localize the Latin and Dutch nomenclature for the Japanese reader.[71] In some sense, therefore, we see here the emergence of a Western-influenced natural history in Japan. Moreover, such a combination of text and image creates a complex semantic field. It could be understood as an example of what Mikhail Bakhtin calls *heteroglossia* (Russian: *разноречие*), i.e., different perspectives or voices within the same work. Another useful term here is *heterosemia*, i.e., different signs, reflecting the fact that such examples include both

---

70 図 is in fact represented here and elsewhere with an older *kanji* 圖, which is no longer in use.

71 Weinmann was a contemporary of Carl Linnaeus, whose binomial genus/species classification would bring order to the disorder of plant classification that had pertained before him. Weinmann does not use the Linnaean system here but does give the plant a binomial. He referred to this plant as 'palma dactilifera', see: http://www.plantillustrations.org/illustration.php?id_illustration=126782 (accessed 6 May 2020). In the Linnaean system, the binomial is 'Phoenix dactylifera', although one of the 'synonyms' is 'palma dactilifera', i.e., the binomial applied by Weinmann.

verbal and pictorial signs.[72] It is certainly more complex than the annotated images in Japanese *honzōgaku* texts such as *Yamato honzō* ('Medicinal herbs of Japan', 1709) by Kaibara Ekiken (1630–1714) with which Japanese readers would have been more familiar. Here, the images are typically accompanied by the name of the plant or animal depicted in Sinitic characters (*kanji*), *kana*, or in a few cases both. One final point in this regard is that one can to some extent apply Foucault's description of natural history to *rangaku*. In other words, this was the nomination of the new objects, ideas and processes that the Japanese encountered as they engaged with and appropriated Dutch and Western scientific knowledge. In some cases, this nomination involved borrowing Dutch or indeed Latin terms, while in other cases it involved forming hybrid words or coining loan translations.

On quite a different note, in response to the perceived threat from foreign vessels in the early nineteenth century, Motoki Shōei compiled a beautifully-illustrated work on Western warships *Gunkan zukai kōrei* ('Examples of Illustrations of Warships', 1808).[73] This is based on several Dutch and French sources. The illustrations are marked with letters corresponding to descriptions in the legend. Some of the descriptions are in *kanji*, while others include *katakana* descriptions of Dutch terms. In one fine illustration of a three-mast ship, item イ／ is identified in *katakana* as the *burōtokamaru*, i.e., the *broodkamer*, where ship's biscuits (*beschuit*) were stored. Item サ is identified as the *kuroitokamaru*, the *kruitkamer*, where gunpowder was stored.

10.4 *Image and Text in Works by Nagasaki Artists*

Kawahara Keiga was a prolific artist who worked closely with several Dutch at Deshima. Some of his pictures have contributed to the image we have of life at the Dutch trading post. In the early nineteenth century, he produced a portrait of the *opperhoofd*, Hendrick Doeff, with the Dutch inscription, *Hendrik Doeff Junior Opperhoofd van ao. 1803 Tot* []. The lack of final date suggests a *terminus ante quem* for the work of 1817, when Doeff left Japan (Narusawa 2007a: 85). Doeff's successor, Jan Cock Blomhoff, brought his wife, Titia Bergsma, to

---

72 A similar example is a multi-volume work on Japanese plants compiled for Von Siebold by his student Itō Keisuke. This is on display in the Sieboldhuis, Leiden (visited 4 January 2020). On each double page there is a dried plant on the left and a corresponding description on the right. One double page is devoted to the dianthus. Next to the dried plant is the Dutch 'Deze wassen zo wel in de wilde als in de hof' ('These grow in the wild as well as in the garden'). This is handwritten, possibly by Keisuke himself. On the same page are the name of the plant in *kanji* and *katakana*, *nadeshiko*. A slip of paper with the Latin name is attached. However, this is probably a later addition.

73 https://schoenberginstitute.org/tag/motoki-shozaemon/. Accessed 7 April 2020.

Deshima, although she was subsequently required to leave. Keiga painted a single-panel screen on silk of Blomhoff and his family which had a Dutch inscription (Narusawa 2007a: 87).[74] Keiga was probably the artist of a drawing in ink on paper of the *hofreis* of 1814 or 1818. There are descriptions in Dutch, such as *opperhoofd* and *schriba* (sic) ('secretary') above their respective palanquins carried by Japanese (Vos 1989: 103). As noted above, in 1820, the Dutch presented a couple of farces at Deshima to mark the departure of the *bugyō*. Keiga painted scenes from the plays and a picture of the curtain. In the centre was the Latin motto of the theatre group, *Ars Longa, Vita Brevis*. On either side of this were two Dutch flags with Dutch mottos. One read 'DAT MEN OP DECIMA OOK OM DE LAUWREN STRYDT' ('Let those on Deshima also compete for the laurel wreath'). The other read 'BY TOHOORONS HIER VERGUND APOLLOE GEWYD' ('Granted by Tohoorons (Thorens?), dedicated to Apollo') (Scholten 1990: 195, 201). Keiga was employed by Von Siebold to produce paintings of Japanese flora and fauna. These have legends in both *katakana* and *rōmaji*.[75] For example, a bird called the 'white eye' has the legend メシロ *Mesiro* (lit. 'white eye').[76] Von Siebold may have added the *rōmaji*. Finally, Keiga had a nickname Toyosuke. He sometimes added a seal to his paintings with *Tojosky* in *rōmaji*.

The Nagasaki artist Ishizaki Yūshi painted portraits of the Dutch, often on silk, and typically adorned with words in Dutch. Several paintings depict members of the Blomhoff family, with their names. One hanging scroll dated 1817 includes his wife, the Dutch servant Petronella Muns holding Jan jr., and the Indonesian servant, Maraty, with all four names in Roman script above (Nagasaki Shiritsu Hakubutsukan 2000: 29).[77] The Nagasaki artist Matsui Keichū (1781/5–1819) produced two works depicting a 'typical' Dutch man and woman with the legends *De Afbeelding van de hollandsche Vrouw* and *De Afbeelding van de Hollander* respectively (Nagasaki Shiritsu Hakubutsukan 2000: 32; Roberts 1974: 74).

Aōdō Denzen (1748–1822) was born in Sukagawa, Fukushima Prefecture. However, according to some sources he may have learnt copperplate etching from a Dutchman at Nagasaki and from Shiba Kōkan. An etching by Denzen

---

74   The inscription runs *De opregte Aftekening van het Opperhoofd J. cock Blomhof. Zijn Vrouw en Kind, die in Ao. 1818 al hier aan gekomen zijn.* It is likely that this was written by a Dutch person, possibly Blomhof himself.

75   Some of these are on display at *Naratakijuku*. Many of Keiga's botanical illustrations would be included in Siebold's *Nippon*.

76   For further examples, see Van Gulik (2000: 27).

77   For another example of a watercolour depicting the same four people and descriptions in Roman script, see Vos *et al.* (1989: 173).

entitled *Meguro hiyokuzuka* ('Lovers' Tomb at Meguro') is of interest for our purposes. It depicts a well-known scene from Japanese theatre in which the lead character commits murder (Katsumori 2007: 116, fig. 15; Roberts 1976: 4). The influence of Dutch can be seen in several ways. First, the writing is in *rōmaji*. Second, there are two words of Dutch in the etching, *Twee jaar*, albeit not correct but comprehensible. They are in the phrase *Boenkwa twee jaar*, which dates the work to the second year of the Bunka (文化) era, 1805. Third, the orthography is influenced by Dutch. In *Boenkwa*, the digraph ⟨oe⟩ points to a Dutch influence. The placename, which in modern transliteration is Michinoku Sukagawa, is given as *MITINOKOE SOEKAGAWA* again using the digraph ⟨oe⟩. *Hiyokuzuka* is rendered as *FIJOKOE TOEKA*. Apart from ⟨oe⟩, the grapheme ⟨j⟩ represents /j/ as is typical in Dutch (Booij 1995: 7; Labrune 2012: 92). There is a sense in which the writing on this etching is Japanese clothed in *rōmaji*.

Nagasaki, and more specifically the Dutch at Deshima, provided inspiration for a collection called *Nagasaki miyage* ('Souvenirs of Nagasaki') by the Edo-born printer, Isono Bunsai (also Nobuharu, ?–1857), published in octavo in 1847. One woodblock print depicts a European man, holding a pocket watch (see fig. 9). The legend refers to a Dutchman (*kōmōjin* (kanji) or *orandajin* (*furigana*)), but the figure may be modelled on the German Von Siebold. In *rōmaji* we read *Hollandsche uurwerk* ('Dutch timepiece'). An inverted VOC insignia is visible on an easy chair on the same print. The book also includes prints of a rather shrivelled elephant and a Dutch woman. These are supplemented respectively by the words in Roman script *OLIFANT* and *Holland vrouw*, the latter example suggesting it was Bunsai who added the Roman script. The running text is in *hiragana-majiri* (a hybrid of *kanji* and *hiragana*), which indicates that the book was aimed at a general public.

Several woodcuts with Dutch writing were made in Nagasaki in the late eighteenth century by local publishing houses. One of these, the *Toshimaya* (or *Tomishimaya* 冨島屋), established by Ōhata Bunjiemon, produced a print of two Dutch East Indiamen in Amsterdam harbour with the words LEYDTSE POORT (Leiden Gate) at the top and in the centre in Dutch and French, MUYDER POORT and LA PORTE DE MUYDEN, i.e., the Muyden Gate, both of these being entrances to the harbour. Boxer suggests that certain features of the print indicate that it may have been made by a Chinese artist in Nagasaki or copied from a Chinese version of a Dutch original (Boxer 1950: 73, 80–81). In the front matter of his book on the Dutch in Japan, Boxer reproduces a Nagasaki woodcut of a Dutch East Indiaman, the *Schellach*, c. 1782. This is one of the variants of a woodcut entitled *Oranda Sen no Zu* (阿蘭陀船之図), or 'Picture of a Hollander Ship' identified with the *Toshimaya* publishing house.

FIGURE 9   A European man holding a pocket watch in *Nagasaki*
miyage (1847)
WUL 文庫 08 B0086

On flags we see the VOC insignia and reference to the Muyderpoort. Around
the ship there is Japanese writing. Above it are three Dutch words, *Son, Maan,*
Sterre ('Sun, Moon, Star'), with the relevant *kanji* above these (日月星). On the
left of the woodcut is a list of the distances from nine places to Japan, mea-
sured in Japanese *ri* 里 (sometimes translated as Japanese leagues). The list
of places includes England, which is rendered *igirisu* (イギリス) (< Portuguese)

(Boxer 1950: 81–83). Other Japanese authors used variations on the Latin name for England, *Anglia*. One version of this print was published in 1782 by Hayashi Shihei (1738–93), a noted Japanese military historian and retainer of Sendai Domain. He wrote an inscription to the print furnished with transcriptions of Dutch words in *katakana*. For example, *retteru* for the Dutch alphabet 'letters' (Dutch: *letter*), *buruku* for 'breeches' (Dutch: *broek*), *rokko* ('coat') (Dutch: *rok*), *skippu* ('ship') (Dutch: *schip*), and *matarosu* for 'sailor' (Dutch: *matroos*) (Boxer: 1950: 177–178).[78] In contrast to Aōdō Denzen's etching where Japanese is clothed in *rōmaji*, here we have Dutch clothed in *katakana*. Another Nagasaki printing house which made similar prints was the *Bunkindō* (文錦堂). The earliest known prints from the *Bunkindō* date from 1802. It would eventually supplant the *Toshimaya* and continue to produce prints until the mid-nineteenth century (Toby 2019: 237; Boxer 1950: 74).

Other Nagasaki prints simply have one or two words in Dutch. The Japanese were taken by creatures imported by the Dutch that they had not seen before. A print from 1821, probably made in Nagasaki by an unknown artist, depicts two camels being led by a Dutchman and a servant. In the top left-hand corner is the Dutch word *KAMEEL* ('camel') and on the left-hand side is the word *kamēru* in *katakana*.[79] This can be seen to stand in the tradition of depicting curiosity or freak shows *misemono* (見世物) in Japanese art. One woodblock print has the Dutch at table at Deshima eating and drinking. The Japanese explains that this is a picture of Dutchmen. At the top in the centre is HOLLAND in Roman script. Finally, a coloured woodblock-print from the early nineteenth century has a Dutch East India ship with the voc letters inverted and a flag with a white 'H' on a red background signifying the Dutch port of Hoorn (Van Gulik 2000: 14, 15).

10.5 *Artworks Made on the* hofreis

Finally, a word is in order about works of art made on the *hofreis* to Edo. Scenes from the 1818 *hofreis* led by Jan Cock Blomhoff were illustrated in a long pencil drawing. The scenes depict the many Japanese who carried the Dutch in their palanquins (*norimono*), as well as provisions and gifts. They are typically annotated in Roman script to indicate the function of the Japanese or what they carried. For example, on one we read *No. 139 is schoenhouder* (shoeholder),

---

78   See http://www.wul.waseda.ac.jp/kosho/imaspdf/pdf/yogaku009.pdf and https://online only.christies.com/s/japanese-art-at-the-english-court/shihei-hayashi-1738-1793-113/13744 for slightly different versions of this print. Accessed 4 May 2020.

79   https://yajifun.tumblr.com/image/60843721309. Accessed 7 April 2020. See also http:// www.nagasaki-keizai.co.jp/data/n003/155_01.pdf for a similar print with the word *kameel*.

No. 131 is tsiabentoo (a portable tea set 茶弁当). It is not clear who added these descriptions, but it is possible that it was a Japanese as the descriptions typically lack an article for the noun, a feature of Japanese (Blomhoff 2000a: 91).[80] One Dutchman who was a gifted artist was the physician Jan Frederik Feilke. During the *hofreis* of 1810 he sketched and signed a view of Mt. Fuji. In the top right-hand corner is an inscription by Hendrick Doeff: *De Foesieberg, zoo als dezelve Zig vertoond, buijten Foetsju. Anno 1810, Hendrik Doeff* ('Mount Fuji, as it presents itself, outside Fuchū 1810. H.D.') (Kobe City Museum 1998: 63).

11   Dutch on Everyday Objects

Dutch words and phrases were added to a range of objects. In some cases, these objects fall into the category of the decorative arts, while in other cases the objects are of a more mundane nature. Most objects, it would seem, were susceptible to the exotic touch that Dutch offered. These examples illustrate that Dutch left its mark not only on fine art, often the preserve of the Japanese elite, but also on Japanese material culture.

Lacquerwork was an important decorative art in Tokugawa Japan. One artist who is only known by the name with which he signed his works, *Sasaya*, produced two plaquettes of lacquerwork with texts in Dutch and French. The plaquettes, which are now in Kobe City Museum, are based on prints by Mathias de Sallieth published in 1782 and depict encounters between Dutch and English ships at Dogger Bank and near Cadiz in 1781 during the Fourth Anglo-Dutch War. Each plaquette carries the Dutch inscription *Verlakt bij Sasaya in Japan Aº 1792* ('Lacquered by Sasaya in Japan anno 1792') (Jörg 2007: 185–187).[81] A chest of drawers finished with lacquerwork and mother-of-pearl inlay depicts the Battle of Kamperduin (1797), during the French Revolutionary Wars. Above the image is a description in Dutch: *Zeeslag tusschen Bataafsche en Engelsche Vlooten op de Hoogte van Egmond den 11 October des Iaars 1797* ('Sea battle between the fleets of the Batavian Republic and Britain near Egmond 11 October in the year 1797'). These words in Dutch were not merely a factual

---

80   One possibility is that the inscriptions were added by Kawahara Keiga, who made works of art for Blomhoff. The problematic Dutch is again illustrated in a drawing with the descriptions *Dit behoort over onderbangjoos* and *Dit is harnaskas en behoort van opperbangjoos* (Blomhoff 2000a: 97) (my bold).

81   Sasaya is mentioned in VOC documents in connection with lacquerwork ordered for the Dutch in Nagasaki and in Kyoto. See also Jörg (2007: 184–185), where ten lacquered medallions made in Japan are depicted which are portraits of prominent Europeans with their names in Roman script. These are based on a French book of engravings.

record, but an addition to the decoration of the chest of drawers (Vos *et al.* 1989: 131).

Ceramics, too, were susceptible to Dutch. Arita-ware bowls with portraits of the Prince of Orange Willem V and his consort, Wilhelmina, were produced on Kyushu in around 1800. One design has the Dutch *Siet wat hier van agteren staat* ('See what is behind this'—i.e., the royal portraits) in blue glaze (Vos *et al.* 1989: 182–183). Contemporary Delftware bowls had the same phrase glazed inside them. On a Nagasaki Kameyama-ware dish, the edge is decorated with the word *JEDOMATI*, a *rōmaji* rendering of *Edo-machi*, a district of Nagasaki, influenced by Dutch orthography (Nagasaki Shiritsu Hakubutsukan 2000: 102). The glazing on Kraak-style plates produced at Arita in the eighteenth century included the insignia of the VOC (Jörg 2007: 175–176). In fact, the VOC insignia pops up elsewhere in Japan. Overmeer Fisscher (1833: 275–176) records that the Japanese who carried the palanquin of the *opperhoofd* had the VOC insignia on their clothing, and the insignia was posted on the Dutch accommodation on the *hofreis*.

Dutch words were painted onto ceramic bottles of sake and soya, called *konpura-bin* (*konpura* < Portuguese *comprador*, *bin* = bottle (瓶, S.-J.)).[82] These were, one assumes, primarily intended for export, although some have been found in excavations at Deshima. The former carried the words *JAPANSCHZAKY* ('Japanese sake') and the latter *JAPANSCHZOYA* ('Japanese soya').[83] Likewise, a *konpura-bin* with the word *MOSTAARD* ('mustard') is in the Siebold collection in Leiden (Nagasaki Shiritsu Hakubutsukan 2000: 42; Vos *et al.* 1989: 141).

In the late eighteenth century, book covers had borders including Dutch words, as this seems to have been visually attractive to Japanese. One example is the cover of a book of illustrated stories published in 1794 by Santō Kyōden (1761–1816), an author of vernacular fiction. The border includes the Latin name of the Flemish botanist, Rembert Dodoens (*Dodonæus*), whose herbal was popular in Japan, along with Japanese words in *rōmaji*.[84] It was common for artists of *ukiyo-e* to feature Western subjects. The *ukiyo-e* painter and print-maker, Keisai Eisen, mentioned above, who would later influence Vincent van Gogh, depicted a view of Mount Fuji from Nihonbashi framed by the Dutch alphabet represented in a somewhat cryptic manner. In some places, we simply

---

82 This is a hybrid loanword—*comprador* is Portuguese (or Spanish) and *bin* is Sino-Japanese.

83 These are on display at the Leiden Volkenkunde (Ethnology) Museum. Visited 26 October 2019.

84 Visit http://www.wul.waseda.ac.jp/kotenseki/html/bunko06/bunko06_00997/index.html. Accessed 4 May 2020. I thank Radu Leca for bringing this example to my attention.

see strings of letters, but the word 'Holland' and the VOC insignia can clearly be made out. This was published in the series 'Famous Places of Edo Framed by Dutch Alphabet' (1830–1844) (Oka 2007: 137; Roberts 1976: 21).

Dutch coins were of course not minted in Japan, but some were brought there. An avid collector of Dutch and other European coins was the *daimyō* Kutsuki Masatsuna. He wrote a book on Western (i.e., European) coins, *Seiyō senpu* ('Notes on Western coinage', 1787, published Edo 1790), many of which he had received from his friend Titsingh. In this woodblock print book Masatsuna presented images of the coins and used these as a motivation for discussing their countries of origin (Lequin 2003: 108–109).[85] This is in fact a treasure trove of information about how Japanese dealt with Western languages in general and toponyms in particular. Most of the images of the coins have Latin inscriptions. However, we also find several examples of German inscriptions, as well as one or two in Dutch and English, and even several in Arabic script. In the last category, on p. 47 there is a coin with 'DUYT IAVAS 1783' on one side and a transliteration of this in Arabic script and the Eastern Arabic numerals for 1783 ١٧٨٣ on the other side (a *duit* was a Dutch coin worth an eighth of a *stuiver*). Some coins have the VOC insignia, minted by order of the VOC for trade. However, perhaps the most interesting example of a Dutch coin is one struck in 1779 to commemorate the 200th anniversary of the Union of Utrecht (p. 30). On one side it has the French motto of the House of Orange, JE MAINTIENDRAI. On the other side is an extensive Dutch inscription, which contains a couple of errors: 'MET HEM HEBBEN WIJ DE EEUWFEESTEN VAN VRIJHEID EN EENDRAGT DIE ZIJNE VADREN EEVESTIGT (sic *recte* GEVESTIGT) HEBBEN GEZIEN MET HEM ZULLEN WIJ ZE BESCHERMEN'. Around the edge of the image are the words 'OP HET TWEEPE (sic *recte* TWEEDE) EEUWFEEST DER UNIE VAN UTRECHT' ('On the second centenary of the Union of Utrecht'). In the accompanying description Masatsuna renders Utrecht in *katakana* as ヲイトレキト (i.e., *woitorekito*). Other European names are transliterated in *katakana*. So, for example, we see *uasuto furisurando* as a transliteration *West-Friesland* (Dutch for West Frisia) and *horurando* for Holland. These Japanese renderings are clearly based on Dutch (see fig. 10).

On a different note, at the foot of Mount Inasa, on land owned by the Goshinji temple, across Nagasaki Bay from Deshima is the Dutch Cemetery, which was used by the Dutch to bury their dead from 1654 to 1870. This has been the subject of several studies, most recently that of Titia van der Eb-Brongersma, a

---

85   Waseda call no. ネ 04 04164 and 文庫 08 B0061.

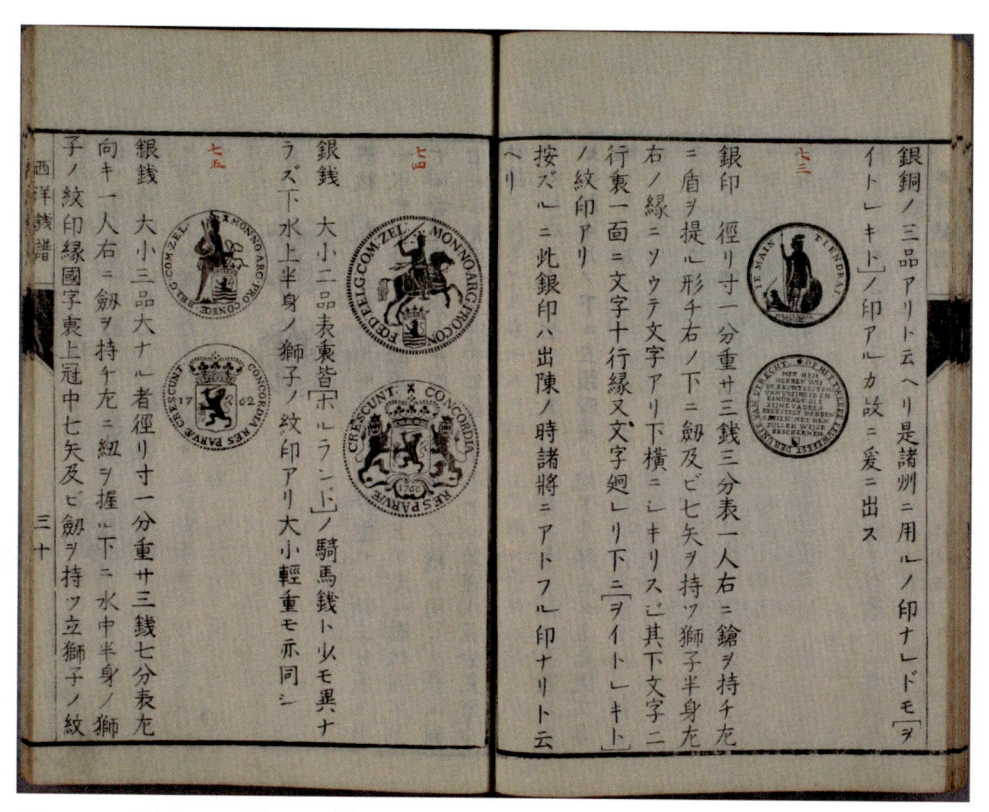

FIGURE 10   *Seiyō senpu* ('Notes on Western coinage', 1787, p. 30) Kutsuki Masatsuna
WUL 文庫 08 B0061

second edition of which was published in 2017.[86] It includes some 41 grave-stones, of which 30 are inscribed with text, although not all of this is legible. One older gravestone on which the Dutch inscription is still legible is that of Hendrik Duurkoop. He was appointed *opperhoofd* in 1778 but died on the ship *Huis ter Spijk* on his way to Deshima. He was therefore buried on arrival.[87] One Dutchman not buried at Goshinji was the *opperhoofd* Gijsbert Hemmij. On the *hofreis* in 1798 he became ill and died. He was buried at Kakegawa on the

---

86   See especially Van der Eb-Brongersma (2017: 82–85) for a useful summary in English. The passage of time will no doubt have made the appearance of the gravestones less attractive, although there have been attempts to maintain them. Overmeer Fisscher (1833: 279) refers to the *fraaije grafzerken en monumenten met Hollandsche opschriften* ('beautiful gravestones and monuments with Dutch inscriptions') on Inasa.

87   See Blussé and Remmelink (2004: xiii) for a full transcription of Duurkoop's grave inscription, although the year of his passing is incorrectly transcribed (see Chapter 5).

Tōkaidō between Edo and Osaka. His grave has a Dutch inscription, to which Overmeer Fisscher (1833: 317) refers in his published account of Japan.

This is by no means an exhaustive list of the objects to which Dutch was added. For example, in the nineteenth century on the *hofreis* at Edo the Dutch would write a few words of their language on the fans or clothing (*kabaai*) of the women they brought back to their quarters to give them something by which to remember their Dutch lovers (Overmeer Fisscher 1833: 307). However, what is clear is that Dutch was used on a range of everyday objects from a lacquerwork chest of drawers to *konpura-bin* in some cases primarily for informational purposes, in other cases to evoke the 'exotic' in Japan, although sometimes for both purposes.

12   Maps and Geographical Texts

The Dutch provided Japan with a window onto the world beyond East Asia. One way in which they did this was to furnish Japanese with world maps and geographical descriptions. Over time, the Japanese themselves made maps based on Dutch and other European maps. Almost unavoidably, the Japanese maps included toponyms taken from the European maps typically rendered in *katakana*. The focus here is on the influence of Dutch on Japanese maps. However, Japanese maps also included toponyms derived from other European languages, above all Latin and Portuguese. One possible reason for this is that Japanese cartographers simply used whatever sources were at hand and were not in a position to use toponyms from one language alone. It is also a function of the fact that some European maps used both Latin and vernacular languages for their toponyms.

Unno Kazutaka asserts that the dominant influence on Japanese marine charts was Portuguese maritime cartography. By the time that the Dutch had become the only Europeans allowed to trade with Japan, Japanese were forbidden from leaving the country and so had little need for new, possibly Dutch charts (Unno 1994: 381). Early navigators on board Dutch ships used portolan charts. For example, two of these brought to Japan by Will Adams on the *Liefde* were charts produced by the Dutch cartographer, Cornelis Doedtsz. of Edam (*fl.* 1600). The toponyms, such as *Iapam* for Japan, are primarily Portuguese (Shapinsky 2006: 15–16).[88]

---

88   Shapinsky (2006: 21–22) also presents valuable research on the hybrid varieties of language that may have been used aboard ships in East Asia. Portuguese, Chinese and Japanese are the three dominant languages in these language varieties. Furthermore,

Early world maps in Japan were of the 'oval' variety which traces its origins back to a map published in Beijing in 1602 by Matteo Ricci (1552–1610) written in Sinitic characters. This continued to influence Japanese world maps into the late eighteenth century (Yamashita 1998: 35). However, by the first half of the eighteenth century, Japanese world maps were also beginning to show the influence of maps and globes imported from Europe. In 1737 the early *ranga-kusha* Kitajima Kenshin completed *Kōmō tenchi nizu zeisetsu* ('Explanation of Dutch celestial and terrestrial globes') based on the globes produced by Gerrit Valck and his son Leonard in 1700 (Unno 1994: 433).[89] Both globes are inscribed in Latin. Kenshin's work consists of two booklets, one for each globe. In the booklet on the celestial globe he gives the names of constellations in *rōmaji*, e.g., *Cancer*, together with *ateji* and *furigana* equivalents (pp. 20–21). In the booklet on the terrestrial globe, he again gives names in Latin. For example, 'Japan' is *Japonia*, rendered in *rōmaji*, *ateji* and *furigana*. However, he also gives what seem to be vernacular alternatives for Japan, *Iapon* and *Iapan* in *rōmaji*, *ateji* and *furigana*. In other cases, such as *Insula Maldiva*, for the Maldives and *Arabia Felix*, Kenshin only gives a Latin form in *rōmaji*, with *ateji* and *furigana*.

Two Japanese works on surveying from the early eighteenth century include the Dutch names for the months of the year. One of these was Hosoi Kōtaku's (1658–1735) *Hiden chiiki zuhō taizensho* ('Complete book of the secret art of surveying and mapping'), a manuscript dating to 1717. The other was Matsumiya Kanzan's (also Toshitsugu 1686–1780) treatise on surveying, *Bundo yojutsu* ('Techniques of protraction', 1728). They list the months in *katakana*, with for example the first three months in Dutch *januari*, *februari* and *maart* being represented as *yanwari*, *befuriwari* and *maruto*.[90] Unno (1994: 394–395) suggests that the names of the months were taught to Japanese sailors by Europeans because of their importance in European navigation in, for example, declination tables. Both works also give names of months derived from Portuguese (e.g., *shanero* for the first month, *janeiro*).

In 1772, Motoki Yoshinaga translated part of a Dutch translation of the German Johann Hübner's (1668–1731) *Kurtze Fragen aus der neuen und alten Geographie* (*Kort begryp der oude en nieuwe geographie*, 'Short Sketch of

---

evidence from Will Adams's 'bouc of remembrance' suggests the use of Cantonese words including the cardinal numbers 1–10 and the cardinal points of the compass. As about half of crews on board VOC ships were not Dutch, such mixed languages are likely to have been used on the ships. It may be that they were also used by crewmembers who came ashore at Hirado and Nagasaki.

89 Keene (1969: 20) has a later date of 1763. Several *daimyō* families owned Valck globes including the Matsūra and Nabeshima on Kyushu.

90 The renderings *yanwari*, *befuriwari* and *maruto* are given by Unno.

Old and New Geography' Amsterdam, 1722) and compiled a booklet entitled *Oranda chizu ryakusetsu* ('Brief Explanation of Dutch Maps') (Unno
1994: 433).[91] In 1773 he completed *Oranda chikyū zusetsu* ('An explanation
in a Dutch atlas of the world'), a translation of the introduction to the *Atlas
van zeevaart en koophandel door de geheele weereldt* ('Atlas of Navigation and
Trade through the whole World', Amsterdam, 1745) by Louis Renard. In the
following year, 1774, Yoshinaga produced *Tenchi nikyū yōhō* ('The use of celestial and terrestrial globes'). This was a translation of a Dutch handbook,
Tweevoudigh onderwiis van de hemelsche en aerdsche globen ('Two-fold instruction on the heavenly and earthly globes', Amsterdam, 1666), the first edition of
which was published by the famous Dutch cartographer, Willem Jansz. Blaeu
(1571–1638) in 1634. Yoshinaga transcribes this in *katakana* as *onderūeisu han
de hēmeru en ārudose gorōben*. It was one of the first works in Japan to explain the Copernican theory of heliocentrism. Yoshinaga's work includes the
first rendering of Copernicus's name in *katakana* (*nikorāsu koperunikyusu*) as
well as other personal names and toponyms such as Blaeu and Amsterdam
(Unno 1994: 433–434).[92]

In 1786, the Edo *rangakusha* Katsuragawa Hoshū produced *Shinsei chikyū
bankoku zusetsu* ('Illustrated explanation of the new map of all the countries
in the world').[93] This work was derived from an explanation attached to Joan
Blaeu's (1598–1673) world map of 1648, the *Nova totius terrarum orbis tabula*
('New Map of the Lands of the Entire World'). Most of Blaeu's toponyms
are in Latin, e.g., *Anglia*, *Gallia* and *Germania*, but some are in vernacular
European languages including Dutch and Frisian.[94] This is an example of how
European maps married Latin and vernacular languages. The explanation
to Blaeu's map is in Dutch. Hoshū rendered several toponyms from the Low
Countries in *katakana* and while some renderings are quite close to the Dutch
(or Flemish) original, others are more distant. He renders *Henegouw* (contrast
French: Hainault) as *henegō*, *Namen* (French: Namur) as *Nāmen* and *Mechelen*
(French: Malines) as *mekeren*. However, he renders the province of Gelderland

---

91   Clements (2015: 151) has the date 1771.
92   See http://www.ndl.go.jp/nichiran/e/s2/s2_2.html. Accessed 7 April 2020. Yoshinaga's
      manuscript is preserved at the Nagasaki Museum of History and Culture. See also
      Goodman (2013: 98). Jacobs (1983: 64) suggests that *Chikyū zu* ('Map of the Globe'), drawn
      by Hayashi Shihei, mentioned above, in Nagasaki in 1775 may have been based on a
      Dutch map.
93   See http://archive.wul.waseda.ac.jp/kosho/bunko08/bunko08_co179/bunko08_co179.pdf.
      Accessed 7 April 2020 (Unno 1994: 434).
94   An example of a Dutch toponym on Blaeu's map is *Noortzee* for North Sea. An example of
      Frisian is *Liewert*, the town known in Dutch as Leeuwarden.

as *geruderurando* and Flanders (Dutch *Vlaanderen*) as *furānderen*, reflecting the Consonant-Vowel (CV) syllable structure of Japanese phonotactics. He renders Artois as *Arutoisu*, taking his lead from Blaeu's use of the French *Artois*, rather than the Dutch *Artesië*. In the French, the 's' is silent, something of which Hoshū seemed unaware.

One of the first maps of Europe to be published in Japan is a woodblock print on page 51 of Kutsuki Masatsuna's book on Western coins *Seiyō senpu* (1787). It gives the names of European countries in *katakana*. While some of these suggest a Latinate origin, e.g., *hisupaniya* for Spain, other names are clearly based on Dutch toponyms. These include *ryusurando* (Russia, Dutch: *Rusland*), *engerando* (England/Britain, Dutch: *Engeland*), *ōsutenreiki* (Austria, Dutch: *Oostenrijk*), *zūeiden* (Sweden, Dutch: *Zweden*), *pōren* (Poland, Dutch: *Polen*) and indeed *horurando* (*Holland*). Germany is indicated with *Doitsu*, from the Dutch for 'German' *Duits*. This is still the standard Japanese word for Germany.

Two years later, in 1789, Masatsuna produced *Taisei yochi zusetsu* ('Illustrated explanation of Western geography'). Sources are likely to include the travel anthology of Abbé Antoine Prévost d'Exiles and work by Johann Hübner (Screech 2006: 33). Volume 15 (*kan* 15) of this impressive work has woodblock prints of Europe and areas of Europe including the Low Countries. Masatsuna adopted several different strategies to render toponyms in Japanese script. The names of towns and provinces are typically transliterated into *katakana*, adapted to Japanese phonology. For example, Brabant is rendered as *burābanto* and Frisia (*Friesland*) as *furīsurando* (Van der Velde 2000c: 133).[95] Rivers are rendered in a combination of *katakana* and *kanji*. The River Rhine (Dutch *Rijn*) is rendered with *rein* in *katakana* and a *kanji* for 'river', viz. レイン河 (pronounced *reingawa*). Seas are typically rendered in *kanji*. The *Zuyderzee* (lit. Southern Sea) is rendered as 南海 (lit. 'South Sea', pron. *nankai*) while the North Sea (*Noordzee* in Dutch) is rendered as 北海 ('North Sea' pron. *hokkai*). This suggests that Masatsuna was able to understand toponyms, as well as transliterate them, possibly with the assistance of Dutchmen such as Isaac Titsingh. Finally, the influence of Dutch toponyms is evident away from the Low Countries. The English Channel is rendered in *katakana* as *kanāru* (Dutch: *het Kanaal*) (see fig. 11).

In the late eighteenth century, Japan started to have more contact with Russia, as its explorers and furriers pushed into East Asia. In 1792, Adam K. Laxman (1766–96?), a Finno-Swede working for Imperial Russia, reached Hokkaido and presented Russian maps to the shogunate (Unno 1994: 435). Japanese

---

95   Van der Velde provides a useful summary of Dutch maps and atlases imported into Japan.

FIGURE 11   *Taisei yochi zusetsu* ('Illustrated explanation of Western geography', 1789), Kutsuki Masatsuna
             kan 15 map of the Low Countries
             WUL ル 08 02859

were interested in, but also wary of, Russia. In 1793 Katsuragawa Hoshū produced *Roshia shi* ('Record of Russia'), based on *Algemeene Geographie, of
Beschryving des Geheelen Aardryks*, a Dutch translation of a geographical work
(*Allgemeine Geographie* referred to by *rangakusha* as *Zeogarahi*) by Johann
Hübner (Clements 2015: 151).[96] Indeed, although the word for Russia in the title
may be derived from one of a number of European languages (the translation
states that Russia is the Latin for the country), in the text there is a rendering in
katakana, *rosorando*, of the Dutch/German word for the country, *Rus(s)land*,

to be found in the Dutch translation (Hübner 1769: IV:327). Other toponyms show a clearer influence of Dutch such as *suwariterosurando* from *Zwitserland* (Switzerland) (contrast German *Schweiz*), which is also in the Dutch translation. Hoshū refers to the Russian Imperial domains as the *keizururureiki tomeinen* ('keizerlijke domeinen') (diacritics are optional), Dutch Hansa towns (*Hanzesteden*) as *nēderurando hansesutēten*, and the Russian Empress as *Katarina*. The islands to the north of Japan were of interest to the Russians and therefore it is understandable that Hoshū would wish to include them in his account. For example, he refers to the island of St. Lawrence as *santo raurensu* in both *katakana* and *ateji*, followed by the *kanji* for 'island' (島).[97] Similarly, Bering Island (*BERINGS-EILAND* in the Dutch) is rendered as *beringesu* in *katakana* followed by 島 (Hübner 1769: IV:412). In the Dutch source, the Kamchatka peninsula retained the German spelling of Kamtschatka (Hübner 1769: IV:404). This was rendered into *katakana* as *kamesukatsutoka*, a good example of how Germanic consonant clusters were converted into CV syllables in Japanese by inserting epenthetic vowels. Hoshū even transliterated the names of smaller places in Eastern Russia that Hübner clearly did not consider so important. For example, he renders Aklanskoi as *akeransuki*, the Penschina river as *benshin* and Anadirskoi as *anadirusuki* (Hübner 1769: IV:402–403). In this work, the running text is a combination of Japanese scripts. In the main, it is in a mixture of *hiragana* and *kanji*, suggesting the book was intended for a general, non-intellectual audience. Foreign toponyms are included either in *katakana* or *ateji* with *furigana*.

In 1792, Shiba Kōkan produced *Yochi zenzu* ('Map of the earth'), the first map to be engraved on copperplate in Japan (Unno 1994: 435). The layout was based on a world map of the Western and Eastern hemispheres reproduced in *Inleidinge tot de geographie* ('Introduction to Geography') (Covens and Mortier, Amsterdam 1730). This in turn was based on a world map by the French cartographer Alexis-Hubert Jaillot (1632–1712) (Loh 2013: 57; Unno 1994: 435).[98] Indeed, many of the toponyms, typically rendered in *katakana*, seem to owe something to Jaillot's French or other Romance languages. However, several of them such as *ruyusurando* (Russia, Dutch: *Rusland*), *sukotsutorando* (Scotland, Dutch: *Schotland*) and *irurando* (Ireland, Dutch: *Ierland*) are probably derived from Dutch. We also find 'Batavia', rendered in *katakana* as *hatahiya*, although this name in turn is derived from the Roman name for the Germanic tribe, the

---

97   In the Dutch text, it is called 'Het Eiland S. LAURENS' or 'TSCHUKOTSKOI- of [or] SCHELAGINSKOINOSS'.

98   There is a copy of the *mappe-monde* in Jaillot's *Nouvelle Introduction a la Geographie pour l'usage de Monseigneur le Dauphin* (Paris: 1692).

Batavii. At the bottom of the map are pictures of exotic plants. One example of the Dutch influence here is the word *safuran* (saffron) in *katakana* next to a picture of the plant (Vos 1963: 170). From the second edition of the map onwards, it was called *Chikyū zu* ('Map of the terrestrial globe') (Unno 1994: 435; Tsukahara 2007b: 197).[99]

Towards the end of the eighteenth century other Japanese maps based on ones imported from Europe were being printed. One such map consists of one large sheet depicting the Western and Eastern hemispheres surrounded by text printed on woodblock in 1796 or 1797. It has the title *Oranda shin'yaku chikyū zenzu* ('New Translation from the Dutch of a Complete Map of the Globe'). The authorship of the Japanese translation is not certain. One possible author is the Osaka *rangakusha*, Hashimoto Sōkichi (1763–1836), while another is a scholar of Chinese, Sotani Ōsei (1738–97).[100] The map gives the names of European countries and cities in *katakana*, although it typically lacks the diacritics found in other maps. Examples of Dutch toponyms clothed in *katakana* are *doitsurando* (Germany, *Duitsland*), *zūeiden* (Sweden, *Zweden*), and *ōsutenreiki* (Austria, *Oostenrijk*). Major seas are also marked. One which catches the eye is the rendering for the Baltic Sea, in Dutch *Oostzee* (lit. 'East Sea'). Here, the author adopts a strategy employed a few years earlier by Kutsuki Masatsuna in *Taisei yochi zusetsu*, combining *katakana* and *kanji* to produce ヲースト海. The *katakana* reads *ōsuto* and the *kanji* represents 'sea' (*kai*). However, the influence of Dutch was not just limited to European toponyms. As is well known, the first Europeans to reach Australia were the Dutch in the middle of the seventeenth century. The Dutchman Abel Tasman named Australia *Nova Hollandia* in Latin, *Nieuw Holland* in Dutch. These names continued to be used until the nineteenth century when they were gradually replaced by the name *Terra Australia* ('Southern Land'), shortened to Australia. In *Oranda shin'yaku chikyū zenzu*, Japanese versions of both *Nova Hollandia* and *Nieuw Holland* are given. The Latin name is rendered in *katakana* as *nōha horurando*. The Dutch name is rendered as 新ヲランダ, which comprises the *kanji* for 'new' 新 and *katakana* for *oranda*. These are followed by the date AD (紀元 (*kigen*)) 1644, the year in which it was named for Holland by the Dutch explorer Abel

---

99   Jacobs (1983: 65) writes that the later states were called *Chikyū zenzu* ('Map of the **whole** terrestrial globe') (my bold).

100   For a discussion of this map and a reproduction of it, see Unno (1994: 437, Fig. 11.65). A copy of the map in Cambridge has Dutch writing embossed on the covers, which, in the view of the Japanologist Radu Leca imitates the look and authority of a Dutch book. This may suggest that Dutch had a certain prestige at this time, at least in relation to maps. I am grateful to Radu Leca for bringing this map to my attention. For an online copy of this map, visit http://lapis.nichibun.ac.jp/chizu/santoshi_2435.html. Accessed 7 April 2020.

Tasman (1603–59). On the left is written *leuin* in *katakana*, a reference to the voc ship *Leeuwin* which reached Australia by accident in 1622.

In 1798, Morishima Chūryō published *Bangosen* ('Lexicon of Barbarian Words'). The final eighteen pages give an extensive range of toponyms in *kanji* (semantograms and phonograms) and *katakana* ordered by continent. Several examples serve to illustrate how Chūryō rendered toponyms from outside East Asia in Japanese. He bases his rendering of the Baltic on the Dutch but does so in a slightly different manner to the author of the map just discussed. Below, he gives *ōsutozē* (Dutch: *Oostzee*) in *katakana* (the 'Barbarian' word). Above this, he gives a *kanji* rendering with *ōsuto* in *ateji* and 海, the semantogram for 'sea'. He does something similar with the Apennine Mountains in Italy. Below, he gives a transliteration of the Dutch in *katakana*, *apenein beruge* (Dutch: *Apennijn Bergen*), and above an *ateji* version of *Apennijn* followed by 山, the semantogram for 'mountain'. Likewise, he renders the Alps in *katakana* as *yarupesu beruge* and above gives the toponym in *ateji* followed by 山. He is not always consistent, though. Below, he renders the Atlas Mountains in North Africa as *atarasu* in *katakana* (no *beruge*) but above adds 山 to the *ateji* rendering. This lack of consistency may in part be due to a lack of consistency in his sources. Ireland is rendered as *īrurando* and Lapland as *rapurando*, both in *ateji* and *katakana* and both suggestive of a Dutch source. Some renderings are clearly drawn from other European languages, such as *sukotsiya* for Scotland (< Late Latin *Scotia*) and *furansu* for France (< French). Toponyms outside Europe, too, point to a Dutch influence. One good example that illustrates that Chūryō is not simply transliterating European renderings concerns the 'legendary' Mountains of the Moon in East Africa. The Dutch is *Maanbergen*. Below, he renders this in *katakana* as *mānberuge*, and above in semantograms as 月 山 ('moon', 'mountain(s)'). Chūryō renders North and South America in a combination of semantograms and phonograms with *furigana*. In each case, the *furigana* is based on the Dutch, viz. *Nōrudo-amerika* (< Dutch *Noord-Amerika*) and *Soido-Amerika* (< Dutch *Zuid-Amerika*). Many of the toponyms from these continents are however based on Spanish and Latin names. In the section on Asia, he gives *batāhiya* for the Dutch/Latin toponym Batavia below in *katakana* and above in *ateji*.

A slightly different example is a Japanese map of Japan in the Leiden University collection. This is annotated in red ink with toponyms in *rōmaji* in the hand of Isaac Titsingh, most likely with the help of Japanese informants. The map has the title *Kaisei Nihon yochi rotei zenzu* ('General map of Japanese Territory. Revised edition') printed 1779 (Serrurier 220a).[101] Titsingh's renderings of Japanese toponyms are typical of those found in Dutch texts. He

---

101   I thank Hans van de Velde for this information.

renders Nagasaki as *Nangasakki*, Hirado as *Firando* and Buzen as *Boezen*. The reasons for these and other renderings of Japanese toponyms by authors of Dutch texts are analysed in Chapter 5. The south-east tip of Korea is depicted in the map and Titsingh even renders a few Korean toponyms in *rōmaji*, e.g., *foesan* for Busan.

The *fūsetsugaki*, the annual reports that the Dutch produced for the *bakufu*, included foreign toponyms based on Dutch names. For example, the 1797 report, signed by Gijsbert Hemmij, includes *katakana* transcriptions for Denmark (*dēnemaruko* < Dutch *Denemarken*) and for North America (*nōrudoamerika* < Dutch *Noord-Amerika*) (Nagasaki Shiritsu Hakubutsukan 2000: 20–21). However, in the first half of the nineteenth century, Japanese texts and maps of the world and Europe often included toponyms drawn from languages other than Dutch. In 1816, the astronomer and *Tenmondai* translator Takahashi Kageyasu (1784/5–1829) produced a map of the world on a hanging scroll, *Shintei bankoku zenzu* ('Newly Revised Map of the World') (Kobe City Museum 1998: 140–141). This was based on a world map by the English mapmaker, Aaron Arrowsmith (1750–1823), but probably other sources as well. The names of several of the countries in Europe are *katakana* versions of Latin names; for example, England is rendered as *angeriya* (cf. Anglia), Scotland as *sukotsia* (cf. Late Latin *Scotia*) and Spain as *isupaniya* (cf. *Hispania*). There is little evidence of a Dutch source, for even Flanders is rendered in *katakana* as *Furanderesu* (Dutch *Vlaanderen*).

As late as 1853, classical or medieval Latin versions of toponyms were still being used in Japanese maps of the world. For example, in Abe Yasuyuki's *Bankoku chikyū yochi zenzu* ('Comprehensive Map of the Myriad Countries of the Globe', 1853) we see *Isupanya* for Spain in *katakana*. The name for Britain, *Igirisu*, comes from the Portuguese *Inglês*, while another toponym, *Poronya* for Poland, may be derived from Latin or Portuguese. Again, there is no evidence of a Dutch influence here. The oval shape of the world map seems to point back to Ricci's 1602 map rather than to the later Dutch maps discussed above (Cortazzi 1983: 118–119).

In concluding this section, several points are in order. First, Dutch toponyms influenced Japanese maps and geographical texts from the early eighteenth century onwards, although it was only towards the end of that century, when *rangaku* was popular and relatively free of official censorship, that this influence was most strongly felt. Second, Dutch was not the only European language to influence Japanese maps. Latin and Portuguese toponyms were also incorporated into Japanese maps. Third, Japanese cartographers adopted several approaches in order to render Dutch (and non-Dutch) toponyms in

Japanese. Kutsuki Masatsuna's *Taisei yochi zusetsu* is an excellent example of this. Given the range of source languages and variety of approaches to rendering European toponyms in Japanese script, we again need to talk in terms of Bakhtin's *heteroglossia* or indeed *heterosemia* with regard to Japanese world-maps in the late Tokugawa period. Fourth, these toponyms appeared in a range of texts from maps to geographical descriptions to the *fūsetsugaki*. Finally, while some Dutch toponyms have subsequently fallen into disuse, others have remained in use in Japanese. For example, whereas in cMJ England is now called *igirisu*, from the Portuguese, Germany is *doitsu* from the Dutch *Duits*.

13   Book Collecting and Reading

While many translations were made from Dutch to Japanese, in other cases Japanese simply collected Dutch books. This does not of course necessarily mean that the books were read, for there were Japanese such as *daimyō* who were wealthy enough to collect Dutch books, without necessarily being able to read them. Nevertheless, the possibility is certainly there, and in some cases the books would have been read by other *rangakusha*. This section analyses who was collecting books, which books they were collecting and how they acquired these books.

The Dutch themselves had a library on Deshima. In his account of his time in Japan in the late 1850s and early 1860s, the Dutch physician Jhr J.L.C. Pompe van Meerdervoort (1970: 87) recorded that there were some 'very fine, elaborate works' on physics and chemistry in the library which he used to explain aspects of these subjects to the Japanese whom he taught. As for Japanese, probably the largest collection of books in Dutch in Japan was, perhaps unsurprisingly, the Momijiyama library, housed at the shogun's castle in Edo (Mervart 2015: 17). Demand for these books was driven by the *bakufu*, which was keen to acquire information useful for the government of the country. This gained impetus after 1684, when the *bakufu* assumed responsibility for the calendar and subsequently established its own astronomical observatory, the *Tenmondai* (天文台), sometimes referred to as the 'Bureau of Astronomy' in secondary literature (Boot 2013: 190; Clements 2015: 156).

Some of those close to the shogun acquired Dutch books. Inoue Masashige, who was variously an intellectual, the government official responsible for keeping an eye on the Dutch (*ōmetsuke* 大目付), Inspector of Religions (*Shūmon aratame no Yaku* 宗門改役) and *daimyō* of Chikugo province, was one Japanese who collected a range of Dutch books as well as some in Portuguese and indeed

Latin (Laver 2011: 65; Screech 2012: 312; Kornicki 2018: 150).[102] Other *daimyō* too actively collected Dutch books. One of the largest collections of Dutch books, possibly even larger than that of the shogun was built up by the Nabeshima *daimyō* (Kornicki 2018: 303). From their base at Saga in western Kyushu, the Nabeshima *daimyō* were *de facto* responsible for the defence of Nagasaki and they therefore acquired many Dutch books on military matters. Matsuda Kiyoshi (2006) has identified some 750 Dutch titles in the Nabeshima-Saga collection. He provides details of more than 150 of these under the heading 'artillery' (*heihōsho* 兵砲書). The collection also includes over thirty books on marine and naval matters (heading: *funegakusho* 船学書), some sixty lexicons, learners and grammars for Dutch and other European languages, 25 books on astronomy (*tenmon* 天文) and geography (*chiri* 地理), a remarkable fifty books on chemistry (*bunrisho* 分離書), sixty books on medicine (*isho* 医書), almost 100 books on geometry, surveying and mathematics (*dogaku heisangaku sho* 度学并算学書), and some forty books on physics (*rigakusho* 理学書) as well as various 'miscellaneous' books.[103]

At the end of the eighteenth century, the *daimyō* and statesman Matsudaira Sadanobu (1758/9–1829) recorded that he had been collecting what he calls 'barbarian books' on a range of subjects including astronomy, geography, military matters and medicine (Boot 2013: 197–198). However, in contrast to the Nagasaki interpreters he expressed disquiet about the potential threat of *rangaku* to Japan. The heads of the Matsūra family were *daimyō* of Hirado. Matsūra Kiyoshi (1760–1841), better known by his pen name, Seizan, was an avid collector of Dutch books and owned one of the largest collections of books in Dutch in Japan, rivalling even that of the Momijiyama library (Boot 2013: 199; Mervart 2015: 16–17). Over one hundred Dutch books and periodicals are still in the Matsūra collection at Hirado today. Some of these are analysed below. Finally, today, the Sanada family still possesses many Dutch books. This is largely due to the efforts of the *daimyō* Sanada Yukitsura (1791–1852) of Matsushiro domain, who actively promoted *rangaku* (Goodman 2013: 148).

Many of these *daimyō* were clearly not simply feudal lords, but notable intellectuals. Other intellectuals and scholars collected Dutch books, too. The shogunal astronomer Takahashi Kageyasu built up a substantial collection of Dutch books (Kornicki 2018: 150). Ogata Kōan, the founder and principal of

---

102   For more on Inoue Masashige, see Blussé (2003a).

103   For the Nabeshima collection and interest in Dutch studies see also Goodman (2013: 154–156); Matsumoto (2000), Michel *et al.* (2014) and Sugitani (2014). Goodman (p. 156) uses a different source and gives precise numbers. I avoid giving precise numbers as several entries in the catalogue are categorized incorrectly. The numbers given above are indicative of where the priorities and interests of the Nabeshima family lay.

the *Tekijuku* Dutch medical school in Osaka, owned many Dutch books, which he allowed his students to consult (Fukuzawa 2007: 344–346). On a slightly different note, in the late eighteenth century, an affluent rice dealer, Yamagata Shigeyoshi, owned what is described as 'a worthy collection of Dutch books and translations of European books' along with other Western objects such as telescopes (Jackson 2016: 46). Kornicki (2001: 303), though, strikes a note of caution, observing that ownership of Dutch books in general amongst Japanese was not as widespread as one might think. He takes the case of the Mitsukuri family as an example, writing 'even the famous family of experts in Western studies, the Mitsukuri, appear to have possessed barely fifty Dutch books of their own, published between 1710 and 1866'.[104] Finally, by the beginning of the eighteenth century the Nagasaki interpreters had begun to assemble a small library of Dutch books at the chambers of the *tsūji nakama* on Edomachi Street, just outside the entrance to Deshima. Clearly, the Japanese mentioned here, including the interpreters, many of whom came from the samurai class, belonged to the upper echelons of Japanese society. Further research may reveal whether Japanese lower down the social order acquired Dutch books.

Auctions of books and other possessions of the Dutch at Deshima were held after they died (Boot 2013: 198–199). Lists of items for auction give us an insight into the books they owned. A good example is the auction after the untimely death of the junior merchant (*ondercoopman*) Cornelis van Brattim in 1761. Besides his material possessions books were auctioned off including a sea atlas, some dictionaries, Kaempfer's work on Japan, books on the lives of Johann van Oldenbarnevelt and the Duke of Alva, and the poems of Jakob Zeeus (Feenstra Kuiper 1921: 253; Blussé and Remmelink 2004: 269). In 1800, an auction was held of the books and other possessions of Gijsbert Hemmij who had died suddenly in somewhat mysterious circumstances while on the *hofreis* (Mervart 2015: 18–19). Seventy-seven titles (195 physical volumes) in several European languages were auctioned off. Hemmij was well-educated, he had studied at Leiden University, and clearly had eclectic interests (Du Rieu 1875: col. 1097). Among the Dutch volumes were Hugo Grotius's introduction to Dutch jurisprudence, *Inleiding tot de Hollandsche Rechtsgeleerdheyt* (The Hague, 1776 edition) and a Dutch translation of François Fénelon's *Aventures de Télemaque* (Amsterdam, 1720). There were also several dictionaries including two copies of Halma's Dutch-French dictionary, a Latin-Dutch lexicon and Sewel's Dutch-English lexicon. His successor, Hendrick Doeff, acquired Dutch, French and English books in the auction including the two Halma lexicons.

---

104 K. Mitsukuri gave a speech entitled 'On the early study of Dutch in Japan' at the Asiatic Society of Japan in 1877, mentioned in the prologue.

He may well have used these as the basis for his own Dutch-Japanese lexicon (Matsuda 1998: 354–362).[105] The *dagregister* provides further details of books in the possession of the Dutch. In 1723, Johannes Thedens (*opperhoofd* 1723–25) recorded that one of the interpreters had given him a Dutch book on navigation and asked him to keep it in his possession (Vermeulen *et al.* 1986–: V:47). There are also several references in the *dagregister* to the fact that the Dutch brought bibles and other religious works into the country sealed in a barrel whenever a ship arrived. However, these would necessarily have had to remain for private use (Vos 1989: 356).

As for what the Japanese were acquiring, one of the earliest books written in Dutch to attract their attention was Rembert Dodoens's famous herbal, *Cruydt-boeck* (first ed. 1554). There were several copies in Japan in the seventeenth century.[106] In the winter of 1682 the *daimyō* and cousin of the shogun, Maeda Tsunanori (1643–1724), who was a scholar and book collector, acquired a copy of the third edition of Dodoens's *Cruydt-boeck*, printed in Dutch in Antwerp in 1644, from the *opperhoofd*, Andreas Cleyer (Matsuda 2001: 192–193; Cleyer 1985: 69). It is also likely that the Japanese herbalist, Kaibara Ekiken, mentioned above, had a copy of Dodoens's *Cruydt-boeck* in his library (Matsuda 2001: 193). One Dutch book that Inoue Masashige borrowed was a copy of Jacob Cats's collection of allegories, *Spiegel van den Ouden ende Nieuwen Tijdt* ('Mirror of the Old and New Time') (1st ed. 1632, The Hague). He was particularly interested in the pictures in this emblem book and informed the Dutch that his interpreter would translate some of the texts into Japanese. Furthermore, he wished to have some of the images copied and put on screens for display in his Edo mansion (Screech 2012: 312; Vermeulen *et al.* 1986–: XII:51, 343).

Timon Screech focusses on the Japanese interest in Western medical books. He asserts that most of the important Western medical books of the early modern period were in Japan. These included 'classics' by Vesalius and Ambroise Paré as well as Dodoens's *Cruydt-boeck*, but also more up-to-date Dutch editions of works by the Germans, Lorenz Heister (*Heelkundige Onderwijzingen* ('Lessons in Surgery'), a translation of Heister's *Chirurgie*), and Johann Woyt (*Gazophylacium medico-physicum*, 1st ed. Leipzig, 1709, Dutch edition Amsterdam 1741) (Screech 2012: 315–316; 2005: 153). In the nineteenth

---

105 Matsuda (1998: 351–379) provides further examples of inventories of books owned by Dutchmen in Nagasaki, which were auctioned off when their owner passed away (Boot 2013: n. 52).

106 Shirahata (2001: 263) argues that Dodoens's book was the most influential book in terms of promoting the rise of *rangaku*.

century many of the books acquired by Ogata Kōan concerned medicine (Fukuzawa 2007: 344–346). On a different note, in the years 1838–42, largely in response to the First Opium War, the *de facto* ruler of Japan, Mizuno Tadakuni (1794–1851) ordered at least 30 Dutch books on military matters (Kornicki 2001: 302–303).

The Matsūra collection at Hirado could be described as eclectic. Among the books in Dutch still in the collection are ones on medicine, Dutch history, a history of the Reformed churches in France (Elias Benoît, *Historie der Gereformeerde Kerken van Vrankrijk*, 1 vol., Amsterdam, 1696), the first fourteen volumes of a commentary on the Bible (Matthew Henry, *Verklaring over den geheelen Bybel of het Oude en Nieuwe Testament*, Delft, 1741–62), the natural world including a Dutch version of Pliny's *Naturalis Historia*, a Dutch translation of Ovid, Kaempfer's book on Japan, and multiple copies of the Dutch periodical *Republyk der Geleerden* ('Republic of Letters') (Matsuda 1998: 427–428).[107] What is perhaps surprising, given the ban on Christianity and the strict control on the import of Christian books, is that several of the Dutch books in the Matsūra collection have Christian content and very obvious Christian iconography. One possibility is that the censors turned a blind eye to a powerful *daimyō* importing such works, while in some cases it may be a function of the fact that the censors in Nagasaki did not read Dutch. Finally, the Ueno collection at the NDL consists of over 3,000 'foreign' books acquired by the *bakufu*, most of which are in Dutch. These books are on a whole range of subjects with those on medicine, military matters and geography as well as learning materials for Dutch particularly well represented.[108]

As for how these Dutch books landed up in Japanese collections, the short answer is that they were imported by the Dutch and either sold to Japanese or given as presents. Let us add some detail to this answer. From the early years of the Dutch presence in Nagasaki, Japanese would ask them to import certain books. For example, in 1660 Joan Boucheljon (*opperhoofd* intermittently 1655–60) records that he sent a copy of Johann Ludwig Remmelin's *Pinax Microcosmographicus* ('Microcosmic Diagrams') to Inaba Masanori (1623–96), *daimyō* of Odawara, which Masanori had ordered along with other imported objects including a Siamese rhinoceros horn! (Vermeulen *et al.* 1986–: XII:407).[109]

---

107 Matsuda's list was published in 1998. For an up-to-date list of the books in the Matsūra library, see the Matsūra Western books catalogue (洋書目録) (unpublished).

108 List of foreign books collected under the Shogunate regime = Lijst van boeken in buitenlandse talen verzameld door het Shogunaat = 江戸幕府旧蔵洋書目録.

109 Masanori is referred to in the *dagregister* by the honorific title *Mino-no-kami* 美濃守.

In a letter in English, Isaac Titsingh writes that he had been supplying the Japanese with books 'particularly on natural history, Botany, Physick & Surgery' (Boot 2013: 197; Lequin 1990: I:450). One of the Japanese that he probably had in mind was his friend, Kutsuki Masatsuna, with whom he regularly corresponded. The books were usually delivered to him by one of the VOC employees at Deshima. In a letter dated 28 May 1785 that Masatsuna wrote from Edo, he thanked Titsingh for various Dutch (and French) learning materials and 'Weimans Kruytboek 8 deelen'. This is a Dutch version of an eight-volume work on flora by Johann Wilhelm Weinmann (1683–1741), *Duidelyke Vertoning Eeniger Duizend in alle Vier Waerelds Deelen wassende Bomen, Stammen, Kruiden, Bloemen, Vrugten en Uitwassen* ('Clear Presentation of several thousand trees, trunks, herbs, flowers, fruits and outgrowths', Amsterdam, 1736–48), which was based on *Phytanthoza Iconographia* (1st ed. Regensburg. 1735).

In the same letter, Masatsuna asks his friend for some more books, which he lists as 'een stel met Lateinsche woordenboek, Jonstons, harentein van 10 deelen [en] Geographie van 6 deelen' (Lequin 1992: 2–3). The first book is a Latin dictionary, the second Jonston's natural history, the third *Oud en Nieuw Oost-Indiën* (1724–26) by François Valentijn (*harentein*) (1666–1727) and the last a six-volume work on geography. Given the vague description of the last item, it may be that Masatsuna had discussed this with Titsingh on another occasion. However, one possibility is that he is referring to Hübner's *Algemeene Geographie*. Masatsuna would send Titsingh rare Japanese and Chinese coins in return. Titsingh sent Dutch books to other correspondents including Katsuragawa Hoshū, Nakagawa Jun'an and Imamura Kinbei (Lequin 2003: 208–209). In his journal for the *hofreis* in 1776, the Swedish physician Carl Peter Thunberg observes that Hoshū and Jun'an had purchased books from the Dutch including Dodoens's *Cruydt-boeck* and Johann Woyt's *Gazophylacium medico-physicum*. In addition, he records that he sold them 'amongst other books, a very fine edition of Muntingius's (Abraham Munting) *Phytographia*'. This was probably the Dutch translation *Naauwkeurige beschryving der aardgewassen* ('Detailed description of plants', Leiden, 1696) (Screech 2005: 153). In *Rangaku kotohajime*, Sugita Genpaku records that he acquired a copy of Adam Kulmus's *Ontleedkundige Tafelen* ('Anatomical Tables') from the Dutch at Edo in 1771. He had been given money by his *daimyō* in order to make the purchase. He would soon find out that Maeno Ryōtaku had acquired another copy of the same book in Nagasaki (Sugita 1969: 25, 28–29). This, it will be remembered, was the source text for *Kaitai shinsho*.

Two dedications on slips of paper, one in a copy of Gerard van Loon's *Beschryving der Nederlandsche Historiepenningen* ['Description of Dutch commemorative coins'] (The Hague, 1723), the other in a copy of Diderot's Encyclopaedia

Recueil des Planches (vol. 6, Paris, 1768), tell us that these books were presents from the *opperhoofd* Johan van Rheede tot de Parkeler given in 1789 to 'de Kooper Raffineerder Jetsmija Kitie Saijemon', i.e., Izumiya Kichizaemon, head of the copper refinery at Osaka. Van Rheede tot de Parkeler visited the refinery during the *hofreis* (Kobe City Museum 1998: 66–67). The fact that the export of Japanese copper formed an important part of Dutch trade with Japan may have been the motivation for this visit and giving of books (Shimada 2006).

Above, mention was made of auctions of books and other possessions after Dutchmen passed away in Japan. However, such auctions often took place without Japanese participation, so it is unclear whether Japanese were able to obtain Dutch books from such auctions. Japanese did, though, sell Dutch books to each other. One Japanese who seems to have been active in this regard was Yoshio Kōgyū. He acquired a copy of Kaempfer's 'History of Japan' from the Dutch and then sold it onto the *daimyō* of Hirado, Matsūra Seizan (Boot 2013: 199; Matsuda 1998: 487–488). Kōgyū also sold a copy of *Heelkundige Onderwijzingen*, the Dutch translation of Lorenz Heister's *Chirurgie*, to Sugita Genpaku and Ōtsuki Gentaku (Van Gulik and Nimura 2005: 15).[110] In fact, he was quite a buyer and seller of Dutch books. He often marked his acquisitions with his *rōmaji ex libris, josiwo*.[111] We find it in Dutch books on the history of the Reformed church in France and on the Princes of Orange, which he passed on or sold to the Matsūra clan (Matsuda 1998: 441, 451). It is also in a Dutch book on Russia in the Ueno collection (no. 567). In 1788, Kōgyū's interest in Dutch books found expression in a work of art. In that year, Shiba Kōkan visited Nagasaki and in the ink wash portrait that Kōkan made of Kōgyū, he depicted him holding a Dutch book (French 1974: 67–68).

Further information about which books the Japanese obtained, and how, is provided in Lists of Requests that they made to the Dutch. From the 1760s onwards, the lists included orders for Dutch books placed on behalf of the Interpreters' Guild (Boot 2013: 199). Lists of books ordered from the Dutch are extant for the years 1810, 1814, 1818–30, and 1844–56; those from the years 1810–30 have been published by Nagazumi Yōko (1998: 9–37; Boot 2013: 199). In these lists, the categories of officials who placed the orders are distinguished as the shogun, Nagasaki magistrates (*daikan* 代官), officials of the Nagasaki *kaisho* (長崎会所, the office that regulated commercial activity in Nagasaki), Nagasaki city elders (*machidoshiyori* 町年寄), and the Interpreters' Guild (*tsūji*

---

110   In *Rangaku kotohajime*, Genpaku records that Kōgyū lent him a copy of *Heelkundige Onderwijzingen* (Ogata 1971: 10).

111   Johannes Broedelet, *Oude en nieuwe staat van 't Russische of Moskovische Keizerrijk; behelzende eene uitvoerige historie van Rusland en deszelfs Groot-Vorsten* NDL 蘭-567.

nakama; sometimes individual interpreters are mentioned by name). A second type of list is the *Meisho-chō* (銘書帳, 'Title ledgers'). These are lists of titles of imported books by the Dutch. They were first drawn up in 1839, in the wake of the crackdown on *rangakusha* (*Bansha no goku* 蛮社の獄) that took place in that year. It was Shibukawa Rokuzō (1815–51) who suggested drawing up these lists to his patron, the Edo city commissioner (*machi bugyō*) Torii Yōzō (1796–1873), who masterminded the crackdown. The lists continued to be made until 1859 and were drawn up in *katakana* (with the odd entry in *kanji*); the lists for the years 1839, 1845, and 1847–59 are still extant. Nagazumi (1998: 43–372) reproduces these yearly lists (3,592 titles in all) and supplements them with indexes of authors and titles. The *Meisho-chō* served two purposes. First, they allowed for the censoring of Dutch books imported at Nagasaki. Second, they enabled those who might be interested in acquiring the books, such as the *bakufu* and *daimyō*, to obtain details of them (Boot 2013: 199). Cornelis Assendelft de Coningh (1856b: 4) recounts his own experience of this system in 1851. The censor or 'boeken-commissaris' ('book commissioner') made a list of books brought ashore. These could not be taken into the Dutch houses. The list was translated into Japanese and sent to the shogun (i.e., *bakufu*) in Edo. About six weeks later, a letter arrived stating which of these books the shogun wanted to acquire. The Dutch were not forced to sell, but often did so. Assendelft de Coningh records that the Japanese wanted above all to acquire Western books on Japan. He had with him a copy of a Dutch translation of Vice Admiral Vasily Golovnin's account of Japan, which the censor was keen to purchase for the shogun.

A full survey of these lists is beyond the scope of this book. It will, however, be instructive to provide a brief analysis of two of the years concerned, 1839 and 1847, to gain a sense of what sort of book was being imported. The list for 1839 (Nagazumi 1998: 46–49) includes 65 books. Several books have not been identified. Of those which have, most have Dutch titles, and most were printed in the nineteenth century. Many of them concern medicine, reflecting the importance attached to Dutch and Western medicine by Japanese. Other subjects include chemistry, an introduction to physics, and astronomy. One book is a copy of Martinet's ever-popular *Katechismus der Natuur*, which was replete with attractive pictures of natural objects. There are two copies of a Dutch spelling guide by Pieter Weiland and a guide to Dutch writing style by Johan Beijer, *Handleiding tot den Nederlandschen stijl* (2nd ed. Rotterdam, 1824).

The list for 1847 includes 126 books (Nagazumi 1998: 68–75). Some books are on medicine, but far fewer than in the 1839 list, a trend that continued in subsequent years. This may be less a function of Japanese losing interest in Western medicine—they were by now producing their own translations of Western medical texts—and more a result of Japanese interest in Western books on other subjects. Several books are on military matters. What is most striking, however, is the range of subjects. Some texts are on weightier matters such as European history, constitutional law and trade, while others concern lighter subjects such as playing cards and gardening. There was even a Dutch translation of a French novel. Three books on Napoleon underline the Japanese interest in the French leader. Details of bilingual books and books in other languages in the lists published by Nagazumi are given in the next chapter. Further details of Dutch learning materials on the list are provided in Chapter 8.

As a footnote to this analysis, the last *opperhoofd* at Deshima, Donker Curtius, acquired over 120 books, most of which relate to *rangaku*. These were shipped back to the Netherlands and are preserved at Leiden University Library (Hoffmann and Serrurier 1882). Many of these books, including Dutch-Japanese lexicons and Japanese translations of Dutch texts, have been consulted in the writing of the present book.

As well as telling us who owned which Dutch books, this section has attempted to provides insights into the circulation of Dutch texts in Japan, with *rangakusha* such as Yoshio Kōgyū acting as nodes for the exchange of Dutch books. In this regard, it may be useful to think of the Dutch language as a *bibliolect*, in other words a language in which information was stored and transmitted in book form.[112] While some of the information transmitted in this manner remained in the Dutch *bibliolect*, other information was translated and activated for use by a new, Japanese readership.

14 Conclusion

There is more work to do on this subject. For example, *rangakusha* often kept scrapbooks, in which they logged examples of Western languages.[113] These offer further *probationes linguae*, to add to those of Maeno Ryōtaku discussed in Chapter 2. Furthermore, our analysis will necessarily remain incomplete, for although the Dutch were meticulous record-keepers, some documents, such as early Hirado *dagregisters*, have been lost or cannot currently be traced. Nevertheless, the analysis in this chapter illustrates that as a result of contact

---

112 This is a re-working of an existing coinage. Holmstedt (2006: 18) uses it in Biblical studies to refer to 'the grammar of each text', which can be used to identify the dating and source of a text.

113 I thank Guita Winkel for this observation.

between Dutch and Japanese, Dutch was used in many ways in Tokugawa Japan. We can perhaps best express this by returning to Bakhtin's notion of *heteroglossia* to describe the different voices, speaking (or writing!) Dutch in a range of registers and through a variety of media.

The Dutch themselves kept extensive records in Dutch primarily in the form of the factory journal, the *dagregister*. They also kept private journals, wrote reports such as the *Oranda fūsetsugaki* and corresponded with other Dutch and Japanese. They gave Japanese associates Dutch, and on occasion Latin, names, and wrote Dutch words for the amusement and occasional edification of Japanese across the social spectrum.

As for Japanese, many collected, read and in some cases translated Dutch scientific texts. We return to translation in Chapter 6. Japanese wrote letters in Dutch, sometimes to other Japanese. Although their written Dutch was by no means perfect, it typically sufficed for the purpose of communication. Several such as Kutsuki Masatsuna used it to obtain books from Dutch associates in order to further their knowledge of Dutch learning. One use of Dutch which this chapter has analysed in detail is for the rendering of toponyms outside Japan on maps and in geographical texts. Masatsuna's *Taisei yochi zusetsu* illustrates the range of strategies that cartographers adopted in order to render names for countries, towns, provinces, rivers and seas in Japanese script. This in some sense mirrors the range of strategies adopted by translators to render Dutch scientific terms in Japanese. Many examples of this are analysed in Chapter 7.

One of the most fascinating aspects of this story is how Japanese appropriated Dutch and used it for their own purposes. In some cases, the use of Dutch was primarily for the purpose of conveying information. Morishima Chūryō's *Kōmō zatsuwa* is a fine example of this. In other cases, there is an element of self-presentation at work. Shiba Kōkan was enraptured by the West. He often signed his work in *rōmaji* and added Dutch text in Roman script or *katakana*. He constructed semantic fields in which he married image and text, creating a whole that spoke in several voices. Here, we might also talk of a visual 'polyphony' (полифония), to borrow from Bakhtin once more, but also of a symphony as the familiarity and strangeness of Japanese scenes depicted in Western perspective mirrored, and in some sense complemented, the use of Japanese script and *rōmaji*.

Artists and artisans often added Dutch for decorative purposes, or to conjure up a sense of the exotic. We see this in the decorative arts, such as lacquerwork and ceramics. Framing this in another way, Dutch was a means to an end, in that it was a vehicle for the mediation of Western knowledge, a metalect if you will. But it was also an end in itself, with its exoticness and otherness being sufficient reasons for its use in fine and decorative art, leaving an indelible mark on Japanese material as well as textual culture.

It is important not to overstate the use of Dutch, for it faced competition from other languages. The case of mapmaking illustrates that Dutch faced competition from Latin and Portuguese. Furthermore, throughout this period, besides varieties of Japanese, literary Sinitic, above all in the form of *kanbun*, continued to play a dominant role in cultural, social and intellectual life in Tokugawa Japan. The competition that Dutch faced from other languages is the subject of the next chapter. As for this chapter, it has illustrated that Dutch was used by various (typically, but not exclusively, well-educated and high-ranking) Japanese in a range of codes and media. Finally, it has attempted to demonstrate that while the use of Dutch in the sphere of learning, i.e., *rangaku*, about which much has already been written, was important, it was by no means the whole story.

CHAPTER 4

Language Contact

1   Introduction

In the prologue, language contact was defined as 'the situation in which languages [...] influence each other synchronically in shared socio-semiotic contexts' (Steiner 2008: 319). It will already be clear that in Tokugawa Japan Dutch was in shared socio-semiotic contexts with varieties of Japanese as well as varieties of several other European and East Asian languages. In some cases, Dutch, if you will, merely 'rubbed shoulders' with other languages, with limited points of contact and no real evidence of influence. In other cases, there is evidence of influence, while in further cases there is evidence of language competition, defined by Peter Burke (2004: 70) as 'the struggle for the centre [involving] attempts to marginalize rivals'. The aim of this chapter is to analyse the languages which functioned in the same socio-semiotic context as Dutch in order to build a picture of the nature of the relationship between them.

In the early years of the Dutch presence in Japan, they traded through Hirado. Clulow (2013: 214) is right to describe it as a multiethnic port city, and one could add multilingual. Here, Dutch faced competition from varieties of Portuguese, but also other languages such as English and Japanese. Hirado had long been a port of entry into Japan for Chinese merchants and so Dutch may have had points of contact with Sinitic varieties as well. From 1641 onwards, after the Dutch move to Nagasaki, the Dutch language continued to face competition from Portuguese, even though the Portuguese themselves had been expelled in 1639. By the end of the seventeenth century, the use of Portuguese had to a great extent receded. In the period of isolation, Dutch faced competition from Malay and Sinitic varieties. Dutch and Japanese authors also used Latin instead of Dutch in certain cases. In the early nineteenth century, as a result of incursions by Russian and British vessels in Japanese waters the *bakufu* ordered interpreters to learn Russian and English to prepare for a possible attack. After the Convention of Kanagawa in 1854, demand for Dutch increased briefly as it functioned as an LWC between Europeans and Americans on the one hand and Japanese on the other hand. Nevertheless, interest in English increased. Furthermore, other European languages, above all German and French, gained ground.

We can get some sense of the demand for these other languages from lists of books ordered by the Japanese from the Dutch at Nagasaki, published by

© CHRISTOPHER JOBY, 2021 | DOI:10.1163/9789004438651_006

Nagazumi (1998). Books written in these languages and learners and dictionaries for students of them preserved in the Ueno collection, although by no means comprehensive, add to our understanding of the competition that Dutch faced.[1] The seals in many of the books tell us that they had previously belonged to institutions such as the *Bansho shirabesho* (蕃書調所, 'Office for the Investigation of Barbarian books'), established in 1856; one of its successor institutions from 1863, the *Kaiseijo* (開成所); and the *Seimikyoku* (舎密局), a chemistry school in Osaka and, later, Kyoto. Several other books in the collection had previously belonged to prominent families active in Dutch studies, such as the Takahashi clan, one of whose members Kageyasu had worked with Von Siebold. During the Meiji period the books belonging to the shogunal institutions had been transferred to the Imperial Library. However, as interest in Dutch had by now diminished, they were soon forgotten. Where appropriate mention will be made of books in the Ueno collection.

Two other languages which functioned in the same socio-semiotic context as Dutch were Korean and Ainu. Here, though, only a few users of Dutch had limited contact with these languages, so there is little or no sense of language competition, let alone influence. In what follows, there is a broadly chronological account of the languages that shared a common socio-semiotic context with Dutch in Japan and the nature of their relationship.

2 Japanese

The language with which Dutch interacted most intensely and for the longest period was Japanese. Chapter 2 analysed one result of contact between varieties of these two languages; namely that many Japanese learnt Dutch. This section analyses whether any Dutch learnt Japanese. It also addresses one other question of interest to linguists: whether any contact variety emerged.

The surviving crewmembers of the *Liefde* remained in Japan, and some become proficient in Japanese. Jan Joosten van Lodensteyn became a merchant in Edo and advisor to the shogun, while Jan Cousynen was employed by the VOC as a Japanese-Dutch interpreter at Hirado. Later, François Caron learnt the language. In 1641, the steward's mate, Hicke Essert, was said to be fairly proficient in Japanese and the merchant Augustijn Muller could speak Japanese with native speakers (Vermeulen *et al.* 1986–: XI:40, 69). However, in

---

1 The information we have on the Ueno books is based on a catalogue of them produced by the National Diet Library (List of Foreign Books 1957). Volumes in this catalogue referred to in this book have the prefix 蘭-/RAN in the National Diet Library catalogue, e.g., 蘭-567.

time an official ban was introduced on the learning of the language by non-Japanese and contact with Japanese was restricted.[2] Thereafter, some Dutch and other Europeans did learn the language, but often with negative consequences. Engelbert Kaempfer studied the language without suffering any such consequences. By contrast, in October 1670 the *opperhoofd* François de Haese recorded that First Assistants Bartram Jansen and Johannes van Beeckhuijsen, Assistant Pieter van Dam and Junior Assistant Jan Jacob van Merwe had been ordered to leave Deshima; the first because he had been in Japan for four years and the other three because they spoke some Japanese (Vermeulen *et al.* 1986–: XIII:366). Similarly, in 1718 the senior surgeon Dr. Willem Wagemans was required to leave Japan because he spoke the language too well (Blussé *et al.* 1992: xix).

Despite the ban, in the eighteenth and nineteenth centuries, a few Dutch and other Europeans did learn Japanese, and in some cases chose to use Japanese instead of a European language. Hermanus Menssingh, having held junior posts at Deshima, was *opperhoofd* intermittently between 1705 and 1710. He was said to be fluent in Japanese (Blussé *et al.* 1992: xxiii). Isaac Titsingh expressed regret that more of his fellow Dutchmen did not try to learn Japanese. He records that this was not for lack of opportunity but rather desire (Vos 1980: 15).[3] Titsingh himself did, however, learn some of the language. We see this in his correspondence with Kutsuki Masatsuna, in which he inserts Japanese proverbs and uses the names of Japanese months in *rōmaji* (Lequin 1992: 42–44). Furthermore, in his diary of the 1780 *hofreis* Titsingh intimates that he and indeed other non-Japanese knew some Japanese when he records that he was aware that the interpreters sometimes did not translate words for him.[4] Titsingh owned several Japanese books. In one of these, an encyclopaedia with the title *Wakan jishi* (= *on*-reading; *kun*-reading *kotohajime* 和漢事始), we see him grappling with the language. On the spine is written *Wa Zi Si* (the second character (*Kan*) is not transcribed). Titsingh notes that *Wa* refers to Japan (*Kan* to China), *Zi* (i.e., *ji*) means *een zaak* ('a thing') and *Si* (i.e., *shi*), *beginsel*, 'principle or origin'. It can be translated as 'Introduction to Japanese and Chinese

---

2 Overmeer Fisscher (1833: 269) wrote 'Geen Hollander kan het Eiland verlaten, zonder de goedkeuring van de Japansche Regering' ('No Hollander (Dutchman) can leave the island without the consent of the Japanese government').

3 Dutch: 'aan de kant van de bediendens niet aan gelegenheid, maar veeleer aan lust ontbreekt tot 't aanleeren der Japansche taal'.

4 In an entry for 31 March 1780, he writes 'niet denkende dat er onder ons waren die zulx verstonden, en vertaalde het mij dierhalven ook niet' ('not thinking that there were any amongst us who understood such things, and for that reason (an interpreter) did not translate it for me') (Lequin 2011: 63).

(Han) Studies'. Titsingh made many other linguistic notes in his copy of the book (Lequin 2003: 80). After leaving Japan, he compiled small lists of Japanese words and phrases (Lequin 2013: 121–122).

Hendrick Doeff was another *opperhoofd* who learnt Japanese. He used his knowledge of the language in the compilation of the Dutch-Japanese lexicon, the *Nagasaki* or *Zūfu Haruma*, analysed in Chapter 2. Doeff also wrote *haiku* poetry. One poem of his was inspired by seeing a lady slicing tofu very quickly as he passed through Gion, Kyoto on the *hofreis*:[5]

> *Inadsma no Kaÿna*
> *Wo karan Koesa*
> *Makura.*

This can be translated as 'Lend me your arms, fast as thunderbolts, as a pillow on my journey'. In his account of Japan, Von Siebold indicates that he knew something of the language while Johannes van Overmeer Fisscher devotes several pages in his *Bijdrage tot de kennis van het Japansche rijk* to a description of the Japanese language, in particular the writing system. Furthermore, he provides seven short dialogues in both Dutch and transcribed Japanese. He does, however, acknowledge his debt to work by Von Siebold and other Europeans (Overmeer Fisscher 1833: 88–115). Nevertheless, he notes, with some humility, that although he had an incomplete knowledge of Japanese words, it was sufficient to make himself understood by those Japanese with whom he came into contact (Overmeer Fisscher 1833: 90–91; Effert 2008: 102–103).

The question of whether a contact variety emerged as a result of contact between Dutch and Japanese is an interesting one. However, there is very little evidence on which to base any firm answers. Often in new contact situations, pidgins emerge. There is no precise definition of a pidgin, but one view is that it is often lexically based on one of the contact languages (the lexifier), with a grammar that is a 'cross language compromise' with 'influence from universals from second-language learning', such as a simplified verb system (Thomason 2017: 64). The Dutch frequently passed negative comments on the Dutch spoken by the Japanese interpreters, although they do not provide concrete examples. Shiba Kōkan's exchange with the surgeon Stützer (a Swede) described in Chapter 3 may give us a hint of how some Japanese and Dutch communicated. Kōkan records Stützer as saying *Minēru komu kāmoru*. Did

---

5   It seems likely that he wrote this in *rōmaji*, although secondary sources are not clear on this (Vos 1989: 360–361). See also http://kulturserver-nds.de/home/haiku-dhg/Netherlands.htm. Accessed 9 April 2020.

Stützer say these actual words, or something closer to *Meneer, kom naar mijn/ de kamer* ('Sir, come to my/the room')? We do not know. Kōkan records his response as *iki kāmoru komu iki kāmoru komu* (roughly: I come to [the] room'). This exhibits features of a pidgin, in that it has Dutch lexical items, but with a Japanese grammatical substratum, i.e., the word order is Subject Object Verb as in Japanese, rather than the Subject Verb Object order of Dutch main clauses (Shiba Kōkan 1927: 100–103; French 1974: 64). However, this is insufficient evidence on which to build the case for a pidgin. One objection is that some Japanese spoke and wrote Dutch quite well, although even the more advanced users sometimes omitted the article (which Japanese lacks) and struggled with word order. Furthermore, we have little idea of the Dutch that native speakers used in communicating with Japanese. They might well have simplified their Dutch, but we do not know, for example, whether they modified their grammar to assist Japanese with understanding. Perhaps what we can say is that the Dutch used by the Japanese varied in quality and that it was influenced by Japanese grammar to varying degrees.

As a result of sharing a socio-semiotic context, there was significant lexical interference by Japanese on the Dutch used in Japan. This is analysed in Chapter 5. Going in the other direction, there was a significant amount of lexical interference in Japanese as a result of contact with Dutch and a more limited amount of syntactic and graphic interference. Examples of these are analysed in Chapter 7.

3   Portuguese

Apart from Japanese, Portuguese was the language with which Dutch had most contact during the early years of Dutch trade with Japan. Indeed, although the Portuguese themselves were expelled from Japan in 1639, their language continued to play an important role in communication between the Japanese and the Dutch for many years thereafter and there is evidence that Portuguese was still used in the early eighteenth century. What follows is an analysis of the relationship between Portuguese and Dutch in Tokugawa Japan, which attempts to posit reasons for the persistence of Portuguese after 1639.

The Portuguese first arrived in Japan in 1543. Thereafter, Portuguese merchants traded with Japan until 1639. Furthermore, there were many Portuguese among the Catholic missionaries, who went to Japan in the wake of the (Spanish-born) Jesuit Francis Xavier (1506–52), who arrived in Kagoshima on Kyushu in 1549. It is reckoned that by 1591 the proselytizing activities of religious orders such as the Jesuits and Franciscans, populated principally by Portuguese, as well as Spanish and Italians, had led to there being some 200,000 Japanese Christian converts (Boxer 1951: 148). One possible reason for the persistence of Portuguese in Japan is its association with religion. This often affords a high status to a language, and in this case, it meant that Portuguese had a certain prestige among some Japanese (Boxer 1950: 58–59; Romaine 2000: 54). This prestige was enhanced by dictionaries and grammars published by the Jesuits, such as the bilingual Japanese and Portuguese lexicon, *Vocabulario da Lingoa de Iapam com a declaração em Portugues* printed in Nagasaki in 1603, and a trilingual Latin, Portuguese and Japanese (in modified Latin script) dictionary (*Dictionarium Latino Lvsitanicvm, ac Iaponicvm*) (Amakusa, 1595), based on the polyglot dictionary of Ambrogio Calepino.[6] The Portuguese Jesuit missionary João Rodrigues (1561/2–1633/4) published *Arte da Lingoa de Iapam*, a sophisticated account on the nature of the Japanese language and its grammar, in Portuguese in Nagasaki in 1604 (Lach 1977: II: 3, 499).[7]

The first Dutch ship, the *Liefde*, had reached Japan four years earlier in 1600. Although the navigation maps used on the ship were printed in Edam in Holland, they were largely based on Portuguese charts and most of the toponyms were Portuguese renderings (Boxer 1950: 2). As noted in Chapter 1, the ship's pilot, the Englishman Will Adams, spoke some Portuguese. This allowed him to speak via a Portuguese interpreter to Tokugawa Ieyasu, when he and other members of the crew met Ieyasu in Osaka (De Lange 2006: 170). Richard Cocks, the head of the English trading post at Hirado from its creation in 1613 until its closure in 1623, observed that many Japanese spoke and wrote Portuguese with great fluency. Boxer (1950: 58) argues that a knowledge of Portuguese or Castilian Spanish was therefore a *sine qua non* for *opperhoofden* at Hirado. Indeed, the Japanese knowledge of Portuguese played a role in the persistence of the language as an LWC between the Japanese and Dutch and other Europeans (Sugimoto 1976–82: v:905).

Portuguese interpreters would continue to play an important role in communication between the Dutch and the Japanese. This was not only on Hirado, where the Dutch had a trading post between 1609 and 1641, but also on the

---

6 *Dictionarium Latino Lusitanicum ac Iaponicum, ex Ambrosii Calepini volumine depromptum* [...] *In Amacusa in Collegio Iaponico Societatis Iesu. Cum facultate superiorum Anno MDXCV* (1595). A typical entry is that for 'dog'. The Latin is given first, with genitive singular inflection, followed by the Portuguese and the Japanese in *rōmaji*, viz. 'Canis, is Lus. Cão. Iap. Inu'. Frellesvig (2010: 304–325) makes the important point that Christian sources printed in Japan provide valuable information about pronunciation of Japanese at the time they were printed.

7 Boxer (1951: 193–197) also provides a good analysis of the learning aids discussed above.

hofreis to Edo, where the Dutch would pay homage to the Tokugawa shoguns. There were exceptions, however, such as Jan Cousynen (De Lange 2006: 215).

Over time, opposition to the Catholic mission increased, fuelled by fears of an invasion by the Portuguese and Spanish. This had led the warlord and unifier of Japan, Toyotomi Hideyoshi (1537–98), to promulgate an edict expelling the missionaries in 1587, and the following year he ordered the crucifixion of 26 missionaries and Japanese converts (Orii 2015: 192).[8] Although official resistance to Christian mission lessened after Hideyoshi's death in 1598, in 1614 the Tokugawa shogunate moved to expel all missionaries.[9] There were further persecutions of missionaries and Japanese converts and finally, in 1639, in the wake of the Shimabara Rebellion that broke out on Kyushu in 1637, all Portuguese including traders were expelled from Japan.

Nevertheless, in the first years after the move to Deshima communication between the Dutch and the Japanese still often took place in Portuguese (De Groot 2005: 24). Indeed, it is likely that some Nagasaki interpreters only spoke Portuguese along with Japanese, although others knew both Portuguese and Dutch (Vande Walle 2001b: 130–131). In 1641, the Deshima *dagregister* records that the interpreter Hideshima Tōzaemon was proficient in Portuguese and fairly competent in Dutch (Vermeulen *et al.* 1986–: XI:25). An interesting insight into the place of Dutch and Portuguese on Deshima is provided in 1646 by Willem Verstegen. He recorded that one evening interpreters arrived with servants, one of whom could speak some Dutch. He notes that they did not therefore need the help of any Portuguese interpreters on this occasion as they could get by with Dutch and Japanese.[10]

In Chapter 2, mention was made of the German physician Caspar Schamberger, who went on the annual *hofreis* to Edo in 1649/50. As a result of his success in curing Inaba Masanori of gout, he was asked to stay in Edo and give instruction in medicine. He did so primarily in Portuguese. The Japanese interpreters working with him gave the students wordlists not only in Portuguese, but also in Dutch.[11] One possible explanation for this advanced

---

8   Toyotomi Hideyoshi's attitude to Christianity did, however, vary over time. In 1591 he reportedly wore a rosary and Portuguese dress. Furthermore, a letter from Padre Pasio in 1594 indicates that some of Hideyoshi's retainers learnt the *Pater Noster* and *Ave Maria* litanies by heart (Boxer 1951: 153, 207). For more on Christianity in early modern Japan, see also Elison (1973).

9   This was through the promulgation of the *Bateren tsuihō no fumi* (伴天連追放之文) (also spelt without 之 *no*) ('Edict on the Expulsion of the Padres') (Morris 2018: 410).

10   'Tegens den avont verschenen de tolcken met de dienaers.... waeronder een dienaer of wasscher welck wat Duyts kon spreken [...] ons waeren oock geen Portugeesche tolcken noodigh, met het Duyts en Japans conden ons wel behelpen' (*Diaries*: X:29).

11   This vocabulary was written in the *katakana* syllabary.

by De Groot (2005: 26) is that at this time the Japanese considered Portuguese and Dutch to be two dialects of the same, general European language. Over time, several manuscripts based on Schamberger's instruction were written and circulated (Michel 1999: 154–155).[12]

Rembert Dodoens's herbal, *Cruydt-boeck*, first printed in 1554, was one of the earliest books written in Dutch to attract the attention of the Japanese. In 1653, Frederick Coyett recorded in the *dagregister* that the *ōmetsuke* Inoue Masashige, prompted by his interest in pharmacognosy (*honzōgaku* 本草学) and indeed his own ailments, had asked whether any of the Dutch could translate Dodoens's book into Portuguese. Coyett informed Masashige in a very polite manner that there was no one at Deshima who could do this (Vande Walle 2001b: 130; Vermeulen *et al.* 1986–: XII:95). Masashige's preference for Portuguese is underlined both by the fact that his interpreters used Portuguese and that he requested a book on anatomy in Portuguese (Michel 1999: 164–165; Vermeulen *et al.* 1986–: XII:41). Furthermore, he owned a copy of the Portuguese-Japanese dictionary, *Vocabulario da Lingoa de Iapam*, mentioned above. In 1652 the shogunal counsellor Andō Ukyō (1600–57) asked for a book on anatomy in Portuguese, as well as one on botany in Portuguese (Vande Walle 2001b: 130). Indeed, as Wim Boot (2013: 196) records, many years after the Portuguese had been expelled from Japan, into the late seventeenth century, the Japanese would often ask the Dutch for the books in Portuguese.

In February 1655 in Edo, Leonard Winnincx (*opperhoofd* 1654–55), was visited by a watchmaker who addressed him in Portuguese. He had in fact been a prisoner, incarcerated because of his Christian faith, but not executed because of his skill as a craftsman (Vermeulen *et al.* 1986–: XII:195). In 1656 Inoue asked the physician Mukai Genshō (1609–77) to collect the medical instructions of the German surgeon on Deshima, Hans Juriaen Hancke.[13] The interpreters translated Hancke's instructions into Japanese and Genshō transcribed what they had written. The *dagregister* does not tell us the language in which Hancke had given his instructions. However, he had to deal with Masashige's Portuguese interpreter, Guinemon or Sinnemon. So, Hancke may

---

12   One example cited by Michel (1999: 154–155) is a manuscript, which he names as *Oranda geka ihō hiden* ('Secret transmission of the medical formulas of Dutch surgery'). This is analysed in more detail below (p. 163). Michel (2005: n. 10) refers to a Dutch glossary compiled by a 'disciple' of Schamberger, Kawaguchi Ryōan in 1660. He cites Kawashima (1992). The interpreter Inomata Denbei (d. 1666) was one of Schamberger's pupils. Along with six other interpreters he wrote a book based on Schamberger's instructions (Van Gulik and Nimura 2005: 38).

13   Hancke came from Breslau (modern-day Wrocław in Poland) http://wolfgangmichel.web .fc2.com/serv/ histmed/dejimasurgeons.html. See also Michel (1995 and 1996).

have switched between Dutch and Portuguese. Currently, we can say nothing more concrete.[14] In Edo in 1663, Hendrick Indijck (*opperhoofd* 1660–61 and 1662–63) reported that he had a conversation in Portuguese with Sinosie, who had been an interpreter to Inoue Masashige (d. 1661), but who now worked for another *ōmetsuke* (Vermeulen *et al.* 1986–: XIII:371).[15]

In 1673, the English tried to start trading again with Japan. Derek Massarella records that English ships under the command of Simon Delboe arrived at Nagasaki furnished with "'Copies of the Articles betweene ye Emperor of Iapaon & and the (English East India) Company in Portuguese and Lattin' and in Japanese, and copies of the king's and Company's letters to the shogun, with duplicates in Portuguese and Latin". The first set of documents dated from 1623, the final year of the English trading post at Hirado. If I read Massarella correctly, the second set would have been in English, Portuguese and Latin. Therefore, even forty-four years after the expulsion of the Portuguese from Japan, the English considered it more appropriate to write to the shogun in these languages rather than in Dutch (Massarella 1990: 356–357). Dutch did, however, play a role in negotiations. Questions were put to Delboe by the Nagasaki *bugyō* in Portuguese, he recorded in his diary. Answers were given in Portuguese or, perhaps surprisingly, Spanish and then translated into Dutch (Vande Walle 2001b: 131). But clearly the dominant European language in these interactions was still Portuguese (Boxer 1950: 59). The English were to fail in their attempts to begin trade with the Japanese, in part because the Dutch told the Japanese that the Queen of England, i.e., Charles II's Queen Consort, Catherine of Braganza, was Portuguese. So, a little ironically, whilst using the Portuguese language was acceptable, trading with a country with connections to Portugal was not.

In the same year, 1673, the Nagasaki *bugyō* finally required interpreters to receive instruction in Dutch from native speakers on Deshima. Even after this, the use of Portuguese in Japan persisted for several decades. Eventually families such as the Nishi family switched from being Portuguese to Dutch interpreters (Sugimoto 1976–82: V:906). However, this process took some time. In the 1670s, one member of the family, Nishi Genpo, the son of Nishi Kichibyōe,

---

14   Genshō's Japanese manuscript was called *kōmōryū geka hiyō*. This means 'Secret summary of red-haired surgery',—'red-haired' because the Japanese saw the Dutch as red-haired (Clements 2015: 155). The dating of this manuscript is, however, slightly problematic. Clements and indeed the NIJL database (ID 2567091) give the date 1654 or early 1655 (Jōō 3), whereas according to Michel (1996), Hancke only arrived in Deshima in late 1655. Further investigation may reveal the reason for this discrepancy.

15   Indijck describes Sinosie as being 'competent' in Portuguese, which may suggest that his own Portuguese was good (p. 373).

knew both Dutch and Portuguese (Iwao 1961: 173–174). He had been a pupil of the Portuguese apostate, Cristóvão Ferreira (c. 1580–1650) (Goodman 2013: 38).

As late as 1695, Imamura Gen'emon, who had been Engelbert Kaempfer's assistant, took an examination in both Dutch and Portuguese (Vande Walle 2001b: 131). So, although by the end of the seventeenth century Dutch was being used by interpreters in communications between the Dutch and Japanese, the use of Portuguese did persist. In the early eighteenth century, Gen'emon visited Edo in the company of an Italian priest, Giovanni Battista Sidotti, who had been secretly dropped off by a Portuguese ship on an island near Kyushu in 1708. In Edo, Gen'emon made the acquaintance of the leading neo-Confucian scholar Arai Hakuseki and provided him with interpreting services and the basis of his description of the Dutch language (De Groot 2005: 35, 38). The hand of both men can be seen in a series of manuscripts containing Dutch, Portuguese and Latin words. However, there is no indication as to which word is from which language (De Groot 2005: 42; 2010: 207).[16]

Some of the servants employed by the Dutch at Deshima were of Javanese origin (Irwin 2011: 36; Vos 2014: 153). Some knew Dutch to a greater or lesser degree, although Low or creolized Portuguese was often used as an LWC among people from the Dutch East Indies. There were also Asian slaves at Deshima (Winkel 1999: 54). Some of these are thought to have spoken Low Portuguese and Low Malay.[17]

Little has been written about the language(s) spoken on board VOC ships. Dutch crew members no doubt used varieties of Dutch. We get the occasional hint from the sources that Portuguese, typically the Low or creolized form of the language, was also spoken on board. Van Rossum (2014a: 143–146) records that one group of Asian crewmembers about which we do know something are South Asian Christian sailors who spoke Portuguese.[18] A case heard in Batavia in 1735 also points to the use of the language on board. A cook's mate from Dresden issued orders in Dutch to a crewmember of Indian origin. The latter swore in bastardized Portuguese, a fight ensued, and he was killed. The cook's mate was found guilty and sentenced to death by decapitation (Van

---

16   De Groot suggests that the reason for the lack of distinction between these languages by Hakuseki is that, in common with other Japanese, he considered them merely to be dialects of one European language. It is thought in fact that his knowledge of Dutch was never more than superficial.

17   Some slaves at Batavia spoke Low Portuguese, whilst others learnt Dutch (Groeneboer 1998: 3, 28).

18   According to Van Rossum, the Portuguese-speaking South Asian Christians are defined in the VOC records as *toepassen matrozen*. *Matrozen* means 'sailors' but precisely what *toepassen* means is not clear.

Rossum 2014a: 139–140). These examples suggest that we need to talk not simply of Portuguese but of Portugueses, with a division of labour between the
Low form of the language, which emerged from trade pidgins, and which was
used on ships and by servants, and something closer to that spoken by educated Portuguese, which was the language of learning and religion (Le Page
and Tabouret-Keller 1985: 26–29).

In Japan, knowledge of Portuguese persisted, although probably only to a
limited extent. In the *dagregister* for September 1734, there is reference to four
interpreters who spoke Portuguese. Two of them, Suenaga Tokuzaemon and
the *naitsūji* Zinnemon, were required to go on the *hofreis* 'to escort the musicians to Edo'. It may be that the musicians were Javanese servants, who spoke
Low Portuguese, and so the interpreters were required to facilitate communication between them and the Dutch (Blussé *et al.* 1992: 434). Another of the
four was a son of Imamura Gen'emon, so he may have picked Portuguese up
from his father (Blussé *et al.* 1992: 556). One final example of its use is seventeen wordlists of Japanese and Dutch (in *katakana*) or Japanese, Dutch and
Portuguese in the so-called *kuchi* group. Few of these are dated so we cannot
be sure when they were compiled. While some are probably from the second
half of the seventeenth century, others are likely to have been written in the
early eighteenth century. One that is dated 1802, the *Orandakuchi iroha wake*,
includes Portuguese words suggesting that some knowledge of Portuguese
did persist, albeit in a limited manner, throughout the eighteenth century (De
Groot 2005: 49).[19]

Finally, a word is in order about why Portuguese persisted to a greater or
lesser extent for over one hundred years after the Portuguese themselves had
been expelled from Japan. One probable reason is that Portuguese had already been established as an LWC for interactions between the Japanese and
Europeans for fifty years before the Dutch reached Japan. Furthermore, during the Hirado period (1609–41), it was used for communication between the
Japanese and Dutch, typically via interpreters. Only from 1673 onwards does
there seem to have been a concerted official effort to shift from Portuguese
to Dutch. So, Portuguese had had well over one hundred years in which to establish itself as a means of communication between Japanese and Europeans,
before official moves to prioritize Dutch. Portuguese had established itself in
other parts of South and East Asia before the Dutch arrived and although the
Dutch managed to eject the Portuguese themselves, their efforts to dislodge
the Portuguese language were for the most part fruitless. Two examples of this
are Ceylon and the Moluccas (Joby 2019b: 123–129).

---

19   *Kuchi* (口) means 'mouth' but here means 'word' or 'language'.

Second, social factors may have been at work. In this regard, Peter Burke writes 'what most concerns a social historian is the use of language to mark differences in social statuses or social situations' (Burke 2014: 34). Portuguese had been brought to Japan by traders, but also by Catholic missionaries. Languages associated with religion often have a high (H) prestige.[20] Dutch, by contrast, had no association with religion. Furthermore, it was used in Japan primarily by merchants. Merchants had a relatively low position in Japanese society and so Dutch was probably seen, in the seventeenth century at least, as having a low (L) prestige. It was, though, the association of Portuguese with religion that would eventually lead to its recession in Japan (Wardhaugh 1987: 9). In 1639, all native speakers were expelled because of their religious affiliation and so thereafter it subsequently lacked a native speaker community in Japan to sustain it.

Third, the persistence of Portuguese was also a product of the slow spread of Dutch. Reasons for this are given in Chapter 2 (p. 52). Fourth, while the Portuguese were pro-active in spreading Western knowledge based on the liberal arts and the languages, primarily Portuguese and Latin, which mediated it, the Dutch were much less pro-active. Indeed, with Dutch it was primarily a case of the Japanese pulling what they needed from Western learning and translating it with the help of the Dutch, rather than any sustained attempt by the Dutch to promote the learning in the books that they imported and the language that mediated it (Vande Walle 2001b: 132–133; Boot 2013: 201). Finally, there may be a more practical reason for the persistence of Portuguese. Interpreters trained in Portuguese worked for the Dutch after the Portuguese had been expelled. Older interpreters may have been loath to, or unable to, switch to Dutch. It may also be that Portuguese persisted as part of a hybrid form of communication, for we have seen several instances of Dutch and Portuguese being used side-by-side.

Contact between Portuguese and varieties of Japanese resulted in many Portuguese loanwords *gairaigo* (lit. 'foreign origin words') entering Japanese.[21] One example is the Japanese word for bread, *pan* (パン), which comes from the Portuguese *pão*, originally introduced as the sacramental bread. Irwin (2011: 29–35) provides an extensive list of such loanwords. In his survey of *gairaigo* in the Nagasaki dialect in the first half of the twentieth century, Koga Jūjirō (2000) records some 3245 Portuguese loanwords, which is no small number,

---

20 Wardhaugh (1987: 9) gives the example of Islam in helping to spread Arabic. See also Ferguson (1982).

21 *Gairaigo* are loanwords which are more or less transliterated or transvocalized. In the literature on this subject they are often described as 'pure' loanwords.

and all the more impressive given that the survey was carried out some 300 years after the Portuguese had been expelled (Irwin 2011: 31).

As for Dutch, one example of the influence of Portuguese is in spelling. Portuguese spellings of place names such as Nagasaki (Nangasacqui), reflecting the prenasalization of 'g', were adopted by authors of Dutch texts (Michel 2012: 112). Several Portuguese words appear regularly in Dutch texts in Japan and can be understood either as loanwords in the Dutch topolect used in Kyushu, or *nesolect* (< Gk. νῆσος 'island') to coin a new term, or as instances of code switching. One example is *comprador* (Portuguese 'buyer'), which appears regularly in Dutch texts. Further examples are given in the next chapter.

The Portuguese language's Iberian neighbour, Spanish, is occasionally mentioned in the sources, although there were always fewer Spanish native speakers and the use of Spanish was more restricted. After the expulsion of Portuguese and other European Catholics in 1639, there is the occasional reference to Spanish in the *dagregister*. In September 1643, Jan van Elseracq (*opperhoofd* 1641–42; 1643–44) records that one of his colleagues at Deshima, Willem Bijlvelt, was fluent in Spanish (Vermeulen *et al.* 1986–: XI:117). In May 1645, Pieter Overtwater (*opperhoofd* 1642–43, 1644–45) records that he had been informed by the interpreter, Nishi Kichibyōe, that the *bugyō* had received a letter written in Spanish. Kichibyōe had been summoned to translate it. It had been written by one of two 'Castillians' imprisoned in Ōmura (Vermeulen *et al.* 1986–: XI:206).

4   Latin

To see Latin as a competitor to Dutch in Japan is perhaps to overstate the case, although in some instances a clear choice was made to use Latin over against Dutch. Nevertheless, it may be more appropriate to see Latin as closer to a companion to Dutch, sitting alongside it, or perhaps slightly above it in a shared socio-semiotic context, as it did in early modern Europe in the intermediate phase of the shift from the dominance of Latin as a written language towards the vernacular. Before the arrival of the Dutch in Japan in 1600, Latin was used extensively by Catholic missionaries. Furthermore, it was taught to Japanese who trained for the priesthood (Boxer 1951: 86–89).[22] In the late sixteenth and early seventeenth centuries, Mass was celebrated in Latin in Japan, with prayers (*oratio*) being chanted in Latin. The Jesuit missionaries imported Latin books into Japan and between 1591 and 1614 they operated a printing press which

---

22   For the teaching of Latin in Japan by Catholic missionaries, see also Taida (2017: 566–586).

produced devotional and linguistic works in Latin and Japanese (Boxer 1951: 191; Joby 2019a). One example of this is the trilingual Latin, Portuguese and Japanese dictionary based on Ambrogio Calepino's lexicon, mentioned above. There were still copies of this lexicon in mid-seventeenth century Japan. The *ōmetsuke* Inoue Masashige owned a copy which he showed to the Swede Olof Eriksson Willman at Edo in 1652 (Willman 2013: 44).

As these details suggest, some knowledge of Latin spread amongst the upper echelons of Japanese society, and furthermore this knowledge persisted after 1639. One striking example of this is recorded in the *dagregister* at Batavia in 1641. Two Japanese, Masashige and the uncle of shogun Iemitsu, had ordered the guide for sea-pilots, "'The Light of Navigation' in Latin" (*'t licht der Zeevaert int latyn*) from the Dutch. *Het Licht der Zeevaert* had been published in Amsterdam in 1608 by Willem Jansz. Blaeu (Boxer 1950: 5).[23] Furthermore, another request was made to Batavia in 1641 for '1 Planeet bouck in Latijn Castiliaens of t Portugees', i.e., a book on the planets in Latin, Castilian Spanish or Portuguese (not Dutch) for the 'Commissaris Tsickingdonne'. Tsickingdonne is probably a corruption of *Chikugo-no-kami*, one of the titles of Inoue Masashige, with the honorific suffix *dono*.[24]

In the second half of the seventeenth century, Japanese physicians translated and transcribed Western medical sources into Japanese. One manuscript, *Oranda geka ihō hiden* ('Secret transmission of the medical formulas of Dutch surgery'), drew on several sources including the 1636 'Pharmacopoea Amstelredamensis'. This includes many transcriptions from Latin, although they indicate that the transcribers did not necessarily understand the source text (Michel 1999: 155–156; 2015: 97).[25] Several VOC employees at Deshima used Latin, sometimes instead of Dutch, sometimes alongside it. The German physician Engelbert Kaempfer wrote letters in Latin to, among others, Willem van Outhoorn (1635–1720), the Governor-General of the Dutch East Indies in Batavia.[26] Van Outhoorn had studied at Leiden University, where Latin was

---

23 Most of *Het Licht der Zeevaert* is in Dutch, with some Portuguese and a little Latin, e.g., for the names of stars. I have not yet identified a Latin translation of this. Indeed, one might ask how much use a Latin edition would be to sea-pilots.

24 MS The Hague, Nationaal Archief, VOC (1.04.02) 1134, fol. 471v. The 'n' before the 'g' is probably another example of prenasalization.

25 This manuscript consisted of words in Dutch, Portuguese as well as Latin. The manuscript is not listed in the NIJL database. There is, however, a manuscript entitled *Oranda geka ihō*. Further investigation may reveal whether this is the same manuscript.

26 Kaempfer informed Van Outhoorn that he was writing from 'Nangasacci Japoniae', i.e., Nagasaki in Japan. On the journey between Batavia and Deshima, Kaempfer kept a journal primarily in German, but also in Latin. The entries for the day of his arrival in Japan and the following day (25 and 26 September 1690) are in German and Latin respectively.

the language of instruction. Kaempfer also wrote in Latin to the mayor of Amsterdam, Nicolaes Witsen (1641–1717), who, like Van Outhoorn, had studied at Leiden (Meier-Lemgo 1965: 27 (Van Outhoorn), 30 (Witsen)). In the *dag-registers* at Hirado and Deshima, we find Latin words and phrases inserted into the Dutch text. Examples of these are provided in the next chapter.

Another VOC employee at Deshima who knew Latin was Adriaan Douw from Dordrecht.[27] After the arrest of the Italian priest Sidotti in 1708, it was recognized that the best way to communicate would be for Douw to speak Latin with him (De Groot 2005: 41, 44). Although Sidotti was subsequently moved to Edo, the need to use Latin in this case rekindled an interest in it amongst Japanese in Nagasaki. On 18 November 1709, Hermanus Menssingh (*opperhoofd* intermittently 1705–10), recorded in the *dagregister* that two junior interpreters (*kotsūji*) were coming to Deshima every day to learn Latin, adding that this was even though their Dutch was very poor. There is another entry for the following day, 19 November, concerning Japanese officials who acted as intermediaries between the Governor of Nagasaki and the Dutch. They went to Deshima with some 'students of Latin' and asked Menssingh 'to teach the students Latin' (Blussé *et al.* 1992: 116).[28] It is not clear if these were the junior interpreters from the previous day, or different students. Menssingh records that he agreed to do so, but without much enthusiasm.

In Chapter 3, we met the *rangakusha* Kitajima Kenshin. Latin features prominently in his work from the middle of the eighteenth century, which indicates that he was one of the first Japanese scholars to take an interest in Western writing systems (De Groot 2005: 41; 2010: 206). After this, there is the occasional mention of Latin in the sources. In 1779 Maeno Ryōtaku translated Latin poems in Ioannes Stradanus's *Venationes Ferarum, Auium, Piscium* ('Hunting of Wild Animals, Birds and Fish') into Japanese.[29] However, most of the engagement with Latin was related to scientific research. In 1784 the Swedish physician at Deshima, Carl Peter Thunberg, made excursions to the area around Nagasaki to do botanical research. He would tell Japanese physicians who accompanied him the names of plants they collected not only in

---

MS London British Library, Sloane 2921, fol. 37r. See also Terwiel (1993) for details of Kaempfer's voyage from Batavia to Japan.

27   Douw was a bookkeeper and assistant at Deshima. http://wolfgangmichel.web.fc2.com/ serv/histmed/dejimasurgeons.html. Accessed 9 April 2020.

28   The Japanese officials were called *nenban tsūji*. In Dutch this term is rendered as *rapporteurtolken*. Sugimoto (1976–82: V:906) gives them the English name, 'annual duty interpreter'. These were the interpreters who led the Guild of Interpreters for that year.

29   The title of Ryōtaku's translation is *Seiyō gasan yakubunkō* (Taida 2017: 580). The NIJL has an earlier date of 1773, ID 1332678.

Dutch but also Latin. The use of Latin may not simply have been a question of language. By this time, Linnaeus had published his *Systema Naturae* in which he set out his binomial genus-species classification of the natural world. If Thunberg was giving the Linnaean *binomina* to the Japanese, this would mark a shift for them away from the plant-classification systems based primarily on properties and use presented in works such as Dodoens's *Cruydt-boeck*. In any case, it is reasonable to assume that this information was of some use to the Japanese. In 1826, members of the *Shōhyaku-sha* (嘗百社), a network of local scholars in Owari Domain (around Nagoya), which included physicians, farmers and bureaucrats, met Philipp von Siebold at the Atsuta Shrine in Owari. The Japanese had brought samples of plants, fruit, minerals and dried fish to the meeting. Von Siebold examined the objects and affixed Dutch and Latin names to them (Fukuoka 2012: 16). He would often attach labels in Latin to plants that he collected and dried in Japan.[30]

Latin was used by other Japanese within the context of *rangaku*. Those who translated Dutch books into Japanese would sometimes be confronted with Latin terms. In this sense Dutch could be understood as the carrier of Latin to Japan, a *linguifer* or *ferolect* if you will. In the 1780s, the interpreter Matsumura Genkō (dates not known) translated an abridged Dutch version of Pliny's *Naturalis Historia* into Japanese for Matsūra Seizan, *daimyō* of Hirado. The autograph manuscript survives, and it shows that Genkō transcribed Latin plant names into *katakana*. For example, he transcribed *Lelium* ('lily') as レ―リョム (*rēryomu*). He gave the *kanji* for this (百合), although the fact that the Dutch name (*lelie*) was provided may have helped him to identify which plant was being described (Matsuda 2001: 196–197). Just as elsewhere I have talked of Dutch clothed in *katakana*, here we have Latin clothed in *katakana*. The abridged Dutch version of Pliny's *Naturalis Historia*, published in Amsterdam in 1662 as *C. Plini Secundi des wijdt-vermaerden natuerkondigers Vijf boecken* ('Five Books of the celebrated natural historian Caius Plinius Secundus'), is still in the Matsūra collection today. It includes references to sources from antiquity, such as 'Augustinus contra Pelagium lib 4' ('Augustine against Pelagius book 4'). This, of course, refers to Christian literature. The fact that this book is a Christianized version of Pliny's work is made clear from the outset, with a picture of Adam and Eve, the serpent and other animals in Eden in the front

---

30   In the Siebold collection in Leiden, a piece of paper on display has the words *Dioscorea Japonica, in monte Higosan legi Julio 21 1825*, i.e., 'I collected *Dioscorea Japonica* (Mountain yam) on Mt. Higo on 21 July 1825'. The paper has the Japanese name *yamaimo* ('mountain tuber') in *katakana*. Von Siebold wrote the Latin in sepia ink. The *katakana* may be a later addition.

matter. This provides further evidence that although Christianity was officially proscribed, powerful Japanese such as the Matsūra family were able to acquire books with Christian content and iconography.

On occasion, we see Latin clothed in *ateji* with *furigana*. There are several examples of this in Ōtsuki Gentaku's *Rokumotsu shinshi* ('New applications for a miscellany of six things', c. 1786). Gentaku refers to agaric (Latin: *agaricus*) in this manner and to Rembert Dodoens (Latin: Dodonaeus), whose *Cruydt-boeck* was one of Gentaku's sources. European coins often included Latin inscriptions. In *Seiyō senpu* ('Notes on Western coinage', 1787), Kutsuki Masatsuna includes images of coins, more than half of which have inscriptions in Latin or a mixture of another European language, such as Dutch, and Latin. For example, on page 25 the face of one coin dated 1775 reads *Res Parvae Crescunt Concordia* ('Small Things Grow from Concord'). In a letter that he wrote in 1785 to his friend, Isaac Titsingh, who was by then stationed in Chinsura, Bengal, Masatsuna asked his friend to send him a Latin dictionary (*Lateinsche woordenboek*). It may be that he wanted to use it to read the Latin inscriptions on these coins (Lequin 1992: 2).

European maps from this period were often primarily or completely in Latin. Several of these reached Japan. In the early eighteenth century, a copper-engraved world map was imported into Japan. This had a Latin heading, *Nova totius terrarum orbis tabula emendata A.N. Visscher* ('New Map of the Lands of the Entire World, Emended (by) A.N. Visscher'). It was a revision from around 1678 of a world-map made in 1648 by the Amsterdam cartographer Joan Blaeu (Boxer 1950: 12; Unno 1994: 435 n. 325). In the late eighteenth century, Katsuragawa Hoshū produced a Japanese translation of the explanation attached to Blaeu's map, *Nova totius terrarum orbis tabula*. Hoshū recorded that the Japanese title that he gave his work *Shinsei chikyū bankoku zusetsu* was a translation of the title of Blaeu's map (Unno 1994: 434–445). The Latin means 'New map of the countries of the whole world', while Hoshū's rendering means '(Illustrated) Explanation of the new map of all the countries in the world', so the translation is a little free, but acceptable.

At this time, too, Japanese maps based on ones imported from Europe were being printed.[31] The Japanese mapmakers often included Latin toponyms in Japanese script in their maps and geographical descriptions. The toponyms in Motoki Yoshinaga's *Oranda chizu ryakusetsu* ('Brief Explanation of Dutch

---

31   The first printed Japanese map of the world to be influenced by *rangaku* was *Yochi zenzu* ('Map of the earth', 1792), a copperplate engraving made by Shiba Kōkan (Unno 1994: 435).

Maps') were both in Latin and Dutch (Krieger 1940: 59).[32] One map to mention is *Oranda shin'yaku chikyū zenzu* (1796/7). Dutch toponyms in this map were analysed in Chapter 3. Here, the use of Latin is analysed. In the text accompanying the map we read (bottom right) 大日本・蘭譯「ヤハン」或「ヤボ—ニヤ」which transliterates as *Dainippon・Ranyaku*「*Yahan*」*aruiwa*「*Yabōniya*」. The first two words translate as 'Great Japan・Dutch translation'. The words in brackets seem to be transliterations of the Dutch word for 'Japan' (*Yahan/Yapan*) (followed by the word for 'or', *aruiwa*) and the Latin word for the country (*Yabōniya*, the New Latin term is often written as *Iaponia*). Another transliteration into *katakana* which seems to be derived from Latin is the term for 'Spain' イスパニア (*Isupania*). This is probably from the Latin *Hispania* rather than the Dutch *Spanje*. Other renderings of toponyms such as *Shīna* (シーナ) for the Great Qing (大清) may be influenced by Dutch or Latin. Many names are Dutch. However, two other terms in the surrounding text (in the section on Europe top middle), are clearly derived from Latin. One is rendered in *katakana* as ゼルマニヤインペリヨル. This transliterates as 'Zerumaniya Inperiyoru', i.e., "Germania Inferior", used by Blaeu to refer to the Seventeen Provinces of the Netherlands (it was the name of the Roman province covering the Low Countries south of the Rhine). The author indicates that he recognizes that this is Latin, by adding 羅甸語 ⟨*ratengo*⟩. The first two *kanji* are used phonetically (*ateji, raten*), while the third is a semantogram meaning 'language' (*on*-reading *go*), so literally 'Latin language'. The author also adds 羅甸語 under two *katakana* renderings of Latin versions of 'Moscow'.[33]

One other map to mention, which has Latin toponyms is the *Atlas contractus* compiled by Petrus Schenck, published in Amsterdam in 1700. The Matsūra family at Hirado possessed a copy of this.[34] Later in this chapter English learners compiled by Japanese in the early nineteenth century are analysed. They often used the word *Angeria* (< Latin *Anglia*) to refer to England rather than *Igirisu*, from Portuguese, which is the standard word for England or Britain in cMJ. This and the other examples presented here illustrate that it was not uncommon for Latin versions of European toponyms to be used during the Tokugawa period. Occasionally, those who translated Dutch texts into Japanese translated Latin words and phrases.

---

32   This was later revised by Matsumura Mototsuna, who, like Yoshinaga, was a Nagasaki interpreter.

33   These are *Mosucopii* and *Myusucopii* (sic), both probably derived from *Moscovia* (used in the Blaeu map of Russia) or a vernacular derivative thereof.

34   Full title: *Atlas contractus sive Mapparum Geographicarum Sansoniarum auctarum et correctarum Nova Congeries* (Matsuda 1998: 431).

Staying with the Matsūra family, another book in their collection was Michel de Marolles' *Tableaux du Temple des Muses tirez du Cabinet de feu Mr. Favereau*, written in French, but interspersed with Latin.[35] This is analysed in more detail below in the section on French. The front matter included a quotation in Latin from the Roman poet, Martial. A Dutchman at Deshima and a Japanese translator worked together to produce a Japanese translation of the Martial quote and the French title (Matsuda 1998: 503–536).[36] In the Matsūra collection there is a full set of the Dutch version of the eight-volume folio edition on flora by Johann Wilhelm Weinmann (*Duidelyke Vertoning* ('Clear Presentation') Amsterdam 1736–48). This includes beautiful copperplate illustrations underneath which are the names of plants in Latin and Dutch.[37]

In the mid-1790s Shizuki Tadao, sometimes referred to as the 'patriarch of Dutch learning', translated into Japanese an appendix to the Dutch translation of Engelbert Kaempfer's 'History of Japan' that belonged to Matsūra Seizan.[38] Tadao had to translate a quotation from Virgil's *Georgics* (I. 54; 57) that the Dutch translator had left in the original Latin.[39] He was able to identify the language as Latin and managed to understand it with the help of a Latin-Dutch dictionary in Seizan's library at Hirado.[40] However, he did not translate the quotation from Virgil into Japanese, but rather into modified literary Sinitic (*kanbun*) (Mervart 2015: 23). This may suggest that Tadao was aware of the prestige that attached to Latin and attempted to reflect this in his translation by using *kanbun*.

---

35   Michel de Marolles, *Tableaux du Temple des Muses tirez du Cabinet de feu Mr. Favereau....* Paris, Nicolas L'Anglois, 1655.

36   Matsuda records that the translation is on a piece of paper preserved at Kyoto University Library. This quotation is from Martial's *Epigrams* (XIV.xciii.1), *Non nostri Gloria Coeli* ('This glory is not from our skies').

37   *Duidelyke Vertoning Eeniger Duizend in alle Vier Waerelds Deelen wassende Bomen, Stammen, Kruiden, Bloemen, Vrugten en Uitwassen* ('Clear Presentation of several thousand trees, trunks, herbs, flowers, fruits and outgrowths'). Numbers 5–1 to 5–8 in the Matsūra collection 洋書目録 ('Western books catalogue').

38   The publishing history of Kaempfer's work is somewhat complex. For our purposes it is necessary to know that Tadao was working with a Dutch version, *De Beschryving van Japan* (Amsterdam: 1733), based on an English version 'The History of Japan' (1727), which was the first published edition, based on Kaempfer's German manuscript and supplemented by appendices from Kaempfer's original Latin (Mervart 2015: 20–21).

39   The quotation from Virgil in the Dutch translation of Kaempfer's work runs, *Hic Segetes, illic veniunt felicius Uvae: India mittit ebur, molles sua thura Sabæi* ('Here corn, there grapes shoot forth more luxuriantly; India sends forth ivory, the soft Sabaeans their frankincense').

40   This was Benjamin Jacques and Samuel Hannot, *Dictionarium Latino-Belgicum* (Rotterdam: Pieter van der Slaart, 1699) (Mervart 2015: 22–23).

Yoshio Kōgyū produced a small book, which included names of plants used for medicinal purposes taken from Dodoens's *Cruydt-boeck* in Latin and Dutch (*Dodoneusu honzō abese ruiju* 'Dodonaeus's ABC of Herb Categorization').[41] On one typical page he writes in Latin and Dutch, *Acorus oft lisch met welriekiende bladeren* ('Acorus or iris with fragrant leaves'). He also provides Japanese renderings of the plant name in *kanji* and *katakana*. In the nineteenth century, Katsuragawa Hoshū II compiled a one-sheet list of medicinal substances.[42] The names are in Latin and English.

In 1804, Sō Senshun (1758–1834) and Shirao Kunihashira (1762–1821) published *Seikei zusetsu* ('Illustrated Encyclopaedia of Agricultural Products'). This collection comprising some 30 volumes is an impressive, richly-illustrated encyclopaedia of native Japanese plants. The woodblock illustrations, which could be coloured at extra cost, are supplemented by Japanese names in *kanji* and *furigana*. Some illustrations carry the binomial Latin names of plants developed within the Linnaean genus-species taxonomy system. One suggestion is that the source of these Latin names was Linnaeus's 'apostle', Thunberg himself, or his *Flora Japonica* (1784) (Chatterjee and Van Andel 2019: 382–383). One example of this is the illustration for the mountain yam. On the top right are Japanese names in *katakana* and *kanji*. The *katakana* reads *yamaimo*, while the *kanji* 薯蕷 can be read as *shoyo* or *joyo* (both *on*-readings). On the bottom right is the Latin name 'Dioscorea Japonica Th[unb.]' (Vol. XXII:p. 21), the 'Th[unb.]' indicating that it was Thunberg who gave this species its Latin binomial.[43] Dutch names are given in the text. Such books, replete with Latin and Dutch terminology, were *loci* for intellectual and linguistic exchange in Tokugawa Japan.

Itō Keisuke from Nagoya was a physician and biologist who studied under and worked with Von Siebold. In Nagoya in 1828 (Bunsei XI), Keisuke published *Taisei honzō meiso* ('Western Plant Taxonomy' (3 vols.)). This was based on Thunberg's *Flora Iaponica*, published in Latin (Taida 2017: 579–580). On woodblock prints, Keisuke gives the binomial Latin Linnaean names for plants, Japanese names in *katakana* and Chinese names in Sinitic characters (occasionally annotated with *katakana* to facilitate reading). A circle was added to indicate that Von Siebold had made the correlation between the Linnaean and Japanese names. While the names are listed in Roman alphabetical order, the

---

41   NDL 特 7-193. See http://www.ndl.go.jp/nichiran/e/data/R/044/044-005r.html. Accessed 9 April 2020.
42   The title *ratengo yakuhinmei* ('Names of Medicines in Latin') seems to be a later addition.
43   This is still the accepted name of this species: http://www.theplantlist.org/tpl1.1/record/ kew-240312. Accessed 5 May 2020.

layout of the pages allows for the Japanese to read from right to left—Chinese name, Japanese name, Latin name (Fukuoka 2012: 68–69). Dutch is largely absent. The title page is, though, in Dutch and there is the occasional note in Dutch to indicate the use of certain plants.[44] On the reverse of the title page, there is a reproduction of a portrait of Thunberg, with an inflected Latin version of his name (*Carolo Petro Thunberg*). Between the name and the portrait are the words *Capensis Thunbergia. Javanica*, which are related to two plant species named after Thunberg, *Thunbergia capensis* and *Thunbergia javanica*, both members of the *Acanthaceae* family.[45] Here again, as with some of the examples presented in Chapter 3, we can talk in terms of *heteroglossia*, as Japanese authors negotiated the space between their European sources and their Japanese readers. The publication of *Taisei honzō meiso* led to the widespread adoption in Japan of the Linnaean binomial classification, which brought order to plant taxonomy (Brown 1976: 47). Keisuke continued to use these Latin terms in works such as *Nihon sanbutsu-shi* ('History of the Products of Japan') (1873–77). For example, in the entry for deadly nightshade we see the Latin binomial *Atoropa Belladonna* (deadly nightshade) in Roman uppercase script. Underneath this in *katakana* is the name *hashiridokoro* and the *kanji* 莨菪.[46] The combination of these three forms of script together with a picture of the plant bespeaks *heteroglossia* once more. A fundamental difference, however, from the example in *Ran'en tekiho* analysed in Chapter 3 was that the *heteroglossia* evinced by Keisuke's works included the voice of Carl Linnaeus. Moreover, returning to Foucault, Keisuke's work provides further evidence of the emergence of a Western-influenced natural history in Japan, but one now based on Linnaean binomials.

Chapter 3 provided details of Dutch names given to Japanese. Several Japanese were given Latin names. In the early nineteenth century, Katsuragawa Hoan was given a Latin name, Wilhelmus Botanicus, reflecting his interest in plants (Winkel 2004: 81; Overmeer Fisscher 1833: 306; Hoffmann and Serrurier 1882: 112–113). In a wonderful example of the cultural and intellectual exchange that took place between Europeans and Japanese, Hoan gave Von Siebold a copy of *Seikei zusetsu* with colour illustrations, which is now in Leiden University Library. In the inside cover of volume 30, he wrote in beautiful cursive Roman script 'Aan de Heer Siebold geschenk door zijn vriend Kaneel

---

44   The title page reads *Naamlyst van Gewassen door den Beroemden Natuuronderzoeker C.P. Thunberg, M.D. op Japan Gevonden. Herzien en met Japansche en Chineesche Namen Verrykt door Itoo Keiske. Te Nagoya, by Boenzy XI* (1828).

45   The *Thunbergia* genus was named in honour of Thunberg by his fellow Swede, Anders Jahan Retzius (1742–1821).

46   According to one dictionary this *katakana* name refers to another plant, the *Scopolia japonica*, sometimes called Japanese belladonna. *At(o)ropa Belladonna* and *Scopolia japonica* belong to the same family, *Solonaceae*, but have different genus and species.

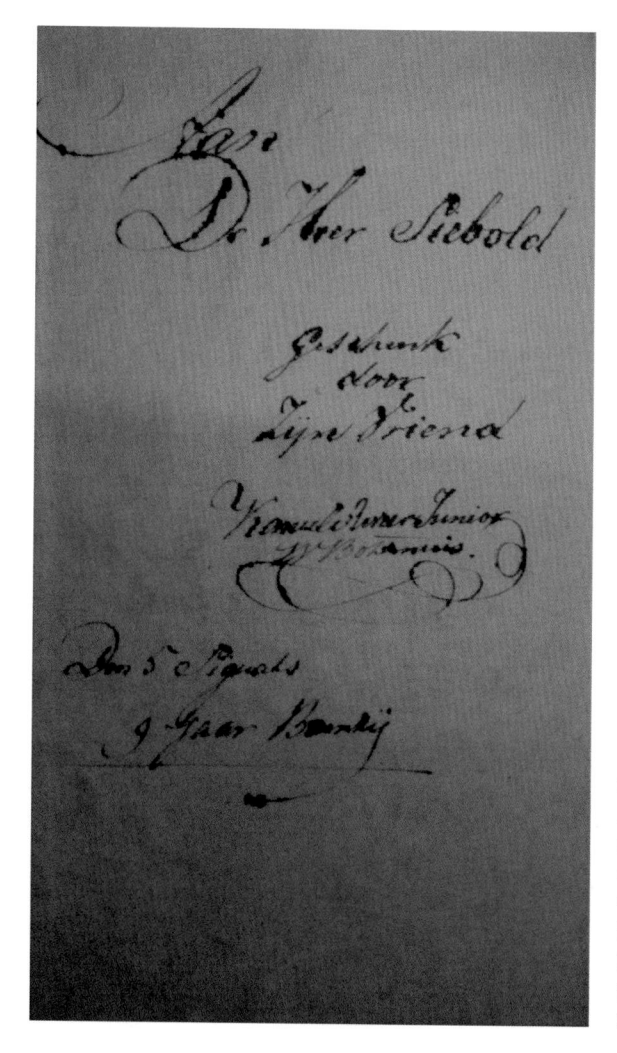

FIGURE 12
A page from *Seikei zusetsu*
('Illustrated Encyclopaedia
of Agricultural Products',
vol. XXX, inside cover)
inscribed by Katsuragawa
Hoan to Philipp von Siebold
LEIDEN UNIVERSITY
LIBRARY, SER. 1042

Rivier Junior (i.e., Katsuragawa) W. Botanicus' ('To Mr. Siebold, present from his friend Cinnamon River Junior, W. Botanicus') and dated it '9 Jaar Boenzij' (i.e., 1826) (see fig. 12).

Von Siebold's confidante Takahashi Kageyasu was given the Latin name Johannes Globius, reflecting his interest in maps. Unfortunately, however, this interest was perilous, for Kageyasu handed Von Siebold maps which the German tried to take out of Japan in 1828, which was forbidden. His failure to do so led to Kageyasu's arrest and execution (Goodman 2013: 108, 186–187).[47] Von Siebold

---

47   On the flyleaf of a copy of a Dutch translation of *Maritime geography and statistics* (1815) by James Kingston Tuckey (*Aardrijkskunde voor zeevaart en koophandel*, Rotterdam, 1819), which Von Siebold gave to Kageyasu, is written 'To Globius, the honourable doctor of

himself was placed under house arrest and then expelled from the country. In a list of European pennames given to Japanese compiled by the *opperhoofd*, Willem de Sturler, there are several other Latin names. Unfortunately, the transcriptions of the Japanese do not always make it clear who is being referred to (Hoffmann and Serrurier 1882: 112–113). 'Narse Ita Ia to', a *daimyō* in Owari domain, was called Johannes Wilhelmus, 'Watanabe Toeij' Johannes Stephanus medicus and 'Ooije Goensij' Jacobus Paracelsus. 'Hajasi Joohakf', the physician to Johannes Wilhelmus was given the name Herman Practicus—was he good at medical practice, one wonders. Finally, the American Ranald MacDonald, who entered *sakoku* Japan by pretending to be a castaway, observed in 1848/9 that as well as learning English, the Nagasaki interpreter Moriyama Einosuke was learning Latin and indeed French (MacDonald 1923: 209–210).

In the late eighteenth and nineteenth centuries, Japanese placed orders with the Dutch for Latin learning and reference material. Lists for 1794–96 include one Latin-Dutch dictionary per year (Nagazumi 1998: 6). Most annual lists that we have for 1810 onwards include at least one bi- or monolingual Latin dictionary. Occasionally, we are told the author; in 1822 a copy of Samuel Hannot's Latin-Dutch dictionary is listed (Nagazumi 1998: 19). Lists of books imported via Deshima in 1860 include four Latin-Dutch dictionaries (Itazawa 1959: 666).

The Ueno collection, too, includes several books involving Latin. Among these are three Latin-Dutch lexicons.[48] One book consists of Dutch and Neo-Latin poems.[49] The Japanese practice of placing a seal on books, similar to the *ex libris* used by European book owners, allows us to trace their ownership.[50] This book has the seal of the *Bansho shirabesho*, but also that of the Takahashi clan. It is likely to have belonged to Takahashi Kageyasu, mentioned above. Whether this indicates that Kageyasu knew Latin, or that it is simply a sign of his friendship with Von Siebold, or another European at Deshima who knew Latin, would require further investigation.

Japanese adopted several Latin loanwords during 'The Christian Century', most of them relating to religion; for example, *oratio* 'prayer' (オラショ, pron.

---

medicine, as a remembrance from Dr. Ph. Fr. Von Siebold, May 7, 1826' in Von Siebold's handwriting in Dutch.

48   L.C.E. Schuessler, *Latijnsch-Nederduitsche Lijst van Naam- en Werkwoorden* ... (Zutphen: A.E.C. van Someren, 1848) (nos. 2275 and 2469); and Karl Ernst Georges, *Handwoordenboek der Latynsche taal, naar de 10de uitgave van het Lateinische-Deutsches Handwoerterbuch* [...], Groningen 1854 (no. 3158).

49   Joanna Koerten, *Het stamboek op de papiere snykunst ... Bestaande in Latynsche en Nederduitsche Gedichten der Voornaamste Dichters*, Amsterdam, 1735 (no. 115). Another book in the Ueno collection, translated from Latin into Dutch, retains a little Latin, August Arnold Sebastian, *Algemeene natuurkunde van den mensch* [...] *uit het Latijn vertaald door J.B. Dompeling* (Groningen: J. Oomkens, 1840) (no. 3349).

50   For more on these seals or *zōshoin* (蔵書印), see Kornicki (2001: 398).

orasho) and *anima* 'soul' (アニマ), are both first attested in a Japanese text in 1591 (Irwin 2011: 32). One other interesting possibility is that the word *tempura* (てんぷら), an intrinsic part of Japanese cuisine, may have a Latin origin.[51] Eylenbosch (1940: 580–581) goes into some detail about how this may have happened, suggesting that it results from the Spanish and Portuguese missionaries eating deep-fried fish on Ember or *Tempora* days, from the Latin *tempus*, *-oris* ('Time').[52] Latin loanwords have survived in the Nagasaki dialect. Koga Jūjirō (2000: 1047–68) has identified 227 such loanwords in the first half of the twentieth century, many of them again relating to religion (Irwin 2011: 31). As for the influence of Latin on Dutch in Japan, this is most evident in the code switching analysed in the next chapter. From the foregoing, several Dutch sources read and translated by Japanese included Latin. Typically, Japanese authors were aware of this and reflected this in their texts, as in the case of Shizuki Tadao using *kanbun* and the author of *Oranda shin'yaku chikyū zenzu*, adding *ratengo* to Latin toponyms.

Finally, a brief word is in order about Ancient Greek. There is very little evidence for the use of Greek in Japan. However, several works originally written in Greek were imported, perhaps most famously, Aesop's Fables, two Japanese versions of which were published. Furthermore, the craze for Hippocrates amongst Japanese physicians in the eighteenth century is another point of contact between Tokugawa Japan and Ancient Greece. However, most if not all of this contact came through Latinized versions of names such as Hippocrates and Aesop, rather than in the original Greek (Joby 2019a).

5 Malay

Along with Portuguese, Malay was an LWC in East Asia from the sixteenth century onwards. Varieties of the language were spoken on the Malay Peninsula and across the Indonesian archipelago, but also elsewhere.[53] Collins (1998: 33) writes that 'at the threshold of the 17th century, Malay dominated the cultural scene of much of Southeast Asia'. Furthermore, it was pluricentric and diffuse. The Dutch language made little headway in the Indonesian archipelago. One possible reason for this is that Malay was too well-established as an LWC for Dutch to dislodge it (Joby 2019b: 123–127). Another view is that the Dutch saw

---

51 *Tempura* is also written 天ぷら or 天麩羅.
52 A Spanish or Portuguese etymology cannot be ruled out (Irwin 2011: 33, 35).
53 See for example, Errington (2008: esp. ch. 6) for a short history of Malay as an LWC across the Indonesian archipelago.

the potential of Malay for communication across East Asia and thus used it for their own purposes (Collins 1998: 41). Timon Screech writes that Dutch seamen spoke it as did many of the populace in Nagasaki (Screech 1996: 14–15). As noted above, some of the Asian slaves at Deshima probably spoke Low Malay. The language is mentioned on several occasions in the records at Deshima. The *Orandayuki* (literally 'the women who go to the Dutch') mixed Malay and Dutch words in their conversation along, one presumes, with Japanese (Harada 1964: 102; Vos 1971: 631; Goodman 2013: 22–23). Cornelis Assendelft de Coningh (1856: 46) observed in 1851 that some Dutch learnt Malay in order to communicate with their 'housemaids' who were often also lovers or concubines, as it was easier to learn Malay than Japanese.

An entry in the *dagregister* for March 1792 seems to indicate that interpreters were expected to translate Malay. Here, Petrus Chassé recorded that the shogun had sent for one of the black slaves at Deshima. Black slaves typically spoke Malay so it was expected that the interpreters would be asked to translate Malay, which made them wary. Eventually, Chassé sent one of his slaves who was conversant in Dutch. He also observes that it would not be necessary to send a Dutchman with the black slave as his Dutch was not much worse than that of the interpreters! (Vermeulen *et al.* 1986–: X:21). The notion that some interpreters knew Malay (albeit it in varying degrees) is strengthened by the fact that two letters from 1748 now in the Deshima archive in The Hague were translated from Chinese into Dutch via Malay.[54] Malay was one of the languages studied by the multilingual *rangakusha* Tsuji Norinobu (Goodman 2013: 144–145).

Contact between Dutch and Malay in Japan and elsewhere in East Asia led to the use of Malay words by the Dutch in Japan. For example, Overmeer Fisscher (1833: 265) refers to the *Kambang-pakhuis* at Deshima. *Pakhuis* is the Dutch for 'warehouse', while *kembang pala* is the Malay word for the spice mace.[55] In 1845, two Dutch-Malay grammars, a manual of Low Malay and a Dutch-Malay dictionary were imported at Deshima. The dictionary is probably an edition of the *Nederduitsch en Maleisch woordenboek* compiled by P.P. Roorda van Eysinga and printed in Batavia (1st ed. 1824). In 1847, another Dutch-Malay dictionary was imported (Nagazumi 1998: 61–65, 75). In the Ueno collection there are thirteen copies of two editions of a Dutch book for learning Malay: J.J. de Hollander, *Handleiding bij de Beoefening der Maleische Taal en Letterkunde* ('Guide to Practising the Malay Language and Literature'), published in Breda

---

54   MS The Hague, *Nationaal Archief*, VOC (1.04.21), 609 (Roessingh 1964: 58).

55   The *kambang*-trade (Dutch: *kambang-handel*) was in fact private trading, so this warehouse may have been used for this purpose.

in 1845 and 1856. There are also fifteen copies of De Hollander's *Handleiding bij de Beoefening der Javaansche Taal en Letterkunde*, printed in Breda in 1848. Javanese, like Malay, is an Austronesian language (List of foreign books 1957: 32).

6 Sinitic Varieties

The Chinese were one of the few peoples apart from the Dutch who were permitted to trade with Japan after 1639. Like the Dutch, the Chinese traders in Japan were confined to an area of Nagasaki and used interpreters, *tōtsūji* (唐通詞), to communicate with Japanese.[56] Our current knowledge does not allow us to state whether there was any competition between the Dutch and Chinese for interpreters. Boxer (1950: 60) observes that communications between the Governor-General at Batavia and the Nagasaki officials or shogunal authorities were often written in Chinese. He suggests that this was possible as there were many Chinese at Batavia and even a few Dutch who had knowledge of the language. They did this in part because of the suspicion that the Nagasaki interpreters might falsify or mistranslate documents sent in Dutch. On a different note, users of Dutch inserted words from Sinitic varieties into their texts. Examples of these are analysed in Chapter 5.

However, it was perhaps in the field of medicine and to some extent other branches of learning such as astronomy where Dutch and literary Sinitic varieties, above all *wényán* (Classical Chinese 文言) and *kanbun* (漢文), a form of literary Sinitic used in Japan, competed most obviously (Clements 2015: 100).[57] One early hint of this was the case mentioned above of the Deshima physician, Casper Schamberger, curing Inaba Masanori, *daimyō* of Odawara, of gout during his visit to Edo in 1650/1 (Michel 1999: 117). This was something which the physicians trained in Chinese medicine had not managed to do. What is of particular interest is that it was the long history of Japanese scholars engaging with texts written in literary Sinitic that would in fact assist the development of Dutch as a language of learning in Tokugawa Japan.

---

56 *Tō* (唐) is derived from the Chinese T'ang dynasty.

57 Very broadly, one might usefully compare the case of *wényán* and *kanbun* with that of Latin in Europe. In this view of things, *wényán* would equate to the stylized written Latin of ancient Rome (which itself was marked by diversity), while *kanbun* would equate with the Latin used by administrators and scholars in medieval and early modern Europe. This, too, was marked by diversity, but importantly, influenced by local vernaculars to a greater or lesser degree.

The Chinese language and culture had influenced Japan for a thousand years before the arrival of the Dutch. Chinese texts were translated into Japanese and the influence of Chinese could be felt in the Japanese writing systems and lexicon, as well as Japanese culture more generally (Clements 2015, esp. Ch. 3). The importation and translation of Chinese texts continued into the Tokugawa period and neo-Confucian scholars continued to read ancient Chinese texts written in literary Sinitic. In 1630, an edict was passed relating to imported books, although as it is no longer extant its precise contents are not known. It is thought likely that the edict introduced a ban on books associated with Christianity, in particular 32 works from China by the Jesuit missionary, Matteo Ricci (1552–1610), and other Europeans (Clements 2015: 145, 181; Kornicki 2001: 326–327).[58] However, in 1716 the new shogun Tokugawa Yoshimune lifted this ban and the reception of books on Western learning in Chinese coincided with a gradually increasing interest in the Dutch books entering Japan.[59] In the eighteenth century and indeed into the nineteenth century it was often scholars trained in reading Chinese texts, who were in the vanguard of attempts by Japanese to engage with the Dutch language. For example, Arai Hakuseki and Aoki Kon'yō, both of whom were ordered by Yoshimune to learn Dutch from the Nagasaki interpreters who visited Edo on the *hofreis*, were neo-Confucian scholars, who had studied the four books and five classics of ancient Chinese literature.[60] In *Rangaku kaitei* ('Guide to Dutch Learning', 1783), Ōtsuki Gentaku describes the process of translating Dutch texts into Japanese and what is clear is that this owes much to the process by which texts written in literary Sinitic were translated into Japanese. First, the translator affixes glosses to the Dutch words, as they often did when translating Chinese texts. The glosses are then re-arranged in order to build a Japanese sentence (Clements 2015: 164–165). Two significant differences between the syntax of Dutch and Japanese are first that in Japanese the verb is invariably sentence-final, whereas in Dutch the finite verb is typically in the second position in main clauses, and, second, prepositions in Dutch are usually rendered by suffix particles in Japanese (e.g., *naar* 'to' is rendered by *-ni* に or *-e* へ in Japanese). Furthermore, when Gentaku felt that the medical explanations of Dutch texts were insufficient, he would have recourse to Chinese texts in order to try and shed light on what he read in the Dutch texts (Macé 2016: 98). Later,

---

58   Keene (1969: 12) argues that as a result of this decree, books already in Japan were burned. He records that these included translations of Cicero's *De Amicitia* and Euclid's *Elements*.

59   Clements (2015: 181) writes that shogun Yoshimune lifted a ban specifically on the works from China by Matteo Ricci in 1721, while Vos (1978b: 217) dates the lifting to 1720.

60   For more on Kon'yō, see De Groot (2005: 101–108).

in 1815, Sugita Genpaku made an interesting contrast in *Rangaku kotohajime* ('The Beginnings of Dutch Learning') between Chinese learning and Dutch learning. He observed that while Chinese was primarily a rhetorical language, Dutch expressed facts and was easier to learn (De Bary *et al.* 2005: 370). It was clearly this aspect of Dutch, or at least the Dutch that he encountered, that attracted Genpaku, a man educated with texts written in literary Sinitic, to the Western language.

If one were to ask the question, how Dutch, as the vehicle for *rangaku*, would have fared if Chinese had not been the dominant language of learning in Tokugawa Japan, one would receive more than one answer. On the one hand, it could be argued that it would have faced less competition as a language of learning—Chinese was still by far the most widely-used language of learning in Tokugawa Japan. On the other hand, however, it may have fared less well as it owed its success in part to its adoption by scholars of Chinese learning. Finally, contact with Sinitic varieties led to lexical interference in the Dutch topolect or *nesolect* in Kyushu. Examples are analysed in Chapter 5.

7   Korean

During the Tokugawa period, one other nation with whom Japan did continue to trade and exchange diplomatic missions was Joseon Korea. There is reference from time to time in the *dagregisters* to the Korean embassies to Edo or Korean ships arriving by design or misfortune in Japan. In the *dagregister* for 1637, there are several references to the Korean embassy in Edo, with Koreans being referred to as *Coreers*. We are told that in one of the Korean palanquins there was a lacquer-work box on a table, in which there were letters to the shogun 'in Coreesche caracters' ('in Korean characters'). We are not told, but these were probably Sinitic *hanja* (漢字/한자) characters rather than *hangeul* (한글) letters (*Diaries*: II:144, 159). In 1639, the *opperhoofd* Caron refers to the Korean 'ambassador' passing through Hirado. It seems they exchanged words, although no details are given of the languages involved. By now Caron spoke some Japanese, so that may have served as an intermediary language (*Diaries*: IV:60).

Sixty merchants from the island of Tsushima, situated between Japan and Korea, were permitted to trade with Korea. A school for learning Korean was established on the island in 1727 and continued to function into the late nineteenth century. It had been established by the Confucian scholar, Amenomori Hōshū (1668–1755), who had visited Korea several times, staying at the 'Japan House', the Tsushima trading post in Busan, and had studied Korean

(Kornicki 2018: 91–92).[61] Tsushima also played the role of intermediary in the importation of Korean medical texts written in literary Sinitic into Japan.

In the late eighteenth century, there are regular reports in the *dagregister* of Korean vessels arriving in and departing from Nagasaki Bay, but no firm evidence of contact between Dutch and Koreans. In the nineteenth century, one European at Deshima who did show an interest in Korea was Von Siebold. In fact, Von Siebold worked with Korean informants, who were survivors of shipwrecks brought to Nagasaki to be repatriated, as well as Japanese interpreters in the service of Tsushima, in compiling knowledge about the language that he presented in his *magnum opus* on Japan, *Nippon* (Osterkamp 2009: 192).[62] Here, he devotes several pages to the Korean language, based on his own observations and those of European scholars using Chinese sources. He notes that already in 1824, he had sent information about *hangeul* to Batavia.[63] He also provides a short vocabulary in German, Sino-Korean and pure Korean words (Von Siebold 1897: II:315, 317–318).

8   Ainu

Ainu is a language isolate, which is currently endangered and may no longer have native speakers.[64] It was spoken on Ezo (Hokkaido) in the north of the Japanese archipelago, and neighbouring islands during the Tokugawa period (Shibatani 1990: 5). There is no evidence of the Dutch having direct contact with Ainu people. Nevertheless, in the Special Collections at Leiden University Library there is a Dutch-Japanese-Ainu vocabulary and a German-Japanese-Ainu lexicon compiled in part by Von Siebold, which require our attention. The Dutch-Japanese-Ainu vocabulary (Ser. 95, Kerlen 1809) consists of 43 woodblock-print sheets (see fig. 13). The introduction, written in Dutch, records that it was based on 'an original publication by a Japanese' ('een Originele uitgave van een Japander'). We do not know when this vocabulary was compiled or who compiled it. However, the copy in Leiden University

---

61   In Korean the 'Japan House' was called *waegwan*, in Japanese *wakan* (倭館).

62   In the collection of the Volkenkunde Museum in Leiden, there is a 'Thousand Character Classic' of Sinitic characters (*Qiānzìwén* 千字文) with equivalents in the Korean alphabet *hangeul*. Von Siebold, we are told, acquired this from Korean sailors shipwrecked on Kyushu. See also Osterkamp (2009: 203).

63   Von Siebold refers to *hangeul* as a syllabary, and presents a chart of *hangeul* open syllables, although it is an alphabet, from which letters are formed into open and closed syllables. This approach may have been influenced by the use of syllabaries in Japanese.

64   For a detailed study of Ainu, see Shibatani (1990: 1–86).

FIGURE 13
A Dutch-Japanese-Ainu
vocabulary, first page
LEIDEN UNIVERSITY
LIBRARY, SER. 95

Library has the *ex libris* 'Uit de Verzam[eling] van Overmeer Fisscher'. This may give us a *terminus ante quem* for publication of 1829, as this was the year in which Johannes van Overmeer Fisscher left Japan.[65] As for the compiler, one possibility is that it was one of the Dutch interpreters sent to Ezo to make contact with Russian sailors, such as Baba Teiyū, discussed in the next section. For each word, from left to right, there is the Dutch term reading horizontally, then vertically the sound of the Ainu equivalent in Latin script (influenced by Dutch spelling) and *katakana*, followed by the Japanese equivalent in *rōmaji* and *kanji*. A detailed analysis of the lexicon is beyond the scope of this book, but a few points are in order. First, some of the words, such as the numbers, are what one might expect to find in such a vocabulary. There is also trading terminology such as the unit of measure the *gantang* (*Ganting* in the vocabulary), but

---

65   Overmeer Fisscher (1833: 85–87) makes a brief reference to the Ainu, their language and customs in his account of Japan.

also *Paap* ('Papist'), a derogatory Dutch term for Catholics. In fact, there seems little logic to the choice and order of the words which may be a function of the resources available. Second, a small sample of words indicate that at least some entries for Ainu differ from those in the Ainu-Japanese-English dictionary published by the English missionary John Batchelor (1855–1944) in 1905. For example, Batchelor gives one, four and five as *shine, ine* and *ashne* (also *ashikne*) (Batchelor 1905: 10 and separate entries). The Leiden Dutch-Japanese-Ainu vocabulary gives (in *rōmaji*) *sinif, jonetsfoe* and *asjiki*. While some words are quite similar, e.g., for 'war' (Dutch *oorlog*) Batchelor has *tumi* and the Leiden vocabulary *tomi*, others are different, e.g., for 'dog' (Dutch *hond*), Batchelor has *seta* and the Leiden vocabulary *sekki*. It may be instructive for a specialist in Ainu to try to explain these differences. Third, the *rōmaji* and *katakana* renderings of the Ainu words are sometimes slightly different. For example, one and four in *katakana* are *shinefu* and *yonetsufu* (in Hepburn). Fourth, the *rōmaji* renderings show the influence of Dutch orthography, e.g., ⟨oe⟩ and ⟨sj⟩. Finally, the Japanese (Yamato) numbers are given rather than their Sino-Japanese equivalents, and the spelling of these in *rōmaji* differs somewhat from modern Hepburn spelling, e.g., 1,2,3 are given as *Fitots, Fitats, Mits* (Hepburn: *Hitotsu, Futatsu, Mittsu*). Reasons for the word-initial ⟨f⟩ in *Fitots*, and the lack of word-final ⟨u⟩ in all three words are discussed in Chapter 5. In short, this is an interesting and possibly unique example of contact between Dutch and Ainu in Tokugawa Japan and deserves further study.

The German-Japanese-Ainu lexicon is an altogether more ambitious project. This was based on a Japanese-Ainu lexicon by the explorer and cartographer, Mogami Tokunai (c. 1754/5–1836), to which Von Siebold, who met Tokunai in Edo, added German equivalents, and the occasional word of Latin, in sepia ink (Von Siebold 1897: 11:253). A few entries have Dutch equivalents in black ink, possibly by a different hand (*broeder* ('brother') is spelt *bloeder*: this hints at a Japanese hand but no more). The lexicon has the title *Ezogashima gengo* ('Ezo Island language', i.e., Ainu). It consists of 134 sheets of German-Japanese-Ainu words and another 41 sheets in Ainu and Japanese. Again, a full analysis of this lexicon is beyond the scope of this book, but a few points are in order. First, it is above all a Japanese-style lexicon. The terms are listed in *iroha* sequence, probably to be read top-down on each page, with Ainu in *katakana* at the top, Japanese in *kanji* with *furigana* in the middle, and Von Siebold's German at the bottom. Second, a brief comparison of the Ainu indicates that some terms are the same as those in the Dutch-Japanese-Ainu vocabulary, while others differ. For example, while 'four' is *yonetsufu* in the Dutch-Japanese-Ainu vocabulary, it is given as *inetsupu* in the Tokunai-Siebold lexicon (compare Batchelor *ine*). 'Tooth' (*Tand*) in the Dutch-Japanese-Ainu wordlist is *nimaki*, but in the

Tokunai-Siebold lexicon (*Zahn*) *imaki*. Batchelor (1905: 84) accepts *nimaki*, but specifically rejects *imaki*, also proposed by a Russian, Dobrotvorsky. 'Two' is *totsufu* (*rōmaji totsoefoe*) in the former, but *zutsufu* in the latter. Batchelor has *tu* in Roman script, but ツ [tsu] in *katakana* (indeed some differences may result from differences in Japanese and European sound systems). 'Six', on the other hand, is rendered as *iwan* (イワン) in both the Leiden works, although the Tokunai-Siebold lexicon also has *iwanbe*.[66] Third, the question arises as to whether Von Siebold's work on Tokunai's lexicon might tell us whether he was involved at all in the production of the Dutch-Japanese-Ainu wordlist. Currently, there is insufficient evidence for this. These few examples indicate that there were some differences in the Ainu. Furthermore, the Dutch wordlist is entirely woodblock-print, while the German lexicon has Von Siebold's handwriting, so it is difficult to make a comparison based on the *rōmaji* in each work. In *Nippon* Von Siebold devotes several pages to analysing the Ainu language (Von Siebold 1897: II:253–256). Finally, Batchelor (1905: 7), sometimes referred to as the 'father of Ainu studies', mentions Von Siebold by name once but does not analyse his lexicon. He implicitly criticizes the accuracy of earlier work on Ainu by Europeans but does not go into detail. I can see no mention of the Dutch wordlist in Batchelor's 1905 English-Japanese-Ainu lexicon. Further study of this and the Von Siebold lexicon may yield useful results about Ainu.

9   German

Von Siebold's involvement in compiling the Ainu lexicon provides a link to German as a contact language for and competitor to Dutch in Japan. Many of the surgeons posted to Deshima were German. Indeed, about half of the surgeons at Deshima in the second half of the eighteenth century were German. However, they were typically, though not always, the only Germans on the island and so would have had little opportunity at least to speak German. Indeed, as German and Dutch are closely related, it would have been relatively easy for them to learn Dutch.

The German soldier and adventurer Caspar Schmalkalden arrived in Japan in 1650, having previously spent a couple of years in Taiwan. At the end of his travelogue, which remained unpublished until 1983, he added some short German-Japanese glossaries (Schmalkalden 1983: 140–149). However, it is likely that he compiled these after returning to Europe, using existing

---

66   The Dutch-Japanese-Ainu wordlist transcribes the *katakana* as *iwang* in *rōmaji* (Batchelor Part II, p. 10 has *iwan*).

published material such as Portuguese-Japanese lexicons as his primary sources (Michel 1986). Several Germans worked on Deshima in the 1670s. Two German pharmacists, Godefried Haeck and Frans Braun, were dispatched to Japan successively in 1669 and 1671 (Michel 2011: 80–81). Mathaeus Hans Otter and Heinrich Muche both worked as junior surgeons on Deshima in the early 1670s.[67] Another German who worked in Japan in the seventeenth century was Andreas Cleyer (*opperhoofd* 1682–83 and 1685–86). He kept the *dagregister* during these periods in Dutch, and probably used Dutch for most of his time in Japan. He did, however, employ a fellow German, the gardener Georg Meister (1653–1713), at Deshima. It seems, however, that Meister did not merely take care of the weeds, but was actively involved in assisting Cleyer with research into Japanese *materia medica*, so there would have been ample opportunity for them to exchange words in German (Michel 2011: 84).[68] Furthermore, it seems that Meister had time to study Japanese for he, like Caspar Schmalkalden before him, compiled some German-Japanese wordlists (Michel 1986: 1).

In the final decade of the seventeenth century, the German physician Engelbert Kaempfer wrote letters in German from Deshima and compiled a Japanese-German glossary.[69] He also annotated his own sketch of a *hofreis* to Edo in German.[70] There is little firm evidence of German in eighteenth-century Japan. However, the records occasionally make mention of German books. In 1778, the senior surgeon Thomas Neegers passed away. One of the books in the inventory made after his death was a copy of the German edition of Adam Kulmus's *Anatomische Tabellen* (Beukers 2000: 114). In March 1792, the interpreter Nakayama Sakusaburō (also Busei) asked Petrus Chassé if a voc employee could translate a German book on military evolution and drills. Chassé refused (most politely) (Vermeulen *et al.* 1986–: x:21).[71]

The *Phaeton* incident of 1808, in which a British frigate, HMS *Phaeton*, entered Nagasaki Bay to ambush Dutch trading ships, resulted in Nagasaki interpreters avidly studying European languages other than Dutch, one of which was German. Some Nagasaki interpreters studied German privately and there

---

67   http://wolfgangmichel.web.fc2.com/serv/histmed/dejimasurgeons.html. Accessed 9 April 2020.

68   For more on Cleyer's life, his time on Deshima and a transcription of his *dagregister* entries for October 1682 to November 1683, see Cleyer (1985).

69   For example, in 1690 he wrote a letter in German to his brother Joachim, who taught law at Leiden (Meier-Lemgo 1965: 292–293). See also Joby (2018: 188).

70   MS London, British Library, Sloane MS. 3060, fol. 502.

71   There were at least eight generations of the Nakayama family who worked as interpreters (Assendelft de Coningh 2012: 47, n. 26). Several of them had the given name Sakusaburō. For this one, see also Screech (2006).

is the occasional German dictionary amongst the books ordered from the Dutch by the Japanese (Nagazumi 1998: 24). Furthermore, the *bakufu* occasionally ordered them to translate German documents. They typically did so with the help of the Dutch at Deshima (Clements 2015: 179 n. 8).[72] The most prominent German in Japan in the first half of the nineteenth century was Von Siebold. He typically used Dutch at his medical school in Narutaki, just outside Nagasaki. In the collection at Narutaki there are documents written by Von Siebold in Dutch such as a letter to his student Kō Ryōsai. In 1861 Von Siebold published a collection of open letters under the title 'Open Brieven' in Dutch, 'Ter Nederlandsche Drukkerij' ('At the Dutch Press') on Deshima. He also wrote in Latin and learnt Japanese. Von Siebold produced a map of Japan and surrounding countries in German, and wrote his great book on Japan, *Nippon*, in German.[73] However, our current state of knowledge does not allow us to say whether and if so to what extent Von Siebold used German in Japan.

In the wake of the Convention of Kanagawa in 1854, Germans were quick to go to Japan and keen to play a role in the country's drive to modernize, particularly in the fields of medicine and law. This led to several German loanwords entering Japanese. For example, the Japanese for 'impotence', *inpotentsu* (インポテンツ), comes from the German *Impotenz*. In other cases, given their similarities German or Dutch may be the source. The Japanese for typhoid *chifusu* (チフス) may come from the German *Typhus* or the Dutch *tyfus* (Irwin 2011: 50–53). There is little evidence for switching between Dutch and German, which is to be expected, as there would have been little motivation for those speaking or writing Dutch to switch to German.

Lists of books ordered from the Dutch by Japanese in the nineteenth century occasionally include requests for German dictionaries (Nagazumi 1998: 21, 25, 34). In the Ueno collection we find several dictionaries including German, and German learners. Two lexicons are bilingual German-Dutch dictionaries again illustrating that other European languages were typically learnt via Dutch: *Nieuw volledig woordenboek. 1ste deel: Hoogduitsch-Nederduitsch, 2de deel: Nederduitsch-Hoogduitsch*, Amsterdam, 1845, 1851 (two copies, nos. 1259, 1260), and Dirk Bomhoff's *Vollständiges deutsch-holländisches und holländisch-deutsches Taschenwörterbuch, 1 Theil. Deutsch-Holländisch*, Leyden, D. Noothoven van Goor, 1846 (827). The second dictionary has the seal of the chemistry school, the *Seimikyoku*. This is but one illustration of how German played a role in the Japanese engagement with Western science in the late Tokugawa and early Meiji periods. As for learners, the Ueno collection

---

72   Clements refers to a Japanese secondary source, Koga Jūjirō (1966: I:esp. 112–119).
73   A copy of the map is preserved at the Seinan Gakuin Museum in Hakata.

includes two copies of H. Weiffenbach, *Leitfaden zum Unterricht in der deutschen Sprache und Literatur 2te Aufl.* printed in Breda in 1853 (nos. 3546, 3575). They have the seal of the censor's office of the Nagasaki Governor. Furthermore, the collection includes a copy of a five-volume German learner by a Swiss, Jakob Kaderly (1827–1874), who taught German in Tokyo. The learner was also produced by a Japanese, Nakamura Yūkichi, and first printed in Tokyo in 1870 (Meiji 3).[74] This has the seal of the *Daigaku Nankō* (大学南校) (lit. university southern school), where Kaderly worked. This was established in 1869 as one of the successor schools to the *Kaiseijo*, the school for foreign studies established by the *bakufu* in 1863. The *Daigaku Nankō* was one of predecessors of Tokyo University. The fact that this book was printed in Tokyo and in German, with no reference to Dutch underlines the shift that was underway in the relative importance of Dutch in the late Tokugawa/early Meiji period. A second edition was printed in Tokyo in 1878 and a third in 1885. Finally, the Ueno collection contains no non-fiction books written in German, but it does contain Dutch translations of German books, for example by the German explorer and scholar Alexander von Humboldt (1769–1859).

10 Russian

As early as 1739, the *dagregister* records reports of Russian ships (some captained by Swedes) being spotted off the northern coast of Japan, even reaching Matsumae *han* in Southern Ezo (now Hokkaido) This was a consequence of Russian expansion into Eastern Siberia, and it raised questions regarding Russian interests in Japan. Indeed, the shogun sent a list of questions to the Dutch about Russia in the wake of this news (Blussé *et al.* 1992: 492–494). In 1771, the ship of Count Moritz Aladar von Benyowsky (1746–86) reached the shores of Japan (Liss 2009: 32).[75] This led to the Japanese beginning to show an interest in the Russian language. A further impetus for this was the return in 1791 of the Japanese merchant Daikokuya Kōdayū (1751–1828) from an 11-year stay as a hostage in Russia.

---

74 Jakob Kaderly, *Lehrbuch der Deutschen Sprache fuer die hoehern Classen der kaiserlich-japanischen Akademie Daigaku Nanko Tokio in Japan mit Beruecksichtigung der meisten Neuerungen bearbeitet von Jakob Kaderly Lehrer der deutschen Sprache und Literatur an obiger Akademie. Gedruckt in der akademischen Buchdruckerei im dritten Jahre Meidschi 1870* (848) (Shirōka 2011: 105–126).

75 See also Vermeulen *et al.* (1986–: X:59) for a report of a Russian ship reaching Matsumae on Hokkaido in 1794.

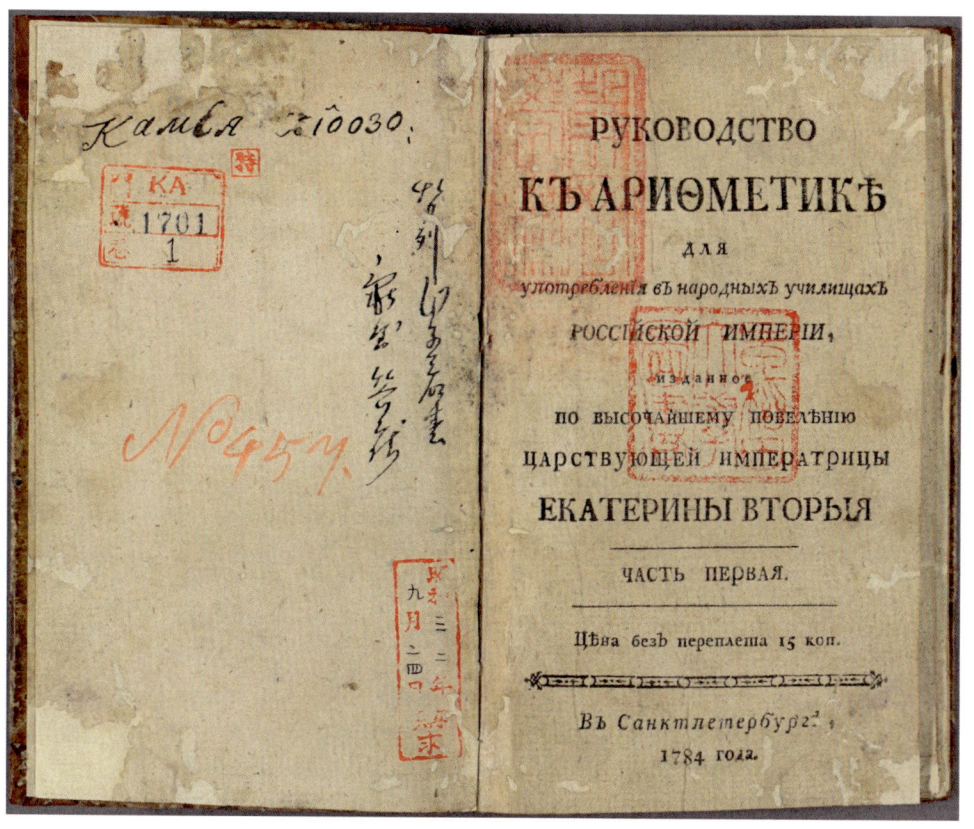

FIGURE 14   A Russian mathematics book brought back to Japan by Daikokuya Kōdayū. Title page
WUL KA 01701

Kōdayū had evidently learnt Russian during his captivity and even produced a map in Japan with Japanese and Russian toponyms. A Russian book on mathematics that he brought back from Russia is now in Waseda University Library (see fig. 14).[76] Kōdayū had been returned to Japan along with two other castaways by Adam Laxman (1766–1806), a Finno-Swedish sailor in the Russian navy. He had hoped that in return for repatriating Kōdayū he could gain trading concessions from Japan (Wells 2004: 32). In 1792, Laxman presented some Russian maps to the shogun. These were translated into Japanese by Katsuragawa Hoshū, who, as we have seen, also invested much time and energy

76   It is catalogued as *Rukovodstvo k arifmetikě dlia upotrebleniia v narodnykh uchilishchakh Rossiiskoi Imperii* ('Arithmethic manual for the use of the public schools of the Russian Empire') printed in St. Petersburg in 1784. http://www.wul.waseda.ac.jp/koten seki/html/ka/ka_01701/index.html. Waseda call no. KA 01701. Accessed 10 April 2020.

in the Dutch language. In translation they became appendices to Hoshū's *Hokusa bunryaku* ('Story of a driftage to the north', 1794), which was based on questioning Kōdayū and his fellow captives (Unno 1994: 436; Katsuragawa Hoshū 1978). The manuscript of *Hokusa bunryaku* was first published in 1937. Of particular interest is Chapter XI, which is the first Russian-Japanese lexicon (Katsuragawa Hoshū 1978: 297–346). The lexicon is arranged thematically, with Russian words rendered in *katakana* and Japanese ones in *kanji*. One other consequence of this contact between Russians and Japanese was that the *opperhoofd* Gijsbert Hemmij produced a short account of Russia in Dutch (*Kort beschrijving van Russland*). This was translated into Japanese by Hoshū (Katsuragawa Hoshū 1978: 325–328; 471).

In 1791/2, Russian texts were brought to Deshima, which were to be translated at the request of the shogun. However, as none of the Dutch knew Russian, the *opperhoofd* Chassé had to decline (again!) in the politest manner possible. The documents, he noted in the *dagregister*, had possibly arrived in Japan as a result of an investigation into whether there were Russian soldiers on the Kuril Islands (Vermeulen *et al.* 1986–: X:25). We even find some Russian dated 1793 in a scrapbook owned by Katsuragawa Hoshū's brother and fellow *rangakusha*, Morishima Chūryō.[77]

In 1804, the Russian ship *Nadezhda*, captained by Ivan Krusenstern and carrying the ambassador Admiral Nikolai Rezanov (1764–1807), arrived in Nagasaki with the aim of entering into diplomatic and commercial relations with Japan, an attempt which failed (Wells 2004: 6, 61; Boot 2008: 104; Goodman 2013: 217). This, together with the *Phaeton* incident of 1808, prompted the *bakufu* to encourage the study of other European languages apart from Dutch, above all Russian, French and English. In 1809, Motoki Shōei and other Dutch interpreters were ordered to study Russian as well as English (Kornicki 2018: 97).

The *Phaeton* incident led to the establishment of the *Bansho wage goyō* ('Office for the Translation of Barbarian Books') in Edo in 1811 within the *Tenmondai* ('Bureau of Astronomy') (Clements 2015: 156). One of those who worked there was the promising Nagasaki Dutch interpreter, Baba Teiyū, a pupil of Shizuki Tadao. One of his first tasks was to decipher letters found on the ship of Vice Admiral Vasily Golovnin (1776–1831), commander of the *Diana*. Golovnin and his crew were held captive in Japan for two years as the Japanese tried to decide whether, as Golovnin claimed, he was simply surveying northern Japan, or whether he was preparing for a full-scale Russian invasion of the country. Baba Teiyū visited Ezo, where he is said to have taken tuition from

---

Golovnin in Russian. Another Japanese who met Golovnin was Murakami Teisuke (1780–1845). According to Golovnin's own account of the affair, Teisuke picked up Russian quickly and conversed with him daily in Hakodate on Ezo. These interpreters' work, and indeed their ability to use Russian, led to the release of the prisoners in 1813 (Cullen 2006: 149–151). Baba Teiyū used his knowledge of Russian to compile *Rogo bunpō kihan* ('Rules of Russian Grammar', 1813) from notes made by Golovnin (Clements 2015: 157).[78] Furthermore, he translated *Tonka hiketsu* ('Preventing Smallpox by Vaccination', 1820) from the Russian (Goodman 2013: 257 n. 20; Akizuki 1989: 150). This was based on one of two books on vaccination that had been brought back to Japan by Nakagawa Gorōji (1768–1848), a *bakufu* guard who had spent five years as a captive in Siberia (Jannetta 2007: 71).

In 1810, a Japanese (we do not know who) placed an order with the Dutch for a book on Russia (Nagazumi 1998: 10). Orders for Russian dictionaries (possibly bilingual) in 1824, 1825 and 1830, and even a French-Russian dictionary (1814) hint at the need of a few Japanese to learn Russian (Nagazumi 1998: 11, 21, 25, 34). In 1855, a Japanese-Russian-Dutch vocabulary *Roshia jisen* was published. This had been compiled by Sakaki Reisuke (1823–94) (see fig. 15). It is a small vocabulary which folds out like a concertina. In the front matter, there is a guide to printed and written Russian letters in upper and lower case with equivalents in *katakana* and Roman script. These are supplemented with the corresponding Dutch letters (*Holl[andsche] letteren*), which act as a pronunciation guide. The words are arranged in three columns. In the left-hand column is a Japanese word in *katakana* and *kanji*. In the middle column are Russian equivalents in Russian cursive script with *katakana* superscript for pronunciation. In the right-hand column is the Dutch equivalent, again with *katakana* superscript. The first words relate to the weather, as in traditional Chinese/Japanese reference works (or more generally sky/heaven). Other words indicate times of the day and family relations, although they do not seem to follow a strict order. The vocabulary concludes with greetings. Finally, although limited in scope (there are fewer than 100 entries), this vocabulary illustrates how Dutch continued to play a role as an intermediate language between Japanese and other European languages after 1854. Two books in the Ueno collection in Russian were printed in St. Petersburg in the 1850s.[79] However,

---

78   For further information see also https://hermes-ir.lib.hit-u.ac.jp/rs/handle/10086/11630. Accessed 12 April 2020.

79   Ueno catalogue no. 3614, *Podarok' mashĩe; knizhechka dlĩa malen'kikh dĩeteĭ* (printed 1856) and no. 3615 (*Nastavlenĩe dlĩa ustroĭstva kozhevennago zavoda i proizvodstva vsĩekh* (printed 1858)). There are also several books on Russia in the Ueno catalogue. One is Johannes Broedelet, *Oude en nieuwe staat van 't Russische of Moskovische Keizerrijk;*

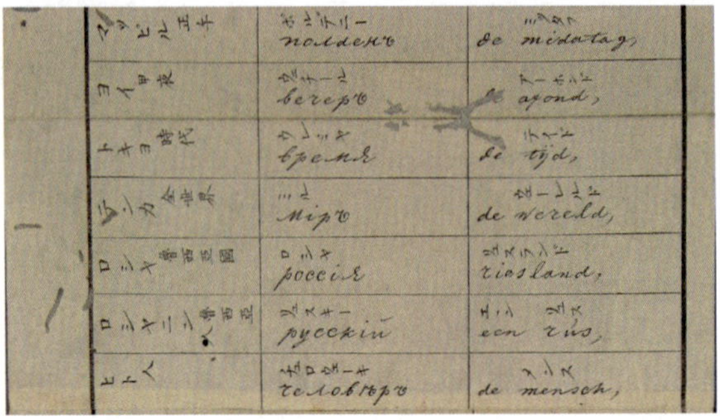

FIGURE 15   Japanese-Russian-Dutch vocabulary *Roshia jisen*,
              1855, Sakaki Reisuke
              WUL 文庫 08 C0838

despite efforts to learn Russian, the future novelist Ivan Goncharov (1812–91), who arrived in Nagasaki in 1853 as a secretary on board the frigate *Pallada*, observed that the interpreters only knew Dutch. He does not, unfortunately, tell us which language(s) were used for communication between the Russians on the *Pallada* and Japanese (Wells 2004: 107). Finally, most Russian loanwords in Japanese date from after our period. However, two Russian loanwords are first attested in 1807: *balalaika* (バラライカ) and *seiuchi* (セイウチ, 'walrus') from the Russian *сивуч* (*sivuch*, 'sea lion') (Irwin 2011: 46).

11   Manchu

Manchu is a Tungusic language, considered by some linguists to be a member of the Altaic language family. Towards the end of the eighteenth century, the *bakufu* was already recognizing the need to learn Manchu, one of the official languages of the Qing dynasty in China, as documents written in Manchu were brought to Japan via Sakhalin and the Kuril Islands. The petitions for trade

---

behelzende eene uitvoerige historie van Rusland en deszelfs Groot-Vorsten (vol. I part II) (no. 567). On p. 817 in the margin there is a red stamp (scored through) 'Josiwo'. 'Josiwo' refers to the Nagasaki *rangakusha* Yoshio Kōgyū. On page 201 a little slip of paper has been inserted on which someone has written *PETURUSU DEN GUROTEN* in *katakana*. This is based on a Dutch version of the Tsar's name, *Petrus den Grooten*, which is in the title of this section. Another book on Russia in the Ueno collection in two volumes is Jacobus Scheltema, *Pieter de Groote, Keizer van Rusland, in Holland en te Zaandam in 1697 en 1717*, 2 dln. Amsterdam 1814 (nos. 1294, 1295). These have the seal of the censor's office of the Nagasaki *bugyō*.

that Admiral Rezanov submitted in 1804 were written in Manchu as well as Japanese and Russian. The Manchu documents would eventually be translated by Takahashi Kageyasu, mentioned above, who worked at the *Tenmondai*.[80] He, along with other officials at the *Tenmondai*, was ordered by the *bakufu* to study Manchu, as well as Russian, in the wake of the *Phaeton* incident in 1808 so as to provide it with expertise regarding the problems emerging on Japan's northern borders (De Bary *et al.* 2005: 363). He would produce a Manchu-literary Sinitic dictionary based on a revised version of the Qing government Manchu dictionary, *Zēngdìng Qīngwén Jiàn* (增訂清文鑑, 'Revised and Enlarged Mirror of Manchu', completed in 1771) (Clements 2015: 183). Another translator at the *Tenmondai* who learnt Manchu was Baba Teiyū, mentioned above, who had been a Dutch interpreter at Nagasaki. One commentator suggests that the knowledge of Dutch 'coloured' the encounter with Manchu of translators and scholars such as Baba Teiyū (Söderblom Saarela 2017: 388). In Nagasaki it was above all the *tōtsūji*, i.e., Chinese interpreters, who were ordered to learn Manchu (Clements 2015: 180–181). In the 1850s, some Nagasaki interpreters learnt Manchu, as it was thought, incorrectly, that this was still the dominant language of Qing China (Kornicki 2018: 97). Nevertheless, their efforts were not completely without rewards as a team of fourteen *tōtsūji* led by Tei Einei (1829–97) produced two Manchu-Japanese dictionaries based on the first edition of the *Qīngwén Jiàn* (清文鑑, 'Mirror of Manchu' 1673–1708) (Clements 2015: 180).

12   French

Prior to the *Phaeton* incident, Japan had little contact with French. The Dutch did, though, send or bring French books to Japan. One of these was a copy of G.W. Knorr's exquisite album of shells, *Les délices des yeux et de l'esprit* (1764–65), which Isaac Titsingh sent to his friend and correspondent, Kutsuki Masatsuna. Another French book that Titsingh sent to Masatsuna was a world atlas compiled by Nicolas Sanson (*Atlas Nouveau / contenant toutes les parties du Monde* [...] Paris: Hubert Jaillot, 1692) (Lequin 2003: 206–207).[81] Furthermore, Masatsuna requested several French dictionaries and learners from Titsingh. One was Chomel's *Dictionnaire Oeconomique*. In a letter from Edo dated 28/5/ 1785 to Isaac Titsingh in Chinsura, Masatsuna thanked his friend for books

---

80   Söderblom Saarela (2017: 392) calls Kageyasu the most productive scholar of Manchu language studies in Tokugawa Japan.

81   This includes a dedication to Masatsuna from his friend, Titsingh.

delivered by 'Heer Ulps' (Lequin 1992: 2–3).[82] These included two French learners, which may suggest that Masatsuna already wanted to study French at this point (p. 3). One was Pierre/Pieter Marin's *Nouvelle méthode pour aprendre les principes et l'usage des langues françoise et hollandoise. Nieuwe Fransche en Nederduitsche spraakwyze, vermeerderd met een uitvoerige syntaxis, of woordenschikking*. This was first published in 1694 and was frequently reprinted in the subsequent 150 years, almost unchanged (Frijhoff 2010: 43–44; Loonen 2000: 326).[83] The other was Louis Cornelle's *Beknopte en klaare leerwyze der Fransche taale* (Rotterdam, 1783) (Lequin 2003: 206).

The question arises as to why Masatsuna would want to learn French. One possibility is that Titsingh, a Francophone and Francophile, had told him of its importance as a language in eighteenth-century Europe. Furthermore, Masatsuna was an avid coin collector. He may have learnt French to be able to read French inscriptions on European coins. Titsingh had supplied many European coins which Masatsuna described and depicted in *Seiyō senpu*.

Another French book that reached Japan was a copy of Michel de Marolles' *Tableaux du Temple des Muses*, mentioned above. The subject of the book is well-known characters, usually mythical, from antiquity, such as Phaeton and Pandora. The book, printed by Nicolas L'Anglois in Paris in 1655, came into the possession of the *daimyō* of Hirado, Matsūra Seizan, at some point between 1785 and 1788 and is still in the Matsūra collection in Hirado.[84] The Japanese scholar Matsuda Kiyoshi has done extensive work on the Matsūra collection and has tried to build a picture of how Seizan might have used this book. He suggests that Seizan asked the *opperhoofd* Van Rheede tot de Parkeler to translate passages of Marolles' book, presumably into Dutch, so that one of the interpreters could translate it into Japanese. Seizan sent Van Rheede tot de Parkeler, via the senior interpreter Narabayashi Shinbei (Eizaemon), three rolls of material and other goods as gifts for his troubles.[85] Van Rheede tot de Parkeler wrote a thank-you letter in Dutch, which Matsuda (1998: 507–508) reproduces, and which he suggests an interpreter would have translated into Japanese.[86]

---

82   This is Hendrick Andries Ulps, who held several junior positions at Deshima.

83   Marin produced *Méthode Familière* (1698) and *Nouvelle Méthode* (1694) for beginner and intermediate level respectively, for Dutch students of French (Loonen 2000: 326).

84   It is no. 37 in the Matsūra Western books catalogue (洋書目録).

85   The following year, Seizan sent Tot de Parkeler another gift of some Hirado ware (Matsuda 1998: 508).

86   Matsuda transcribes the Tot de Parkeler letter as follows: *de drie rollen stoffen die den Landsheer van firando de goedheijd gehad heeft aan den ondergeteekenden hollandschen Capitain tot een vriendelijk geschenk toe te zenden, zin hem door den oppertolk Jeseijmon behoorlijk ter hand gesteld de Capitain bedankt zeer hartelijk voor dit aangenaame present en heeft de Eer na welmeent aanbod van weederdienst, den Landsheer Een Langleeven. Een*

Another French book that reached Tokugawa Japan was an illustrated French edition of Aesop's Fables, *Fables d'Esope* (Paris, 1810). The Edo artist Ishikawa Tairō owned a copy of this and it is likely that it passed on to the *ukiyo-e* artist Utagawa Kuniyoshi (1798–1861) on his death in 1817 (Katsumori 2007: 109, 113).

A word is in order about the Dutch-Japanese lexicon the 'Edo Halma' (*Edo Haruma*) completed in 1796 after thirteen years' work under the leadership of Inamura Sanpaku. This was based on the French-Dutch dictionary compiled by the Utrecht bookseller and Huguenot refugee, François Halma, first published in 1717. The *Zūfu Haruma*, analysed in Chapter 2, was also based on Halma's dictionary (Doeff 1833: 244; Goodman 2013: 141).[87] After the *Phaeton* incident, the Japanese set about increasing their knowledge of French as well as Russian and English. An early fruit of their engagement with French was a Japanese-French glossary *Furansu jihan* ('Glossary of French') produced by Motoki Shōei, mentioned above.[88] He had learnt French from Hendrick Doeff, who also taught the language to other Japanese (Clements 2015: 179; Kornicki 2018: 97). In the preface to *Furansu jihan*, Shōei, perhaps with Doeff looking over his shoulder and even dictating, writes:

> *Moi, Shohei, Motoki, voulant apprendre (la langue française) depuis long-temps, consulte toujours le dictionnaire rédigé par un Hollandais, Pieter Marin [...]*

> [I, Shohei, Motoki, having wanted to learn (the French language) for a long time, always consult the dictionary edited by a Dutchman, Pieter Marin [...]]

Indeed, as Yoshioka Akiyoshi argues, the principal source for *Furansu jihan* was the 1775 edition of Pierre Marin's *Nouvelle Méthode*. Shōei then expresses sadness that he had to put aside his study of French, which he calls *une langue élégante*, while he compiled an English-Japanese dictionary. However,

---

aanhoudende gesondheijd en Een bestending voorspoed toe te wenschen en zig in de vriend-schap van den Landsheer te recommandeeren decima den 1 november off 11 Siuguats 1786.

87   Another French-Dutch dictionary, Pierre Marin's *Groot Nederduitsch en Fransch Woordenboek, Grand dictionnaire hollandois & françois*, was used in the compilation of an early Dutch-Japanese lexicon by the interpreter referred to as Zenzaburō. By his death, however, he had only completed the first few letters of the alphabet (De Groot 2004: 162; Blussé and Remmelink 2004: 859).

88   The manuscript is undated but given Shōei's dates must have a *terminus ante quem* of 1822.

he had eventually been able to return to taking lessons in French (Yoshioka 1965: 24–26):

During Admiral Rezanov's embassy to Japan in Nagasaki in 1804, Hendrick Doeff had exchanged letters with him in French (Doeff 1833: 93–94). If this had happened during the seventeenth century, the exchange between Doeff and Rezanov, born in St. Petersburg, might have been in Dutch, as this was typically the maritime *lingua franca* in the Baltic region. However, this time had now passed. Shortly before he left Deshima in 1817, Doeff was called on to translate a document in French found on board Vice Admiral Golovnin's ship. He later recalled in his memoir that the document could be interpreted as proof that the Russians were at least eager to take control of the Kuril Islands and Sakhalin, in which, it suggested, the Japanese had shown no interest. Doeff wrote, *ik verzachtte de uitdrukkingen zo veel mogelijk* ('I softened the expressions as much as possible'), to minimize the possibility that the Japanese would feel threatened by the Russians and act accordingly (Doeff 1833: 158–159).

Murakami Hidetoshi (1811–90), born in Sakuyama, has been described by one commentator as 'the first serious student of French'. He was a friend of the *rangakusha* Sakuma Shōzan (1811–64) and seems to have acquired a basic grasp of French by means of an old Dutch-French dictionary, possibly the Halma. By 1854 he had compiled a three-volume quadrilingual Japanese-French-English-Dutch lexicon *Sango-benran* ('Trilingual Manual') in octavo.[89] The words are grouped by theme in the order of traditional Chinese reference works, i.e., *ten—chi—jin* (天地人)—heaven, earth, mankind. Each entry has four rows, from top to bottom with Japanese at the top (*kanji* (meaning) and *katakana* superscript (pronunciation)), followed by French, English and Dutch. The French, English and Dutch words were also furnished with equivalents in *katakana*. So, for example, above the French word *aigre* ('sharp') was written a *katakana* transliteration *aigure*, above *grec* ('Greek') *gireki*, etc. The use of *katakana* transliteration would have meant that the Japanese pronunciation of French would have been difficult to understand for native speakers. Similarly, the *katakana* next to the Dutch is some way from Dutch pronunciation, for example, *ster* ('star') is written as *suteru*.

In Edo in 1864, Hidetoshi published his *Grand Dictionnaire*, the bilingual (French-Japanese) *Futsugo-meiyō* ('A Handbook of French') (Irwin 2011: 48, 217; Sims 1998: 270). In the preface to *Futsugo-meiyō*, Hidetoshi tells us why he began learning French. He wrote that although the use of Dutch for the study of science was well developed (Yoshioka 1976: 54):

---

89   Kerlen (no. 1382) gives a date of publication of 1856.

Je n'entends personne parler ou lire le français. C'est ainsi que je me suis décidé à apprendre cette langue il y a déjà quelques années.

[I do not hear anyone speak or read French. That is why I decided to learn this language a few years ago.]

However, he admits that it was by no means straightforward, but eventually it served its purpose:

Ce fut très pénible et, trois fois, j'ai été au bout de ma patience, mais enfin, grâce à mon assiduité, je suis parvenu à le maîtriser et à pouvoir publier ce dictionnaire français-japonais.

[It was very annoying and three times I was at the end of my tether, but finally, thanks to my diligence, I finally mastered it and have been able to publish this French-Japanese dictionary]

The structure of *Futsugo-meiyō* differs significantly from that of *Sango-benran*. While the words in the latter were in the *ten—chi—jin* order of Chinese reference works, this was arranged in Roman alphabetical order with French on the left and Japanese on the right. Furthermore, in contrast to *Sango-benran* the French words in *Futsugo-meiyō* were not furnished with *katakana* pronunciation guides. A possible reason for this shift is that in 1854 priority was given to educating Japanese in the reading and speaking of French, while by 1864 the aim was to provide a resource for Japanese translators of imported French books. This case also provides another example of how contact with Western languages prompted a re-ordering of Japanese lexicons, something we saw in Chapter 2 in relation to the *Haruma* dictionaries. Hidetoshi would subsequently produce many other works and acquired a reputation as the founder of the study of French in Japan. From 1860 onwards he taught French at the *Bansho shirabesho*. Other Japanese would later join him, including in 1861 Irie Bunrō (1834–78), who had learnt the elements of French from Hidetoshi's works and taken lessons from a French legation official, Henri Weuve. By 1868 it is reckoned that there were some 200 students of French at the *Kaiseijo* (Sims 1998: 270; Tanaka 2017: 11).

Private schools were established to cope with the demand for French, as well as other Western languages. In 1871–72 there were five private schools in Tokyo teaching French, four exclusively. One of them, Hidetoshi's *Tatsuridō* (達理堂) had 429 students between 1868 and 1877. In about 1875, Nakae Chomin, who had studied French at Nagasaki and Yokohama established a private academy, the *Futsugakujuku* (仏学塾). In twelve years, it trained nearly two thousand students (Sims 1998: 272).

Lists of books that the Japanese ordered from the Dutch in the nineteenth century suggest an increased interest in French, although details are often partial. The first comprehensive list that we have is from 1810, but even prior to this French learning material was being imported. This includes six copies each of the Halma and Marin French-Dutch dictionaries ordered between 1793 and 1809 (Nagazumi 1998: 6–8). Editions of both lexicons appear regularly in lists for subsequent years. In the Ueno collection there are nineteen lexicons in which French is one of the languages.[90] Typically these are French-Dutch dictionaries, suggesting that in the first instance the Japanese learnt French through Dutch. One of the dictionaries is Kilian's trilingual German, Latin and French lexicon, *Kilianus Auctus seu Dictionarium Teutonico-Latino-Gallicum*, printed in Amsterdam in 1642 (no. 3579).[91] The book has the seal of the Fukuyama clan in present-day Hiroshima prefecture. It is not clear when they purchased the book, but it would have been some time in Edo period. It is likely to have been used in the *Fukuyama seishikan* (福山誠之館), the official school of the Fukuyama *han* which operated from 1846 to 1872. Another of the dictionaries is French-English (A. Spiers, *Dictionnaire abrégé anglais-français et français-anglais*. 15 éd. Paris 1867) (no. 824). This has the seal of the Numazu military school near Yokohama. We do not know when the book reached Japan. This combination of languages is to be expected as French and English, rather than Dutch, were the languages of instruction at Numazu, although there are also French-Dutch lexicons in the Ueno collection with the Numazu seal.

---

90 These are Abraham Blussé's French-Dutch *Dictionnaire Portatif* (undated) (825); two copies of an undated French-Dutch dictionary by D. Bomhoff (760, 761); several copies of Halma's French-Dutch lexicon (87, 993–996) including Halma, *Le Grand Dictionnaire François et Flamand* (with the seal of the Numazu military school near Yokohama) (996), Pieter Marin, *Nederduitsch en Fransch woordenboek* 6de druk. Amsterdam 1793 (with the seal of the Numazu military school) (821), Pieter Marin, *Groot Nederduitsch en Fransch Woordenboek 2dln 2e druk* (Dordrecht, 1730) (with the seal of the *Kaiseijo* and the *kyuki* seal indicating that the book was previously in the collection of the Takahashi clan) (84–86); S.J.M. van Moock, *Nieuw Fransch-Nederduitsch en Nederduitsch-Fransch woordenboek. II deel (A–G), II deel, III stuk (O–R)*, Arnhem 1833–38. (nos. 2919, 2920), M.P. Poitevin, *Nouveau dictionnaire universel de la langue française*. Paris, 1860 (*Kaiseijo*) (747). One other dictionary, entirely in French, is dedicated to marine terminology, *Dictionnaire de la terminologie et des locutions de la marine à voile et à vapeur* (no. 3365). This was printed in St. Petersburg in 1853.

91 The catalogue has 'Williamus' instead of Kilianus, but this is incorrect. A sample entry is 'eighth' 'achtste octavus le huictiesme'.

The Ueno collection also includes several French learners and grammars. One that catches the eye is listed as *Livre pour l'instruction dans l'école Kaiceizio à Yedo 1. édition. Yedo. En l'an 2. Kei-au* (no. 3611). This was printed in Edo for the teaching of French at the *Kaiseijo*.[92] This suggests that at a certain point demand for learning French outstripped the ability to import French learners. 'Kei-au' or Keiō (慶応) 2 is 1866/7, so this is only twelve years after the Convention of Kanagawa. Finally, the Ueno collection includes several books in French. Some of these are on law, reflecting the Japanese desire to adopt a Western legal framework.[93] Other books do not easily fall into common categories, ranging from a history of France to an atlas of Java and a book on physics.[94]

13   English

Prior to 1800, English was a relatively unknown language in Japan. The pilot of the first Dutch ship to reach Japan, *De Liefde*, was the Englishman, Will Adams. He is unlikely to have used much English in the early years of his time in Japan. He knew Portuguese, probably some Dutch, and learnt Japanese. Nevertheless, he used English with employees of the English East India Company, not least Captain John Saris, whom he helped to obtain a trading

---

92   Other French learners and grammars in the Ueno catalogue are: four copies of the French learner: Pieter Marin, *Méthode familière pour ceux qui commencent à s'exercer dans la langue française, 9de druk.* Arnhem, 1851 (nos. 119, 578, 2584, 3097); Pieter Marin, *Nouvelle méthode pour apprendre les principes & l'usage des langues; Françoise et Hollandoise* door P. Marin en J.J. Gilbert. Amsterdam, 1790 (Seal of the *Bansho Shirabesho*) (117); M. Noël, *Nouvelle grammaire Française.* Paris 1862 (3612); and R. van der Pijl, *Fransch lees-vertaalboekje. 7de en 18de druk.* Dordrecht, 1853, 1859 (135, 136). This has the seal of the *Yōsho shirabesho* (洋書調所, 'Office for the Investigation of Western Books'), the successor to the *Bansho shirabesho*.

93   M. Eschbach, *Introduction générale à l'Etude du droit, 3 ed.*, Paris, 1856 (no. 3606), two copies of H. Wheaton, *Elements du droit international 2 tomes. 4ᵉ ed.* Leipzig. 1864 (3190, 3191), and M. Ortlan, *Explication historique des Instituts de l'Empéreur Justinien, 2 tomes, 8ᵉ ed.* Paris, 1870 (3101). These all have the seal of the *Daigaku Nankō*, one of predecessors of Tokyo University, mentioned above.

94   Pierre Braff, *Principes d'Administration Communale* (2nd ed., 1869) (no. 806); V. Duruy, *Histoire de France*, Paris, 1868 (no. 855, 3102); A. Ganot, *Traité Elémentaire de Physique 13ᵉ ed.* Paris, 1868 (seal of the *Daigaku Nankō* and the Tokyo *Kaiseijo*) (3111); François Noël and Michel de la Place, *Leçons françaises de littérature et de morale*, Brussels, 1857 (Seal of the censor's office of the Nagasaki *bugyō* and of the *Daigaku Nankō*) (3162), T.S. Raffles, *Carte de l'Ile de Java*, 2 toms. Brussels 1832 (Seal of the *Bansho shirabesho*) (831, 832).

pass from the shogunate. The English operated a trading post at Hirado for ten years from 1613. However, it was not commercially successful, and the trading post was closed in 1623 (Satow 1900).[95]

As noted above, in 1673, the English tried to start trading again with Japan. This attempt was unsuccessful and certainly did not lead to Japanese learning English. However, in the wake of the *Phaeton* incident in 1808 the Japanese authorities did begin to require interpreters to learn English.[96] The following year the *bakufu* ordered Motoki Shōei and other Nagasaki *tsūji* to study English (and Russian).[97] They learnt English from Jan Cock Blomhoff, who had served in England with his army regiment (Blomhoff 2000b: 10–11). Blomhoff's first turn of duty at Deshima was from 1809 to 1813. He would later serve as *opperhoofd* at Deshima from 1817 to 1823. In 1811, Shōei produced a ten-volume English learner and lexicon, *Angeria Kōgaku Shōsen* ('First Steps in the Study of English'), also called *Angeria Kokugo Wage*.[98] It begins by presenting the English alphabet with *katakana* superscript and then gives English words and phrases with Japanese equivalents.

The words are ordered thematically in the style of traditional Chinese reference works. On each page the words are in two columns. On the left of each column is an English word with *katakana* superscript to aid pronunciation with the Japanese equivalent in *kanji* on the right. So, for example, the first entry is 'Heaven' with *hēhen* (no diacritics and no 'v' in Japanese) above it, with 天 (*ten*, 'heaven') to the right. The phrases are written in cursive English with *katakana* superscript and *kanji* for meaning below (Kobe City Museum 1998: 82). As with Dutch learners supplemented with *katakana*, the *katakana* transcriptions of English words do not give a particularly close rendering of English pronunciation. For example, 'Sir, I thank you an eternal friend ship and whish ijou alwaijs to suplij fortune, fare well' (p. 415) is rendered in *katakana* as *Siru ai chanki yuu en eterunaru furinto shibbu ento wisu yuu aruweisu to shubburai horuteyun hare weru*. In the preface Shōei noted the similarity between written

95 See also Thompson (1883) and Farrington (1991). For a recent account of the English trading post, which challenges existing perceptions of the failure of this project, see Clulow (2013).

96 For a detailed account in Japanese of the study of English in Japan, see Toyoda (1969). See also Clements (2015: 178–179).

97 Cobbing (1998: 12) writes that six Nagasaki interpreters were ordered to learn English.

98 In 1825, Takahashi Kageyasu published *Angeriajin seijō shi* ('Account of the Nature of British People'), where *Angeriajin* combines the Latin word for 'England/Britain' and *jin*, the Sino-Japanese for person/people (Vanoverbeke 2016: 160). https://taweb.aichi-u.ac.jp/hayakawa/e-jdic.html provides a chronological list of Japanese-English dictionaries. Accessed 10 April 2020.

and spoken English (Twine 1991: 27).[99] In 1814, Shōei produced an expanded Japanese-English vocabulary *Angeria Gorin Taisei* ('Great Collection of English Vocabulary') (Clements 2015: 179). Neither work was published. Nowadays, the standard Japanese word for 'England' and indeed Britain is *Igirisu* (英吉利). However, in both cases *Angeria* (rendered as 諳厄利亜 in *ateji*) is used, which is presumably derived from the Latin *Anglia*.

Those who learnt English would have opportunities to use the language in the following years as ships from Anglophone countries probed Japanese shores. In 1818, Baba Teiyū was dispatched because of his knowledge of English when the British ship *The Brothers* entered Uraga Bay, near Tokyo, while in 1824 Takahashi Kageyasu was given the task of interrogating British whalers at Hitachi (Clements 2015: 156; Cobbing 1998: 13). Already in 1810, a Japanese placed an order with the Dutch for a bilingual English-Dutch dictionary. In 1814 orders were placed for four English dictionaries and three English grammars in Dutch, and in 1819 for two copies of Willem Sewel's Dutch-English dictionary (Nagazumi 1998: 10, 11–12, 15). In Batavia in 1830, the English missionary W.H. Medhurst (1796–1857) published an English-Japanese/Japanese-English vocabulary. He admits on the title page and in the introduction that he based his lexicon on 'native books' but provides no further details. The order of the words requires comment. In the English-Japanese section, they are grouped in the traditional Chinese *ten—chi—jin* order. The order from left to right is English word then Japanese in *rōmaji*, *katakana* and *kanji*, e.g., 'Heaven *Ten* テン 天'. The Japanese-English section is in *iroha* sequence, reading from left to right, Japanese *katakana*, some entries with *kanji*, a *rōmaji* transcription, followed by the English translation. So, while the Dutch and *rangakusha* lexicographers discussed in Chapter 2 were moving away from traditional modes of ordering words, Medhurst was keen to affirm them. There is a copy of the 1830 edition in the National Diet Library in Tokyo.[100] Further research may reveal when it was imported into Japan.[101]

One informative example of a *rangakusha* who would later learn English is that of Fukuzawa Yukichi. In his autobiography (Fukuzawa 2007), having described how he learnt Dutch in Nagasaki and then studied Dutch medicine at the *Tekijuku* in Osaka, he recounts how, having moved to Edo in the late 1850s he realized that English was becoming the most important European language.

---

99   Earns (1993: 135–139) provides a short overview of *Angeria Kōgaku Shōsen* and further examples of English phrases rendered in *katakana* in a similar manner.

100   NDL shelfmark 833-cM48e.

101   A copy in Leiden University Library belonged to Von Siebold (shelfmark 863 F 34). It includes German translations of the entries, possibly in the hand of J.J. Hoffmann, who owned it until it was acquired by Leiden University Library.

He therefore set to work learning that language through Dutch.[102] Another example of how quickly English became an important language in Japan after 1854 concerns Hayashi Michisaburō (林道三郎). He was one of a long line of Chinese interpreters who could trace their descent to a Chinese, Lin Gongyan (林公琰, 1598–1683) (Lin and Hayashi are the Chinese and Japanese readings respectively of 林), who arrived in Nagasaki as part of the Fuqing diaspora (Jiang Wu 2015: 104–105). Michisaburō, who died in 1873, learnt English as well as Chinese (Kornicki 2018: 93).

As Japan opened up after 1854, further aids to learning English were developed such as 'A New Familiar Phrases of the English and Japanese Languages', compiled anonymously and printed in Nagasaki in 1859. The focus, as the title suggests, is on everyday phrases such as 'Good day' and 'What will you buy?' though the English is sometimes a little awkward, as witnessed by a phrase such as 'I come to buy something'.[103] The learning of English in the first few years after 1854 was still somewhat limited. In 1858, there were about a dozen students learning English at the *Bansho shirabesho*. In Nagasaki only three or four *bakufu* interpreters were learning the language from Dutch interpreters. At *han* level, an early example of English tuition was in Hizen near Nagasaki, which was underway by 1859 (Cobbing 1998: 174). The Dutch physician Pompe van Meerdervoort recorded that in the early 1860s some English and American missionaries were giving English lessons.[104] At this time, Christianity was still officially banned, so missionaries probably used the provision of language lessons as a cover for their proselytizing work. The publication of an English-language newspaper, 'The Nagasaki Express', began weekly in 1870.[105]

Branches of the Asiatic Society in Japan opened in Tokyo, Yokohama and elsewhere, which seem to have been predominantly Anglophone. As noted in the prologue, on 14 February 1877 Mr. K. Mitsukuri gave an address to the Asiatic Society in Japan in Yokohama. He was a member of the famous Mitsukuri family of scholars that included the late Edo *rangakusha* Mitsukuri Genpo (1799–1863). The speech was entitled 'The early study of Dutch in Japan' and was subsequently published in English. There is no indication that this

---

102   See also Rubinger (1982: 136–152).

103   The subtitle was 'General Use for the Merchant of the Both Countries' (Earns 1993: 139–143; Sugimoto 1989: 170–172).

104   It is not completely clear if Pompe van Meerdervoort (1867–68: 1:287) is referring to Edo or Nagasaki here, but it seems to be the former.

105   Van der Velde (2000: 27) refers to an article (by a Dutchman in English) dated 29 January 1870, giving a *terminus ante quem* for the start of the 'Nagasaki Express'.

is a translation, so the possibility is there that we have a Japanese addressing Britons and Americans in English in 1877.[106]

The Ueno collection contains a significant number of English lexicons, learners and grammars, often in Dutch, illustrating the shift from Dutch to English and that knowledge of English was often acquired through Dutch. Furthermore, it includes several books in English. I have identified twenty-two lexicons in the Ueno collection in which one of the languages is English. Most of these dictionaries are bilingual with the other language being Dutch.[107] One dictionary is French-English, to add to the one mentioned above, and another is a quadrilingual English, Dutch, French and German dictionary.[108] Most of the dictionaries have the seal of the *Bansho shirabesho* and its successor institutions such as the *Kaiseijo*.

The collection also includes almost thirty English learners and grammars. Several of these are in Dutch, again illustrating that English was often taught

---

106 Mitsukuri (1877). In the introduction to the journal in which Mitsukuri's speech is published, there is a list of members of the Asiatic Society of Japan in 1877/8. We only find a few Japanese names in a list of over 100 members.

107 D. Bomhoff, *Nederlandsch-Engelsch & Engelsch-Nederlandsch zakwoordenboek. 2de druk*, Arnhem, 1857 (no. 826); Bomhoff, *A New Dictionary of the English and Dutch Language*, *4th ed.*, Nijmegen, 1851 (677); two copies of Bomhoff, *Nieuw Grootwoordenboek der Nederlandsche Taal*, Leiden, 1858 (673, 676); two copies of William/Willem Sewel, *A Compleat Dictionary English and Dutch*, Amsterdam, 1766 (48, 49); Sewel, *Groot woordenboek der Nederduitsche en Engelsche taalen*, Amsterdam, 1708 (75); two copies of Sewel, *A Large Dictionary, English and Dutch, 2 dln, 4de druk.* Amsterdam, 1749 (73, 74); two copies of John Holtroy, *English and Dutch dictionary; Engelsch en Nederduitsch woordenboek*, Amsterdam, 1823–24 (3099, 3098); A. Jaeger, *New dictionary of the English and Dutch, and Dutch and English languages*, Gouda (undated) (95); B. Janson, *New pocket-dictionary of English and Dutch languages*, Dordrecht, 1881 (3350); three copies of. H. Picard, *A New Pocket Dictionary of the English and Dutch languages*, 2nd ed. Zalt-Bommel, 1857 (90, 3595, 3596); A.J. Hillebrand, *Woordenboekje voor landverhuizers; of eerste beginselen om het Engelsch te leeren spreken, 2nd ed.*, Groningen, 1848 (2562, 2566); N.S. Calish, *A New Dictionary of the English and Dutch Languages*, The Hague, 1855 (no. 88); *Nieuw woordenboek der Nederduitsche en Engelsche taal [...] Op nieuw bewerkt en aanzienlijk vermeerderd door D. Bomhoff II. Deel Nederduitsch-Engelsche vierde uitgave*, Nijmegen, 1851 (no. 92). This includes the seal of the *Kanagawa Kaisho* ('Office'), the censor for books imported through nearby Yokohama.

108 J. Wilson, *French and English dictionary*, London, 1867 (seals of the *Kaiseijo* and the Numazu military school) (748), and the quadrilingual *Nieuw Woordenboek der Nederduitsche, Fransche, Hoogduitsche en Engelsche Talen, tweede Uitgave vermeerderd en verbeterd door N.S. Calisch*, The Hague, 1854 (no. 89). This has the seals of the *bakufu* and the Tokyo *Kaiseijo*, which followed on from the *Bansho shirabesho* and was a forerunner of Tokyo University.

and learnt through Dutch in the years following 1854.[109] Of particular note are eight copies of *Engelsche spraakkunst* ('English grammar') (6th edition, 1852) by Lindley Murray and Frederick Cowan;[110] three copies of each of two editions of J.J. de Hollander's *Handleiding bij de beoefening der Engelsche Taal* ('Manual for practising the English language') (1850s) (nos. 1403, 1673, 1674, 2298, 2610 and 2653); three copies of each of the first and second courses of E. Gerdes, *Nieuwe Leerwijze der Engelsche Taal* ('New Method for Learning the English Language') printed in Amsterdam in 1854 and 1855 (nos. 1114, 2439, 2453, 2437, 2438, 2452); and five copies of *Nieuwe Engelsche spraakkunst* ('New English grammar'), based on an English grammar by H.E. Lloyd (Arnhem, 1855, nos. 2290–2294). Also of note are editions of Roelof van der Pijl's English learner and grammar printed in Dordrecht.[111] The 1854 Dutch edition was re-printed in Nagasaki in 1857. The Ueno collection has one copy of the Nagasaki re-print.[112] The collection includes three copies of Reinier van der Pijl's *A practical grammar of the Dutch language* (Rotterdam, 1819) (nos. 1750, 2002, 2126). There are no seals in the copies of this book, so we do not know when they reached Japan, but it is certainly interesting and unexpected that the collection includes a Dutch learner in English. Over time, it is likely that Dutch no longer played a role in the acquisition of English. This may explain the presence of four copies of G.P. Quackenbos's *First book in English grammar* (New York, 1867, nos. 3507, 3508, 3605, 3632) in the Ueno collection.

Several of the Dutch books in the Ueno collection were translated out of English. There are also many books in the collection written in English. The earliest date of publication is 1828, although we often do not know when books reached Japan. This is *The nautical almanac and astronomical ephemeris* for

---

109 K.G. Clairmont, *Handboek tot het Voeren van Engelsche Gesprekken*, Amsterdam, 1861 (no. 680), H.A. Hamelberg, *Beknopte Engelsche spraakkunst*, Dordrecht, 1845 (no. 2949), T. Knuivers, *Beknopte orthoepie of uitspraakleer der Engelsche taal*, Amsterdam, 1862 (no. 2473), Willem Locke, *Spiegel der Engelsche taal; of students wegwijzer*, Rotterdam, 1801 (131), E. Peel, *Nieuwe practische en gemakkelijke leerwijze ter beoefening der Engelsche taal. iste deel*, Utrecht, 1855 (2651).

110 The eight copies of *Engelsche spraakkunst door Lindley Murray en F.M. Cowan 6de druk*, Zalt-Bommel. 1852, have the Ueno collection numbers, 110, 118, 130, 813, 1911, 1209, 1896 and 1904. The collection also includes Lindley Murray's, *English grammar*, London, 1861 (no. 749).

111 R. van der Pijl, *Gemeenzame leerwijs, voor degenen, die de Engelsche taal beginnen te leeren. 2de uitgave*, Dordrecht, 1822 (644); *Van der Pijl's gemeenzame leerwijs, voor degenen die de Engelsche taal beginnen te leeren, door R. van der Pijl verbeterd door H. Schuld*, Dordrecht, 1854 (no. 118).

112 *Van der Pijl's gemeenzame leerwijs, voor degenen die de Engelsche taal beginnen te leeren.* Dordrecht, 1854. *Nagedrukt te Nagasaki in het 4de Jaar van Ansei* (1857) (no. 639). This has the seals of the Nagasaki Censor (*bugyō*'s office), the *Kaiseijo* and the *bakufu*.

the year 1828 (no. 243). Another volume in this series, published in 1829 (244), is also in the collection. Both volumes were published in London, as was Robert Chambers's *Political Economy for use in schools and for private instruction* (undated) (3594). Typically, however, the books in English in the Ueno collection were printed in the United States, above all New York and Washington. Several books relate to U.S. government and military matters, including *Ordnance instruction for the United States Navy* (4th ed. New York, 1866) (3514), *Reports of the Commissioner of Patents, agriculture*, for the years 1850–1858 and an army pay table (1862, no. 962), all printed in Washington. Several books provide introductions to various branches of science, while others deal with a range of topics such as the American Civil War, civil government and commercial navigation.[113] The catalogue of the library of the Asiatic Society in Tokyo compiled in 1878 includes several books for learning Japanese as well as a Japanese-English dictionary by Hepburn (Transactions of the Asiatic Society of Japan 1877–1878: 6(3), 536).

Figures presented by Shibatani (1990: 148) indicate that the influence of English on Japanese was rapid. By the Taishō era (大正, 1912–25), over half of the *gairaigo* in Japanese were English (51.9%), while just over a quarter (27.8%) were Dutch. The rapid rise in English, along with French and German, was mirrored by an equally rapid decline in the use of Dutch in the early Meiji period. This decline or shift and the reasons for it are analysed further in Chapter 8.

14 Conclusion

Despite the extensive range of languages analysed in this chapter, this may not necessarily be a complete list of languages that functioned in the same socio-semiotic context as Dutch. At Nagasaki, as well as *tōtsūji* for Chinese, there were also *tonkintsūji* for Vietnamese, *shamutsūji* for Thai and *mōrutsūji* for a

---

113 The books on science are William G. Peck, *Introductory Course of Natural Philosophy for the use of Schools and Academies*, New York, 1868 (3110); Benjamin Silliman, *Principles of Physics*, 2nd ed., Philadelphia, 1869 (3179); three copies of J.F. Johnson, *The Chemistry of Common Life*, 12th ed. New York, 1870 (3245, 3638, 3629); and D.A. Wells, *The Science of Common Things; familiar explanation of the first principles of physical science*, New York, 1865 (788). The other books are Frank Moore, *The Rebellion Record*, New York, 1861 (381, 380) (on the American Civil War); Calvin Townsend, *Analysis of Civil Government. 2nd ed.* New York, 1870 (3177); Homans J. Smith, *A Cyclopaedia of Commerce and Commercial Navigation*, New York, 1859 (400). Other books in English in the collection are Charles Davies, *Elements of descriptive geometry*, New York, 1870 (3521), Amos Dean, *Bryant and Stratton's commercial law for business men*, New York, 1868 (3225), and J. Haven, *Mental Philosophy; including the intellect, sensibilities, and will*, Boston, 1869 (3178).

language used by the Mughals.[114] Further investigation may reveal whether and to what extent there were points of contact between Dutch and these other languages, and if so, what the nature of that contact was.

This chapter has analysed twelve languages with which Dutch had a shared socio-semiotic context to a greater or lesser degree in Tokugawa and early Meiji Japan. While in some cases, there were few points of contact, in other cases we can talk of influence and indeed competition. In the case of Korean and Ainu, contact was limited and there is no evidence of influence. One might talk of competition to the extent that one user, Von Siebold, was using these languages instead of Dutch, but not competition in the sense generally understood by linguists. The case of Manchu is slightly different in that according to one scholar the manner in which translators such as Baba Teiyū approached Manchu was 'coloured' by their encounter with Dutch (Söderblom Saarela 2017: 388). There was not, however, influence in the form of lexical or syntactic interference.

Contact with Portuguese, Sinitic varieties and Japanese did result in influence. Users of Dutch inserted words from each of these in their texts. The influence of Chinese was, however, most keenly felt in the manner in which Japanese translators approached Dutch texts. As for competition, two points are in order. First, the languages that competed with Dutch changed over time. While some of these slowed its initial spread, others contributed to its decline. In the early years of the Dutch presence in Japan, the European language that provided Dutch with its strongest competition was Portuguese. Indeed, Portuguese continued to compete with Dutch for many years after the expulsion of native speakers in 1639. In the early nineteenth century, as a result of the perceived and actual threats posed by various European powers and America, Japanese began to learn European languages other than Dutch, above all English, French and Russian, but also Manchu. This is some sense foreshadows the eventual eclipse of Dutch in the early Meiji period analysed in Chapter 8.

Second, Dutch faced competition from different languages in different social spheres or domains. In the domain of commerce, it initially faced competition from Portuguese and later from other European languages. However, in the domain of learning, it was above all varieties of literary Sinitic that offered Dutch most competition. Nevertheless, it was often scholars trained in reading and translating Chinese texts, who were behind developments in *rangaku*.

---

114   Kornicki (2018: 94) suggests that this was a mixture of Persian and Hindi. One possibility is that this is a variety of Urdu. He also observes that having such interpreters was based on a perceived rather than actual need, primarily to deal with cases where ships might be blown off course.

This illustrates well the sometimes complex nature of the relationship between Dutch and other languages.

One final point is that a feature of the complex language environment in which Dutch functioned is that it came into contact with more than one variety of several languages. The case of Sinitic varieties points in this direction. Furthermore, while Low or creolized Portuguese was used (alongside Low Malay) among slaves and servants at the Dutch trading posts and onboard voc ships, something closer to the language of educated Portuguese was used for communication between Dutch and Japanese for much of the seventeenth century. Although it is a somewhat contested term, we can perhaps talk here of 'diglossia' in the sense of two varieties of a language being used in the same community (Joby 2015: 98; Burke: 2014).

In conclusion, the picture that emerges in this chapter is that Dutch had shared socio-semiotic contexts not only with Japanese, but also with several European and non-European languages. In other words, for much of the history of Dutch in Japan it functioned in a polyglossic or multilingual, rather than simply a monolingual or bilingual, environment. Subsequent chapters provide further examples of the outcomes of this contact. Contact with Japanese led to extensive interference from Dutch on a lexical, syntactic and indeed graphic level. Examples of this interference are analysed in Chapter 7. Contact between Dutch and the language varieties analysed in this chapter led to lexical interference in the Dutch used in Japan, primarily but by no means exclusively from Japanese. This is the subject of the next chapter.

Interference in Dutch Texts

1   Introduction

This chapter analyses the effect of contact with other languages on Dutch in Tokugawa Japan. Broadly speaking the linguistic phenomena resulting from such language contact can be called influence or 'interference' (Adams 2003: 27). Two types of interference in Dutch texts and utterances, produced by both native and non-native speakers, are code switching and 'gap-filling'.[1]

Code switching is a common feature of language contact situations (Schendl 2012: 523). It is, however, a linguistic phenomenon that is by no means easy to define, with one commentator going so far as to say that it can mean whatever we want it to mean (Gardner-Chloros 2009: 10–11). Nevertheless, several other commentators have attempted to define code switching. Simply put, it is the insertion of words or phrases from one language into an utterance that is primarily in another. Charlotte Hoffmann (1991: 110, quoted in Adams (2003: 19)) defines it as 'the alternate use of two languages or linguistic varieties within the same utterance or during the same conversation'. James Adams (2003: 19) uses the term 'to describe a full-blown switch from one language into another within one person's utterance or piece of writing'. A more complex definition is provided by Lim and Ansaldo (2015: 40–41). They define code switching as 'an alternation of languages within a conversation, usually at semantically or sociolinguistically meaningful junctures, which is associated with particular pragmatic effects, discourse functions, or associations with group identity'. Other commentators, too, focus on the 'discourse functions' of code switching. Taking his lead from work by Carol Myers-Scotton, Simon Swain (2002: 144) views code switching as part of an author's discourse strategy, expressing identities that he or she may wish to advance in an attempt to distinguish him or herself from other users of the language. In other words, in many cases code switching is a choice, rather than evidence of inadequate linguistic control (Swain 2002: 128). In his analysis of code switching in antiquity, Adams (2003: 410–413) writes that there was nothing accidental or unintentional about the switching between Latin and Greek in Cicero's correspondence with Atticus.

---

1 Another related term which could be used here is 'cross-linguistic influence' (Winford 2003: 12).

© CHRISTOPHER JOBY, 2021 | DOI:10.1163/9789004438651_007

Implicit in such code switching is the fact that the author or speaker is bilingual to a greater or lesser extent. A desire to exhibit this forms part of the discourse strategy.

As for 'gap-filling', this occurs where terms do not currently exist in the matrix language, in this case Dutch, for things such as new technologies or concepts (Swain 2002: 143–144). This is also one of the motivations for loanword borrowing. One difference between loanwords and many of the examples presented below is that while loanwords can be inserted by users of the matrix language who do not have any level of bilingualism, those who inserted non-Dutch words in their Dutch texts in Japan were often to some extent bilingual (Swain 2002: 143–146). Some of the examples below occur regularly and over an extensive period and seem to have become 'embedded' in the variety of Dutch used on Deshima. Others, by contrast, may only have been used a few times for a short period. However, given the fragmentary nature of the available evidence, the extent of usage is difficult if not impossible to judge. Therefore, there will only be the occasional attempt to make a firm distinction between loanwords and other lexical interference for the purpose of gap-filling (Adams 2003: 18–19).

It could be argued that the gap-filling analysed in this chapter is a subset of code switching. However, in what follows, they will be treated separately, with code switching being used for instances of interference which are part of a discourse strategy. Nevertheless, here too the distinction is not absolute and there will be a certain amount of overlap. In some cases, it will be argued that authors engaging in gap-filling could have used a Dutch term or a circumlocution. For example, several authors insert the Japanese word *hayafune*, a type of fast boat, into their texts. They could have used a Dutch circumlocution such as 'snelle boot' ('fast boat'), but chose to use the Japanese term, perhaps simply to indicate that they knew this. In this regard, 'gap-filling' is part of an author's discourse strategy. Part of the problem here is terminology, and this study is by no means alone in this regard. As Suzanne Romaine (1995: 180) writes 'Problems of terminology continue to plague the study of language contact phenomena with terms such as code-switching, mixing [and] borrowing not being used by all researchers in the same way or even defined at all'. In this chapter, gap-filling in Dutch texts will be analysed thematically. Authors of these texts inserted words for objects which can be categorized as, for example, musical instruments, coins, weights and measures, items of clothing, food and drink and modes of transport.

In analysing the lexical interference in Dutch texts, several issues arise. One of these is that Dutch came into contact with more than one language. While most of the examples analysed involve interference from Japanese, this is by no means the whole story. Latin, Portuguese, Sinitic varieties and Malay are among the other contact languages concerned, and examples of interference from each are given below in section 2. With reference to interference from Japanese, another issue is phonology. To what extent were Japanese words integrated into the Dutch sound system and to what extent did authors of Dutch texts need to accommodate their orthography to account for differences in the respective sound systems? And how did they do this? In trying to answer such questions, we face several challenges. One is a lack of orthographical consistency between authors and even within texts written by the same author. Another is that authors did not necessarily accurately represent what was said. On the other hand, certain orthographical patterns emerge which tell us something about how Japanese words were pronounced and how this varies from modern pronunciation. Here, work on renderings of Japanese toponyms in early modern Western maps of Japan by Michel (2012) will be instructive, as will work on Japanese phonology by Labrune (2012) and Frellesvig (2010).

Another issue concerns morphology. To what extent and how did authors integrate words from other languages into the Dutch morphological system? Did they, for example, give words from Japanese and other languages Dutch plural and case suffixes, and if so which ones? Or did they leave these words uninflected? These and other questions are addressed in section 7 on morphological integration.

Much of the secondary literature on these language contact phenomena focusses on the spoken language. This chapter, however, analyses interference in written texts. One problem with referring to the secondary literature on switching and other contact phenomena in speech is that this often analyses cases where there is one matrix and one donor language. In the present context, there were several donor languages. Furthermore, whereas the analysis in studies of the spoken language is typically quantitative, given the nature of the available sources the analysis below will necessarily be predominantly qualitative. This is something we find in analyses of interference in other written texts (e.g., Adams 2003). On the other hand, an analysis of written sources overcomes one of the major obstacles faced by those who investigate switching in speech, namely 'the observer's paradox' (Swain 2002: 145). It almost goes without saying that those who wrote the Dutch sources discussed below did not anticipate that their language would be analysed for instances of language interference. An important contribution to the study of contact phenomena in written sources is James Adams's (2003: esp. Ch. 3) analysis of bilingualism and code switching in ancient Latin texts.[2] Adams analyses code switching in these texts by motivation, which in some sense flows from the notion that this phenomenon is part of an author's discourse strategy. In the present chapter, too, code switching is analysed by motivating factors. These include switching for the purpose of dating texts, quoting direct speech and giving a proverb in another language.

1.1 Sources

Many of the examples analysed in this chapter come from the *dagregisters*, the factory journals kept meticulously by the *opperhoofden* at Hirado and Deshima, or, in his absence, his deputy. The code switching in the *dagregisters* conforms to a more general pattern observed by Schendl (2012: 527) that historically administrative texts have often included code switching. Other sources include correspondence, such as that between Isaac Titsingh and the *rangakusha* Kutsuki Masatsuna, and personal accounts of life in Japan. These include journals written by Titsingh and later, in the years after 1854, by the diplomat Jonkheer Dirk de Graeff van Polsbroek. As this is a historical study, we only have written evidence for code switching. The occasional metalinguistic comment, however, is suggestive of switching in speech.

An attempt is made, as far as possible, to use only sources written in Japan. In some cases, however, above all those involving private published journals, it is not clear to what extent texts were composed inside or outside Japan. One pertinent example is Johannes van Overmeer Fisscher's *Bijdrage tot de Kennis van het Japanse Rijk*, which has been described as 'a descriptive ethnographic study of Japan'. Overmeer Fisscher, who had worked at Deshima for most of the 1820s, made extensive notes during his time in Japan including the 1822 *hofreis*, which features prominently in his book (Effert 2008: 88, 103, 106). On his return to the Netherlands, he worked these notes into a catalogue for an exhibition of the objects that he had brought back from Japan. This catalogue formed the basis of the *Bijdrage*, which he published in Amsterdam in 1833. Therefore, in this and similar cases, judicious reference is made to such sources.

Other cases are more clear-cut. The letters that Isaac Titsingh wrote to Japanese associates after he had left Japan are one salient example. Many of these are masterpieces of code switching, driven by his thirst for knowledge about all things Japanese. So, although many of his letters have been excluded, I have made one or two exceptions. A good example of Titsingh's switching is a letter that he wrote from Chinsura, Bengal in 1785/6 to several of his interpreter-*rangakusha* friends in Nagasaki (Lequin 1990: 11:550–557). He asks

---

2 See also Joby (2014: esp. Ch. 6).

his correspondents to give him the name of the new era (*Nengo* 年号) in Japan, if there is one: 'Indien de *Nengo* verandert wordt gelieft my de naam van de nieuwe op te geeven' (my italics). He also asks them to explain names 'in het tweede boek van de Nifonki', i.e., in the second book of the *Nihon Shoki* (日本書紀, 'The Chronicles of Japan', also called *Nihongi*). He then produces a 75-line riot of code switching between Dutch and Japanese in *rōmaji*, e.g., 'het zwaard *Tosoeka no Tsoerogi*.... de boom *Iasoe* ... wat verstaad men door de visch *akama*' (my italics for Japanese). Further examples abound. It is tempting to think that Titsingh had conversations with the interpreter-*rangakusha* replete with similar switching, but currently we have no firm evidence for this.

2   Contact Languages Other than Japanese

Most of the examples of language contact phenomena analysed in this chapter involve Japanese words and phrases. However, Dutch authors did switch into or borrow from other languages to fill gaps including Latin, Portuguese, varieties of Chinese (Sinitic varieties) and Malay.

2.1   *Latin*

Some of the senior employees at the Dutch trading post had a classical education. Occasionally, they insert a Latin word or phrase into their Dutch, something authors in the Dutch Republic did, too. For example, it was common at least in the early years of the *dagregister* for authors to begin entries with *Adij*. This is a corruption of the Latin *Ad diem* 'on this day'. In the late 1640s, Dirck Snoeck (*opperhoofd* 1648/49) wrote *Adij 28en. 's Morgens quamen alle de tolcken, demptis Dimbe*, i.e., 'On this day, the 28th, in the morning, all the interpreters came, except Dimbe' (probably Inomata Denbei (also transcribed Denbē)), where *demptis* is a Latin word used to mean 'except' (the alliteration may have appealed to Snoeck) (*Diaries*: XI:145).[3] 'Year' was often written with the Latin *A*[*nn*]*o* ('in the year').

Other *opperhoofden* also peppered their Dutch with Latin. Willem Verstegen (*opperhoofd* 1646–47) inserted *de novo* (Latin, 'once again') into his Dutch text in 1646 (*Diaries*: X:4). Dirck Snoeck begins an entry in 1649 'Quamen de tolcken *in omnibus*', i.e., 'all the interpreters came' (*Diaries*: XI:185). Several Dutch authors insert Latin quotations into their texts. In the *dagregister* for 1654,

---

3   *Demptis* is in fact an ablative plural past participle. It is rarely used in this manner as a preposition.

Gabriel Happart (*opperhoofd* 1653/54) quoted the second line of a distich from *Collectio distichorum vulgaris* (II.18) ('The Common Collection of Distiches'), traditionally ascribed to Cato the Younger because of his censorious reputation, although the actual authorship is not known (Vermeulen *et al.* 1986–: XII:133).[4] The context was a discussion of the civilities such as bowing and stooping that he and his companions were required to perform when they arrived in Edo. The full distich runs:

> Insipiens esto, cum tempus postulat aut res:
> Stultitiam simulare loco, prudentia summa est.
>
> [Act the fool, when time or circumstance require,
> To fake stupidity at the right moment is the most prudent thing to do.]

The *Collectio* was a compendium of practical ethics considered to be 'safe-reading' for young students of Latin in the Middle Ages and Renaissance. So, Happart probably encountered it at Latin school in the Dutch Republic (Duff and Duff 1934: 585).[5] It may be its apophthegmatic quality that appealed to Happart. A little further on, he inserts another Latin apophthegm: in Edo he was given a gift of thirty gowns, which, it was expected, he and his fellow Dutchmen would wear. In recounting this clothes switching, he also engaged in code switching, writing 'Si fueris romae, romano vivito more' ('If you are in Rome, live in the Roman manner': in other words, 'When in Rome ...'), part of a saying ascribed to St. Ambrose (4th C. AD). The people most likely to read the *dagregister* were Happart's successors as *opperhoofd*, who consulted previous entries when deciding how to deal with questions and challenges posed by Japanese. One reason for switching into Latin was to emphasize the shared educational background of author and reader (Joby 2014: 271). Happart had matriculated at Leiden University to read philosophy in April 1632 (Du Rieu 1875: col. 242). Furthermore, an element of self-promotion was probably also at work, in other words it was part of his discourse strategy. A later Dutch author who switched into Latin for the purpose of quotation was the merchant Cornelis Assendelft de Coningh, who was in Yokohama in around 1860. He wrote to the Dutch consul that he could not expect to be greeted with 'Ave

---

4 Happart's version runs 'Stultitiam simulare loco est summa prudentia'.
5 Little seems to be known about Happart, but it is likely he came from a family of Protestant ministers.

consules' in Yokohama and then send him to Kanagawa like a gladiator of the Caesars sentenced to death (Assendelft de Coningh 2012: 44).[6]

One Japanese who switched into Latin was the Nagasaki interpreter, Narabayashi Jūbei. Some code switching involves the addition of a tag or formula to a statement in another language (Adams 2003: 21–24). This, unsurprisingly, is referred to as 'tag-switching'.[7] Jūbei seems to include a tag-switch in a letter to the learned Dutchman, Isaac Titsingh, when he signs off with *'door groot haast, vaale'*, i.e., 'in great haste, *vale*' ('goodbye' in Latin) (Lequin 1990: 1:12). He may have learnt this word from Titsingh and switching to Latin would have been a way to seal the bond of friendship.

2.2   *Portuguese*

Although the Portuguese were expelled from Japan in 1639, we still find traces of their language in Dutch texts after this date. In early Dutch versions of the *Oranda fūsetsugaki*, the annual report on external affairs, which the Dutch compiled for the Japanese authorities, we regularly find the word *novos* for 'news' from the Portuguese (Iwao 1976–79: II:275, 24 July 1641). In the 1647 version of the *fūsetsugaki*, the word *novelles* (probably from French or another Romance language) is used (Iwao 1976–79: II:278). In 1646, Willem Verstegen refers to the interpreters being sent to the Governor of Nagasaki 'met *complementos* van danckbaarheyt' (lit. 'with complements of gratitude'). *Complementos* is a Portuguese word for 'complements' (*Diaries*: x:4). Earlier, in 1634 the *opperhoofd* Nicolaes Couckebakker referred to a Portuguese nobleman in Japan using the appropriate Portuguese word *fidalgo* (*Diaries*: I:195). In the previous year, 1633, when discussing Tonkin (in modern-day Vietnam), Couckebakker wrote *dit landt meest geregeert werdt van* **cappados** *die geen kinderen genereren* ('this country is mainly ruled by eunuchs who have no children') (*Diaries*: I:7, my bold).[8] Why Couckebakker used the Portuguese word for 'eunuchs', *ca(p)-pados*, is not clear, given that Dutch has several words for them, such as *castraat* and *eunuch*.[9] One possibility is that it was for the purpose of euphemism, i.e., he wanted to avoid the directness of the term in his own language, although another possibility is simply that the Portuguese term had entered the

---

6   This is probably a reference to the apocryphal 'Ave Caesar, morituri salutamus' ('Hail Caesar, we who are about to die greet you').

7   Similarly, intrasentential switching takes place *within* the boundaries of a sentence or clause, while intersentential switching, which takes place *at* the boundaries of sentence or clause.

8   Couckebakker also wrote *kapade* and *kapado*, a good example of how spelling at this time was by no means standardized.

9   Spanish also has *capados*. However, given the greater presence of the Portuguese in Japan, it is more likely to have been borrowed from their language, rather than Spanish.

common currency of European languages in Japan.[10] Both of these examples may also suggest that Verstegen and Couckebakker switched into Portuguese from time to time when speaking.

Given that the Portuguese were the first Europeans to trade with Japan and other countries in East Asia, it is to be expected that some of the commercial vocabulary that the Dutch used was borrowed from Portuguese. One example is *pancado*. Originally, this referred to buying and selling wholesale, but it came to refer specifically to the determination of the fixed price at which raw Chinese silk was purchased in Japan, *ito wappu* (糸割符) in Japanese (Blussé and Remmelink 2004: 809). In 1633, Couckebakker wrote 'de *pancado* van de rouwe zijde was geslooten' ('the *pancado* of raw silk was fixed') and complained about having to sell silk at a low price *onder pancado* (below the *pancado*) (*Diaries*: I:11, 58). The Dutch continued to use the term after the Portuguese had been expelled. In 1649, Dirck Snoeck switches from Dutch to refer to the fixing of the *pancado* (he writes *pencado*) (*Diaries*: XI:185). In 1647, the word is rendered *pankado*, which in some sense integrates it into the orthography of Dutch, as 'k' is typically not used in Portuguese orthography (*Diaries*: X:153). One form of lexical interference that occurs quite often in Dutch texts is hybrid words, where, typically, one part is Dutch and the other Japanese. However, there are other language combinations. For example, one hybrid word formed with *pancado* was *pancadozijde* (pancado-silk), which combines the Portuguese *pancado* and the Dutch *zijde* (*Diaries*: X:210).

A related word of Portuguese origin in the early *dagregisters* is *bietcho*. This comes from *bicho* (*da seda*), which means 'silkworm'. It is used in the collocation *premiere bietcho* which refers to the best silk in a harvest (*Diaries*: I:288).[11] *Barigo/a* is the Portuguese or Spanish for a type of silk from Southern India sold by the Dutch in Japan (*Diaries*: XII:196). The word *comprado(o)r*, from the Portuguese meaning 'buyer', is used in Dutch texts to mean both 'merchants', who belonged to the *konpura nakama* (コンプラ仲間, 'Guild of Compradors') and, in the singular, the Nagasaki *bugyō*. He was appointed by the shogun to ensure that income from trade went directly to his master and was not distributed locally. Authors of the *dagregister* typically use it to refer to merchants with whom they trade: the *opperhoofd* Andreas Cleyer (1985: 77) refers to *compradoors* on 1 January 1683. The word seems to have become embedded in the Dutch used on Deshima. In 1851 on his first visit to the island,

---

10   For further examples of code switching for the purpose of euphemism, see Joby (2014: 229–231).

11   Also spelt *bitjos* (*Diaries*: I:11).

Assendelft de Coningh noted its use, asserting that it specifically referred to the Japanese merchants who were permitted to trade with the Dutch (Assendelft de Coningh 1879: 19; 2012: 18–19). Several early authors switch to refer to a *feetor* (spelt variously). This comes from the Portuguese *feitor* and means 'factor' (*Diaries*: III:63).[12] The Portuguese had built up their commercial empire in the sixteenth and seventeenth centuries using *feitorias*.

On the *hofreis* of 1647, the *opperhoofd* Verstegen was interviewed by several senior Japanese about the Netherlands and above all medicine. Verstegen records that the Japanese wanted to know about the healing properties of bezoar and *pedroporck*. This is a corruption of *pedra de porco*, the Portuguese term for the gallstone of a pig, which was known as an antidote (*Diaries*: x:80). In the early *dagregisters*, the word *caseres* is inserted in the Dutch text. This refers to assistants of the *otona*, the local official with oversight of the Dutch trading post at Deshima. This probably comes from the Portuguese *caseiro*, someone who does work in the house (*casa*) (*Diaries*: v:147).[13] Several toponyms are referred to by names given by the Portuguese. One of these is an alternative name for Taiwan, Formosa, from the Portuguese *Ilha Formosa* ('Beautiful island'). Another is the name for islands to the west of Taiwan. They are sometimes called the Penghu Islands, a corruption of the Southern Min name for them. However, the Dutch often used the name 'Piscadores', from the Portuguese *Ilhas dos Pescadores* ('Islands of the Fishermen') (*Diaries*: x:32). In 1650, Antonio van Bronckhorst (*opperhoofd* 1649/50) refers to the island of Iōjima (伊王島), which is a small island at the entrance to Nagasaki Bay. He calls it *Ilies Cavale*, from the Portuguese *Ilha(s) dos cavalhos*, meaning 'island(s) of horses' (the plural may cover the neighbouring Okino Island as well) (*Diaries*: XII:77; Boxer 1951: 412). Some of the words just mentioned could be Portuguese or Spanish. One term that is clearly Spanish is *Mestre del Campo* ('Field general'). In 1649, Willem Verstegen inserts it into his Dutch text to refer to Ōno Harunaga (1569–1615), a general in the army of Toyotomi Hideyoshi, Lord of Osaka (*Diaries*: XI:128).

2.3   *Sinitic Varieties*

Dutch authors occasionally switched into Sinitic varieties. This was above all in relation to commercial activities involving Chinese merchants, and so these were probably vernacular varieties rather than the literary Sinitic varieties

---

12   For the use of this term in Portuguese commercial expansion, see Subrahmanyam (2012: 49–52).

13   The Japanese word for the *caseres/caseros* is *kumigashira* (組頭) (Blussé and Remmelink 2004: 805).

discussed in Chapter 4.[14] A *sampan* (三板) is a small vessel used to transport goods between ships at anchor and Deshima. It comes from a Sinitic variety, possibly Cantonese.[15] Dirck Snoeck refers to an *oude champan* ('old sampan'), which the *bugyō* was planning to replace (*Diaries*: XI:34). We cannot be certain how he would have pronounced the word-initial consonant, but one possibility is as the unvoiced fricative /ʃ/. If so, he may have derived his rendering from contact with Chinese merchants in Kyushu speaking northern Sinitic varieties. In *pinyin*, one rendering of the word is *shānbǎn*.

A word of Chinese origin for a medium-sized sea-going junk is often inserted into Dutch texts in a Malay form, *wankang* (Blussé and Remmelink 2004: 412).[16] Here, the boundaries between code switching and borrowing become blurred. In the prologue, I introduced the notion of 'Dutches' (Burke 2005: 5). The lexicon of the Dutch used on Deshima differed somewhat from that of the Dutches used in the Low Countries. As I have already suggested, we could view this variety as a Dutch topolect or *nesolect* ('island language'), used on Deshima or Kyushu, or even a *polilect* (< Ancient Greek πόλις 'town'), i.e., the Dutch spoken in Nagasaki, including Deshima. In this view of things, *wankang* was often used in Dutch texts written in Japan and so could be understood as an example of a Chinese loanword in the lexicon of this Dutch *nesolect*. Pushing this idea a little further, we could talk in terms of a Dutch *emporiolect* (trading language) or *thalassolect* (sea language) in East Asia, in which *wankang* could also be viewed as a loanword. Another type of Chinese ship to which the Dutch referred were 'junks'. Some authors, such as Andreas Cleyer, rendered these as *joncq* (Cleyer 1985: 67). However, several other authors refer to *jonckjens*, which would appear to be a Dutch plural diminutive form (*-jens*), while elsewhere we find the diminutive form *jonckje*, which illustrates that code switching was by no means consistent (*Diaries*: X:8 (*jonckjens*); XI:140 (*jonckje*)). The etymology of the word is unclear. According to the *WNT* it was originally a Javanese word (*djong*).

The Dutch needed to render Chinese toponyms. One example is 'Hocchio'. This refers to Fuzhou/Foochow (福州), a port in Southern China facing Taiwan (*Diaries*: X:8). Another example is 'Siousan', which refers to Zhoushan (舟山), a port near Shanghai (*Diaries*: XI:140). 'Amu' and 'Aijmuij' render Amoy in

---

14 For the contrast between literary and vernacular Sinitic varieties, see Clements (2015: 99–102).

15 Cantonese 三板 = 'three planks' (Blussé and Remmelink 2004: 811).

16 The precise origin of the term is not clear. One possibility is that it comes from the Sinitic *huáng chuán* or *gāng* (艎舡).

Southern China. This is the Hokkien name for the port city known in Mandarin Chinese as Xiamen (廈門) (*Diaries*: X:127; I:12).

2.4 *Malay and Persian*

Other languages into which authors of Dutch texts switched include Malay and Persian. One word borrowed from Malay was *kuli*, rendered by Dutch authors as *koelie*, which refers to a day labourer. Overmeer Fisscher (1833: 279) records that on the 9th and 11th days of the ninth month *kugatsu* (九月) (he writes *Kfoeguats*), *de geringste Koelie is dan als een Heer* ('the lowest coolie is treated then as a Lord'). In fact, it seems Malay derived *kuli* in turn from an Indian language, possibly Tamil.[17] A *gantang*, which appears regularly in the *dagregister*, is a unit of volume for rice and wet goods, such as wine. This derives from Malay or Javanese (Lohanda *et al.* 2018: 64; *WNT*; Vermeulen *et al.* 1986–: XIII:372–374). On a different note, Vos (1971: 631) asserts that as well as adopting Western manners such as shaking hands, using Western umbrellas and drinking coffee, *Orandayuki* would mix Dutch and Malay words in their conversation along, one presumes, with Japanese.[18] Finally, although Dutch did not have contact with Persian in Japan, trade with Persia inevitably meant that Persian words would become part of the VOC vocabulary. One example is *takht-i-rawan*, a movable throne, which the Dutch were planning to order. This was inserted into the Dutch of the *dagregister* by Gabriel Happart in November 1653 (Vermeulen *et al.* 1986–: XII:125).

3   Phonological Issues

In what follows, most of the examples involve Japanese words, or hybrid words of which one component is Japanese. While a detailed account of the phonological issues arising from this switching is beyond the scope of this book, a word is in order about issues arising from how authors of Dutch texts graphically realized Japanese terms. Here, work by Michel (2012) on how Japanese toponyms were graphically realized in early modern Western maps of Japan will be instructive.

First, several phonological traits suggested by the Dutch renderings of Japanese words have disappeared in cMJ or are limited to dialectal varieties. One example is that for most of the Edo period (1603–1868) the word-initial sounds 'ha', 'he' and 'ho' were produced as voiceless bilabial fricatives, i.e.,

---

17   In Tamil, *kūli-k-kāraṇ* means 'day labourer' (Lohanda *et al.* 2018: 96). See also *WNT*.
18   See also Assendelft de Coningh (1856: 46).

[ɸ].[19] So, Willem Verstegen rendered Hakata as *Facatta*, Hirado as *Firando* and the name of the interpreter (Namura) Hachizaemon as Fatsesaymon (*Diaries*: X:9, 13). Likewise, Nicolaes Couckebakker rendered the name Machiya Hachiroemon as 'Matsia Fatseraijemon' (*Diaries*: 1:8).

The rendering of Hirado as *Firando*, with the insertion of the grapheme ⟨n⟩, illustrates another feature of early modern Japanese, which was a tendency to nasalize vowels before voiced plosives like g, d, b, giving rise to prenasalization (e.g., *Diaries*: X:13). This explains why Hida is rendered as *Finda* and Edo, *Yendo*.[20] Likewise, Dirck Snoeck renders the name of the interpreter (Shizuki) Magobē as Mangabe and Antonio van Bronckhorst as Mangobe, and there are many similar examples (*Diaries*: X:33; XII:4). This phenomenon can still be observed among some current speakers of Japanese, but it is not reflected in Japanese script or the Hepburn romanization system. One keen observer of Japanese pronunciation was the German physician, Engelbert Kaempfer, who worked at Deshima from 1690 to 1692. As noted in Chapter 1, Kaempfer made observations on the phenomenon of prenasalization in 'The History of Japan' (1727: 414, quoted in Michel 2012: 113). He suggested that the Japanese frequently 'add to some syllables the letter n [...] for the sake of an easier and more agreeable pronunciation'. A different perspective is, however, offered by Morishima Chūryō in *Kōmō zatsuwa* ('Red-haired miscellany', 1787). He suggests that the Dutch call Nagasaki *Nangasaki* because they want to transform it into a word that sounds like one in their language (Winkel 2004: 60).[21]

Another feature of early modern Japanese is the initial consonantal sound in the syllable 'wo', often realized graphically as ⟨vo⟩ or ⟨wo⟩. We see this in the rendering of the family name of Ōno Harunaga as *Vono*. A slightly different case is that of a weakening of the vowels 'i' and 'u' between unvoiced consonants and after unvoiced sibilants from around the sixteenth century onwards. This is reflected in Dutch renderings, but not in the Jesuit or Hepburn transliteration systems. One frequent example is the rendering of Japanese months. In the Hepburn system, the months take the form *Xgatsu*, where X is the relevant cardinal number (occasionally concatenated). So, whereas the third month is now transliterated *sangatsu*, in Dutch texts we

---

19 Historically, in Japanese phonology the only CV combination in which the C[onsonant] has been and is still realized as /ɸ/ is *fu* (Labrune 2012: 25). /ɸ/ is described as bilabial rather than labio-dental, as it was probably produced by rounding the lips rather than by placing the top teeth on the bottom lip and aspirating.

20 Another example is *Fingo* for Higo in the journal of Olof Eriksson Willman (2013: 77).

21 There may be some truth in this, for Dutch does not have the [g] sound as in the English 'goal', so it may be that native Dutch speakers used ⟨ng⟩ to indicate the velar nasal ([ŋ] of 'thing') as this is relatively close to [g]. I thank Marc van Oostendorp for this observation.

typically find *sanguats* (Michel 2012: 109). In his record of the *hofreis* of 1646, Willem Verstegen renders *Kusatsu* as 'Coesats', and *Minakuchi* as 'Minacuts' (*Diaries*: X:58). Both are towns in Ōmi province. One Japanese author who frequently does not write a word-final 'i' or 'u' not only after sibilants, but also unvoiced consonants, is Kutsuki Masatsuna. He renders months as *Xguats*, e.g., the ninth month *kugatsu* as *Koeguats*, and the eras of *genroku* (元禄) and *shōtoku* (正徳) as *genrok* and *siotok* respectively (Lequin 1992: 10–11). Similar forms were still in use in 1861, when they appear in the *Nederlandsche en Japansche Almanak* printed at Deshima. For example, the second month is given as *Nigwats* (modern form Nigatsu) and the ninth month as *Koegwats*.

Second, the Dutch rendering of Nagasaki as *Nangasaki*, *Nangasacqui* and variants thereof may point to the adoption of Portuguese spellings by Dutch authors (Michel 2012: 112). For example, the place where the lexicon *Arte da Lingoa de Iapam* was printed in 1604 is given in Portuguese as *Nangasaqui*, i.e., Nagasaki.[22] Returning to Ōno Harunaga, in 1649 Willem Verstegen referred to him as *Vono Xuriddonne* (*Diaries*: XI:128). *Xuriddonne* is formed from his title 'Shuri-no-suke' and the honorific suffix *dono*. The initial 'x' in Verstegen's rendering for /ʃ/ is based on the Jesuit transliteration system. The use of ⟨x⟩ to represent /ʃ/ is found in early Dutch renderings of Japanese toponyms such as *Meaxima* for the island Meshima (女島), one of the Danjo Islands (男女群島) to the west of Kyushu (*Diaries*: IX:64). Luís Teixeira's map of Japan *Iaponie Insulae Descriptio* (1595), on which Abraham Ortelius based his 1598 map *Iaponia Insula*, refers to Hirado as *Firando* and Hizen as *Figen*. These renderings may have influenced Dutch spelling (Cortazzi 1983: 91–93).[23]

Third, issues arise as a result of Dutch and Japanese having a different set of native phonemes. Two examples serve to illustrate this. First, Dutch has two alveolar liquids, /l/, and /r/, both of which are realized in more than one way (Booij 1995: 7–8). Japanese, however, only has one liquid, /r/. Although this can be realized as [ɾ] or [l], it is this difficult for a European listener to pick up this distinction.[24] In this regard, in 'The History of Japan' Kaempfer (1727: 382, quoted in Michel 2012: 113) writes that the Japanese pronounced 'Holanda' as

---

22   Other variants are *Nangasacq* or *Nangazackij* (*Diaries*: I:8; Lequin 1990: I:4). 'n' is inserted before 'g' in other toponyms, viz., Nicolaes Couckebakker renders Shinagawa as *Sinangauw*, Frederick Coyett renders Kamagari as *Camangary* and Andreas Cleyer refers to Saga as *Sanga* (*Diaries*: I:28; XI:5; Cleyer 1985: 85).

23   See also Michel (2012: 111) for a map of Kyushu by Christophorus Blancus (1617) with Portuguese renderings of Japanese toponyms.

24   Again, a full analysis of Japanese phonology is beyond the scope of this book. However, to expand slightly on the above, phonologists seem to agree that there is one Japanese liquid /r/. This is usually realized as an apico-alveolar flap or tap [ɾ], but in certain cases such as before palatalized vowels [e.g., rya, ryu, ryo], it is realized as an apico-alveolar lateral [l] (Labrune 2012: 92).

'Horanda'. On the same subject, Overmeer Fisscher (1833: 99) described the problems that the Japanese had with certain Dutch sounds, saying that they make 'mistakes' pronouncing R and L (and H and B). Modern spellings tend to render this liquid as ⟨r⟩, whereas authors of Dutch texts often render it as ⟨l⟩. For example, Nicholas Couckebakker renders the name of the interpreter (Sadakata) Riemon as 'Liemon' (*Diaries*: 1:25). Likewise, over two hundred years later, the physician Pompe van Meerdervoort (1970: 84) rendered the name of Matsumoto Ryōjun, as Mats-Moto-Lyozun. Ryōjun was a future imperial court physician sent to Nagasaki to supervise the teaching of medicine. Nevertheless, in these cases at least, as a result of the phonetic environment, the sound produced was possibly closer to [l] than [ɾ] (Labrune 2012: 92).

The second example is of Dutch lacking native phonemes found in Japanese. For example, in Dutch there is no voiced postalveolar affricate /dʒ/, as in the 'j' in the English 'jump' (Booij 1995: 7).[25] This makes it difficult to render the Japanese toponym *Fuji(san)*. Overmeer Fisscher (1833: 301) is one author who does so with 'de Foegieberg', although in Dutch the grapheme ⟨g⟩ is usually realized as a velar fricative, [ɣ] or [x] (Booij 1995: 7–8). Kutsuki Masatsuna renders the twelfth month *junigatsu* as *dzuniguats*, while other Japanese authors render the tenth month *jugatsu* as *zuuguats*. This probably also explains why the interpreter Hori Monjūrō signs himself 'FL MONSURO' (Lequin 1992: 11; 1990: 1:13). Similarly, Dutch lacks the voiceless postalveolar affricate /tʃ/, a word-initial and word-final sound in the English word 'church'. This is sometimes rendered with the digraph ⟨ts⟩. Overmeer Fisscher (1833: 264) rendered the Nagasaki district of Edo-machi as *Jedomatsi*. Isaac Titsingh rendered this as *Jedomats* and the town of Togawa-machi (*machi* (町) is Japanese for town) as *Ogauwamatz* (the word-final 'i' after a sibilant is weakened) (Lequin 2011: 68–71). We find this in the rendering of personal names, too. In 1668 Constantin Ranst (*opperhoofd* 1667–68) referred to the Nagasaki interpreter Nishi Kichibei as *Niis Kitsibeoye* (Michel and Sugitatsu 2003: n. 34). One Japanese author who followed this practice was Kutsuki Masatsuna. In a letter to Isaac Titsingh in 1786, he provides a list of coins that he is sending to his friend who was by now working in Bengal. Among the coins he lists are several *Jtsib*, i.e., *ichibu* (一分) (Lequin 1992: 9–11).

Fourth, some authors of Dutch texts added ⟨f⟩ after 'k' in Japanese words, something that Michel (2012: 114) suggests reflects a friction of breath by Japanese speakers. When quoting a Japanese proverb, Isaac Titsingh renders *mattaku* (全く) ('exactly') as *mattakf* (Lequin 1992: 53). In his discussion on learning Japanese, Overmeer Fisscher (1833: 100) transcribes the word for 'I' as *watakfs*. This probably renders the first-person singular pronoun *watakushi*,

---

25 Combinations of Dutch letters are used in loanwords containing this consonantal sound.

which is more formal than the better-known *watashi* (私).[26] One hint at why he renders it thus comes from a comment by Pompe van Meerdervoort (1867–68: I:284–285) in his account of his time in Japan. He writes 'ik, Wa-ta-ku-si (in de gewone taal als wa-taks uitgesproken) wordt met 4 karakters geschreven' ('I, Wa-ta-ku-s(h)i (in everyday language pronounced wa-taks) is written with four characters', i.e., in *kana*).

Finally, we need to account for the fact that Dutch orthography differs from the orthography of most transliteration systems, such as the Hepburn system, which is largely based on English. For example, the palatal glide /j/, which is typically graphically realized as ⟨y⟩ in English is realized as ⟨j⟩ in Dutch (Booij 1995: 7). In 1646 Willem Verstegen renders the Yokotagawa River (横田川) as 'Jockotanguwa' (*Diaries*: X:58). The vowel /u(:)/ is graphically realized as ⟨u⟩ or ⟨oo⟩ in English, but typically as ⟨oe⟩ in Dutch. Furthermore, although there is some consistency in spelling, we do find orthographical variation between authors and even from the same author on the same page. In 1647, Verstegen renders the name of the island Iōjima, mentioned above, as 'Uwos', while Dirck Snoeck a few years later renders it as 'Ouvos' (*Diaries*: X:36; XI:169). Verstegen clearly had difficulties rendering the title of the Japanese official Inoue Masashige, which was *Chikugo(-no-kami)*, to which the honorific suffix *-dono* was often added. He rendered this in several ways, such as 'tZikkingodonne, Sickingodonne, Zickingodonne and Tsickingodonne. These variant renderings reflect the lack of the affricate /tʃ/ in Dutch and the prenasalization of /g/ in Japanese (*Diaries*: X:27).

4   Code Switching by Motivation

Among the motivations for code switching are switching at the beginning and end of texts, including for the purpose of dating a text, in some cases in Japanese, in other cases in Latin; quoting speech; providing information; and giving a proverb. In most cases, this switching forms part of the author's discourse strategy.

4.1   *Switching at the Beginning and End of Texts*
One motivation for code switching, which can be further categorized as tag-switching, is switching at the beginning or end of a Dutch text, often for the purpose of dating it. This is something we often see in correspondence and

---

26   In both cases, 'k' is followed by 'u'. The 'u' is pronounced 'weakly', i.e., voiceless. This is acoustically like /f/. I thank Marc van Oostendorp for this observation.

is part of a more general pattern whereby code switching was considered socially acceptable in early modern personal correspondence (Schendl 2012: 525). In Europe, it occurs in the correspondence of learned men such as the Dutch statesman and man of letters, Constantijn Huygens (1596–1687), who took their lead from ancient exemplars such as Cicero (Joby 2014: 220–250).[27]

In the Hirado period, the merchant and survivor of the *Liefde* shipwreck Jan Joosten van Lodensteyn begins a letter in Dutch to a fellow Dutchman with a Latin tag *Laus deo den 18. Meij Anno 1615* ('Praise to God ...') (Wieder 1923–25: 102). Above, mention was made of the word *Adij*, a corruption of the Latin *Ad diem*, i.e., 'on this day'. Many of the early entries in the *dagregister* in the 1630s and 1640s begin with *Adij* followed by the date number and *dito*. An early entry, from 1633, begins *Adij 6e d[it]o* (*Diaries*: I:3); *6e* is the Dutch ordinal (*zesde*); while *dito* (from Latin *dictus* via Italian *ditto*) means 'the aforesaid' (a note indicates that 'the above' was the eighth month, *hachigatsu*). A slightly different example from the late 1640's begins *Primo April* ('First of April') before switching into Dutch, while a later entry begins *Ultimo ditto* ('Last of the above', i.e., June) (*Diaries*: XI:127, 145). Entries in the trading book at Deshima begin with several of these Latin words. The entry for 1 November 1642 runs *Laus Deo adij P^{mo} November anno 1642 In 't Comptoir Nangasacki* (*Diaries*: VII:236).

Switching into Latin for this purpose was common practice in Europe. However, in Japan authors writing in Dutch also switch into Japanese to render dates. In 1633, Nicolaes Couckebakker rendered the first month of the lunar year, *shōgatsu* (正月), as *Songuats* (*Diaries*: I:55). Willem Verstegen renders *shōgatsu* as *Sionguats*, while Andreas Cleyer renders it *songuats* (in both cases the ⟨n⟩ suggests that the 'g' is a prenasalized consonant) (*Diaries*: X:14–15; Cleyer 1985: 77). While Isaac Titsingh typically, though not always, dated his letters to Japanese correspondents in Dutch, his Japanese correspondents, such as Nishi Kichibei, Narabayashi Jūbei and Kutsuki Masatsuna, often dated their letters in Dutch to Titsingh with transliterated versions of Japanese names for months, e.g., *senguats* for the third month and *rokguats* for the sixth month (*sangatsu* and *rokugatsu* respectively in modern Japanese transcription). For example, Masatsuna dates one letter to Titsingh *Jedo den 1 Rokguats van het 6 jaar der Nengo Tenmy*, i.e., the first of *rokugatsu* of Year 6 of the Tenmei (天明) era (*nengo* 年号) (Lequin 1990: I:34). On a different note, Baba Teiyū wrote the

---

27 Switching for the purpose of dating is something that we often see in texts written in other languages. Authors in ancient Rome would often date Greek texts in Latin and Renaissance humanists often switched language to date texts (Joby 2014: 224–225; Adams 2003: 390–393).

preface to *Imonsuchi Orandago hōkai* in 1815 in Dutch. He concludes it with the date 'den vijf en twintigste van fatiguats in het jaar boenkwa twaalfde' ('25th of the eighth month (*hachigatsu*) in Year 12 of the Bunka era (1804–18)') switching between Dutch and transcribed Japanese.

In some cases, authors date texts in a combination of modified Japanese, Dutch and Latin. Masatsuna concludes another letter to Titsingh, *Jedo den 1 senguats int 5de Jaar der Nengo Tenmij of A° 1785*, i.e., 'Edo 1 *sangatsu*, Year 5 of the Tenmei era or A[nn]o 1785' (Lequin 1992: 1).[28] The interpreter Hori Monjūrō dated a letter to Isaac Titsingh in these three languages, giving both a modified version of the Japanese month and the European equivalent: *Bij ons* ('chez nous') *den 7e Zuuquats off den 22e November A° 1789*, i.e., '7th *jūgatsu* (10th month) or 22nd November A[nn]o 1789' (Lequin 1990: 1:132). The graphic realization of /ʤ/ as ⟨z⟩ again reflects the lack of this phoneme in the native Dutch sound system. One probable reason for authors giving the Japanese and Dutch names of months is that there was not an exact correspondence between the Dutch solar and Japanese lunar calendars. In this regard, there is an element of 'gap-filling' at work.

Taisei honzō meiso ('Western Plant Taxonomy') by Itō Keisuke gives the names of Japanese plants in Latin, Japanese and Chinese. The title page is in Dutch. At the bottom, the place and date of publication are given: *Te Nagoja by … Boenzy XI (1828)* (see fig. 16). The Japanese era *Boenzy* (note the influence of Dutch orthography) is nowadays rendered *Bunsei* (文政, 1818–30). We find another example of switching to give a trilingual date at the end of a document for the import of cloves signed by the Nagasaki interpreters in 1784: *Collegie den nen zuiguats 4e jaar der Nengo Tenmio Ao 1784*. This means 'The College [of interpreters] 11 *shōgatsu* 4th year of the Tenmei [Era (nengo)] Anno 1784'.[29] One other interesting piece of switching in a date comes at the end of a letter to Titsingh from Imamura Kinbei in 1786. At the end of the date, he writes *6de jaar van temmij moema, of paardjaar*, '6th year of Tenmei …'. *Muma*, or here *moema* (with the Dutch digraph ⟨oe⟩), represents an old way of pronouncing 'horse' (馬) in Japanese. In cMJ, the *kun*-reading is typically 'uma'.[30] *Paard(en)-jaar* is Dutch for 'year of the horse' (Lequin 1990: 1:43–45).

A word is in order about switching to give the date *in* the text. An early example of this occurs in the *dagregister* in January 1649. Here, Dirck Snoeck writes

28 The Tenmei Era lasted from April 1781 to January 1789. The European date is 9 April 1785.
29 MS, The Hague. *Nationaal Archief*, VOC (1.04.21), 614.
30 Broadly speaking there are two ways of reading *kanji*, *on*-reading (*on'yomi*) and *kun*-reading (*kun'yomi*). The former, literally 'sound-reading' is the Sino-Japanese reading, whereas the latter, literally 'meaning-reading' is the 'native' Japanese reading.

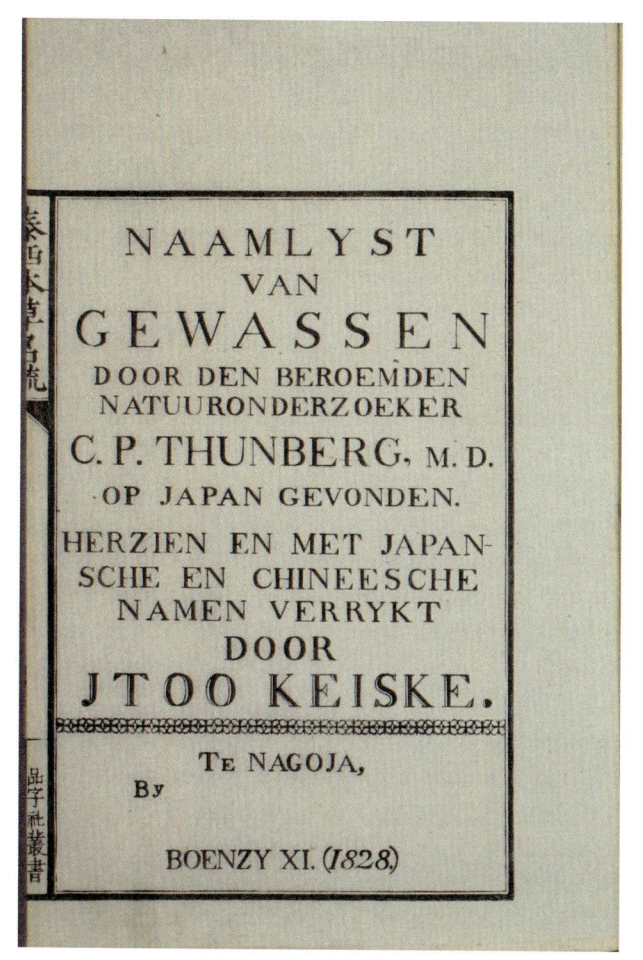

FIGURE 16
Taisei honzō meiso
('Western Plant
Taxonomy', 1828), Itō
Keisuke, title page in
Dutch
WUL 二 14 00793

'de Japanze 8en mane, fatsinguats', i.e., the Japanese eighth month (*Diaries*: XI:113). *Fatsinguats* is now rendered *hachigatsu* (八月), with the word-initial 'f' reflecting the tendency to pronounce 'ha' as /fa/ and the 'n' suggesting that the 'g' was a prenasalized consonant (Michel 2012:109). In the 1644 *dagregister*, Jan van Elseracq refers to the arrival of 54 Chinese junks in Nagasaki from *eersten dagh des Japanschen **songuats** ende Nieuwejaer, dat den 8en. Februarij passado is geweest* (my bold). *Songuats* graphically realizes *shōgatsu* (正月, New Year and by extension the first month) again with a prenasalized 'g'. In his journal of the *hofreis* in 1780, Isaac Titsingh renders *shōgatsu* as *sjoguats*, while his correspondent Kutsuki Masatsuna renders it *Siuguats* (Lequin 1992: 1). ⟨sj⟩ is often used in Dutch to graphically realize the non-native phoneme /ʃ/ in loanwords (Booij 1995: 7). In a letter to Titsingh, Masatsuna gives details of when coins, which he is sending to his friend, were minted. He switches from Dutch to render the ninth month *kugatsu* (九月) as *Koeguats* and the twelfth month *junigatsu* (十二月) as *dzuniguats*, ⟨dz⟩ being a fair attempt to realize graphically /dʒ/. Japanese and Dutch authors are consistent in graphically realizing 'gatsu' as ⟨guats⟩, a function of the weakened 'u' after a sibilant. The fact that both sets of authors used this modified form for months may point to a pattern of negotiation and accommodation between them to overcome the fact that they did not share a common first language. Authors switched to render Japanese eras, too. In a description of a coin that he sent to Titsingh in 1786, Masatsuna refers to the Japanese era of *Hōei* (宝永, 1704–11) as *Fooiiy* (Lequin 1992: 11).

Switching at the start or end of a text was not always for the purpose of dating. A complex example of switching at the start of a text is to be found in *Hakkō shōran, shokō* (八紘勝覧初稿), the Japanese translation of *Merkwaardigheden uit elk land van Europa* ('Wonders from every land in Europe') (Amsterdam, 1827), itself a translation by Johannes Olivier of *Scenes of Europe* written by Isaac Taylor.[31] On the title page, the translator Mitsukuri Genpo interspersed the details of the Dutch edition in Roman script with Japanese equivalents in *kanji*. The rest of the translation is in Japanese littered with *katakana* renderings of European terms.

4.2   *Quoting Direct Speech*

Dutch authors switched into Japanese to quote direct speech. In the *dagregister* for January 1647, Willem Verstegen records that on the *hofreis* in Edo he was called to the residence of the *ōmetsuke*, Inoue Masashige. He writes that Masashige said to him 'Capitaijn Woiensamma fumbeets sinday mimaista'. Immediately after this there is a translation in Dutch which means 'The captain (*opperhoofd*) has seen the Shogun at his pleasure, I was happy'. If one were looking for a discourse strategy here, Verstegen might be trying to indicate that he understood some Japanese (*Diaries*: X:92).[32] Of course, Masashige, who spoke Portuguese, may have told him what this meant, or there was an interpreter present, although none is mentioned. The *dagregister* for 1655 switches to Japanese to report that when Leonard Winnincx (*opperhoofd* 1654–55) went into the presence of the shogun, the counsellor Andō Ukyō shouted *Oranda Kapitan*, i.e., 'the Dutch *opperhoofd*', both words being Portuguese loanwords

---

31   八紘 means 'whole world'. Literally, it means 'eight crown chords', but was used to refer to the whole world: 勝覧 'nice view', and 初稿 'first draft'. *Hakkō shōran shokō* is not listed on the NIJL database. See http://www.ndl.go.jp/nichiran/e/s2/s2_2.html. Accessed 6 May 2020.

32   Verstegen's version is not entirely accurate. One suggestion as to the original words is *Uesama funbetsu shidai mimaishita* (*Diaries*: X:92 n. 348).

in Japanese (Vermeulen *et al.* 1986–: XII:197).[33] Adriaen van der Burgh (*opperhoofd* 1651–52) switches to quote the same words in 1652 (Vermeulen *et al.* 1986–: XII:44). Spellings vary. The *dagregister* for March 1651 records this exclamation as 'Olande capitayn' and 'Olanda capitan'. It glossed the command 'den Hollandtschen capiteyn doet reverentie' ('the Dutch *opperhoofd* pays homage') (*Diaries*: XII:138).

In the *dagregister* for 1745 Jacob van der Waeijen quotes himself in transcribed Japanese saying to the Governor of Nagasaki 'ietsman gosin fake' ('15000 boxes [of copper]'). In modern standard Japanese these words would be transcribed as 'ichi man gosen hako' (Blussé and Remmelink 2004: 69). In *ichi* ('one'), 'ch' is graphically realized as ⟨ts⟩ as Dutch lacks /tʃ/, while 'ha' in *hako* is likely to have been realized as [ɸa], hence *fake* (Booij 1995: 7; Michel 2012: 109). In his journal, Dirk de Graeff van Polsbroek refers to a ceremony that was conducted before he and others left on the *hofreis*. He writes that the shout went out: 'werd steeds geroepen Stanie! Stanie! Kniel, kniel neder!' *Stanie* is a corruption of the Japanese 'Shita ni!' (下に, lit. 'go down') (De Graeff van Polsbroek 1987: 34). In his account of life in Japan, Overmeer Fisscher wrote that when an official arrived on Deshima, this was 'aangekondigd door het schreeuwen van "Oeidi di goezarimasi" hetwelk beteekent "hij komt!"' ['announced by the cry of "Oeidi di goezarimasi", which means "he comes!"']. A little later, he describes a Buddhist ceremony and refers to participants shouting repeatedly, '*Namoe Amida outs*! hetwelk beteekent "God AMIDA! bid voor hem"'. It is likely that '*Namoe Amida outs*!' refers to the chant *Namu Amida Butsu* (南無阿弥陀仏) which means 'Pray for/hail Amitabha Buddha' (Overmeer Fisscher 1833: 268, 280).

4.3 Switching to Provide Information

Chapter 1 introduced a case of switching by the Swedish physician and botanist, Carl Peter Thunberg. He would conduct botanical research away from Deshima with two Japanese physicians. They would tell him the Japanese names for plants, and he would tell them the Dutch and Latin names (Thunberg 1784: xviii; Screech 2005: 153). This example of switching language to provide information is based on metalinguistic comment. A slightly different case of

---

33   Winnincx adds what he thinks this exclamation really meant 'He (the *opperhoofd*) is lying there and is paying homage to your Majesty, with a presentation of gifts'. Japanese had adopted *Kapitan* (カピタン) from the Portuguese *capitão* ('captain') as a name for the *opperhoofd*. The Japanese used the form 'Oranda' (there are several renderings of this in *ateji* including 和蘭 and 阿蘭陀) rather than 'Holanda', again borrowed from the Portuguese ('Olanda').

switching from Dutch to Latin to give information occurs in the *dagregister* for March 1645. Some Japanese brought a print of the Annunciation to the Virgin Mary to the *opperhoofd*, Overtwater. He told them it was a Flemish print, for it included the words of Luke 1: 28 in Dutch. He then informed them that it was better known to them in Latin, *Ave Maria gratia plena* ('Hail Mary, full of grace'), suggesting they were Christian converts (*Diaries*: IX:46).

We also find instances of switching into Japanese for this purpose. In the *dagregister* for December 1784, Hendrik Romberg discusses measures that had been taken to prevent coolies from stealing from Chinese junks. They had to wear short sleeves and on the back of their garments, the words 'TODA ARATIEMIE' had to be written in large characters. *Aratiemie* or *aratame* comes from the Japanese verb *aratameru* (改める), which can mean 'to inspect'. Toda (Ujiharu) was the name of the Nagasaki governor, and it is not clear why his name was mentioned, although it may simply be that he gave this instruction. So, the phrase could be translated '([On the order of] Toda, inspect me' (Vermeulen *et al.* 1986–: IX:76, 94). Similarly, in his journal in 1858, when referring to the lanterns on the side of the palanquins (*norimono*) carried on the *hofreis*, Dirk de Graeff van Polsbroek (1987: 34) writes, "De lantaarns waren van rood, wit en blauw papier, waarop in het Japansch geschreven was 'Wolands Taisho' (Hollandsche Groote Heer)". A modern transcription is *Oranda taishō* which means 'The Dutch Great Lord', i.e., the *opperhoofd*. De Graeff van Polsbroek records that the words 'Wolands Taisho' were written 'in Japanese', but does not tell us in which script. One possibility is that they were written in *rōmaji*.[34] If so, the 'wo' in 'Wolands' might indicate that some Japanese still pronounced the first syllable of *Oranda* as 'wo'. The word-final 's' is a Dutch genitive suffix.

4.4   *Giving a Proverb*

Educated Romans often inserted Greek proverbs into their Latin texts and in the early modern period educated authors did something similar, engaging in *imitatio* of their ancient exemplars (Adams 2003: 335–336; Joby 2014: 232). In Japan, we find several examples of this in the correspondence of Isaac Titsingh. In a letter to Hori Monjūrō, Titsingh observes that other Japanese correspondents had been complaining that the present regime in Japan, above all the Governor of Nagasaki, was not to their liking. In *rōmaji* he cites a Japanese proverb, *tokakoe oekijo wa mama naranoe* ('things in this world never go as one would like'). In trying to offer consolation, Titsingh recalls the proverb *Aketje*

---

34   The words may also have been written in *katakana*, in which case 'wo' would be rendered with ⟨ヲ⟩. However, if so, the transcription 'wolands' would be problematic, above all in relation to the consonant cluster ⟨nds⟩.

no tenka mika. This means 'Aketje only ruled for three days', a proverb meaning that some things last only a short time, and in this case, he hopes, the tenure of the present Governor (Lequin 1990: II:682).[35] Titsingh may have picked up the first of these proverbs from a letter dated 4 April 1789 from Kutsuki Masatsuna (Lequin 1990: I:102). As usual Masatsuna asked Titsingh to correct his Dutch and return the letter to him. When Titsingh did so, a couple of years later in February 1791, he added his own response to *tokakoe oekijo wa mama naranoe*, which was *sawari ni naranoe kotto wa koraje rarejo*. This can be translated as 'Don't worry about things that do not cause [you] a problem' (Lequin 1990: II:677).

In a letter to Masatsuna from Amsterdam dated 4 June 1807, Titsingh recalls an aphorism from the Analects of Confucius (he calls him *Kon-foe-tsoe*, which is closer to the Chinese *Kǒng Fūzǐ* 孔夫子 than to the Latinate Confucius), which his friend had quoted, writing it in *rōmaji: Itsoe wari wo / fito ni wa i ute / tsoe mi no besi / kokoro no towaba ikaga kota i in* (Lequin 1992: 53; 1990: I:460–461). This translates as 'It is an easy thing to tell lies, but how is one's conscience to be made clear'.[36] Touchingly, Titsingh then quotes a line from the Analects which he notes was Masatsuna's favourite line from the philosopher: *genko mattakf seijo*, i.e., 'one's words must equal one's actions' (Lequin 1992: 53).[37] One possible reason for Titsingh and Masatsuna switching for the purpose of quotation is to create or re-create a bond by referring to proverbs with which they are both familiar and which in some cases they exchanged face-to-face. Indeed, Titsingh recalls that the first proverb was expressly recommended to him by Masatsuna on many occasions (*my door u zo vaak met nadruk aangepresen*).

---

35   'Aketje' is a corruption of Akechi (Mitsuhide), who murdered the sixteenth-century *daimyō*, Oda Nobunaga (1534–82). In modern Japanese the proverb runs 明智の三日天下 'Akechi-no-mikka tenka'.

36   Winkel (2004: 77) has the reading *Itsoe wari wo fito ni wa iute tsoe mi no besi kokoro no towaba kokoro no towaba* (sic) and suggests a current reading is probably *Itsuwari o hito ni wa iute tsumi nobesu kokoro no towaba ikaga kotaen*. MS London British Library Add. MS 9393 fols. 2r–3v includes an English translation of this letter which seems to have been made by Titsingh, who lived in London for some time. If I read a note to the translation correctly, a Dutch translation was made of a book printed by Masatsuna on ancient Chinese copper coins (fol. 3v). This was possibly *Shinsen senpu* ('Newly selected manual of numismatics') (Titsingh refers to this in his letter to Masatsuna as *Sin-sen-sen-poe*). See also Boxer (1950: 182–183). Titsingh was clearly taken by this proverb, for he repeated it in a letter to his brother from Chinsura in 1790. Here he explains the meaning as 'men kan een ander ligt onwaarheeden wys maaken, maar hoe zal men dan zyn ygen hart gerust stellen' (Lequin 1990: I:176).

37   This proverb from Confucius is rendered in Japanese script as 言行全（く）正常. This is pronounced 'Genkō matta(ku) seijō' with a *kun*-reading of 全く (*mattaku* ('exactly')) (*on*-reading of 全 is 'zen'). This helps to explain Titsingh's version. The ⟨kf⟩ combination may be a function of aspiration after the 'k' cf. *watakfs* discussed earlier in this chapter.

How much Japanese Titsingh knew is not clear (he certainly knew some), but by inserting Japanese proverbs into his Dutch texts, he could engage with the language without having to write an entire text in it.[38]

In March 1787, Titsingh wrote to the interpreter Nishi Kichirōbei (he calls him Heer Kitsrofe) from Chinsura (Lequin 1990: 1:54). In the Dutch text he inserted two Japanese proverbs in *rōmaji*. One he rendered as *Dakarete neroe zo ta no skede*. A closer rendering is *Dakarete neroe zo tanoshikere*. This means 'Sleeping next to someone is pleasant'. Titsingh is clearly aware of this for he adds a Dutch equivalent *het bijslapen is aangenaam*.[39] He asks Kichirōbei to translate some lines of Japanese and then adds a second proverb, *sussee soereba nani gotomotassoe*. A closer rendering is *Shussei soereba nanigoto mo tassoe*. It means 'If you do your best, you can achieve anything'.[40]

A different example of switching for the purpose of giving a proverb can be found on the grave inscription of Hendrik Duurkoop (Blussé and Remmelink 2004: xiii). This begins with the Latin proverb *Mora sine volat hora* ('Time Flies Without Delay') before switching into Dutch to give the details of Duurkoop's life and death. It concludes *in den schoot der rust aanbetrouwd den XV Aug A° MDCCLXXVIII*—laid to rest on 15 August 1778, with the Roman numerals framing the epitaph along with the Latin proverb.[41]

4.5   No Motivation

In some cases, there is no clear motivation, apart from, perhaps, an author wishing to demonstrate that he knew a word or phrase. In 1646, Reijnier van Tzum (*opperhoofd* 1645–46) reported that a Japanese would return 'als (jangatte), dat is metterhaest ofte binnencorten' (*Diaries*: IX:129). *Jangatte* is his rendering of the Japanese *yagate* (やがて/軈て, 'soon'), something Van Tzum makes clear in his Dutch gloss. It may be that the Japanese said this, although the author does not state this. If this is so, then it is an example of switching for the purpose of quoting direct speech. Things are a little clearer when Peter Sterthemius (*opperhoofd* 1650–51) inserts *jangatti* in a *dagregister* entry on 19 March 1651 (*Diaries*: XII:137). Like Van Tzum, he notes it means 'metterhaest' and that the interpreters had often used it, in this case telling the

---

38   Titsingh translated some short Japanese verses somewhat loosely into Latin. Again, this does not tell us *per se* how well he knew Japanese but does suggest that he engaged with it to a significant extent (Screech 2006: 163–170).

39   In Japanese script this is rendered: 抱かれて寝るぞ楽しけれ. *Bijslapen* is often used as a euphemism for having sex.

40   In Japanese script this is rendered: 出精すれば何事も達す. I thank Professor Shimizu Makoto for helping me to identify these two Japanese proverbs.

41   Blussé and Remmelink (2004: xiii) give MDCCLXXVII, but this is incorrect.

Dutch that they were soon to have an audience with the shogun and should therefore hurry up!

5 'Gap-Filling'

In some sense, these are examples of Japanese being clothed in Roman script. One of the most common reasons for interference from other languages in Dutch texts was the lack of an appropriate term in Dutch, or 'gap-filling'. In some cases, authors would simply give a description or circumlocution in Dutch. In other cases, however, they rendered Japanese terms in Roman script, providing further examples of the re-clothing of Japanese, although, to push this metaphor a little further, the choice of clothes was not always consistent, with the same term being graphically realized in several ways. 'Gap-filling' was used for objects such as Japanese musical instruments, coins, weights and measures, and everyday objects such as items of clothing and food and drink. Dutch authors also inserted the titles and occupations of Japanese with whom they had dealings. It will be instructive to analyse examples of 'gap-filling' thematically.

5.1 Musical Instruments

The naval officer Willem Huyssen van Kattendyke (1860: 188) who was in Japan in the late 1850s records that after a meeting with some Japanese, he received a sword while a colleague was given 'een blaas-instrument, *Soe* genaamd, ten geschenke' ('a wind instrument, called a *Soe*, as a present'). A *sō* (笙, also read *shō*) is a traditional Japanese wind instrument resembling pan pipes. Overmeer Fisscher (1833: 278) refers to 'het geluid van *samsies*, trommels en andere muzijkinstrumenten'. A *samsie* (三味線, pron. *samisen*) is a three-stringed Japanese guitar. In theory, Overmeer Fisscher could have used the word *gitaar* ('guitar'), although this may not have had the same effect on Dutch readers. In other words, another motivation for code switching here may be to bring Japan to the reader's mind, or even to transport the reader to Japan in his or her mind.[42] At one point in his account of life in Japan, Overmeer Fisscher (1833: 291) refers to a Japanese *Sakki-partij* where some *samsiespeelsters* were playing. Both are examples of hybrid words comprising Dutch and Japanese morphemes. *Sakki* refers to the well-known Japanese rice wine *sake* (酒) and *samsiespeelsters* are female players (Dutch 'speelsters') of the *samsie* (see fig. 17).

---

42 For more on code switching for the purpose of evocation, see Joby (2014: 243–244) and Adams (2003: 403–405).

FIGURE 17   A Japanese woman tuning a *samisen*, Yashima Gakutei, c. 1825–c. 1829, colour woodcut
RIJKSMUSEUM, AMSTERDAM

5.2 Coins

One coin to which frequent reference is made in Dutch texts is the *ichibu* (一分) (*ichi* means 'one'), the smallest Japanese coin, worth a quarter of one *koban* (小判) (Blussé and Remmelink 2004: 804).[43] In the *dagregister* for 1633, Nicolaes Couckebakker refers to it as *een Itchebo*, while in his informal *hofreis-journaal* for 1780 Isaac Titsingh writes *een Itzebo* (*Diaries*: 1:29; Lequin 2011: 70). In a list accompanying coins that he sent to Titsingh in 1786, Kutsuki Masatsuna refers to this coin as *Jtsib* (Lequin 1990: 1:23). In his account of Japan, Overmeer Fisscher (1833: 318) refers to '*itsjiboe's*, of stukjes goud van circa drie gulden waarde' ('Ichibus or pieces of gold worth about three guilders'). These examples also illustrate that authors of Dutch texts graphically realized the same word in different ways.

In a description of a coin that he sent to Titsingh in 1786, Masatsuna refers to the character inscribed on the coin as *fon*, i.e., *hon* (本) (Lequin 1992: 11). In the *dagregister* for 1782 Titsingh refers to a *koban* (小判), mentioned above. It is a small oval gold coin worth about one seventh of an *ōban* (大判), a large gold coin used only among *daimyō* (Blussé and Remmelink 2004: 463, 808, 809; see fig. 18).[44] Masatsuna refers to this coin as a *Cobang*, while he refers to the *ōban* as *Oobang* (the 'oo' reflecting the fact that the word-initial vowel has two *morae*) (Lequin 1992: 2).[45] The question arises as to whether the word-final ⟨ng⟩ in Masatuna's renderings tells us that speakers may have produced a word-final velar nasal /ŋ/. This is currently thought to have emerged in Japanese around the eighteenth century, but according to Labrune (2012: 78–79) is only found word-internally. If not, further investigation would be required to establish whether the word-final ⟨ng⟩ and the graphic alternative ⟨n⟩ represent the same pronunciation. Japanese coins are mentioned in the *dagregister* in relation to payment for goods. One example is Couckebakker mentioning 'Japansche senes' (*Diaries*: 1:176). 'Senes' is a rendering of a plural for *zeni* (銭), a round coin with a square hole in the middle. Finally, several of these coins including *itsibu* and *koban* are inserted in a section on Japanese coins in the Dutch text of the *Nederlandsche en Japansche Almanak*, printed on Deshima in 1861.

5.3 Weights and Measures

When he mentions *een Itchebo*, Couckebakker gives an equivalent as *1½ taijl*. Later, in 1783, Hendrik Romberg records that while rice is very cheap in

---

43 This is sometimes referred to as *Boontje* ('little bean') in Dutch texts (Blussé and Remmelink 2004: 804).

44 A *koban* was equal to one *ryō* (両).

45 Andreas Cleyer (1985: 65) refers to *coubanghs*.

FIGURE 18   A Japanese *koban* with a stamp (the coat of arms of Holland) applied in Batavia, 1690
RIJKSMUSEUM, AMSTERDAM

Nagasaki it is expensive in Edo, costing *1:6 tael per gantang* (Vermeulen *et al.*
1986–: XI:49). According to the *WNT*, *tael* (of which *taijl* is an orthographical
variant) was originally a Malay word borrowed by Dutch via Portuguese. In
Malay it means 'weight', but it came to be used as both a unit of weight and
currency in Dutch. Here it is used for currency.[46] As noted above, *gantang* also
seems to derive from Malay or Javanese.[47] Another example of a unit of measure inserted into a Dutch text is *ikken* (一間), a unit of length equating to six
Japanese feet (c. 1.81 m).[48] In the 1633 *dagregister*, in relation to the sale of cloth
to Japanese, this is rendered as *ijckien* and *ickge* (viz. *een ickge geel laecken*—
an *ikken* of yellow cloth') (*Diaries*: I:51). In 1646, Willem Verstegen gives the
length of pieces of cloth as *10½ ickjen* (*Diaries*: X:7). In his 1780 *hofreisjournaal*, Titsingh refers to the wall of a castle, a few *ikken* (*eenige ikies*) of which
had been burnt away in a fire (Lequin 2011: 87). In 1787, in relation to damage
to a roof at Deshima, Hendrik Romberg refers to an area two *ikken* long and
one *ikken* wide (Vermeulen *et al.* 1986–: IX:136). In 1818, Blomhoff (2000a: 79)

---

46   In the early 1600s it was equivalent to about 3.5 *gulden*, but by 1783 it was equivalent to
1.65 *gulden* (Clulow 2013: 224 n. 71; Blussé and Remmelink 2004: 812).

47   In 1782, Titsingh placed an order for 2,000 *gantang* of rice at market price (Vermeulen
et al. 1986–: IX:31).

48   In the *Nederlandsche en Japansche Almanak voor het Jaar 1861*, 1 *ken* (*ikken*) is given as
2.0862 English yards.

described some bridges on the *hofreis* route as '30, ja 100 Ikjes, somwijl 200 Ikjes lang'. These authors could have used a Dutch unit of length but chose to use this Japanese term. This suggests that there were certain core Japanese terms, which formed an intrinsic part of the lexicon of users of Dutch in Japan. It is probably this unit of measure that is being referred to with the word *jokken* in an annotation of a depiction of a Russian ship that reached Japan (undated). The measurements given are *Lanck omtrent 15 jokken wijte 4 jokken*, i.e., around 15 *ikken* long and 4 *ikken* wide. It has been suggested that errors in the inscriptions on the picture indicate that they were probably written by an interpreter (Blussé *et al.* 1992: vii–viii).

The *koku* (石) is a unit for measuring rice roughly equivalent to five bushels, on which income was assessed. This is rendered as *cockjens* in a report that François Caron wrote in 1636, while still a merchant, to Philips Lucasz., Directeur-Generaal in Batavia.[49] By extension, the *koku* was used to indicate the area of land on which this rice was grown. Caron tells Lucasz. how many *koku* are owned by leading Japanese, adding *sijnde ijeder cockjen weerdig in Japan thien Carolus guldens Nederlands* ('each *koku* (*cockjen*) is worth in Japan 10 Dutch Carolus guilders'). A unit of measure based on the *koku* was the *mangoku* (萬石 (modern *kanji* 万石)), used for large quantities of rice equating to some 49,000 English bushel. An entry in the *dagregister* for 1638, which refers to an area of land on which this amount of rice could be grown, renders this as *mangock* (*Diaries*: III:164). Three other units of weight in Dutch texts are the *catty* (1¼ Amsterdam pounds), *mas* (1/10 *tael*) and *picol* (100 catties). Jan Joosten van Lodensteyn mentions all three in letters that he wrote in 1616 in relation to his work as a merchant. He refers to *10:000 catty copers* (10K catty of copper); *3 a 4.000 maes* and *200 picol peper, 10 a 15 picol note muscaten om aen die Spaengiaers te vercoopen* ('200 picols of pepper and 10–15 picol of nutmeg to sell to the Spanish') (Wieder 1923–25: 112–113). The Dutch kept detailed records of goods in and goods out in the *negotie journaal*. These units of weight are frequently used for dry goods here (*Diaries*: VII:234–322). *Catty* and *picol* are Malay or Javanese words, possibly adopted in Dutch via Portuguese (WNT *kati* and *pikol*). These examples concerning weights and measures illustrate well the range of source languages for terminology used in Dutch texts in Japan and the range of graphic forms in which individual terms were realized.

---

49   MS Leiden, LUB D H 213. *Verklaringh op verscheyden Vragen 't Japance Rijk concernerende door den Edele Heer Philips Luijcasz, Directeur-Generaal wegens den nederlanschen Stand in India voorgestelt ende door den Edele President François Caron beantwoord.*

5.4   *Clothing and Portable Objects*

In the *dagregister* in 1784 Hendrik Romberg switches to refer to *kabaaien*. A *kabaai*, here inflected with the Dutch plural suffix -*en*, was a garment worn in Asia. It comes from the Persian *kabâi* via the Malay *kabája*. (*WNT*; Vermeulen *et al.* 1986–: IX:76). Albert Bauduin (1829–90), a Dutchman who arrived in Nagasaki in 1859, wrote of the *kabaaijen* that both men and women wore in Japan (Moeshart 2001: 27). Blomhoff (2000a: 60–61) renders this as *cabaij* in his *hofreisjournaal* of 1818. This word could be seen as a loanword as it is included in several citations in the authoritative *Woordenboek der Nederlandsche Taal*, taken from Dutch texts written in the Low Countries and East Asia. Furthermore, we can talk here in terms of the 'circulation of loanwords', whereby a word is loaned from one language to another often undergoing phonological changes in the process. The early *dagregisters* contain much information about goods bought and sold by the Dutch, often necessitating switching into another language. For example, there is frequent reference to *catabers*. This is a Dutch rendering of *katabira* (帷子), a light kimono (*Diaries*: II:214–215). Several authors refer to *kappakagos*, a small bamboo basket for carrying a raincoat. This is a hybrid word from the Portuguese *capa* ('cape') and the Japanese for basket c/*kago* (籠). Blomhoff (2000a: 61) refers to these as *capagagos* (essential on the *hofreis*), while Overmeer Fisscher (1833: 275) refers to *Kappa Kago's*.

Authors of Dutch texts switched to render Japanese items that were carried on the person. In 1609, Nicolaes Puyck kept a private journal in Dutch throughout his journey to and from Sunpu, the small town in modern Shizuoka prefecture where the retired shogun, Tokugawa Ieyasu, had established his court (Clulow 2014: 49). He writes that the shogun, referred to by the title Gohijsamme (comprised of *gosho* (御所) a word for 'shogun' and the honorific suffix *sama* (様)), honoured them 'met een schoone gatane' ('with a beautiful *gatane*'). *Gatane* is now rendered *katana* (刀) and refers to a type of sword (Van Opstall 1972: II: 352). An object for which Overmeer Fisscher (1833: 309–310) switched in his account of Japan was 'pajong'. He writes 'een paar bedienden, welke den *pajong* boven het hoofd dragen' ('a few servants, who carry the pajong above the head'). A *pajong* was an umbrella or parasol, with the colour indicating the rank of the person for whom it was being carried (*WNT*).[50] There may be an element of switching to add local colour, or for the purpose of evocation, at work here. After all, there were perfectly good Dutch words for 'umbrella'.

---

50   The origin of the word is unclear. It is possibly from an Indonesian language or Tagalog. Bahasa Indonesia, a standardized form of Malay, has the word *payung*.

5.5   Food and Drink

In the *dagregister* in 1646, Willem Verstegen refers to *wijn ende sackana* ('wine and sackana') (*Diaries*: x:4). *Sa(c)kana* (肴) is food taken with *sake*. On the *hofreis* in March 1741, Jacob van der Waeijen records that the Dutch treated their Japanese companions to *sakana* (Blussé and Remmelink 2004: 3). One hybrid word including *sackana* is *saccane-bereyder*, someone who prepares and serves (Dutch: *bereider*) the *sackana* (*Diaries*: x:129). The Dutch were no strangers to *sake*. Van der Waeijen records that he and his colleagues received a gift of dried fish and a barrel of *sake* for providing hospitality to the Lord of Karatsu (Blussé and Remmelink 2004: 41). They also drank tea in Japan. The modern Dutch word for 'tea' is *thee*. This comes from the Southern Chinese Hokkien dialect word for 'tea', which the Dutch encountered in Java and introduced to Europe in around 1620 (*WNT*). However, in the late sixteenth and early seventeenth centuries, some Dutch authors such as Jan Huygen van Linschoten used *tsia* or variants thereof.[51] This is based on the Japanese *cha* (茶), which comes from Mandarin Chinese.[52] This is realized graphically in different forms. In 1643 on the *hofreis*, Johan van Elseracq refers to *sia*, while in 1683 Andreas Cleyer refers to drinking *een coppie gemaalen chiaa* ('a cup of ground (green) tea') (*Diaries*: IX:28; Cleyer 1985: 87). On a different note, in 1783, Isaac Titsingh referred to a quantity of Cantonese *sum* (蔘) that had been confiscated from the Chinese. Cantonese *sum* is a type of ginseng (Vermeulen *et al.* 1986–: IX:37).

A word is in order about soy or soya (Dutch *soja*) from the Japanese *shōyu* (醤油, 'bean paste oil'). Authors frequently insert this word in their Dutch texts in Japan (e.g., Blussé and Remmelink 2004: 63), and as we saw in Chapter 3 *konpura-bin* were made for exporting soya bearing the word JAPANSCHZOYA ('Japanese soya'). However, it was already being used by Dutch authors in the Dutch Republic in the late seventeenth century, so in that context it could be treated as a loanword (*WNT*). Furthermore, it was borrowed by other languages via Dutch. As early as 1679 the English philosopher John Locke was referring to *saio* (OED). Frisian has adopted Dutch hybrid words such as *sojakoek* ('soya biscuit') and *sojaboon* ('soyabean') as *sojakoeke* and *sojabean* (*WFT*). Van der Sijs (2010: 593) provides extensive details of languages which have borrowed this word via Dutch, illustrating once more how contact between Dutch and Japanese has contributed to the 'circulation of loanwords'.

---

51   Van Linschoten uses the variant *cha* in his *Itinerario* (36a, 1596) (*WNT*).
52   Most European languages take their word for 'tea' from Hokkien, a southern Sinitic variety, while Portuguese is one language that borrows from Mandarin (viz. *chá*), originally a northern Sinitic variety.

Authors of Dutch texts switched to render containers for food and drink. In 1646, in listing a bill of lading Willem Verstegen refers to a 'matsinbo of [or] *tsia*-pot'. As the Dutch gloss suggests, a *matsubo* (真壺) is a highly-prized type of jar used to store tea leaves or ground tea (*Diaries*: X:37). The additional 'n' in Verstegen's rendering suggests that the 'b' was a prenasalized consonant (Michel 2012: 109). In the *dagregister* in 1649, a *gioubackje* is mentioned several times. This is a *jūbako* (重箱) or multi-tiered food box which was used to store food on excursions (*Diaries*: XI:145). A word-initial 'g' in Dutch is typically pronounced [ɣ] or [x], but ⟨gi⟩ may be used to represent a sound closer to the Italian 'gi', as the initial consonant in Modern Japanese is pronounced [dz] (Booij 1995: 7; Labrune 2012: 67). Another rendering in the *dagregister* in 1649 is *sjoebaxkens*, which seems to include a diminutive and plural suffix (-*ken-s*) (*Diaries*: X:55). Again, the word initial ⟨sj⟩ which probably represents the non-native phoneme /ʃ/ is another attempt to approximate the word-initial sound in Japanese. In his 1818 *hofreisjournaal*, Blomhoff (2000a: 60) refers to 'De *tiabinto* van het *opperhoofd*'. *Tiabinto* is now transcribed as *chabentō* (茶弁当) and refers to a portable tea-set, which was very useful on the long journey to Edo.

5.6 *Japanese Writing Systems*

In his account of learning in Japan, Overmeer Fisscher (1833: 89) switches to give the names of different writing systems in Japanese. He writes 'Het alphabet [...] bekend onder de namen van het Katakane, Hiragane, Manyokane en Jamatogane', i.e., 'The (Japanese) alphabet is known by the names of *Katakane, Hiragane, Manyokane* and *Jamatogane*'. The first two, *katakana* and *hiragana*, are well known to the reader. 'Manyokane' refers to *Man'yōgana* (万葉仮名), the first writing system using Sinitic characters to represent Japanese phonetically. By 'Jamatogane' Overmeer Fisscher is probably referring to an older form of *hiragana* and *katakana*. *Yamato* (大和) is an ancient word for Japan (日本 (*Nihon*) is Sino-Japanese), while 'gane' or 'kana' (仮名) refers to a syllabary.

5.7 *Modes of Transport*

Dutch texts include renderings of Japanese modes of transport, which provide further examples of words inserted for the purpose of gap-filling. Overmeer Fisscher (1833: 283) refers to two types of chair in which people were carried. He describes one as 'een' *Cango* of draagstoel' and the other as 'een *norimond* of palankijn'. *Cango* probably refers to a *kago* (輿, 'a palanquin'), providing another example of a prenasalized consonant, realized as /ŋ/ (Michel 2012: 109). The second example, which occurs frequently in the *dagregister*, is often written *norimon*, although the *kun*-reading in Japanese is *norimono* (乗り物).[53]

---

53   The graphic form *norimon* suggests that the final 'o' was unstressed.

Several hybrid words were formed consisting of *norimon* and a Dutch word or morpheme. For example, in the *dagregister* for December 1646, Willem Verstegen refers to a *norimon-drager*, i.e., a 'palanquin-bearer', where *drager* is the Dutch for 'bearer' (*Diaries*: x:58). Other Dutch authors such as Isaac Titsingh also used this term.[54] Overmeer Fisscher (1833: 284) refers to *een norimonds-oppasser*. *Oppassen* is the Dutch for 'to look after', so this was someone who took care of the *norimono*.

Dutch authors inserted the names of types of Japanese boat in their texts. These include the *hayafune* (早船), a fast type of boat used on the *hofreis*, and the *tentōbune* (天道船). Willem Verstegen refers to the *hayafune* as *fayfenees* (plural) and *phayofne* (*Diaries*: x:128, 127), while Nicolaes Couckebakker rendered *hayafune* as *faija fenne* (*Diaries*: I:208). These renderings reflect the tendency in the Edo period to pronounce a word initial 'h' as [ɸ] (Michel 2012: 109; Frellesvig 2010: 386–387). The *tentōbune* is described by François Caron as *een expres cleen roeijvaertuijch* ('a small, quick rowing boat'), with a shortened or clipped form, *tentho* or *tento* (*Diaries*: I:191; IV:167). This shortened form may suggest that it was a term with which the Dutch were familiar and that it had been shortened through regular usage. In an account of visits to the Goto Islands by some Dutch at Hirado, Couckebakker (*Diaries*: I:164) notes that they travelled 'met een *coebaij*', i.e., a *kobaya* (小早), a small wooden boat. Later, Verstegen refers to *coebays* (plural) (*Diaries*: x:128). Finally, a barge used on part of the *hofreis* was named *hiyoshi maru* (日吉丸). This seems to have been taken from a pet name for Toyotomi Hideyoshi, rather than referring to a specific type of boat. Dutch authors realized this graphically in various ways including *Fiooosmaar* and *Fijoschima* (Blussé and Remmelink 2004: 806–807).

Although a distinction has been drawn between switching as part of a discourse strategy and switching for gap-filling, these examples illustrate that this is not an absolute distinction. These authors could, of course, simply have written a Dutch word or circumlocution, such as *snelle boot* ('fast boat') for a *hayafune*, but chose instead to refer specifically to the Japanese name for the boat. One possibility is that it was part of a discourse strategy to illustrate their familiarity with the Japanese terms, to use, as it were, *le mot juste* (Adams 2003: 337–340; Joby 2014: 248–250). Evocation, too, is probably at work here: the desire to create a certain image in the mind of the reader, which a Dutch circumlocution would not achieve.

Finally, Dutch authors did occasionally use Dutch words or Dutch coinages to refer to modes of transport in Japan. For example, several Dutch authors such as Hendrik Romberg used the coinage *hofreisbark*, i.e., the barque or boat for the *hofreis* (Vermeulen *et al.* 1986–: IX:77). In the loanword typology

---

54   Titsingh refers to *norimondsdragers* (Lequin 2011: 69).

of Winford (2003: 42–45), discussed in more detail in Chapter 7, this can probably be categorized as a native creation in Dutch, i.e., it had no direct no counterpart in Japanese.

5.8   *Other Objects*

Authors of Dutch texts switched for the purpose of 'gap-filling' for objects which do not neatly fit one of the above categories. The *dagregister* for 1663 records that a cargo on ships bound for the Dutch Republic included pieces of porcelain decorated with *Fatsenbacks*, i.e., *hasamibako* (挟箱), covered boxes typically of decorated lacquered wood carried on a pole on journeys (Volker 1971: 149). Moreover, the Japanese word is given a Dutch plural suffix -*s*, and so has undergone morphological integration, a phenomenon described in more detail in section 7. Overmeer Fisscher (1833: 284) refers to *twee hassambakkodragers* (cf. norimon-*drager*), another example of a Japanese-Dutch hybrid word, with a Dutch plural suffix. *Goza* (茣蓙) is a Japanese word for rush matting. In 1646, Willem Verstegen refers to 'een fijne mat, off gosa' ('a fine mat, or *goza*') (*Diaries*: X:245). At Kanzaki, which Dirk de Graeff van Polsbroek (1987: 34) records as Tanzakki, he writes that in the evening, 'om 7.30 was het al tamelijk donker geworden en werden mitsdien de tojiengs, papieren lantaarns, aangestoken' ('it had already become quite dark at 7.30 and so the tojiengs, paper lanterns, were lit'). It is not clear, however, which Japanese word De Graeff van Polsbroek is trying to render with *toijeng(s)*. One possibility is *chōchin* (提灯), a word for paper lanterns, while another is *tōshin* (灯心), the wick inside paper lanterns. *Toijeng* is, though, not a close match to either word. In a letter addressed to Isaac Titsingh in 1785, the interpreter Hori Monjūrō writes that a woman, 'Sakragi San' (sic), probably an *Orandayuki*, was now living with her mother and father in a 'roephuijs, of ageja' (Lequin 1990: 1:14). An *ageja* (揚屋) was a high-class pleasure house, to which outside prostitutes were invited. A *roephuis* is usually simply a small building where someone stands to proclaim news (*roepen* means 'to call'), so why Monjūrō connects these words is not clear. It may be that the Dutch used this as a euphemism.

5.9   *Words Relating to Religion*

In his 1636 report to Philips Lucasz., François Caron wrote that one of the movements within Buddhism was the 'Icko ofte [or] Ickois'. This 'sect' as he calls it was the most superstitious ('het superstitienste') of all those in Buddhism (Caron refers disparagingly to Buddhists as *papen* ('Papists')). This is more properly the *ikkōshū* (一向宗), often viewed as a small, militant Buddhist movement.[55]

---

55   MS Leiden, LUB D H 213.

In 1647 Dirck Snoeck refers to a *bōzu* (坊主) or Buddhist monk (*Diaries*: XI:131). He renders this as *bonzo*, which suggests that in this case 'z' is a prenasalized consonant. If so, then one might tentatively suggest that prenasalization occurs not simply with voiced plosives such as /g/, but with voiced obstruents, a group which includes both plosives and fricatives such as /z/.

Overmeer Fisscher (1833: 138) discusses Japanese religion in some detail in his account of Japan. At one point he refers to 'de Hemelgoden, of *Cami's*'. As the Dutch gloss, which literally means 'gods of heaven', suggests, the 'Cami' or *kami* (神) are the Japanese gods or spirits (another name for *Shintō* (神道) is 'kami-no-michi' (神の道, 'way of the gods')). A little later he writes, 'Tot de secte der *Sintoïsten* behooren ook de *Jamabosi's* of Sintoïstische kluizenaars' ('The yamabosi's or Shintō hermits also belong to the Shintō sect') (Overmeer Fisscher 1833: 144). In a note, Overmeer Fisscher writes '*Jamabosi* beteekent bergsoldaat' ('Yamabushi' means 'mountain soldier'). *Yamabushi* (山伏) are primarily ascetic, often itinerant, mountain hermits. In the *dagregister* for 1646 they had been described as *berghpapen* ('mountain papists'). This is in some sense is a loan translation, although the use of *papen* in this manner gives it an element of native creation (*Diaries*: X:64). Overmeer Fisscher (1833: 142) also inserts hybrid compound words into his Dutch text, consisting of both Dutch and Japanese morphemes. At one point he refers to the 'Dayrie, of het hoofd der Sintō-secte', i.e., 'the Shintō-sect', and on several occasions to 'deze Sinto-leer', by which he means 'the Shintō religion'.

5.10 *Japanese Titles*

Another motivation for Dutch authors switching was to render the title of Japanese dignitaries. In the text just quoted, Overmeer Fisscher mentions the *dayrie*, now rendered as *dairi* (内裏). This refers to the Imperial Palace in Kyoto (Miaco) and by extension the Emperor himself. In his report to Lucasz., Caron refers to *den daijro*, as does Nicolaes Couckebakker in 1634, while in 1663 Hendrick Indijck writes *Dairi* or 'Japanese Pope' (*Diaries*: I:86; Vermeulen *et al.* 1986–: XII:66).[56] Putting aside the anti-Catholic slant to this reference, it does point to the fact that during the Tokugawa period, the Emperor in Kyoto was largely a religious figurehead. This contrasts with the shogun in Edo, who was a temporal, military leader (Blussé and Remmelink 2004: 805). Isaac Titsingh makes this distinction in his 1780 *hofreisjournaal*. He records that he had received news of the death of 'den Daijri of geestelijken Keiser' ('the Dairi or spiritual Emperor') Go-Momozono (1758–79). He notes that some believed

---

56 MS Leiden, LUB D H 213.

that 'den wereldlijken Keizer' or 'secular Emperor', i.e., the shogun had died, although this was not the case (rather it was his heir apparent, Tokugawa Iemoto (1762–79)) (Lequin 2011: 68).[57] One other use of *dairi* is to refer to the dolls of the emperor and empress used during the doll festival of *Hina matsuri* (雛祭り) on 3 March. The Emperor was also referred to as Mikado (帝). Overmeer Fisscher writes (1833: 137) 'zoo lang zij toch in hunnen *Mikaddo* of *Dayrie* den waren afstammeling van den eersten stichter huns volks TENZIO DAYZIN erkennen'.[58] *Tenzio Dayzin*, sometimes transliterated as *Tenshō daijin* (天照大神), is a name for the sun goddess *Amaterasu* (天照), from whom according to Japanese mythology the Emperor was said to be descended. The temporal counterpart of the Emperor, the shogun, is referred regularly in Dutch texts in a variety of graphic realizations. In his report to Philips Lucasz., Caron writes *siugaan*.[59] Over time, this has become a Japanese loanword in Dutch, *sjogoen* ('shogun') (Van der Sijs 1996: 450–451).

When rendering the names of other important Japanese, the Dutch often added the relevant honorific suffixes, such as *dono* (殿). In 1633, Couckebakker refers to 'de Raedtsheer [counsellor] *Oijed[on]o* (*Diaries*: I:13). This is Doi Toshikatsu (1573–1644), a counsellor to the shogun, who had the title 'Ōi-no-kami'. *Oijed[on]o* is formed by adding the honorific suffix *dono* to the first part of his title. In 1649, Willem Verstegen refers to Ōno Harunaga, mentioned above, as *Vono Xuriddonne*. *Xuriddonne* is formed from *Shuri* in Harunaga's title 'Shuri-no-suke' (the ⟨x⟩ influenced by Portuguese orthography) and the honorific suffix *dono* (*Diaries*: XI:128). Likewise, Couckebakker added this honorific to the name of Ryūzaki Shichirōemon, rendering it as 'Streumondono' (*Diaries*: I:13). Another honorific suffix, *-sama* (樣 (modern *kanji* 様)), is also used by authors of Dutch texts. In 1633, Sakai Tadayuki, who had the title 'Awa-no-kami', is recorded as *Sacaija Auanomanijsamma* (sic). On the very next folio, four Japanese are listed with the same honorific suffix (*Diaries*: I:36–37). The *dagregister* for the 1651 *hofreis* names two of the shogun's counsellors as Sannickasamma and Insiesamma (*Diaries*: XII:138). On the *hofreis* in 1655, Leonard Winnincx adds the suffix *-sama* to the name of the shogunal counsellor Andō Ukyō (Vermeulen *et al.* 1986–: XII:197). In the 1683 *dagregister*, Andreas Cleyer (1985: 78, 64, 69) refers to one of the shogun's advisors, Hotta Masatoshi (1634–84), Lord of Chikuzen, as *Tzickuzeen-samma*, the

---

57   The *opperhoofd* Andreas Cleyer (1985: 107) refers in the *dagregister* to 'den ambassadeurs van den Dairo'. He is probably referring to the ambassadors of the *dairo* in Kyoto, although possibly to the shogun.

58   Trans: 'as long as they recognize in their Mikado or Dayrie the true descendant of the first founder of their people Tenzio Dayzin'.

59   MS Leiden, LUB D H 213.

Governor of Nagasaki as *Kinmot-samma*, and the *daimyō* Maeda Tsunanori, also known as Matsudaira Kaga-sama, as Matzendairo Cange-zamma.[60] In the last example, the voiced plosive 'd' was probably a prenasalized consonant (as was 'g') (Michel 2012: 109).

In his 1780 *hofreisjournaal*, Isaac Titsingh renders several Japanese titles in transcription. He refers to the *daimyō* of Numazu-*han* (沼津藩), Mizuno Tadatomo (1731–1802), as *dewa-no-kami* (出羽守), which was an honorific title given to *daimyō* of Numazu-*han* from the Mizuno clan (*kami* (守) is often translated as 'Lord'). Titsingh describes Kanō Hisakata (1711–86) as *Totomi no kami*, *Tōtōmi* (遠江) being the name of a province in Japan (Lequin 2011: 71; Blussé and Remmelink 2004: 849). Kutsuki Masatsuna sometimes signed his letters to Isaac Titsingh with his title *Koetski* (i.e., Kutsuki) *Okinocami*, reflecting his position as *daimyō* of Oki province. He also rendered Japanese titles in his letters. In one dated 1789, he refers to *TaijCoo FideJosi*. *FideJosi* is his rendering of (Toyotomi) Hideyoshi, the sixteenth-century Japanese warlord. He was given the extremely rare and exalted title *Daijō Daijin* (太政大臣, 'Chancellor of the Realm'), the first part of which Masatsuna renders as *TaijCoo*, possibly modifying it in *rōmaji* in an attempt to make it comprehensible for his Dutch correspondent (Lequin 1992: 31).

5.11 *The Names of Japanese Officials, Occupations and Institutions*

A slightly different case is switching in Dutch texts to give the job title of Japanese officials and others with whom the Dutch had contact. The *ot(t)ona* (乙名) were the heads of wards in Nagasaki. The *otona* of Deshima had oversight of the island with responsibility for the cleaning and repair of its buildings (Blussé and Remmelink 2004: 809). Overmeer Fisscher (1833: 265) picks this up when he writes 'Ottona's of Burgemeesters van het eiland' ('Otonas or Mayors of the island'). The term *bongiois* and variants thereof is used in Dutch texts to refer to those entrusted with guard and inspection duties. Willem Verstegen rendered it as *bongioys* and Dirck Snoeck as *bongeois* (*Diaries*: X:4; XI:115). In the one surviving letter in Dutch by Will Adams we read *Bon Jous* (Wieder 1923–25: 77). Hybrid forms for senior (*opper-*) and junior (*onder-*) *bongiois* also emerged. Isaac Titsingh refers to *Onderbanjoosen* (Lequin 2011: 69–70). In 1683 Andreas Cleyer (1985: 79) mentions *bongoisen* and *opperbongoisen*. In his 1818 *hofreisjournaal*, Blomhoff (2000a: 56–57) refers

---

60   There is a long list of Japanese names with both honorific suffixes in the 1633 *dagregister* (*Diaries*: 1:37).

to *Opper* and *onder banjoos*.[61] The etymology of the term, however, remains unclear.[62] Another term for a Japanese official with which the Dutch formed similar hybrid words was *bugyō*. In a list of Japanese who accompanied the *hofreis* in 1780, Titsingh refers to *een Opperbugio* and *twee Onderbugios* (Lequin 2011: 69–70). The Japanese word *bugio* (i.e., *bugyō*) usually refers to the Governor of Nagasaki or his counterpart in Edo. Here, however, it seems to refer to officials working for the *bugyō*.

In his account of his time in Yokohama (c. 1860), Assendelft de Coningh (2012: 36) switches to refer to *Jakoni*. A modern rendering is *yakunin* (役人) (/j/ is graphically realized as ⟨j⟩ in Dutch). They were government officials, whom Assendelft de Coningh refers to as sword-bearers, which reflects the fact that they were drawn mainly from the samurai class. Overmeer Fisscher (1833: 281) refers to *yakunin* as *Jakfnins*, adding a word-medial ⟨f⟩ to reflect aspiration and inflecting the word with the Dutch plural suffix -*s*.

Authors switched to render less salubrious job titles or social positions. Assendelft de Coningh (2012: 46) refers to the *rōnin* (浪人, masterless samurai) as *loonings*.[63] Dirk de Graeff van Polsbroek (1987: 37) discusses the Japanese *publieke huizen*, i.e., brothels in Shimonoseki, a stopover on the *hofreis*. He notes that the younger girls served the older prostitutes 'als [as] Kamoetoe of [or] Kabroes'. *Kabroes* is a corruption of *kaburos* (*kaburo* 禿 + Dutch plural suffix -*s*), young girls working for high-class prostitutes. Van Polsbroek continues 'Op huwbaren leeftijd ... ontvangt ze van het huis ... prachtige *kirimons* en haarspelden', i.e., 'when they are of marriageable age, they receive beautiful kimonos (*kirimons*) and hairpins from the house' (my italics).[64] A little later he writes 'De meeste dier vrouwen hebben ook hun eigen Okiaks of mainteneur' *Okiaks* is a corruption of *Okyaku sama* or *san* (お客様), i.e., 'an honoured guest', i.e., a 'customer' who only goes to one woman.

A slightly different example is the word *Keesje(n)s*, which literally means 'little Keeses', but was used to refer to the prostitutes who visited the Dutch at

---

61   Blomhoff also writes *opper Bangooshen* on the 1818 *hofreis*. MS Leiden, LUB BPL 3651.

62   One suggestion is that it comes from *banshū* (番衆), an archaic Japanese term for a guard in the service of local government (*Diaries*: 1:4). Another is that it comes from the Japanese *gobanjōshi* (Blomhoff 2000a: 56–57), while another is that it derives from *bugyō shū* (奉行衆), officers of the Nagasaki government (Blussé and Remmelink 2004: 804).

63   It was common for the Dutch to refer to them as *lonings* (De Graeff van Polsbroek 1987: Introduction). A little later, Assendelft de Coningh switches again with the word *toojing* (i.e., *tōjin* 唐人, 'Chinese (T'ang) person'), often used for any type of foreigner.

64   It does seem strange that Van Polsbroek recorded *kirimons* for 'kimono(s)'. He did know some Japanese but was not fluent. He has probably made a mistake here, but it is not currently possible to explain why.

Deshima.[65] As early as 1676, this appears in a Dutch travelogue in the phrase, 'De vrouwen die zij Keesjens noemen' ('the women they call Keesjens') (*WNT*) (Struys 1676: 66). One possibility is that this is a Dutch version of *geisha*. However, it is more likely to be derived from the Sino-Japanese *keisei* (傾城). This originally meant 'a woman who is a beauty' but came also to mean a leading courtesan or prostitute (Vos 1971: 615 n. 8).

Authors of Dutch texts used other strategies to refer to Japanese officials. These include coining loan translations and 'native creations', as well as extending the meaning of existing Dutch terms (Winford 2003: 42–45). Loan translations or calques are morpheme-by-morpheme translations from the donor language, in this case Japanese. One set of loan translations that the Dutch coined were applied to the various grades of interpreter (*tsūji*), who were employed, at their expense, to facilitate their communication with other Japanese. Dutch authors referred to the senior interpreters (*ōtsūji*) (大通詞, ō (大) means 'big' or 'senior') as *oppertolken* (*opper* = upper/senior, *tolk* = interpreter), and junior interpreters, *kotsūji* (小通詞) ('junior interpreter'), quite logically, as *ondertolken*.[66] The Japanese term for the body to which the interpreters belonged was the *tsūji nakama* (通詞仲間). The Dutch translated this as *tolkencollege*, i.e., college of interpreters.

Other terms for Japanese officials were 'native creations', i.e., terms coined by the Dutch using Dutch morphemes, which have no direct equivalent in Japanese. For example, many Dutch authors referred to the *dwarskijker*, a compound formed from *dwars* ('at a right angle') and *kijker* ('looker'). This rendered the Japanese *metsuke* (目付), officially a supervisor or inspector, but someone who the Dutch felt, not without justification, was spying on them on behalf of the Japanese authorities. The *WNT* records that this term was first used in the Dutch East Indies. In 1787 Hendrik Romberg used it in the *dagregister*. Unfortunately, the *WNT* does not give a date for the first use, but one possibility, which requires further investigation, is that it was used in Japan before being used in the Dutch East Indies.[67] Romberg also used the terms *opperdwarskijker* and *grootdwarskijker* to refer to the inspector general, the *ōmetsuke* (大目付) (Vermeulen *et al.* 1986–: IX:136). On a different note, another native creation by Dutch authors is *Opperpaap*. This literally means 'senior Papist' and was sometimes used to refer to the senior priest at a local temple or shrine.

---

65   Kees is in turn an affective form of Cornelis.

66   Another rank was the *nenban tsūji*. As noted above (Ch. 4, n. 28), these were the interpreters who were in charge of their fellow interpreters for that year. The term was rendered in Dutch as *rapporteurtolk*. Sugimoto (1976–82: V:906; Vermeulen *et al.* 1986–: III:192).

67   The first citation that the *WNT* gives by an author in the Netherlands is dated 1868 (J.T. Buys, *Studiën over Staatkunde en Staatsrecht*).

It reflected the Calvinist orientation of the Dutch, and their negative view of Roman Catholicism and Japan religions (e.g., Blomhoff 2000a: 54).

Extensions are a type of lexical contact phenomenon whereby the meaning of an existing native word is extended as a result of contact with another language (Winford 2003: 45). A couple of examples serve to illustrate this. The Dutch word *Keizer* means emperor. As noted above, Dutch authors sometimes referred to the shogun as the secular 'Keizer'. However, other authors simply described the shogun as the 'Keizer'. For example, Overmeer Fisscher (1833: 308) refers to an 'audientie bij den Keizer van Japan', i.e., an 'audience with the Emperor (the shogun) of Japan'. As the Dutch were well aware, however, the shogun was not the Emperor or even an Emperor, rather he was a military leader. The Emperor, who lived in Kyoto during the Tokugawa period, was largely a ceremonial and religious figure, with whom the Dutch had little contact. One Dutch term used to refer to more than one official Japanese position is *burgemeester*, which usually translates as 'mayor' in English. In some cases it referred to the city's four (later six) *machidoshiyori*, who reported directly to the *bugyō*.[68] A variant on this is *stads burgermeester* ('town mayor'). In a letter to Titsingh in 1775, Hori Monjūrō tells his friend of two newly-appointed *stads burgermeesters* (Lequin 1990: 1:14).[69] In other cases, *burgemeester* referred to the Japanese term *ot(t)ona*, mentioned above, who had oversight of the island of Deshima. For example, in a *dagregister* entry for 1646, he is referred to as 'den burgemeester van 't eylant' ('the mayor of the island') (*Diaries*: x:6). The *bugyō* is often referred to by authors of Dutch texts as the *Gouverneur* ('Governor') of Nagasaki (e.g., *Diaries*: XI:3–5).

On a slightly different note, one other example of an extension concerns the Dutch term *Geldkamer*. This literally means 'money chamber', and was a standard word used in Low Countries Dutch.[70] Dutch authors in Japan used this term to refer to the *Nagasaki kaisho*. This literally means the 'Nagasaki meeting place'. However, it was the institution in Nagasaki, through which foreign traders, i.e., the Chinese and the Dutch, were required to sell their goods to Japanese merchants, and which distributed income from this trade to the citizens of Nagasaki. Therefore, this extension of an existing Dutch term captures well the function of the institution rather than providing a literal translation of its Japanese name (Blussé and Remmelink 2004: 806).[71]

---

68   Hesselink (2005: 516) and Screech (2005: 279) suggest that 'ward elder' is an appropriate translation for *machidoshiyori*.

69   *Burgermeester* is an older form of *burgemeester*.

70   The one example cited in the *WNT* refers to it as a place where books, paper and money were stored in an orphanage.

71   For more on the *Nagasaki kaisho*, see Shimada (2006: 165).

5.12 *Japanese Festivals*

In the *dagregister* for June 1647, Willem Verstegen refers to the 'Japance sik'. This is a seasonal festival now rendered *sekku* (節句). In August 1647, Verstegen refers to the 'Japansche bon', where *bon* (盆) was a Buddhist festival of the dead lasting several days (*Diaries*: X:155, 187). However, some authors insert loan translations of these names (Winford 2003: 45). A couple of examples serve to illustrate this. In 1781, the *opperhoofd* Arend Willem Feith recorded on a given day that it was the Japanese *Popjesfeest*. This is a literal translation of the Japanese *Hina matsuri* (雛祭り), which means 'doll festival' (Blussé and Remmelink 2004: 810). In the summer of the same year, Feith refers to the *Sterrefeest* ('Star Festival'). This is a loan translation of *Hoshi matsuri* (星祭り), the 'Star festival', which is also called the *Tanabata matsuri* (七夕祭り) (Vermeulen *et al.* 1986–: IX:6, 10). In other cases, Dutch authors used hybrid words to denote the names of Japanese festivals. In the late 1640s, Dirck Snoeck referred to the *Sannits-feest*, which is a combination of the Japanese festival *Sannichisai* held on the third day of the third month and the Dutch word for festival, *feest* (*Diaries*: XI:129). Finally, one text in which there is regular switching to insert the names of Japanese festivals is the *Nederlandsche en Japansche Almanak* printed at Deshima in 1861. Some of the renderings given here differ from those in other Dutch texts. *Hina matsuri* is referred to by another of its names, *Momo no sek'*, i.e., *Momo-no-sekku* (桃の節句, 'Peach Festival'), while the *Tanabata matsuri* is referred to as the *Starrenfeest* (*Sitsiseki*). *Sitsiseki* renders *Shichiseki*, an old reading of 七夕, the Sinitic characters used in Chinese for the festival.

6 Toponyms

The question of whether the insertion of Japanese toponyms in Dutch texts constitutes interference is not an easy one to answer. One could argue, however, that because this occurs as a result of language contact, it does indeed constitute a form of interference. Examples are legion. For example, Isaac Titsingh mentions over 170 Japanese place names in his 1780 *hofreisjournaal* alone (Lequin 2011: 63). As already noted, Michel (2012) provides extensive details of how Japanese toponyms were rendered in early modern Western maps of Japan (see fig. 19). However, a few points are in order here.

First, at a basic level, one could view the insertion of Japanese toponyms as 'gap-filling'. However, in some sense it also formed part of an author's discourse strategy. By rendering these toponyms in *rōmaji* authors demonstrated (probably intentionally) a certain familiarity with them, although the accuracy

FIGURE 19 A map of Japan with Dutch renderings of toponyms, Adriaan Reeland,
Jan Goeree, 1737–1750
RIJKSMUSEUM, AMSTERDAM

with which they rendered them varied. Second, as Michel has demonstrated, the insertion of Japanese toponyms provides us with useful information about how the Dutch and indeed Japanese may have pronounced these names. The frequency with which authors begin toponyms with ⟨f⟩, which are now rendered with a word-initial ⟨h⟩, does suggest that at some point pronunciation was closer to /f/ (realized as [ɸ]) than /h/. This supposition is supported by observations by Europeans in Japan. In an essay on the Japanese language, the Swede Thunberg (1792, quoted in Frellesvig 2010: 386–387) often writes ⟨f⟩, where today there is a ⟨h⟩, e.g., *fanna* ('flower') (Hepburn: *hana*), but observes that words written with ⟨f⟩ are sometimes read or pronounced with ⟨h⟩. Von Siebold wrote such words with ⟨h⟩ but noted that they were often pronounced with an 'f'. In 1636 François Caron refers to Hakata as 'Fackatta'.[72] In 1647, Frederick Coyett refers to Hibi in Bizen province as 'Fiby' (*Diaries*: XI:5). In his 1780 *hofreisjournaal*, Isaac Titsingh refers to the mountains of *Hakone* as 'het Faconies gebergte' (*gebergte* is the Dutch for mountains) (Lequin 2011: 68–71).[73] In his private journal on the *hofreis* of 1818, Jan Cock Blomhoff (2000a: 107) renders Himeji as Fimegi, Hakone as Fakonis and Hizen as Fiseeng. Similar examples abound. Frellesvig (2010: 386–387) observes that the change from /f/ to /h/ took place during the period of Modern Japanese (from c. 1600 onwards) and that by the middle of the nineteenth century, such words would typically be written with 'h', except before 'u', where it is 'f' reflecting the fact that here /h/ is realized as [ɸ].

Third, another strategy that authors adopted was to give Dutch names to Japanese places, above all topographical features, in some sense domesticating them. In 1643, Dutch ships explored the northern coast of Japan (manned by Hesselink's 'Prisoners of Nambu'). They devised Dutch names for promontories, mountains, islands, etc., such as Wolvis-boght, Caap de Kennis and Sand-duynige hoek near Edo. These appear in a 1783 map of Korea and Japan published by Louis Brion de la Tour. On the expedition, Captain Maerten Gerritsz. Vries (1589–1646/47) named the strait between Kyushu and Tanegashima as Straat van Diemen, in honour of (and to win favour with?) the Governor-General of the Indies, Antonio van Diemen (1593–1645) (Michel 2012: 120–121). One example of a Dutch name for a topographical feature lasting well into the nineteenth century and used by many authors is *Papenberg* (lit. 'Papist mountain'), the name for a hill or mountain on Takaboko Island (高鉾島) at the entrance to Nagasaki Bay.[74] In the typology of Winford (2003: 45), *Papenberg*

---

72   MS Leiden, LUB D H 213.
73   Writing in Swedish, Olof Eriksson Willman (2013: 41) refers to Hakone as *Fauckonij*.
74   W.J.C. Huyssen van Kattendyke (1860: 4–5) observes that it was thought that the mountain gained the name *Papenberg* as Portuguese missionaries were forced to jump from it

could be classified as a 'purely native creation', i.e., there was no equivalent in Japanese. Furthermore, the use of *Papenberg* in some sense forms part of a discourse strategy in identifying with the anti-Catholic sentiments implicit in the Dutch name.

7 Morphological Integration

Most of the lexical items inserted into Dutch texts in the section on 'gap-filling' are nouns. In the related contact phenomenon of loanword borrowing, open-class content items such as nouns and adjectives lend themselves more easily to borrowing than closed-class function items, such as pronouns and conjunctions. By contrast, verbs tend to be borrowed less than other open-class items, in part because of their increased morphological complexity and their centrality to the syntax of a sentence (Winford 2003: 51–52). Authors of Dutch texts in Japan sometimes made the nouns they inserted plural, diminutive or genitive. In a few cases they made adjectives from them. They inflected these words according to the rules of the matrix language, Dutch, in order to integrate them morphologically into that language. It will be instructive to see how this did this.

7.1 *Plural Forms*

First, as regards making nouns plural, broadly speaking Dutch uses two suffixes, *-en* and *-s* (Van Wijk 2007: 30–33).[75] There are other suffixes for limited groups of nouns, such as *-eren* (e.g., *kind, kinderen* (child(ren)), and plurals where the stem undergoes change, such as Latin loanwords (e.g., *museum, musea*). Today the rules for when to use which ending are quite well established, with phonological factors playing an important although not necessarily determinative role (Van Wijk 2007: 32). In the seventeenth century, the use of *-s* was more common than now and the choice of suffix was to some extent dependent on

---

to their deaths (see Chapter 3). He doubts this, suggesting rather that it gained its name as it looked like a monk's skull cap.

75   The manner in which plurals are formed in Japanese is quite different from that used in Dutch. There are several plural suffixes, such as *-tachi*, but these are typically limited to words denoting humans. Otherwise, rather than plurals *sensu stricto*, count words are used to denote the number of an item (one or more than one) on the basis of certain qualities that it possesses. For example, flat objects take the count word or suffix *-mai*, while large animals take *-tō*. The native Japanese number for four is *yon*, so four flat objects is *yonmai*, while four large animals is *yontō*. I have come across no examples of authors of Dutch texts switching into Japanese and forming plurals in this manner, or indeed using the Japanese plural suffixes for humans (Kaiser *et al.* 2013: 465–466, 348–349).

the author (Weijnen 1968: 45). In the nineteenth century, the rules were still less well established than they are now. An edition of Weiland's *Spraakkunst* published in Amsterdam in 1805 identifies *-s*, *-en* and *-n* as the plural suffixes (p. 55), but offers little firm advice as to when each should be used. It might then be too much to expect all native users of the language, let alone Japanese, to be consistent in their use of these suffixes.

Let us look at some examples. The *yamabushi* (山伏), ascetic mountain hermits, mentioned above, are referred in the *dagregister* for 1646 as *jammabosen*, with the Dutch plural suffix *-en* (or possibly *-n*) (*Diaries*: X:64). *Bongioys/bongeois* is written with the Dutch plural suffix *-en*, as in *bongeoisen*, used by Dirck Snoeck (*Diaries*: XI:5).[76] In 1768 Jan Crans (*opperhoofd* intermittently 1763–69) refers to *bongioisen* (Blussé and Remmelink 2004: 327). Another spelling variant is *banjoost*. Several authors refer to the junior ranks as *Onderbanjoosten*.[77] The example of *kabaaien*, as a plural of *kabaai*, was given above. In his private journal of 1609, Nicolaes Puyck refers to *fumen* ('boats'), giving the Japanese *fume/fune* ('boat') the Dutch plural ending *-n* (viz. 'met 18 fumen') (Van Opstall 1972: 352). One example of another author using an alternative plural form is Nicolaes Couckebakker, who in 1637 referred to *pheijfenes*, a plural form of *hayafune* ('fast boat') with *-s*, watching a Chinese junk sailing past Hirado Bay (*Diaries*: III:13). In his informal *hofreisjournaal* for 1780 Isaac Titsingh rendered the Japanese word *nagamochi* (長持ち) ('a long oblong chest carried on poles') as *nagamoetsen*, giving it a Dutch plural form (Lequin 2011: 78). It is possible that he considered the singular to be *nagamoets* (with a weakened word-final 'i' after a sibilant) and added the plural suffix *-en*. In the 1630s Couckebakker was entertained *met saccaenen ende wijn* and *wijne ende sackanen* (*Diaries*: I:58; III:150). The singular for *saccaenen/sackanen* (items of food eaten with sake) is typically rendered *sakana*. One possibility is that Couckebakker considers the final vowel to be a schwa and adds the plural suffix *-n*. If not, then he is modifying the stem.

In other cases, Dutch authors used the suffixes *-s* and *-'s*. In 1636, Nicolaes Couckebakker refers to '2000: goude *coebans*', i.e., 2000 golden *koban* (小判) (*Diaries*:II:43). In the same year, the senior merchant (*oppercoopman*) Hendrick Hagenaer wrote a letter from Hirado to colleagues on the *hofreis* referring to 'valsche silvere *coebans*' ('false silver *koban*') (*Diaries*: II:76). The unit for measuring rice, *koku* (石), was rendered as *cockjen* by François Caron. Couckebakker

---

76 Snoeck describes them as 'stadsdienaers off rackers', i.e., low-ranking employees of the city.

77 See Overmeer Fisscher (1833: 280) for this form. In his 1780 *hofreisjournaal*, Titsingh writes the plural form *Onderbanjoosen* (Lequin 2011: 69).

gave it the plural form *kockiens* (*Diaries*: 1:70). Dutch authors often referred to *norimons* ('litters'). In his *hofreisjournaal* Isaac Titsingh writes *onse norimons* ('our litters'), adding a Dutch plural suffix -*s* to the Dutch rendering of the Japanese word *norimono*, possibly influenced by the fact that Dutch nouns ending in an unstressed -*en* typically take -*s* for the plural (Lequin 2011: 69).

In Late Modern Dutch, words ending in -a, -i, -o, -u and -y are given the plural suffix -'s (the apostrophe indicates that the final open vowel should remain open). These are typically (though not always) loanwords such as *firma, taxi, auto, paraplu* and *baby*. Grammars such as Weiland's *Spraakkunst* (1805) and Roelof van der Pijl's 'A Practical Grammar of the Dutch Language' (Rotterdam, 1819) make no mention of words with these endings or how they are made plural (pp. 34–39). Nevertheless, authors of Dutch texts in Japan used both -'s and -s to form plurals for such words. As noted above, Couckebakker and other authors make the Portuguese word *capado* ('eunuch') plural by adding -*s* (*cap(p)ados*) (*Diaries*: 1:7; III:196). In 1649, Antonio van Bronckhorst (*opperhoofd* 1649–50) refers to the *casera's*, i.e., house servants, who served the Dutch with 'saccanen ende wijn' (*Diaries*: XII:13). Ships from China often brought silkware. In 1646, junks from Nanjing brought *fabitaas/fabitas*. These are 'pieces (*pees*)' of *habutae* (羽二重), fine Chinese silk (*Diaries*: IX:138–139). In 1636, Hendrick Hagenaer switched to refer to 'itsseboos', a plural of the coin *ichibu* (一分) (*Diaries*: II:76). In the nineteenth century, Assendelft de Coningh (2012: 48) refers to *itzeboes*. Overmeer Fisscher (1833: 318) refers to *itsjiboe's*, which is but one example of how there was little consistency in the formation of plurals.

Elsewhere in his account of Japan, Overmeer Fisscher (1833: 270) refers to '*Tjaya's* of theehuizen'. *Chaya* (茶屋) is a Japanese word for a place where one can go to drink tea.[78] He also refers to *Kappa Kago's* (baskets for raincoats), and *hassambakko's* (small boxes), both of which were carried in the train of the *opperhoofd* (Overmeer Fisscher 1833: 275–276, 312). However, he is not always consistent. In another passage he refers to 'twee paar *Hassambakkos*' ('Two pairs of *hassambakkos*') (p. 285). For the plural of *sami*, the three-stringed guitar mentioned above, Overmeer Fisscher uses *samies* (p. 278). Overmeer Fisscher (1833: 138) refers to the Japanese gods as *Cami's*. This is a plural form of 'Cami' or *kami* (神). Another Japanese term that occurs regularly in the *dagregister* is *ot(t)ona*. Overmeer Fisscher (1833: 265) typically gives this the plural 's viz. *ottona's*, while other Dutch authors give this form or *ottonas*. One interesting exception occurs in the *dagregister* for 1635. In the entry for 30 March, Couckebakker uses the form *ottenae*. This is probably a Latin plural of a word

---

78   According to the *WNT*, *theehuizen* is sometimes used by the Dutch to refer to brothels.

being treated as a first declension masculine noun, cf. *poeta, poetae* (*Diaries*: 1:213). An example of a word from Portuguese being inflected with a Dutch plural is *complemento's*, from the Portuguese for 'complements' (the Portuguese plural is '-os') (*Diaries*: VIII:188–189).

7.2   *Diminutive Forms*

In seventeenth-century Dutch, a variety of suffixes were used to form the diminutive. These include *-ken, -sken, -ie, -tje* and *-tge* (Weijnen 1968: 53–54). In Late Modern Standard Dutch, diminutives are formed with the suffix *-je*, which has the plural *-s*, e.g., *lampjes* ('small lamps').[79] In earlier texts, several suffixes have been used to form diminutives. In the late eighteenth and early nineteenth centuries, while Siegenbeek preferred *-je*, Bilderdijk opted for *-jen* (Van der Horst 2008: 1:1640).

The question arises as to whether authors of Dutch texts made diminutives from Japanese words in their texts. Above, it was suggested that several authors make diminutives of the word *jonck* ('junk'). Two further examples relate to *jūbako* (重箱), the multi-tiered food box used to store food on excursions. In the *dagregister* in 1649, this is referred to several times as *gioubackje* (*Diaries*: XI:145). The *-je* ending is suggestive of a diminutive. In the *dagregister* for 1649, we find *sioubacxkens*. This seems to be a diminutive (*-ken*) rendering of *jūbako* with the Dutch plural suffix *-s*. It may be modelled on *barckxkens* ('small boats') which appears in the previous sentence (*Diaries*: X:46). The form *sjoebaxkens* occurs a few pages later (*Diaries*: X:55). Another word which seems to be a diminutive is *cockjen*, a rendering of *koku* (石) by both François Caron and Nicolaes Couckebakker (*kockiens*).

One final example concerns the Japanese unit of length, the *ikken* (一間). This is rendered in several forms in Dutch texts including *ijckien, ickge, ikies* and *ikjes*. These forms are suggestive of Dutch diminutives and may reflect an attempt by Dutch authors to 'domesticate' this Japanese term.[80] However, here we need to strike a note of caution. In the 1861 *Nederlandsche en Japansche Almanak* in the section on Japanese weights and measures, the entry for *ikken* adds '*vulgo* ikje'. If I read this correctly, it is saying that the 'common' Japanese pronounced *ikken* as *ikje*. If so, then forms such as *ikies* and *ikjes* may simply be renderings of the Japanese 'vulgar' form with a Dutch plural suffix. On the

---

79 There are variants on this rule. However, these are beyond the scope of the current analysis. Other endings such as *-ke* and *-ken* are still used in dialectal varieties of Dutch.

80 One other possibility, particularly concerning the forms where there is an 'i' or 'j' before the 'e' is that this represents a weak 'i' before an 'e', which has now disappeared (Michel 2012: 109).

other hand, it may be that authors of Dutch texts viewed these as diminutive forms and inflected them as such.

7.3 Genitive Forms and Adjectives

Another feature of Dutch noun morphology is the addition of -s or -'s for the genitive singular of nouns. In the seventeenth century, this feature was much more common than it is now and was used to inflect most if not all classes of noun, e.g., 'den strael *des goetheyts*' ('the ray of goodness') in P.C. Hooft's 'Granida' (l. 492) (my italics) (Weijnen 1968: 43). In Late Modern Dutch, its use is largely restricted to proper nouns and family relations as well as set phrases. Several authors of Dutch texts in Tokugawa Japan inflect non-Dutch words with these suffixes, i.e., according to the rules of the matrix language. In a letter to Isaac Titsingh in 1785, Narabayashi Jūbei refers to *de daijrijs doctor*, i.e., 'the physician of the Emperor' (Lequin 1990: I:11). This may also be at work in the reference by Motoki Yoshinaga to *eenige Firandoos porcelein werken* in a letter to Titsingh in 1786 (Lequin 1990: I:41). Here the genitive suffix may be attached to the toponym *Firando* (Hirado). Alternatively, Yoshinaga may be using an adjective, formed in the manner of other Dutch toponymic adjectives, e.g., *Amsterdams(ch)* or *Utrechts(ch)*. We see this more clearly in the phrase 'eenige Firandosche burgers' ('some citizens of Firando') in the 1640 *dagregister* (*Diaries*: IV:321).[81] A similarly clear example is provided by Namura Katsuemon, who in a letter written in quite comprehensible Dutch to Titsingh in 1786 refers to *een stel **Miacosche** knoopen* that he is sending his correspondent. Miaco is another name for Kyoto, so he is sending a set of buttons from Kyoto (Lequin 1990: I:37). In 1645, Jan van Elseracq formed the adjective *Miaecse (prijs)* referring to the price of silk in Miaco (*Diaries*: IX:42). Similarly, in 1649 Dirck Snoeck makes a Dutch adjective from the toponym 'Nagasaki' when he mentions Sacquemondonne (Takagi Sakuemon), 'den eersten der **Nangasacquise** borgemeesteren', i.e., the first of the Nagasaki 'mayors' (*Diaries*: XI:185).[82] Van Elseracq had earlier referred to the '**Nangasackyse** marckt' (market for silk) (*Diaries*: IX:42, my bold) The use of -s(ch)e to make an adjective from a toponym was not limited to Japanese names. Junks from Nanjing in China were referred to as *Nankijnse joncken* (the 'k' is a feature of southern Sinitic varieties) (*Diaries*: IX:138; X:153).

---

81 Another example is *Firandees* (*seecker Firandees coopman* 'A certain Hirado merchant') (*Diaries*: IV:132).

82 As noted above, Dutch authors typically use 'burgemeester' to refer to the *machidoshiyori* of Nagasaki (Blussé and Remmelink 2004: 804).

7.4   *Demonyms*

The suffix *-er* is often used in Dutch to create demonyms, i.e., to denote someone from a particular place. For example, someone from Japan is a *Japanner*.
In seventeenth-century Dutch, there is evidence in other types of word for
d-insertion between a nasal consonant and 'er', e.g., /n—ər/. Two examples are
gheender (an inflected form of *geen* 'not, no') and *fijnder* ('finer') (Weijnen 1968:
34). In Dutch texts written in Japan, we also find d-insertion in demonyms,
for example in the form *Japanders* (e.g., *Diaries*: IX:12).[83] In his preface to
Imonsuchi Orandago hōkai in Dutch, Baba Teiyū refers to *Japanders*. Likewise,
in the 1646 *dagregister*, there is reference to *Nankinders/Nanquinders*, i.e., people from Nanjing (*Diaries*: IX:154; XI:28).

7.5   *Concluding Remarks*

Thus, we can conclude that authors of Dutch texts integrated non-Dutch
words, primarily nouns, morphologically, into the matrix language, to form
plurals, diminutives, genitives, toponymic adjectives and demonyms. While
most of the examples presented were written by native speakers, a few examples were written by Japanese, suggesting that they had at least a basic command of Dutch noun morphology.

8   Conclusion

This chapter has employed the resources of several sub-disciplines within linguistics including phonology, morphology and sociolinguistics in order to analyse the insertion into Dutch texts of words and phrases from other languages,
and related phenomena such as native creations, semantic extensions and hybrid words, broadly referred to as 'interference', that resulted from language
contact in Japan.[84] The picture that has emerged is that this was a frequent
and, from the evidence presented in this chapter, necessary phenomenon in
texts written in Dutch. It is marked by both homogeneity and heterogeneity.

First, while most of the instances of interference can be categorized as either switching as part of a discourse strategy or 'gap-filling', these categories
can be further analysed into several sub-categories. Almost all the examples
of 'gap-filling' were nouns. In this regard, it has something in common with

---

83   In Late Modern Dutch, there is d-insertion in the sequence /r—ər/, e.g., *donkerder*
      ('darker'), not **donkerer* (Booij 1995: 74).

84   Another term for these phenomena is 'outcomes of contact' (Winford 2003: 42).

loanword borrowing, in that open-class content items such as nouns and adjectives lend themselves more easily to borrowing than closed-class function items (Winford 2003: 51–52). While switching has been analysed by motivation, 'gap-filling' has been analysed into twelve themes. Furthermore, instances of interference have been analysed by language. Inevitably, many examples of switching and gap-filling involved Japanese words and phrases. However, other languages, too, provided instances of interference in Dutch texts including Latin, Portuguese, Sinitic varieties and Malay.

Second, the chapter has drawn examples from a range of sources and authors. The sources include the *dagregister*, private journals, correspondence and commercial documents. They are spread across the Dutch period in Japan. Nicolaes Puyck's 1609 journal was written almost at the dawn of this period, while the journals of Dirk de Graeff van Polsbroek and Cornelis Assendelft de Coningh were written as the sun was starting to set on Dutch as a contact language in Japan. Dutch, non-Dutch European and Japanese authors have been cited. There is a sense in which the insertion of non-Dutch words and phrases helped to create a bond between author and reader; for example, Isaac Titsingh and Kutsuki Masatsuna, developing and drawing on a common translingual lexicon. Certain social categories, above all women, are almost completely absent from this analysis (the *Orandayuki* being one exception), but this is a function of the social context rather than a deliberate choice on the part of this author.

Third, while the same word might be rendered differently by authors and even by the same author, there is some element of consistency. Two examples are the use of the grapheme ⟨f⟩, where cMJ typically has a word-initial 'h', and the insertion of ⟨n⟩ before voiced obstruents indicating a prenasalized consonant. These both suggest that the Japanese that the Dutch heard was somewhat different from cMJ, a point supported by contemporary sources.

Fourth, most of the examples analysed under the heading 'gap-filling' are more or less accurate graphic realizations of Japanese terms, involving 'total morphemic importation' to borrow from Winford (2003: 45). Authors of Dutch texts did, however, use other types of lexical contact phenomena, including loan translations, hybrid words and native creations. Fifth, some words may have been inserted only once or twice in Dutch texts, whereas others were inserted more frequently and for a significant period. For example, in the case of gap-filling to render Japanese coins, while *ichibu* (and orthographical variants) was used by both Dutch and Japanese authors of Dutch texts from the seventeenth to the nineteenth centuries, there was much less evidence for the use of *zeni*.

Sixth, the insertion of these words in Dutch texts means that the lexis of the Dutch written in Japan differed somewhat from the lexis of Low Countries varieties of Dutch. As a result, I have tentatively posited the notion of a Dutch topolect or *nesolect*. On the one hand, this notion gains support from the use of core terms for some two hundred years, which were not used in Low Countries varieties of Dutch. On the other hand, I recognize that this proposal is problematic, as for example, there were few native users in Japan at any one time; most of them stayed in Japan for several years at most; and they probably used different varieties of Low Countries Dutch. Despite these objections, it may, nevertheless, be instructive to place this variety in the framework for analysing the effects of language contact developed by Thomason and Kaufman (1988: 74–76). The interference in this variety of Dutch is limited to borrowing non-essential lexical items, which equates to level 1 on the scale of 1–5 proposed by Thomason and Kaufman. 'Borrowing' needs to be understood broadly here, for as already noted the focus in this chapter is on 'interference' in general rather than merely on borrowing *sensu stricto*.

Seventh, the question arises as to whether the evidence analysed in this chapter allows us to draw any conclusions about the Dutch spoken on Deshima. In one sense, it does, for we know that the *dagregister* was often dictated by the *opperhoofd* to a clerk (*scriba*). Therefore, the *opperhoofd* is likely to have inserted non-Dutch words and phrases in his Dutch as he dictated. Given the extent to which authors of Dutch texts switched, it is probable, although not certain, that they did so in other spoken utterances. Furthermore, the phonological information contained in the graphic realizations of these non-Dutch words at least hints at how the Dutch pronounced, or perhaps tried to pronounce, them. Therefore, while it is not possible to draw firm conclusions, I would argue that the written sources do nevertheless give us some sense of which non-Dutch words were inserted in Dutch utterances, how they were pronounced, and indeed how they might have been morphologically integrated into these utterances.

Finally, one future research possibility is the analysis of switching into Dutch in Japanese texts. This is often seen as the first step towards full borrowing of loanwords. Several examples were given in Chapter 3. However, more work could usefully be done on this subject. Dutch words that have become embedded in Japanese are analysed in Chapter 7. As for this chapter, it has, one hopes, illustrated that many European and Japanese authors writing in Dutch in Tokugawa Japan inserted words and phrases from Japanese and other languages both as part of their discourse strategies and for the purpose of 'gap-filling'. Furthermore, it is to be hoped that this analysis adds to the literature on code switching, above all on switching in written sources.

CHAPTER 6

Translation from Dutch

1 Introduction

In the last chapter, the focus was on the effect of language contact on Dutch in Tokugawa Japan. In this chapter and the next chapter, attention shifts to the effect of contact with Dutch on Japanese. This chapter focusses on aspects of the translation of Dutch books in Japan, while Chapter 7 analyses the effect of this contact on Japanese on a lexical, syntactic and graphic level.

Probably the most significant effect of language contact between Dutch and other languages in Tokugawa Japan was the proliferation of translations, which were typically, although not always, made from Dutch to Japanese. More than 1,000 of the books that the Dutch imported were translated into Japanese (Clements 2015: 147, 150). These translations would help to develop Japanese knowledge in several fields of enquiry such as medicine, astronomy and botany, and towards the end of the Tokugawa period military matters, and they would therefore exercise a significant influence on Japanese society.[1] In fields such as anatomy, plant classification and astronomy one can even assert that a paradigm shift took place as a result of translations from Dutch.

Before we go any further, however, a word is in order about what we mean by the term 'translation'. Theo Hermans gives a good definition of the contemporary understanding of translation when he describes it as 'a transcendental and utopian conception of translation [in which] the original, the whole original, and nothing but the original [is reproduced]' (Hermans 1985: 9, quoted in Clements 2015: 11–12). However, in many of the cases analysed in this chapter, translation was understood rather as a means by which to extract information from a source text and language and produce a new text incorporating that information in the target language. This information was sometimes gathered from a variety of sources, both oral and written, and rather than translate an entire source text, Japanese translators would often only translate parts of the source text that they considered useful. In this regard, as Boot observes, we should view this process from a Japanese viewpoint, rather than a European one: 'our perspective should not be the *spread* of European *science*, but the *reception* of [...] European *knowledge*' in Japan. In other words it was the Japanese who were deciding what they needed to add to their existing knowledge

---

1   For an extensive list of Dutch medical books translated into Japanese, see Miyasita (1975).

systems that determined what was translated, rather than the Dutch trying actively to advance Western learning in Japan (Boot 2013: 201; Vande Walle 2001b: 132–133). One might usefully contrast this state of affairs with that which pertained in the late sixteenth and early seventeenth centuries when it was Catholic missionaries who promoted translations into Japanese. It was, typically, they who decided what they wanted to be translated, rather than the Japanese (Clements 2015: 146). The variety of approaches to translation, not simply of Dutch texts, but also Chinese and older Japanese texts, is reflected in the plethora of terms for translation in pre-modern and early modern Japan. Clements (2015: 11) lists twenty-two such terms.

Another distinction to be made concerns who produced these translations. In early modern Europe, while some translations, for example those of the Bible from classical into vernacular languages, were collaborative enterprises, most translations were undertaken by individuals (Burke 2007: 11). By contrast, many of the translations analysed below, particularly those made in the earlier part of the Tokugawa period, were the result of collaboration between several individuals. One of the reasons for this is that few individuals had all the necessary language skills to translate from Dutch to Japanese on their own. For example, early manuscript translations on the surgery performed by the Dutch at Deshima were the product of collaboration between the Japanese physician Mukai Genshō (1609–77), Japanese interpreters and Dutch and German surgeons at Deshima (Michel 2010b; Clements 2015: 155).

Valuable work has been done in this field before. Japanese scholars such as Sugimoto Tsutomu and Tasaki Tetsurō have highlighted the critical role of Nagasaki interpreters in the development of translations from Dutch to Japanese, which had previously been seen as peripheral (Clements 2015: 147).[2] Wolfgang Michel and Rebekah Clements have presented this scholarship and their own in European languages. Michel and Clements will be important conversation partners in this chapter. Clements blends cultural history with translation studies in her analysis of the nature and influence of translation in early modern Japan. Similarly, this chapter employs the resources of these disciplines, drawing on work by, *inter alios*, Peter Burke and Pierre Bourdieu. Furthermore, it makes use of entries in Dutch primary sources, above all the *dagregister*, which to date have received relatively little academic attention.

---

2 Honma Sadao argues that the contribution of the Nagasaki interpreters to *rangaku* has been deliberately ignored by Japanese historians, who continue to 'perpetuate the myth that the Edo scholars were far superior to the Nagasaki interpreters in their ability to translate Dutch' (Jannetta 2009: 178). Another scholar who has highlighted the role of the Nagasaki interpreters is Annick Horiuchi.

These give us a window onto translations other than those of Dutch scientific books, for example, of letters and official documents, which also form part of our story.

Burke has done much work on early modern translation studies. He frames his discussion of cultures of translation in early-modern Europe as a series of responses to the questions: Who translates? What is translated? For whom? In what manner? and With what consequences? (Burke 2007: 7–38). It seems appropriate to frame the analysis of translation from Dutch in Tokugawa Japan as responses to the same questions.

2 Who Translates?

2.1 Cristóvão Ferreira/Sawano Chūan

As already noted, early translations were often a collaborative enterprise between various Japanese and Dutch or Germans.[3] One other person who seems to have played an important role in this regard is the Portuguese apostate, Cristóvão Ferreira (c. 1580–1650), who had taken the Japanese name, Sawano Chūan (Elison 1973: 208–209).[4] As a Jesuit he had a limited interest in surgery (Michel 2001: 3). However, as an apostate he could take a more active interest in it. He attended early Dutch medical interventions in the 1640s, taking notes on Dutch surgeons' activities.[5] Elison asserts that Ferreira/Chūan passed on the knowledge he obtained from the Dutch to Japanese physicians. The notes that he took survive in manuscripts under several titles. Cook (2007: 346)

---

3 As Clements (2015: 147) has observed, the view that the translation of Dutch texts was initiated in the early eighteenth century by Edo scholars after the lifting of a ban on Western books by shogun Yoshimune, which several scholars (e.g., Rubinger (1982: 102–103)) put forward, has since been proven incorrect. There was nevertheless a ban on certain books, above all, Chinese translations of Christian works by, among others, Matteo Ricci. This was introduced in 1630 but relaxed in about 1720 (Ōba 2012: 40–68).

4 For a summary of the practice of Western medicine during the Portuguese period in Japan, and further reading on the subject, see Michel (2001: esp. 5–7).

5 Ferreira/Chūan's name (referred to by the Dutch as s'Jouan) appears frequently in the *dag-register* in the 1640s, for example on 29 June 1641, when he is referred to as an apostate 'den renegaert s'Jouan' (*Diaries*: V:90), and on 17 November 1646 where he is described as the former head of the Jesuits in the area (*Diaries*: X:25). On 26 July 1648 he attended an operation on one of Inoue Masashige's servants. Three months later, on 26 October, in deepest secrecy he brought to the Dutch what he thought was the horn of the beast the *eenhorn*, thinking this was a unicorn. However, a pharmacist from the Dutch ship happened to be present and Chūan was surprised to hear that what he actually had in hand was the horn of a rhinoceros (*renocerhoorn*) not of a unicorn (Elison 1973: 208, 448 n. 66; Vermeulen *et al.* 1986–: XI:326; *Diaries*: XI:65).

gives the title of one as *Nanbanryū geka hidensho* ('Secret transmission of the Southern Barbarian Style of Surgery').[6] The title refers to 'Southern Barbarian' (*Nanban*) as this name was often used by the Japanese to describe Iberians such as Ferreira/Chūan. When the manuscript was published in 1696 and again in 1705, this association was removed from the title, being replaced by one referring to the Dutch, *Oranda-ryū geka shinan* ('Introduction to the Dutch style of surgery'). In truth, it must be admitted that the extent to which the Dutch language was involved in this process is unclear and it may be that Chūan communicated with the Dutch surgeons in Portuguese.

2.2   *Japanese Translators of Caspar Schamberger's Medical Instructions*

Japanese, too, were beginning to take an interest in the activities of the Dutch medical staff at Deshima. The barber surgeon Juriaen Henselingh taught surgery to Japanese in the early 1640s (*Diaries*: V:195; VI:38). In 1648 Dutch surgeons cured two Japanese (Vermeulen *et al.* 1986–: XI:317; *Diaries*: XI:36). It is certainly possible that Japanese were translating the oral instructions of the surgeons at this time. However, we need to wait until 1649–50 for the first concrete evidence of this. One of the representatives of the Dutch trading post on the *hofreis* to Edo in 1649–50 was the German physician Caspar Schamberger. As noted in Chapter 2, he was able to cure one of the shogun's advisors, Inaba Masanori of gout, something which Japanese physicians trained in Chinese medicine had been unable to do (Michel 1999: 117). With their own eyes, the shogun and his courtiers could see that Dutch (and German) medicine might be of use to them and so Schamberger was invited to stay in Edo and give lessons in Western medicine. It is likely that he gave instruction primarily in Portuguese. However, the interpreters who worked with him provided students with wordlists in Dutch, as well as Portuguese.[7] His teachings were translated and compiled by Inomata Denbei, with the help of other interpreters (Michel 2010b: 385). Over time, several manuscripts were written based on Schamberger's teaching. One, compiled by Denbei's pupil Kawaguchi Ryōan, whom Michel describes as an 'adherent' of Schamberger, was given the title

---

6   I have not identified this title in the NIJL database. A work with a similar title which is in the database (ID 3704129) is *Nanban geka hidensho* ('Secret transmission of the Southern Barbarian Surgery'). This also has the title *Nanbanryū gekasho*. János (2012: 276) gives the title of another similar manuscript as *Nanban Chūan hidensho*.

7   De Groot (2005: 26) suggests that this was because Portuguese and Dutch were considered by the Japanese to be two dialects of the same (general European) language.

Kasuparu denpō ('Transmitted Recipes of Caspar', 1661) (Cook 2007: 347).[8] Another manuscript had the title *Oranda geka ihō hiden* ('Secret transmission of the medical formulas of Dutch surgery').[9] It included words in *katakana* that correspond to medical terms and medicaments in Dutch, Portuguese and Latin. Besides the oral teaching, Michel identifies the 1636 'Pharmacopoeia Amstelredamensis' as a source for Japanese renderings in this manuscript of Western remedies primarily in Latin (Michel 1999: 154–156; 2015: 97). Although this does not conform to translation as we typically understand it today, it is an early example of the incorporation of Dutch (and other European) terms from a Dutch source into a Japanese text. One book based on Schamberger's teaching and treatments that appeared in print was *Kōmō hiden geka ryōjishū* ('Collection of secretly transmitted red-haired surgical healing methods') replete with illustrations by Nakamura Sōyo, published in Kyoto in 1684.[10]

2.3 *Inoue Masashige, Mukai Genshō and Arashiyama Hoan*

An important figure for the Dutch in the early years of their presence in Nagasaki was Inoue Masashige, *daimyō* of Chikugo province, whom we met previously in this book. He was the government official responsible for keeping an eye on the Dutch (*ōmetsuke*). He also had a personal reason for taking an interest in the activities of the Dutch, as he suffered from a number of ailments including bladder stones, haemorrhoids and catarrh (Michel 1995: 109). One of the books that the Dutch had imported to Deshima was Pliny the Elder's *Naturalis Historia*. In February 1652, the *dagregister* records that Masashige wanted all the names in Pliny's work to be transcribed for his interpreter to translate them into Japanese. Unfortunately, the *dagregister* does not tell us the language in which this copy of Pliny's work was written. The first Dutch version was published in 1610, so it could have been the Dutch or Latin version.[11] Shortly afterwards, the *opperhoofd* Adriaen van der Burgh

---

8   The NIJL database lists カスパル伝方 *Kasuparu denpō* ID 2204162. Here, on p. 7, Schamberger is described as an *Orandajin*, i.e., a Dutchman. More precisely, he is referred to as a 紅毛人 (*Kōmōjin*) 'red-haired person' which has the *furigana Oranda(jin)*. This hints at the more general point that even though he was German, he was considered as Dutch by the Japanese. A later copy of this is preserved in the Fujikawa Collection in Kyoto University Library, record no. RB00001584. See also Michel (1999: 292).

9   A manuscript with this title is not listed in the NIJL, although there are other manuscripts with very similar titles.

10   There is a copy of this work in the Bayerische Staatsbibliothek in Munich. This is available on google books. Accessed 6 May 2020. Michel (2001: 11 n. 10) refers to *Oranda hiden geka ryōjishū* based on Schamberger's teachings. This may be the same work, particularly as the *kanji* for *Kōmō* 紅毛 were sometimes read 'Oranda'.

11   I have not yet identified a Portuguese translation from this period.

recorded that he and his colleagues had assisted Masashige's interpreter with translating the names of animals in Pliny's work into Japanese (Vermeulen *et al.* 1986–: XII:51–52; Vande Walle 2001b: 130). Masashige's interest in Pliny's work was in part driven by the long tradition in Japan of the study of *materia medica*, pharmacognosy (*honzōgaku* 本草学 in Japanese). An important book in this tradition is Li Shizhen's (1518–93) *Běncǎo Gāngmù* 本草綱目 ('Compendium of *Materia Medica*') (late 1500s), introduced into Japan in the early seventeenth century (*Honzō kōmoku* in Japanese) (Marcon 2015: 7). This interest led Masashige to ask the Dutch in January 1653 if they could translate Rembert Dodoens's famous herbal, *Cruydt-boeck* (1st ed. 1554), from Dutch to Portuguese. However, on this occasion, the *opperhoofd* Frederick Coyett had to turn down Masashige's request politely, saying there was no-one at Deshima who could do this (Vermeulen *et al.* 1986–: XII:95). Dodoens's herbal was particularly popular with Japanese, not least because of its detailed illustrations. There were several copies in Japan in the seventeenth century.[12]

Wolfgang Michel records that although the Japanese had contact with Dutch physicians on the *hofreis* to Edo, as well as at Deshima, Masashige was not satisfied with what had been learnt from them.[13] In 1656 he therefore ordered the physician Mukai Genshō from Hizen Province to visit Deshima and record the medical instructions of the Breslau-born senior surgeon at the Dutch trading post, Hans Juriaen Hancke, and to enlist his help in preparing medicines for Masashige.[14] Genshō duly visited Deshima along with some interpreters and took notes on Hancke's instructions. The question arises as to which language, or languages this instruction would have been given in. At this time, many interpreters spoke Portuguese, although some also knew Dutch. The German Hancke, who had trained as a barber-surgeon, had worked for the

---

12 In 1659, the *opperhoofd* had presented the shogun with a copy of Dodoens's *Cruydt-boeck*. In 1682 a copy of the 1644 edition was acquired by the *daimyō* of Kaga, Maeda Tsunanori (1643–1724). This was an answer to the Japanese request for books with many illustrations. Boot (2013: 196), Vande Walle (2001a: 17), and Shirahata (2001: 263), among others, argue that Dodoens's book was the most influential book in terms of promoting the rise of *rangaku*.

13 He had, for example, been treated by the Dutch surgeon in Edo on 23 February 1655. The surgeon had summarized several cures for Masashige's ailment, which had been written down. Earlier, on 17 February his interpreter, Guinemon (also Sinnemon), had visited the surgeon to write down some remedies, with the help of the surgeon, from Galen and Paracelsus (Vermeulen *et al.* 1986–: XII:198, 195).

14 Michel (1995: 109) observes that Masashige's motivations were in part political, he was responsible for gathering information from overseas, including Western medicine, and in part personal, due to the ailments from which he suffered. See also Michel (1996) and Vermeulen *et al.* (1986–: XII:254).

VOC at Batavia since 1647 and, given the closeness of German to Dutch, was probably fairly comfortable with the latter. As for Genshō, besides Japanese, he may have had a smattering of Portuguese, but is unlikely to have spoken any Dutch, therefore communication would have been problematic to say the least. These difficulties would have been exacerbated by the fact that the conceptual framework within which Western physicians such as Hancke operated would have been very different from that with which Japanese physicians were familiar, grounded as it was in Chinese philosophy. One is left to wonder how the interpreters, who themselves probably knew little about medicine, translated concepts such as Yin and Yang, themselves Chinese in origin, into European languages (Michel 1995: 110). Nevertheless, despite these obstacles it seems some progress was made. Genshō returned at the start of the following year with one original and one copy of a Japanese manuscript, based on Hancke's oral instruction and translated into Japanese with help of interpreters (Vermeulen *et al.* 1986–: XII:282, entry for 14 January 1657).[15] Hancke and Zacharias Wagenaer (*opperhoofd* 1656–57, 1658–59) were required to sign the translations to indicate that the instructions to Genshō were given sincerely and to the best of Hancke's knowledge 'based on the works of several authors', The *dagregister* does not tell us which authors, although one possibility is Galen.

In November 1657, Genshō returned to Deshima with some interpreters and informed the Dutch that he had been asked by the Governor of Nagasaki, Kainoshō Masanobu (in office 1652–60), to write a book on medicine in Japanese. The new senior surgeon at Deshima, Steven de la Tombe, was sent for and Genshō spent several days with him gaining instruction in medicine. He said he would write to Masanobu, who had departed for Edo, when he had completed his book. Unfortunately, there is no trace of Genshō's book, but the fact that he was planning to write one, at the request of a powerful Japanese, indicates how seriously Dutch medicine was taken even at this early stage (Vermeulen *et al.* 1986–: XII:330–331). It also illustrates once more that it was the Japanese who were deciding what to translate rather than the Dutch. Despite the lack of book, several manuscripts emerged from Genshō's investigations including *Oranda-den geka ruihō* ('Assorted formulas of Dutch external medicine') and *Oranda geka ihō* ('Medical formulas of Dutch external

---

15 Michel (1995: 112) records that Genshō returned in 1656. However, it must have been in 1657, as he met Zacharias Wagenaer, who only became *opperhoofd* in November 1656 (Vermeulen *et al.* 1986–: XII:272). The entry in the *dagregister* confirms this.

medicine').[16] In 1670 Genshō's work reached a wider public when parts of it were incorporated in Yamawaki Dōen's *Oranda geka ryōhō* ('Good formulas of Dutch External Medicine') (Michel 1995: 112; 2010b: 385). As a consequence, Michel argues that Genshō would come to dominate the reception of Western medicine in Japan for the next 100 years.

A non-interpreter physician Arashiyama Hoan (1633–92/3) underwent surgical training from the Dutch on Deshima. In the early 1660s, he was instructed by Herman Katz, senior surgeon at Deshima from October 1660 to May 1662, and his successor, Daniel Busch. Hoan was presented with a certificate of medical proficiency by Busch. He would later write a work based on Dutch medicine *Bankoku chihō ruiju* ('An Explanation of the Medical Practices of Barbarian Countries', 1683). Again, we do not know in which language he was instructed. Portuguese and possibly Dutch may have been used, although we can currently say nothing more concrete (Van Gulik and Nimura 2005: 14; Goodman 2013: 40).[17] Finally, in 1672, six Japanese interpreters translated the instructions given by the German pharmacist Frans Braun at Deshima, sketching the equipment he used. The report was subsequently leaked and frequently copied (Michel 2001: 12). Parts of it were incorporated in early prints such as *Oranda geka shinan* ('Compass for Dutch surgery', 1696) (Michel 2015: 99).[18] This is not an exhaustive account of works based on the oral instructions of surgeons at Deshima, but illustrates well that they functioned as an important source for early medical translations in Japanese.

2.4   *Hōjō Ujinaga and Juriaen Schedel*

Away from medicine, on the *hofreis* of 1649–50 the (Swedish-born) mortar-gunner Juriaen Schedel was required to stay in Edo for an extra three months to give instruction on ballistics to high-ranking Japanese. They included the *bakufu* official Hōjō Ujinaga (1610–70). He produced a treatise based on Schedel's extensive instructions, with the title *Oranda yuriamu sōden kōjōhō*

---

16   *Oranda-den geka ruihō* is the title on the inside of a manuscript. On the outside the title is *Oranda geka seiden* ('Correct Transmission of Dutch Surgery') (Michel 1995: 112).

17   Another Japanese who took instruction from Katz was Kawaguchi Ryōan, mentioned above (Michel 1999: 170). The NIJL database lists a work by Ryōan with the title *Arumansu denpō* アルマンス伝方 ('Transmitted Recipes of Herman', ID 1943722). This was published in 1746. *Arumansu* seems to be a Japanese version of 'Herman'. Michel gives *Harumasu* (sic) as an alias for Ryōan. These two observations are not necessarily mutually exclusive.

18   http://base1.nijl.ac.jp/iview/Frame.jsp?DB_ID=G0003917KTM&C_CODE=XSI6-001012. Accessed 12 April 2020. NIJL ID 1053174. In the NIJL database *Oranda geka shinan* is ascribed to Cristóvão Ferreira/Sawano Chūan. In the database, an alternative name is *Oranda-ryū geka shinan*, mentioned above (p. 258).

('Transmission of the Dutch Juriaen's Siege Method', dated 1650). The Waseda University Library collection includes *Kōjō oranda yurian sōden* ('Transmission of the Dutch Juriaen's Siege Method') by Ujinaga. This is most probably another manuscript copy of the same text.[19] It is certainly on the same theme with Schedel named as the principal source. It includes diagrams of Western star-shaped fortresses, suggesting a written source as well, such as Simon Stevin's *De Sterctenbouwing* ('The construction of fortifications', Leiden, 1594).[20] Finally, it has been suggested that Ujinaga's cartographical surveys of Edo and other areas were relatively accurate as a result of Schedel's instruction (Willman 2013: 84 n. 33).

2.5 *Motoki Ryōi and* Pinax Microcosmographicus

The Nagasaki interpreter Motoki Ryōi made one of the earliest translations into Japanese based on a written as opposed to an oral Dutch source. In around 1682, he completed his translation of the Dutch version of a book on anatomy, *Pinax Microcosmographicus* ('Microcosmic Diagrams') by the German physician and author, Johann Ludwig (Johannes) Remmelin (1583–1632). This was first published in Latin in Amsterdam in 1634 (Clements 2015:148; Miyasita 1975:16). The Dutch version *Ontleding des menschelyke lichaems* ('Anatomy of the human body') was first published in Amsterdam in 1667. Ryōi's original translation no longer survives, but a copy of it does, entitled *Oranda keiraku kinmyaku zōfu zukai* ('Dutch Illustrations of Nerves, Muscles and Intestines') (Matsuda 2001: 196). It should, though, be admitted that it was far from a complete translation of the original text with Michel referring to it as a 'simple summary'. In fact Ryōi only translated the anatomical terms which provided explanations of the illustrations in the original text. Furthermore, it had little impact at the time, circulating in a number of manuscripts for the next ninety years (Michel 2001: 16). Finally, in 1772 (Meiwa 9), it was published by Suzuki Soūn with the title *Oranda zenku naigai bungōzu* ('Dutch Diagrams of the External and Internal Parts of the Human Body').[21] The Motoki family would produce several generations of interpreter-translators stretching into the nineteenth century.

---

19   Waseda call no. 文庫 o8 C0289. The NIJL does not refer to the Waseda copy. The NIJL does not provide scans so a visual comparison of the two copies is not possible.

20   Another related title is *Oranda yuriama kōjōden* ('Siege Method of The Dutch Juriaen') (Willman 2013: 84 n. 33). Again, this may be another title for the same work, or another work based on Schedel's instructions.

21   Copies were made by Hara Sanshin, physician to the *daimyō* of Fukuoka (Michel 2001:16). See also Clements (2015: 148). The NIJL (ID 753004) has the title as *Oranda zenku naigai bungōzu oyobi kengō*. See also Boot (2013: 197).

Rebekah Clements (2015: 145) observes that between the last of the Catholic mission translations in the early seventeenth century and the emergence of translations within the field of *rangaku* in the eighteenth century, there was a 'scarcity of translations', which was due to the combined effects of 'a lack of linguistic expertise and an absence of any strongly perceived reason to engage in translation'. From the evidence above, I would suggest that these comments need to be nuanced somewhat. It is certainly true that in comparison to what came later, there were relatively fewer translations. However, in the second half of the seventeenth century, there was clearly a reasonable amount of translation activity with the oral instructions of Dutch and German physicians or Dutch and Latin texts as the source and Japanese as the target language. Already in the 1640s, but certainly from 1650 onwards there was a recognition that the Dutch had something to offer in the field of medicine and so several Japanese undertook translations based on oral and written sources. What is true, and possibly what Clements is alluding to, is that in this period, unlike the earlier and later periods, there was limited use of written sources and there were few *published* translations. However, Japanese had already identified a reason to engage in translation and, despite the obstacles involved, including linguistic ones, undertook several translation projects.

2.6   Eighteenth-Century Translators

In the eighteenth century, those who translated Dutch texts into Japanese can be divided into two main groups. First, there was a small number of Nagasaki interpreters whose language skills were sufficient to allow them to translate works written in Dutch. It was by engaging with these interpreters that a second group, scholars in Edo, became interested in the knowledge that they were gaining from the Dutch and eventually translated Dutch texts.[22] Details of members of both groups are now provided. Where relevant, details of their translations are given below.

At the end of the seventeenth century, Nishikawa Joken (1648–1724) wrote *Kaitsūshōkō* ('An Investigation of Trade between China and Barbarian lands'), based on Chinese and European sources, including information provided by the Dutch. The first edition was published in 1695 and a revised enlarged edition in 1708 (Clements 2015: 174). In the first half of the eighteenth century, Nagasaki interpreters continued to make translations. Two of them, Narabayashi

---

22   Furthermore, Clements (2015: 149) notes that a key step in helping Dutch knowledge to move beyond the confines of Nagasaki was the observation by interpreters of Dutch, and I would add German, doctors treating patients in Nagasaki. This continued a pattern that began to emerge in the second half of the seventeenth century.

Chinzan and Nishi Gentetsu (1681–1760), both produced Japanese texts based on *De Chirurgie* ('Surgery') by Ambroise Paré (c. 1510–90). Chinzan studied under Willem Hoffman, senior surgeon at Deshima from 1671 to 1676 (Van Gulik and Nimura 2005: 14). His work, entitled *Kōi geka sōden* ('Transmission of Red-haired Barbarian (i.e., Dutch) Surgery') and consisting of three fascicles, was completed in 1706, although it was never published (Clements 2015: 148 n. 31; Boot 2013: 197–197).[23] An entry in the *dagregister* for 1724 records that another Nagasaki interpreter, Namura Hachizaemon, had been ordered by the Governor of Nagasaki, Kusakabe Hirosada (in post 1717–27) to ask the Dutch whether Paré's work *De Chirurgie* contained remedies against cervical tumours. He then translated several chapter headings and part of Paré's book into Japanese (Blussé *et al.* 1992: 288–289).

Another Nagasaki interpreter who translated from Dutch to Japanese was Engelbert Kaempfer's protégé Imamura Gen'emon. One of his translations, *Oranda basho* ('A Book on Dutch Horsemanship', 1729), was prompted by shogun Yoshimune's interest in improving horses and horsemanship in Japan (Clements 2015: 148). This interest led to the importing of horses and an invitation to the German-born equestrian expert Hans Jurgen Keijser (1697–1735) to come to Japan to teach Western horsemanship and horse veterinary medicine.

Another member of the Motoki Nagasaki interpreter family, Yoshinaga (1735–94), produced translations and works in Japanese based on Dutch geographical and astronomical sources. The Nagasaki-born astronomer Kitajima Kenshin (*fl.* 1719–38) was also interested in Dutch works on geography. He produced a map *Oranda shintei chikyū zu* ('World map based on a Dutch source', undated) and a booklet *Kōmō tenchi nizu zeisetsu* ('Detailed Explanation of Red-haired (Dutch) celestial and terrestrial Globes', 1737) based on the Valck globes of 1700 (inscribed in Latin). Goodman (2013: 98) describes Kenshin as the interpreter Nishi Zenzaburō's 'brilliant pupil' and it is thought that Zenzaburō worked with Kenshin on his translation projects (Unno 1994: 433).

Occasionally, we get a sense of the excitement and urgency that interpreters felt as they pushed forward their knowledge and that of fellow Japanese with translations. In a letter to Isaac Titsingh in 1785, the Nagasaki interpreter Hori Monjūrō refers to several translation projects underway in Japan. He tells Titsingh that 'De vertaaling ('translation') van het boek gempirok door de Kosak is bewerkt'. 'Kosak' refers to the Nagasaki interpreter, Yoshio Kōgyū or Kōsaku. *Gempirok* probably refers to *Genpiroku*, which means 'Top secret record'. One possibility is that this is a work that Titsingh refers to as *Kindai Genpiroku*, which he used as a source for what Screech calls his *magnum opus*

---

23   Gentetsu's text was entitled *Kinso Tetsuboku Ryōji No Sho* (Van Gulik and Nimura 2005: 14).

on Japanese history (Screech 2006: 66–68).[24] *Kindai Genpiroku* is probably Titsingh's name for *Kindai Kōjitsu Genpiroku* ('Top secret record of public affairs of modern times', 1754), a record of anecdotes concerning Tokugawa shoguns by Baba Bunkō (1718–59), of whom we know little beyond the fact that he was an excellent raconteur.[25] If I am right, then this indicates that Kōgyū, well known for his skills as an interpreter, was translating from Japanese to Dutch and not vice versa. Monjūrō continues by referring to two books 'bij mijn zeer haastig en zeer grof vertaalt voor 't vertrek van 't schip', i.e., translated very quickly and very roughly before the ship left Nagasaki (Lequin 1990: 1:14–15).

2.7   Edo-Based Scholars

So far, many of the translations discussed have been the work of one or more Nagasaki interpreters, underlining their contribution to the development of the Japanese understanding of Western learning. This undermines the claim made by Sugita Genpaku (1969: 37) in *Rangaku kotohajime* ('The Beginnings of Dutch Learning') that the story of *rangaku* started in Edo. In time, however, scholars elsewhere in Japan, above all Edo, would play an increasingly significant role in translating Dutch texts. In 1713 the Edo neo-Confucian scholar Arai Hakuseki, who had contact with the Nagasaki interpreter Imamura Gen'emon, published *Sairan igen* ('Various sights and strange words'). This was a compilation from various sources including conversations with the Italian Jesuit missionary Giovanni Battista Sidotti (1668–1714), who had entered Japan illegally in 1708 (Clements 2015: 151). Hakuseki questioned the *opperhoofd*, Hermanus Menssingh, in order to check whether what Sidotti had told him was true (Krieger 1940: 7). Several Dutch loanwords appear for the first time in a Japanese text in *Sairan igen*. It also includes the names of many countries in *ateji* and *furigana*. Most names seem to owe something to Latin or Italian, such as *Idāriya* (Italy) and *Serumania* (i.e., Gerumania, Germany), although the form for Japan *yāpan* may be based on the Portuguese, *Japam*, or even, given the word-initial /j/, the Dutch *Jappan*.

However, it was not until the second half of the eighteenth century that the first significant translation project was undertaken by Edo-based scholars. This

---

24   This was first published in French in Paris 1820 as *Mémoires et anecdotes sur la dynastie régnante des djogouns*. An English version, 'Illustrations of Japan', was published in 1822.

25   If I understand Monjūrō's commendable, but slightly opaque, Dutch, correctly, he seems to contradict himself, for just before writing that Kōgyū was translating 'gempirok', he writes that he asked several fellow interpreters including Kōgyū about 'het boek Gempirok'. They responded that they had not heard of it. One possible explanation is that he is referring to another work by Baba Bunkō, *Kinsei Kōjitsu Genpiroku* (Screech 2006: 66–68).

was the translation of the Dutch translation by the Leiden surgeon, Gerard Dicten (*Ontleedkundige Tafelen*, 'Anatomical Tables', 1734), of a work originally published in German (*Anatomische Tabellen*, 'Anatomical Tables', 1st ed. 1722) by Johann Adam Kulmus (Clements 2015: 146; Beukers 2000). As with previous translations, this was a collaborative effort, primarily involving Maeno Ryōtaku, a pupil of Aoki Kon'yō, who had an excellent knowledge of Dutch, Sugita Genpaku, who had trained in Chinese medicine, and the physician and *rangakusha*, Nakagawa Jun'an. The project to translate this book took almost three and a half years to complete at a rate of ten lines per day and was eventually published in 1774 as *Kaitai shinsho* (lit. 'New Text on Anatomy'). Unfortunately, the translation was so full of errors that it could not, in fact, be used as a guidebook for dissection (De Groot 2005: 7). Nevertheless, the need to grapple with a text on anatomy led the translators to coin loan translations derived from Dutch anatomical terms, which are still in use in cMJ. Some of these are analysed in Chapter 7.

Towards the end of the eighteenth century, Genpaku and his pupil Ōtsuki Gentaku translated *Heelkundige Onderwijzingen* ('Lessons in Surgery'), a Dutch translation of a German surgical textbook by Laurens Heister.[26] They had acquired the Dutch translation from Yoshio Kōgyū, who had bought it for 20 barrels of not simply sake, but Sakai sake, a superior quality of sake, so keen was Genpaku to lay his hands on the book (Sugita 1969: 18–19).[27] In 1815, Genpaku wrote *Rangaku kotohajime*, in which he describes the trials and tribulations of translating from Dutch to Japanese. However, he observed that although the translation had been difficult, Dutch was easier to learn than Chinese. This, he admits, may have been because learning Chinese 'had prepared the Japanese mind' for Dutch (De Bary *et al.* 2005: 370).

An important step in the development of the Japanese understanding of the body was made by the translation of Johannes de Gorter's *Gezuiverde Geneeskonst* ('Purified Medicine' Amsterdam, 1744) by the Edo-born physician Udagawa Genzui (1755–97). Genzui's translation, *Seisetsu naika senyō* ('Synopsis of Internal Medicine', 1792), was the first to investigate internal medicine. He also made a translation of Petrus Nyland's *Der Nederlandtse Herbarius of Kruydt-boeck* ('The Dutch herbal', Amsterdam, 1670), giving it the title *Ensei yakukei* ('Far Western *Materia Medica*'). This was not, however,

---

26   *Chirurgie, in welcher alles was zur Wund Arztney gehöret, nach der neuesten und besten Art, gründlich abgehandelt wird usw.* (Van Gulik and Nimura 2005: 15). See also http://www.encyclopedia.com/people/medicine/medicine-biographies/lorenz-heister. Accessed 14 April 2020.

27   The Japanese translation of this was completed in 1790 (Van Gulik and Nimura 2005: 15).

published (Marcon 2015: 256; Sugita 1969: 55).[28] Genzui was the first of several *rangakusha* from his family who undertook important translation projects from Dutch to Japanese. His son, Udagawa Genshin (1769–1834) made the translation *Ensei ihan* ('Medical precepts of the Far West' 1804–18). He also produced the 36-volume medical work, *Ensei ihō meibutsukō* ('Reflections on Well-Known Far Western Medical Cures'), based on various Dutch sources and Weinmann's *Phytanthoza Iconographia* (1st ed., 1735).[29] Genzui's grandson, Udagawa Yōan (1798–1846), contributed to Japanese knowledge of Western pharmacology through *Oranda yakukyō* ('The Mirror of Dutch Medicine') (with his father), Western botany through *Shokugaku keigen* ('The Revelation of Botany'), and Western chemistry through the multi-volume *Seimi kaisō* ('Principles of Chemistry'). *Seimi kaisō* is based on many sources, but above all a Dutch translation of 'An Epitome of Chemistry' (1st ed., 1799), a work by the British scientist William Henry (1774–1836). This is turn was a simplified version of Antoine Lavoisier's 'Traité élémentaire de chimie', 1789.

A word is also in order about the Nagasaki-born interpreter-turned-*rangakusha*, Shizuki Tadao. One work that he produced, *Rekishō shinsho* ('New Writings on Calendrical Phenomena') (1798–1802), was based on several Dutch texts including *Inleidinge tot de waare Natuur- en Sterrekunde* ('Introduction to the True Physics and Astronomy'), a Dutch translation by Johan Lulofs (1st ed. 1741) of John Keill's *Introductiones ad veram Physicam et veram Astronomiam* (Leiden, 1725) (Clements 2015: 151–152). Tadao also translated an appendix of a Dutch translation of Engelbert Kaempfer's 'History of Japan' (Boot 2008: 94).

Other Edo scholars who produced many translations were the brothers Morishima Chūryō and Katsuragawa Hoshū I. While some such as Hoshū's *Oranda yakusen* ('Selected Dutch Drugs'), a translation of a Dutch pharmacopoeia were not published, others such as Chūryō's *Kōmō zatsuwa* were published (1st edition 1787) (Sugimoto and Swain 1989: 330, 385; Sugita 1969: 59).

2.8   The Nineteenth Century

As the eighteenth century turned into the nineteenth century, interest in the knowledge mediated by Dutch increased, as did the number and quality of translations. Four translators to mention here are Baba Teiyū, Takano Chōei, Ogata Kōan, and Fukuzawa Yukichi. Baba Teiyū was one of the most

---

28   In *Kōi geka sōden* (1706) Narabayashi Chinzan comments that he abbreviated the part on Dutch internal treatment in his Dutch source, as this was deemed inappropriate for the Japanese (Krieger 1940: 5).

29   He may have used the Dutch translation of Weinmann's work, *Duidelyke Vertoning* ('Clear Presentation') Amsterdam, 1738–48.

successful Nagasaki interpreters, so much so that having risen quickly through the ranks in Nagasaki he was summoned in 1808 to work as a translator at the *Tenmondai* ('Bureau of Astronomy') in Edo. For several years, translations from Dutch into Japanese had been made by personnel at the *Tenmondai* to assist in maintaining a correct and reliable calendar (De Groot 2005: 4; Clements 2015: 181–182). This illustrates well how the Japanese interest in Dutch books on astronomy played an important role in the development of *rangaku*. In 1811, the *Bansho wage goyō* ('Office for the Translation of Barbarian Books') was established within the *Tenmondai*, at Asakusa, a district of Edo (Vos 2014: 156; Clements 2015: 156).[30] This acted as the official body for the translation of Dutch books into Japanese and represented an attempt by the *bakufu* to exert control on translation activity. Baba Teiyū was seconded to work on translation projects there. It is reckoned that he translated some 48 works into Japanese. While the source language for a few of these is Russian, for most of them it is Dutch (Clements 2015: 156–157).

Takano Chōei, from Sendai *han*, went to Nagasaki to study Dutch and would learn Dutch medicine under the German physician, Philipp Franz von Siebold, at the *Narutakijuku*. He received financial support from several rich patrons, which allowed him to devote time to producing Japanese medical texts based on Dutch sources. These include *Ransetsu yōjōroku* ('Record of Dutch Theories on Prolonging Life', 1827), which he translated with Oka Kenkai (1799–1839), and *Igen sūyō* ('Fundamentals of [Western] Medicine'), the first part of which was published in 1832 (Clements 2015: 160–163).[31]

Ogata Kōan is probably best known as the founder and head of the *Tekijuku* medical school in Osaka (see fig. 20). He was, however, also a translator. One

---

30 The *Tenmondai* was a gift from the shogun to the man who in 1684 had provided him with a new and improved calendar, Shibukawa Shunkai (1639–1715). Initially it focussed on astronomy, but over time undertook the study of cosmology, mathematics, surveying and cartography (Boot: 2014). In this regard, although the *Tenmondai* refers to the astronomical observatory in Edo and *Tenmonkata* to the 'astronomy officers', a firm distinction between these two terms is not always made in the secondary literature. The corresponding institutions were the *Wagaku kōdansho* for Japanese studies, and the *Shōheizaka Gakumonjo* for Chinese studies. There was also the medical institute, the *Igakkan*. Those who studied and worked at these institutes belonged to the intellectual elite in Tokugawa Japan. Furthermore, each institute had its own publication project. The principal work that the *Bansho wage goyō* translated into Japanese was *Algemeen huishoudelijk-, natuur-, zedekundig- en konst-woordenboek* (Leiden, 1778–93), a Dutch translation of Noël Chomel's French *Dictionnaire oeconomique* (1709). In fact, only a partial translation into Japanese was achieved. This was given the title *Kōsei shinpen* ('A New Compendium for Health').

31 Nakamura (2005: 32–37) refers to this work as **Seisetsu** *igen sūyō* ('Fundamentals of **Western** Medicine', my bold). It was in part based on Dutch translations of medical works originally written in German and French.

FIGURE 20   *Tekijuku* medical school, Osaka
AUTHOR'S OWN COLLECTION

book that he translated from Dutch to Japanese was H.H. Hageman's *Enchiri-dion Medicum: handleiding tot de geneeskundige praktijk* (Amsterdam, 1838), itself based on Christoph Wilhelm Hufeland's German text, *Enchiridion Medi-cum: oder Anleitung zur medizinischen Praxis* (Berlin, 1836). Kōan's translation was published in Edo in 1857 as *Fushi keiken ikun* ('The Handed-Down Teach-ings of (the late) Mr. Hufeland'). His student at *Tekijuku*, Fukuzawa Yukichi, would make many translations during the Meiji period. His initial interest in Dutch was not so much driven by a desire to learn about Western medicine, but rather about ballistics and other sciences which would help to defend Japan in the wake of Commodore Perry's arrival in the 1850s. In his autobiography, he describes how he secretly copied and then translated C.M.H. Pel's *Handleiding tot de Kennis der Versterkingskunst* ('Guide to the Knowledge of Fortification', Den Bosch, 1852) (Fukuzawa 2007: 48, 343).

Finally, while most translators were from the upper echelons of Japanese society, there were exceptions. Ozeki San'ei (also Koseki, 1787–1839) was from peasant (*nōmin* 農民) stock. He studied Dutch in Edo and would later prac-tise as a doctor of Dutch medicine. Among the translations he produced are *Taisei naika shūsei* ('An Anthology of Western Internal Medicine', 1832), which was based on a work by the German physician, Georg Wilhelm Consbruch (Clements 2015: 158).[32]

Other Japanese made translations of Dutch texts.[33] From the above, the Nagasaki interpreters both translated works into Japanese and gave instruction to others who wanted to do so. Over time, Edo scholars such as Sugita Genpaku undertook translation work and by the nineteenth century other scholars such as Takano Chōei and Fukuzawa Yukichi, who went to Nagasaki to study Dutch, would also produce translations in Japanese based on Dutch source texts. The picture that has also emerged is that a translation was often the work of more than one person and was a collaborative effort rather than an individual one. Furthermore, while some translators had no family background in Dutch studies, others came from families with several generations of translators, such as the Nagasaki-based Motoki and Edo-based Udagawa families.

3   What Was Being Translated?

Translation reveals what one culture finds of interest in another (Burke 2007: 20). In the present context, we have already identified that many of the translations into Japanese from oral and written sources concerned medical matters, for it was Dutch medicine above all that clearly caught the attention of the Japanese, and filled what they considered to be a 'gap' in their understanding of the world. It is worth contrasting this with the situation in early modern Europe, where many of the most important translation projects were religious ones (Burke 2007: 16). Indeed, of the more than one thousand translations made under the aegis of Dutch Studies or *rangaku* in Tokugawa Japan roughly one half did concern medicine.[34] However, this is not the whole story.

---

32   The NIJL database attributes 14 works to San'ei, for most of which he is identified as the translator.

33   For other translators, discussed by domain, see Goodman (2013: 148–174). For translators of medical texts in the nineteenth century, see also Mieko Macé (2016).

34   Miyasita (1975: 10) provides details of 473 Japanese books and manuscripts translated from 189 Dutch books. In fact, as Miyasita observes, four of the 'Dutch' books were not Dutch: two were Latin, one Russian and one English. It would probably be impossible to say precisely how many translations were made. Clements (2015: 142) talks of 'thousands' in both print and manuscript, while graphs seem to indicate that the figure is between one and two thousand (pp. 147, 150).

3.1   *Jonston's Natural History and Dodoens's* Cruydt-boeck

In the previous section, mention was made of translations of subjects as varied as astronomy, fortifications and horsemanship. One book that caught the attention of shogun Yoshimune (ruled as shogun 1716–41) was a Dutch translation of Johannes Jonston's work on quadrupeds, originally written in Latin.[35] This had been given to the shogunate by Hendrick Indijck in 1663 but had lain in the shogunal library largely ignored by Yoshimune's predecessors. While certainly no Greenblattesque 'swerve', the identification of Jonston's work was an important step in the development of *rangaku*, which took Japanese scholars and scholarship in a new, unexpected direction.[36] It was above all the illustrations in this book that caught Yoshimune's attention, a fact which leads Timon Screech to observe that the importance of the pictures in the Western books in Japan cannot be underestimated. In April 1717, Yoshimune asked Joan Aouwer (*opperhoofd* intermittently 1716–20) to translate the names of the animals in (the Dutch translation of) Jonston's book. Christiaen van Vrijberghe[n] (*opperhoofd* 1717–18) recorded in March 1718 that he had translated the names of several animals and their places of origin from the copy of Jonston's book which had been shown to Aouwer the previous year (Vermeulen *et al.* 1986–: IV:116–17 and 132–133). Yoshimune also commanded several Edo scholars to learn Dutch and the 'horizontal script' in which it was written (Screech 2012: 319–320).[37] In 1741, the shogun's personal physician visited the *opperhoofd* Jacob van der Waeijen in Edo with the Indijck copy of Jonston's book and asked him to translate some of the comments by the author. Van der Waeijen passed this task to the interpreter Yoshio Tōsaburō (?–[1742]). A few days earlier the same physician had brought with him a folio book by Emanuel Sweerts, probably his *Florilegium* (Frankfurt, 1612), and asked for the names of some of flowers and trees depicted in the book. Van der Waeijen was able to oblige with the help of the book's register (Blussé and Remmelink 2004: 5).

---

35   The Dutch version was entitled *Naeukeurige beschrijving van de natuur der vier-voetige dieren*, first published in Amsterdam in 1660.

36   In 'The Swerve' (2011), Stephen Greenblatt argues that Poggio Bracciolini's (1380–1459) discovery of the sole surviving manuscript of Lucretius's *De Rerum Natura* in a German monastery was a key moment in the emergence of the European Renaissance. His thesis has, however, been criticized by several scholars.

37   In 1721 Yoshimune lifted a ban imposed in the previous century on works from China by Matteo Ricci and other Europeans (Clements 2015: 145, 180). While this did not have an immediate effect on the volume of translations (Clements (2015: 150, fig. 7) has calculated that about a dozen Western works were translated into Japanese between 1700 and 1750), it is suggestive of a more receptive official policy towards Western learning in eighteenth-century Japan.

Japanese had shown an interest in Rembert Dodoens's *Cruydt-boeck* since the mid-seventeenth century. It had something in common with popular books on pharmacognosy such as Li Shizhen's *Běncǎo Gāngmù*, although it was smaller in scale. Towards the end of the eighteenth century, the *daimyō* and senior counsellor to the shogunate, Matsudaira Sadanobu planned a complete translation of *Cruydt-boeck*. The first translator, Ishii Shōsuke, was originally a Nagasaki interpreter who moved to Edo and had assisted Inamura Sanpaku with the compilation of the *Edo Haruma* (Sugita Genpaku 1969: 58–59). Shōsuke made much progress, but died before he could complete it, being replaced by Yoshida Seikyō, who eventually finished the translation in 1823. Unfortunately, many of the 170 volumes of manuscript translation that they made were lost in the great fire of Edo of 1829, though some which survived are now in Waseda University Library (Shirahata 2001: 269).

3.2 Physics and Chemistry

Non-medical Western scientific texts were translated into Japanese. One of Yoshio Kōgyū's students in Nagasaki was Hiraga Gen'nai. It is said that he was so taken by Dutch learning that he sold his furniture in order to buy Dutch books. He was something of a Renaissance man. Among his achievements was the making of an *elekiter* (エレキテル, *erekiteru*), a static electricity generator, based on one imported from the Dutch Republic. In 1765 he published a short work on asbestos *Kakanpu ryakusetsu* ('Brief explanation of asbestos'), based on the article on asbestos in the Dutch translation of Johann Jacob Woyt's *Gazophylacium medico-physicum* (1st ed. Leipzig 1700) (Goodman 2000: 191–192).

Above, mention was made of Udagawa Yōan's major work on chemistry *Seimi kaisō*, which can trace its origins back via Dutch and English translations to Antoine Lavoisier's 'Traité élémentaire de chimie'. An earlier work by Yōan *Kōso seimika* ('Chemistry of the Element of Light', 1830) explains light and heat reactions with substances. This is based on a paragraph of the Dutch edition of Lavoisier's seminal work on chemistry. In truth, Lavoisier did not understand these reactions so well, a fact reflected in Yōan's translation (Siderer 2017). Although Yōan is usually considered to be in some sense the 'father of Japanese chemistry', other Japanese were also translating Western texts on chemistry before or at about the same time as Yōan. Hidaka Ryōtai (1797–1868) produced a manuscript on chemistry in c. 1820–30, which drew on several Western sources including possibly a Dutch translation of Antoine-François de Fourcroy's *Système des Connaissances Chimiques* (Paris, 1801–2). Fujibayashi Fuzan, whom we met in Chapter 2, produced a manuscript on chemistry entitled *Rigō genpon* (lit. 'Source book on dividing and joining'). The primary source for this work is *Grondbeginselen der scheikunde, of oversicht over alle de vakken der scheikunde* ('First Principles of Chemistry, or overview of all the disciplines within chemistry', Amsterdam, 1803), a Dutch translation of a Latin work by the Austrian, Joseph Jacob von Plenck. A third early manuscript on chemistry is *Seiren hatsumō* (1829) by Tsuboi Shindō.[38] One possible source for this is *Bataafsche Apotheek* ('Batavian Phaemacopoeia', Amsterdam, 1807) by Sebaldus Justinus Brugmans *et al.*, which was a translation from Latin. Each of these works attempted to grapple with the new words and concepts that emerged from the Chemical Revolution in late eighteenth-century Europe mediated to Japan in Dutch. For each author, as for Yōan, the study of chemistry was essentially for practical reasons as Japanese explored the potential of developing new pharmaceutical drugs (Tsukahara 2000a). Of these, however, Yōan's *Seimi kaisō* was the only work to be published and so would have the greatest influence on the subsequent development of chemistry in Japan.

3.3   *Cartographical, Geographical and Astronomical Works*

To the works on cartography and geography mentioned above, we can add further translations. In 1772 Motoki Yoshinaga completed *Oranda chizu ryakusetsu* ('Brief Explanation of Dutch Maps') (Unno 1994: 433).[39] Two years later he produced *Tenchi nikyū yōhō* ('The use of celestial and terrestrial globes'). This was a translation of a Dutch handbook, the first edition of which was published by Willem Jansz. Blaeu in 1634.[40] It explained the Copernican theory of heliocentrism, and is a good example of how such translations not merely brought new knowledge to Japan, but prompted paradigm shifts in the 'Japanese mind', to borrow from Thomas Kuhn (Goodman 2013: 98; Unno 1994: 434). Another early work, which advocated the Copernican theory, was Shiba Kōkan's *Tenkyū zenzu* ('Complete Illustrations of Heaven's Sphere', 1796). In this work, consisting of twelve pages, Kōkan presents a copperplate engraving of an orrery, or globe illustrating the heavens. He gives his source for information about this device as *Ūhensukōru*. This is a rendering of the Dutch *oefenschool* ('practice school') from *Algemeene oefenschoole van konsten en weetenschappen* ('General practice school of arts and sciences'), the title of a multi-part work published by Pieter Meijer in Amsterdam (1763–) (Screech 1996: 248–249).

---

38   Tsukahara (2000a: 209) explains the meaning of *Seiren hatsumō* as refining by the use of fire or a heating process. A slightly different interpretation is that it means 'Enlightenment on the production of medicines'. I thank Professor Shimizu Makoto for this information.

39   Clements (2015: 151) has the date 1771.

40   The source text was Blaeu's *Tweevoudigh onderwiis van de hemelsche en aerdsche globen* (Amsterdam, 1666 [first edition, 1634]) (Unno 1994: 434).

Another product of the Japanese interest in Western astronomy was *Taiyō kyori rekikai* ('Solar declination (lit. distance) calendar'), the translation of a *Graadboeck* or solar calendar by Motoki Yoshinaga and Matsumura Genkō in 1774. As the title suggests it is largely comprised of declination tables. It includes Latinate Dutch terms that are transcribed into *ateji* with *furigana* such as *dekirināshī* (Dutch: *declinatie* = declination) and *afūaikingi* (Dutch: *afwijking* = deviation) (Kobe City Museum 1998: 112).

What Unno Kazutaka describes as the earliest work of a cartographic nature by a Dutch scholar in Edo was *Shinsei chikyū bankoku zusetsu* ('Illustrated explanation of the new map of all the countries in the world'), completed by Katsuragawa Hoshū I in 1786. His translation was derived from the topographical explanation attached to Joan Blaeu's world map of 1648, the *Nova totius terrarum orbis tabula* ('A New Chart of the Lands of all the World'). In 1793 Hoshū produced *Roshia shi* ('Record of Russia'), based on *Algemeene Geographie, of Beschryving des Geheelen Aardryks* (Amsterdam, 1769), a Dutch translation of a geographical work by the German, Johann Hübner (Clements 2015: 151). Hoshū based his *Hokusa bunryaku* ('Story of a driftage to the north') largely on conversations with the Japanese merchant Daikokuya Kōdayū and his fellow sailors, who had been held captive in Russia.[41] However, he also included a translation of a short description of Russia written by Gijsbert Hemmij, based on a Dutch book (Katsuragawa Hoshū 1978: 471).

In about 1785, Motoki Yoshinaga produced a translation of the *Nieuwe Atlas* (1730, Amsterdam, Johannes Covens and Cornelis Mortier), giving it the title *Oranda zensekai chizusho yaku* ('Translation of a Dutch atlas of the world'). In addition to these works, he produced *Seijutsu hongen taiyō kyūri ryōkai shinsei tenchi nikyū yōhōki* ('The ground of astronomy, newly edited and illustrated; on the use of celestial and terrestrial globes according to the heliocentric system' 7 vols., 1792–93). This was based on a Dutch book *Gronden der starrenkunde* ('Principles of astronomy', Amsterdam 1770/1), which was itself a translation by Jacob Ploos of 'A Treatise Describing and Explaining the Construction and Use of New Celestial and Terrestrial Globes' (London, 1766) by George Adams (c. 1709–73), instrument-maker to King George III (Unno 1994: 434; Kobe City Museum 1998: 113).[42]

One translation of a geographical text from the nineteenth century is *Hakkō tsūshi* (八紘通誌, 'Journal of the Whole World'), published by Mitsukuri

---

41   For more on *Hokusa bunryaku*, see Winkel (2004: 126–138).

42   The full title of the Dutch translation is *Gronden der starrenkunde, gelegd in het zonnestelzel, bevatlijk gemaakt; in eene beschrijving van 't maaksel en gebruik der nieuwe hemel- en aard-globen.*

Genpo in 1851.[43] Genpo used several foreign sources including N.G. Kampen's *De Aarde Beschouwd in Haren Natuurlijken Toestand en Verdeeling* ('The Earth Viewed in its Natural State and Division', Haarlem, 1816–17). The first volume is divided into three parts. The second part provides details of Netherlands, Belgium, Germany and Austria. As one might expect, toponyms from Netherlands and Flanders are in Dutch. The name given for Austria in *katakana* is *Ōsutenreiki*, which is probably derived from the Dutch *Oostenrijk* rather than the German *Oesterreich*. This would be an important book for Japanese understanding of the world in the years after 1854.

3.4   *Translations on History and Politics*

To these we can add translations on European history and foreign affairs. Most of the works that Ozeki San'ei translated were related to Western medicine. One exception was *Naporeon den* ('A Biography of Napoleon', 1837, see fig. 21), printed posthumously in 1857. This was based on a Dutch translation of a French source.[44] One possible reason for this choice is that there was quite an interest in Napoleon in Japan (Clements 2015: 151, 159; Ravina 2017: 112–113).

Japanese became increasingly interested in Dutch books and other material on military matters as the nineteenth century progressed. Several authors produced annotated diagrams of warships based on Dutch models (Kobe City Museum 1998: 122–123). In 1808 Motoki Shōei compiled a work on Western warships entitled *Gunkan zukai kōrei* ('Examples of Illustrations of Warships'). This beautifully-illustrated work was based on Dutch and French sources. In 1856, Ōtsuka Dōan's (1795–1855) translation of the third part of the Dutch work *Reglement op de exercitien en manoeuvres der infanterie* (Breda, 1855), was published posthumously with the title *Oranda kangun batteira gakkō zensho* ('Complete course of Exercises by Battalion of the Dutch Army'). Such was the demand for military works that the Dutch version was reprinted in Nagasaki in 1857 (Ser. 536, Kerlen 1316). Another example is Fukuzawa Yukichi's translation of a Dutch book on fortifications.

3.5   *More General Translations:* Kōmō zatsuwa *and* Kōsei shinpen

Other translations were of a more general nature. In 1787 Morishima Chūryō published *Kōmō zatsuwa* ('Dutch (lit. Red-haired) miscellany') in five volumes,

---

43   Hakkō (八紘) literally means 'eight crown cords', an old expression referring to the whole world. I thank Prof. Shimizu Makoto for this information.

44   Clements (2015: 159) names the Dutch source as 'The Life of Bonaparte', (*Het Leven van Bonaparte*, 1801). This was a translation from an as yet unidentified French source by Johannes van der Linden (1756–1835). The NIJL database (ID 395299) gives the author of the Dutch source as Van der Linden.

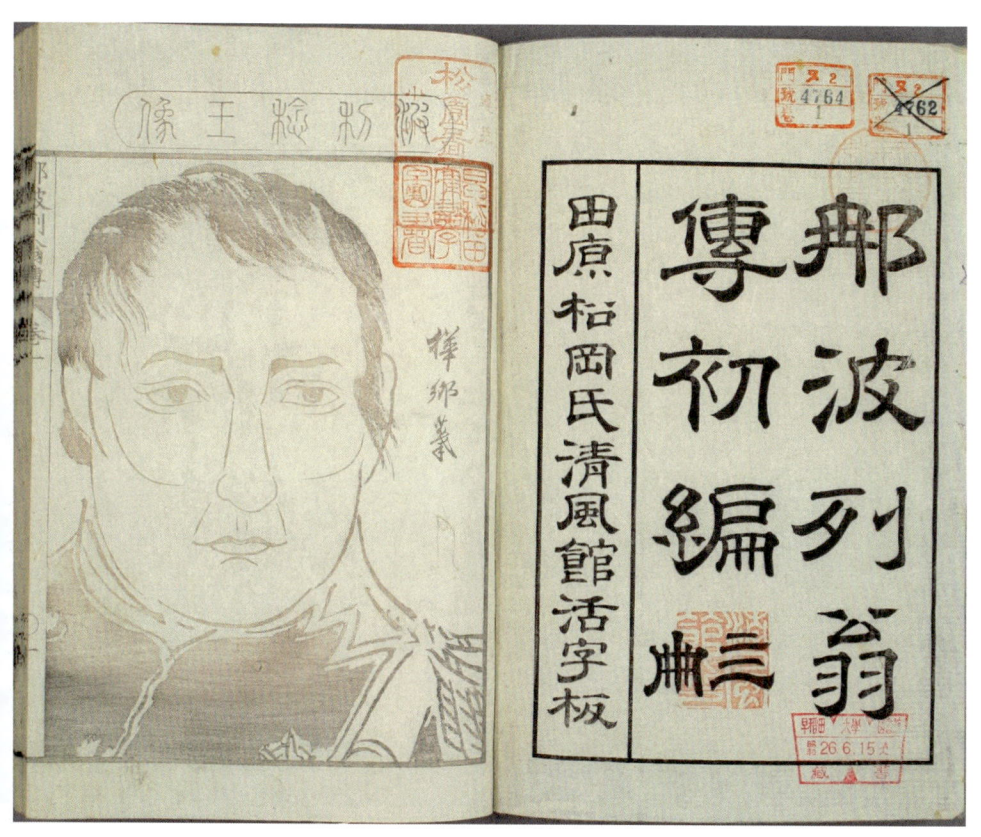

FIGURE 21   *Naporeon den* ('A Biography of Napoleon', 1837), trans. Ozeki San'ei. Title page
WUL 又 02 04764

which was re-printed four times between 1796 and 1829 (Clements 2015: 151, see
fig. 22). Timon Screech (2012: 319) describes it as 'the first best-seller of popular-
izing rangaku'.[45] This is underlined by the use of *hiragana*, alongside *kanji* and
katakana for loanwords, which was used for non-serious literature. This book
was primarily a description of daily life on Deshima, based on observations
of friends and *rangakusha* who came into contact with the Dutch at Nagasaki
or Edo. However, it also included descriptions of European institutions such
as hospitals and almshouses (Winkel 1999: 44).[46] One Dutch source on which

---

45   Screech notes that *kōmō* (meaning literally 'red fur', although here and elsewhere typically translated as 'red-haired') refers to Europeans more generally rather than simply the
Dutch. It was a Chinese, and therefore academic sounding, term for Europe and therefore
not intended to sound rude.

46   For a detailed account of *Kōmō zatsuwa*, see Winkel (2004: 46–72).

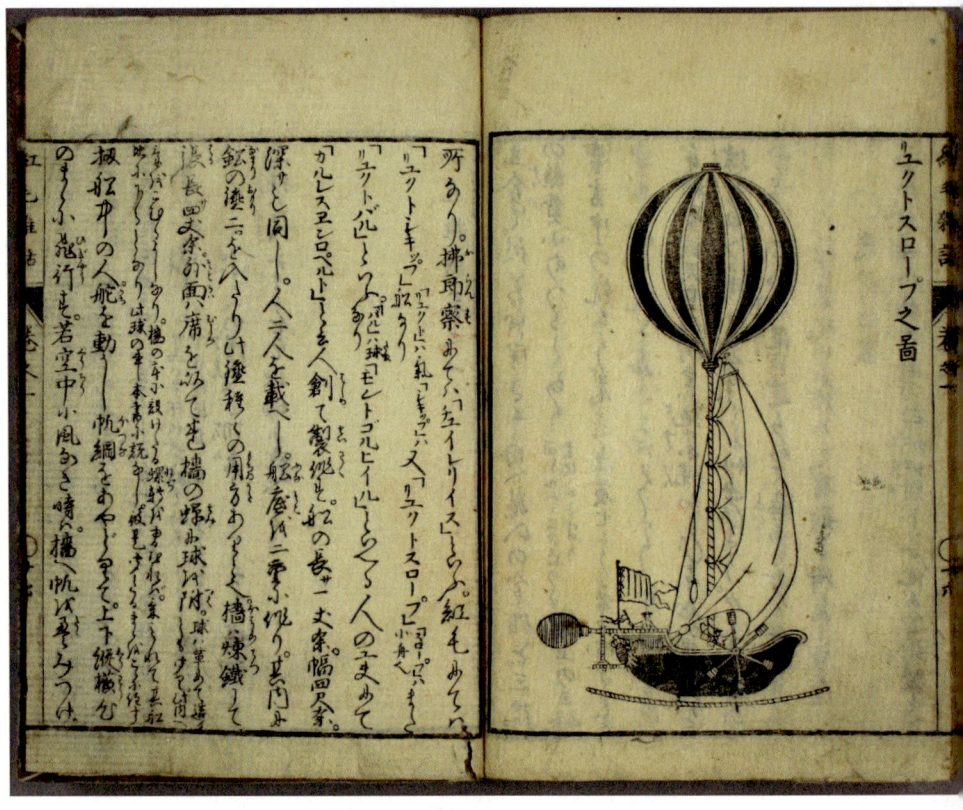

FIGURE 22   An airship (リュクトスロープ *ryukutosurōpu* < *luchtsloep* 'air sloop') in *Kōmō zatsuwa* ('Red-haired Miscellany', 1787), Morishima Chūryō, vol. I WUL 文庫 17 W0217

it draws is Gerard de Lairesse's treatise on art, *Het Groot Schilderboek* (1707). Chūryō refers to this work in order to inform his readers how to draw in the Western manner (Screech 2012: 321).

One translation project on which Baba Teiyū worked at the *Bansho wage goyō* was a translation of the seven-volume *Algemeen huishoudelijk-, natuur-, zedekundig- en konst-woordenboek* (1778–93). This was a Dutch translation of Noël Chomel's French *Dictionnaire oeconomique* ('The Family Diction-ary', Lyon, 1709).[47] The Japanese translation was given the title *Kōsei shinpen*

---

47   Although Chomel's dictionary is typically translated as 'The Family Dictionary', it dealt with subjects as diverse as animal husbandry and technology and the art of commerce. 'The Dictionary of Household Management' may be a more appropriate translation.

('A New Compendium for Health') (Clements 2015: 156).[48] The manner in which the translators rendered Dutch terms in *katakana* was often quite different from the Dutch renderings. This is, at least in part, explained by the differences in the Dutch and Japanese phonological systems analysed in Chapter 5. In one volume we find transliterations in *katakana* of the Dutch for Poland (*Polen*) *pōren* and Lithuania (Dutch *Litouw(en)*), *Ritauhen*. The entry for a type of wading bird *strandloopers* in the Dutch translation of Chomel is quite extensive.[49] The Japanese translators render this as *sutorando rōperusu*, perhaps not realizing the Dutch word is a plural. They render 'mastic' (Mastik in the Chomel) as *masuchiko*, reflecting the lack of the phoneme [ti] in the Japanese sound system, and the plant 'apocijnum' (apocynum) in the Chomel dictionary as *aposēnyumu*.[50] 'Conger eel', rendered as *Konger-aal* in the Dutch translation, is given in *katakana* as *kongeruāru*. The Dutch translation has the entry for 'salmon' under *Salmen* (*WNT* plural). *Kōsei shinpen* follows suit by rendering it as *sarumen* in *katakana*. Other fish to which it refers are herring (*hāringen*—in the Dutch translation *haaringen*), a fish given in the Dutch translation as *meirslangen* and in Japanese *katakana* as *meirusurangen*, i.e., a member of the genus 'cobitis' in Latin, or 'spiny loach', and the *sutekerubarusen*, i.e., the *stekelbaars* or stickleback.[51] All are given in the plural as they are in the Dutch translation. Chomel's work was also used as a source for Chūryō's *Kōmō zatsuwa*. For example, he reproduced a figure of a spring-loaded gun trap, annotating it in Japanese (Screech 2006: 23, 25). Some of these entries were extremely unusual, but this did not necessarily concern the translators. Part of the motivation in translating Chomel's encyclopaedia was to gain access to 'all' Western knowledge, before considering the relative importance of the information.

3.6 Rangaku *Translations: General Comments*

It will already be clear that although the Japanese were translating from Dutch, most of the works they translated were not originally written in Dutch. In fact, a survey of books translated between 1706 and 1852 indicates that of 213 books for which the original language is known, only 20, or just under 10%, were originally written in Dutch. The most common original language was German, accounting for 113 or 53% of the total. The other 37% of books are roughly split

---

48 For more on this translation, see Fukuoka (2012: 43–51).
49 This is probably the dunlin in English.
50 http://dl.ndl.go.jp/info:ndljp/pid/2545247/15. Accessed 13 April 2020.
51 The *stekelbaars* does not have a lemma in the Dutch translation of Chomel, but the authors of *Kōsei shinpen* may have found it under another entry.

equally between Latin, French and English. Many books had therefore been translated out of another language before being translated into Dutch and so had gone through two or three translations before being clothed in Japanese. Thus, some Japanese texts are likely to have differed quite significantly from the original European source text (Clements 2015: 153).

The volume of translations is difficult to gauge not least because many circulated in manuscript and may no longer survive. By the end of the eighteenth century about ten works were being translated each year from Dutch to Japanese. By about 1820, some 20 translations a year were being made. This number fell in the next twenty years or so as opposition to Western learning grew but recovered in the period 1840–60 when at its peak nearly 60 translations a year were being made (Clements 2015: 147).

3.7   The Translation of Administrative, Legal and Commercial Documents and Correspondence

It was not only books relating to learning that were being translated between Dutch and Japanese. Other documents such as official orders, trading documents and correspondence were also being translated. VOC documents needed to be translated into Japanese for the *bakufu*. Two VOC letters from 1630 and 1644 tell us, as Adam Clulow (2014: 101–102) argues, that the position of the Dutch in Japan was in some sense akin to that of vassals of the shogun. In early 1644 the Dutch received an order from the shogun which was to be read out and translated into Dutch, after which the *opperhoofd* Jan van Elseracq would be questioned to ensure that he understood it. Amongst other things the order told the Dutch that if they heard of any Portuguese or Spanish priests planning to come to Japan or any Iberians plotting attacks on Japan, they should inform the shogun of this (Vermeulen *et al.* 1986–: XI:152–153). On 15 July 1668 two Dutchmen were summoned to the governor's house to help translate some papers written in Dutch which had been found on Chinese junks (Vermeulen *et al.* 1986–: XIII:305).

In July 1775 Daniel Armenault (*opperhoofd* intermittently 1770–75) recorded that orders given by Japanese officials, which had to be observed during the trading season, were interpreted imperfectly. He therefore demanded a written translation in Dutch. This was granted, but he said that he would have it copied and checked before signing it. Requests for translations were not, however, always fulfilled. In April 1775 the *dagregister* states that the interpreter Namura Shinpachi (also Katsuemon) was asked to provide a written translation of an order against smuggling. Katsuemon tried to delay doing it because he was unable to translate it. He was therefore called incompetent (Blussé and Remmelink 2004: 388, 386).

One particularly important set of documents was the *Oranda fūsetsugaki* ('Dutch Book of Rumours').[52] These were reports compiled typically annually by the Dutch consisting of news of events outside Japan. The first such report was produced in 1641, after the Dutch move to Deshima.[53] The final report is thought to have been made in 1859, the year before the Dutch trading post at Deshima was closed. The reports were translated into Japanese for use by the shogun and the Nagasaki *bugyō*.[54] From 1840, the Governor-General in Batavia began supplementing the Dutch text for the *Oranda fūsetsugaki* with a yearly report focusing on the impact of the First Opium War on East Asia.[55] This was translated into Japanese with the title *Betsudan fūsetsugaki* ('Special [Dutch] Book of Rumours'), and was then presented to the *bakufu* (Matsukata 2012). Also in 1840, the *bakufu* ordered the Nagasaki *bugyō* to submit to Edo the original Dutch of the *fūsetsugaki* together with the Japanese translation (Matsukata 2011: 102).

In 1844, a letter dated 15 February was sent by King Willem II of the Netherlands to the shogun. It was written in Dutch, having been prepared by the king's advisor, Von Siebold, who had been expelled from Japan for attempting to take maps of the country to Batavia. The letter was sent without an accompanying Japanese translation. However, three contemporaneous Japanese translations survive, and a modern Japanese translation has been published, too (Matsukata 2011: 109).[56] In the early 1860s, the *Bansho shirabesho* ordered

---

52   In Dutch, the *Oranda fūsetsugaki* was referred to as *Gewoon Nieuws* ('Normal News') (Matsukata 2011: 102).

53   Editions of these reports have been published by Iwao (1976–79). The reports were not the only channel by which news of Europe reached Japan. The Chinese brought news from the Europeans such as Jesuit missionaries who were still active in China. See also Matsukata (2007) for Japanese versions of many of the early *Oranda fūsetsugaki*. The first such report was compiled on 2 May 1641 (p. 39). A page from the *fūsetsugaki* for 1797, signed by the *opperhoofd* Gijsbert Hemmij, is given in Nagasaki Shiritsu Hakubutsukan (2000: 20).

54   There are 55 extant copies of Dutch and 272 Japanese versions of the *fūsetsugaki* (Iwao 1976–79: II:25–26). Iwao observes that in the wake of the First Opium War, further copies of the *fūsetsugaki* were distributed across the country. Tsukahara (2007b: 197) reports that *rangakusha* such as Shiba Kōkan also had access to the *fūsetsugaki*.

55   From 1850 to 1854, this was given the title *Apart Nieuws* ('Special News'). See MS The Hague, *Nationaal Archief*, VOC (1.04.21), nrs. 1703–1706 for the *Apart Nieuws* reports for 1850, 1852, 1853 and 1854.

56   *Bakufu* communications with the Dutch were translated into Dutch. For example, we have a Dutch translation of a communication made on 17 September 1842 concerning the Order for the Provision of Firewood and Water (薪水給与令, *shinsui kyūyorei*), an edict which signalled a softening of the Japanese approach to dealing with foreign ships entering their waters (Matsukata 2011: 104).

translations to be made of the *Javasche Courant*, a Dutch-language newspaper published in Batavia. The translations were made for a broad educated public in what Clements (2015: 207) describes as 'simple academic Japanese written in a mixture of Sinitic characters (*kanji*) and cursive *kana*'. Non-Japanese names were rendered in *katakana*, which would have led Japanese readers to pronounce them somewhat differently from the original.

Letters to and from the Nagasaki *bugyō* and indeed the shogun were translated between Dutch and Japanese. Occasionally, the Dutch were called on unexpectedly to translate documents. On the *hofreis* in 1780, Isaac Titsingh encountered a Japanese who handed him two documents that had been written in 1625 in the language of the Dutch court (*in de Hoftaal geschreven*). They turned out to be trading licences that had been written by the *opperhoofd*, Cornelis van Nijenroode, for one of the forefathers of the Japanese in question. The documents were translated into Japanese, probably by one of the interpreters in Titsingh's party (Lequin 2011: 76).

Although the focus of this chapter is on translations from Dutch to Japanese, a word is in order about a small number of translations from Japanese, which remained in manuscript, that Titsingh himself seems to have made, with the aid of native speakers. One of these is a draft translation of an extract from 'Gjoofirok', a work compiled in secret by 'Baboen Koo' on events at the Shogunal Palace. Despite the differences in spelling, 'Gjoofirok' may well refer to (*Kindai Kōjitsu*) *Genpiroku* and 'Baboen Koo' to Baba Bunkō, discussed above. If so, this may add something to our knowledge of Bunkō, as Titsingh describes him as a servant of the grandfather of the present Tokugawa shogun ('een Dienaar van de grootvader van deeze Kyser'). Another example is a translation of a Japanese work entitled 'Lyky', but we have no further details (Lequin 2003: 179). Again, with the help of an interpreter, Titsingh translated a Japanese work on indigenous plants, *Kai* ('Types of flowers', Kyoto 1765) by Shimada Mitsufusa and Ono Ranzan (Lequin 2003: 128–129).[57]

In the nineteenth century, Dutch legal texts were translated into Japanese. Prior to the nineteenth century, the translation of legal texts into Japanese had solely been from Chinese (Verwayen 1998: 337). In 1841, the high-ranking court official (*Rōjū* 老中) Mizuno Tadakuni (1794–1851) ordered scholars attached to the *Bansho wage goyō* in Edo to translate Dutch law codes imported into the country (Verwayen 1996: 61–63, quoted in Boot 2013: 205 n. 51).[58] This would

---

57 On the manuscript, the Japanese book is referred to as 'kwaji of Kruydboek'. Lequin gives the first name as Shimada Shigefusa. Mitsufusa is given in the NIJL database (ID 235767).

58 Verwayen concludes that it cannot be established when or how the law codes were imported.

help the *bakufu* to understand the Dutch legal system. Among the translations made were those of the Dutch Constitution, the Dutch Criminal Code and Code of Criminal Procedure and Code of Civil Procedure (Verwayen 1998: 340).

3.8 Works of Fiction

So far, this analysis has focused on non-fiction Dutch texts. Works of fiction, too, were imported in Japan, and although there is little firm evidence for the translation of them into Japanese, there are a few exceptions, as illustrated by the following examples from the beginning and end of our period.[59] In the mid-seventeenth century, the *ōmetsuke* Inoue Masashige, mentioned above, was able to consult a copy of Jacob Cats's emblem book, *Spiegel van den Ouden ende Nieuwen Tijdt* ('Mirror of the Old and New Time') (1st ed. 1632). This contained several references to the Christian God (Vermeulen *et al.* 1986–: XII: 51–52). In 1652, Masashige asked the Dutch to copy the names in Cats's book and informed them that his interpreter would then translate these into Japanese. It would have been interesting to learn of Masashige's response to Cats's book, for part of his brief was to conduct the anti-Christian campaign in the 1640s and 1650s. Unfortunately, the *dagregister* does not give any further details.

In 1820, two plays were performed by the Dutch at Deshima. The departing *bugyō*, Tsutsui Masanori, was so impressed that he ordered the interpreters to make a summarized version of them in Japanese, which would in fact go on to enjoy some success (Scholten 1990: 190). In 1848, the first Japanese translation of Daniel Defoe's 'Robinson Crusoe' was made, based on a 1720 Dutch translation of the work (*Het leven en de wonderbaare gevallen van Robinson Crusoe*, Amsterdam). The translation was made in the literary Sinitic mode *kanbun*. The title character's resoluteness and self-sufficiency were attractive to Japanese readers. Another translation of Defoe's story was made in 1857 by Yokoyama Yoshikiyo (1826–79) in informal Japanese using *hiragana-majiri*. In this case, the Dutch source was a later translation, *Beknopte Levensgeschiedenis van Robinson Crusoe* ('Concise Life-history of Robinson Crusoe') (Amsterdam, c. 1850), which was explicitly aimed at younger readers. Yoshikiyo gave his translation the title *Robinson hyōkō kiryaku* ('Concise account of the castaway adventures of Robinson'). The Dutch title is reproduced in the front matter in upper-case Roman script along with several illustrations of the eponymous castaway. The Dutch source text was used by Itō Keisuke when giving Dutch lessons in Nagoya in around 1858 (Matsuda 2000: 127; Bownas 2005: 232).

---

59 In a lecture given in Seoul on 16 May 2017, Prof. Olf Praamstra stated that books by P.C. Hooft, Wolff & Deken, Bosboom-Toussaint and Hendrik Tollens had been imported into Japan.

A Dutch science-fiction novel, *Anno 2065 Een Blik in de Toekomst* ('The Year 2065, A Look in the Future') published by Pieter Harting (a.k.a. Dr. Dioscorides 1813–85) in Utrecht in 1865, was translated into Japanese by Kondō Makoto (1831–86) in 1868 with the title *Shin-mirai-ki* ('New chronicle of the future'). However, the translation was not published until 1878 (Scholten 1990: 190).[60]

One other Dutch fiction author to be translated into Japanese was Jan Bastiaan Christemeijer (1794–1872). Christemeijer's books are the forerunners of the modern detective novel. In 1861 two of his detective stories were translated by Kanda Takahira (1830–98), who had studied *rangaku* and taught at the *Bansho shirabesho*. He was a member of the Edo salon group of *rangakusha* in the late Tokugawa period, which centred around the house of a later member of the illustrious Edo family, Katsuragawa Hoshū 11, and which would also include Fukuzawa Yukichi (Scholten 1990: 199–200).

One of Christemeijer's stories that Kanda translated was *De Jonker van Roderijcke of een dubbele moord, door de titel van een blijspel ontdekt*. A copy of a collection of stories by Christemeijer is on an import list in Nagasaki in 1854, and it may be that this was Kanda's source. Kanda gave his translation the title (*Yonkeru fan rodereiki ikken*). The first three words are a transliteration of the name of the subject ('Jonker (squire) van Roderijcke'), while *ikken* (一件) means 'one case'. The other story was *De blauwe ruiter en zijn huisgezin* ('The blue horseman and his household'). His translations are both accurate, although not entirely without error, and impressive in their rich vocabulary (Scholten 1990: 202). Kanda translated both works privately, not intending to publish them. However, the author and scholar Narushima Ryūhoku (1837–84) published Kanda's translation of *De Jonker* in instalments in *Kagetsu shinshi* (花月新誌) a literary journal, modernizing Kanda's Japanese in the process. Narushima suggested that the Japanese took to Christemeijer's works as he gave a very close description of crimes, something that Japanese authors did not do (Scholten 1990: 204).[61] He therefore filled a gap in Japanese literature and this can be seen as a good example of Itamar Even-Zohar's polysystems theory, whereby translations are often made to fill a gap in the culture of the target language (e.g., Even-Zohar 1990).

Finally, Dutch songs and poems were translated into Japanese. Sugimoto (1980) provides details of several of these. To give one example here, he presents a drinking song, 'drink lied'. This is written in Roman script with

60   https://dl.ndl.go.jp/info:ndljp/pid/768374. Accessed 13 April 2020.

61   The stories were published in 1891 under the title *Oranda bisei roku* ('A Dutch Record of Good Governance') (Clements 2015: 217). There is, though, an entry for this work with Christemeijer listed as one of the authors in *worldcat* dated Meiji 20 (1887).

katakana superscript. The Roman script seems to have been copied by the Edo scholar and early *rangakusha*, Aoki Kon'yo, for his own amusement. He added *katakana* superscript and translated the song into Japanese. The transcription was not without error. In line four of the first verse, we read 'cam me ratie'. This may be a misspelt version of the French *camaraderie* ('comradeship') but is certainly not 'good' Dutch. The *katakana*, as usual, means that Japanese pronunciation differs significantly from the Dutch—e.g., *tot* ('until') is rendered *totto* and *druppelen* ('drops') as *doropperen*. Sugimoto also records that on an earlier *hofreis* Engelbert Kaempfer (*kenperu*) had sung a song and danced at Edo Castle and that the song was translated (Sugimoto 1980: 156–157).

4   For Whom?

Many of the translations throughout this period were made for Japanese officials including the Nagasaki *bugyō* and those working for the *bakufu*. The recording and translation of the oral instructions of Dutch surgeons and physicians by Mukai Genshō were made at the request of the *ōmetsuke* Inoue Masashige. The annual *Oranda fūsetsugaki* and later the *Betsudan fūsetsugaki* were translated for the *bugyō* and the *bakufu*. In the nineteenth century, as fears grew of a possible foreign invasion, the *bakufu* ordered scholars to translate works on military matters. Other works were translated specifically at the request of the *bakufu*. One example is Motoki Shōei's illustrated book on Western warships, *Gunkan zukai kōrei* ('Examples of Illustrations of Warships', 1808). In 1841, scholars attached to the *Bansho wage goyō* were ordered to translate a Dutch book on naval artillery (Verwayen 1998: 337).[62]

Sometimes it is not clear for whom a translation was made. Famously, Shizuki Tadao made a translation of an appendix of the Dutch translation of Engelbert Kaempfer's 'Description of Japan'.[63] He may initially have made it

---

62   Going in the other direction, translations, such as those of shogunal orders, were made from Japanese to Dutch for the leaders of the Dutch trading post at Deshima or for senior VOC officials in Batavia.

63   The publishing history of Kaempfer's work is somewhat complex. For our purposes it is necessary to know that Shizuki Tadao was working with a Dutch version, *De Beschryving van Japan* (Amsterdam: 1733), based on an English version 'The History of Japan' (London, 1727), which was the first published edition, based on Kaempfer's German manuscript and supplemented with appendices translated into Dutch from chapters of Kaempfer's Latin publication *Amœnitates exoticae* ('Exotic Delights', 1712). The appendix that Shizuki Tadao translated was the chapter 'Relatio XIV' in *Amœnitates exoticae* (Boot 2008: 88; Mervart 2015: 20).

for himself, or at the request of Matsūra Seizan, *daimyō* of Hirado, whose copy of Kaempfer's work Tadao is likely to have used as his source text (Boot 2008: 90–91).[64] Some Japanese clearly did produce translations for themselves. Teachers of *rangaku* made translations for their own use, a point I return to below. The translations of Jan Bastiaan Christemeijer's stories by Kanda Takahira do seem to have been, at least initially, for private use. Later, Narushima Ryūhoku's publication of his revised version of Kanda's translation of *De Jonker* in a literary journal brought the story to its well-educated readership.

Many of the translations that come under the heading of Dutch learning were aimed at the scholar/interpreters at Nagasaki and scholars at Edo who were interested in the relevant subjects. One exception to this is *Kaitai shinsho* ('A New Treatise on Anatomy'). Clements observes that this was not simply aimed at medical experts, but 'at a more general readership of educated samurai'. However, the target language of the translation was not Japanese, but *kanbun* (the form of literary Sinitic used in Japan), and so it was criticized by some for not being sufficiently accessible (Screech 2005: 51; Clements 2015: 148). Others who could make use of specific translations were physicians, educated laymen and landowners trying to improve the yield from their land.

Finally, other works were clearly for a more general readership. Such books were often written in a combination of *hiragana* and *kanji* (*hiragana-majiri*). Isono Bunsai's *Nagasaki miyage* ('Souvenirs of Nagasaki', 1847) and Ōtsuki Gentaku's *Ransetsu benwaku* ('A clarification of misunderstandings in theories about the Dutch', 1797) are two examples of books written in this script which aimed to bring information about the Dutch and Dutch learning to a wider audience. *Shin-mirai-ki*, Kondō Makoto's translation of Harting's *Anno 2065 Een Blik in de Toekomst*, and Yokoyama Yoshikiyo's version of Robinson Crusoe are two examples of translations of works of fiction written in *hiragana-majiri*.[65]

5   In What Manner?

Here, we can explore several topics concerning the process of translation. Among these are the question as to whether translations were individual or group projects, the nature of sources, the relationship between source and target texts, the source-target language combinations, the 'mechanics' of how

---

64   Boot also notes that Seizan had acquired a second copy of the Dutch translation from the Nagasaki interpreter, Yoshio Kōgyū.

65   These works contain *hiragana* characters, which are no longer used, referred to as *hentaigana* 変体仮名 or 変体がな.

Japanese translators rendered a source text in the target language, the aids to translation such as lexicons which translators used, and the form in which translations were circulated.

5.1 Individual or Group Projects

Some translations, such as those by Kanda Takahira of Christemeijer's detective stories, were essentially individual efforts. The interpreter Matsumura Genkō undertook translation projects on his own (Goodman 2013: 157). Two of these are *Shinzō bankoku chimei kō* ('Newly enlarged list of geographical names in the world', 1779), and a map of the Western and Eastern hemispheres. However, he also undertook translation projects with his close friend, Motoki Yoshinaga, such as *Oranda chizu ryakusetsu* ('Brief Explanation of Dutch Maps', 1772), based on Johann Hübner's *Kort begryp der oude en nieuwe geographie* (Amsterdam, 1722) and *Oranda chikyū zusetsu* ('An explanation in a Dutch atlas of the world', 1773), one of whose sources was *Atlas van Zeevaart en Koophandel door de geheele weereldt* (Amsterdam, 1745), itself a translation from a French work by Louis Renard (Unno 1994: 433–434). An example of a word that needed to be rendered in Japanese was *dampkring*, the Dutch for 'atmosphere'. This was rendered in *katakana* as *danpukiringi* (Kobe City Museum 1998: 108).

Other translation projects were also collaborative efforts. The early translations made by Mukai Genshō involved not only him, but also interpreters and the principal sources, the senior surgeons at Deshima, Hans Juriaen Hancke and later Steven de la Tombe. The translation project that produced *Kaitai shinsho* was a collaborative effort involving the Edo scholars Maeno Ryōtaku, Sugita Genpaku and Ōtsuki Gentaku, with the last two working together again to translate another medical text, *Heelkundige Onderwijzingen* ('Lessons in Surgery'). Sometimes collaboration took the form of financial support. Takano Chōei translated his work on prolonging life *Ransetsu yōjōroku* under the patronage of Kumatani Gorōzaemon (dates unknown) (Clements 2015: 161). In truth, some translation projects were both individual and group enterprises. Although Shizuki Tadao undertook his translation of Kaempfer's work largely on his own he was to some extent reliant on Dutch informants. Tadao was clearly not entirely happy with his translation, blaming its quality on 'the obtuseness of his Dutch informants' (Boot 2008: 92).

5.2 The Nature of the Sources

As for the nature of the sources, while for most translations they were written, for others they were oral. Mukai Genshō's translation and other early translations based on the instructions of physicians and surgeons at Deshima fall into the latter category. Some later translations do so as well. Noro Genjō based his book *Oranda kinjū chūgyo zu wage* ('Illustrations of Dutch Birds and Animals, Insects and Fish, explained in Japanese', 1741) on interviews, via an interpreter, with the Dutch on the *hofreis* at Edo, armed with a copy of the Dutch translation of the Latin work on quadrupeds by Johannes Jonston, mentioned above (Shirahata 2001: 267–268). Kornicki (2001: 302) observes that by 1750 Noro Genjō had applied the same method to producing a Japanese version of Dodoens's herbal. In 1800, Yoshio Kōgyū published a book containing information that he had gleaned from the Swedish physician, Carl Peter Thunberg. It was entitled *Kōmō hijiki* ('A Record of Dutch (lit. Red-haired) Secrets') and contained among other things information from Thunberg on the treatment of syphilis (Screech 2005: 34).

5.3   *Source and Target Languages*

The most common combination of source and target languages for *rangaku* was Dutch as source and Japanese as target. However, there were other combinations. There is a strong possibility that some of the medical instructions which formed the basis of early translations were in Portuguese or a combination of Portuguese and Dutch. On occasion, Japanese translators had to translate from Latin. The most famous example of this concerns Shizuki Tadao.

Although he based his Japanese translation of an appendix of Kaempfer's book on a Dutch translation (*De Beschrijving van Japan*), he had to translate several words and phrases from Latin. One notable example involves two lines from Virgil's *Georgics* Book I that the Dutch translator had left in the original Latin.[66] As noted in Chapter 4, Tadao was able to identify the language as Latin and managed to understand and translate it with the help of a Latin-Dutch dictionary that sat in a library in Hirado.[67]

The same passage in Virgil's *Georgics* from which these two lines were taken (I: 54–61) had been used by Hugo Grotius in *Mare Liberum* ('The Free Sea', Leiden, 1609) in support of free commercial exchange. An interesting footnote to Tadao's translation is that he rendered the title of Kaempfer's appendix, which in English was 'An Enquiry, whether it be conducive for the good of the Japanese Empire to keep it shut up, as it now is, and not to suffer its inhabitants to have any commerce with foreign nations, either at home or abroad',

---

66   The two lines from Virgil's *Georgics* Book I in the Dutch translation of Kaempfer's work are 54 and 57: *Hic Segetes, illic veniunt felicius Uvae: India mittit ebur, molles sua thura Sabæi* ('Here corn, there grapes shoot forth more luxuriantly; India sends forth ivory, the soft Sabaeans their frankincense').

67   This was Benjamin Jacques and Samuel Hannot, *Dictionarium Latino-Belgicum* (Rotterdam: Pieter van der Slaart, 1699) (Mervart 2015: 22–23).

simply as 'Essay on a Closed Country'. In Japanese this is *Sakoku-ron*. *Ron* (論) means 'essay' or 'argument'. *Sakoku* is a neologism coined by Tadao.[68] It literally means 'chained or closed kingdom', corresponding to the Latin *regnum clausum*, but came to mean 'national isolation' and in the nineteenth century was used widely to describe the period during which Japan was deemed to have closed itself from the outside world, although it did in fact remain open to a limited extent through 'the four gates' (*yottsu no kuchi*) (Mervart 2015: 27–28).[69] *Sakoku* (鎖国) has subsequently been adopted by Mandarin Chinese (pronounced *Suǒguó*). This refers not only to Japan's period of isolation but also to other countries which close themselves to the outside word.

Tadao translated the couplet from Virgil not into Japanese, but rather into *kanbun*, the form of literary Sinitic used in Japan. In doing so, he was 'proposing something of a functional parallel between the two bodies of authoritative classics' (Mervart 2015: 23). Similarly, the translators of *Kaitai shinsho* also chose to translate their work into *kanbun* rather than Japanese (Screech 2005: 51; Clements 2015: 148–149).[70] A key reason for the choice of literary Sinitic in this case was that this was the authoritative language for medical texts in Japan. Works in literary Sinitic were typically addressed to other scholars. However, although this book was intended for a general readership of educated samurai, Shiba Kōkan complained about 'the needless difficulty of the book's language' (Screech 1996: 268 n. 104). He also argued that its use was 'a plot to frighten the illiterate' (Clements 2015: 169).

Some texts were translated into Japanese using a combination of Sinitic characters (*kanji*) and *katakana*, the square-form Japanese syllabary. One example of this is the last volume and final version of *Rekishō shinsho*, a three-volume work on Western physics and astronomy translated by Shizuki Tadao (Clements 2015: 168–169). Likewise, Itō Genboku (1801–71) produced *Iryō seishi* ('Correct Beginnings of Medical Treatment', 1835) using a mixture of *kanji* and *katakana* (Clements 2015: 196).[71] The target audience here consisted of students and interested lay people, who did not have a sufficiently good reading knowledge of literary Sinitic. As noted above, other texts were also translated into Japanese using a combination of Sinitic characters and *hiragana*, the cursive Japanese syllabary. These were typically texts of a less serious nature. Texts

---

68   *Sakoku* consists of two *kanji* (鎖国). The second *kanji*, *koku*, means 'country' with the first *kanji*, *sa*, which literally means 'chain', giving the sense of closure. See also Keene (1969: 76) and Miao-Ling (1990: 228–229 n. 1).

69   Miao-Ling (1990) provides a nuanced account of Japan's relations to the outside world in the Tokugawa period.

70   For more on *kanbun* see Steininger (2017: 12–13).

71   This was based on a work by the Austrian physician, Ignaz Rudolf Bischoff (1784–1850).

in these 'mixed' forms of written Japanese, known respectively as *katakana-majiri* and *hiragana-majiri*, were composed according to the standard grammar of classical Japanese.

5.4 The Process of Translation

As for the 'mechanics' of how Japanese translators rendered a source text in the target language, there was some variation. Several accounts give us insights into how many of the texts would have been translated. These can be analysed at three levels: word, sentence and text. It should be noted that much of what follows is derived from the processes developed for translating texts written in literary Sinitic into Japanese. This is to be expected given that many of the *rangakusha* were intellectuals who had been trained to read and translate Chinese texts. To borrow from Pierre Bourdieu these processes can perhaps be understood as the 'habitus' of the Japanese translators, i.e., the skills that they had built up by translating Chinese texts, which they could apply to translating Dutch texts (Bourdieu 1972, quoted in Burke 2007: 25).

Let us take the level of word first. In the translators' preface to *Kaitai shinsho* ('A New Treatise on Anatomy') three types of translation of Dutch terms are described. The first of these is 'equivalent translation' (*hon'yaku* 翻訳) (*yaku* (訳) means 'translation' or 'version'), which is used when an equivalent term exists in the target language. The second type is 'translation of meaning' (*giyaku* 義訳). This typically refers to the translation of the constituent parts of a compound word in Dutch to give a new compound word in the target language. The translators of *Kaitai shinsho* coined several *giyaku*, which are morpheme-by-morpheme translations, or loan translations, of Dutch terms, e.g., *ko-maku* (鼓膜) for the tympanic membrane. This and other examples of loan translations are analysed in Chapter 7. A slightly different instance of *giyaku* is the translation of *Gemeenebest* ('commonwealth'), a form of government unfamiliar to East Asia, by Shizuki Tadao in his translation of an appendix to Kaempfer's 'History of Japan'. Tadao chose to translate this with the phrase *dōkō gōitsu* (同好合一) which has the sense of a 'unity (*gōitsu*) of friendly communion (*dōkō*)'. He also provided a gloss giving further insight into this somewhat alien term (Mervart 2015: 27–28). The third type is 'direct translation' or transliteration (*chokuyaku* 直訳). This is used where there is no equivalent in the target language and where the meaning cannot be inferred from the Dutch etymology. For example, the Dutch *klier* (Eng. gland) is rendered as *kirīru* using the *ateji* 吉里爾 (phonograms as opposed to semantograms) (Clements 2015: 166; Vande Walle 2001b: 135). These words produced by *chokuyaku* equate more or less to *gairaigo*.

This is not the end of the matter, for another way in which translators could render Dutch words into Japanese was to form new *kanji*. Here again, we can refer to a rendering of the Dutch *klier* in Japanese. Whereas the authors of *Kaitai shinsho* used *ateji*, in 1805 Udagawa Genshin used a new *kanji sen* (腺) for his medical translation *Ihan teikō* ('Concise Model of [Western] Medicine', publ. 1845). This was composed of the radical for 'meat', also used for parts of the human body, and a phonetic element, which had the meaning 'spring'. So, 'gland' was translated as 'the spring inside the human body (meat)'. This was later adopted by Chinese (Kuiper 1993: 123).

In his introduction to *Kōi geka sōden* (completed 1706), Narabayashi Chinzan comments that in order to compose the book, all Dutch words were transcribed and then translated into Japanese. Furthermore, in some cases only the Dutch words were used (Krieger 1940: 5). Another translator, Motoki Yoshinaga, was said to be 'overwhelmed' by phonological differences between Dutch and Japanese. For one translation, he used Chinese characters to be read in the Chinese manner from the Song dynasty (960–1279 AD) and thereafter, a system referred to as *tō-on* (唐音). He did this because he felt that *katakana* even with its markings did not represent Dutch closely enough. So, he used what is essentially a non-phonetic writing system to resolve issues around phonological differences between Dutch and Japanese. It may also be that the prestige of Chinese script played a role here (Vande Walle 2001b: 136). For his translation *Tenchi nikyū yōhō* ('The use of celestial and terrestrial globes'), mentioned above, he used a mixture of literal translation, translation of meaning (*giyaku*), transliteration and indeed abbreviation (Vande Walle 2001b: 134).

At sentence level, several strategies may have been adopted. In *Rangaku kaitei* (1783), Ōtsuki Gentaku describes the approach that he used. There were two stages. First, the translator should translate individual words and phrases, affixing his translations at word and phrase level as glosses. He can then move onto understanding sentences and translating these into the target language with the necessary adjustments to word order. The process of translation using these glosses was known as *kun'yaku* 訓訳 (Clements 2015: 163–164).[72]

A similar translation method was adopted at the *Bansho wage goyō*. First, the Dutch text was provided with marks in order to show how the word order should be changed to conform to Japanese grammar and syntax.[73] Second, the

---

72 This term is related to *kundoku*, the process by which texts written in literary Sinitic were read by Japanese.

73 Marks known as *kaeriten* (返り点) were written alongside characters in literary Sinitic texts to indicate the order for reading them in Japanese.

Dutch text was translated word for word into Japanese, after which one assumes a final translation at sentence level was produced. While such an approach was adequate for translating texts written in literary Sinitic, it resulted in the loss of some of the 'grammatical coherence' of the Dutch texts (Verwayen 1998: 339).

An example from the pen of Shizuki Tadao shows us, as it were, the translator at work. This can be found in the entry for *Het Republyk der geleerden* ('The Republic of Letters') in the catalogue of the Matsūra Rakusaidō library at Hirado.[74] Under each Dutch word is a rendering in *katakana* to assist the Japanese reader in pronunciation. For example, if we take the word 'der' ('of'), the phonetic equivalent of the *katakana* applied by Tadao is *deru*. Above each Dutch word is the *kanji*, so above *der* is the possessive particle 之 (Mervart 2015: 36). Likewise, below *geleerden* is *gerēruden* in *katakana* and above it is the Japanese equivalent in *kanji*, 学者 ('gakusha'). Tadao then rearranged the words to form the appropriate Japanese phrase. We return to this phrase shortly. Differences between Dutch and Japanese syntax, some of which were touched on in Chapter 4, mean that the re-ordering of words was not straightforward.

At the level of text, several approaches were adopted. One was to provide a rendering in the target language as close as possible in scope and meaning to the original text. In other cases, as a result of the Japanese emphasis on extracting information from source texts rather than producing complete translations, it was common for translators to produce target texts based on one or more source texts, often simplifying them in the process (Clements 2015: 169–171). As Vande Walle (2001b: 144) succinctly puts it, 'Most translations were adaptations involving omissions as well as additions'.

In the first category we can place official documents, such as orders given to the Dutch by the *bakufu* and documents prepared by the Dutch destined for Japanese officials. A complicating factor in the early years of the Dutch presence was that documents would need to be translated via Portuguese (Clulow 2014: 275 n. 68). Although Shizuki Tadao only translated an appendix to Engelbert Kaempfer's 'History of Japan', his *sakoku-ron* was nevertheless quite a close translation of the source text (Boot 2008: 94). Indeed, Boot (2008: 94–96) observes that it was a 'complete and literal' translation and that it therefore marked a shift from translations upto this point as it had been usual merely to 'translate the captions under the illustrations, or give a paraphrase or a partial translation of the parts he happened to understand, c.q. found interesting'. This meant that he had to struggle with each word and

---

74 Matsūra Seizan's library at Hirado contained copies of a journal entitled *Het Republyk der Geleerden*. These are items 51–1 to 52–22 in the Matsūra collection Western books catalogue.

individual phrase, rather than simply avoid them. Examples of those he found difficult to translate are the Dutch equivalents of 'force of gravity' and 'adverb'. Mervart (2015: 9–10) observes that Tadao's frustrations were similar to those of his contemporary Shingū Ryōtei (1787–1854), who composed a short poem in Classical Chinese, emulating models from the High T'ang dynasty, in which he bemoaned the difficulty of translating Dutch texts, something of which only 'the night rain outside' was aware. Boot (2008: 94) remarks that Tadao undoubtedly knew Dutch well, although realizes his knowledge of the language is not perfect. He concludes,

> There are a few mistakes due to misapprehension of the Dutch source text, but these are rare. As a translation of nineteen folio pages of stilted Dutch, which is the translation of an English translation of a Latin original, this is not a bad score.

It is not simply a translation, but also includes seven prefatory notes and well over one hundred intra-textual notes to help the reader understand the text. Tadao frequently distinguishes between Netherlands and Japan with the words 'over there' (*kanata*) and 'here' (*konata*). One of the most challenging features of the translation is the fact that he was often working with Japanese concepts that were now written in the Latin alphabet. How, he asks, do you translate back into Japanese the phrase 'Nippon means origin of the sun', or 'their beer they call sacki'? He resolves the problem by taking advantage of the fact that Japanese has two syllabaries, *katakana* and *hiragana*. Whereas most Japanese scholars prefer *katakana*, Tadao uses what Boot refers to as the more 'frivolous' *hiragana*, reserving *katakana* for the transliteration of Dutch words and sounds (Boot 2008: 95). The intra-textual notes are of two types; those inserted in the text and those added to the end of a section. In the former, he sometimes inserts Kaempfer's original notes, in which case he introduces them with the phrase *Kenperu jichū iwaku* ('Kaempfer's own note says'), giving us, in passing, an indication of how he and other Japanese might have pronounced Kaempfer's name, but also underlining his own diligence. Boot concludes his excellent account of Tadao's translation of Kaempfer's work by reflecting on why he chose to translate it. One interesting suggestion is that he did so because he wanted to show that Dutch could be mastered and that he was one of the few Japanese who could master it.

By contrast to his translation of Kaempfer's appendix, Tadao based *Rekishō shinsho* ('New Writings of Calendrical Phenomena', 1798–1802) on several Dutch sources, primarily *Inleidinge tot de waare Natuur- en Sterrekunde* (1741), the translation of John Keill's *Introductiones*. Likewise, Ōtsuki Gentaku's translation *Rokumotsu shinshi* ('New applications for a miscellany of six things'), probably completed in about 1786, drew on several Dutch sources, including Rembert Dodoens's *Cruydt-boeck*, and a Dutch translation of Johannes Jonston's illustrated Latin work on quadrupeds, *Naeukeurige beschryving van de natuur der vier-voetige dieren* ('A precise description of the nature of quadruped animals').[75] Morishima Chūryō based *Kōmō zatsuwa* ('Dutch (lit. Red-haired) miscellany', 1787) on various Dutch and Japanese sources. Udagawa Yōan cites more than twenty-five books of foreign authors as sources for his *magnum opus* on chemistry *Seimi kaisō* (Siderer 2017). Finally, as the material was often new to readers, it was common for early translations to be introductions to their subject.

Another example of a book that was not a translation in the late modern sense described by Theo Hermans, but rather the product of extracting useful information and presenting it in Japanese was *Dodoneusu honzō abese ruiju* ('Dodonaeus's ABC of Herb Categorization'), edited by Yoshio Kōgyū. The NDL has an autograph by Kōgyū. This was given by Kōgyū's son, Joen (or Gonnosuke), to Itō Keisuke (1802–1901), the grandfather of the famous Japanese botanist Itō Tokutarō (1866–1941), and a student of Von Siebold at the *Narutakijuku*. Kōgyū's work includes the Dutch names of plants, occasionally with Latin equivalents from Dodoens's *Cruydt-boeck*. He also provides Japanese names in *katakana*, with further details in Japanese script. For example, one page has 'winter groen oft pijrola'. *Wintergroen* ('Winter green') is the Dutch name and 'pyrola' the Latin species name for an evergreen herbaceous plant in the family Ericaceae. Kōgyū gives a Japanese equivalent *kitsukausau* in *katakana*.[76] This probably acted as something of a key for Japanese readers of the *Cruydt-boeck*. Another page has 'lijnen oft vitalba'. *Lijnen* is an old Dutch name (now *bosrank*) and *vitalba* the Latin species name for the flower 'traveller's joy'. Japanese equivalents in *katakana* are added with further description in *kanji*. Several pages give the names of varieties of iris (*lis(ch)*). One refers to 'another type of iris' (*ander gedaente van lisch*) and gives the Japanese in *katakana* as *kakitsubata* (*kanji*: 杜若). This is the Japanese name for the 'Iris laevigata'. Further work would be required to ascertain how well Kōgyū matches the plants described by Dodoens to Japanese equivalents. The use of several languages in this manner brings to mind Bakhtin's notion of *heteroglossia*,

---

75 Copies of both books were owned by the shogunate. Jonston was born in Poland of Scottish heritage.

76 *Dodoneusu honzō abese ruiju*, edited by Yoshio Kōgyū. Autograph. 2 v. NDL <Call number 特 toku7-193>. A modern Japanese dictionary gives *Ichiyakusō* for Pyrola. *Kitsukausau* is not listed.

described in previous chapters. One difference, though, with *Taisei honzō meiso* ('Western Plant Taxonomy'), Itō Keisuke's work to which this term was applied in Chapter 4, is that Keisuke uses the binomial Linnaean plant names based on species and genus, rather than the species names in Dodoens's *Cruydt-boeck*. This is true of other botanical works by Itō Keisuke such as *Nihon sanbutsu-shi* (Vande Walle 2001a: 19). So, as Kōgyū's book, which looked back to Dodoens, passed to his son and onto Keisuke and his grandson Tokutarō, the Japanese mind went through another paradigm shift, the re-ordering of a system of knowledge, in this case mediated by Latin.

5.5 Translation of Cultures

A word is in order about the difficulties that translators faced as a result of the often very significant differences between their own culture and the one in which the source texts had been written. Above, mention was made of the challenges that Mukai Genshō is likely to have faced in translating the instructions of Hans Juriaen Hancke as a result of the significant differences between the Eastern and Western philosophies that informed their respective medical traditions. For a second example, let us return to the phrase *Het Republyk der Geleerden* ('The Republic of Letters'), which Shizuki Tadao was required to translate into Japanese, itself a translation of the Latin *Respublica Literaria*. As well as being a phrase in the catalogue of the Matsūra library at Hirado, it was one that he encountered when translating the Dutch translation of Engelbert Kaempfer's 'History of Japan' into Japanese. As noted above, the concept of *geleerden* 'the learned' was not a difficult one for Tadao and he rendered it as *gakusha* (学者, 'scholar'). The reader will note the similarity between this word and *rangakusha*, i.e., 'those engaged in Dutch learning'. However, it was the notion of 'republic' that proved trickier for Tadao, as it was a type of polity not found in East Asia. His solution was to appropriate a recent coinage, *kaidoku*. This is composed of two Sinitic characters (会読), which mean 'encounter' or 'meeting', and 'reading'. In Tadao's time it was used to refer to gatherings which involved learned interchange. Thus, Tadao rendered *Het Republyk der Geleerden* as *gakusha no kaidoku* (学者之会読), which means 'the collective reading session of the learned'.[77] This captures something of the activity and purpose of *Het Republyk der Geleerden* and the sense of equality amongst its

---

77   *No* is a Japanese particle indicating belonging or possession. A later rendering of 'the republic' in 'the Republic of Letters' was *kyōwakoku* (共和国). This was coined in the 1840s by Mitsukuri Shōgo (1821–47) and means 'the polity of agreeing together'. It tries to capture the sense of men attempting to understand the world better by discussing a matter and through debate coming to an agreed position on it (Mervart 2015: 29).

members, although it suggests something different from the long-distance intellectual community in early-modern Europe held together by the exchange of letters and other texts (Mervart 2015: esp. 29).

Third, despite an official ban on Christianity, many of the books imported by the Dutch contained references to this religion. These books probably managed to get past censors as they could not read Dutch. Translators were faced with the question of what to do with the Christian material in their source texts. The Edo scholar, Arai Hakuseki, for instance, wrote a book on Christianity. Hakuseki's book, which for many years circulated only in manuscript form, was entitled *Seiyō kibun* ('Western journal', 1714) and was based on several texts and interviews with the Italian Jesuit priest, Giovanni Battista Sidotti, whom we met earlier in this chapter (Goodman 2013: 45–46). Hakuseki's work contained several Latin words and expressions traditionally used in Christian texts: for example, he writes 'Deusu, Kan ni tenshu to yakusu' ('Deus, in China translated as *tiānzhǔ*'), *Deusu* being the word used for God by Japanese Christians, and 'anima wa tamishii nari' ('anima is soul') (Kaiser 1996: 22–24). He borrowed terms from Buddhism to help explain the meaning of these and other Christian terms. The philosopher Miura Baien (1723–89) wrote an anti-Christian treatise, *Samidare-shō* ('Extract of the Summer Rain', 1784), using information on Christianity supplied to him by the Nagasaki interpreter, Matsumura Genkō (Boot 2013: 196). Some Japanese authors, however, took a different approach, avoiding references to Christianity in Western books altogether. This was the case with *Kaitai shinsho*, which was a Japanese translation of a Dutch translation of a German work by Johann Adam Kulmus (Clements 2015: 146). In his work Kulmus had wanted to reconcile the revelation of the Bible with the new knowledge of anatomy, drawing amply on biblical texts. The Japanese translators, however, only translated the notes accompanying the plates, leaving the biblical texts untranslated (Vande Walle 2001b: 142).

A fourth example of the problems faced by translators as a result of cultural differences concerns the translation of Dutch legal texts into Japanese by Mitsukuri Genpo. He had originally studied Chinese medicine and would subsequently translate part of the Dutch Code of Civil Procedure. A fundamental problem in this case was the difference between the nature and purpose of the law as it was understood in the Netherlands and in Japan. In this regard, Verwayen (1998: 343) observes that whereas in the Dutch legal system, the concept of the 'rule of law' is fundamental, in the legal system of Tokugawa Japan, it was, rather, the concept of 'rule of status'. In other words, in the Netherlands, the law was a means by which an abstract notion of justice could be realized. By contrast, in Japan the law was the means by which the stratified social order could be maintained.

Another difference was that whereas in the Netherlands there was a division of labour between those who made the law and those who administered it, i.e., the legislature and the judiciary, in Japan there was not such a clear-cut distinction. Such fundamental differences in the purpose and administration of the law would necessarily create difficulties for translators tasked with rendering Dutch legal texts into Japanese. Two examples illustrate this. The first is Genpo's rendering of the Dutch *vonnis* ('judgment'). Genpo renders this in Japanese as *zaika* (罪科), which is more properly 'punishment'. Verwayen (1998: 345) ascribes this error in part to the relatively undeveloped distinction at this time in the Japanese legal system between criminal and civil law. A second example is how Genpo translated the Dutch term *beroep* ('appeal'). In fact he uses more than one Japanese term to translate *beroep*, but the principle that seems to underlie each of them is that, as he understands it, it is the judge who makes this appeal, rather than the plaintiff or defendant who feels that justice has not been properly administered. Genpo's misunderstanding may well arise from the fact that it was very rare in Japan for a plaintiff or defendant to be able to complain about how justice was administered, unless there was a suspicion of corruption. Furthermore, Genpo did not always grasp the meaning of non-legal terms. One example is *behoudens*, which means 'except for'. Genpo's inability to fully to understand such terms had consequences for his comprehension of the logic of the text (Verwayen 1998: 348–353).

5.6   *Aids to Translation*

Over time, translators were able to avail themselves of increasingly sophisticated learning aids. Chapter 2 analyses how reference material for translating Dutch and Japanese developed. First, translators compiled simple word lists, often not making a clear distinction between words from different European languages. These were often ordered in the purely Japanese *kana*-based *iroha* sequence. Subsequently, lexicons were developed along the lines of Chinese reference works with words ordered by theme (*ten—chi—jin* (天地人)— heaven, earth, mankind). Morishima Chūryō's *Bangosen* is one such lexicon. Others such as *Rango yakusen* used a combination of these systems of lexicographical ordering. Finally, with the advent of the *Haruma* lexicons, translators from Dutch to Japanese could look up Dutch words listed in Dutch alphabetical order and find Japanese equivalents for them. One can imagine how this change will have facilitated and speeded up the laborious task of looking up words in the source language in the early phase of the translation process. I do not think it is going too far to view this lexicographical re-ordering as another paradigm shift, in which for practical reasons words were ordered on the basis of word-initial phonograms of the Dutch/Latin alphabet, rather than the semantograms of Sino-Japanese characters or the word-initial phonograms of Japanese *kana*.

Another example of how developments in lexicons assisted translation concerns the *Oranda jii* ('Dutch vocabulary'), which was based on the *Zūfu Haruma*. This was published between 1855 and 1857, some fifteen years after Mitsukuri Genpo had run into some difficulties in translating part of the Dutch Code of Civil Procedure. Entries for legal terms in the *Oranda jii* indicate that the Japanese understanding of Dutch concepts had developed significantly, something of which subsequent translators of Dutch legal texts would be able to take advantage (Verwayen 1998: 339, 356). Similarly, Ōtsuki Gentaku's primer *Rangaku kaitei* ('Guide to Dutch Learning') helped translators better to understand the grammar of the Dutch language (De Groot 2005: 55–71).

5.7 *The Form in Which Translations Circulated*

Finally, a word is in order about the form in which translations were circulated. Despite the many books that were published, the vast majority of translations from Dutch texts circulated in manuscript throughout Japan during the Tokugawa period (Clements 2015: 149). For example, Shizuki Tadao's translation *Sakoku-ron* based on a work by Engelbert Kaempfer was transmitted in a great number of manuscripts. Recent research has identified at least ninety manuscripts of the work, indicating that it was very popular. However, since it concerned the foreign policy of the *bakufu*, Boot asserts that printing it would have been 'unthinkable' (Boot 2008: 5).

There were other reasons why translations remained in manuscript. One reason may simply be that printing costs were prohibitive. Another reason, advanced by Clements, is that where the subject was medical, the contents of the translation might be seen as threat to Chinese medicine. A third reason is that some teachers of *rangaku* made their own translations of Dutch texts, but seem only to have used them for their own teaching with no intention of publishing.[78] One other possible reason for not printing translations was that they were viewed as intellectual property and restricting access to them was part of the long tradition of *hiden* (秘伝, 'secret transmission' (the word occurs in the title of several early works analysed in this chapter)), in which specialist knowledge was transferred from master to initiate. However, it is probable that this became less of an issue as the Edo period progressed (Kornicki 2001: 101; Clements 2015: 149–150). To a great extent, translations under the broad aegis

---

78   One example is Takahashi Keisaku, a physician and teacher who studied under Takano Chōei (Nakamura 2005: 93).

of *rangaku* were made within existing modes of cultural production. What was different was the content of these translations.

6 With What Consequences?

Indeed, this content and the concomitant translation activity affected life in Japan in several ways. First, it introduced knowledge which was to have a significant effect on Japanese society. Second, it provoked responses and had several consequences in the political sphere in Japan. While some, such as certain *daimyō* and other prominent Japanese, actively supported *rangaku*, others opposed the influence of this 'foreign' learning. This led to the infamous *Bansha no goku* ('Gaoling of the Society for Barbarian Studies') incident of 1839. Third, the sheer quantity of translations and the range of subjects with which they dealt left their mark on the Japanese language and learning materials for it.

6.1 Knowledge and Society

Simply put, the most significant consequence of the translation activity was that it vastly increased Japanese knowledge of developments outside the country in a whole range of fields. Apart from Chinese translations of European works, the books imported into Japan by the Dutch and the knowledge that the Dutch themselves imparted were more or less the only way that Japanese could find out about what was happening outside East Asia. The *Oranda fūsetsugaki* and later the *Betsudan fūsetsugaki* were the primary means by which the Japanese authorities learnt about events beyond their shores. In the field of learning, translations from Dutch, both published and unpublished, provided Japanese with information about developments in a range of disciplines including medicine, astronomy, physics, geography, and later military matters. In medicine above all translation had a profound effect. For example, the translators of *Kaitai shinsho* realized the accuracy of Johann Kulmus's charts of the body and included copies of them in their publication. One consequence of this was that it helped to discredit Chinese medical opinion (Clements 2015: 149). In 1804, Hanaoka Seishū (1760–1835) performed the first successful operation under general anaesthetic not merely in Japan, but in the whole world (Kornicki 2001: 304).

We must be careful not to overstate the number of people who had access to the information mediated by translations, which was limited in part by the fact that many of them circulated in manuscript. Nevertheless, nothing short of a revolution occurred in several fields of learning as a result of these translations. It was through translations such as Motoki Yoshinaga's *Tenchi nikyū yōhō* that Japanese learnt about concepts such as the Copernican Revolution and Newton's physics and his theory of gravity.[79] Translations by Itō Keisuke such as *Taisei honzō meiso* ('Western Plant Taxonomy'), marked an important shift away from the tradition of *honzōgaku* (本草学) in which plants were grouped by features such as physical characteristics, source and medicinal use of a plant towards Linnaeus's binomial taxonomy in which plants were classified by genus and species and which gave order to a previously somewhat unsystematic nomenclature. As we shall see shortly, engaging with texts on the Dutch language and coining Japanese equivalents led to a shift in how parts of speech were ordered, and, as we have just seen, the translation of Dutch bilingual dictionaries led to a move away from traditional lexicographical methods. In short, the translation of Dutch texts radically altered how Japanese viewed the world and how they produced and ordered their knowledge of it.

Those who engaged with and translated Dutch, such as Sugita Genpaku, did so for practical reasons. In other words, they used or instrumentalized the language to solve practical as well as social problems. Takano Chōei made a translation of a work on theories on prolonging life and published works on the relief of famine and avoidance of epidemic diseases. Sugita Ryūkei (1786–1846) sought to take advantage of Western learning on ophthalmology. He therefore translated a Dutch book on eye diseases, which itself was a translation by Martinus Pruys of a Latin work by Joseph Jacob von Plenck. He gave the book the title *Ganka shinsho* ('New Book of Ophthalmology', 1815) (see fig. 23). On a different note, Fukuzawa Yukichi translated a book on fortifications as his contribution to addressing concerns over a possible foreign invasion. In this regard, Tetsuo Najita has written 'Dutch was a language to translate, not to theorize with' (Najita 1991: 634, quoted in Nakamura 2005: 3). Furthermore, Dutch was a 'metalect' in Japan, i.e., a language that mediates knowledge. Sugita Genpaku observed in a similar vein that Dutch was a language that expressed facts (De Bary *et al.* 2005: 369–371). This clearly had much to do with the type of book that he and other *rangakusha* were translating into Japanese.

As the translators studied the source text and tried to render it in Japanese, they necessarily increased their own knowledge of the subject. In this sense, translation was a form of research method. While some of the knowledge they acquired stayed within relatively limited social confines, other knowledge was spread more widely. Ellen Nakamura's study of the effect of Dutch medicine on rural communities in Japan is one example of this. This spread of knowledge beyond the social elite and beyond the intellectual nodes of Edo, Nagasaki

---

79   Newton's *Principia* was not translated into Japanese until 1930 (Clements 2015: 152).

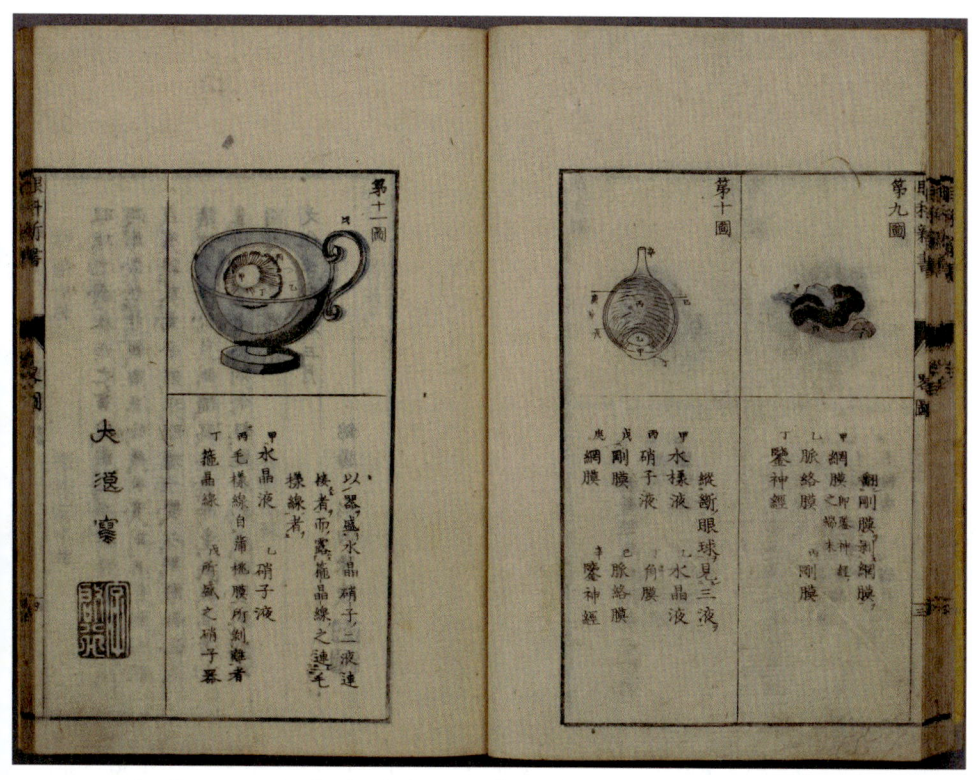

FIGURE 23 Eye diagrams in *Ganka shinsho* ('New Book of Ophthalmology', 1815), trans. Sugita Ryūkei, vol. I
WUL 文庫 08 C0225

and in time Osaka and Kyoto gave rise to *zaison no rangaku*, i.e., 'the study of Western learning in the countryside' (Nakamura 2005: 2).

Those who made translations often underwent a cultural translation. Yoshio Kogyō had a Dutch-style house in Nagasaki. Several translators, such as the brothers Katsuragawa Hoshū and Morishima Chūryō, used the Dutch names given to them by their Dutch associates. Whether they ever dressed in a Western style—moving in the other direction to, say, Matteo Ricci in China—would require further investigation (Burke 2007: 15). However, for some Japanese translating was not merely a dry exercise in rendering source texts into a target language, but an engagement with and appropriation of the culture which had mediated those texts. In this sense we can view Japanese translators such as Hoshū and Chūryō as linguistic or cultural bridges—*gengo-no-kakehashi* (言語の架け橋) or *bunka-no-kakehashi* (文化の架け橋) to coin Japanese words.

In short, translation between Dutch and Japanese had a significant effect on Japanese society in a variety of spheres, although it is important not to overstate how many people came into contact with it or directly benefitted from it. Perhaps in concluding this section we can state that although this translation did not bring Japan into the era of modernity, or at least to any significant degree, what it did do was prepare many people for modernity when, like Hokusai's great wave, it crashed onto the shores of Japan in the 1850s. One might usefully make a contrast between Japan and China at this point. While Japan was largely able to defend itself militarily, and yet engage with modernity, in the century between the start of the Opium Wars and the end of World War II, China, in what rhetorically became known as 'the century of humiliation', had been more or less at the mercy of Western powers, and indeed Japan, as it had not engaged with the developments in Western learning with which Japanese had become familiar through translations of Dutch texts.

6.2   Politics

Translation from Dutch texts had several consequences in the political sphere in Japan. One of these was that through the *Oranda fūsetsugaki* and later the *Betsudan fūsetsugaki*, Dutch reports of events in the outside world could be brought to the attention of the *bakufu*. The information was not always accurate or timely, but in the nineteenth century it offered the *bakufu* a means of understanding the frequent incursions in its waters. The 1852 *Betsudan fūsetsugaki* included a warning that the Americans would soon arrive in Japanese waters. The *bakufu* was slow to react to this and so even though the Japanese had been warned, they were still somewhat surprised by the arrival of Commodore Perry and the 'black ships' in 1853 (Tsukahara 2007b: 196).

As *rangaku* gathered pace in the late eighteenth and early nineteenth century, while some welcomed the advances in science that it brought with it, others were opposed to its importation of alien ideas into Japanese society.[80] The establishment of the *Bansho wage goyō* in 1811 could be seen as an official attempt to control and manage the spread of Dutch learning by bringing at least some translation under its control. Indeed, the growth of *rangaku* was a continuing cause for concern amongst neo-Confucian scholars and *bakufu* officials. One manifestation of this is the famous 'Siebold affair' (1829), named after the German physician and scholar, Von Siebold. He was found to be in possession of maps of Japan, which were considered forbidden material. Japanese teachers and students who had been in contact with Von Siebold, including Takahashi Kageyasu (Von Siebold's Globius), a translator at the *Bansho wage goyō*, were arrested and imprisoned, and Von Siebold himself was placed

---

80   For more on anti-Western sentiment and *rangaku* in nineteenth-century Japan, see Wakabayashi (1986: 9).

under house arrest and then expelled from the country. Ten years later, in 1839, the 'Gaoling of the Society for Barbarian Studies' incident (*Bansha no goku*) was another strike against *rangaku*. This was the result of an investigation into the activities of *rangakusha* by the Edo city commissioner and the *metsuke*, Torii Yōzō, the leader of a conservative faction within the *bakufu*. The main charge was that there had been public criticism of the *bakufu* in the form of tracts over its handling of the Morrison Incident in 1837. The *Bansha no goku* was also a result of personal rivalries and an attempt to stifle *rangakusha* working outside official institutions. Among those imprisoned was Takano Chōei (Clements 2015: 190–191; Nakamura 2005: 39). In the 1840s, in a further move prompted by conservative forces, the *Bansho wage goyō* undertook a censorship role (Montgomery 2000: 215).

On the other hand, after 1840, as news of the First Opium War filtered into Japan, there was an increase in translation activity. Whereas in the twenty years prior to 1840 there had been a gradual decrease in the annual number of translations relating to *rangaku*, thereafter there was a sudden surge reaching almost sixty a year by the mid-1850s. In broad terms, this reflects the recognition that Japan needed Western knowledge in order to defend itself against a possible invasion from Western countries. However, by far the largest number of translations between 1840 and 1855 were of medical texts, followed at a distance by works on foreign matters and military affairs. These reflect a desire among Japanese to learn more about the outside world and to improve Japan's defence capabilities. The large number of medical translations may simply reflect the fact that many *rangakusha* were primarily interested in Western medicine (Clements 2015: 151–152).

As noted above, those who defended *rangaku* could point to the fate of China in the Opium Wars and argue that it was only by keeping up with Western technological advances, mediated by books in Dutch, that Japan could fend off potential invaders. One telling statistic about the scale of this enterprise is that the library of the Japanese National Diet houses approximately 3,600 books that previously belonged to the *Bansho shirabesho*, founded in 1857, a successor to the *Bansho wage goyō* and other, successor organizations.[81] Most of these books are in Dutch.

---

81 *List of foreign books collected under the Shogunate regime = Lijst van boeken in buitenlandse talen verzameld door het Shogunaat* = 江戸幕府旧蔵洋書目録. Another successor organization was the *Kaiseijo*, a school for foreign studies founded in 1863. After the Boshin War (1868–69), it was renamed, and became the *Kaisei gakkō* (開成学校) As the *Kaisei gakkō*, the institute became one of the organizations that subsequently merged to form Tokyo University.

6.3 Language

A third consequence of translation between Dutch and Japanese concerns language. In the early days of *rangaku*, translation was an important means of getting to grips with the Dutch language (Clements 2015: 165). Indeed, the very process of translation requires one to pay close attention to the source (as well as the target) language, and so will have helped translators increase their knowledge of the language. It was the need of translators to understand better the lexis and grammar of Dutch that led to the compilation of important works such as the *Edo Haruma* and *Zūfu Haruma* dictionaries and Mitsukuri Genpo's *Oranda bunten zenpen*, a Japanese edition of Matthijs Siegenbeek's *Grammatica of Nederduitsche Spraakkunst* (2nd ed. Leiden, 1822) (De Groot 2016: 74).

The translation activity also affected the lexis and grammar of the Japanese language. One set of words introduced into Japanese as a result of translation activity were terms for the parts of speech. In *Oranda bunten zenpen*, Genpo used terms for the parts of speech, such as *daimeishi* (代名詞) for 'pronoun', many of which form the basis of modern Japanese grammatical terminology. Although not unique in this regard, one advantage that Dutch has is that many of its lexical items have a high degree of 'morphosemantic transparency', i.e., it readily forms compound words, the meaning of which can be deduced from its separate morphemes. If one takes the Dutch word for 'participle', *deelwoord*, it consists of two morphemes, *deel* ('part') and *woord* ('word'). This is rendered in Japanese as *bunshi* (分詞), again literally 'part-word'. However, if a translator had come across the English term, it would have been more difficult to analyse it and provide a Japanese equivalent on a morpheme-by-morpheme basis.[82] Further examples of grammatical terms coined by Genpo in this manner are analysed in Chapter 7. Translations from Dutch to Japanese also led to the coining of many new words relating to the sciences. In *Rekishō shinsho* ('New Writings on Calendrical Phenomena', 1798), Shizuki Tadao introduced new terms for physics, such as *jū-ryoku* for 'gravity', still the standard term in cMJ, while Udagawa Yōan did something similar for chemistry in *Seimi kaisō* ('Principles of Chemistry', 1837–49).[83] However, this is by no means the whole story. Translating a text by Engelbert Kaempfer resulted in Tadao having to coin Japanese words for concepts such as 'commonwealth' and most

---

82 This fits into the pattern of *giyaku* discussed above. *Bunshi* appears in an 1871 grammar by Nakagane Masahira, inspired by Mitsukuri Genpo's model (Vos 2000a: 103).

83 *Jū-ryoku* (重力), literally 'heavy power', is derived from the Dutch word for 'gravity', *zwaartekracht* ('weight power'). Further examples are provided in Chapter 7.

famously *sakoku*, by which he rendered the concept of the 'closed kingdom' in Japanese.

As for the influence of this translation activity on Japanese grammar, translators needed to develop or re-deploy particles in order to fill gaps in the Japanese grammatical system. Two examples are *tokoro-no* (ところの), the equivalent of a relative pronoun used in adnominal clauses, and the use of the compound suffix *ni-yotte* (によって) in passive sentences. Above all in the case of *ni-yotte*, usage has broadened and indeed been modified since the end of the Tokugawa period. These along with other linguistic consequences of translation such as the broadening of the use of pronouns and the use of abstract nouns as the subject of a sentence, are analysed in detail in Chapter 7. One final point, which is also developed further in the next chapter, is that many loanwords resulting from translations of Dutch texts into Japanese were re-borrowed by languages which came into contact with Japanese. For example, Kuiper (1993) has identified at least 90 such loanwords in Mandarin Chinese. Taiwanese Hokkien and Korean are other language varieties affected in this manner. Here, we can talk in terms of the circulation of loanwords, often driven in this context by translation activity.

7 Conclusion

In conclusion, the translation of Dutch texts over the course of some 200 years in Tokugawa Japan is marked by its diversity and its impact on Japanese society and culture. First, a word is in order on sources. While printed Dutch texts did form the source material for most translations, for others oral instructions and conversations were an additional or primary source. Dutch was not the only source language. Early oral instructions are likely to have included Portuguese. Translators needed to negotiate words and phrases, and in at least one case lines of verse, written in other languages such as Latin for which Dutch in some sense acted as a *linguifer*. This was often a function of the fact that many of the books translated by Japanese were originally written in a language other than Dutch. The books translated into Japanese or, on occasion, literary Sinitic, some of which had undergone several translations before being translated in Japan, form part of the international circulation of literature.

Second, mention of oral instruction reminds us that in this context we need to understand translation in a broad sense. Few of the works discussed in this chapter, above all in the early Tokugawa period, were translations as we might understand the term today. Rather they were projects, whose objective was to mine sources in Dutch for useful information and to render this into Japanese. Here, I have coined the term *metalect* to describe the function of Dutch as a medium for the transmission of knowledge, often from another European language, into Japanese.

Third, while many of the translators were either Nagasaki interpreters or Edo scholars, others were not. Increasingly, during the nineteenth century translators such as Fukuzawa Yukichi came from elsewhere in Japan, although they typically studied Dutch at Nagasaki or Edo. While many translators came from samurai stock, some high, some low, Ozeki San'ei is one translator who came from peasant stock. On the other hand, from the evidence available, some social groups, such as women, were excluded from this activity altogether.

Fourth, whereas some translations were in essence individual efforts, with recourse to Dutch informants when necessary, others were the product of small groups working together. *Kaitai shinsho* is perhaps the most well-known example of this, although there are many others such as the early manuscript-translations, which were the fruit of collaboration between the Japanese physician Mukai Genshō, Dutch surgeons and Japanese interpreters made at the request of a high-placed Japanese official. With Tessa Morris-Suzuki we can speak of 'social networks of innovation' (Morris-Suzuki 1994: 7, 18). Such networks begin with the arrival of new experts and result in the transmission of expertise from one society to another. Here, the new experts, the Dutch and German physicians at Deshima, formed new networks with the Japanese interpreters, physicians and political leaders. Such a pattern of collaboration involving Japanese scholars, interpreters, leaders and financial backers such as *daimyō*, on occasion working with Dutch informants, is one that we have often seen in this chapter.

Fifth, a word is in order about Chinese. Scholars who made translations were trained in reading texts written in literary Sinitic, in particular the canonical 'four books and five classics'. Furthermore, they were trained in translating texts from literary Sinitic to Japanese. This provided them with the 'habitus', to return to Bourdieu, that they applied to translating Dutch texts. However, the translation of Dutch medical texts would provide a direct challenge to the position of Chinese medicine, and perhaps Chinese learning more generally. This is vividly illustrated in an essay by Sugita Genpaku that remained in manuscript. In the essay, entitled *Kyōi no gen* ('The Words of a Mad Doctor', 1775), Genpaku challenges the orthodox view in Japan of the superiority of Chinese culture. He uses this as a pretext to argue that Dutch medicine is in fact superior to Chinese medicine and underpins his argument by stating that he had seen this with his own eyes (empirical evidence!) by being able to confirm the accuracy of Dutch anatomical charts (Boot 2011). Despite such voices, which could be heard more frequently in the nineteenth century, the volume of Dutch texts in circulation in Japan and of translations from Dutch was much smaller than that of Chinese texts and translations. Nevertheless, the impact of the Dutch texts on Japanese society was significant.[84]

Sixth, this impact could be framed in terms of paradigm shifts in several fields of enquiry. Here, the translations often went hand-in-hand with the introduction by the Dutch of 'new' material artefacts such as globes, telescopes, maps and anatomical charts. In the field of human medicine, there was a shift from focusing on the whole body to the part. The adoption of Dutch surgical techniques necessitated giving names to parts of the body that had previously not been seen by Japanese eyes. Some of these are analysed in Chapter 7. In botany, there was a shift from categorizing *materia medica* by features such as characteristics and source to adopting the Linnaean binomial classification based on genus and species; the Linnaean revolution if you will. This provided botanists and others with a common language to denote plants and would eventually allow Japanese to talk in this shared language with colleagues from outside Japan. In the fields of geography and astronomy, translations of Dutch books and maps allowed Japanese eyes to see the world beyond East Asia more accurately, and from a different perspective—China, the Middle Kingdom (中国) was no longer in the middle! Meanwhile, translations of Dutch scientific texts transmitted the Copernican and Newtonian revolutions to Japan. Furthermore, the needs of translators to be able to look up Dutch words in alphabetical order provoked a shift in Japanese lexicography. Although these shifts took place slowly, as they did in Europe, and often involved *kaitei* backwards as well as sideways, they provoked nothing less than a revolution in the Japanese mind, with paradigmatic revolutionaries such as Sugita Genpaku, re-ordering and re-conceiving the world, in the vanguard.

Seventh, translators used a range of registers to give form to the material they translated. While the translators of *Kaitai shinsho* chose *kanbun*, Shizuki Tadao used *katakana-majiri* for *Rekishō shinsho* and Morishima Chūryō *hiragana-majiri* for *Kōmō zatsuwa*. Each author aimed to communicate some aspect of Dutch or Western learning to a different audience. In some sense the body of knowledge described as *rangaku* was a composite semiotic system consisting of different registers or codes, scholarly and vernacular, of Japanese and literary Sinitic (Fukuoka 2012: 53).

---

84 Much material relating to *rangaku* has been preserved at Waseda University Library. For an introduction to this material and images of it, visit http://www.wul.waseda.ac.jp/ kotenseki/ga_yogaku/index_en.html. Accessed 14 April 2020. For more on the translation of Chinese texts in Tokugawa Japan, see Clements (2015: Ch. 3).

Finally, placing this chapter in a broader context, it provides an interesting case-study of how contact between two cultures can result in extensive translation activity as the knowledge and technology of one culture is transferred or translated into another culture. Apart from official documents, orders and letters, there was relatively little translation from Japanese to Dutch. It was the Japanese who identified what 'gaps' they needed to fill in their knowledge of the world and it was this, above all in fields as diverse as medicine, astronomy and geography and later military matters, that was the motivation for the re-clothing of Western knowledge in the Japanese language.

Lexical, Syntactic and Graphic Interference by Dutch in Japanese

1 Introduction

Chapter 5 analysed how contact between Dutch and other languages, above all Japanese, led to interference in Dutch. This chapter goes in the other direction, focussing on the interference in Japanese resulting from this contact. Probably the most significant element of this interference was lexical. Much, although by no means all, of this was a consequence of the translations from Dutch to Japanese analysed in Chapter 6. Differences in the syntax of Dutch and Japanese led translators to develop slight modifications to Japanese syntax. A third way in which this contact led to interference in Japanese was the use of *rōmaji* by Japanese authors.

The chapter makes a start by reviewing previous work on the lexical outcomes of contact with Dutch in Japanese.[1] These have been analysed by both Western and Japanese scholars. One Dutch scholar who made a significant contribution to our understanding of this subject is the former Professor of Japanese at Leiden University, Frits Vos (1918–2000), who published an extensive article on it in 1963 (republished in 2014). On the Japanese side, a book by Saitō Shizuka published in 1967 is important, as it provides details of Japanese sources for the early use of these lexical contact phenomena. These and other authors often give a figure for the number of words in Japanese resulting from contact with Dutch. This chapter does the same but makes clear that for several reasons giving a precise figure is difficult if not impossible.

Before analysing these words, the chapter addresses several methodological issues. One of these concerns giving the earliest date for the use of a contact-induced word in a Japanese text. While in some cases this is relatively straightforward, as we know the Japanese text in which a word first appeared, in other cases it is clearly less so with authors of secondary literature giving widely differing dates. Another problem is that it is not always easy to distinguish

---

[1] Terminology in this field is not always applied consistently. As far as possible, I use 'loanwords' to refer to words that have been borrowed directly from Dutch with a greater or lesser degree of phonemic substitution. I use other terms such as 'lexical contact phenomena' to refer to the broader category of words in Japanese that are the result of contact with Dutch.

between words used once or twice and those which have become embedded in the recipient language, a subject touched on in Chapter 5. As far as possible this chapter focusses on those which have become embedded, although again no absolute distinction is made. Another question that arises is whether these words are in fact outcomes of contact with Dutch. In some cases, such as the loan translations for parts of the anatomy coined by the translators of *Kaitai shinsho* (1774), the matter is clear. However, in other cases, above all where a Dutch word has cognates in other contact languages such as English and German, the matter is less clear. Where possible, such cases will be highlighted.

The fact that there were no 'rules' as to how Japanese authors incorporated lexical contact phenomena into their texts has several consequences for this analysis. One of these is that there was often more than one contact-induced word in circulation for a given concept or object. This is another reason why giving a precise number of contact-induced words is almost impossible. Yet another complication is that many words were only borrowed into Japanese dialects. A full analysis of dialectal borrowings is beyond the scope of this chapter. However, details are given of a study of 'pure' loanwords from Dutch in the Nagasaki dialect, which may indicate that the total number of contact-induced words in this and other varieties of Japanese is well in excess of 1000. What is beyond doubt is that contact between Dutch and Japanese had a much greater effect on the lexis of the latter than the former, not least because the Dutch introduced many new objects as well as processes and ideas into Japan.

Lexical contact phenomena are typically the result of actions by those who know the donor as well as the receiving language. For our purposes, this suggests a certain degree of Japanese-Dutch bilingualism (Adams 2003: 29). These lexical outcomes of contact with Dutch took various forms. Some are in effect transliterations of Dutch words, which have undergone phonological adaptation to a greater or lesser degree. In this chapter, these are typically referred to as 'pure' loanwords or *gairaigo* to use the Japanese term.[2] Other contact phenomena include 'loan translations', where the Dutch terms have been translated on a morpheme-by-morpheme basis, and extensions, where the meaning of existing Japanese words has been extended as a result of contact with Dutch. Whereas many of these lexical items are the direct result of contact during the Tokugawa period, some have emerged after this period as contact-induced morphemes have continued to be productive. In this chapter, these words will be analysed using the typology for lexical contact

---

2   *Gairaigo* is the term used in Japanese for loanwords. Irwin (2011: 10) defines it as 'a foreign word which has undergone adaptation to Japanese phonology, has been borrowed into Japanese after the mid-16th century and whose meaning is, or has been, intelligible to the general speech community'. For a full analysis of the term *gairaigo*, see Ishiwata (1985).

phenomena proposed by Winford (2003).[3] In general borrowing takes place in given spheres of activity. Japanese borrowing from Dutch is no different in this regard, and so the lexical contact phenomena will be further categorized by theme, such as food and drink, seafaring, and sciences including botany, chemistry, medicine and physics. The Japanese words resulting from contact with Dutch were themselves often outcomes of contact with other languages such as Latin, French and German. In turn, some of the contact-induced words in Japanese were subsequently borrowed by other contact languages in East Asia, above all Sinitic varieties and Korean. Here, the shared use of Chinese or Sinitic characters facilitated borrowing. This re-borrowing can be understood as part of the 'circulation of loanwords'.

In the process of translating from Dutch to Japanese, Japanese translators needed to re-deploy parts of speech to bridge the gap between Dutch and Japanese syntax. Two examples are the complementizer *tokoro-no* (ところの) and the use of the compound suffix *ni-yotte* (によって) in passive sentences. Above all in the case of *ni-yotte*, usage has broadened since the end of the Tokugawa period. Other examples of syntactic contact phenomena are the use of the pseudo-copula *de aru*; using inanimate things as the subject of a transitive verb; and the increased use of pseudo-pronouns.

A third way in which contact with Dutch interfered with Japanese was in the script used by Japanese authors. Whereas the first two consequences analysed, i.e., the influence on a lexical and syntactic level, were in some sense clothed in Japanese script, the use of *rōmaji* took Japanese in the other direction, making the interference very visually obvious. The use of *rōmaji* in Tokugawa Japan, albeit limited, provoked fierce debate, with some authors even advocating that it should replace Japanese script. Others viewed it as a 'barbarian' influence. Therefore, in some sense, the debate in Tokugawa Japan regarding Dutch, and more generally Western, influence crystallized in the arguments around which script to use.

In short, this chapter analyses the extent to which Dutch interfered with or influenced Japanese on a lexical, syntactic and graphic level. Almost all the influence of Dutch on Japanese resulted from contact between the languages in the Tokugawa period. The lexical outcomes of contact are linguistic signs or tokens of Japanese efforts to try to bridge the divide between Dutch/Western culture and Japanese culture. They are in some sense emanations of the attempt by Japanese to understand and assimilate the culture mediated by the Dutch. As Burke (2007: 9) observes, 'understanding itself is a kind of translation, turning other people's concepts and practices into their equivalents in our own "vocabulary"'. Some of the lexical outcomes of contact with Dutch

---

3   For another very detailed and effective loanword typology, see Van der Sijs (1996: 9–29).

have since been replaced in Japanese by words induced by contact with other languages, such as English, or by Sino-Japanese coinages. Nevertheless, much of the influence of Dutch on the Japanese lexis, and to a lesser extent the syntax, is still observable in standard contemporary Modern Japanese.[4]

2   *Status Quaestionis*

Several non-Japanese and Japanese scholars have analysed the lexical influence of Dutch on Japanese. Frits Vos suggests that during the Tokugawa period there were more than 300 Dutch loanwords in Japanese. Writing in 1963, he asserted that more than 160 Dutch loanwords were still in use in modern standard Japanese. These figures, however, relate to 'pure loanwords', a point Vos recognizes when he states that they exclude words of 'doubtful origin' (possibly from another language), dialectal words and 'translation loan-words' (loan translations). Therefore, by Vos's own admission, the number of words in the Japanese lexis resulting from contact with Dutch is much higher than 300 (Vos 2014: 178). In her evaluation of the influence of Dutch on the Japanese lexis, Isabel Tanaka-van Daalen (2000) suggests that during the Tokugawa period some 350 Dutch loanwords were adopted by Japanese, a number similar to that given by Nicoline van der Sijs, both of whom, it would seem, are referring to 'pure' loanwords (2006: 117). The Japanese scholar Saitō Shizuka (1967), who does include many loan translations in his analysis, lists more than 600 Dutch words, which have been adopted in a variety of forms by Japanese. Some of these, however, may only have been used for a short period and in a few cases Saitō refers to two separate Dutch words from which one Japanese loanword has emerged.

According to one estimate by a Japanese scholar the number of Dutch loanwords in Japanese reached some 3,000 in the period after 1750 when the study of *rangaku* really took off (Sonoda 1975: 9, quoted in Sakagami 2000: 25). Here, reference is made to *gairaigo*, the term usually reserved for 'pure' loanwords or what are more or less transliterations of foreign words. This does seem somewhat high, particularly if *gairaigo* is being used in this sense. It may be that some of these words were used just a few times rather than becoming fully embedded in Japanese. On the other hand, some words introduced into Japanese and used for a significant period have subsequently fallen into disuse. If, however, *gairaigo* is being used more broadly (and somewhat loosely), then it may include other types of lexical interference such as loan translations and

---

4   For a periodization of Japanese, see Frellesvig (2010: 1–3). Modern Japanese begins in around 1600.

hybrid words derived from Dutch words, which are not included in some of the totals given above. I return to the question of how many Japanese words are outcomes of contact with Dutch in the conclusion.

One of the earliest Western scholars to analyse Dutch loanwords in Japanese was the Jesuit priest and Professor at Sophia University, Tokyo, Joseph (J.M.) Eylenbosch (1940: 224–228). He, however, provides a largely descriptive account, which is limited to *gairaigo*, and so makes no attempt to use a loanword typology. In 1963, Vos published his analysis of Dutch lexical contact phenomena in Japanese which is more systematic and does use a loanword typology. He divides them into 'Genuine Dutch words' (i.e., 'pure' loanwords), of which he lists 322; 'Portuguese and Spanish Loan-Words "Reinforced" by Borrowings from Dutch' (20); hybrid words, where one element is Dutch (32); 'words of doubtful origin', which may in fact have been borrowed from other languages such as German or English (6); dialectal words (23); and 'Japanese translations of Dutch words', i.e., loan translations. Vos lists 22 examples of this last type but acknowledges that 'a very large number' of Dutch words have been translated into Japanese on a morpheme-by-morpheme basis in the fields of science, medicine and anatomy. One of the aims of this chapter is to analyse a significant number of such loan translations.

Vos's systematic approach to the analysis of contact-induced words marks an important step forward in this field. His 1963 article was re-published in 2014, suggesting it still has some currency. However, it does have a few drawbacks. Probably the most significant of these is that Vos does not give his sources. In a few cases, he provides a date for first use, but again without reference to sources. Furthermore, the dates that Vos gives occasionally differ from those given by other authors. Nevertheless, Vos's article makes a significant contribution to this field and this chapter makes frequent reference to it.

One author who does mention sources is the Leiden Sinologist Koos Kuiper. His 1993 article focusses on borrowings from Dutch that have been (re-)borrowed by Mandarin Chinese via Japanese. He identifies about ninety such words. Not only does Kuiper mention sources, where they can be identified, but he also gives the rendering of the loanword in Sinitic characters, something that Vos does not do. This article will be of use not only for the section in this chapter on Dutch loanwords in Sinitic varieties, but also for our understanding of the different strategies that Japanese authors adopted to incorporate borrowings from Dutch in their texts.

The Dutch etymologist Nicoline van der Sijs (2010: 84–85) provides a useful summary of previous work on Dutch loanwords in Japanese, placing it in the broader context of Dutch loanwords in languages worldwide. Her detailed loanword-by-loanword analysis of which languages have borrowed which Dutch words illustrates that while some Japanese borrowing, such as that of *matroos* ('sailor'), fits into a broader pattern of other languages adopting Dutch nautical terms, other outcomes of contact, such as scientific terms, are more specific to the case of Japanese.

Mark Irwin (2011) on the other hand analyses only loanwords from Dutch and other languages in Japanese. He provides several useful tables of 'pure' Dutch loanwords by theme together with a year for their first use in a Japanese source. However, I have several concerns regarding Irwin's approach. First, in almost all cases he cites secondary rather than primary sources (Irwin 2011: 25). These are above all the multi-volume Japanese lexicon, *Nihon kokugo daijiten* (NKD) and Arakawa Sōbei's loanword lexicon *Gairaigo jiten dai 2 ban* (2nd ed., Tokyo: Kadokawa, 1977). These are written in Japanese and so, even though Irwin writes in English, if a scholar who does not read Japanese wanted to check Irwin's primary source and date, s/he would find it difficult if not impossible to do so. Many of his dates are the same as those given in other secondary sources, but some are not, a point I return to shortly. Second, his tables include only a selection of 'pure' loanwords (*gairaigo*) and so do not give a comprehensive picture of the extent and thematic diversity of these loanwords. Third, by including only 'pure' loanwords, Irwin does not analyse other types of lexical outcomes of contact between Dutch and Japanese. In truth, his primary concern seems to be the phonological integration of 'pure' loanwords into Japanese.

Japanese authors, too, have analysed the lexical outcomes in Japanese of contact with Dutch. In 1935, Saitō Shizuka produced an early article entitled 'The Dutch Influence on Japanese'. His 1967 book, *Nihongo ni oyoboshita Oranda-go no eikyō* ('The Influence of Dutch on Japanese'), is a much more ambitious account of the Dutch influence on the Japanese lexis, analysing not only 'pure' loanwords, but also other lexical outcomes of this contact.[5] In many cases, he gives his source with a date and gives the borrowings in Japanese script. One drawback is that Saitō does not categorize these words, but instead lists them in Dutch alphabetical order (although not in alphabetical order within each letter). Furthermore, there are some notable omissions from his analysis, such as *kokku* ('cook' from the Dutch *kok*). Nevertheless, the fact that Saitō often reproduces the texts in which these words were first used is important and this chapter makes frequent reference to Saitō's 1967 work and the primary sources that he cites.

Other Japanese scholars have analysed the Dutch influence on specific areas of the language. In 1929 Isomura Shūsaku (quoted in Umegaki 1963: 68 and

---

5   日本語に及ぼしたオランダ語の影響. Earns (1993: 38) writes that Saitō gives 740 Dutch words with Japanese equivalents. However, some words are duplicated and for others there is little evidence that they became embedded in Japanese.

Sakagami Shizuka 2000: 25) analysed the influence of Dutch on Japanese engineering terminology and identified 86 Dutch loanwords used in this field.[6] This study is, however, now almost a century old, so further investigation would be required to identify how many of these terms are still current. Many Japanese words in the field of chemistry derived from contact with Dutch were first used by Udagawa Yōan in *Seimi kaisō* ('Principles of Chemistry', 1837–49), a work in which the author Yōan demonstrates his skills in coining new Japanese terms (Siderer 2017). A detailed analysis of these words was made in a 1975 edition of Yōan's work (Udagawa Yōan *et al.* 1975).

Other Japanese scholars have analysed the influence of Dutch on the dialect of Nagasaki, where the Dutch had their trading post for over two hundred years. Irie Ichirō records in *Nagasaki hakurai kotoba* ('Nagasaki Loanwords' 1987: 52) for example, that whereas in cMJ we find the English loanword *kureen* (クレーン) for 'crane' (the lifting device), the Nagasaki dialect has adopted the form *karan* from the Dutch *kraan* ('crane'). Indeed, in his dictionary of loanwords in the Nagasaki dialect, Koga Jūjirō (2000) lists some 1,520 words of Dutch origin.[7] Further examples include *hīru* (ヒール, four) from the Dutch *vier* and *kōningi* (コーニンギ) from the Dutch *koning* ('king'). Unfortunately, Koga does not give a sense of how frequently these words are used, which both have Japanese and Sino-Japanese equivalents (Koga 2000: 899, 974). Given the orality of dialect, it is of course difficult to list sources. However, this does make it difficult to verify Koga's account. Clearly, this number of loanwords is far greater than the numbers given by scholars such as Vos, although he specifically notes that he excludes dialectal words in his tally.

The aim of the present chapter is to provide a synthesis of this previous work on Dutch loanwords in Japanese by both Japanese and non-Japanese scholars and new, original research, providing instances of early, and, where possible, the earliest use of these loanwords in Japanese texts. It does so by employing a loanword typology developed by Winford (2003: 42–45), which is somewhat more rigorous than the typology used by Vos (1963) and closer to that used by Kuiper (1993).[8] It also analyses the methodological issues associated with lexical contact phenomena, some of which, such as the lack of citations in earlier publications, have already been touched on. Furthermore, it analyses re-borrowing into contact languages with Japanese, above all, Korean and Sinitic

---

6   Although he does not make it explicit, Umegaki (1963) seems to be an important source for Vos (1963). The copy in Leiden University Library, shelfmark LUB 2352 F 04, has Vos's signature on the title page.

7   Koga also records words of Portuguese and Latin origin still used in the Nagasaki dialect. He lists 3245 words of Portuguese origin and 227 words of Latin origin (Irwin 2011: 31).

8   In Vos's defence, it should be noted that the analysis of lexical contact phenonema was still to some extent in its infancy when he wrote his 1963 article.

varieties, contributing to our understanding of the circulation of loanwords. This is supplemented by an analysis of the influence of contact with Dutch on Japanese at a syntactic and graphic level.

3   Methodological and Terminological Issues

Before analysing the lexical outcomes in Japanese of contact with Dutch, we need to address several methodological and terminological issues, some of which have been introduced above. These include the dating of the first use of words in Japanese; the distinction between borrowing and code switching; sources; how words were incorporated into the Japanese lexis; and the lexical contact phenomena in Japanese dialects.

3.1   *Dating of First Use*

As noted above, several authors provide details of when a contact-induced word was first used in a Japanese text. While this can be useful in identifying how, as well as when, a word entered Japanese, for example, the chemical terms coined by Udagawa Yōan in *Seimi kaisō*, it does generate several problems. First, the use of a non-Japanese word in one text is not proof *per se* that it has become integrated or 'embedded' in the target language. The case of 'coffee' is instructive in this regard. Irwin (2011: 41) gives a date of 1615 for the first use of 'coffee' (< Dutch *koffie*) as a *gairaigo* in Japanese. He refers to Arakawa Sōbei's loanword lexicon, *Gairaigo jiten dai 2 ban* (1977) as his source. If this reference is correct, then this seems very early in terms of the history of coffee in Japan, and indeed of the Dutch in Japan (only six years after the trading post at Hirado was opened), and may only be an isolated example. Yoshizawa and Ishiwata (1979: 193) state that while coffee was brought to Europe by a Venetian merchant in 1615, in Japan it was in the Tenmei era (天明, 1781–89) that coffee was mentioned in a document entitled 'Red-Haired (Dutch) Medicinal herbs' (*Kōmō honzō* 紅毛本草).

This brings us to a second problem associated with giving the date of first use; namely that secondary sources give different dates. Vos (2014: 168) gives a later date of 1797 for 'coffee'. However, Vos does not give his source. Saitō Shizuka (1967: 110–111) gives an even later date of 1811.[9] An interesting instance

---

9   The copy of Saitō Shizuka's *Nihongo ni oyoboshita Oranda-go no eikyō* ('The Influence of Dutch on Japanese') in Leiden University Library has Frits Vos's *ex libris*. However, as it was published in 1967, he could not have referred to it for his 1963 article. For example, Vos's date of 1797 for 'coffee/koffie' does not appear in this book.

of coffee being mentioned in Japan, which has so far not been reported in secondary sources, comes in the *dagregister* entry for 7 February 1706. Here, the *opperhoofd* Hermanus Menssingh reports that a Japanese invited him and fellow Dutchmen to a Japanese meal in Nagasaki. He wrote 'Curiously enough coffee was included in [the meal]'. Although the text is Dutch, the context is Japanese. It is not in a Japanese text, but seems to indicate, surprisingly as Menssingh observes, that a Japanese was already serving coffee to his guests in 1706 (Blussé *et al.* 1992: 74). In March 1722, the *dagregister* reports that Imamura Gen'emon was drinking coffee with Hendrik Durven (*opperhoofd* 1721–23) (Blussé *et al.* 1992: 263).

A full analysis of the Japanese texts where this and other loanwords are written is beyond the scope of this book. However, the example of 'coffee' illustrates well the problems associated with dating the first use of such loanwords. That is not to say that the first date is unimportant, and where this is known it will be stated, along with the source. However, it needs to be treated with some caution. There are two final points to make here. First, some of the works in which contact-induced words appeared for the first time were published over several years. The earliest date of publication is given, but this does not necessarily mean that the word itself appeared in that year. A case in point is *Kōsei shinpen* ('A New Compendium for Health'), the Japanese translation of the Dutch translation of Noël Chomel's *Dictionnaire oeconomique*. Although words appearing in this work are given the date 1811, this was in fact published between 1811 and 1839. Second, before a word appeared in a Japanese text, it may have circulated for several years either in the spoken language or in manuscripts that are now lost. Saitō (1967) provides some help here by including references to Dutch texts imported into Japan in which words subsequently adopted by Japanese appear.

3.2   *Borrowing and Switching*

In Chapter 5, it was stated that there would be no attempt to make an absolute distinction between 'borrowing' and switching'. There, where the focus was on interference in Dutch texts, the emphasis was on switching, in part because of the incompleteness of source data. In this chapter, where the focus is on interference in Japanese, it is somewhat easier to talk in terms of borrowing in relation to 'pure' loanwords. This is partly because many of the words analysed are still in current use and have become firmly embedded in the recipient language, Japanese. However, other cases are less clear cut. For example, *aarudoapperen* ('potatoes'), from the Dutch *aardappel(en)*, is first attested in a Japanese text in *Kōsei shinpen* (the Dutch plural *-en* is imported without modification). This appears in other texts until at least 1844 (Saitō 1967: 9–10).

However, the word only appears in texts for a period of probably no more than thirty years, so the question arises whether we can talk of it being embedded in Japanese. It is certainly no longer in use.

Pictures of inventions imported from Europe were often accompanied by Japanese renderings of Dutch words. For example, *sutōmo bōto* ('steamship') appeared on woodblock prints in the 1830s (Tsukahara 2007b: 200). Already in 1851, a Sino-Japanese loan translation *kisen* (汽船, lit. 'steamboat') was in use (Saitō 1967: 221). We currently have no other evidence to indicate who used *sutōmo bōto*, whether they were bilingual or not, or for how long it was used. Therefore, it is difficult to say with certainty whether it became embedded in Japanese.

The same question arises for another type of lexical contact phenomenon, hybrid words. In the Tokugawa period, there were many hybrid words, the first morpheme of which was *Oranda* or a shortened form, *Ran* or *Oran*. It is likely that they were once used frequently but have subsequently fallen into disuse. For example, 'strawberry' (Latin: *Fragaria x ananassa*) was *oranda-ichigo* (オランダいちご), but now simply *ichigo*.[10] Feenstra Kuiper (1921: 259) suggests that in the Nagasaki dialect *Oran* became a prefix for anything from Europe, for example *orangasa* referred to a Western umbrella (Japanese *kasa* (傘) = 'umbrella').[11] Most of these are no longer used. So, while the emphasis in this chapter is on contact-induced words that have become embedded in Japanese, given such concerns, no absolute distinction will be made between words that are embedded and those which are instantiations of switching. Nevertheless, conduct-induced words that are still in use will be marked with an asterisk.

3.3   *Loanword Source*

Another issue hinted at by Vos, which makes it difficult to give a firm answer to the question 'How many Japanese words are outcomes of contact with Dutch?' is that some 'pure' loanwords may have been 're-inforced' or replaced by words from other languages, such as English or German, which are phonetically and morphologically similar to Dutch words. A simple example of what Vos refers to as 'words of doubtful origin' is the modern Japanese word for 'gallon', *garon* (ガロン). In Dutch *gallon* is an English loanword, embedded in Dutch since the middle of the nineteenth century (*WNT*). So, it may have been incorporated into Japanese from English or Dutch (Vos 2014: 174). As there is no clear

---

10   Here the word is written in *katakana* and *hiragana*, but it can also be written in *katakana* and *kanji* (オランダ苺).

11   Further research may reveal the extent to which the prefix *Oran-* was used in Nagasaki and elsewhere in comparison with related prefixes *Oranda-* and *Ran-*.

answer regarding which language it was borrowed from, we cannot answer the question whether hybrid creations including *garon* ガロン such as *garonbin* (ガロン瓶, 'gallon bottle') are the result of Dutch contact with Japanese. The origin of other words is clearer. However, we are still left with the question of whether they can be counted as 'lexical outcomes of contact with Dutch'. For example, the loanword *kapitan* appears in a Japanese text as early as 1610 (see below). Another early use of *kapitan*, rendered in *ateji* (phonetic *kanji*) as 甲比丹, was in a *hokku* (later called *haiku*) composed in 1678 by the famous Japanese poet Matsuo Bashō (1644–94), in which he paid mock tribute to the shogun:

kapitan mo
tsukubawasekeri
kimi ga haru

[The *kapitan*, too,
lies prostrate before Him,
Spring of the Shogun's reign.][12]

Kapitan (甲比丹; カピタン) was originally derived from the Portuguese *capitão* ('captain [of a ship]'). It came to refer to the *opperhoofd* of the Dutch trading post (Sugimoto 1976–82: V:905). Vos (2014: 172) suggests that its use in Japanese was 'reinforced' by the borrowing of the Dutch word, *kapitein*. So, one could argue that this is a Portuguese loanword, but that Dutch played a role in its continued use. It is therefore a moot point as to whether it should be included in an overall figure for outcomes of contact with Dutch in Japanese, or indeed in the figure for 'pure' loanwords.

In the nineteenth century, terms relating to chemistry were borrowed by Japanese. Many of these were first published in works by Udagawa Yōan. He typically relied on Dutch sources, although these were often translations of texts written in other European languages. Furthermore, in the early Meiji period, German became one of the principal languages or metalects in which the knowledge of chemistry was communicated in Japan. The Dutch word for potassium *kalium*, still used in Japanese in the form *kariumu* (カリウム),

---

12   甲比丹も/つくばはせけり/君が春 (Matsuo Bashō 2004: 23). Numata (1992: 32) translates the *hokku* more freely, 'When the *opperhoofd* arrives, it too has arrived, spring for our lord.' See also Screech (1996: 16). *Kapitan* also appears in a *kyōka* verse by Shōjūdō Shunkō inscribed on an illustration of the *Nagasakiya* in Edo by Utagawa Hiroshige (Screech 1996: 25).

is a German loanword (from Neo-Latin and Arabic before that). It entered Japanese via a Dutch text, but its use may have been 'reinforced' in the early Meiji period. It has been included in the list below, but there is a strong influence of German on this and other chemical terms.

3.4 *Inconsistency in Borrowing*

The identification of lexical contact phenomena in Japanese is made more difficult by the fact that authors were not consistent in their borrowing. In other words, there were no hard and fast rules about which source language to borrow from and how to render contact-induced words in Japanese. For example, there were at least four words from three different languages used to render 'England' or 'Britain' during the Tokugawa period. Two of these were borrowed from Dutch. One was *Egeresu* (エゲレス), from the Dutch *Engels(ch)* meaning 'English'. It was used in the 1678 *Oranda fūsetsugaki* (Iwao 1976–79: 1:96). In his book on Western coins *Seiyō senpu* (1787: p. 51), Kutsuki Masatsuna gives the names of the countries in Europe in *katakana*. He renders 'England' as *engerando*, probably from the Dutch, *Engeland*. *Angeria*, a modified version of the Latin 'Anglia', is found in the title of several early works on English, such as Motoki Shōei's Japanese-English vocabulary *Angeria Gorin Taisei* (1814). *Angeriya* is given by Morishima Chūryō in *Bangosen* ('Lexicon of Barbarian Words' 1798). Chūryō also gives *gorōto boritaniya* from the Dutch for Great Britain, *Groot-Brittannië*. Throughout the Tokugawa period, *Igirisu* (*katakana* イギリス *ateji* 英吉利) from the Portuguese for 'English', *Inglês* was also used.[13] This is the standard word for England in cMJ.

Another instructive example is 'chemistry', for which Japanese coined several terms. In the 1820s Hidaka Ryōdai (also Ryōtai) produced a manuscript on chemistry in which he referred to the science as *bunri gakuritsu* (分離学律). *Bunri* means 'separation' or 'analysis' while *gakuritsu* means the study of law and order, or research of rules, so this was in some sense a circumlocutory rendering of chemistry as 'the study of separation'. We do not know precisely which sources Ryōdai used, but this in fact corresponds quite closely to the Dutch word for chemistry *scheikunde*, the knowledge (*kunde*) of division (*scheiden*). This work remained in manuscript, so the coinage *bunri gakuritsu* probably had limited use (Tsukahara 2000a: 196–201). Another early term for 'chemistry' was *rigō* (離合), literally 'dividing and joining'. This appears in an

---

13   *Igirisu* is used in a Japanese memorandum (*oboe*) addressed to the Dutch dated to 1621. Viallé and Cryns (2018: 26). Despite the *katakana* spelling, Labrune (2012: 80) writes that the 'g' is prenasalized. This brings it closer to the first syllable of the Portuguese *Inglês*, from which *Igirisu* is derived.

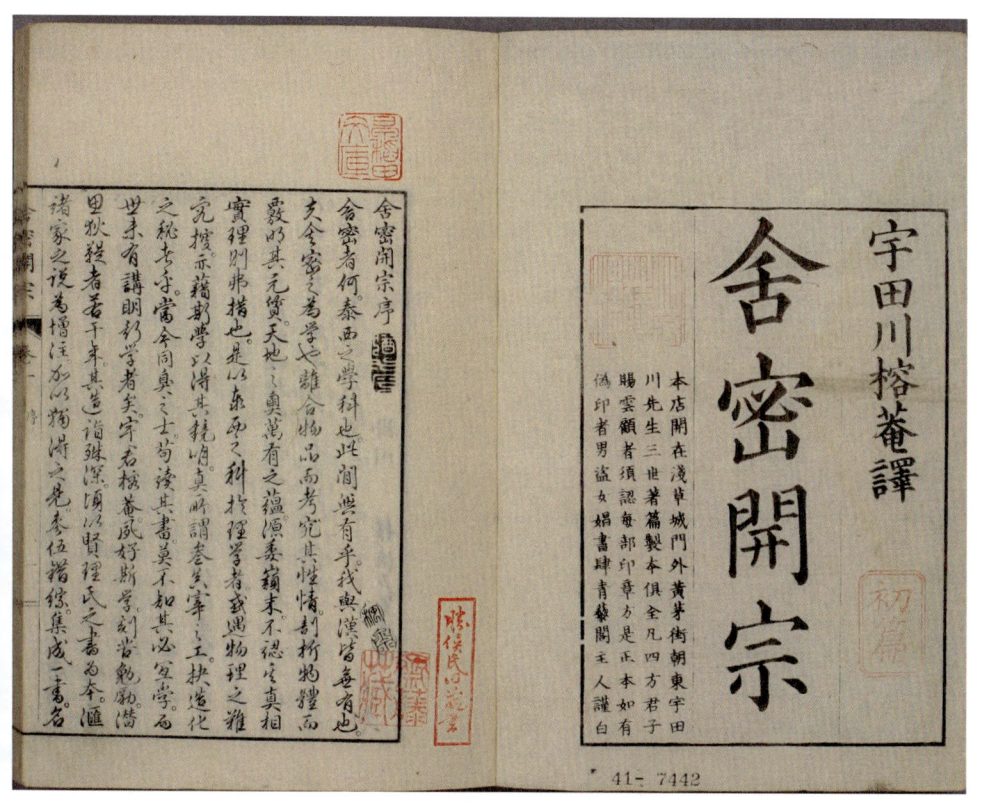

FIGURE 24   *Seimi kaisō* ('Principles of Chemistry', 1837–49), Udagawa Yōan, title page
WUL 文庫 08 C0057

undated manuscript by Fujibayashi Fuzan, *Rigō genpon* 離合源本 ('Source book on dividing and joining') (Tsukahara 2000a: 201–208). Around 1830, *seimi* from the Dutch *chemie* ('chemistry') rendered in *ateji* as 舎密 began to be used.[14] This appeared in the title of a translation of a Dutch work on chemistry, *Seimi kaisō* (舎密開宗 'Principles of Chemistry', 1837–49) by Udagawa Yōan (Clements 2015: 152, see fig. 24). Yōan's work was published, giving *seimi* traction in the late Tokugawa period. Indeed, we see it in the name of the *Seimikyoku* (舎密局), a chemistry school in Osaka and Kyoto, founded in 1869 by the Dutchman Koenraad Gratama (1831–88) (Beukers 2018: 98). It also appears in the title of a chemistry learner *Seimi kaitei* (舎密階梯, 'A Guide to Chemistry') published in 1876 by Harada Michiyoshi. However, *seimi* has now

---

14   Irwin (2011: 40) gives the first attestation for *seimi* as 1833. However, it appears in the title of Yōan's *Kōso seimika* (光素舎密加, 'Chemistry of the Element of Light'), dated to 1830.

been replaced by the Sino-Japanese *kagaku* (化学), or 'the study of change', which is based on a Chinese coinage (Van Sterkenburg *et al.* 1994: 134). In fact, there was a period of overlap. In 1867, a book was published entitled *Kagaku nyūmon* (化学入門, 'Introduction to Chemistry').

In the typology used in this chapter, while *bunri gakuritsu* is a loan translation, *seimi* is an example of 'total morphemic integration'. One question this example raises is whether these count as two contact-induced words, or different renderings of the same donor-language word. The picture is further complicated by the fact that Dutch itself has two words for 'chemistry', *chemie* and *scheikunde*. Here, as the emphasis in on interference in the recipient language, *bunri gakuritsu* and *seimi* are viewed as two contact-induced words, but one could also argue that they represent two phases of the same contact phenomenon. Another salient example is the Japanese borrowing of the Dutch word *klier* 'gland'. In 1774, the authors of *Kaitai shinsho* rendered *klier* ('gland') as *kirīru* using *ateji* (phonograms as opposed to semantograms) (Clements 2015: 166). Some thirty years later, in 1805 Udagawa Genshin created a new *kanji, sen* (腺), to render *klier* in Japanese (Kuiper 1993: 123). This is still in use. So, although there is only one source word, there is more than one rendering of it in the recipient language. Again, these are treated as two contact-induced words, not least because they are different types of word, but it could be argued they are simply different manifestations of the same concept in the recipient language.

3.5 *Borrowings in Japanese Dialects*
The Japanese of the Edo period was marked by its dialectal diversity (Labrune 2012: 5; Frellesvig 2010: 377).[15] As noted above, Koga Jūjirō (2000) lists some 1,520 words of Dutch origin in the Nagasaki dialect. Clearly, this dialectal variety is likely to have more words induced by contact with Dutch than other dialectal varieties of Japanese, as the Dutch were based in Nagasaki Bay for over 200 years. However, other dialectal varieties have borrowed words from Dutch. One example is *garasu* (< Dutch *glas* 'glass'). In and around Itoigawa in Niigata Prefecture, *garasu* and modified forms *gasu* and *gasa* are used to refer to a thin ice that people see in the early winter (Tokugawa 1979: 513–515).

Another example concerns dialectal words for 'potato'. In his treatise on preventing famine, *Kyūkō nibutsukō* ('Treatise on two things for the relief of famine', 1836), Takano Chōei refers to *appura* for 'potato', which he states is probably a corruption of the Dutch word for 'potato' *aardappel*. He writes that *appura* was used in 'a dialect of the hinterland', which suggests that was

---

15   Frellesvig (2010: 377–379) places the Japanese of the Tokugawa/Edo period at the beginning of Modern Japanese.

a variety of Japanese far away from the urban centres where the Dutch stayed or visited. However, the question of whether it had become embedded in this variety is difficult to answer (Nakamura 2005: 190). More promising are two dialectal words listed by Vos (2014: 176), viz., *afura*, used in Kawanobe County, Akita Prefecture, and Ojika County, Miyagi Prefecture; and *anpura* used in Akita Prefecture. Tokugawa (1979: 69) confirms this giving both *anpura* and *appura* in the Oga peninsula in Akita Prefecture. He also notes that *anpura* was a dialectal word in Fukushima. *Appura-imo* is a hybrid dialectal word, *imo* being the Japanese for 'tuber', used in Ibaraki Prefecture, to the north of Tokyo. In a distribution map of words for 'potato' in Japanese dialects, Tokugawa (1979: 69) gives *Oranda-imo* for 'potato' in and around Nagasaki and on the nearby Goto Islands. He also gives *kapita-imo* used in Shinshū (Nagano) in central Honshu. The first morpheme is the Portuguese/Dutch loanword 'kapitan' These last three examples in some sense mirror the modern standard Japanese word for 'potato', *jagaimo* (じゃが芋), itself a hybrid. Of particular note is the geographical spread of the dialectal forms.

These examples provide a small window onto Dutch loanwords in Japanese dialects. However, given that dialects are often not written down, the task of identifying all Dutch loanwords in Japanese dialects would be a Sisyphean one, all the more so for the Dutch loanwords in dialectal varieties in the Tokugawa period, when there was less standardization of the language. It may therefore have been quite wise of Vos to exclude dialectal words in his overall tally of Dutch contact-induced words in Japanese. This does, however, mean that we do not know how close to the 'real' figure his number is.

Vos does, in fact, mention several other contact-induced dialectal words. One example is *dontaku* (ドンタク), which is derived from the Dutch word *zondag*, meaning 'Sunday' (Vos 2014: 165, 176–177). *Dontaku* has been adopted by a range of dialects with a range of meanings from 'stupid' in the Hiroshima dialect to 'hunting cap' in Shimane and Ōita, and even 'menstruation' in Ihara County, Shizuoka Prefecture. However, the most common meaning is 'holiday' or 'free day'. For example, there is a triptych print by Utagawa (Gountei) Sadahide (1807–79) from 1861, *Yokohama dontaku no zu* (横浜鈍宅之図, 'Picture of a free day in Yokohama'), which depicts a typical Sunday, a free day, in the treaty port of Yokohama.[16] It is with this meaning and the related idea of a holiday festival that it persists in its most well-known form in modern Japan,

---

16   This is reproduced in Vande Walle (ed.) (2016: 398–399). The names of the countries represented are given in *hiragana*, e.g. *igirisu(jin)* for English(person). *Dontaku* is rendered in *ateji* 鈍宅.

Hakata dontaku, a festival held each May in the city of Hakata on Kyushu.[17] A related dialectal hybrid creation is *handon* (半ドン), which means 'Saturday' or 'half-day holiday', whereby one might leave work early to fulfil personal duties. The first element, *han* (*kanji* 半), is the Sino-Japanese word for 'half' and the second element, *don* (*katakana* ドン), is the first syllable of *dontaku*.[18] Other dialectal loanwords listed by Vos include *furaho* (< Dutch *vlag* 'flag') used in several prefectures, and *pottoru* (< Dutch *potlood* 'lead-pencil'), used in Shizuoka. Vos has clearly gone to great lengths to identify contact-induced words in Japanese dialects, and has provided some very interesting examples. However, his list is not exhaustive. In short, from the foregoing, it will be clear that providing a definitive number of contact-induced words in Japanese is difficult to say the least.

4   The Categorization of Contact-Induced Words

Before analysing contact-induced words in Japanese, a few points are in order about the methodology to be used, the fact that most of the words are nouns, and that they fall into certain thematic categories.

4.1   *Methodology*

Winford (2003: 42–45) provides a typology for lexical contact phenomena based on that of Haugen (1953), which will be used to analyse words in Japanese induced by contact with Dutch. Winford distinguishes between 'lexical borrowings', which in some way imitate the donor model, and 'native creations', 'which are entirely native and have no counterpart in the donor language'. 'Lexical borrowings' can be further subdivided into 'loanwords' and 'loanshifts'.[19] 'Loanwords' can be divided into two categories, 'pure loanwords' and 'loanblends'. In broad terms, 'pure loanwords' fall into one of two categories. First, those in close imitation of foreign items, for example *rendezvous* from French to English. This is characterized by 'total morphemic importation'. Second, items transformed in shape, such as the Costa Rican Spanish *chinchibi*

---

17   *Hakatadontaku* is written in *kanji* and one of the Japanese syllabaries, *hiragana* (博多どんたく). This suggests that it is most probably not considered to be a loanword (Vos 2014: 165, 175).

18   *Handon* can also be written in *kanji* and *hiragana* (半どん). Normally, *hiragana* is not used to render words or morphemes that originate from Western languages.

19   'Loanshifts' are those words in which 'the morphemic composition of the item is entirely native, though its meaning derives at least in part from the external source language' (Winford 2003: 43).

from English *gingerbeer*. This involves some level of phonemic substitution. 'Pure loanwords' may undergo semantic shift. For example, the general Dutch word for 'knife', *mes*, was borrowed by Japanese as *mesu*, but with the specific meaning of 'scalpel'. As for 'loanblends', these are a combination of native and imported morphemes. They involve the transfer of part of the donor model and the reproduction of the rest. They are subdivided into 'compound blends' and 'derivational blends'. Compound blends consist of an imported stem and a native stem. Derivational blends consist of an imported or native stem plus a native or imported affix.

As for 'loanshifts', their morphemic composition is entirely native, although the meaning derives, at least in part, from the donor language. Winford divides 'loanshifts' into 'extensions' or 'semantic loans' and 'loan translations' or calques (Winford 2003: 43–45). 'Extensions' involve a shift in the semantics of a native word under the influence of a foreign word. There are several examples of this in relation to words borrowed by Japanese from other languages such as Spanish and Portuguese, with a subsequent semantic shift as a result of contact with Dutch. One example is the Japanese *kapitan*, derived from the Portuguese *capitão* ('captain [of a ship]'). This meaning was extended to refer to the *opperhoofd* of the Dutch trading post (Sugimoto 1976–82: V:905). The second type of loanshift, 'loan translations', involve a combination of native morphemes in imitation of a foreign pattern. These form a large group of Dutch loanwords in Japanese. Many scientific terms in Japanese are 'loan translations' from Dutch. Typically, the morphemes in these words are Sino-Japanese.

The second main category of lexical contact phenomena identified by Winford are 'native creations', which have no equivalent in the donor language, in this case Dutch. He subdivides these into 'purely native creations', 'hybrid creations' and 'creations using only foreign morphemes'. 'Purely native creations' are 'innovative uses of native words to express foreign concepts'. 'Hybrid creations' involve the combination of native and foreign morphemes to express foreign concepts. During the Tokugawa period, the prefix *Oranda*, itself a Portuguese loanword, was often applied to devices of foreign origin. For example, the *Oranda megane* (和蘭眼鏡) was a device which allowed viewers to see pictures in Western-style perspective. Finally, there are words which are creations using only foreign morphemes. Many of these have emerged since the Tokugawa period, using morphemes borrowed during this period. There are some twenty such cases which include the morpheme *kōhī* (< Dutch *koffie* 'coffee'), for example *kōhīshoppu* (コーヒーショップ) ('coffee shop') and *kōhīkappu* (コーヒーカップ) ('coffee cup'), the second half of both words being derived from English. These contact-induced words will be analysed thematically, of which more below. Finally, while the categorization of most words is clear, in a few cases it is less clear. For example, the Japanese word for grammatical article is *kan-shi* (冠詞). This literally means 'crowning word'. This renders into Japanese the Dutch *lidwoord* which literally means 'joint word' (< Latin *articulus*). While *kan-shi* is not a direct morphemic translation, i.e., loan translation, of *lidwoord*, it is perhaps going too far to say that it is a 'purely native creation'. In such cases, mention is made of questions regarding categorization.

4.2   'Borrowability'

Winford notes that there is a 'well-known' 'hierarchy of borrowability' according to which open-class content items such as nouns and adjectives lend themselves more readily to borrowing than closed-class function items such as pronouns, conjunctions and prepositions. Furthermore, verbs tend to be borrowed less than other open-class items, in part because of their increased morphological complexity and their centrality to the syntax of a sentence (Winford 2003: 51–52). Words in Japanese induced by contact with Dutch are no different from other contact-induced words in this regard, in that the vast majority are nouns, alongside a few adjectives. I would argue that one of the reasons that Japanese borrowed so many Dutch scientific terms as loan translations is the high degree of 'morphosemantic transparency' of such terms. For example, Japanese derives its term for 'gravity' *jū-ryoku* (重力, 'heavy power') from the Dutch *zwaartekracht*. *Zwaarte* means 'weight' and *kracht* 'power' (Saitō 1967: 290). This is more transparent than, say, the English term, the meaning of which cannot be easily derived by dividing it into its constituent morphemes. In some sense, Japanese translators took their lead from the books on anatomy mediated in Dutch; they dissected the Dutch scientific terms they encountered with a pen rather than a *mesu*, and then replaced the Dutch morphemes with corresponding Japanese ones.

4.3   Themes

Contact-induced words often tend to fall into certain thematic categories. Given the history of the Netherlands as a seafaring nation, it is not surprising that Dutch has loaned out many nautical terms to other languages (Van der Sijs 2010). Japanese is one language which has adopted some of these terms. These include *dekki* (デッキ) (Dutch *dek*, 'deck'), *dokku* (ドック) (Dutch *dok*, 'dock'), *masuto* (マスト) (Dutch *mast*, 'mast'), and *tarappu* (タラップ) ('ship's ladder' or 'gangway') from the Dutch *trap* ('staircase'). The Dutch word for 'sailor', *matroos*, has been adopted by Japanese in a number of phonetic variants such as *madorosu* (マドロス).[20] It appears in Morishima Chūryō's *Kōmō zatsuwa* ('Dutch miscellany', 1787) as *matorosu* (Winkel 2004: 49). In some cases, this

---

20   There was also a loan form *matarosu*.

borrowing may be a result of 'gap-filling'. In other cases, these terms may have been adopted as part of a discourse strategy, where language users adopted foreign words to distinguish themselves from other users. These imported words 'complement the existing language with a high degree of synonymity' (Swain 2002: 144). Many of the cases below involve 'gap-filling'.

Japanese also borrowed heavily from Dutch scientific vocabulary, often in the form of loan translations. Mention has already been made of the large number of Dutch loanwords in the field of chemistry.[21] Many of these words for chemical elements, compounds, instruments and processes derive from works by members of the Udagawa family. These include *Ensei ihō meibutsukō* ('Reflections on Far Western Medical Terminology', 1822) by Udagawa Genshin and his son, Udagawa Yōan, and *Seimi kaisō* ('Principles of Chemistry', 1837–49) by Yōan. Other sciences which adopted Dutch loanwords include physics, botany and medicine. Other thematic categories where Japanese borrowed from Dutch are food and drink (the Dutch introduced beer and coffee to Japan) and everyday items. Finally, while in most cases, the thematic category to which a word belongs is clear, in some cases it may belong to more than one category. Plant names are typically categorized under 'botany', but those with medicinal qualities could also be included under 'medicine'.

4.4 Sources

Below, I give a date of first use. Most of these are cited in Saitō (1967). A sample number of 30 references given by Saitō have been checked in primary sources and with one or two exceptions detailed in notes below, they have been found to be accurate. Furthermore, references in *Seimi kaisō* have been checked in the source text. In the Index of Japanese Primary Sources by Title, the NIJL ID is given along with the reference in the Kerlen and Serrurier catalogues of Japanese books in Netherlands and Leiden University library respectively. The dates given in the wordlists below refer to more than 70 Japanese works as follows:

1695   *Kaitsūshōkō* 華夷通商考 ('An Investigation of Trade between China and Barbarian lands'), Nishikawa Joken.

1709   *Yamato honzō* 大和本草 ('Medicinal herbs of Japan'), Kaibara Ekiken.

1713   *Sairan igen* 采覧異言 ('Various sights and strange words'), Arai Hakuseki.

1714   *Seiyō kibun* 西洋紀聞 ('Western journal'), Arai Hakuseki.

1719   *Zōho jikinshō* 増補地錦抄 ('Overview of the Ornament of the Terrestrial Globe: Supplement'), Itō Ihei IV.

---

21   One source (Udagawa Yōan *et al.* 1975) lists as many as 1,000 borrowings in *Seimi kaisō*. However, it does not state how many of these have become embedded in the Japanese lexis.

1724   *Oranda mondō* 和蘭問答 ('Dutch questions and answers'), Imamura Ichibei (Gen'emon).

1750   *Kōmō-yaku-mondō* 紅毛訳問答 ('Red-haired Translation Questions and Answers'), Ogura Yoshinari (otherwise unknown).[22]

1757   *Kai-yaku fu* 会薬譜 ('Tables of Medicines'), Hiraga Gen'nai.

1763   *Butsurui hinshitsu* 物類品隲 ('The Products of Nature Arranged by Class'), Hiraga Gen'nai *et al.* A six-volume work consisting of an overview of 360 types of agricultural products from a selection of some 2000 such products.

1765   *Oranda banashi* 紅毛談 ('Dutch Tales' or 'Red-haired Stories'), Gotō Mitsuo.

1774   *Kaitai shinsho* 解体新書 ('New Treatise on Anatomy'), Sugita Genpaku *et al.*

1783   *Rangaku kaitei* 蘭学階梯 ('Guide to Dutch Learning', publ. 1788), Ōtsuki Gentaku.

1784   *Kyūryoku hōron* 求力法論 ('Essay on the Laws of Forces'), Shizuki Tadao.

1786   *Seikō kaikoku heidan* 精校海国兵談 ('Carefully Collated Discussion of the Military Problems of a Maritime Nation'), Hayashi Shihei.

1787   *Kōmō zatsuwa* 紅毛雑話 ('Dutch (lit. Red-haired) miscellany'), Morishima Chūryō.

1795   *Oranda iji mondō* 和蘭医事問答 ('Dutch Medical Practice Questions and Answers'), Takebe Seian, Sugita Genpaku.

1798   *Bangosen* 蛮語箋 ('Lexicon of Barbarian Words'), Morishima Chūryō.[23]

1798b   *Seiiki monogatari* 西域物語 ('Tales of the West'), Honda Toshiaki.

1798c   *Rekishō shinsho* 暦象新書 ('New Writings on Calendrical Phenomena', 1798–1802), Shizuki Tadao.

1798d   *Ruiju kōmōgoyaku* 類聚紅毛語訳 ('Thesaurus of translations of Red-haired (Dutch) terminology'), Morishima Chūryō.

1799   *Ransetsu benwaku* 蘭説弁惑 ('A clarification of misunderstandings in theories [about] the Dutch'), Ōtsuki Gentaku.[24]

---

22   Only 3 mss. of this are listed in the database of the National Institute for Japanese Literature (NIJL) or *Kokubunken*.

23   This was originally called *Ruiju orandago yaku* (類聚紅毛語訳, 'A Categorized Collection of Translated Dutch Words') (De Groot 2005: 55–71); See also De Groot (2016). Screech (2012: 325) has the date 1788.

24   Saitō gives a date of 1788. This was when the woodblocks were cut, but the work was not published until *Kansei* 11 (1799) (Goodman 2013: 124).

1799b *Narabayashi zatsuwa* 楢林雑話 ('Narabayashi Miscellany'), Tachihara Suiken.[25]

1802 *Zōtei sairan igen* 増訂采覧異言 ('Various sights and strange words. Revision'), Arai Hakuseki, Yamamura Masanaga.

1804 *Seikei zusetsu* 成形図説 ('Illustrated Encyclopaedia of Agricultural Products'), Sō Senshun, Shirao Kunihashira.

1804–14 *Tenba ibun* 天馬異聞 ('Curious Tale of the Flying Horse'), Yoshio Joen/Gonnosuke.

1805 *Ihan teikō* 医範提綱 ('Concise Model of [Western] Medicine'), Udagawa Genshin.

1809 *Buppin shikimei* 物品識名 ('The Nomenclature of Objects of Natural History'), Okabayashi Kiyotatsu.

1811 *Kōsei shinpen* 厚生新編 ('A New Compendium for Health'). Published between 1811 and 1839. Baba Teiyū *et al.*

1811b *Seibun kihan* 西文規範 ('Examples of Western Texts'), Baba Teiyū.

1814 *Teisei rango kyūhinshū* 訂正蘭語九品集 ('Revised collection of the nine parts of speech of the Dutch language'), Shizuki Tadao, Baba Teiyū.

1815 *Ganka shinsho* 眼科新書 ('New Book of Ophthalmology'), Sugita Ryūkei.

1822 *Ensei ihō meibutsukō* 遠西医方名物考 ('Reflections on Far Western Medical Terminology'), Udagawa Genshin and Udagawa Yōan.

1822b *Naikasen'yō* 内科撰要 ('Compilation of Essential Internal Medicine'), Johannes de Gorter, Udagawa Genzui. (NIJL ID 1043001 compiled 1792).

1822c *Botanika-kyō* 菩多尼訶經 ('The Sutra of Botany'), Udagawa Yōan.

1823 (*Rigaku nyūshiki*) *ensei kanshō zusetsu* (理学入式) 遠西観象図説 '(Introduction to Physics) Illustrated Explanations of Western Astronomical Observations', Yoshio Shunzō, Kusano Yōjun.

1823–28 *Genshin shinsho* 玄真新書 ('New writings of Genshin'), Yoshio Bō.

1825 *Kikai kanran* 気海観瀾 ('An Overview of Nature'), Aoji Rinsō.

1826 *Jūtei kaitai shinsho* 重訂解体新書 ('Revised New Treatise on Anatomy'), Sugita Genpaku *et al.*, revised by Ōtsuki Gentaku.

---

25 Suiken was a prolific writer, having 75 titles to his name. This *zatsuwa* ('Miscellany'), however, was not a success; only two ms. copies are listed. This is likely to be a collection of works by the Nagasaki interpreter family, the Narabayashi, including the illustrious Chinzan (楢林鎮山, 1649–1711).

1828(–1830) *Oranda yakkyō* 和蘭薬鏡 ('Mirror of Dutch Medicine'), Udagawa Genshin and Udagawa Yōan.

1833 *Shokugaku keigen* 植学啓原 ('The Revelation of Botany'), Udagawa Yōan.

1833b *Kakubyō ron* 各病論 ('Essay on Diseases'), Takano Chōei.

1834 *Taisei hōkan* 泰西方鑑 ('Survey of Western Medicine'), Komori Tōu.

1835 *Iryō seishi* 医療正始 ('Correct Beginnings of Medical Treatment'), Itō Genboku.

1837 *Seimi kaisō* 舍密開宗 ('Principles of Chemistry', 1837–49). Also SK. Udagawa Yōan.

1837b *Taisei yaku-mei hayabiki* 泰西薬名早引 ('A Simple dictionary for [looking up] the names of Western medicines'), Yokoi San.

1842 *Oranda bunten zenpen* 和蘭文典前篇 ('Dutch Grammar, First Part'), Mitsukuri Genpo.

1844 *Ran'yaku tebikigusa* 蘭薬手引草 ('Illustrations of Western medicinal herbs'). Ishiwara Yasushi (NIJL has 1845).

1848 *(Kaisei)bangosen* (改正) 蛮語箋 ('Revised Lexicon on Barbarian Words'), Morishima Chūryō. Revised ed. by Morita Goichirō, publ. 1850.

1850 *Rangaku chōhōki* 蘭学重宝記 ('Record of Things Useful for Dutch Studies'), Udagawa Yōan (published posthumously).

1851 *Kikai kanran kōgi* 気海観瀾広義 ('Expansion on An Overview of Nature'), Kawamoto Kōmin.

1854 *Ensei kikijutsu* 遠西奇器述 ('Stories about marvellous instruments from the Far West'), Kawamoto Kōmin.[26]

1854b *Sango-benran* 三語便覧 ('Trilingual Manual'), Murakami Hidetoshi.

1855 *Oranda jii* 和蘭字彙 ('Dutch vocabulary'), Hendrick Doeff, Katsuragawa Hoshū II.

1855b *Byōmei yakumei wayō benran* 病名薬名和洋便覧 ('Western handbook of the names of illnesses and the names of medicines'), Izawa Tomijirō. Not on the NIJL database.

1856 *Wātoru yakushōron* 窊篤児薬性論 ('(Van de) Water's Essay on the properties of medicine'), Johannes van de Water, trans. Hayashi Dōkai.

1856b *Sanpeitakuchiiki* 三兵答古知幾, Takano Chōei, trans. of *Taktiek der drie wapens* ('Tactics of the three weapons').

---

26 This book discusses new inventions such as the daguerreotype, telegraphy and steam engines.

1856c   *Oranda bunten jirui* 和蘭文典字類 ('Dutch grammar and vocabulary'),
Iizumi Shijō (*zenpen* 前編 front part).

1857   *Fushi keiken ikun* 扶氏経験遺訓 ('The Handed-Down Teachings of (the
late) Mr. Hufeland'), Christoph Hufeland, trans. Ogata Kōan.

1857b   (date given by Saitō) *Ika hikkei* 医家必携 ('Essentials for Physicians'),
Tsuboi Shindō.

1857c   *Yakken* 訳鍵 ('Keys to Translation') (first ed. 1810), Fujibayashi Fuzan.

1858   *Banpō tamate bako* 万宝玉手箱 ('Small box for 10,000 treasures'),
Sugita Seikei.

1858b   *Fushi shindan* 扶氏診断 ('Diagnosis of Mr. Hufeland'), Christoph
Hufeland, trans. Yamamoto Muneyoshi.

1862   *Seimikyoku hikkei zenpen* 舎密局必携/前編 ('Manual of the School of
Chemistry, Part I'), Ueno Hikoma.

1866   *Naigai shinpō* 内外新法 ('New Internal and External Principles'),[27]
Ogata Kendō.

1866b   *Iryō shinsho* 医療新書 ('New Book on Medicine'), Tsuboi Hōshū.

1867   *Kagaku nyūmon* 化学入門 ('Introduction to Chemistry'), Takehara
Heijirō.

1869   *Rika shinsetsu* 理化新説 ('New Theories on Physics and Chemistry'),
K.W. Gratama, and Misaki Shōsuke.

1875   *Kaibō jisho* 解剖辞書 ('Dictionary of Dissection').[28]

1897   *Kō Nihon bunten* 広日本文典 ('Comprehensive Japanese grammar'),
Ōtsuki Fumihiko (Vos 2000a: 104).

5   Lexical Contact Phenomena in Japanese Resulting from Contact with Dutch

The words analyzed below are divided according to the typology proposed by
Winford. A word marked with an asterisk (*) signifies that it is still in use (cf.
Vos 1963; 2014). 'Vos' indicates that the word is listed in Vos (1963, 2014), 'Van
Sterkenburg' that it is listed in Van Sterkenburg *et al.* (1994), and 'Saitō' that it
is listed in Saitō (1967). Where appropriate, the date is given of the first use of
the word in a Japanese text as listed by Saitō and Van Sterkenburg *et al.* or from
my own research. 'SK' indicates that the word appears in *Seimi kaisō* (1837–49).
On occasion, the earliest date is given as 1837, the date of the publication of

---

27   NIJL (ID1043090) renders the title in *hiragana* as *naige shinpō*. The fourth *kanji* can be 報.

28   This is not on the NIJL database. Saitō may have meant *Kaibō shinsho* 解剖新書 ('New
Book on Dissection') ID 2167160, but this requires further investigation.

the first volume of *Seimi kaisō*. Where a contact-induced word has been superseded by another word, 'ns.' (nowadays) is used (cf. Vos 1963; 2014). (J.) indicates that a word is a *Yamato kotoba* (大和言葉) or *wago* (和語) i.e., a 'native' Japanese word. (S.-J.) refers to Sino-Japanese or *kango* (漢語) words.

I list 577 Japanese words that are lexical outcomes of contact with Dutch. 383 of these are marked with an asterisk, indicating they are still in use in cMJ, although this use may be restricted to certain social domains. Other lexical outcomes of contact are not included, primarily for lack of space. For example, eleven grammatical terms are listed (5.1.2.2.2), but there are at least a further 16 such terms that are also lexical outcomes of contact with Dutch. Twenty 'creations using only foreign morphemes' are listed (5.2.3), although the total is much higher. Indeed, a figure of double the 577 words listed is probably not an underestimate, and that is without counting dialectal words. On the other hand, the figure for 'pure loanwords', 315, is close to that given by other authors and is probably fairly close to the 'true number' of such borrowings; it is loan translations and hybrids that make the overall total shoot up.

5.1 *'Lexical Borrowings' (Modelled on the Donor Language) (488 Words)*
5.1.1 Loanwords (361 Words)
As noted above, 'loanwords' can be divided into 'pure' loanwords (5.1.1.1) and 'loanblends' (5.1.1.2). The 'pure' loanwords are examples of *gairaigo*, which are, in general, words borrowed by Japanese since the sixteenth century (Labrune 2012: 16–20).

5.1.1.1 *'Pure' Loanwords (315 Words)*
Winford makes a distinction between those 'pure' loanwords where there is some element of phonemic substitution and those where this is negligible or non-existent. However, given the differences between the Dutch and Japanese sound systems, there are very few cases, where there is what Winford refers to as 'total morphemic integration', i.e., where there is very little or no phonemic substitution, as in the English adoption of the French words *rendezvous* and *entourage*.[29] Some of the differences between the Dutch and Japanese sound systems analysed in Chapter 5, section 3 of this book influence how Dutch words were adopted by Japanese. Vos (2014: 160–163) provides a useful summary of the Japanese sound system as well as a summary of the most important changes that Dutch words underwent when they were adopted by Japanese. Let us take a closer look at several of the most significant of these:

---

29 Even in the case of *rendezvous*, as Winford admits, there is arguably very slight phonemic substitution.

1. Japanese and Dutch phonotactics differ significantly. In classical Japanese words, the structure of the basic prosodic unit is V(owel) or C(onsonant) V(owel) (Labrune 2012: 16).[30] Dutch words, by contrast, often include consonant clusters and can have one or many word/morpheme-final consonants. Many Dutch words borrowed by Japanese have therefore undergone epenthesis (Winford 2003: 47). For example, the Dutch *matroos* ('sailor') was adopted as *matorosu* or *madorosu* in Japanese. Another example is the Dutch *blik* (tin) becoming *buriki*, where *blik*, which is CCVC, has been modified to the trisyllabic (or tri-moraic) *buriki*, which is CVCVCV (Shibatani 1990: 121–122).[31] In some cases, the additional epenthetic vowels in question are the result of anticipatory replication, while in others they are the result of perseverative replication. For example, Japanese adopted the Dutch *glas* ('glass') as *garasu* (ガラス). The first 'a' is an example of anticipatory replication (Irwin 2011: 111; Vos 2014: 165, 171). In modern loans, anticipatory replication seems to play a less prominent role. The English glass has been incorporated as *gurasu*, reflecting the fact that in cMJ, the main epenthetic vowel is /u/ (Labrune 2012: 29). One example of perseverative replication is *sutorikinīne* (ストリキニーネ), a Japanese rendering of the Dutch *strychnine* ('strychnine') (Irwin 2011: 112; Vos 2014: 171).[32] Here, the second, epenthetic 'i' replicates the first one.

2. Dutch has two alveolar liquids, /l/, and /r/, both of which are realized in more than one way whereas Japanese has only one liquid, /r/. This helps to explain why, for example, the Dutch *leeuw* ('Leo', 'lion') is rendered *rēyū* in the Hepburn transliteration system.

3. The native Japanese sound system lacks certain phonemes present in Dutch, for example /v/. Nowadays in loanwords this is typically rendered graphically as ⟨b⟩ and realized as [b]. However, in the Tokugawa period,

---

30 The (C)V pattern was supplemented as a consequence of the flood of Chinese loanwords adopted by Old and Middle Japanese. This introduced new syllable types, such as the syllable-final nasal in, for example, *hon* (本), which is the second part of the Sino-Japanese word for 'Japan' *nihon* (日本). The morpheme-final /n/ is realized in several ways in Japanese, depending on the phonetic environment in which it is situated. For more on this, see Labrune (2012: 132–134).

31 In Japanese, the three syllables of *kiruku* are also considered to be independent moraic units, where a *mora* is a phonological unit that can be represented by one letter of the *kana* syllabary. For example, *shinbun* ('newspaper') has two syllables, but four *mora*, shi n bu n. Shibatani (1990: 158).

32 See also Saitō (1967: 224–225). In modern Japanese there is also the rendering *sutorikinin* (ストリキニン) loaned from English.

the Dutch /v/ was rendered graphically as ⟨h⟩ or ⟨w⟩.[33] For example, the Dutch 'vet' ('fat') was incorporated as *hetto* (ヘット) in Japanese.

4. Historically, the combinations *[du] and *[di] have not existed in spoken Japanese.[34] Before *u*, /d/ has been realized as [z] or [dz] and before *i* as [z] (word-internally and -initially) and [dz] (word-initially). This helps to explain why the Dutch word for 'canvas' *doek* was adopted by Japanese as *zukku* (ズック) and the surname of Hendrick Doeff was rendered as *(d)Zūfu* (ヅーフ). Likewise, the unvoiced equivalents, [tu] and [ti], are not in the native Japanese sound system. Before *i* /t/ is realized as [tɕ]. So, the Dutch *typhus* is rendered in Japanese in *ateji* or *katakana* as *chifuzu* (Labrune 2012: 62–63).

Finally, when these words were first used in Japanese texts, they were written in either *ateji* (phonograms) with *furigana* or in the *katakana* syllabary. Nowadays, loanwords are typically, although not always, rendered in *katakana*. Arai Hakuseki (1657–1725) was the first Japanese to render loanwords consistently in *katakana*.

5.1.1.1   Botany (63 Words)

In the text of the 30-volume *Seikei zusetsu* ('Illustrated Encyclopaedia of Agricultural Products', 1804), there are 103 Dutch names for the native Japanese plants depicted in the illustrations (Chatterjee and Van Andel 2019: 382). While few if any of these Dutch names are used in Japanese today, the question arises as to whether they were in common use in the nineteenth century and if so to what extent any of them could be considered loanwords. It is likely that they were used in intellectual exchange, perhaps amongst *rangakusha*, but currently we can say nothing more concrete. One example is *rāpu*, written in *katakana*, from the Dutch *raap*. This referred to the turnip (Vol. XXI: p. 35). Other words derived from Dutch relating to botany are:

1   *adamusuapperu* < Dutch *adamsappel* ('Adam's apple'). Saitō (gives the earliest date of use as) 1826.

2   **akashia* < Dutch *acacia* ('acacia'). Vos, Saitō 181.

---

33   For a summary of Japanese phonemes, see Vos (2014: 160–161). Some Japanese may pronounce foreign words with 'v' as [v], although [b] is more typical. Labrune (2012: 97) makes two important points in this regard. First, those who do pronounce [v] have a particular sociolinguistic profile, i.e., urban, educated and female. Second, even though [v] is represented in *katakana* (ヴ), actual pronunciation is more conservative and does not always reflect the *kana* spelling.

34   Since the Edo period, [di] and [du] have been used to render the foreign combinations *di* and *du*.

3   *amanderen* < Dutch *amandelen* ('almonds'). Saitō 1826. Vos (2014: 172) writes that the forms **amendō* and *anmendō* were Portuguese loanwords reinforced by the Dutch *amandel*. ns. *āmondo* (Eng.).

4   *ananasu* < Dutch *ananas* ('pineapple'). Vos, Saitō 1811. ns. *painappuru* (Eng.).

5   *aneisu/*anisu* < Dutch *anijs* ('anis'). According to Vos (2014: 172) this is a Portuguese/Spanish loanword reinforced by Dutch. Saitō *aneisu* 1822.

6   **arabiagomu* < Dutch *Arabisch gom* ('gum arabic'). Vos, Saitō 1811. ns. also *arabiagamu, arabiyagomu*.

7   **aroe* < Dutch *aloë* ('aloe'). Vos, Saitō 1811.[35]

8   **arunika* < Dutch/Latin *arnica* ('arnica'). Vos, Saitō 1837b.

9   *arutā* < Dutch *althea* ('althaea'). Saitō 1811.

10   **barusamu* < Dutch *balsem* ('balm', 'balsam'). Vos, Saitō 1799.

11   *barusamu han (van) pērū* < Dutch *balsam van Peru* ('balm', 'balsam from Peru'). Saitō 1811.[36]

12   **bīto* < Dutch *biet* ('beet'). Vos.

13   *garubanumu* < Dutch *galbanum* ('galbanum'). Saitō 1837.[37]

14   *genisuda, enisuta* < Dutch *genista* ('Scotch broom', *Cytisus scoparius*). Saitō *enisuta* 1719 (p. 6) and *genishida* 1828. Vos. ns. *enishida*, possible influence of Spanish *hiniesta*.

15   **genchiana* < Dutch *gentiaan* (< Latin *gentiana*) ('gentiana'). Saitō 1822.

16   *gēru* < Dutch *chijl/gijl* ('chyle'). Saitō 1774, ns. *niyūbi* 乳糜 (S.-J.).

17   **harogen* < Dutch *halogen* (plural *halogenen*) ('halogen'). Saitō (*harogenen*) 1867.

18   *harusu* < Dutch *hars* ('resin'). Van Sterkenburg 1822; 1854, II, p. 18.

19   *henrūda* < Dutch *wijnruit* ('rue', *Ruta graveolens*). Vos, Saitō 1757.

20   **hisoppu* < Dutch *hysop* ('hyssop', *Hyssopus officinalis*). Vos. Saitō *hīsoppu, heisoppusu* (< Latin) 1837b; *hisoppu* 1857b.

21   **hiyosu, hiyosuyamosu* < Dutch *hyoscyamus* ('henbane', *Hyoscyamus niger*). Vos, Saitō *hiyosushiami* 1822; *hiosu* 1857.[38]

22   *hokushia* < Dutch *foksia* ('fuchsia', *Fuchsia hybrida*). Vos. ns. *fukushia, fukushiya* (Eng.).

23   **hoppu* < Dutch *hop* ('hop', *Humulus lupulus*). Van Sterkenburg, Saitō 1822.

---

35   *Aroe* is also given in *Bangosen* (1798).

36   The Latin *balsamum peruvianum* occurs in the *dagregister* in 1788 (Blussé and Remmelink 2004: 562).

37   ns. *fūshikō* 楓子香 in online dictionary www.jisho.org. Accessed 16 April 2020.

38   The loanword seems to have undergone the syllabification of the initial glide here (Winford 2003: 47).

24 *horuko, hoko* < Dutch *vork* ('fork'), 1798, 1799. ns. *fōku* (Eng.).

25 **jigitarisu* < Dutch *digitalis* ('foxglove', *Digitalis purpurea*). Vos *jigitarisu*, Saitō *jikitarisu* 1844.

26 *jira* < Dutch *dille* ('dill'). Saitō 1822. ns. *inondo* (Sp.).

27 **kamitsure, kamirure* < Dutch *kamille* ('camomile').[39] Vos, Saitō *kamirure* 加密列 (カミツレ) (*ateji* with *furigana*) 1822.

28 **kanfuru, kanpuru, kanheru, kanpora* < Dutch *kamfer* ('camphor'). Vos, Van Sterkenburg 1713, Saitō *kanpuru* 1713, SK *kanpura, kamupora* (Udagawa Yōan *et al.* 1975: 560, 451). ns. also *shōnō* 樟脳 (S.-J.).

29 *karūei* < Dutch *karwij* ('caraway', *Carum carvi*). Vos, Saitō 1811. ns. *karauē*, *kyarauei* (Eng.) or *hime-uikyō* 姫茴香 (J., S-J.).

30 **kayupute* < Dutch *kajapoet* ('cajeput', *Melaleuca cajuputi*). Vos, Saitō 1815 (*ateji* and *furigana*) (Appendix, p. 15) (< Malay *kayu*, 'wood'; *putih*, 'white').

31 **kerupu* < Dutch *kelp* ('kelp'). SK *ateji* with *furigana* (Udagawa Yōan *et al.* 1975: 560, 99).

32 **kino* < Dutch *kino(gom)* ('kino gum' (resin)). Vos, Saitō *kinogomu* 1822.

33 **koendoro* < Por. *coentro* reinforced by Dutch *koriander* ('coriander', *Coriandrum sativum*). This plant had ceased to exist in Japan and the seeds were often imported by the Dutch from the Mediterranean (Vos 2014: 172). Saitō records that in *Buppin shikimei* (1809: p. 122), *koentoro* (*katakana*) is given as 蛮語 (*bango*, i.e., Portuguese) with *korianteru* as a 'modified pronunciation' (written as ノ転ナリ). ns. also *koriandā* (Eng.).[40]

34 *komein* < Dutch *komijn* ('cummin', *Cumimum cyminum*). Vos. Saitō 1834. ns. *kumin* (Eng.), *kyunmeru* (< German *Kuemmel*).

35 **koruku, kiruku, kiruko* < Dutch *kurk* ('cork'). Vos *koruku* 1759; Saitō *kyoruko* 1763, 1799.[41]

36 *kuwasshia* < Dutch *kwassie[hout]* ('quassia', 'bitterwood'). Vos, Saitō *kuwasushia* 1834. ns. *niga-ki* 苦木 (J.)

37 **merissa* < Dutch *melisse*/Latin *melissa* ('melissa [officinalis]', 'balm-mint'). Vos, Saitō 1822.

38 **opopanakkusu* < Dutch *opopanax* ('opopanax'). Vos. Saitō 1834.

39 *orēifu* < Dutch *olijf* ('olive'). Vos, Saitō 1774. ns. *orību* may be of Eng. or Fr. derivation.

---

39 The syllable *tsu* ツ in *kamitsure* was originally used in writing in order to indicate the doubling of the *l* (cf. the syllable *ru* in *kamirure*) (Vos 2014: 166 n. 43).

40 The *dakuten* which indicates voicing was not always used.

41 Saitō gives 平賀品随 as his source for 1763, but this does not appear on the NIJL database. It may well be an alternative name for *Butsurui hinshitsu* 物類品隲 by Hiraga Gen'nai.

40 *pokkuhouto* < Dutch *pokhout* ('guaiac', *Lignum vitae*). Vos, Saitō 1822.

41 *ponpūn* < Dutch *pompoen* ('pumpkin'), 1804, XXVII, pp. 16–17. ns. *tōnasu* 唐茄子 or *kabocha* 南瓜.

42 *porīgara* < Dutch *polygala, kruisbloem* ('milkwort', *Polygala sibirica*). Vos, Saitō *porīgara* 1834. ns. *hime-hagi* 姫萩 (J.).

43 *rabarubaru* < Dutch *r(h)abarber* ('rhubarb', used as a medicine *Rheum officinale*). Vos, Saitō 1828. ns. *rubābu* (Eng.), *daiō* 大黄 (S.-J.).

44 *rāhenderu* < Dutch *lavendel* ('lavender', *Lavandula officinalis*). Vos, Saitō 1811. ns. *rabendā* (Eng.).

45 *ratania* < Dutch/Latin *ratanhia* ('ratanhia'/'rhatany', genus *krameria*). Saitō 1822.

46 *raurīru* <Dutch *laurier* ('laurel', 'bay', *Laurus nobilis*). Vos, Saitō 1822. ns. *rōreru. gekkēju* 月桂樹 (S.-J.).

47 *raurīru-kerusu* < Dutch *laurierkers* ('cherry-laurel'). Vos, Saitō 1837.

48 *sabajira, **sebajira, sabajirura* < Dutch *sabadilla* (*Schoenocaulon officinale*). Vos, Saitō 1837b.

49 *safuran < Dutch *saffraan* ('saffron'). Vos, Saitō 1763. Irwin 1705.

50 *santori* < Dutch *santorie* ('centaury', *Erythraea centaurium*). Vos, Saitō *santorī* 1822.

51 *sarubia < Dutch *salvia* ('salvia'). Saitō *saruhia* 1822.

52 *sarusaparirura*, *sarusa < Latin/Dutch *sarsaparilla* (*Smilax officinalis, Smilax medica*). Vos, Saitō 1822.

53 *sassafurasu < Dutch *sassafras* (*Sassafras albidum*). Vos, Saitō 1822.

54 *semenshina < Latin/Dutch *semen cinae* ('santonica', *Artemisia cina*). Vos, Saitō 1822.

55 *senega < Dutch *senega* ('senega', *Polygala senega*, 'milkwort'). Vos.

56 *senna, senneburāden* < Dutch *sennebladen* ('senna leaves'). Saitō 1822. ns. *sena*.

57 *serupentaria* < Dutch *serpentaria/slange(n)wortel* ('serpentaria'). Saitō 1822.

58 *suponsu* < Dutch *spons* ('sponge'). Saitō 1765. ns. *suponji* (Eng.).

59 *tamarindo < Dutch *tamarinde* ('tamarind-tree', 'tamarind-fruit' *Tamarindus indica*). Vos, Saitō 1834.

60 *terebin, terebintēna* < Dutch *terpentijn* ('turpentine'). Vos notes that *terebin* is a 'continuation of Portuguese'. Saitō *terementei* < Dutch *termentijn* 1695, *terementeina* 1763, *terupentein* 1799. ns. *tāpentain*.

61 *torumenchirura* < Dutch *tormentilla* ('tormentil', *Potentilla tormentilla*). Vos, Saitō 1834.

62 *yarappa < Dutch *jalappe* ('jalap', *Exogonium purga*). Vos, Saitō *yārappa, yārappe* 1822.

63   *yasumein* < Dutch *jasmijn* ('jasmine', *Jasminum oficinale*). Vos, Saitō *yasumein* 1833. ns. *jasumin* (Eng.).

5.1.1.1.2   Chemistry (*SK* = Seimi kaisō) (80 Words)

1   *amejisuto, ameshisuto* < Dutch *ametist* ('amethyst') SK *ateji* with *furigana* (Udagawa Yōan *et al.* 1975: 563, 228).

2   *anchimonī* < Dutch *antimonie* ('antimony'). SK *katakana* (Udagawa Yōan *et al.* 1975: 563, 361). Vos, Saitō 1837. ns. also *anchimon* (Vos 2014: 164).

3   *anjaberu, anjelier* < Dutch *anjer, anjelier* ('carnation', 'pink'). Vos, Saitō *anjaberu* 1799. ns. *kānēshon* (Eng.).

4   *anmonia,* *anmoniya, amemonia* < Dutch *ammonia* ('ammonia'). SK *katakana* (Udagawa Yōan *et al.* 1975: 563, 329), Vos.

5   *anmoniaka* < Dutch *ammoniak* ('ammoniac'). Saitō 1837b.

6   *arukari* < Dutch *alkali* ('alkali') SK, the *ateji* now used (亜爾加里) are the same as those in *Seimi kaisō*, although now this word is usually written in *katakana* (Udagawa Yōan *et al.* 1975: 563, 222). Vos, Saitō 1822.

7   *arukōru, arukōu, arukohoru* < Dutch *alcohol* ('alcohol') Vos, Saitō 1844, Van Sterkenburg 1822.

8   *asubesuto* < Dutch *asbest* ('asbestos'). Van Sterkenburg *asubesutosu* 1765; SK *ateji* with *furigana* (Udagawa Yōan *et al.* 1975: 563, 199).

9   *bengara* < Dutch *Bengalen* (Bengal) refers to 'Indian red', 'red iron oxide' or 'red-ochre rouge'. This it was imported by the Dutch from Bengal. Vos. ns. also *benigara*.

10   *berensu* < Dutch *Berlijns [blauw]* ('Prussian blue'). Vos. Van Sterkenburg *berensuburāu* 1763, Saitō *berurin burāu* 1811. Screech (2012: 299) *bero*. ns. also *purushian burū, berurin ao, mirorī burū* and *konjō* 紺青 (S.-J.).

11   *bisumitto* < Dutch *bismuth* ('bismuth'). Vos, Saitō 1837. ns. *sōen* 蒼鉛 (S.-J.) or *bisumasu*.

12   *buriki* < Dutch *blik* ('tin plate'). Vos. In *Bangosen* (1798) it is described as a 'thin metal used for making containers'.[42] Saitō *burikki* 1811. Used in collocations e.g. *buriki-no-omocha* ('tin toys').

13   *burūdosutēn* < Dutch *bloedsteen* ('blood-stone'/'haematite'). Saitō 1811. ns. *kesseki* 血石 (S.-J.) or *buraddosutōn* (Eng.).

14   *chinki* < Dutch *tinctuur* ('tincture', 'solvent'). Vos, Saitō *chinki* 1828.

15   *ekisu, ekisutarakuto* < Dutch *extract* ('extract'). Vos, Saitō *ekisu* 1822; *ekisutarakuto* 1828. SK *oitoterekisuru* < Dutch *uittreksel* ('extract').

---

42   Eylenbosch (1940: 586), writes that a Japanese word derived from this is *burikiya* (ブリ キ屋), which means 'tin shop'.

16   *erasuchikku, erasuchika, erasuteikku* < Dutch *elastiek* ('a piece of elastic') Saitō *erasuchika* 1837. ns. *erasuchikku* is used for 'elastic fabric'. Vos (2014: 176) *erasuchika* is a dialectal word for rubber band in Fukui City.

17   *erubiumu, *erubyumu* < Dutch *erbium* ('erbium'). Saitō *erubyumu* 1862.

18   *furinto-garasu* < Dutch *flintglas* ('flint glass'). Vos. Saitō 1837. Udagawa Yōan *et al.* 1975: 214.

19   *furiorine* < Dutch *fluorine* ('fluorine'). Vos *furiyūorine* 1862. Saitō *furiorine* 1837: SK *ateji* with *furigana* (Udagawa Yōan *et al.* 1975: 198). ns. *fusso* フッ素 (S.-J.) and *furōrin*.

20   *furyūoru* < Dutch *fluor* ('fluorine'). Vos.

21   *garasu* < Dutch *glas* ('glass', 'plate glass'). Vos 1763, Saitō, Van Sterkenburg 1799, also 1798. Here, Vos's date may be correct, although he does not name a source. The form *garasu* is given in *Butsurui hinshitsu* (e.g. 1:50) 1763.

22   *garena* < Dutch *galena* ('galena' lead (II) sulfide (PbS)). SK *ateji* with *furigana* (Udagawa Yōan *et al.* 1975: 561, 341). ns. *hōenkō* 方鉛鉱 (S.-J.).

23   *Garuhani batterii* < Dutch *Galvanische batterij* ('Galvin battery'). SK *ateji* with *furigana* (Udagawa Yōan *et al.* 1975: 561, 54).

24   *garuhanisumiyusu* < Dutch *galvanismus* ('Galvanism'). Saitō 1851, XI, p. 16.

25   *gasu* < Dutch *gas* ('gas'). Vos 1822. Saitō 1811.

26   *gipusu* < Dutch *gips* ('gypsum', 'plaster cast'). Saitō 1837.

27   *giyaman, jiyaman* < Dutch *diamant* ('diamond'). Vos, Saitō *giyaman* 1765.[43] Possible Spanish or Portuguese origin. ns. *daiya[mondo]*, *daia-mondo* (Eng.).

28   *gomu* < Dutch *gom* ('gum', 'rubber'). Vos 1847, Saitō 1798 *giutte gomu* (*guttegom* WNT), 1822 *gomu*. SK (Udagawa Yōan *et al.* 1975: passim, e.g. 453).

29   *irijiūmu* < Dutch *iridium* ('iridium'). Vos, Saitō 1837; 1851, III, p. 23.

30   *ittoriumu* < Dutch *yttrium* ('yttrium'). SK *ateji* with *furigana* (Udagawa Yōan *et al.* 1975: 562, 225). Yōan renders yttrium ore as *itoruārudo* (< Dutch *ytteraarde*) in *ateji* with *furigana*.

31   *kadomiumu* < Dutch *kadmium* ('cadmium'). Vos, Saitō 1837.

32   *kantarisu* < Dutch *kantharis* pl. *kanthariden/s* ('cantharides', 'Spanish fly'). Vos, Saitō *kantaridesu* 1837.

33   *karāto* < Dutch *karaat* ('carat'). Saitō 1837. SK *ateji* with *furigana* (Udagawa Yōan *et al.* 1975: 561, 251). The modern word is *karatto* (short 'a') possibly influenced by English.

---

43   *Giyaman* is given as the *furigana* reading in *Bangosen* (1798) suggesting it had become embedded by this time. The Dutch is given as *jiyamanto*.

34   *kariumu < Dutch kalium ('kalium/potassium'). Vos, Saitō 1833, SK ateji
     with furigana (Udagawa Yōan et al. 1975: 561, 64). Yōan writes karimetāru
     < Dutch kali-metaal). The shortened form kari is in use today in ateji
     加里 or katakana. He also writes pottāsumetāru, i.e., potash metal (<
     Dutch potas-metaal). ns. also called potashūmu (Eng.).

35   *karomeru, karōmeru < Dutch kalomel ('calomel' Mercury (I) Chloride).
     Vos, Saitō karomeru 1815, karōmeru 1822. ns. also 甘汞 kankō (S.-J.) (see
     below).

36   karorimētoru < Dutch calorimeter ('calorimeter'). SK ateji with furig-
     ana (Udagawa Yōan et al. 1975: 560, 184). ns. netsuryōkei 熱量計 (S.-J.),
     karorimētā (Eng.).

37   *karuki < Dutch kalk ('lime'). Vos, Saitō 1833. SK ateji (Udagawa Yōan et al.
     1975: 561, 199).

38   *karumein, *karumin < Dutch karmijn ('carmine') Vos, Saitō karumein,
     karumin 1811, karumein 1837. ns. also kāmain (Eng.).

39   *karushūmu < Dutch calcium ('calcium'). Vos, Saitō ateji 1862. ns. also
     karushiumu.

40   *kasutoryūmu < Dutch castoreum ('castor'/'castoreum'). Vos, Saitō 1822.
     ns. kairi-kō 海狸香 (S.-J.).

41   *katēteru < Dutch katheter ('catheter'). Vos, Saitō 1811.

42   kereito < Dutch krijt ('chalk'). Vos 1822, Saitō 1811. ns. hakuboku 白墨 (S.-J.)
     and chōku (Eng.).

43   *kereosōto < Dutch c/kreosoot ('creosote'). Vos, Saitō kereosoto 1856. ns.
     also kureosōto

44   *kobaruto < Dutch kobalt ('cobalt'). Vos, Saitō kobaruto 1811. SK ateji and
     katakana, koboruto (Udagawa Yōan et al. 1975: 559, 369, 370).

45   *kochinūru < Dutch cochenille SK ateji with furigana (Udagawa Yōan et al.
     1975: 560, 346).

46   korojion < Dutch collodium ('collodium'). Vos, Saitō 1862.

47   korokinto < Dutch kolokwint ('colocynth', Citrullus colocynthis). Vos, Saitō
     1822. ns. koroshinto (Eng.).

48   korōn-garasu < Dutch kroonglas ('crown-glass'). Vos, Saitō 1851. ns.
     kuraun-garasu (Eng. + Dutch).

49   *kuromu < Dutch chroom ('chromium'). SK ateji (Udagawa Yōan et al.
     1975: 561, 379).

50   *maguneshia, maguneshiya < Dutch magnesia ('magnesia'). Vos, Saitō
     1834, SK maguneshia in katakana (Udagawa Yōan et al. 1975: 560, 199). ns.
     also kudo 苦土 (S.-J.) and san-ka-maguneshiumu 酸化マグネシウム (S.-J. +
     Dutch hybrid) = magnesium oxide.

51   *maguneshiumu < Dutch magnesium ('magnesium'). Vos, Saitō 1822.

52   *mangan < Dutch mangaan ('manganese'). Vos, Saitō 1822.

53   mayorana < Dutch/Latin majoraan/majorana ('marjoram'). Saitō 1815, Appendix, p. 17. ns. mājoramu (Eng.).

54   menī < Dutch menie ('minium', 'red lead'). Vos, Umegaki (1963: 68), ns. entan 鉛丹 (S.-J.).

55   *moribudēn, moreibudāniumu < Dutch molybdeen, molybdenum ('molybdenum'). Saitō moribudēn 1837; Udagawa Yōan et al. 1975: 375 (SK).

56   *nafuta < Dutch naphtha ('naphtha'). Vos, Saitō nafutā 1834, nafuta 1837b.

57   *natoriumu < Dutch natrium ('sodium'). Saitō 1862.

58   *natoriumuranpu < Dutch natriumlamp ('sodium vapour lamp').

59   *nikkeru < Dutch nikkel ('nickel'). Vos, Saitō 1837.

60   *onsu < Dutch ons ('ounce') Vos 1822, Saitō 1822. SK ateji (Udagawa Yōan et al. 1975: 561, 252).

61   *opāru < Dutch opaal ('opal'). Vos, Saitō 1837. SK ateji with furigana (Udagawa Yōan et al. 1975: 562, 498).

62   *osumiumu < Dutch osmium ('osmium') Saitō 1837.

63   parurajiumu < Dutch palladium ('palladium'). Vos, Saitō 1837. ns. parajiumu.

64   *purachina < Dutch platina ('platinum'). Vos, Saitō purachina, hakkin 白金 (S.-J.), lit. 'white gold' 1822.

65   rakkamūsu < Dutch lakmoes ('litmus'). Vos, Saitō 1837. ns. ritomasu (Eng.).

66   *retoruto < Dutch retort ('retort', a glass vessel used for distillation). Vos, Saitō (retoruta in ateji) 1811, retoruto in ateji and furigana 1815 Appendix, diagrams (zusetsu), p. 4.

67   *richiumu < Dutch lithium ('lithium'). Vos, Saitō 1837.

68   rōdogarasu < Dutch loodglas ('lead/flint glass'). Saitō 1862. ns. kurisutarugarasu (garasu is the Dutch loan form), kurisutarugurasu, kurisutaru.

69   rōdosoikuru < Dutch loodsuiker ('lead acetate' or 'sugar of lead'). Saitō 1822.

70   sahhiru < Dutch saffier ('sapphire'). SK (Udagawa Yōan et al. 1975: 229). ns. safaia, safaiya.

71   seimi < Dutch chemie ('chemistry'). Vos, Irwin 1833. Used in Udagawa Yōan's Kōso seimika (光素舎密加, 1830). ns. kagaku 化学.

72   *semento < Dutch cement. Vos, Saitō 1811.

73   *sōda < Dutch soda. Vos, Saitō 1822.

74   sōjiumu < Dutch sodium. Vos sojūmu. Saitō 1822. ns. sodiumu (ソディウム).

75   surangasuten/sutein < Dutch slangsteen ('serpentine stone'). Vos, Saitō 1750. ns. jamonseki 蛇紋石 (S.-J.).

76   *sutorikinine* < Dutch *strychnine* ('strychnine'). Saitō 1837. SK *sutorikinine*,
      ateji with *furigana* (Udagawa Yōan *et al.* 1975: 556, 402).

77   *teru, tēru, teiru* < Dutch *teer* ('tar'). Vos, Saitō *teru* 1799b, *tēru* 1822, ns. *tāru*
      (Eng.).

78   *terumomētoru, tarumomētoru* < Dutch *thermometer* ('thermometer').
      Saitō *terumomeitoru* 1799; SK *terumomētoru, ateji* with *furigana* (Udagawa
      Yōan *et al.* 1975: 561, 16). ns. *kandankei* 寒暖計, *ondokei* 温度計 (S.-J.).

79   *worupuramu* < Dutch *wolfram* ('tungsten'), possibly reinforced by
      German. SK *ateji* (Udagawa Yōan *et al.* 1975: 562, 380). Yōan also renders
      'tungsten' in *katakana* as *teyungusuteen metaaru* (< Dutch *tungsteen-
      metaal*). ns. *tangusuten*.

80   **yojiumu* < Dutch *jodium* ('iodine'). Vos, Saitō *yojūmu*, SK *ateji* with *furi-
      gana* (Udagawa Yōan *et al.* 1975: 563, 375), 1837, 1854, p. 1. ns. also *yōdo* and
      yōso.

5.1.1.1.3   Food and Drink (20 Words)

1   **arakku, araki* < Dutch *arak* ('arrack'). Vos.

2   **bīru* < Dutch *bier* ('beer'). Vos 1724, Van Sterkenburg 1724, 1798, Saitō 1799
     (*hiragana*). 1799 (*Ransetsu benwaku*) also has *bīru-garasu* ('beer glass').

3   **bisuketto, besukoito* < Dutch *beschuit* ('rusk'). Saitō *besukoito* 1848. Vos:
     ns. also used for biscuit in general and for crackers. The word might be a
     'continuation' or 'reinforcement' of *bisukōto* (Port. *biscoito*).

4   **bonbon* < Dutch *bonbon* ('sweet', 'sugar-plum'). Vos. French loanword in
     Dutch, but already used in Dutch by 1785 (*WNT*).

5   *bōtoru, bōtoro* < Dutch *boter* ('butter'). Vos. ns. *batā* (Eng.).

6   *doroppu* < Dutch *drop* ('liquorice'). Vos.

7   **hamu* < Dutch *ham* ('ham'). Saitō 1798. In *Bangosen* (1798), the Japanese
     equivalent is given as *rakan*, a kind of smoked ham.

8   **kakao* < Dutch *cacao* ('cacao'). Vos. ns. also as an ingredient *kakaomasu*
     ('cacao mass').

9   *kāzu* < Dutch *kaas* ('cheese'). Vos, Saitō 1822. ns. *chīzu* (Eng.).

10   **kōhī, kohhī* < Dutch *koffie* ('coffee'). Vos 1797; Saitō *kōhī, kohhī* 1811. SK *kōhī*
     (Udagawa Yōan *et al.* 1975: 559, 204).[44] Dutch books imported into Japan

---

44   A word is also in order about the adopted Japanese pronunciation. According to Sugimoto
      (quoted in Sakagami 2000: 26), the Dutch *koffij* (*sic*) is only used in the Kansai region
      around Osaka. He argues that it is the later introduction of the English 'coffee' that gave
      rise to the standard Japanese *kōhī* which emerged from the Tokyo dialect. Unfortunately,
      he offers no evidence for this. However, if he is right, it may explain why the Japanese
      rendering has a long 'o', possibly under the influence of American English, where it is
      sometimes pronounced with a long 'o', rather than British English, which has a short 'o' for

in the eighteenth century, such as Chomel (1778–93) had the form *koffy/coffy*. The *dagregister* mentions Japanese using coffee in 1706 and 1722.

11   **kōhī-shiroppu* < Dutch *koffiesiroop* ('coffee syrup'). Vos.

12   *meruki* < Dutch *melk* ('[mother's] milk'). Vos. Van Sterkenburg 1822 (vol. 3). This was adopted despite the fact that there is a Sino-Japanese word *bonyū* (母乳), and a Japanese word *chichi* (乳) for breast milk (*bonyū* is more common). ns. for cow's milk *miruki* (Eng.) and *gyūnyū* (牛乳) (S.-J.).

13   *ponsu* < Dutch *pons* ('punch' alcoholic and non-alcoholic: 'squash'). Vos; Umegaki (1963: 68). ns. *ponchi, panchi* (Eng.).

14   *rimonāde* < Dutch *lemonade* ('lemonade'). Vos, Saitō 1822. ns. *remonēdo* (Eng.).

15   *sago* < Dutch *sago* ('sago'). Saitō 1709. (Also used in Li Shizhen's *Běncǎo Gāngmù* 本草綱目 introduced into Japan in the early seventeenth century as *Honzō kōmoku*.)

16   *sarādo* < Dutch *salade* ('salad'). Vos, Saitō 1811. ns. *sarada* (Port.).

17   **shiroppu* < Dutch *siroop* ('syrup'). Vos, Saitō 1815 (Appendix, p. 24).

18   *soppu* < Dutch *sop, soep* ('soup', 'broth'). Vos, Van Sterkenburg, Saitō all 1787. ns. *sūpu* (Eng.).

19   *wāheru* < Dutch *wafel* ('waffle'). Vos and Saitō 1855. ns. *waffuru* (Eng.).

20   *zeneifuru* < Dutch *jenever, genever* ('gin'). Vos. ns. *jin* (Eng.).

5.1.1.1.4   Mathematics (2 Words)

1   *ahuterekkingusu teken* < Dutch *aftrekkingsteken* ('minus sign'). Saitō 1850. ns. *mainasu-kigō* マイナス記号 (Eng. + S.-J.).

2   **konpasu, konpattsu* < Dutch *kompas* ('[a pair of] compass[es]'. Vos 1837; Saitō *konpassu* 1713, *konpattsu* 1765. ns. also *enki* 円規 (S.-J.). *Konpasu* is slang for legs, found in the phrase *kompasu ga nagai*, 'to have long legs', 'to walk with long strides' (Vos).

5.1.1.1.5   Medicine (35 Words)

1   *ādorurāten* < Dutch *aderlaten* ('vein-letting'); or *burūdorāten* < Dutch *bloedlaten* ('blood-letting'). Saitō 1811. ns. *hōketsu* 放血 (S.-J.), also *shaketsu* 瀉血 (S.-J.).

2   *āmubaien* < Dutch *aambeien* ('piles'/'haemorrhoids'). Saitō *āmubeien* 1811. ns. *ji* 痔 (S.-J.).

---

coffee. Dutch versions of the word invariably seem to have a short 'o'. One other possibility in this regard is that the 'o' may be long as this gives the word four *morae*, to which some Japanese words tend. I thank Takashi Chiba for this suggestion.

3 *chifusu, chipyusu* < Dutch *typhus* ('typhus'). Vos, Van Sterkenburg *teipyusu* 1833b, Saitō *chihyusu* (*ateji* and *furigana*) 1856, IX, p. 41, *chifusu* 1858b.

4 *dokutoru* < Dutch *doktor* ('medical doctor'). Vos, Van Sterkenburg and Saitō *dokutofuru* 1799, *dokutoru* 1848. ns. *dokutā* (Eng.), *isha* 医者, *ishi* 医師 (S.-J.).

5 *gasutohoisu* < Dutch *gasthuis* ('hospital'). Saitō 1787.

6 *hetto* < Dutch *vet* ('fat'). Vos, Irwin (2011: 41), Saitō *heto* 1774, *hetto* 1798. ns. *hetto* is specifically applied to beef dripping.

7 *hipokonderī* < Dutch *hypochondrie* ('hypochondria'). Vos. ns. *shinkishō* 心気症 (S.-J.).

8 *hipokonderu* < Dutch *hypochonder* ('hypochondriac'). Vos. Saitō *ipokonderu* 1822b, *hipokonderu* 1857.

9 *infuryuensa* < Dutch *influenza* ('influenza'). Vos, Saitō 1835.

10 *kataru* < Dutch *catarrh(e)* ('catarrh') (Kuiper 1993: 125).

11 *kina* < Dutch *kina* ('cinchona', 'quinine'). Vos, Saitō *ateji* and *furigana* 機那 (*kina*) 1815 Appendix p. 19, 規那 (*kīna*) 1822, 規那 (*kina*) 1851, II, p. 18.

12 *kinīne* < Dutch *kinine* ('quinine'). Vos, Saitō *ateji kuinīne* 1837, *ateji kinīne* 1856.

13 *kirīru* < Dutch *klier* ('gland'). 1774 (*Kaitai shinsho*).

14 *kirishisu* < Dutch *crisis* ('crisis' specifically of an illness). Vos 1834, Saitō 1834. ns. *kiki* 危機 (S.-J.) and *tōge* 峠 (J.).

15 *kirisuteru* < Dutch *klisteer* ('enema', 'clyster'). Vos, Saitō 1795. ns. *kanchō* 浣腸 (S.-J.).

16 *korera* < Dutch *cholera* ('cholera'). Vos 1822.

17 *koroido* < Dutch *colloïde* ('colloid'). Vos.

18 *korojion* < Dutch *collodion* ('collodion'). Vos.

19 *mararia, marariya* ('malaria') Vos lists this as a Dutch loanword but gives no source. The first Japanese source given by Saitō is dated 1904, 36 years after the end of the Tokugawa period. Saitō (1967: 141) concludes that more research needs to be done to identify when and how this loanword was first used in Japanese.

20 *masuchikku* < Dutch *mastiek* ('mastic'). Vos, Saitō *masuchiki* 1837b.

21 *merankoria* < Dutch *melancholie/melancholia* ('melancholy'). Vos, Saitō 1822. ns. *merankorī*.

22 *moruhine* < Dutch *morfine* ('morphine'). Vos, Saitō 1837.

23 *narukochine* < Dutch *narcotine* ('narcotine'). Vos, Saitō 1856, VII, p. 20. ns. *narukochin* (Eng.).

24 *pappu, *happu* < Dutch *pap* ('cataplasm', 'poultice'). Saitō 1822b in *ateji* (琶布).

25   *pepushine* < Dutch *pepsine* ('pepsin'). Vos. Saitō 1867. ns. *pepushin* (Eng.).

26   **pesuto* < Dutch *pest* ('plague'). Vos 1856, Saitō 1834. ns. also *kokushibyō* 黒死病 (S.-J.), 'the disease of the black death' (a translation from Dutch or Eng.).[45]

27   **pinsetto* < Dutch *pincet* ('a pair of tweezers'). Vos, Saitō 1848.

28   **ransetto* < Dutch *lancet* ('lancet'). Vos, Saitō 1799, also 1798. This is a 'continuation' of *ransetta* from the Portuguese *lanceta* (Vos). The primary use now is for the medical journal.

29   **repura* < Dutch/Latin *lepra* ('leprosy'). Vos, Saitō 1857. ns. also *rai-byō* 癩病 (S.-J.) and *hansen-byō* ハンセン病) (Eng. and S.-J. hybrid, cf. Hansen's disease).

30   *reumachisu, reyumachisushusu* < Dutch *re(u)matijs, r(h)eumatismus* ('rheumatism'). Saitō *reyumachisushusu* 1848, *reumachi* 1856. ns. *riumachi*.

31   **rinpa* < Dutch *lymfe* ('lymph'). Vos, Saitō *rīnpa* 1856, XIII, p. 16.

32   *santonīne* < Dutch *santonine* ('santonin'). Vos. ns. *santonin* (Eng.).

33   **supoito* < Dutch *spuit* ('syringe'). Vos, Saitō 1795, Van Sterkenburg 1773 (private letter). *Supoito* also referred to a water pump (1804, XII, p. 42).

34   **sutorikinīne* < Dutch *strychnine* ('strychnine'). Vos, Saitō *sutorīshinine* 1837, *sutorīkunine* 1844.

35   **teriaka* < Dutch *triakel* ('theriac'). Saitō 1695.

5.1.1.1.6   Physics, incl. Meteorology, Metrology and Astronomy (27 Words)

1   *baromētoru* < Dutch *barometer* ('barometer'). Vos, Van Sterkenburg *baromeiteru* 1798c, Saitō 1848. ns. *baromētā* (Eng.) or *seiukei* 晴雨計 (S.-J.).

2   **ereki, erekiteru, erekishiteito* < Dutch *electriciteit* ('electricity'). Vos, Saitō *erekiteri* 1765. *erekiteru* used in the Edo period for electricity generator. ns. *denki* 電気 (S.-J.).

3   *erekiterumētoru* < Dutch *elektrometer* ('electrometer'). Saitō 1837. ns. *den'ikei* 電位計 (S.-J.), *erekiterumētā* (Eng.).

4   **eru* < Dutch *el* ('ell', 'yard'). Vos.

5   **ēteru, āteru* < Dutch *ether, aether* ('aether'). Vos. Saitō *aeteru* 1811, *āteru* 1837, *ēteru* 1869.

6   *garamu* < Dutch *gram* ('gram'). Vos. ns. *guramu* (Eng.).

7   *gerein* < Dutch *grein* ('grain'; as a weight). Vos, Saitō 1822.

8   **gurosu, gorosu* < Dutch *gros* ('gross', twelve dozen). Vos.

9   *hauhenhaito, hārenhaito* < Dutch *Fahrenheit* ('Fahrenheit'). Saitō 1822. ns. *ka-shi* 華氏 (S.-J.).

---

45   *pesuto* is given in *Bangosen* (1798).

10   *hēguromātoru* < Dutch *hygrometer* ('hygrometer'). Saitō 1822, SK
     (Udagawa Yōan *et al.* 1975: 558, 59). ns. *shitsudo-kei* 湿度計 (S.-J.) *shitsudo*
     'moisture', *kei* 'meter'.

11   *hekuto* < Dutch *hektometer* ('hectometre'). Saitō *hekuto* (*ateji*) 1862;
     hekutomēteru 1869. ns. *hekutomētoru*.

12   *kērukiringu* < Dutch *keerkringen* ('tropics'). Saitō 1823. ns. *kaikisen* 回帰線
     (S.-J.).

13   *kērukiringu han stēnbokku* < Dutch *keerkring van (den) steenbok* (lit.
     'tropic of goat', i.e., capricorn). Saitō 1823. ns. *minami kaikisen* 南回帰線
     (J. and S.-J.).

14   *kiro[garamu]* < Dutch *kilo[gram]* ('kilogram'). Saitō 1862. The subsequent
     influence of other West European languages on the use of *kiro[garamu]*
     must be acknowledged. ns. *kiroguramu*.

15   *kiro[mēteru]* < Dutch *kilo[meter]* ('kilometre'). Saitō 1862. The subsequent
     influence of other West European languages on the use of *kiro[mēteru]*
     must be acknowledged. ns. *kiromētoru*.

16   *magunēto* < Dutch *magneet* ('magnet'). Vos. ns. *magunetto* (Eng.) and
     ji-shaku 磁石 (S.-J.).

17   **manteru* < Dutch *mantel* ('mantle', 'cloak'). Vos, Saitō, Van Sterkenburg,
     mantoru 1713, *manteru* 1848. ns. also *manto* from French *manteau*, pos-
     sibly also influence of Portuguese *manto*.

18   *marusu* < Dutch *Mars* ('Mars'). Van Sterkenburg 1787. ns. *ka-sei* 火星.

19   **mētoru* < Dutch *meter* ('metre'). Vos, Saitō 1862. ns. also *mētā* (E.).

20   *mirurigaramu, miruri* < Dutch *milligram* ('milligram'). Vos, Saitō *miruri*
     1850. ns. *miriguramu*.

21   *mirurimēteru* < Dutch *millimeter* ('millimetre'). Saitō 1862. ns. *mirimētoru*,
     miri.

22   **pondo* < Dutch *pond* ('pound' (weight)). Irwin 1637, Vos 1781, Saitō *pondo*
     1804–14, *pon* 1822b.[46]

23   **ranpu* < Dutch *lamp* ('lamp'). Vos, Saitō *gasuramupu* ('gas lamp') 1851,
     VII, p. 9.

---

46   Irwin (2011: 39) gives his source as the NKD. This in turn records that *pondo* is mentioned
     in *Tenba ibun* (天馬異聞) by Yoshio Joen (vol. 18, p. 254), based on an account of the
     Shimabara Rebellion originally written by Nicolaes Couckebakker in 1637/8. One problem
     here is that Yoshio Joen (also Gonnosuke) compiled *Tenba ibun* in the early nineteenth
     century (this is Saitō's source). So, the question arises as to whether *pondo* was mentioned
     in a Japanese text in 1637, or rather in a Dutch text (as *pond*), which was only subsequently
     translated into Japanese. This is not clear and requires further investigation.

24 *renzu* < Dutch *lens* ('lense'). Vos.[47]

25 *ryukutoponpu* < Dutch *luchtpomp* ('air pump'). Saitō 1798c. ns. *kūkiponpu* 空気ポンプ (S.-J./Dutch hybrid).

26 *ryukutoshikippu* < Dutch *luchtschip* ('air ship'). Van Sterkenburg 1787, Saitō 1798c. ns. *kikyū* 気球 (S.-J.).

27 *senchimētoru* < Dutch *centimeter* ('centimetre'). Vos. Saitō 1850. ns. abbreviated to *senchi*.

5.1.1.1.7 Seafaring (11 Words)

1 **bui* < Dutch *boei* ('buoy'). Vos. ns. also *fuhyō* 浮標 (S.-J.) (lit. floating sign).

2 *dekki* < Dutch *dek* ('deck'). Vos, Irwin 1857.

3 **dokku* < Dutch *dok* ('dock'). Vos 1854. Saitō 1855.

4 **kīru* < Dutch *kiel* ('keel of a ship'). Vos. ns. also *ryūkotsu* 竜骨 (lit. dragon's (spinal) bone).

5 **konpasu* < Dutch *compas* ('[a mariner's] compass'). Vos 1837, Saitō 1798b, 1798. ns. also *rashinban* 羅針盤 (S.-J.).

6 **madorosu, matorosu* < Dutch *matroos* ('sailor'), Van Sterkenburg *matarausu* 1750; *matarosu* 1787.

7 **masuto* < Dutch *mast* ('mast'). Vos 1848, Saitō 1848.[48]

8 *okutanto* < Dutch *octant* ('octant') Vos, Saitō 1798c. ns. *hachibungi* 八分儀 (S.-J.).

9 *sutōmu bōto* < Dutch *stoomboot* ('steamship') 1830s (Tsukahara 2007b: 200). ns. *kisen* 汽船 (S.-J.), lit. 'steam boat'.

10 *sutōmu shikippu* < Dutch *stoomschip* ('steamship'). Saitō 1854, p. 30. ns. also 蒸気船 *jōkisen* (S.-J.).

11 *tarappu* < Dutch *trap* ('staircase'), used in sense of 'ship's ladder' or 'gangway'). Vos.

5.1.1.1.8 Engineering (Umegaki 1963: 68, from Isomura 1929) and Weaponry (21 Words)

1 **baito* < Dutch *beitel* ('bite' as a tool). Vos. ns. also used as an abbreviation of *arubaito* (< German, Arbeit), 'side-work'.

2 *bakku* < Dutch *bak* ('cistern', 'tank'). Vos. ns. *tanku*.

3 *bōtō* < Dutch *bout* ('bolt'). Vos. ns. *boruto*, also 'volt'.

---

47 *Renzu* occurs in *Saikoku risshihen* (1870–71) by Nakamura Masanao. This was based on an English work by Samuel Smiles. Irwin (2011: 39) gives a date of 1785 but does not give a primary source.

48 *Masuto* is given in *Bangosen* (1798). The Japanese equivalent is given as *hobashira* in *kanji* (帆柱) and *furigana*.

4   *darai < Dutch draaibank ('lathe'). Saitō darāibanku 1862. ns. also darai-
     ban ダライ盤 (Dutch draai ('turn') + S.-J. ban) and senban 旋盤 (S.-J.).

5   fusuke < Dutch hoekijzer ('angle iron').[49] Vos. ns. angurubarokku ('angle
     block').

6   hakka < Dutch haak ('hook'). Vos.

7   *karan < Dutch kraan ('tap', 'cock', 'faucet'). Vos 1854. Saitō peirukarān
     (pijlkraan) (kanji and furigana 1854, p. 22). ns. also (suidō no) ja-guchi
     (水道の) 蛇口 (lit. (water supply) snake mouth).

8   keitoru < Dutch ketel ('steam-boiler'). Vos. ns. boirā (Eng.).

9   kereppu < Dutch klep ('valve'). Vos.

10   ketchin < Dutch ketting ('chain'). Vos. ns. chēn (Eng.).

11   mōru < Dutch moer ('nut' a negative screw). ns. neji 螺子 (S.-J.); natto
     ('nut') (Eng.). Vos.

12   moruchūru, mortier ('mortar' (gun)). Vos. ns. morutaru (Eng.).

13   passuru < Dutch passer ('a pair of compasses'). Vos. ns. kompasu (Eng.).[50]

14   patoron, hatoron < Dutch patroon ('paper cartridge'). Vos.

15   peresu < Dutch pers ('press'). Vos.

16   *ponpu < Dutch pomp ('pump'). Vos, Saitō, Van Sterkenburg all 1798c.

17   *rosutoru < Dutch rooster. Vos 1. gridiron (still in use for this); 2. grate of
     a stove.

18   *sāberu < Dutch sabel ('sabre', cavalry sword). Vos.

19   sukoine < Dutch schuin ('sloping', 'slant'). Vos.

20   sukorufu < Dutch schroef ('screw'). Vos. ns. sukuryū (Eng.).

21   supī < Dutch spie ('pin', 'wedge', 'peg'). Vos. ns. kī (Eng.).

5.1.1.1.9   Positions Held by Europeans at Deshima (7 Words)
These are listed by the Edo-born printer Isono Bunsai in Nagasaki miyage
('Souvenirs of Nagasaki', 1847). Written in katakana.

1   deisubenshiru < Dutch dispencier ('storehousekeeper')

2   hofumēsutoru < Dutch hofmeester ('steward')

3   kabitain < Dutch opperhoofd (kabitain from Portuguese)

4   konsuttēburu < Dutch constabel ('constable')

5   ondorumēsutoru < Dutch ondermeester ('junior merchant')

6   roitonanto < Dutch luitenant ('lieutenant')

7   teinmeruman < Dutch timmerman ('carpenter')

---

49   I have only found this example in Vos. The metathesis of k and s/z is unexpected.
50   Passuru is used for a wire-device for fishing.

5.1.1.1.10   Miscellaneous (49 Words)

1   *afutēkeningu* < Dutch *aftekening* ('drawing') (1805, IX, p. 15)

2   **dansu* < Dutch *dans* ('dance'). Vos.

3   *doitsu* < Dutch *Duits* ('German') (Irwin, 1725).[51] Used in Japanese for 'Germany'. 1798 (*Bangosen*) gives *Zerumaniya* (< Latin) or *hōgodoitsu* (< Dutch *Hoog-Duits* 'High German') for 'Germany'.

4   *donkurukāmuru* < Dutch *donkere kamer* (lit. 'dark room', *camera obscura*). Van Sterkenburg 1798, Saitō 1799. See also Screech (1996: 57). ns. *anbako* 暗箱 (S.-J. + J.)

5   **dontaku* < Dutch *zondag* ('Sunday' see above). Vos.

6   **erikishiru, erikisuru* < Dutch *elixir* ('elixir'). Vos, Saitō 1828.

7   *ettsen* < Dutch *etsen* ('etching'). Saitō 1811. ns. *etchingu suru* (Eng. + J.).

8   **furan'neru, furano* < Dutch *flanel* ('flannel'). Vos, Saitō 1856, XIII, p. 3. Also abbreviated as *neru*, an example of 'clipping' (Winford 2003: 50).

9   *gatto* < Dutch [*man*]*gat* ('manhole'). Vos, Umegaki (1963: 69). ns. *manhōru* (Eng.), *jinkō* 人孔 (S.-J.).

10   *gorofuguren* < Dutch *grofgrein* ('grosgrain'). Vos, Saitō 1799.

11   *gyuruden* < Dutch *gulden* ('guilder'). ns. *girudā* (Eng.).

12   *hōgorō, bōgoru* < Dutch [*struis*]*vogel* ('ostrich'). Vos. ns. *dachō* 駝鳥 (S.-J.).

13   **hokku* < Dutch *hoek* ('hook', 'clasp', 'hook-and-eye'). Vos.

14   *hottentotto* < Dutch *hottentot* ('hottentot'). Khoikhoi Africans. Saitō 1855.

15   **inku, inki* < Dutch *inkt* ('ink'). Van Sterkenburg 1798d, Vos *inki* 1800, Saitō *inkito* 1837; *inki* 1848; *inku* 1854b.

16   **kaban* ('bag' or 'satchel') < Dutch *kabas* meaning 'basket' or 'sack'. Vos.[52]

17   **kamereon* < Dutch *kameleon* ('chameleon'). Vos, Saitō *kameron* 1799b.

---

51   With reference to the NKD Irwin (2011: 41) gives 1725 as the first attestation of *doitsu*. See also Vos (2014: 163). *Doitsu* also occurs in Kutsuki Masatsuna's *Seiyō senpu* (1787).

52   Vos (1963: 363) writes that *kaban* derives from the Dutch *kabas*. There is reference to 'harte-vellen *cabesses*', i.e., deerskin bags/sacks, on a bill of lading at Nagasaki from October 1646 (*Diaries*: x:8), and to *zijdecabessa* ('bag of silk') on a bill of lading reproduced by the *opperhoofd* Andreas Cleyer (Cleyer 1985: 72), which seem to support this view. However, in a later article Vos (2000b: 300) recognizes that viewing *kaban* as a direct loanword from Dutch is problematic. For example, one might expect it to be adopted into Japanese as *kabasu* or *kabase*, etc. Vos suggests that it was a reading of Sinitic characters as *kabansu*, with the final -*su* being dropped, which might have led to the form *kaban*. Another possibility is that it evolved from one or both Chinese words 夾板 (Jap. *kyōban*, Ch. *jiábǎn*) or 夾慢 (*kyaman/jiāmàn*), and possibly reinforced by the Dutch *kabas*. In time the character 鞄 (Mandarin *páo*) which refers to tanned leather, was applied to it. However, one is then left to ask why the character for *páo* was used and not the characters for the other Chinese words. Vos concludes by asking whether this could be a case of 'contamination of *kabas* with *jiaban*'? He does not, however, answer the question. The fact that *kaban* has been written with *katakana* is suggestive of some Dutch influence, although again not conclusive. Finally, this word has been adopted by Korean as *kabang*.

18 *kan < Dutch kan ('can', 'tin'). Vos, Ishiguro (1963: 32).

19 kanon < Dutch kanon ('cannon'). Van Sterkenburg 1714. Saitō 1786. ns. kyanon (Eng.). See also kanon-hō below.

20 *kantera, kanteira < Dutch kandelaar ('candle-stick'), used in the sense of 'metal hand-lamp'. Vos, Van Sterkenburg kantera 1719, Saitō kantera, kanderrāru 1799. Possible influence of Portuguese candeia.

21 kapperu < Dutch kachel ('stove'). In the Nagasaki dialect, this was formerly called kāheru. Vos.

22 *kokku < Dutch kok ('cook'). Vos 1615.

23 komuma < Dutch komma ('comma'). Vos, Saitō 1783 (publ. 1788). ns. konma.

24 *koppu < Dutch kop ('cup') (also influence of Port. copo). Vos 1617, Saitō 1724. In Bangosen (1798), this appears in the hybrid Japanese word 臺コップ t/dai-koppu, which is given the Dutch equivalent kerukei (< Dutch kruk 'jug').

25 *manna < Dutch manna ('manna'). Saitō 1822. Written in katakana and ateji 満那.

26 *mesu < Dutch mes ('scalpel'). In Dutch mes is a general word for knife, but in Japanese it is specifically used for a surgical instrument. Vos, Saitō 1799. Van Sterkenburg 1798.

27 *morumotto < Dutch marmot ('marmot', 1. marmot, 2. guinea pig). Vos. ns. 1. māmotto (Eng.), 2. morumotto.

28 *musuku < Dutch musc/Latin muscus ('musk'). Vos, Saitō musuku 1713. ns. jakō 麝香 (S.-J.).

29 *orugōru, orugoru, orukoru, orukōru < Dutch orgel ('organ'). Van Sterkenburg 1802. Vos. ns. only used in the sense of 'music box'. The word for a 'standard' organ is orugan.

30 *paretto < Dutch palet ('palette'). Vos, Saitō 1811. Originally for art, but also now for shipping pallet.

31 *pen < Dutch pen ('pen'). Van Sterkenburg 1798b. Here, in Seiiki monogatari ('Tales of the West') Honda Toshiaki observes that in the West the brush is called a pen.

32 *penki, pekki, pikki < Dutch pek, pik ('pitch', 'tar'). Vos. ns. only used in the sense of 'paint'.[53]

33 *perikan < Dutch pelikaan ('pelican'). Vos.

34 *pisutoru < Dutch pistool ('pistol'). Vos 1837, Saitō pesutoru 1713, pisutōru 1837. ns. also kenjū 拳銃 (S.-J.).

35 pottorōdo < Dutch potlood ('lead-pencil'). Vos. ns. enpitsu 鉛筆 (S.-J.).

---

53 The 'n' in penki may be the result of prenasalization.

36   *raketto < Dutch raket ('racket' (for sport)). Van Sterkenburg 1787.

37   *randoseru < Dutch ran(d)sel ('knapsack', 'satchel'). Vos, Van Sterkenburg 1856b. ns. specifically backpack for school children.

38   *raten, ratein < Dutch Latijn ('Latin'). Vos, Saitō raten-no-go ラテンの語 1714. ns. also Dutch + S.-J. hybrid raten-go ラテン語 (lit. Latin + language).

39   reiperu < Dutch lepel ('spoon') 1799. ns. supūn (E.) and saji 匙 (J.).

40   *retteru < Dutch letter ('letter', i.e., character). Vos, Saitō 1811. ns. only used in the sense of 'label'.

41   rēyū < Dutch leeuw ('Leo'). Saitō 1848. ns. also reo < Latin leo and shishi-za しし座 (S.-J.).

42   rūpuru, rūfuru < Dutch roeper ('trumpet'—used for a loudspeaker or megaphone). Vos, Van Sterkenburg 1750.[54] ns. megahon (Eng.).

43   Shina. In the later Edo period, Japanese authors rendered 'China' with the word Shina, rather than the more normal Chūgoku (中国), from the Chinese Zhōngguó. One such author was Sugita Genpaku in his essay 'The Words of a Mad Doctor' (Kyōi no gen) (1775) (Boot 2011: 45 n. 12). Towards the end of the Edo period, a Japanese nationalist thinker, Ōkuni Takamasa (1792–1871) rendered 'China' in kanji as Shina (支那) rather than Chūgoku (中国) (lit. 'the middle (of the world) kingdom'). Kornicki suggests that this probably reflected Takamasa's knowledge of the pronunciation of 'China' in Dutch. His aim was to indicate that China was a country like any other, shorn of its privileged position in East Asian history. The term was used widely in Japan until the end of the Second World War, but subsequently fell into disuse as it was perceived to be derogatory (Kornicki 2018: 13). A Korean equivalent written in hanja (also 支那) was used from the end of the nineteenth century.

44   *sukoppu < Dutch schop ('shovel', 'scoop') Van Sterkenburg 1848. ns. shaberu or shoberu (< Eng. shovel) is more common.[55]

---

54   There is a picture of a rūpuru in Kōmō zatsuwa (Morishima Chūryō and Ōtsuki Gentaku 1972: 62). This was sounded when Dutch ships entered Nagasaki Bay. Irwin (2011: 41) writes that the Japanese rappa ('trumpet') is a loanword from the Dutch roeper with a date of first use as 1684. However, it is more likely to be a borrowing from the Chinese 喇叭 lăba. The same characters are used in Japanese. The rectangles indicate these are phonograms. The word probably came as a loanword from Mongolian into Chinese and then to Japanese. The Chinese author Qi Jiguang (1528–88) used it to refer to a sort of military musical instrument. However, unusually for loanwords from Chinese, it is often written in katakana in Japanese, viz. (ラッパ).

55   Irwin (2011: 41) gives a much later date of 1905. However, it is unlikely that a Dutch loanword would have been written for the first time at such a later date.

45 *tāfuru, tāheru* < Dutch *tafel* ('table'), both in the sense of a piece of furniture and in the sense of a tabulated statement. Vos 1615, Saitō 1615.[56]
Saitō 1750. ns. *tēburu*.

46 *wātorureideingu* < Dutch *waterleiding* ('plumbing') (1804, XII, p. 36).

47 *wātorumōren* < Dutch *watermolen* ('watermill') (1804, XII, p. 40).

48 *zeneraru* < Dutch *generaal* ('general', 'field officer'). Van Sterkenburg 1695.

49 **zukku, doukku, jukku* < Dutch *doek* ('canvas'). Saitō 1855. ns. *zukku*.
Vos suggests that the word-initial 'z' is the result of progressive assimila-
tion. It is also a function of the fact that historically Japanese has lacked
*[duɯ].

5.1.1.2   'Loanblends' (46 Words)
5.1.1.2.1   Compound Blends (Imported Morpheme and Native Morpheme)[57]
5.1.1.2.1.1   Botany (6 Words)

1 **aroe-nankō* アロエ軟膏 'aloe oil' < Dutch *aloë* + S.-J. *nankō* 'ointment'/'salve'.

2 **barusamu-momi* バルサム樅 'balsam fir' < Dutch *balsem* + J. *momi* 'fir
tree'.

3 **koruku-gashi* コルク樫 'cork oak' < Dutch *kurk* + J. *kashi* 'oak tree' (k > g
between vowels)

4 **koruku-nuki* コルク抜き 'corkscrew' < Dutch *kurk* + J. *nuki* 'drawing out'.
Vos.

5 *koruku-soshiki* コルク組織 'cork tissue' < Dutch *kurk* + S.-J. *soshiki* 'tissue'.

6 **koruku-zōri* コルク草履 'cork-soled sandals' < Dutch *kurk* + S.-J. *zōri* 'traditional sandals'.

5.1.1.2.1.2   Chemistry (18 Words)
The names of many chemical elements in Japanese are Dutch loanwords.
Therefore, many chemical compounds are compound blends. The follow list
is not exhaustive.

1 **en-ka-kobaruto* 塩化コバルト 'cobalt chloride' < S.-J. *en* 'salt' + *ka* 'change'
+ Dutch *kobalt*.

---

56   Saitō gives his source as *Nagasaki miyage* 長崎土産. There is more than one work with
this title, but he gives the author as Isono Nobuharu (磯野信春), an alternative name
for Isono Bunsai (文斎). His *Nagasaki miyage* was published in 1847. Saitō does not give
a page number. There is mention of *tāfuru* on p. 27, but no mention of the date 1615 (NIJL
ID 48613, Kerlen 1098, Ser. 303).

57   Contact-induced words in Japanese which consist of morphemes drawn from more than
one language are called *konshugo* (混種語) (Irwin 2011: 14).

2   *fūzeru-yu フーゼル油 'fusel oil' < Dutch foezel[olie] + S.-J. yu 'oil'. Vos. Saitō 1862.

3   *kadomiumu-chūdoku カドミウム中毒 'cadmium poisoning' < Dutch kadmium + S.-J. chūdoku 'poisoning', also 'addiction'.

4   *kasei-arukari 苛性アルカリ 'caustic alkali/lye', < S.-J. kasei caustic + Dutch alkali. Often shortened to kasei-kari.

5   *kei-san ケイ酸 'silicic acid' < Dutch kei(aard) 'silica' + S.-J. san 'acid'.

6   *kei-seki ケイ石 (also 珪石) 'silica', < Dutch kei(aard) 'silica' (kei = 'rock'/'hard') + S.-J. seki ('stone'). Saitō kei-to 珪土 1822; kei-to 珪土 (keiārudo) < Dutch keiaard 1837; kei-to 珪土 (kīseruārudo) < Dutch kiezelaard 1862.

7   kobaruto-ka コバルト華 'cobalt bloom' < Dutch kobalt + S.-J. ka 'flower'.

8   *moribuden-kō モリブデン鋼 'molybdenum steel' < Dutch molybdeen + S.-J. kō 'steel'.

9   *nikkeru-kō ニッケル鋼 'nickel steel' < Dutch nikkel + S.-J. kō 'steel'.

10   Raiden-bin ライデン瓶 'Leyden or Leiden jar' < Dutch Leiden + S.-J. bin 'jar/bottle'. Saitō 1851, XI, p. 11.

11   *richiumu-denchi リチウム電池 'Lithium battery' < Dutch lithium + S.-J. denchi 'battery'.

12   *sanka-kuromu 酸化クロム 'Chromium oxide' < S.-J. san 'acid' + ka 'change' + Dutch chroom.

13   *suiso-gasu 水素瓦斯 (ガス gasu in katakana) 'hydrogen gas' < S.-J. sui 'water' + so element + Dutch gas < Dutch waterstofgas. Saitō 1822.

14   *tansan-gasu 炭酸ガス 'carbonic acid' < S.-J. tan 'carbon' + san 'acid' + Dutch gas (based on Dutch koolzuurgas/koolstofzuregas (coal + sour (acid) + gas)). Saitō 1822. This is a combination of a loan translation (tansan) and a 'pure loanword' gasu. Likewise, the next two.

15   *tansan-kariumu 炭酸カリウム 'potassium carbonate' < S.-J. tan 'carbon' + san 'acid' + Dutch kalium (potassium) (Kuiper 1993: 127).

16   *tansan-karushūmu 炭酸カルシウム 'Calcium carbonate $CaCO_3$' < S.-J. tan 'coal' + san 'acid' + Dutch calcium.

17   *terebin-yu テレビン油, terupenyu テルペン油 'oil of terpentine' < Dutch terpentijn + S.-J. yu 'oil'. Vos.

18   toshigasu 都市ガス 'town/municipal gas' < S.-J. toshi 'town' + Dutch gas.

5.1.1.2.1.3   Medicine (6 Words)

1   *akiresu-ken アキレス腱 'Achilles' tendon' < Dutch Achilles(pees) ('Achilles' tendon') + S.-J. ken 'tendon'. Vos, Saitō akirisu-ken 1774.

2　*eusutakisu-kan エウスタキス管 'Eustachian tube' < Dutch Eustachius + S.-J. kan ('tube'), (Dutch: Eustachiaanse buis). Vos, Saitō 1811. ns. S.-J. jikan 耳管 and eusutakio-kan.

3　*hosshin-chifusu 発疹チフス 'typhus epidemic' < S.-J. hosshin 'rash' + Dutch typhus ('typhus').

4　*pappu-zai パップ剤 'cataplasm' < Dutch pap ('cataplasm') + S.-J. zai 'medicine'.

5　*rinpa-sen リンパ腺 'lymph gland' < Dutch limfe + sen (kanji for Dutch klier—gland—see above).

6　*rui-sen 涙腺 'tear gland', S.-J. rui 'tear' + sen kanji < Dutch klier. (Other glands are formed in a similar fashion in Japanese).

5.1.1.2.1.4　Miscellaneous (16 Words)

1　*doitsu-bunka ドイツ文化 'German culture' < Dutch Duits ('German') + S.-J. bunka culture.

2　*doitsu-go ドイツ語 'German language' < Dutch Duits + S.-J. go language.

3　*doitsu-jin ドイツ人 'German person' < Dutch Duits + S.-J. jin person.

4　*garasu-bari ガラス張り 'glass-sided', 'above board' < Dutch garasu ('glass') + J. hari 'to stretch'.

5　*garasu-e ガラス絵 'stained glass' < Dutch garasu + J. e 絵 'art'.

6　*han-don 半ドン 'Saturday', 'half-day holiday' < S.-J. han half + Dutch zon(dag) 'Sunday'. Vos. Used in Kyoto Prefecture and the Kansai region.

7　*hatoron-shi ハトロン紙 'kraft paper' < Dutch hatoron (patroon 'paper cartridge') + S.-J. shi paper. So-called as kraft paper resembles that used for paper cartridges. Vos.

8　*inu-safuran 犬サフラン 'meadow saffron (Colchicum autumnale)' < J. inu dog + Dutch saffraan saffron.

9　*kanon-hō カノン砲 'cannon' < Dutch kanon cannon + S.-J. hō cannon, gun. ns. taihō 大砲 (S.-J.). Vos.

10　*kan-zume 缶詰 'canned food' < Dutch kan + J. zume packing/stuffing. Vos.

11　kōhīmame コーヒー豆 'coffee bean', < Dutch koffie + J. mame bean.

12　*men-furan'neru 綿フランネル 'cotton flannel' < S.-J. men 'cotton' + Dutch flannel.

13　*men-neru 綿ネル 'cotton flannel' < S.-J. men 'cotton' + Dutch (flan)nel.

14　*penki-nuri ペンキ塗り 'painting (of buildings)' < Dutch pek 'pitch' + S.-J. nuri 'to coat'.

15　*penki-ya ペンキ屋 'painter (of buildings)' and 'paint shop' < Dutch pek 'pitch' + S.-J. ya (shop and person who sells).

16   *zukku-gutsu ズック靴 'canvas shoes' < Dutch *doek* 'canvas' + J. *kutsu* 'shoes'.

5.1.2   Loanshifts (127 Words)

5.1.2.1   'Extensions' (5 Words)

1   *byō* 秒 (S.-J.) 'second'. Saitō 1798c. In Chinese, this character was used for various types of measures, but by the Song dynasty it was used to refer to a small angle.[58] In *Rekishō shinsho*, Shizuki Tadao wrote that there were 60 秒 in one 分 (see below), and so it came to mean 'second'.

2   *fun* 分 (S.-J.) 'minute'. Saitō 1798c. *Fun* means 'part'. It was used to indicate that there were 60 分 to one hour by Shizuki Tadao in *Rekishō shinsho*, and so it came to mean 'minute'.

3   *toki* 時 (J.) *ji* (S.-J.) 'hour'. Saitō 1798c. In *Rekishō shinsho*, Shizuki Tadao writes that in one 時 there are 60 分. 時 has also been applied to grammatical tense, possibly derived from the Dutch *tijd* 1856c. ns. *jisei* 時制 (S.-J.).

4   *kaku* 格 (S.-J.) 'grammatical case'. Saitō 1811b. The core meaning of *kaku* is 'law' or 'method'. In older Dutch grammars, nouns have four cases. In 1856c, the four cases are rendered in Japanese using *kaku* for 'case' (Dutch *naamval*).

5   *kapitan* < Portuguese *capitão* ('captain [of a ship]'). Extension to mean Dutch *opperhoofd*. In 1610, *kapitan* is used for Jacob Jansz. Quaeckernaeck in the official Japanese record, *Zōtei ikoku nikki shō* ('Selections from the diary on foreign affairs'). This is the first use of the term in a Japanese text relating to the Dutch, although Quaeckernaeck was not in fact the *opperhoofd* but rather the captain of the *Liefde* (Jacques Specx was *opperhoofd*) (Saitō 1967: 103). By the late seventeenth century as evidenced by Bashō's *haiku* (1678) it was being used by Japanese to refer to the *opperhoofd*.

5.1.2.2   'Loan Translations' (122 Words)

5.1.2.2.1   Chemistry (32 Words)

In several books published in the first half of the nineteenth century, authors such as Udagawa Genshin and his son, Udagawa Yōan, present words for chemical terms, which are loan translations or calques based on Dutch terminology. For example, in 1822 they presented the word *suiso* (水素) in *Ensei ihō meibutsukō* ('Reflections on Far Western Medical Terminology'). *Suiso* means

---

58   Shen Kuo 沈括 (1033–97) used it in this manner in *Mèng Xī Bǐtán (xiàngshù, èr)* 梦溪笔谈 (象数, 二). I thank Koos Kuiper for this information.

'hydrogen'. The Dutch term is *waterstof*, literally 'water matter/element'. *Suiso* is a morpheme-by-morpheme translation of this: *sui* water, *so* element. This again illustrates that it is often easier to determine the constituent morphemes of a Dutch word than of, say, the English or French equivalent.

In 1837, Yōan began to publish the multi-volume *Seimi kaisō* ('Principles of Chemistry'). This presented for the first time many words associated with chemistry, which are still in use in cMJ, appeared. A modern edition of *Seimi kaisō* gives some 1,000 entries which include 'pure loanwords' as well as loan translations. While some may owe something to Latin as well as Dutch, if this figure is relatively accurate it would mean that the total figure of 3,000 mentioned above is not so exaggerated as it at first seems (Udagawa Yōan *et al.* 1975: 550–63). The list below includes loan translations for chemistry, which are Sino-Japanese. Many of these are drawn from *Ensei ihō meibutsukō* (1822) and *Seimi kaisō* (1837).

Two morphemes that occur in several words are *-so* (素) 'element(ary)' and *-san* (酸) 'acid'. As a result of the translation of Dutch chemistry texts, they became established as affixes and are still productive in Japanese (Earns 1993: 61–64).

1   *aen-ka 亜鉛華 'zinc powder', *aen* zinc + *ka* flower < Dutch *zinkbloem* ('zinc powder'—lit. 'zinc flower'). Saitō 1822, 1828 (*furoresu shinki* < Latin: *Flores zinci* 1811).

2   *chisso 窒素 'nitrogen', *chitsu* obstruct + *so* element < Dutch *stikstof* (lit. 'choke' + 'matter'). Saitō 1822.

3   *en-san 塩酸 'hydrochloric acid', *en* salt + *san* acid < Dutch *zoutzuur* ('salt' + 'acid'). Saitō 1837.

4   *gen-so 元素 'element', *gen* origin + *so* elementary < Dutch *grondstof* + *hoofdstof* ('principal' + 'matter'). Saitō 1822. Here, alongside *genso, hoofdstof* is rendered in *katakana* as *hōfudosutofu*.

5   *gi-san 蟻酸 'formic acid', *gi* ant + *san* acid < Dutch *mierenzuur* ('ant' + 'acid'). Saitō 1857.

6   *hō-so 硼素 'borium', *hō* 'borax' + *so* element' < Dutch *boraxstof* ('borax' + 'matter') (Udagawa Yōan *et al.* 1975: 552, 179–180).

7   *in-kyoku 陰極 'cathode', *in* negative + *kyoku* pole < Dutch *negatieve pool* ('negative pole') (Kuiper 1993: 129 n. 28).

8   *iō-ka 硫黄華 'sublimed sulphur', *iō* sulphur + *ka* flower < Dutch *zwavelbloem* or *bloem van zwavel* (*zwavel* = sulphur, *bloem* = flower). Saitō 1834.

9   *jōryū-sui 蒸留水 'distilled water', *jōryū* distillation + *sui* water < Dutch *overgehaalde water* ('distilled' + 'water'). Saitō 1834.

10   *jū-do 重土 'barium oxide', 'heavy clay', jū heavy + do earth < Dutch zwaaraarde ('heavy' + 'earth'). Saitō 1822. Also ns. sanka-bariumu 酸化バリウム (loan translation + gairaigo)

11   kan-kō 甘汞 'calomel', 'Mercury (I) Chloride', kan sweet + kō mercury < Dutch zoete-kwik ('sweet' + 'mercury'). Saitō 1811.

12   *ka-yō 可溶 'soluble', ka can + yō dissolve < Dutch oplosbaar ('dissolve' + 'able'). Saitō 1837.

13   *kin'iō 金硫黄 'red sulphur', kin gold + iō sulphur < Dutch goudzwavel ('gold' + 'sulphur'). Saitō 1828.

14   mukiseitai 無機性体 'inorganic body' < Dutch onbewerktuigde Lichaam. Saitō 無機性体 onbewerukitoigude-tai 1833. ns. mukishitsu 無機質 used for inorganic matter.

15   *niyō-san 尿酸 'uric acid', niyō urine + san acid < Dutch piszuur ('urine' + 'acid'). Saitō 尿酸 1837, 尿酸 pisushūru 1862.

16   *rai-gin 雷銀 'fulminating silver', rai thunder + gin silver < Dutch donder-zilver ('thunder' + 'silver', a precipitate formed by a reaction of silver and ammonia) (Udagawa Yōan et al. 1975: 277).

17   *rin-san 燐酸 or リン酸 'phosphoric acid', rin phosphorus + san acid < Dutch phosphorzuur ('phosphorus' + 'acid'). Saitō 1822.

18   *ryū-dō-tai 流動体 'liquid', ryū flow + dō move + tai substance < Dutch vloeistof ('flow' + 'matter'). Saitō 1825.

19   *ryū-san 硫酸 'sulphuric acid', ryū sulphur + san acid < Dutch zwavelzuur ('sulphur' + 'acid'). Saitō 1822.

20   *saku-san 酢酸 'acetic acid', saku vinegar + san acid < Dutch azijnzuur ('vinegar' + 'acid') (Udagawa Yōan et al. 1975: 559).

21   *san-so 酸素 'oxygen', san acid + so element < Dutch zuurstof ('acid' + 'matter'). Saitō 1837.

22   *sei-bun 成分 'component', sei consist of + bun part < Dutch bestanddeel ('complete' (see WNT) + 'part') (Udagawa Yōan et al. 1975: 400), Saitō 1837.

23   *shō-san 硝酸 'nitric acid', shō nitrate/saltpeter + san acid < Dutch sal-peterzuur ('saltpeter' + 'acid'). Saitō 1833, 1837 (Udagawa Yōan et al. 1975: 162).

24   *shu-seki 酒石 'tartar', shu alcohol/sake + seki stone < Dutch wijnsteen ('wine' + 'stone'). Saitō 1822.

25   *shu-seki-san 酒石酸 'tartaric acid', shu alcohol/sake + seki stone + san acid < Dutch wijnsteenzuur ('wine' + 'stone' + 'acid'). Saitō 1834.

26   sui-en 水鉛 'molybdenum', sui water + en lead < Dutch waterlood ('water' + 'lead'), an old Dutch word for molybdenum.

27 *sui-so 水素 'hydrogen', sui water + so element < Dutch waterstof ('water' + 'matter'), Saitō 1822.

28 *tan-san 炭酸 'carbonic acid', tan carbon + san acid < Dutch koolzuur ('coal' + 'acid'). Saitō 1822.

29 *tan-so 炭素 'carbon', tan carbon + so element < Dutch koolstof ('coal' + 'matter'). Saitō 1822.

30 yashi-yu 椰子油 'palm oil', yashi palm + yu oil < Dutch palm-olie ('palm' + 'oil'). Saitō yashi-yu 椰子油 also parumu ōrī 1828. Now used for coconut oil.

31 *yō-kai 溶解 'dissolution, chemical solution', yō dissolve + kai untie < Dutch oplossen. Saitō 溶解 oppurossen (oplossen) 1837. This has an element of native creation.

32 *yō-kyoku 陽極 'anode', yō positive + kyoku pole < Dutch positieve pool ('positive pole') (Kuiper 1993: 129 n. 28).

5.1.2.2.2   Grammatical Terms (11 Words with Reference to a Further 16)

Prior to the nineteenth century, Japanese translators had not yet devised equivalents for Dutch grammatical terms. When translating a Dutch translation of a work by Engelbert Kaempfer at the very start of the nineteenth century, the accomplished rangakusha Shizuki Tadao struggled to render the Dutch equivalent of 'adverb' in Japanese (Mervart 2015: 9).[59] At this time, other Japanese translators became aware of the need to study Dutch grammar more closely and they began to develop Japanese equivalents for Dutch parts of speech such as 'adverb'. Some early attempts were rather unwieldy but by the middle of the century, loan translations had been developed which are still used in standard contemporary Modern Japanese.

Several rangakusha coined grammatical terms based on those in Dutch grammars that circulated in Japan. Mitsukuri Genpo coined loan translations which form the basis of the modern Japanese names for grammatical terms. Genpo based these on terms in Siegenbeek's Grammatica of Nederduitsche Spraakkunst, which he re-printed in 1842 with the Japanese title Oranda bunten zenpen ('Dutch grammar Part I') (5,000 copies were printed). In 1856, Oranda bunten jirui 和蘭文典字類 (zenpen 前編) was published by Iizumi Shijō (1856c, see fig. 25). This contains a small grammar which includes many of the terms coined by Genpo. Genpo's terms were published with refinements by Nakagane Masahira (dates unknown) in Yamatogogaku tebikigusa ('Guide for the study of the Japanese language', 1871), and by Ōtsuki Fumihiko (1847–1928) in Kō Nihon bunten ('Comprehensive Japanese grammar', 1897). This cemented

59   The Late Modern Dutch for 'adverb' is bijwoord.

their place in the Japanese lexis (Vos 2000a: 103–104). While these terms have been categorized here as loan translations, some of them, such as *kanshi* (article) are not close translations but have an element of native creation.[60]

1 **dai-mei-shi* (代名詞) 'pronoun', *dai* stands for/substitutes + *mei-shi* noun < Dutch *voornaamwoord* (instead of + noun), c. 1800, used by Genpo 1842.[61] 1856c lists six types of pronoun, which include *dai-mei-shi*, e.g. **jin-dai-mei-shi* 人代名詞 for personal pronoun (人 *jin* = person (S.-J.)).

2 **dō-shi* (動詞) 'verb' *dō* movement/action + *shi* word < Dutch *werkwoord* (work + word). Genpo 1842, 1856c. There are also compound words of which *dō-shi* is a component. 1856c has eight such words, e.g. **sai-ki-dō-shi* 再帰動詞 'reflexive verb' < Dutch *wederkeerig werkwoord*.

3 **fuku-shi* (副詞) 'adverb', *fuku* aiding + *shi* word < Dutch *bijwoord*. Genpo 1842, 1856c.

4 **ji-dō* (自動) 'intransitive (verb)', *ji* self + *dō* move < Dutch *bedrijvende* or *onzijdige* (*werkwoord*) (terms used by the grammarians Sewel and Weiland). Saitō 1811b. ns. *ji-dō-shi* 自動詞.

5 *jo-shi* (助詞) 'auxiliary verb', *jo* help + *shi* (詞) word < Dutch *hulpwerkwoord* (lit. 'help work-word') 1856c. The meaning of *jo-shi* has changed over time, and it now refers to 'enclitic non-inflected bound elements' or 'grammatical particles' (Miller 1967: 315). Other grammatical terms have been developed of which *jo-shi* forms a part, for example *kaku-jo-shi* 格助詞 for 'case-marking particle'.

6 **kan-shi* (冠詞) 'article', *kan* capping/crowning + *shi* word < Dutch *lidwoord* (joint word). Genpo 1842, 1814 (Kuiper 1993: 133). 1856c has Japanese words for 'definite article' and 'indefinite article', which are still used today, viz. *tei-kan-shi* 定冠詞 (Dutch *bepaald lidwoord*) and *fu-tei-kan-shi* 不定冠詞 (Dutch *onbepaald lidwoord*). It is probable that the Japanese terms are based on the Dutch terms.

7 **kei-yō-shi* (形容詞) 'adjective', *kei* form + *yō* appearance + *shi* word < Dutch *bijvoeg(e)lijk naamwoord* (added [to] noun). Genpo 1842, 1856c.

8 **mei-shi* (名詞) 'noun', *mei* name + *shi* word < Dutch *naamwoord* (lit. name word). Genpo 1842, 1857c (*jitsu*) *meishi* (true noun) < Dutch *zelfstandig naamwoord* (lit. 'independently-existent name-word'), Ōtsuki Fumihiko *mei-shi* 1897.

---

60 For a detailed account of the development of grammatical terms in Japanese see Saitō (1985: 77–217).

61 Miller (1967: 315) records that the word *daimeishi* (代名詞) was first used in Japanese in around 1800.

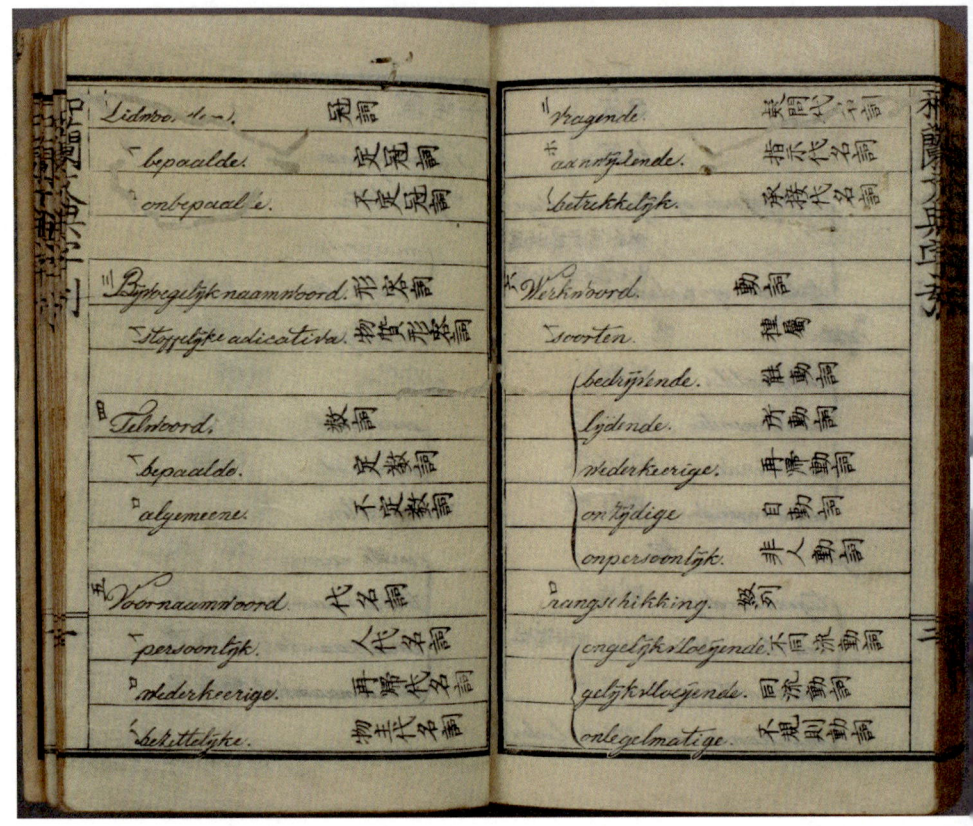

FIGURE 25   Dutch grammatical terms with Japanese equivalents. *Oranda bunten jirui* 和蘭文典字類
(*zenpen* 1856c). Iizumi Shijō
WUL 文庫 08 C0538

9   *setsuzoku-shi* (接続詞) 'conjunction', *setsuzoku* connection + *shi* word <
Dutch *voegwoord* (join word). Genpo 1842, 1856c.

10   *sū-shi* (数詞) 'numeral', *sū* 'count/number' + *shi* word < Dutch *telwoord*
(count/number word). Genpo 1842, 1856c.

11   *zen-chi-shi* (前置詞) 'preposition' *zen* before + *chi* placed + *shi* word
< Dutch *voorzetsel* (a particle placed before (a noun)). Genpo *zenshi*
(before-word) 1842. 1856c has *zen-chi-shi*.

5.1.2.2.3   Medicine and Anatomy (53 Words)

1   *bi-yoku* 鼻翼 'nostrils', *bi* 'nose' + *yoku* 'wing(s)' < Dutch *neusvleugels*
(nose + wings). Saitō 1875. ns. also *kobana* 小鼻, *bikō* 鼻孔.

2   *bo-han* 母斑 'birthmark', *bo* 'mother' + *han* 'spot' < Dutch *moedervlek*
(mother + spot). Vos, Saitō 1815, I, p. 13.

3   *byō-in 病院 'hospital', byō 'illness' + in 'public building'. Vos.[62]

4   *chi-kotsu 恥骨 'pubic bone', chi 'shame' + kotsu 'bone' < Dutch *schaamte-been* (shame + bone). Saitō 1826.

5   *chō-shinkei 聴神経 'auditory nerve', chō 'to hear' + shinkei 'nerve' < Dutch *gehoorzenuw* (hear + nerve) (Kuiper 1993: 128).

6   *dō-myaku 動脈 'artery', dō 'move' + myaku 'vein' < Dutch *slagader* (beat + vein). Saitō 1774.

7   *gi-maku 偽膜 'pseudo-membrane', gi 'false' + maku 'membrane' < Dutch *schijnvlies* (apparent + membrane). Saitō 1866b.

8   *hen-tō-sen 扁桃腺 'tonsils', hen-tō means 'almond' < Dutch *amandelen* (tonsils) + sen 'gland' (Kuiper 1993: 128).

9   *i-eki 胃液 'gastric juice', i 'stomach' + eki 'juice' < Dutch *maagsap* (stomach + juice) (Kuiper 1993: 128).

10   *i-tsū 胃痛 'gastralgia/stomach cramp', i 'stomach' + tsū 'pain' < Dutch *maagkramp* (stomach + cramp). Vos, Saitō 1866. ns. also fuku-tsū 腹痛 (S.-J.) for a general abdominal pain.

11   ji-kai 耳介 'auricle', ji 'ear' + kai 'shellfish' < Dutch *oorschulp* (ear + scallop). Vos, Saitō 1826. ns. also jikaku 耳殻 (S.-J.).

12   *ji-shi 示指 'index finger', ji 'indicate' + shi 'finger' < Dutch *wijsvinger* (point + finger). Saitō 1774. ns. also hitosashiyubi 人差し指 (J. more common in general usage).

13   *jūni-shi-chō 十二指腸 'duodenum', jūni 'twelve' + shi 'finger' + chō 'intestine' < Dutch *twaalfvingerige darm* (twelve-finger + intestine (bowel), i.e., 'duodenum'). Vos, Saitō 1774.

14   *kagyū-kaku 蝸牛殻 'cochlea', kagyū 'snail' + kaku 'husk/shell' < Dutch *slakkenhuis* (snail + house). Saitō 1826.

15   *kai-ketsu-byō 壊血病 'scurvy', kai 'break' + ketsu 'blood' + byō 'sickness' < Dutch *scheurbuik* (break + stomach). Saitō 1815, I, p. 8.

16   *kaku-maku 角膜 'cornea', kaku 'horn (anatomy)' + maku 'membrane' < Dutch *hoornvlies* (horn + membrane). Saitō 1815, I, short desc. p. 3.

17   *kan-shi 環指 'ring finger', kan 'ring' + shi 'finger' < Dutch *ringvinger*. Saitō 1774. ns. also kusuri-yubi 薬指 (J.)

---

62   In *Kōmō zatsuwa* (1787), Morishima Chūryō quotes a Chinese translation of the equivalent of the Dutch *gasutohoisu*: *Minjin byōin to yakusu* (明人病院と訳す, 'The Ming Chinese translate it as *byōin*'). How this Chinese translation came to replace the Dutch *gasutohoisu* in the Japanese lexis would require further investigation (Kaiser 1996: 24; Morishima Chūryō and Ōtsuki Gentaku 1972: 27). It does also at least raise the question of whether Vos is right to assert that this is a Dutch loan translation in Japanese. Unfortunately, he gives no source with which to explore this matter further.

18   *ka-soku 加速 'acceleration', ka 'addition' + soku 'speed' < Dutch versnelling (making quicker, i.e., acceleration) 1798c (Aikawa et al. 2007: 28).

19   *kekkyū 血球 'blood cell', ketsu 'blood' + kyū 'ball' < Dutch bloedbolletje (little blood ball). Saitō 1822b, Kuiper (1993: 128 n. 26).

20   *ken-shi 犬歯 'canine tooth', ken 'dog' + shi 'tooth' < Dutch hondstand (dog + tooth). Saitō 1826b.

21   *ketsu-maku 結膜 'conjunctiva', ketsu 'bind' + maku 'membrane' < Dutch bindvlies (join + membrane). Saitō 1774.

22   *ko-chō 鼓脹 'tympanites, flatulence', ko '(hand)drum' + chō 'intestines' < Dutch trommelzucht (drum + swelling). Saitō 1822b.

23   *ko-maku 鼓膜 'eardrum, tympanic membrane', ko '(hand)drum' + maku 'membrane' < Dutch trommelvlies (drum + membrane). Saitō 1774.

24   *kō-sai 虹彩 'iris', kō 'rainbow' + sai 'colouring', < Dutch regenboogvlies (rainbow + membrane). Saitō 1815. This has an element of native creation.

25   *kō-tō 喉頭 'larynx', kō 'throat' + tō 'head' < Dutch strottenhoofd (throat/gullet + head). Saitō 1811.

26   *kyō-maku 鞏膜 or 強膜 (ns. more usual) 'sclera', kyō 'hard/strong' + maku 'membrane' < Dutch hardevlies ('hard' + 'membrane'). Saitō 強膜 1774, 鞏膜 1826 also in katakana harude furīsu (no 'v' in Japanese).

27   *kyō-maku 胸膜 'pleura', kyō 'breast' + maku 'membrane' < Dutch borstvlies ('breast' + 'membrane'). Saitō 1774.

28   *kyō-sui-byō 恐水病 'hydrophobia', kyō 'fear' + sui 'water' + byō 'illness' < Dutch hydrophobie, watervrees (water + fear). Saitō kyōsuibyō 1828, haidorohobia, watoru furēsu 1822b. ns. also kyōsuishō 恐水症 shō 'symptom' (S.-J.).

29   *kyū-shinkei 嗅神経 'olfactory nerve', kyū 'small' + shinkei 'nerve' < Dutch reukzenuw (smell + nerve). Saitō 1826.

30   mekura-ji 盲痔 'anal fistula', mekura 'blind' + ji 'anal fistula', < Dutch blinde fistel (blind + fistula) Vos. Saitō 盲痔漏 mekura-ji-rō (no date).

31   *mō-chō 盲腸 'appendix', mō blind + chō intestine < Dutch blinde darm (lit. 'blind' + 'intestine'). Vos, Saitō 1774.

32   mō-jō-kan 毛状管 'capillary tube', mō 'hair' + jō 'form' + kan 'tube' < Dutch haarbuis(je) (hair + tube (dim.)). Saitō 1851. ns. mō-sai-kan 毛細管.

33   *mō-maku 網膜 'retina', mō 'net' + maku 'membrane' < Dutch netvlies (net + membrane). Saitō 1774.

34   *mon-myaku 門脈 'portal vein', mon 'door' + myaku 'vein' < Dutch poortader (gate/door + vein). Saitō 1774.

35   *nan-kotsu 軟骨 'cartilage', nan 'flexible' + kotsu 'bone' < Dutch kraakbeen (crack + bone). Saitō 1774.

36   *nen-eki-shu 粘液腫 'myxoma', nen 'sticky' + eki 'fluid' + shu 'tumour/swelling' < Dutch slijmgezwel (mucus + swelling). Saitō 1822b.

37 *nen-maku 粘膜 'mucous membrane', nen 'sticky' + maku 'membrane' < Dutch slijmvlies (mucus + membrane). Saitō 1774.

38 *nō-maku 脳膜 'cerebral membrane' nō 'brain' + maku 'membrane' < Dutch hersenvlies (brain + membrane). 1805 (Kuiper 1993: 128).

39 *roku-maku 肋膜 'pleura', roku 'rib' + maku 'membrane' < Dutch ribbevlies (rib + membrane), Saitō 1811.

40 *rui-kan 涙管 'tear duct', rui 'tear' + kan tube < Dutch traanbuis (tear + tube). Saitō 1815.

41 *rui-sen 涙腺 'tear gland', rui 'tear' + sen 'gland' (see above) < Dutch traanklier (tear + gland). Saitō 1815.

42 ryō-tō-kin 両頭筋 'biceps', ryō 'both' + tō 'head' + kin 'muscle' < Dutch tweehoofdige spier (two-headed + muscle). Saitō 1774. ns. nitōkin 二頭筋 (S.-J. 1875).

43 *san-han-ki-kan 三半規管 'semi-circular canals' (in the inner ear), san 'three' + han 'half' + kikan 'round tube' < Dutch driehalfrondebuizen ('three semi-circular tubes'). Saitō 1774, 1826 hankisankan.

44 *shak-kotsu 尺骨 'ulna', shaku Japanese foot (as a measure, in the sense of the Dutch 'el') + kotsu 'bone' < Dutch elleboogsbeen ('elbow bone', i.e., 'ulna'). Vos.

45 *shi-kaku 視角 'optic angle', shi 'vision' + kaku 'angle' < Dutch gezichtshoek ('vision' + 'angle').

46 *shi-shinkei 視神経 'optic nerve', shi 'vision' + shinkei 'nerve' < Dutch gezichtszenuw (vision + nerve) (Kuiper 1993: 128).

47 *shojo-maku 処女膜 'hymen', shojo 'virgin' + maku 'membrane' < Dutch maagdevlies (maiden/virgin + membrane). Vos, Saitō 1857.

48 *shō-nō 小脳 'cerebellum', shō 'small' + nō 'brain' < Dutch kleine-hersenen ('small-brain'). Saitō 1826.

49 *shōshi-tai 硝子体 'vitreous humour' shōshi 'vitreous' + tai 'substance' < Dutch glaslichaam ('glass body'). Saitō 硝子液 (shōshi-eki 'vitreous fluid') 1815, I, p. 5. ns. also garasu-tai ガラス体 (loanblend).

50 taiki-no-atsuryoku 大気の圧力 (shortened to taikiatsu 大気圧) 'atmospheric pressure' taiki 'atmosphere' + no (of) + atsuryoku 'pressure' < Dutch luchtdruk/atmospherische druk. Saitō 1822. ns. kiatsu 気圧.

51 *tsuchi-kotsu 槌骨 'malleus', 'hammer' (bone in inner ear), tsuchi hammer + kotsu bone < Dutch hamer. Saitō 1826.

52 *ya-mō 夜盲 'nightblind(ness)', ya 'night' + mō 'blind' < Dutch nachtblind (night + blind). Saitō 1855b. Often used with shō 症 (symptom): yamōshō 夜盲症.

53 *za-yaku 座薬 'suppository', za 'seat' + yaku 'medicine' < Dutch zet-pil ('place pill'). Saitō 1822b. ns. also za-zai 坐剤.

5.1.2.2.4 Physics, Mathematics and Astronomy (17 Words)

1. *ba-riki 馬力 'horsepower', ba 'horse' + riki 'power' < Dutch paardenkracht (horse + power). Saitō 馬ノ力 1851, X, p. 19.

2. *bun-shi 分子 'molecule', bun 'part' + shi 'child' (diminutive) < Dutch molecule/molecuul (molecule). Saitō 1798c.

3. bun-shi-riki 分子力 'molecular force', bun 'part' + shi 'child' (diminutive) + riki 'force/power' < Dutch moleculaire kracht. Saitō 1869. bunshikanryoku 分子間力 (intermolecular force) is still used.

4. *chō-ryoku 張力 'tension', chō 'snap' + ryoku 'power' < Dutch veerkracht (spring + power). Saitō 1798c.

5. *dan-ryoku 弾力 'elasticity', dan 'stretch' + ryoku 'power' < Dutch uitzettingsvermogen (expansion + power). Saitō 1822.

6. *enshinryoku 遠心力 'centrifugal force', en 'distant' + shin 'heart'/'centre' + ryoku 'force' < Dutch middelpuntvliedende kracht (centre-fleeing + power). Saitō 1798c.

7. *futtō-ten 沸騰点 or futten 沸点 'boiling point', futsu 'boil' + ten 'point' < Dutch kookpunt, kokendpunt (boiling + point). Saitō futtō-ten 1833; futten 1854.

8. *in-ryoku 引力 'gravitation', 'attraction', in 'pull' + ryoku 'power' < Dutch aantrekkingskracht (drawing + power). Saitō 1798.

9. *jitsu-dō 実動 'real motion', jitsu 'truth' + dō 'motion' < Dutch ware beweging (true + motion). 1823.

10. *jū-ryoku 重力 'gravity', jū 'heavy' + ryoku 'power' < Dutch zwaartekracht ('weight power'). Saitō 1798c.

11. *ka-fu 加符 'plus sign +', ka 'addition' + fu 'sign' < Dutch optellingsteken ('addition sign'). Saitō opputeruringusu tēken 1850, ka-fu 1858.

12. *kan-sei 慣性 'inertia', kan 'to accustom' + sei 'nature' < Dutch traagheid ('slowness'). 1823–28 (Kuiper 1993: 130).

13. *kenbi-kyō 顕微鏡 'microscope', ken 'appear' + bi 'minuteness' + kyō 'glass'. Dutch mikroskoop. Saitō 1822 (1787 mikorasukōbyun) (see fig. 26).[63]

14. *kikai-gaku 機械学 'mechanics', kikai 'instrument' + gaku 'study' < Dutch werktuigkunde ('instrument science'). Saitō 1851, VII, p. 12.

15. *kōsei-jitsu 恒星日 'sidereal day', kōsei 'fixed star' + jitsu 'day' < Dutch sterredag (star + day). Saitō 1798.

---

63. The katakana ヒ is marked with a dakuten. In cMJ, this would necessarily be voiced, i.e., [bi]. It is possible however that a speaker of Japanese would have known that it should be unvoiced, i.e., [pi]. The handakuten, which indicates an unvoiced consonant, had been introduced by the Portuguese in the sixteenth century, but was only gradually adopted by Japanese authors (Frellesvig 2010: 165).

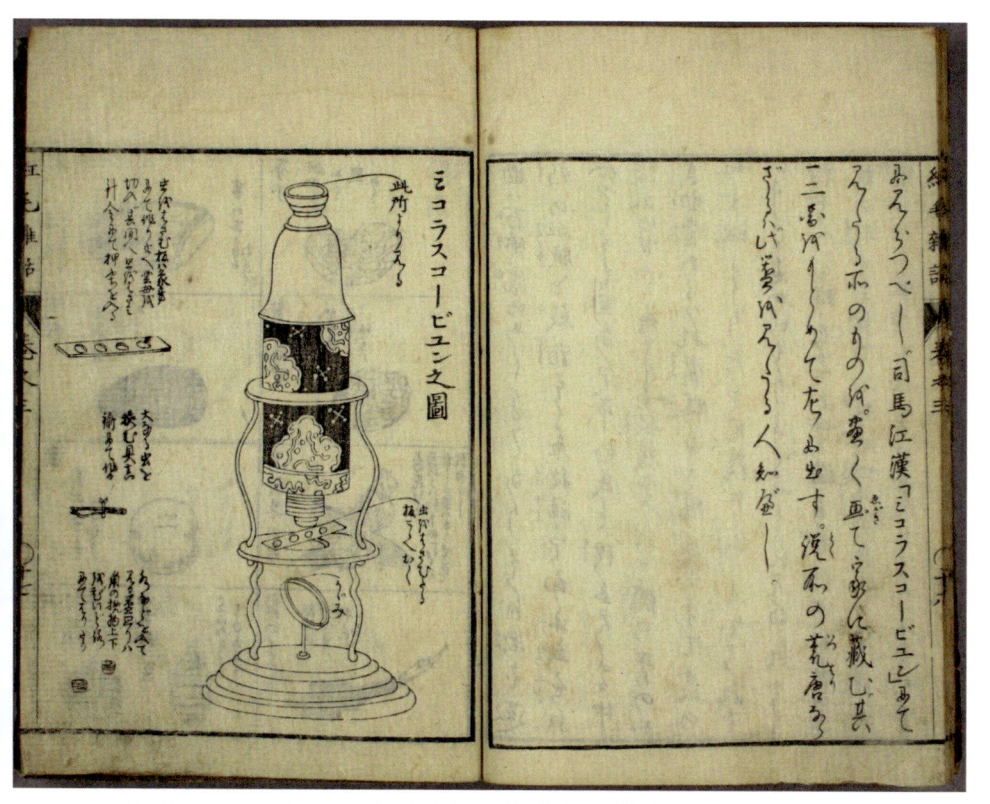

FIGURE 26   A microscope with the word in *katakana* (ミコラスコービュン, *mikorasukōbyun*) in *Kōmō zatsuwa* ('Red-haired Miscellany', 1787), Morishima Chūryō, vol. 3
WUL 文庫 17 W0217

16   *kyūshin-ryoku 求心力 'centripetal force', *kyū* 'seek' + *shin* 'heart'/'centre' + *ryoku* 'force' < Dutch *middelpuntzoekende kracht* (lit. 'centre-seeking power'). Van Sterkenburg *mitterupunto sūkende karakuten* 1784; Saitō 1798c.

17   *shi-dō 視動 'apparent motion', *shi* 'seeing' + *dō* 'motion' < Dutch *schijn-bare beweging* (apparent + motion). Saitō 1823.

5.1.2.2.5   Miscellaneous (9 Words)

1   *jū-tai* 獣帯 'zodiac', *jū* 'animal' + *tai* 'belt' < Dutch *dierenriem* (animals + girdle ('zodiac')). Vos; Saitō 1823 also gives *jūren rīmu* (from *dierenriem*).

2   *kai-gun 海軍 'navy', *kai* 'sea' + *gun* 'armed force' < Dutch *zeemacht* (sea + power). Vos.

3   *kai-sō 海葱 'sea onion', *kai* 'sea' + *sō* 'onion' < Dutch *zeeajuin* (sea + onion). Saitō 1822.

4 *nyū-san 乳酸 'lactic acid', nyū 'milk' + san 'acid' < Dutch melkzuur (milk + acid). Saitō 1866.

5 *nyū-tō 乳糖 'lactose', nyū 'milk' + tō 'sugar' < Dutch melksuiker (milk + sugar). Saitō 1822.

6 *nyū-zai 乳剤 'emulsion', nyū 'milk' + zai 'dose'/'emulsion' < Dutch melk drank (milk + drink). Saitō 1828.

7 *shiki-so 色素 'pigment', shiki 'colour' + so 'matter' < Dutch kleurstof (colour + matter) (Kuiper 1993: 128).

8 *shoku-min 植民 'colonization', shoku planting + min people < Dutch volk(s)planting (people + planting). Vos pre-1801. (Kuiper 1993: 131).

9 *sōzō-ryoku 想像力 'power of the imagination', sōzō 'imagination' + ryoku 'power' < Dutch verbeeldingskracht (imagination + power). Saitō 1857.

5.2 Native Creations (89 Words)
These have no counterpart in the donor language, i.e., Dutch.

5.2.1 Purely Native Creations (22 Words)
5.2.1.1 Miscellaneous (16 Words)
1 *bō-en-kyō 望遠鏡 'telescope', bōen 'far off'/'distance' + kyō mirror < Dutch verrekijker, telescoop (viewer + afar). Vos, Saitō 1765 (device referred to by circumlocution), 1798 bōenkyō and furukeikeru (verrekijker in katakana). ns. also teresukōpu (Eng.).

2 *bu-dō-shu 葡萄酒 'wine', budō 'grape' (ateji, but also written in hiragana) + shu 'alcohol' < Dutch wijn (wine). Saitō 1713. ns. wain (Eng.) more common.

3 chū-tō 柱頭 'stigma (top of pistil in a flower)', chū trunk + tō head < Dutch stempel ('stigma'), 1822c (Kuiper 1993: 132).

4 *dai-ki 大気 'atmosphere', dai 'big' + ki 'air', Saitō 1822, 1851 (x, p. 19), to render Dutch atmosfeer (Kuiper 1993: 132).

5 dōkō gōitsu 同好合一 'commonwealth', dōkō 'friendly communion' + gōitsu 'unity' so 'unity of friendly communion', coined by Shizuki Tadao to render the Dutch gemeenebest ('commonwealth') into Japanese, when translating an appendix to Engelbert Kaempfer's history of Japan from Dutch into Japanese (Mervart 2015: 27–28). ns. renpō 連邦 (S.-J.).

6 ka-chū 花柱 '(flower) style', ka flower + chū trunk/post < Dutch stijl ('style') 1822c (Kuiper 1993: 132).

7 mizu-sama-ha 水様波 'aqueous humour', mizu water + sama like + ha wave < Dutch waterachtig (oog)vocht (water-like + (eye)moisture). Saitō 1774. ns. bōsui 房水 (S.-J.).

8   *on-do 温度 'temperature', on warm + do degree, to render Dutch *tempe-ratuur* (Kuiper 1993: 132).

9   *sa-koku 鎖国 sa chain + koku country, coined by Shizuki Tadao to ren-der the Latin *regnum clausum* ('closed kingdom') into Japanese, a phrase used in an appendix to Engelbert Kaempfer's history of Japan to refer to Japan's isolation.

10   *sa-kotsu 鎖骨 'clavicle', sa chain + kotsu bone < Dutch *sleutelbeen* (key + bone). Saitō 1826.

11   *san-ka 酸化 'oxide' (san acid + ka change) is a Japanese native creation based on the Dutch *oxyde*. It was used by Udagawa Yōan in *Shokugaku keigen* (1833), and again in *Seimi kaisō* (1837) (Saitō 1967: 184; Udagawa Yōan *et al.* 1975: 558). There are many oxides of which this forms a part, e.g., sanka-dō 酸化銅, copper oxide; ni-sanka-tanso 二酸化炭素 carbon di-oxide; sanka-tetsu 酸化鉄 iron-oxide (Saitō 1822).

12   *sen 腺 (new *kanji*) 'gland' < Dutch *klier*. Saitō 1805, p. 109. This *kanji* is a combination of two meanings: 'spring (inside the human body)' and 'meat' (Kuiper 1993: 123; Earns 1993: 51).

13   *sen-i 繊維 'fibre', sen 'cloth woven from tree fibres' + i 'fibrous tree' < Dutch *vezel* (fibre). Saitō 1805.

14   *sha-shin-jutsu 写真術 'photography', sha 'copy' + shin 'true' + jutsu 'art/skill'. Saitō 写真鏡 (lit. 'photo mirror') 1851. Van Sterkenburg: first use of *fotogarahī* in 1858; Saitō 撮影術 *fotogarapī* 1862. ns. also *shashin*.

15   *shin-kei 神経 'nerve'. This word was coined by Sugita Genpaku to trans-late the Dutch *zenuw*. It means 'spiritual meridian', suggesting that nerves were in some sense the meridian paths along which the *shin* or spirits that controlled the body passed. Saitō, Van Sterkenburg 1774.

16   *shō-ka 昇華 'sublimation', shō rise up + ka flower (Dutch = *sublimeeren*). Saitō 1837.

5.2.1.2   *Zodiac Signs and Constellations (6 Words)*

Japanese authors created several words based on terms in Western languages used for both zodiac signs and constellations, such as Capricorn and Taurus. Initially, one term with the suffix -kyū 宮 denoting 1/12 of the sun's orbit was used. In time, another term with the suffix -za 座 emerged. These can be used somewhat interchangeably for the zodiac signs and constellations, although -za 座 is more common.

1   *hakuyōkyū 白羊宮 'Aries', 'the Ram'. haku white + yō sheep + kyū zodiac sign < Dutch *ram*. Saitō 1823. ns. also *ohitsujiza* 牡羊座 (J. + S.-J.)

2   *jinbakyū 人馬宮 'Sagittarius' jin person + ba horse + kyū zodiac sign < Dutch *schutter* ('archer'). Saitō 1811. ns. also *iteza* 射手座 (J. + S.-J.).

3 *kin'gyūkyū 金牛宮 'Taurus', kin gold + gyū cow + kyū zodiac sign < Dutch
   stier. Saitō 1765 taurisu, 1823 金牛宮 (suchiru (stier) in katakana). ns. also
   oushiza 牡牛座 (J. + S.-J.).

4 *makatsukyū 磨羯宮 'Capricorn' < Dutch steenbok. Saitō 1811. ns. also ya-
   giza 山羊座 (J. + S.-J.).

5 *sōgyokyū 双魚宮 'Pisces', sō pair + gyo fish + kyū zodiac sign < Dutch
   Vissen. Saitō bishisu < Dutch visschen (fish) 1765. ns. also uoza 魚座 (J. +
   S.-J.), paishīzu.

6 tenkatsukyū 天蠍宮 'Scorpio', ten heaven/sky + katsu scorpion + kyū zodiac sign < Dutch schorpioen. Saitō 1823. ns. also sasoriza 蠍座 (J. + S.-J.).

5.2.2   Hybrid Creations (Used to Express Foreign Concepts) (47 Words)
5.2.2.1   Food and Drink (3 Words)
1 *jaga-imo じゃが芋 'potato' < Jaga(tara) (Jakarta) whence the Dutch
   brought potatoes to Japan + imo (J.) 'tuber'. Saitō 1836, Nakamura (2005:
   190).[64]

2 *kinka-hamu 金華ハム 'Jinhua ham' < kinka (S.-J.) 'Jinhua' + Dutch ham.

3 *renzu-mame レンズ豆 'lentil' < Dutch lens + mame 'legume' (J.).

5.2.2.2   Oranda[65] (35 Words)
In Tokugawa Japan, many hybrid words were formed with the morpheme
Oranda, or a shortened form, Ran or Oran. These morphemes were used not
only to identify things from or related to Holland, but also to Europe more generally or even outside East Asia. Strictly speaking, Oranda is in fact a Portuguese
loan-morpheme. However, words incorporating it are included here as they
are closely related to the story of the Dutch in Japan. Here are some examples
of each:

5.2.2.2.1   Oran (1 Word)
1 Orangasa Western umbrella, J. kasa 傘 'umbrella' (Nagasaki dialect)
   (Feenstra Kuiper 1922: 259); Vos (2014: 156) has rangasa in the Kagoshima
   and Okinawa Prefectures.

---

64 Assendelft de Coningh (1856: 44) refers to potatoes that were imported into Japan as
    'Java-aardappelen'.

65 Oranda (written in hiragana) is used in a Japanese memorandum (oboe) addressed to the
    Dutch dated to 1621 (Viallé and Cryns 2018: 26).

FIGURE 27   A Dutchman (*Orandajin/ooranwdazin*) on horseback, Utagawa Yoshifuji, 1861
RIJKSMUSEUM, AMSTERDAM

5.2.2.2.2   *Oranda* (24 Words)

In earlier texts, *Oranda* was rendered using the *ateji* 阿蘭陀. This form gradually fell out of favour to be replaced by 和蘭 although the first form was still used in titles (De Groot 2005: 48 n. 8).[66] In more modern usage, it is rendered with *katakana*, viz. オランダ語 (*oranda-go* 'Dutch language'). In what follows only the suffixes are rendered in Japanese script.

1   *Oranda-ahiru* 家鴨 'Dutch duck'. Vos.

2   *Oranda-ayame* 菖蒲 'Dutch iris' (Iris x hollandica)'.[67]

3   **Oranda-bashi* 橋 'Dutch bridge' in Hirado.

4   **Oranda-bei* 塀 'The Dutch Wall' used to separate the Dutch trading post in Hirado from the prying eyes of local residents.

5   *Oranda-genge* a type of clover. ns. *kurōbā* クローバー (Dutch) clover (Irie 1987: 26).

6   **Oranda-go* 語 'Dutch language'. *Oranda* + S.-J. *go* language.

7   *Oranda-hakka* 薄荷 'spearmint (Mentha spicata)'.

8   *Oranda-ichigo* 苺 (Fragaria x ananassa). ns. *Ichigo*.

9   *Oranda-imo* 芋 'potato' (Irie 1987: 26).

10   **Oranda-jin* 人 'Dutchman/woman'. In Nagasaki it denotes a foreigner (Vos). See fig. 27.

11   *Oranda-kijikakushi* 雉隠 'asparagus' (Irie 1987: 26).

12   **Oranda-mame* 豆 'Dutch beans' = French beans/haricots in Fukushima.

13   *Oranda-megane* 眼鏡 'Dutch glasses', a device which allowed viewers to see pictures in perspective.

14   *Oranda-mitsuba* 三葉 'celery'. ns. *serori* or *serorī* (Eng.). Vos.

15   *Oranda-ō-me* 大目 'Dutch big eyes'. In his account of Japan, Thunberg refers more than once to the fact that the Japanese described Europeans with this phrase on account of what they perceived to be their large and round eyes (Screech 2005: 88).

16   *Oranda-sekichiku* 石竹 'Dutch pink'. Carnation (Irie 1987: 26).

17   *Oranda-shiru* 'Dutch/Western style' (Irie 1987: 26).

18   *Oranda-shōgatsu* 正月 'Dutch New Year' (the solar as opposed to the lunar New Year, Irie 1987: 26).

19   *Oranda-suisen* 'A beautiful woman' (Irie 1987: 26).

20   *Oranda-sumi* 墨 'ink' (Irie 1987: 26).

21   *Oranda-tōji* 冬至 lit. Dutch winter solstice. Irie (1987: 26) equates this to Christmas.

---

66   In some cases, only 蘭 was used. In *Nagasaki miyage*, this *kanji* is employed as an affix with the *furigana oranda*.

67   Also used for gladiolus.

22   *Oranda-yuki* 行 'girls who go to the Dutch', i.e., the prostitutes who visited the Dutch at Deshima.

23   *Oranda-zaka 坂, or 'Dutch slope' in Nagasaki.

24   *Oranda-zeri 芹 lit. Dutch parsley (Dutch *peterselie Petroselinum crispum*). Vos, Saitō 1828. In *Oranda yakkyō* (1828–30) it was written 洋芹 *yō-seri* ('Western parsley') in *kanji*, but *oranda-seri* in *furigana*, which is an example of how in the Japanese mind, Dutch equated to Western. ns. also *paseri* (Eng.).[68]

The morpheme *Oranda* continues to be productive in Kyushu. In Hirado, *Oranda* is used as a prefix for several toponyms including roads and walkways and the recently-opened *Oranda Shōkan* (オランダ商館) ('Dutch factory') museum.[69]

5.2.2.2.3   *Ran* 蘭 (10 Words)

1   *Ran-ga 蘭画 'Dutch art'. E.g. *Akita-ranga* 秋田蘭画, the Akita-school of Dutch/Western art.

2   *Ran-gaku 蘭学 'the study of Dutch or Western learning more generally'.

3   *Ran-gaku-sha 蘭学者 'students of *rangaku*'.

4   *Ran-go* 蘭語 an older name for the Dutch language.

5   *Ran-kiku* 蘭菊 chrysanthemum. Vos.

6   *Ran-peki* 蘭癖 (those who were 'crazy' about things Dutch such as the *ranpeki-daimyō* 蘭癖 (らんぺき) 大名).

7   *Ran-pō 蘭方 Western medicine.

8   *Ran-pō-i 蘭方医 Doctor practising Western medicine.

9   *Ran-pō kakeru* (to apply the Dutch method) means 'to blast rocks with dynamite'. In Kanoashi County (Shimane Pref.), Ōshima (Yamaguchi Pref.) and Saga Pref. (Vos).

10   *Ran-setsu* 蘭説 'Dutch theories', a word that appears in a number of translations of Dutch texts.

5.2.2.3   *Yaesu-* (2 Words)

In Tokyo, several toponyms include a Japanese version of a Dutch name. One of the first Dutchmen in Japan was Jan Joosten van Lodensteyn (1556–1623). He arrived in Japan in 1600 aboard the *Liefde*. Over time, Jan Joosten moved

---

68   *Oranda-zeri* is listed by Wiersema and León (2013: 1279).

69   Once a month in Hirado there is a festival called the *Hirado Zondag* (Dutch *zondag* = Sunday). This is held on every third Sunday of the month. Here, the local women dress up in Dutch clothing and tea is served free. There may be an element of trying to attract tourists here, but it is perhaps also part of a move to remind people of the important role of Hirado in the history of Japanese-Dutch and indeed Japanese-European relations.

FIGURE 28
Yaesu kitaguchi ('Yaesu North
Entrance'). Tokyo Station, Japan
AUTHOR'S OWN COLLECTION

to Edo and became a merchant and an advisor to the shogun. A Japanese version of his name was given to the area of Edo or Tokyo where he was granted a house by the shogun. This was *Yaesu* (八重洲).[70] Still today, it can be found in hybrid toponyms in and around the Central Station in Tokyo, which is in the area where Jan Joosten lived, for example:

1   *Yaesu chikagai 八重洲地下街 Yaesu underground shopping centre; and
2   *Yaesu kitaguchi 八重洲北口 Yaesu North Entrance (see fig. 28).

5.2.2.4   *Miscellaneous (7 Words)*[71]

1   *bōru-ban ボール盤 'drilling machine', 'drill press' < Dutch *boor* ('drill')
    + S.-J. *ban* ('board', 'tray') < Dutch *boormachine*. The Dutch suffix *bank*
    ('bench') as in *boorbank* also contributes to the use of *ban* 盤 in Japanese.
    Vos.
2   *gasu-dai ガス台 'gas cooker' < Dutch *gas* ('gas') + S.-J. *dai* ('stand').
3   *gomu-dan ゴム弾 'rubber bullet' < Dutch *gom* ('rubber') + S.-J. *dan*
    ('bullet').
4   *gomu-in ゴム印 'rubber stamp' < Dutch *gom* ('rubber') + S.-J. *in* ('stamp').
5   *gomu-naga ゴム長 'rubber boots' < Dutch *gom* ('rubber') + J. *naga* ('long').
6   *gomu-te-bukuro ゴム手袋 'rubber gloves' < Dutch *gom* ('rubber') + J.
    te-bukuro ('glove').
7   *keshi-gomu 消しゴム 'eraser' < S.-J. *ke(shi)* to cancel + Dutch *gom*
    ('rubber').

---

70   *Yaesu* comes from *Yayosu*, which in turns comes from *yan yōs'ten*, both Japanese versions
     of Jan Joosten. His house in Edo was known as *Yayosu-gashi* ('Jan Joosten's Riverbank')
     (Vos 1980: 14).

71   An example of a miscellaneous hybrid creation no longer in use is *karakun-chō* カラク
     ン鳥 'turkey (bird)' < Dutch *kalkoen* ('turkey') + S.-J. *chō* ('bird'). Vos. Saitō *karukufūn*
     < Dutch *kalkhoen* 1750; *karakun-chō* 1855. ns. *shichimenchō* 七面鳥 (S.-J.) (lit. seven-faced
     bird).

5.3.3 Creations Using Only Foreign Morphemes (20 Words)

1   *aroe-crīmu* アロエクリーム 'aloe moisturising cream' < Dutch *aloe* + English 'cream'.

2   **barūnkatēteru* バルーンカテーテル 'balloon catheter' < Dutch *katheter* (catheter) and English 'balloon'.

3   **buriki-kan* ブリキ缶 'tin can' < Dutch *blik* and *kan* (or English 'can').

4   **garasu-etchingu* ガラスエッチング 'glass etching' < Dutch *glas* + English 'etching'.

5   **gasu-sutōbu* ガスストーブ 'gas stove' < Dutch *gas* and English 'stove'.

6   *gasu-tēburu* ガステーブル 'gas range' < Dutch *gas* and English 'table'.

7   **gomu-bando* ゴムバンド 'rubber/elastic band' < Dutch *gom* + English 'band'.

8   **hamu-eggu* ハムエッグ 'ham and eggs' < Dutch *ham* + English 'egg'.

9   **hamu-sando* ハムサンド 'ham sandwich' < Dutch *ham* + English 'sandwich'.

10 **hamu-sarada* ハムサラダ 'ham salad' < Dutch *ham* + Port. 'salada'

11 **kōhī-kappu* コーヒーカップ 'coffee cup' < Dutch *koffie* and English 'cup'

12 **kōhī-shoppu* コーヒーショップ 'coffee shop' < Dutch *koffie* and English 'shop'.

13 **kōn-shiroppu* コーンシロップ 'corn syrup' < English 'corn' and Dutch *siroop*.

14 **kuraun-garasu* クラウンガラス 'crown-glass' < English 'crown' + Dutch *glas*.

15 **madorosu-paipu* マドロスパイプ 'sailor's pipe' < Dutch *matroos* and English 'pipe'.

16 **mēpuru-shiroppu* メープルシロップ 'maple syrup' < English 'maple' and Dutch *siroop*.

17 **pappu-tesuto* パップテスト 'smear test' < Dutch *pap* ('cataplasm') + Eng. 'test'.

18 **paretto-naifu* パレットナイフ 'palette-knife' < Dutch *palet* and English 'knife'.

19 **pinto-gurasu* ピントグラス 'focussing glass' < Dutch (*brand*)*punt* ('focus') + English 'glass'. Vos. (Dutch *glas* was usually rendered *garasu* in Japanese).

20 *pōku-hamu* ポークハム 'pork ham' < English 'pork' and Dutch *ham*.

5.3   *Contact-Induced Words since the End of the Dutch Period in Japan*

Finally, a word is in order about what has happened to these contact-induced words since Dutch and Japanese ceased to have intensive contact in the early Meiji era. First, research has been carried out which sheds light on the fate of lexical outcomes of contact with Dutch in comparison with that of contact-induced words from other languages that have been adopted by Japanese.

The data from this research is presented by Shibatani (1990: 148–149), who notes that most of the 'foreign words' analysed are *gairaigo*, although a very small number are hybrid words. A survey of 'foreign words' used in the Taishō era (1912–25) has been made although the sample is relatively small (162 words). Just over a quarter of these words (27.8%) were Dutch.[72] This was almost double the number of Portuguese loanwords (14.2%), but about half the number of English loanwords (51.9%). French, German and Spanish each had less than 4%.[73] Shibatani suggests that one reason for the quick and deep shift from Dutch to English is the number of English and Americans employed by the early Meiji government. Of 214 foreign employees in 1872, 119 were English, fifty French and sixteen Americans. Only two were Dutch and one Portuguese (Shibatani 1990: 148). By 1964, the position of Dutch loanwords among 'foreign words' in Japanese was even weaker. Here, a survey of nearly 3,000 foreign words in ninety varieties of magazine found that English was again in first place with 80.8%. French was now second with 5.6%. German (3.3%) and Italian (1.5%) were third and fourth, while Dutch was in fifth place with 40 words or 1.3% of the total (Shibatani 1990: 148–149).

The frequency with which Dutch loanwords are used also decreased. An analysis in 2006 of NINJAL, a large magazine corpus which includes text from advertisements, indicates that French and English loanwords are the most commonly used 'foreign words'. The five most frequently occurring Dutch loanwords were *renzu* ('lens'), *garasu* ('glass'), *bīru* ('beer') *gasu* ('gas') and *ekisu* ('extract'). However, their frequency is about one tenth of the frequency of the most-commonly occurring *gairaigo* (Irwin 2011: 27–28).[74] It should, though, be emphasized that these analyses exclude the many loan translations adopted in the Japanese lexis, which form the basis of discipline-specific terminology in several scientific fields.

Second, many of the contact-induced words analysed above have undergone some form of morphological integration as they have become embedded in Japanese. Two examples of this are contact-induced words which have undergone 'clipping', a form of morphological integration common in contact-induced words in Japanese, and those which form *no*-adjectives in Japanese

---

72   Frellisvig (2010: 404) notes that the term was first used in the Meiji period by the linguist
      Ueda Kazutoshi in 1895 after a period of study in Germany. Frellisvig suggests it is closer
      to the German *fremdwort*, i.e., 'alien, foreign word', rather than *lehnwort* or 'loanword'. It
      does not for example include Sino-Japanese loanwords.
73   Shibatani takes these figures from Ueno (1980).
74   See also Irwin (2011: 26) for a summary of surveys of *gairaigo* by donor language,
      1872–2000.

(Winford 2003: 50; Kaiser *et al.* 2001: 5). Regarding the former, the Dutch *flanel* ('flannel') was adopted as *furan'neru* which has been abbreviated to *neru*. Further examples are *ekisu* from the Dutch 'extract' and *hekuto* < Dutch 'hektometer', each example including epenthetic vowels. Several of the dialectal words derived from the Dutch word for 'potato', *aardappel*, also exhibit clipping. Regarding the latter, these are words which have an adjectival meaning but behave grammatically like a noun (Kaiser *et al.* 2001: 5). When preceding nouns, they do not add the adjectival inflections '-i' or '-na', but assume the form (*no*-adj.) + *no*(の) + noun. Some *no*-adjectives have been formed from Dutch loanwords in Japanese. For example, the loanword *gomu* ゴム has given rise to the *no*-adjective *gomujō* ゴム状 (状 *jō* = 'form'), which can be translated as 'rubbery'. So, one can write in Japanese *gomujō-no-mono* ゴム状のもの ('rubbery things/things made of rubber'). Another example of a *no*-adjective is the Japanese word for 'lenticular' レンズ状 *renzu-jō*, formed from the Dutch loanword *renzu* レンズ ('lens') and *jō* 状 'form'.

6   Lexical Contact Phenomena in Other Languages via Japanese

6.1   *Sinitic Varieties*

For much of its written history, Japan has been heavily influenced by Chinese culture and language. However, as a result of the modernization of Japan, heralded by *rangaku*, in the second half of the nineteenth century and the twentieth century, China borrowed much from Japan, including vocabulary to express things and ideas associated with modernity. Many of the Japanese loanwords adopted by Chinese were in turn Dutch loanwords in Japanese. Kuiper (1993) analyses some ninety Dutch loanwords in Japanese adopted by standard Chinese, often referred to as Mandarin (see also Van der Sijs 2010: 57–58). Furthermore, as a consequence of the Japanese occupation of Taiwan between 1895 and 1945, several Dutch loanwords were adopted by another Sinitic variety, Taiwanese Hokkien.

6.1.1   Mandarin Chinese

Further investigation is required to ascertain whether Chinese borrowed any Dutch loanwords via books translated from Dutch to Japanese subsequently translated into Chinese. However, there were other channels for Dutch loanwords in Japanese to be adopted by Chinese. These include Chinese students studying in Japan, other Japanese books being translated into Chinese and lexicons which incorporated the Japanese neologisms, written in more or less the same characters as the Chinese would use (Kuiper 1993: 137–139).

Taking his lead from earlier work on loanwords in Chinese by Zdenka Novotná, Kuiper (1993) identifies six types of loanword that Mandarin has borrowed from Dutch via Japanese. These closely mirror the general categories of borrowing identified by Winford (2003). The first category is 'phonemic loans'. One example is the Chinese word for 'gas' 瓦斯 (pronounced wǎsī). Japanese adopted the Dutch word *gas* ('gas') as *gasu*. Initially this was rendered in *kanji*, based not on meaning, but on sound (*ateji*) as 瓦斯, and it was adopted in this form by Chinese, with phonetic adaptation. As with other phonemic loans from Dutch, this is now written in Japanese with *katakana*, viz. ガス (Kuiper 1993: 125; Saitō 1935: 26).

A second type of loan is the 'graphic loan'. Here, it is the written form rather than the phonemic shape that is borrowed. In fact, as Chinese and Japanese both use Sinitic characters all the loanwords discussed here are of this type. The third category is hybrid words, which consist of a native and loaned morpheme. For example, a Chinese word for 'silica' is *guīshí*. This derives from the Japanese hybrid *keiseki* (珪石). *Kei* comes from the Dutch *kei* ('cobble') and *seki* ('stone') is the *on*-reading of 石. This word appears in Udagawa Yōan's *Seimi kaisō* (Kuiper 1993: 126).

The fourth type of borrowing is the loan translation. Here, the Japanese borrowing consists of Japanese, or very often, Sino-Japanese morphemes, which are translations of the morphemes of a Dutch word. For example, the Dutch word for the appendix in the stomach is *blindedarm*, which literally means 'blind intestine'. This was adopted by Japanese as *mōchō* (盲腸), which also literally means 'blind intestine'. Chinese adopted the same *kanji* (Chinese: *hànzì*), but pronounces them *mángcháng*, again literally 'blind intestine'. As one might expect, the Chinese for 'appendicitis' *mángchángyán* (盲腸炎) is also derived from this loan translation.[75] In Dutch, the 'blind' element refers to the fact that the intestine is closed at one end. This is, however, lost in the Japanese and Chinese loan translations (Kuiper 1993: 127). This category includes loanwords relating to several subjects, not only medicine, but also chemistry, physics and linguistics. In the last category, several grammatical terms adopted by Japanese from Dutch as loan translations were subsequently borrowed by Chinese. Two examples are 'verb' (Chinese *dòngcí* < Japanese *dōshi* (動詞) lit. 'move-word' < Dutch *werkwoord*) and 'pronoun' (Chinese *dàimíngcí* < Japanese *daimeishi* (代名詞) < Dutch *voornaamwoord*). In each case, the separate morphemes

---

75   Korean also adopted this loan translation as *maengjang* and appendicitis as *maeng-jangyŏm*.

are Sino-Japanese, so these are examples of morphemes which have been exported separately, but later imported by Chinese in compound words.

The fifth category of borrowing is the 'semantic loanword'. This refers to words in Japanese texts that had been drawn from Chinese classics and which were then subsequently borrowed back into Chinese. For example, *Kaitai shinsho* ('A New Treatise on Anatomy') was written in *kanbun*. Its authors, or rather translators, used 軟骨 (*nankotsu*) to translate the Dutch *kraakbeen* ('cartilage'). This has been re-appropriated by modern Chinese with the same characters, read as *ruǎngǔ* (Kuiper 1993: 131).

The sixth category is termed 'induced new creations'. They are new coinages, which are descriptive rather than having a morphemic connection to the foreign words that inspired them (Kuiper 1993: 118). One example is *xiānwéi* (纖維), which means 'fibre'. In Japanese this is *sen'i* (same characters), which was 'induced' by the Dutch word *vezel* in a Dutch source text used by Udagawa Genshin for *Ihan teikō* ('Concise Model of [Western] Medicine', 1805).

This is not quite the end of the matter, for in addition to these six types of loanword, there is the rare case of Chinese needing to adopt new characters to assimilate borrowings. As noted above, in *Ihan teikō*, Udagawa Genshin used a new *kanji sen* (腺) to translate the Dutch *klier* ('gland'). This was later adopted by Chinese (Kuiper 1993: 123).

Kuiper (1993) is an extremely detailed analysis of Dutch loanwords in Japanese re-borrowed by Mandarin Chinese. In the light of the research presented in this chapter, it may be useful for Sinologists to investigate whether other Dutch loanwords in Japanese, above all loan translations, have also been borrowed by Mandarin Chinese.

6.1.2 Taiwanese Hokkien

The Japanese loanwords in Mandarin Chinese, borrowed or 'induced' from Dutch, have, of course, not only been used in mainland China, but also in other parts of the world where Mandarin is spoken such as Singapore and Taiwan. After the First Sino-Japanese War (1894/5), Japan occupied Taiwan from 1895 to 1945. Japanese was the official language in Taiwan. Taiwanese were obliged to learn Japanese at school, and it was a high prestige language. As a result, Japanese loanwords were adopted by the Taiwanese Hokkien or Minnan (臺灣閩南語) Sinitic variety. This derives from Fujian province on mainland China and was brought to Taiwan by settlers from the seventeenth century onwards. In 2011, the R.O.C. government made a list of 172 commonly-used Japanese words in Taiwanese Hokkien, several of which are loanwords from Dutch. One is 'beer' (MTL transcription *bielux/bieluq*), In standard Chinese, the word *píjiŭ* (啤酒) is used for 'beer'. Two others are 'gas' (*gafsuq*) and 'cup' (*khokpuq*).[76]

6.2 Korean

Because of the historical relationship between Japan and Korea, Dutch loanwords in Japanese have been adopted by Korean. It is not always clear when Korean adopted these loanwords, but particular points of contact arose when Koreans studied in Japan in the late nineteenth century and Japan occupied the Korean peninsula between 1910 and 1945. Two authors who have analysed these loanwords are Sohn Ho-Min (1999) and Frits Vos (1963, 2000b). Sohn (1999: 118, 120) asserts that there are sixty-five Dutch loanwords in standard Korean although he adds that some of these may not have come via Japanese. He observes that most of the borrowings relate to clothing, medicine and science and lists examples such as *alkhol* ('alcohol'), *ammonia* ('ammonia') *matolosu* ('sailor' < Dutch *matroos*), which are given above as Dutch loanwords in Japanese. Sohn limits his analysis to 'pure' loanwords.[77] The same is true of the first publication in which Vos analyses these loanwords, his 1963 article, re-published in 2014, quoted frequently above. Here, he lists twenty-seven Dutch loanwords in Korean via Japanese, although not all of these are in common usage (Vos 1963: 384–386). However, in his later article, published in 2000, he is more ambitious, listing 51 'pure' Dutch loanwords, which have entered Korean via Japanese. He does, though, strike a note of caution for in the late nineteenth and early twentieth centuries American missionaries were very active in Korean education. Indeed, many leading Korean universities were established by these missionaries. For our purposes, one consequence is that loanwords such as *ak'asia* ('acacia') may come from English or from Dutch via Japanese. Among those which without doubt came via the latter route, we can

---

76 臺灣閩南語常用詞辭典 [Dictionary of Frequently-Used Taiwan Minnan] (in Taiwanese Hokkien and Chinese). Ministry of Education R.O.C. http://taioaan.org/wiki/images/f/ fe/DFT_172_loanwords_from_Japanese_4_columns.pdf. Accessed 12 August 2020. See also Kloeter (2005: 22) for gas and beer. Taiwanese has up to 8 tones, so I have not included the tone markings. MTL stands for the 'Modern Taiwanese Language' orthography. Taiwanese Hokkien also has *khabarng* 'bag' from the Japanese *kaban*. The extent to which this may be a Dutch loanword is analysed above (p. 349, n. 52).

77 Sohn adopts the Yale system of transliteration from Korean. His transliterations often differ from those of Vos who uses the McCune-Reischauer system. I report Sohn's examples using the Yale system, but elsewhere follow Vos in using the McCune-Reischauer system. Many of these words entered Korean when Sinitic characters (*hanja*) were still be used extensively, above all by educated Koreans. The *hangeul* alphabetic system was also in use, although to a far lesser extent than today. Vos (2000b) provides a glossary of these loanwords with *hanja* and *hangeul* renderings.

mention *mesŭ*. This comes from the Japanese *mesu* (メス), which is a loanword derived from the Dutch *mes*, meaning 'knife'. However, both the Japanese and Korean renderings have the specific meaning of 'scalpel' rather than 'knife' in general.[78] This is likely to be because it was Dutch medicine and more specifically surgery that first attracted the attention of the Japanese. This is an example of a loanword that has undergone a semantic shift. Another example is *pirŭ* (also *piru*) for 'beer' from the Japanese *bīru* which in turn comes from the Dutch *bier*. However, the standard word for 'beer' in Korean is now the Sino-Korean *maekchu*. It would have been useful to compare Sohn's list of loanwords with that of Vos, but Sohn does not list all his 65 and so this is not possible. Nevertheless, the number of 'pure' loanwords that he gives is of the same order as that given by Vos (65 v. 51). Where Vos takes this subject further in his second article is in the analysis of loan translations that have entered Korean from Dutch via Japanese. He lists 44 of these, but the 'true' number of these is probably much higher (Vos 2000b: 303–305). As Sinitic characters were still being used extensively in Korean until at least 1945, these were probably 'graphic loans', i.e., with the same characters being used in Korean, but read in a (Sino-)Korean manner, rather than a (Sino-)Japanese manner (Kuiper 1993: 117). One set of words most probably adopted in this way refers to types of membrane. The Dutch *vlies* was incorporated in Japanese in loan translations as *maku*. These were adopted by Korean as *mak*. For example, 'retina' in Dutch is *netvlies*. In Japanese, this became *mō-maku* (網膜) and in Korean *mang-mak*. Vos lists 7 such words.

One group of loan translations to which Vos pays special attention are grammatical terms. He lists eight of these. The Korean Yu Kil-chun (1856–1914) studied in Japan in the early 1880s under the famous *rangakusha*-turned-Anglophone, Fukuzawa Yukichi. It is likely that he read modern grammatical studies of Japanese incorporating Dutch loan translations and coined terms which are still used today for parts of speech in Korean. Two examples are the Korean terms for 'noun' and 'verb'. The Dutch *naamwoord* ('noun') was adopted by Japanese as *meishi* (名詞). This was adopted in Korean as *myŏngsa* (with the same two morphemes and Sinitic characters read in a Sino-Korean manner). Likewise, Japanese adopted the Dutch *werkwoord* ('verb') as *dō-shi* (動詞), which was in turn rendered as *tongsa* in Korean. There were various attempts to replace these with 'native' Korean terms, but these did not 'catch on'.

---

78   It is often preceded by the adjective *oekwayong* (외과용) ('surgical'). This use of *mesŭ* was vividly brought home to me as I sat in a dentist's chair in Korea in 2014 and heard the dentist ask his assistant for the *mesŭ*. See also Eylenbosch (1940). The final vowel in *mesŭ* is a schwa.

In total, Vos (2000b) lists 103 contact-induced words, which with one or two possible exceptions, have been adopted by Korean from Japanese and before that Dutch. Given that Sinitic characters were used much more in Korean prior to 1945 than today, it is likely that there are other 'graphic loans' which have taken this path. Therefore, the 'true' figure for Dutch loanwords in Korean is probably much higher. This offers an interesting opportunity for further research.

6.3 *Ainu*

One other language which has had significant contact with Japanese is Ainu. This has historically been spoken on Hokkaido (formerly Ezo) and adjoining islands, but with the advance of Japanese, it is now an endangered language, which may no longer have any native speakers. It is generally agreed that Ainu is genetically unrelated to Japanese, but as a result of language contact it has adopted loanwords from its neighbour. Three Portuguese loanwords which have entered Ainu via Japanese are *pan* ('bread') from the Portuguese *pão*, *pindoro* ('glass') from the Portuguese *vidro* and *tampako* ('tobacco') from the Portuguese *tabaco*.[79] Using Batchelor's 1905 English-Japanese-Ainu lexicon, I have not yet identified any Japanese loanwords in Ainu, which were borrowed from Dutch. On the other hand, Batchelor does not include entries for certain words that Japanese borrowed from Dutch, such as coffee and potato. Further investigation may reveal evidence for Ainu borrowing such loanwords.

7 The Influence of Dutch on Japanese Grammar

So far the focus has been on lexical interference. An analysis of morphemes with Dutch roots such as *gomu*, *hamu* and *kōhī* and several contact-induced Sino-Japanese morphemes such as *-so* (素) and *-san* (酸) (for 'element' and 'acid' respectively) that have been and still are productive straddles the realms of lexical and grammatical influence. In this section, there is further analysis of the influence of contact with Dutch on Japanese grammar, above all on its syntax. As Japanese and Dutch syntax are very different it was necessary for Japanese translators of Dutch texts in the Tokugawa period to assign new

---

79   I thank Elia da Corso for the final example. In the Ainu rendering there is the insertion of a nasal *m* before the labial occlusive [b], which is a common modification of loanwords borrowed by Ainu (prenasalization). A similar phenomenon may well be at work in the insertion of 'n' before the voiced alveolar stop [d] in *pindoro*. For more on the Ainu sound system, see Shibatani (1990: 11–16).

functions to existing particles and parts of speech in order to render Dutch texts in Japanese. These are examples of what Florian Coulmas (1989) refers to as 'language adaptation'.

Thomason and Kaufman (1988: 74–76) have developed a 5-level borrowing scale whereby they attempt to equate the intensity of language contact with the type of borrowing (lexical, structural, etc.). In the case of Dutch and Japanese, there has been slight structural borrowing in the field of 'conjunctions and adverbial particles'. In broad terms, such borrowing is associated with level 2 of the Thomason and Kaufman scale. Here, the contact is slightly more intense than that associated with level 1, where there is only lexical borrowing (Winford 2003: 30). Importantly, the structural borrowing is largely a function of translation from Dutch to Japanese. It is a commonplace in linguistics that translations can affect the grammatical structure of the target language. In such cases either linguistic features of the source language are introduced into the target language as new linguistic features, or existing norms for linguistic features in the target language are redefined to fit a new communicative task (Baumgarten and Özçetin 2008: 294). In what follows, an example of the former is the increased use of pronouns in Japanese resulting from translation, while an example of the latter is the innovative use of the complementizer *tokoro-no* (ところの) for a new communicative task.

7.1   Tokoro-no

Tokoro-no (ところの) is the equivalent of a relative pronoun used in adnominal clauses, or in other words a complementizer used 'between adnominal clause and head noun' (Frellesvig 2010: 358). It consists of two parts, *tokoro*, which means 'place' and the particle *no*. In Old Japanese (up until c. 800) there were no relative pronoun equivalents in relative clauses. The Japanese translators of Dutch texts probably appropriated this part of speech from *kanbun*, the form of literary Sinitic used by well-educated Japanese (Earns 1993: 92–95; Frellesvig 2010: 1). In *kanbun*, *tokoro-no* fulfils the function of a relative pronoun that always refers to a head noun as the direct object of a clause. We see this in the following example (1),

(1) *Hossuru*   *tokoro-no*   *mono*
    want   that   thing
    'The thing that one wants (to have)'

The relative pronoun, expressed as *that* in English, is the direct object of the relative clause. Gradually, however, *tokoro-no* began to fulfil other functions.

Earns gives the earliest recorded use of it in 1730 in an astronomical text (2) (1993: 58).[80]

(2) *Kōmōjin*   *mochi wataru*   *tokoro-no*   *sei-zu*
     Dutch   bring in/across   which   star-chart
     'The star chart which the Dutch bring in'

This is very early in the history of the Japanese translation of Dutch texts, given that the first of these were only made in the second half of the seventeenth century. In 1812, the translator of *Oranda gohō kai* ('Interpretation of Dutch grammar'), Fujibayashi Fuzan, used sentences with *tokoro-no*, in which the relative pronoun referring to a head noun is the subject and not the direct object of the relative clause (3) (Earns 1993: 94; 1996: 66–67).[81]

(3) *Kore* *o*   *setsumei-suru*   *tokoro-no* *bunpō*   *o*   *iu-nari*
     This   OBJ   explanation-do   which   grammar   OBJ   refers to
     'It refers to the grammar which explains this.'

Here, *tokoro-no* ('which') refers to 'grammar' and is therefore the subject of the relative clause. Importantly, this is not a translation of a Dutch sentence but Japanese commentary added by Fuzan. Up to the end of the Tokugawa period the use of *tokoro-no* was limited to works which were Japanese translations of Dutch texts. Only in the Meiji period was it used in other contexts in Japanese (Martin 1975: 862). Nevertheless, its use in modern standard Japanese seems to be very limited as other constructions can perform this function, although Frellesvig notes that it may still be used in written language (Frellesvig 2010: 358; Matsumoto 2018).

7.2   *Ni-yotte*

Another example of how Japanese grammar was adapted as a result of translations from Dutch is the use of the compound suffix *ni-yotte* (によって) in passive

---

80   Earns refers to the source text as *Dairyaku tenmon meimokusho* (Earns 1993: 39), but I
      have not yet been able to find this text. It may be another name for *Tairyaku tengaku
      myōmokushō* (大略天学名目鈔, 'Brief Extract of Astronomical Names') (1729) compiled
      by Nishikawa Seikyū (or Chūjirō 1693–1756) (Goodman 2000: 53). NIJL ID 5356. However,
      this sentence is not on the page given by Earns. *Kōmōjin* (紅毛人) literally means 'red-
      haired people'.

81   Clements (2015: 26) gives the year 1811 for the publication of *Oranda gohō kai*. NIJL gives
      Bunka 9 (1812).

sentences. Before the Dutch came to Japan, the suffix *ni* (に) was already used in Japanese to indicate the agent in passive sentences. *Ni-yotte* is found in poetry from the eighth century with the meaning 'cause/reason' (Iwasaki 2018: 547). Towards the end of the Tokugawa period Japanese translators of Dutch texts employed *ni-yotte* to translate the Dutch word *door* ('by').[82] According to Kinsui Satoshi (1997: 772–773) one of the earliest examples of a passive sentence in which *ni-yotte* was used in this manner is a Japanese translation of the second edition of the Dutch grammar, *Grammatica of Nederduitsche Spraakkunst*, by Matthijs Siegenbeek, which was published in Leiden in 1822.[83] The Japanese translation by Ohara Tōru, published in Edo in 1856/7, had the title *Sōyaku Garamachika* ('The *Grammatica*—with translation', 1856).[84] The relevant sentence in paragraph 32 is (4):

(4) Er zijn echter eenige algemeene regelen en waarnemingen hieromtrent door kundige Taalbeoefenaars voorgesteld.

['But there are some general rules and observations about this which have been established by expert practitioners of language']

Door kundige Taalbeoefenaars voorgesteld ('established by expert practitioners of language') was initially glossed by Tōru as follows (5):

(5) **Yotte**   *takuminaru*   *gogakusha-ni*   *sadamer-are-taru*
     Door   kundige   Taalbeoefenaars   voorgesteld

Yotte was represented in Japanese script as 因テ. The Japanese would then be arranged into a clause conforming to Japanese syntax (6):

---

82 *Ni-yotte* consists of two parts: the postposition *ni* に and *yotte* (よって). *Yotte* (よって) is the conjunctive or -*te* (テ) form of the verb *yoru* which has a number of meanings, including 'to be caused by' (Kinsui 1997: 770–772).

83 The *Grammatica* was also printed in Deventer and Groningen.

84 *Sōyaku Garamachika* reproduced the Dutch text with Japanese equivalents in *katakana* or *kanji* written in superscript. Kinsui (1997: 772, 779) identifies two other early translations of Siegenbeek's work, in which *niyotte* is used: *Oranda-Bunten Tokuhou* (1856. Kyoto: Katsumara Jiemon) and *Garamachika Kun-yaku* (1857. Edo: Sakakibara). I have identified earlier translations from Dutch in which *ni-yotte* is used. Further investigation including a comparison with the Dutch source text would be required to establish whether these instances are analogous to the ones analysed by Kinsui.

(6) *takuminaru*   *gogakusha-ni*   *yotte*   *sadamer-are-taru*
     kundige   taalbeoefenaars   door   voorgesteld
     expert   practitioners of language   by   establish-(*r*)*are*-PST
     'established by expert practitioners of language'

It is this final step that brought together *ni*, indicating the passive agent, and *yotte*, used to translate *door* to form the compound suffix *ni-yotte*. For our purposes it is not necessary to discuss the entire history of the development of the use of *ni-yotte*. However, although after the beginning of the Meiji period Dutch became less important in Japan, *ni-yotte* continued to be used to indicate the agent in passive sentences translated from other European languages such as English and gradually it began to be used more widely in Japanese (Frellesvig 2010: 410).

Iwasaki (2018) identifies three types of passive construction in cMJ: direct and indirect, where the agent marker is typically *ni*, and the *ni-yotte* construction. However, it does seem that the conditions for the use of *ni-yotte* are not absolute. One use of *ni-yotte* proposed by Iwasaki (2018: 546–547) is in passive sentences with an inanimate subject. Such sentences were introduced in Japanese as a result of the translations from Dutch, a point I return to below. This may help to explain why *ni-yotte* is used in the following sentences (7 + 8):

(7) *Ibento ni-yotte rentaikan ga uma-re-ru*
     Events by   solidarity SBJ create (inf. neg./*nai*-form stem)-PASS-PRS
     'Solidarity is created by [holding] events' (Kaiser *et al.* 2013: 104).

(8) *Kono   e   wa   Pikaso   ni-yotte kaka-re-ta*
     This   picture TOP   Picasso by   paint (inf. neg. stem)-PASS-PST
     'This picture was painted by Picasso' (Makino and Tsutsui 2009: 366).[85]

One may contrast this with sentence (9) where the passive subject (teacher/ *sensei*) is animate:

---

85 Iwasaki (2018: 547) states that *ni-yotte* is used in passive sentences with an inanimate subject. Frellesvig (2010: 410) refers to the condition of the agent being inanimate. However, in this case, the agent, Picasso, is animate. It seems more likely that Iwasaki is correct here. Another example is provided by Makino and Tsutsui (2009: 367) who write that **Kawamoto-san wa itsumo shigoto ni yotte owarete iru* ('Mr. Kawamoto is always kept busy by his work') is 'unacceptable under normal circumstances'. This is because the subject, Mr. Kawamoto, is animate, so *ni-yotte* cannot be used.

(9) *Sensei   wa   Jon   ni   muzukashi   shitsumon   o*
Teacher   TOP   John   by   difficult   question   OBJ
sa-re-ta
do(<*suru*)-PASS-PST
'The teacher was asked a difficult question by John' (Makino and
Tsutsui 2009: 367).[86]
Note: *Shitsumon-suru* means 'to ask a question'. *Sareta* is the past passive
form of *suru*.

Iwasaki (2018: 535) observes that another use of *ni-yotte* is in sentences where
the subject is not directly affected by an action. For example, in the sentence
'the teacher was adversely affected by a student crying in his/her class', the
teacher is directly affected and so 'by a student' is rendered in Japanese as
gakusei-ni (*gakusei* = student). By contrast, in the sentence 'The teacher was
criticized by a student', the teacher may not be directly affected by the criticism and so 'by a student' is rendered as *gakusei-ni-yotte*. However, Iwasaki
(2018: 547) notes that the distribution of *ni-yotte* in modern Japanese is skewed.
For example, as a result of its association with translations, it is used more in
formal writing and much less in informal speech.

7.3   Other Influences of Dutch on Japanese Grammar

Three other ways in which Japanese grammar was modified as a result of translating from Dutch were the use of the pseudo-copula *de aru* at the end of a
sentence; the use of inanimate things as the subject of a sentence; and the
increased use of pseudo-pronouns.

First, as in the case of *tokoro-no* and *ni-yotte* in written Japanese the use of
the pseudo-copula *de aru* (である) was more or less limited until the end of
the Tokugawa period to translations from Dutch into Japanese.[87] In fact it was
not used very frequently in the Tokugawa period. Earns (1993: 77–88) argues
that the origin of its use in Japanese texts can be traced to the *Zūfu Haruma*
lexicon, compiled under the supervision of Hendrick Doeff and completed in
1833. Indeed, we find sentences in this lexicon which use *de aru* in order to
translate the Dutch copula. For example, the Dutch sentence 'Hij is nog een

---

86   The Japanese particle *wa* is the topic marker. In English it can be rendered by 'as for' but
is often left untranslated. Note also that Japanese nouns do not have articles.

87   According to Vos (2014: 179 n. 91) this pseudo-copula was occasionally used towards the
end of the Muromachi period (室町時代, 1336–1573), but thereafter it was used very
rarely until the advent of the translation of Dutch texts into Japanese.

abcling [sic], of nieuweling in de welenschappen (sic)' ('he is still new to the sciences') is rendered in Japanese as (10):

(10) *Kano* *hito* *wa* *mada* *gakumon-ni* *irihana* **de-aru**
That person TOP still sciences-in beginner COP-PRS
'That person is still a beginner in the sciences'.

Interestingly, there was already a copula in classical Japanese *nari* (也, 'to be'), so the question arises as to why the Japanese assisting Doeff did not use this form. Earns posits two reasons. First, one of the guiding principles of the Doeff lexicon was that the Japanese should be close to the spoken language, a point made in Chapter 2 of this book. Here, Earns notes that she is in agreement with Sugimoto (1983: 74). However, whereas Sugimoto argues that the form was drawn from the vernacular language of the Nagasaki interpreters, she suggests instead that it was a feature of the Edo dialect. The interpreters, she posits, would have been familiar with the language of Edo as, despite the distance, there was frequent contact between the two places. She provides sample sentences from drama scripts in the Edo dialect to support her argument.[88] In cMJ, '(noun+) *de aru*' has established itself as an assertive sentence-final copula in the written language (Kishimoto 2018: 306).

Second, prior to contact with Dutch, Japanese did not employ inanimate things as the subject of transitive verbs. This changed as a result of the translation of Dutch scientific texts (Iwasaki 2018: 547). For example, in *Seimi kaisō* Udagawa Yōan makes 'water' (*mizu*) the subject of a transitive verb (Earns 1993: 44) (11):

(11) *Mizu* *wa* *yoku* *mono* *o* *yōkai-su*
Water TOP well thing OBJ dissolving-do
'Water dissolves things well'.

What seems to be a related point is made by Vos (2014: 178–179), namely that as a result of translations from Dutch, the use of abstract terms as the subject of the sentence emerged in Japanese. We see this in another sentence in the *Zūfu Haruma* lexicon in which *de aru* translates the Dutch copula: *yonjūku-no heihōkon-wa shichi-de aru*. This means 'the square root of 49 is 7' or literally

---

88 Earns (1993: 86) quotes six lines from drama scripts to make her point, although each instance has a slight variant on *de aru*, e.g. *de aro* and *de arō*. *De aru* (or *de ar*) occurs frequently in the transcribed Japanese in seven parallel dialogues in Dutch and Japanese in Overmeer Fisscher's account of Japan (1833: 100–115). His source is likely to have been the Nagasaki interpreters.

'49's square root-"as for" 7 is'. Vos argues that an abstract term such as *heihōkon* ('square root') could not have been the subject of a Japanese sentence before the influence on Japanese of translations from Dutch.

Third, before the emergence of *rangaku*, pronouns were not used frequently in Japanese as the person or thing to which a verb referred could be deduced from the context. However, Japanese translators were often faced with Dutch sentences containing pronouns and they needed to gloss these with Japanese words. Two 'pseudo'-pronouns that emerged as a result were *kare* (彼) and *kanojo* (彼女). Originally, *kare* was used as a demonstrative pronoun, but it came to be used for 'he'. *Kanojo* can literally be translated as 'that woman', but has come to mean 'she' (Vos 2014: 179; Earns 1993: 73–75; Frellesvig 2010: 410). It may also be the case that the need to translate Dutch plural prounouns such as *zij* ('they') led to the emergence of the plural pronoun suffix -*ra*, e.g. *karera* (彼ら/彼等, 'they'). It is certainly used in translations from Dutch in the Tokugawa period. However, more work needs to be done on this before firm conclusions can be reached (Earns 1993: 47–48).

Based on a survey of 29 translations from Dutch to Japanese between 1730 and 1869, Earns suggests that several other features in Japanese emerged as a result of these and other translations. First, she argues that the concept of comparative degree, e.g. 'lower', 'better', etc. 'must have been introduced for the first time in the Edo period'. In Classical Japanese, comparison of the form 'A is … than B' was expressed with the construction 'A wa B yori adj.' where *yori* ('than') was almost always used with 'B'. However, as a result of the translation of Dutch texts, *yori* came to function separately with the meaning 'more' (Dutch meer/ -er). Certainly in cMJ we find 'yori yoi より良い + N' ('a better N'), e.g. *yori yoi tatemono* (*desu*) (より良い建物 (です) '(it is a) better building') used as an incomplete comparison and similar constructions.[89] However, Earns (1993: 57–58, 91–92) provides little direct evidence from her data that this shift was induced by translations from Dutch.

Another possible influence of Dutch is the use of sentence-initial connectives such as *shikaredomo* (然れども, 'however'). Certainly, Japanese has historically tended to place connectives at the end of subordinate clauses. For example, a sentence with a causal connective such as 'because it was hot, (I) opened the window' would be rendered (12):

(12) *Atsu-katta*   *kara*   *mado*   *o*   *ake-ta*
     hot-PST   because,   window   OBJ   open-PST

---

89   For further examples of *yori*+adjective to form a comparative, see Kaiser *et al.* (2001: 67–68).

It is suggested that under the influence of Western languages, including Dutch, but also English, it is now also possible to say (13),

(13) *Atsu-katta.*   *Dakara*   *mado*   *o*   *ake-ta*
      hot-PST.   Therefore   window   OBJ   open-PST

In the *rangaku* translation *Naikasen'yō* (1822b) Earns records that there is a sentence beginning with the qualifying connective *shikaredomo* (Earns 1993: 52–53, 89–91) (14):

(14) *Sore* (ns. *sono*)   *chi*   *wa*   *junkan-su.*   *Shikaredomo* [...]
      That   blood   TOP   circulation-do.   However [...]

This translates the Dutch 'Het bloed wordt rond gevoerd, *welker* [...]' lit. 'The blood is circulated, which [...]'. In the Dutch *welker* ('which') is used as a connective. This is translated as *shikaredomo* in Japanese. Whilst one can appreciate the logic of Earns's argument, again more evidence is required before we can draw firm conclusions about the role of translations from Dutch in the emergence of this phenomenon. Any research on this subject would also need to investigate whether contact with other European languages might have contributed to the emergence of this phenomenon.

Probably Earns's boldest claim is that the introduction of sentences with clear punctuation is a consequence of *rangaku* translation. This claim is not without foundation, for in classical Japanese there was no punctuation and the reader had to determine from the context where to make a break. The constant parsing and glossing of Dutch sentences by Japanese translators may thus have contributed to the division of Japanese texts into sentences with the use of punctuation (Earns 1993: 54–55). As with these other suggestions, Earns may well be right, but needs to provide more examples before firm conclusions can be reached. In this regard, it would be instructive not only to add more translations to the corpus (29 from over 1,000 is under 3%), but also to provide examples from contemporary texts which were not translations in order to make any contrast clear.

In concluding this survey of the influence of translating Dutch texts on Japanese syntax, several points are in order. First, in some cases, such as the use of *ni-yotte* and *de aru*, the increased use of subject pronouns and the emergence of inanimate items as the subject of transitive verbs, there is sufficient agreement amongst scholars to conclude that these changes were outcomes of translation from Dutch to Japanese. In other cases, such as those just mentioned, our current state of knowledge does not allow us to draw firm conclusions. This is not to reject these suggestions, but merely to argue that more work needs to be done on them.

Second, while some of these changes, such as the re-assignment of *tokoro-no* have a very restricted use, others such as *ni-yotte* have spread beyond the original use assigned by translators and form an intrinsic part of the syntax of standard contemporary Modern Japanese. Third, it was the application of techniques developed by translators of texts written in literary Sinitic to the process of translating Dutch texts that gave rise to this syntactic interference. The affixing of glosses to each word in the Dutch text in some sense forced the translators to develop equivalents for parts of speech such as pronouns and *ni-yotte* for *door* (Frellesvig 2010: 410). This illustrates well the point made in Chapter 4 that although literary Sinitic provided competition to Dutch in the domain of learning, it was scholars such as Sugita Genpaku, who were experienced in translating Chinese texts, who could apply the same skills (Bourdieu's *habitus*) to engage with and translate Dutch texts. Finally, we can place these findings in a broader research context with reference to work by Werner Koller on how translations can affect the structure of the target language. He distinguishes two ways of triggering this kind of language variation and change in the target language; 'innovations on the level of the language system' (*Systeminnovationen*) and 'innovations on the level of norms or use or stylistic innovation' (*Norm-/Stilinnovationen*). For our purposes, the latter are of most interest. These can be further subdivided into qualitative and quantitative norm innovations. With the former, qualitative, the first occurrence of a linguistic item, feature or structure in a particular use can be traced back to a translation. This is the case for *ni-yotte*. With the latter, quantitative, the item, feature or structure is found in both translations and original texts in the target language—however, its occurrence in translations is triggered by a similar structure in the source texts and is found more frequently in translations than in original texts produced in the target language. This was the case in the late Tokugawa period for *tokoro-no*, drawn from *kanbun*, and *de aru* from everyday speech (Koller 2000, quoted in Baumgarten and Özçetin 2008: 294).

8   The Use of *rōmaji* in Japanese Texts

Contact between Dutch and Japanese inevitably led to a mutual interest in each other's writing systems. Although the learning of Japanese by foreigners was officially forbidden, some of them engaged with and learnt Japanese script.

In his account of Japan, Engelbert Kaempfer reproduces several Japanese syllabaries and *kanji*, the character-based writing system derived from Chinese script, while Johannes van Overmeer Fisscher reproduces the *katakana* syllabary. Philipp von Siebold seems to have been able to write in *kanji*.

In the other direction in the second half of the sixteenth century, the Jesuits devised a system of romanization of Japanese, which achieved some success (Shibatani 1990: 128). During the Tokugawa period, there was intermittent interest in the use of the Latin script or *rōmaji*.[90] In the eighteenth and first half of the nineteenth century several Japanese scholars commented on the ease of use of the Western writing system. In *Rangaku kaitei* ('Guide to Dutch Learning', 1783), Ōtsuki Gentaku observed how easily it could be learned, while Shiba Kōkan praised the ease with which Western writing could be read.[91] In *Seiiki monogatari* ('Tales of the West', 1798), Honda Toshiaki even recommended the use of the Western writing system. Twine concludes that comments such as these sowed the seeds of ideas that would later lead to the establishment of the Rōmaji Club and Kana Club. While the latter, established in 1885, supported a full-scale switch to the Western system, the Kana Club set up in 1881, as the name suggests, advocated the use of the *kana* syllabaries only, i.e., *hiragana* and *katakana*, and no longer using *kanji* (Twine 1991: 225).

Some Japanese, though, were less than enthusiastic about the use of *rōmaji*. The Late Mito (水戸) thinker, Fujita Tōko (1806–55), reflecting the considerable anti-foreigner sentiment in late-Tokugawa Japan, was said to detest all the 'barbarians' who used 'crab writing' letters running sideways (Elison 1973: 243–244). A telling quotation in this regard is 'Lands with letters running sideways all belong to the jashūmon; and the intent of the jashūmon is to drag members of other religions into that same faith and step by step to convert the entire world' (Elison 1973: 244).[92]

Despite such reservations there is plenty of evidence for the use of *rōmaji*. The Portuguese used *rōmaji* extensively in the books they printed in Japan,

---

90   Lach (1977: II:3, 499) writes that the romanization of Japanese devised by the Jesuits was made possible by the practice of writing Chinese characters along with *kana* in the order of its syllabary. We see this in a dictionary of Chinese characters (with *kana*) called *rocuyoxu* (*rakuyōshū*) printed by the Jesuits at Nagasaki in 1598–99. In this regard, Wardhaugh (1987: 10) makes a useful comment, '[there is a] relationship between the spread of religions and the scripts in which various languages are written'.

91   Twine records that Kōkan does this in *Oranda tensetsu* ('Tales of Holland', 1796). However, *Oranda tensetsu* (和蘭天説) should more properly be translated as 'Dutch Explanation of Heaven'). One possibility is that Twine is referring to another work by Kōkan, *Oranda zokuwa* (阿蘭陀俗話, 1798), which does translate as 'Tales from Holland' (NIJL ID 753026).

92   It is not clear to whom Elison attributes this quotation, but it may be Tōko's *daimyō*, Tokugawa Nariaki. It is taken from the *Mitogaku taikei* ('Outline of the Mito School') (V:227–228) (Elison, p. 459 n. 107).

such as the first edition of Aesop's Fables in Japan printed on the Jesuit printing press at Amakusa in 1593 under the title *Esopo no Haburasu* ('Aesop's Fables').[93] *Rōmaji* was also used on material objects such as Christian gravestones.

Several Japanese wrote their language in *rōmaji* in the eighteenth and nineteenth centuries. The *daimyō* of Satsuma, Shimazu Shigehide, would occasionally use Dutch letters and words in his correspondence and kept a diary in Romanized Japanese, probably in order to keep its contents secret. Japanese who corresponded with Dutch associates used *rōmaji* to render the Japanese names for months and eras when dating their letters. We see this most vividly in the letters that Kutsuki Masatsuna wrote to Isaac Titsingh.[94] Masatsuna also inserted the names of Japanese coins and even a Japanese proverb in *rōmaji*. Of course, this was in part to accommodate the fact that Titsingh's ability to read Japanese was probably limited, but it also demonstrates a willingness and even desire to embrace this alien script.

In the late eighteenth century, *rōmaji* became particularly fashionable, for it was considered exotic. This led to the production of works of art incorporating *rōmaji*. In Chapter 3, we saw examples of this in the work of Shiba Kōkan and Aōdō Denzen influenced by Dutch orthography. I suggested there that at least in the case of Kōkan, it conjured up a sense of the exotic or 'other' and allowed him to identify himself in some sense as a Dutch or Western artist. Further examples of *rōmaji* can be found in the decorative arts. It was used on the covers and in illustrations of books translated from Dutch to Japanese (Screech 2001). The vernacular fiction author Santō Kyōden (1761–1816) used *rōmaji* to decorate the borders of the cover of one of his illustrated stories in 1794.[95] Japanese were also interested in the different ways of writing Roman script. In 1765 Gotō Mitsuo published *Oranda banashi* ('Dutch Tales'), which discusses various aspects of the Netherlands such as its customs and flora and fauna. For our purposes it is interesting that it presents the Western alphabet in several styles including Gothic and italics. Under each Western letter is a *kana* from the *katakana* syllabary. In some cases there is no significant difference between the two systems. For example, Mitsuo renders the Dutch 'b' which is pronounced [be:] as ベ [be]. However, he renders the Dutch 'v' [ve:] as イユ, which is pronounced [iyu] (there is no native 'v' in Japanese) (see fig. 29). Such differences contributed to the difficulty the Japanese had in pronouncing Dutch.

---

93   This is rendered in more than one way in transcriptions: however, I follow the example of Ōtsuka Mitsunobu. For a recent work in Japanese on this, see Ōtsuka and Kita (1999).

94   For example, Masatsuna concludes one letter by writing *Nengo Tenmia*. *Nengo* (present-day transcription *Nengō*) (年号) is the Japanese for 'era name'. *Tenmia* is often rendered as *Tenmei* (天明) (1781–89) (Lequin 1992: 10).

95   *Mikenjaku san'nin namaei*. WUL 文庫06 00997.

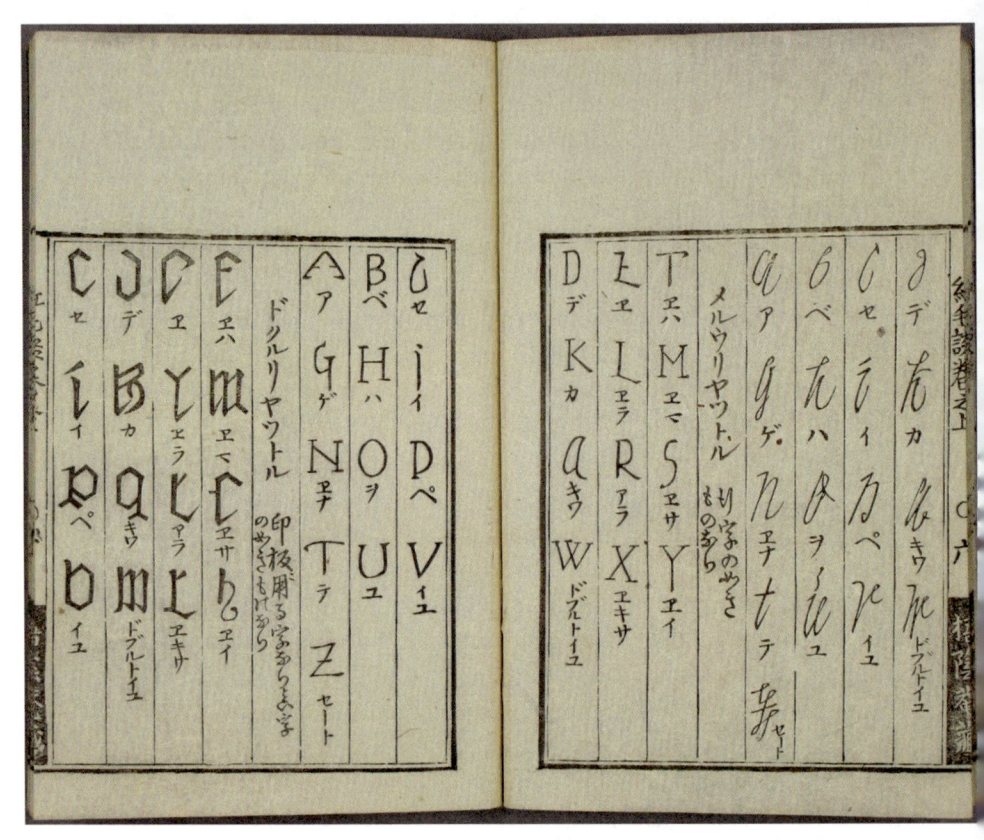

FIGURE 29   Western scripts in *Oranda banashi* ('Dutch Tales', 1765), Gotō Mitsuo. Vol. 1 of 2
WUL 文庫 08 C0200

So, Japanese used *rōmaji* for several reasons. For some, it was the sense of the exotic and 'other' that it conjured up, while for others it provided a means of communication with those who did not read Japanese or Japanese script. Some, such as Honda Toshiaki, recommended that it should replace Japanese script, while others such as Fujita Tōko saw it as a sinister symbol of unwanted 'barbarian' influence.

9   Conclusion

Contact between Dutch and Japanese in the Tokugawa and early Meiji period affected Japanese on a lexical, syntactic and graphic level. Interference on the lexical level was probably the most profound. There are many lexical outcomes of contact between Dutch and Japanese, which have typically been adopted for the purpose of 'gap-filling'. Adapting the loanword typology of Winford (2003) to the Japanese situation, this chapter has illustrated that authors adopted a range of strategies in order to incorporate and embed words based on Dutch models into the recipient language. Many of the examples presented in this chapter are 'pure' loanwords, most of which have undergone some level of phonemic substitution as a result of differences between the Dutch and Japanese sound systems. Another type of contact-induced word of which examples abound in Japanese is the 'loan translation'. Many of these were created in the sciences such as chemistry, medicine and physics. This allowed Japanese to frame the new knowledge from Europe and their own scientific discoveries in terms which were familiar to them. This framing gave rise to *rangaku*, which, as I suggested in Chapter 3, is in some sense the nomination of the new objects, ideas and processes which the Dutch introduced into Japan (cf. Foucault 1994: 132). A third category comprising many words is hybrid creations. Examples of these are also found in the sciences, but some have been formed using morphemes for everyday objects such as *gomu* ('rubber'), *hamu* ('ham') and *kōhī* ('coffee'). These and other contact-induced words have become part of the 'morphemic inventory' of Japanese (Winford 2003: 58). Furthermore, some contact-induced words have undergone processes of morphological integration such as clipping and the formation of *no*-adjectives.

In some sense, these contact-induced words represent a verbal *Wunderkammer*, an eclectic mix of words formed in various ways in the crucible of contact between Dutch and varieties of Japanese, marked by their thematic diversity. Moreover, they can be seen as semiophores, not simply words, but signs that bring the past into the present, telling us something about the nature of the interactions between the Dutch and Japanese languages and those who spoke and wrote them: above all, what the Japanese found interesting and novel in the Dutch language and the culture that it mediated.[96]

Returning to the question of how many words have been adopted by Japanese as a result of contact with Dutch, it will be clear that it is difficult to give a precise answer. In the case of 'pure' loanwords, or *gairaigo*, this chapter in common with other analyses has given a figure of around 300. However, for other types of lexical contact phenomena the matter is less clear. While many of these have been analysed above, the list is not exhaustive. Furthermore, the answer to this question differs depending on whether one is referring to the late Tokugawa period or the present day. In the late Tokugawa period, given

---

96   'Semiophore' is a term coined by Krzysztof Pomian (1990) initially to museum objects as mediators of the past. I use it here to refer to the Dutch loanwords in Japanese as mediators of the past.

the large number of contact-induced words in the sciences, an answer well in excess of 600 is not unreasonable. If we add Koga Jūjirō's c. 1520 dialectal words in the Nagasaki dialect alone, then the figure rises to well over 2,000, although *caveats* have been entered in this regard.[97] As for nowadays, in this chapter more than 380 contact-induced words have been marked as still in use standard contemporary Modern Japanese. Again, taking dialects into account the real figure will be higher. While on the one hand, the analysis presented by Shibatani (1990) indicated that *gairaigo* from Dutch are used less frequently than other *gairaigo*, on the other hand, some other lexical outcomes of contact with Dutch continue to be very productive morphemes in Japanese. Work on the productivity of imported morphemes by Dalton-Puffer suggests that those with high semantic and morphotactic transparency tend to be most productive (Dalton-Puffer 1996: 224, quoted in Winford 2003: 58). Loan morphemes such as *gomu*, *hamu* and *kōhī* score highly on both semantic and morphotactic transparency, which helps to explain why they have formed new words in Japanese and will probably continue to do so. Therefore, while on the one hand, I do not intend to give a definitive figure for the total number of lexical outcomes of contact with Dutch in Japanese, I hope that this chapter has given the reader a sense of the quantity and diversity of these words and of the issues involved in analysing them.

This chapter has, however, also illustrated that there have been other outcomes of contact with Dutch in Japanese. Attention has also been paid to the influence of Dutch via Japanese on the lexis of Sinitic varieties and Korean, part of what I have termed the 'circulation of loanwords'. Work by Kuiper (1993) and Vos (2000b) indicates that around 100 words in Mandarin Chinese and Korean have resulted from this influence. Here, the shared use of Sinitic characters facilitated borrowing. However, in each case, there is little doubt that more work needs to be done to give a more complete picture of the lexical outcomes of this influence in modern Chinese and Korean.

As for the influence of language contact on Japanese grammar, in order to render Dutch texts in Japanese, translators needed to modify Japanese syntax in several ways. Perhaps the most interesting finding here is that innovations such as the use of *ni-yotte* did not simply die out at the end of the Tokugawa period, but rather spread out beyond translations and became an intrinsic part of the grammar of modern Japanese. Some of the suggestions made by Earns require more work, which may produce interesting results.

Furthermore, this chapter analysed the graphic influence of Dutch on Japanese in the form of the use of Latin script or *rōmaji* by Japanese authors.

---

97   See also Tokugawa (1979).

Some Japanese gave serious consideration to replacing *kanji* and *kana* with *rōmaji*, although these ideas did not gain wider acceptance. The use of *rōmaji* by Japanese artists such as Shiba Kōkan is noteworthy, for it conjures up a sense of the exotic. This takes writing beyond the merely functional graphic recording of language and points to its semiotic value as an indicator of a desire to engage with and even embrace 'the other'.

In conclusion, contact with Dutch in the Tokugawa period led to several types of interference in Japanese. While some of this interference has disappeared, other forms have emerged such as the spreading of grammatical particles and the emergence of new hybrid words including Dutch loan morphemes. It is probable that some of this interference has become 'submerged' by the subsequent rise of two other West Germanic contact languages in Japan, English and German. Nevertheless, the evidence presented in this chapter illustrates that although there were only ever some twenty Europeans at the Dutch trading post western Kyushu, the influence of the Dutch language on Japanese, through the introduction of new objects and ideas, and the reading and translation of Dutch texts, has been and continues to be significant.

Language Shift and Recession

1   Introduction

'With English as yet scarcely studied by the natives', and 'with the foreigners who speak Japanese to be counted on the fingers of one hand,' affairs had to be conducted through hastily recruited speakers of Dutch. So wrote Sir Ernest Satow (1921: 169, quoted in Bownas 2005: 229), who worked as interpreter at the British Legation in Edo/Tokyo between 1862 and 1869, and who would later become a leading historian of Japan. Furthermore, Satow recorded in his memoirs that his first act in Japan in 'sweeping away all the cobwebs of the old Dutch diplomacy' was to learn Japanese. Satow's recollections of his time in Japan neatly sum up the position of Dutch in the last chapter of our story, which analyses the shift away from the language, which meant that by about 1900 it had more or less ceased to be used in Japan. In the years immediately following 1854 when Commodore Perry had obliged the Japanese to sign the Convention of Kanagawa, there was an initial increase in the use of Dutch, for as Satow observed, it initially became the Language of Wider Communication (LWC) between Japanese and Europeans as the latter sought to gain trading rights and influence in late Tokugawa Japan. However, for several reasons, such as the realization amongst the Japanese that the Dutch were by no means the most powerful Western nation, other languages soon competed to replace Dutch as the dominant European language in Japan. Some Westerners, though, made efforts to learn Japanese. For example, when Sir Ernst Satow temporarily left Japan in 1869, he was commended by the Japanese Foreign Minister on the 'extreme facility' with which he spoke Japanese (Bownas 2005: 229).

This chapter analyses the shift away from Dutch following a broadly chronological order. Here, I should note that the term 'language shift' is used slightly differently to how it is applied in other literature on language contact. Typically, in sociolinguistics it refers to the gradual replacement of the main language (L1) of a speech community by another language (L2) in all spheres of usage. It can either be intra-generational or intergenerational. It is often observed in migrant communities which make the shift from their heritage language to that of the recipient culture (Pauwels 2016: 18–19). In the case of Dutch in late Tokugawa and early Meiji Japan, the shift involved Japanese forsaking Dutch as their L2 (or perhaps L3 after Chinese) for other European languages, above all German, French and English. As a result, Dutch receded as an LWC between

Japanese and Europeans, to be replaced by these other European languages, or in some cases Japanese. Furthermore, the focus in this chapter in on matters external to language, such as the cultural, social and political context in which it was embedded, rather than internal matters such as syntax and morphology (Burke 2005: 7).

It is difficult to identify one historical moment when this shift began, for we need rather to talk in terms of a process rather than a decisive event, but the response to the *Phaeton* affair of 1808, perhaps influenced by earlier incursions of Russian ships such as the *Nadezhda* in 1804, indicates that from that point onwards Japanese recognized that a knowledge of Dutch would be insufficient to deal with the increasingly frequent arrival of European and American vessels in their waters.[1] The arrival of Perry's 'black ships' in 1853 marked the end of the first phase of this shift. However, as already suggested, perhaps somewhat counter-intuitively, this initially provided a boost for Dutch. Dutch experts such as J.L.C. Pompe van Meerdervoort arrived to help Japan modernize. In 1860, the trading post at Deshima was closed and replaced by a vice-consulate at Nagasaki (De Groot 2005: 2). The Dutch in some sense lost their privileged position and became but one of several Western countries vying for trade and influence in Japan. The 1860s in Japan would be marked by a struggle between those who wanted to hold on to the ways of the past and those who sought to modernize the country, not least in order to prevent any possible foreign invasion. The modernizers won the day and in 1868 the shogunate was abolished and the Meiji era or Restoration (*Meiji ishin* 明治維新) ushered in. After this there was an accelerated shift away from Dutch in the third and final phase of this process. It is not possible to be categorical, but it is likely that one of the reasons for the rapid demise of Dutch was its association with the old regime. It is striking how quickly Dutch was replaced by other European languages in particular in the field of learning and this may in part be attributed to the fact that Dutch had little or no place in the new Japan of the Meiji Restoration. During the 1870s and 1880s, other European languages continued to gain ground. In 1888 a dictionary of physics was published in Japan which included terms in Japanese and three European languages, but not Dutch. This would have been unthinkable thirty, perhaps even twenty years earlier, but by now the time of Dutch as the primary European language in Japan had passed and the embers of the language which had burnt so brightly at many points in the previous three centuries were almost extinguished.

---

1 For a brief account of American ships in Japanese waters since the end of the eighteenth century, see Tsukahara (2007b: 196–197).

2   1808–1853

As Chapter 4 illustrates, Dutch had faced competition from other European languages prior to 1808. Leaving aside its long struggle to replace Portuguese as the dominant European language in Japan, Dutch had also faced competition from German, French and, increasingly, Russian. Perhaps what was different about the *Phaeton* incident of 1808 was the Japanese response, for the fact that the British frigate, HMS *Phaeton*, could enter Nagasaki Bay unchallenged, was a clear indication that Japan could be attacked by European navies. The *bakufu* ordered interpreters to study other European languages, in particular English and Russian. The move to learn Russian was in part inspired by the arrival in Nagasaki Bay four years earlier of the Russian ship *Nadezhda* and earlier incursions by Russian ships in Japanese waters (Boot 2008: 104; Goodman 2013: 217; Kornicki 2018: 97). Furthermore, some Nagasaki interpreters studied German privately and there was also a move to increase Japanese knowledge of French.

2.1   *Ranald MacDonald*

The learning of English was facilitated by the fact that some Dutch, such as Jan Cock Blomhoff, knew the language. Towards the end of the period of *sakoku*, help came from an unexpected quarter, in the form of the American, Ranald MacDonald (1824–94) (Nishikawa-van Eester 2017: 251–254). He had entered Japan illegally on Rishiri Island (利尻島), Hokkaido in June 1848. On his return to the USA, MacDonald wrote a book on his experiences, 'Japan: Story of Adventure'. This was not published until 1923 (MacDonald 1923). From Hokkaido he was sent to Nagasaki at the other end of the country to be repatriated, where he spent several months before leaving on a Dutch ship in 1849. In early encounters with Japanese, MacDonald benefitted from the fact that Joseph Levijsson (*opperhoofd* 1845–50) spoke English. He therefore acted as a linguistic go-between for MacDonald and the Dutch interpreters at Nagasaki, few of whom spoke English (Schodt 2013: 262). One exception was Moriyama Einosuke (1820–72). He spoke Dutch well and according to MacDonald spoke English 'pretty fluently, and even grammatically'. He had a Dutch dictionary, but also a Dutch-English one and 'showed a great desire to learn English'. When pressed by MacDonald about how he had learnt English, Einosuke was not so forthcoming, but MacDonald intimates that he had acquired some of it from shipwrecked Anglophone sailors. On occasion, when MacDonald needed to communicate with the other interpreters, he was given a Dutch-English dictionary in order to show them the Dutch word. While in Nagasaki, MacDonald taught English to some of the interpreters: he lists fourteen of them, including Einosuke (MacDonald 1923: 226). The interpreters would read English to him one at a time and he would correct their pronunciation. He records that the interpreters found it difficult to pronounce some English consonants and that some consonant combinations were practically impossible for them. In particular, he noted that the interpreters had problems pronouncing [l] so that his own name in the mouths of the Japanese sounded more like 'Ranardu MacDonardo'. They also tended to add 'o' or 'i' after consonants (MacDonald 1923: 209, 226; Kawamoto 1998: 153). MacDonald's English lessons did, however, prepare interpreters to some extent for the rapid shift to English after 1854. In fact, several interpreters, such as Einosuke, were called upon when Commodore Perry arrived in Japan.

MacDonald made other notes of relevance to our story. He records that on January 1, 1849, Levijsson gave him some English language material: 68 editions of the 'London Atlas' newspaper and 'Weekly Despatch'. He picked up Japanese words from the interpreters and noted that they said 'pan' for 'bread' (from the Portuguese *pão*) and 'boutre', from the Dutch 'butter' (*boter*) (MacDonald 1923: 243). In his book on Japan MacDonald included a glossary of Nagasaki dialect vocabulary, although the accuracy with which he recorded what he heard has been questioned (MacDonald 1923: 287–302; Kaiser 1996: 9). Nevertheless, he provides us with some interesting insights into the knowledge and use of English in Japan prior to 1853.

2.2 Cornelis Assendelft de Coningh

In 1851, as the captain of the 'Joän', the Dutchman Cornelis Assendelft de Coningh reached Deshima, where he remained for three months.[2] He later published a record of his experiences on Deshima in *Mijn Verblijf in Japan* ('My Stay in Japan'), first published in Amsterdam in 1856. In this book Assendelft de Coningh makes several observations which are of interest for our purposes. He notes that like MacDonald, although not a native speaker, he gave English lessons to the interpreters. He observes that one had already made great advances, possibly a reference to Moriyama Einosuke (Assendelft de Coningh 1856: 41). As for the interpreters' Dutch, he makes a distinction between their qualities as translators and as speakers of the language. While the best ones were very good at translating from Dutch to Japanese, he describes how they spoke and wrote letters as risible (*kluchtig*). He quotes examples of the 'risible' Dutch of the interpreters from messages that they wrote to him. One ran 'Asjeblief, ik verzoek u een fles odeklonje, ik zal zeer verblijd zijn'. While the Dutch is by no means perfect, it is understandable, although this does not tell us how the Japanese

---

2   When he first visited Nagasaki Bay in 1845, he was a sailor and so did not disembark (Assendelft de Coningh 2012: xiv).

would have pronounced such a sentence (Assendelft de Coningh 1856: 37; 1856b: 5). He also gives us an insight into the background and training of the interpreters. All of them, he writes, are the sons of other interpreters (some were in fact adopted sons). When they were five years old, as samurai, they got a sword and began to learn Dutch. They attended the *tolkencollege* and the best junior interpreters accompanied the more senior interpreters as they interpreted for the Dutch and Japanese, in order to learn about the job. He also observes that the *opperhoofd* had six servants, four cooks and other staff. He notes that the six servants were all Japanese (*Japanners*) whose Dutch was better than that of the interpreters (Assendelft de Coningh 1856: 39).

The term *comprador* for the Japanese merchants who could trade with the Dutch was still in use. Assendelft de Coningh (1879: 11:19) observes that they all spoke Dutch, by no means perfectly, but good enough to do business with.[3] He notes that on returning to his lodgings he found a gift with a tag in Dutch reading 'Geschenk van Compradoors' ('Present from Compradors'), and viewed this as a direct attempt to bribe him. Another observation by Assendelft de Coningh concerns the housemaids of the Dutch on Deshima to whom he refers as 'tajoz'.[4] Many if not all of these became lovers or concubines of the Dutch, and were in some sense the final emanation of the *Orandayuki*. He notes that in one case a Dutchman would speak Dutch to his 'tajoz' and she would reply in a mixture of Dutch, Malay and Japanese (Assendelft de Coningh 1856: 46). As in the case of MacDonald, these metalinguistic comments by Assendelft de Coningh contribute to our understanding of the knowledge and use of Dutch on Deshima as well as its relation to other languages just a couple of years before Perry and his black ships arrived in Japan.

2.3 Bansho wage goyō

The *Phaeton* incident led to the establishment in Edo in 1811 of the *Bansho wage goyō* ('Office for the Translation of Barbarian Books') within the *Tenmondai* (Clements 2015: 156). One of the first tasks of one of its employees, Baba Teiyū, was to translate letters found on the Russian ship *Diana*. However, Dutch was still the primary European language from which employees of this institution made translations. Indeed, one of the reasons for the establishment of the *Bansho wage goyō* was to translate the Dutch edition of Noël Chomel's

---

3 'Die lieden spraken allen Hollandsch, 't was er wel na, maar toch overvloedig genoeg om zijne zaken met hen te bespreken'.

4 Elsewhere, Assendelft de Coningh (1856b: 9–11) refers to *tayor*. Both forms come from *tayū* 太夫. Although this originally referred to high-ranking courtesans, over time it was used for *geisha* and other similar lower-ranking women.

Dictionnaire oeconomique into Japanese (Goodman 2013: 130–131). This, it was thought, would provide the Japanese with an as yet unparalleled understanding of Western societies and culture. Bilingual Dutch-Japanese learning materials and lexicons continued to be produced, but perhaps a hint of the future came in 1856. In that year, Murakami Hidetoshi, described as 'the first serious student of French', who had been working at the *Bansho wage goyō* since 1853, published a three-volume quadrilingual (Japanese-French-English-Dutch) lexicon (*Sango-benran*, 'Trilingual Manual') in octavo, described in detail in Chapter 4. The words are ordered in the manner of traditional Chinese/Japanese encyclopaedias and lexicons, rather than according to the Latin alphabet. The arrangement of each entry has symbolic has well as practical value. The words are ordered from top to bottom with Japanese at the top in *kanji* with *furigana*. Below the Japanese are French and English in the middle and finally Dutch at the bottom. One interpretation might be that this dictionary put French, English and Dutch on an equal footing. However, another might be that Dutch was already being relegated to the bottom of the Japanese page, below other European languages, although it was admittedly compiled by the Francophile Japanese, Hidetoshi.

2.4 *Imported Dutch Learning Material*

Chapter 4 gave details of books imported in the nineteenth century via Deshima in languages other than Dutch. The titles were written in *Meisho-chō* ('Title ledgers') by the Japanese censors. There was still demand for Dutch learning material. The 1847 list includes several books for students of Dutch, some of which point beyond the basic acquisition of Dutch and an interest in more advanced subjects. Among these are two spelling guides by Siegenbeek, one by H. Kroeze Ramaker (*Korte schets van de Nederduitsche taal en spelkunde*, 1841), another by Derk Bomhoff (*Nieuw handwoordenboek voor de spelling der Nederduitsche taal*, 1846), and one by Pieter Weiland. The list includes other books compiled by Weiland including a copy of his grammar *Nederduitsche Spraakkunst* and four copies of his lexicons. Another book is on noun genders. The author is given in *katakana* as モイト (*moito*). Nagazumi (1998: 68–69) does not transcribe this, but it is likely to be Pieter Muyt and the book *Handwoordenboek der meestgebruikelijke Nederduitsche zelfstandige naamwoorden met aanwijzing van derzelver bijzondere geslachten* ('Manual of the most common Dutch nouns, with an indication of their gender'), printed in Zaltbommel in 1824. We have no further details, but this is perhaps suggestive of a well-developed interest in Dutch grammar among some Japanese and furthermore a desire to produce correct Dutch. Learning the gender in order to determine which article and what grammatical agreement to use would have been quite difficult for Japanese. First, there is no grammatical article, or indeed grammatical gender, in Japanese. Second, whereas contemporary standard Dutch has two grammatical genders, common and neuter, in the nineteenth century standard Dutch still had three genders, masculine, feminine and neuter, a fact reflected in Muyt's manual.[5] Other books suggestive of a desire to develop Dutch skills further are a manual on Dutch style, Johan Beijer's *Handleiding tot den Nederlandschen stijl* (2nd ed. Rotterdam, 1824) and a manual on Dutch synonyms.

In 1852, on the eve of Perry's arrival, Dutch learning material was still being imported. On the *Meisho-chō* for that year there are three copies of Weiland's *Kunstwoordenboek* ('Dictionary of Technical Terms', The Hague, 1824), which as the subtitle indicates, contains explanations of 'all sorts of foreign/strange words' (*allerlei vreemde woorden*) in Dutch (Nagazumi 1998: 126–137). There is also a spelling guide by Weiland and a copy of the Dutch translation of Chomel's *Dictionnaire oeconomique*. However, the 1852 *Meisho-chō* also lists bilingual learning material, where one language is Dutch. This in some sense heralds the intermediate stage in the post-1854 shift, whereby Dutch was used by Japanese to acquire other European languages. The list includes five Dutch-English dictionaries, a manual for reading and practising English and other material in or on English (described simply as 'Engels' or Engelsche Taal').

2.5   *The Nabeshima Collection*

The Nabeshima-Saga collection included over 700 books in Dutch (Matsuda 2006). Some thirty of these books were Dutch learners or lexicons. These include Weiland's grammar, *Nederduitsche spraakkunst* (Dordrecht, 1839) (370), two copies of H. Martin's Dutch lexicon *Beredeneerd Nederduitsch Woordenboek* ('Comprehensive Dutch Dictionary' 376a,b) and Dutch lexicons by Weiland and Bomhoff (377, 378). However, there were also about thirty books comprising learning material in more than one European language, such as a quadrilingual (Dutch, French, English, German) dictionary (The Hague, 1847–48) (371), a French-Dutch dictionary for the artillery (The Hague, 1811) (372), Halma's French-Dutch dictionary (373), an English-Dutch dictionary (Dordrecht, 1823–24) (374), a Malay learner and dictionary (367a,b), a German-Dutch pocket dictionary (382) and even a small Latin-Dutch dictionary and Latin grammar (375, 392). As with the later *Meisho-chō*, the catalogue of the Nabeshima-Saga collection points both to a continued demand for monolingual Dutch

---

5   Some dialectal varieties of Dutch, such as West Flemish, still identify three grammatical genders in the indefinite article.

learning material, but also to an interest in other European languages, mediated by Dutch.

2.6   *Volume of Translations*

In the period 1820–1840, the number of translations from Dutch to Japanese fell as opposition to Western learning grew. This pattern was reversed in the early 1840s as news of the First Opium War reached the shores of Japan. While some argued that Japan should respond by restricting Western learning, others argued that on the contrary Japan needed Western knowledge in order to defend itself against a possible invasion from Western countries (Clements 2015: 141, 150). The latter view clearly achieved some traction for in the years after 1840 there was a sudden surge of translation activity. The number of translations reached almost sixty a year by the mid-1850s, as Dutch gained an increasingly important place in Japanese intellectual life (Clements 2015: 147, fig. 6). It is of course at this point that the worst fears of some Japanese were realized as Commodore Perry sailed into Edo Bay, changing not only the course of Japanese history, but also that of the Dutch language in Japan. In 1854 the Convention of Kanagawa was concluded between America and Japan, a key step in the opening up of Japan to other Western countries. The treaty was drawn up in four languages, Japanese, Chinese, English and Dutch (Beasley 1973: 96).[6]

2.7   *Concluding Remarks for the Period Prior to 1854*

So, in the period prior to the arrival of Perry, several forces were at work. First, there was an increased interest in European languages other than Dutch, above all English, Russian and French, but also German. Second, some Japanese argued for a restriction on the import of Western books. This had an effect on the number of these books imported in the period 1820–1840. Furthermore, after 1839, imported books were subject to increased censorship. However, how effective this censorship was is not clear and one might certainly raise questions about the ability of the censors to read not only Dutch, but also other Western languages. Third, there was a continued demand for books in Dutch in the period prior to 1853. However, this was not only driven by an interest in Dutch *per se*, but also because it provided access to other Western languages. Here, I would like to introduce the notion of Dutch as a *thuralect*—from the Greek θύρα ('door'). In some sense it acted as a door or portal, through which Japanese could learn other languages.

---

6 Beasley (p. 96 n. 52) gives sources for the texts in Japanese, Chinese and English, but not for the text in Dutch.

3   1854–1868

As Reinier Hesselink (2001: 208) has argued, the arrival of the Commodore Perry and other Americans who followed in his wake did not immediately signal the end for the Dutch language and *rangaku* in Japan. On the contrary, he writes,

> The arrival of Commodore Perry boosted the importance of the role of *rangaku*. This was not limited to the reading of books in Dutch, but expanded to include highly visible careers for countless men in *bakumatsu* and Meiji society, who had, like Sakamoto Ryoma and Fukuzawa Yukichi, started their careers as *rangakusha*.[7]

In 1859, Cornelis Assendelft de Coningh returned to Japan, this time as a merchant staying until 1861. He arrived at Deshima and later moved to the treaty port of Yokohama (see fig. 30). The record of his third visit to Japan, *Ontmoetingen ter zee en te land* ('Encounters at Sea and on Land'), provides some useful insights into the use of Dutch in the years after 1854. At Deshima he notes that a Japanese servant said 'Opperhoofd is nog boven' ('The *opperhoofd* is still upstairs') in 'fairly good Dutch' (*vrij goed Hollandsch*) (Assendelft de Coningh 1879: II:13). On the other hand, he observed that the interpreter 'Saknozio' spoke in 'painfully corrupted Dutch' (*deerlijk gehavend Hollandsch*). This was in fact Yoshio Sakunojō who had worked on the translation of Chomel's *Dictionnaire oeconomique* (Assendelft de Coningh 1879: II:21). In his account of his time in Yokohama, Assendelft de Coningh provides examples of Japanese writing to him in Dutch (like Doeff he refers somewhat disparagingly to *Japansch-Hollandsch*), as he had done in *Mijn Verblijf in Japan*. He was clearly not impressed by the quality of the Dutch, recording that 'the meaning is so out of hand' (*zoo voor de hand weggegrepen*) Two were signed by 'Inomata'. This may be Inomata Dennosuke, who had been an interpreter at Nagasaki when Ranald MacDonald was there in 1848/9 (MacDonald 1923: 226; Assendelft de Coningh 1879: II:102–104; 2012: 86–87). With the changes now afoot, Dutch interpreters needed to be re-deployed within Japan. One interpreter whose spoken Dutch was not altogether beyond the pale for Assendelft de Coningh was 'Tenasabro'. He spoke 'very bookish' (*zeer boeksch*) Dutch,

---

7   *Bakumatsu* refers to the closing days of the Tokugawa shogunate. This was followed by the Meiji period.

FIGURE 30　A Dutch family (*Orandajin*, ヲランダ人) taking a walk at Yokohama, Utagawa Sadahide, 1861
RIJKSMUSEUM, AMSTERDAM

and with 'the wisdom of a teacher' (*met een schoolmeesterachtige wijsheid*) (Assendelft de Coningh 1879: II:59).[8]

3.1   *Learning Dutch*

Japanese continued to learn Dutch. Indeed, Fukuzawa Yukichi, whom we met in Chapter 2. began to learn Dutch in Nagasaki precisely because of Perry's arrival. He wanted to use his Dutch to acquire a knowledge of gunnery in order to help defend his country against foreign incursions (Fukuzawa 2007: 21–22). In this regard, as previously noted, one of his early translations was of a Dutch book on fortifications.

Dutch involvement with the establishment of the Japanese navy also strengthened the position of the Dutch language. With the assistance of the *opperhoofd* at Deshima, a Dutch gunboat from the East Indies naval squadron, the *Soembing*, was presented to the Japanese in the mid-1850s. This was the first boat in the Japanese navy. For our purposes, the instruction of Japanese naval cadets by Dutch naval personnel in Nagasaki from 1855 to 1857 is of interest. This was given in Dutch and translated into Japanese by interpreters (Huyssen van Kattendyke 1860: 201). In the late 1850s, the Dutch school of naval studies in Nagasaki attracted over 150 samurai students from several *han*. Two-thirds of the students had completed a two-year intensive training course in the Dutch language. One of these was the future commander of the modern Japanese navy in the early Meiji period, Katsu Kaishū (1823–99) (Duke 2009: 26). Dutchmen were also involved in construction projects that formed part of the Japanese modernization programme. The Dutch naval engineer, Hendrick Hardes, took charge of constructing a naval repair yard at Nagasaki, and another Dutchman, J.L.C. Pompe van Meerdervoort, a naval medical officer, who lectured in Dutch for several years to naval cadets, oversaw the construction of the first military hospital in Japan (Blussé *et al.* (eds.) 2000: 183; Pompe van Meerdervoort 1970: 85). When Pompe van Meerdervoort left after the end of his five-year contract he was replaced by Toon Bauduin (1820–85), who likewise stayed in Japan for five years. Toon Bauduin was the brother of another Dutchman in Japan, the merchant and diplomat, Albert Bauduin (Moeshart 2001: 33–34).

The Dutch government also played a rôle here. In the first years after 1854, the Dutch ministry of colonies took pro-active steps to maintain the position of Dutch as the primary LWC in Japan. The *opperhoofd* Donker Curtius was asked in private letters to prepare a Japanese grammar (in Dutch) for distribution in Japan. The result was *Proeve eener Japansche spraakkunst* ('Model

---

8   Ranald MacDonald (1923: 226) mentions Shioya Tanesaburō.

of Japanese grammar'), which was edited by the Professor of Chinese and Japanese at Leiden University, J.J. Hoffmann, and printed by Sythoff in Leiden in 1857 (Kuiper 2015: 387–388).

3.2 Dutch Books

After 1854 Dutch books continued to be imported and translated, but also printed in order to cope with the sudden increased demand. The number of Dutch books entered on the *Meisho-chō* by the Japanese censors varied from year to year. In the mid-1850s as Japan signed treaties with Western powers access to Dutch books again became easier (Kornicki 2001: 303). In 1855, more than 300 Dutch books were listed. In 1856, the number dipped to 240. In 1857 it rose sharply to 550, but in 1858 sank to 150 (Nagazumi 1998: 182–261). Nevertheless, in these four years some 1250 Dutch books were imported into Japan. There was still demand for Dutch learning material. The *Meisho-chō* for 1855 include two Dutch spelling guides by Siegenbeek and one spelling guide by Weiland as well as three Dutch dictionaries by Weiland. There was also a copy of Barthold Lulofs' guide to Dutch grammar and style *Over Nederlandsche spraakkunst, stijl en letterkennis* (Groningen, 1831), and an 1839 edition of Beijer's manual on Dutch style. The lists for 1858 include two Dutch grammars by Weiland, seven Dutch dictionaries, four spelling guides and another copy of Beijer's style manual. In 1858, an office for the sale of Dutch books was opened in Edo by the agency permitted to sell imported goods from Nagasaki (Kornicki 2001: 303–304). To meet the sudden increase in demand Dutch books were hastily re-printed in Nagasaki and Edo.

Books on physics were in demand. At least two re-prints of *Natuurkundig schoolboek* ('Schoolbook on physics') by Johannes Buijs (1st ed. Amsterdam, 1800) were made in Japan in the second half of the 1850s, with the addition of a title page in Japanese.[9] Another popular book on physics by Buijs, *Volks-natuurkunde* ('Popular physics'), originally printed in Amsterdam in 1811 for the *Maatschappij tot Nut van 't Algemeen* was reprinted (the title page has *nagedurkt* instead of *nagedrukt*) in Nagasaki in 1858.[10] Dutch military books were also in demand. In the second half of the 1850s a three-volume Dutch military work *Reglement op de exercitien en manoeuvres der infanterie* ('Code

---

9   NIJL ID 4402849 (1856) and WUL 文庫 08 C1141 (1858).

10   Ueno collection number 3161. This has the seals of the Nagasaki *bugyō*'s censor's office, the *Bansho shirabesho* and the *Kaiseijo*. Another re-print of *Volks-natuurkunde* was made in 1856, although the place of publication is not given on the Japanese title page, WUL 文庫 08 C1143.

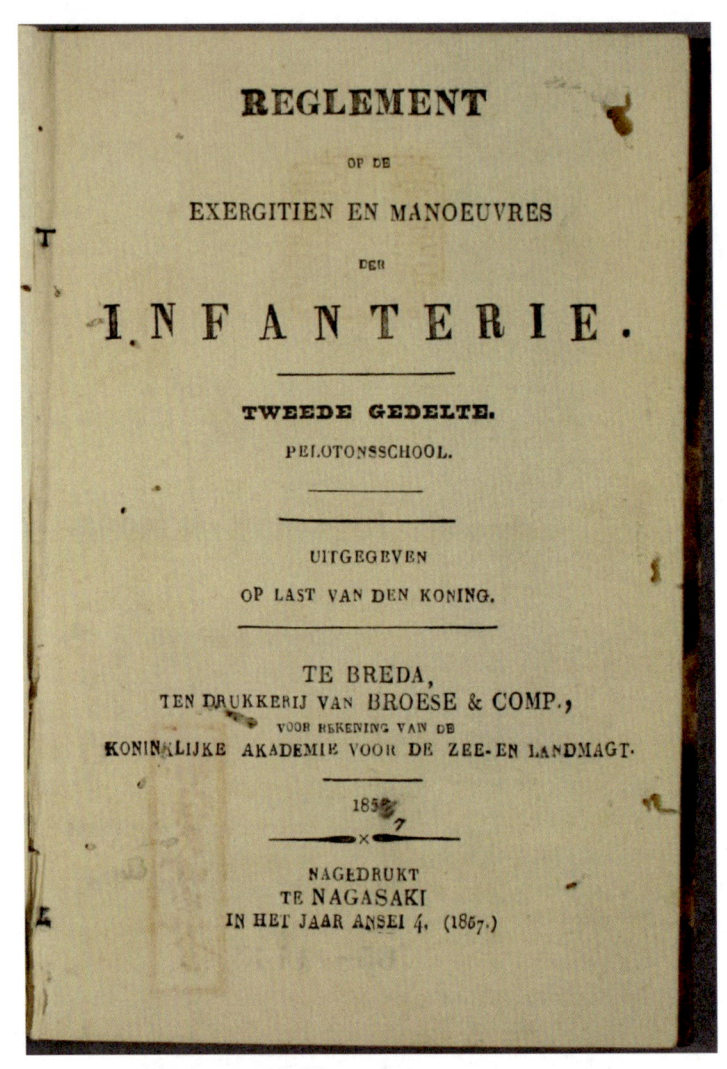

FIGURE 31   The title page of Part II of *Reglement op de exercitien en manoeuvres der infanterie* ('Code for infantry drills and manoeuvres'), re-print, Nagasaki, 1857
WUL 文庫 08 C1153

for infantry drills and manoeuvres') was reprinted in Nagasaki (see fig. 31).[11]
A Dutch book on gunnery, *Voorschrift omtrent de wapens, de munitie en de schietoefeningen der infanterie* ('Instructions on the weapons, munitions and

11   There are six copies of this in the Ueno collection. Number 629 has the shogunal seal. The Ueno collection also includes copies of several editions of the volumes printed in the Netherlands.

firing practice of the infantry'), originally printed in The Hague in 1852, was also reprinted in Japan.[12] In Edo in 1857 a re-print was made of *Algemeene Voorschriften omtrent het Tirailleren en het Defileren der Korpsen Infanterie* ('General Instructions on Skirmishing and Marching of the Infantry Corps'), first printed in Utrecht in about 1830.[13] On the title page of the re-print *Kolpsen* instead of *Korpsen* and *Hoornbrlazers* (sic) instead of *Hoornblazers* ('Buglers') hint at Japanese intervention.

A copy of a treaty (*traktaat*) concluded between the last Dutch *opperhoofd*, Jan Hendrik Donker Curtius, and Japanese officials in Nagasaki was printed at Deshima in 1858. After 1854, the German physician Philipp Franz von Siebold had finally been allowed to return to Japan, which he did in 1859. In 1861, he published a collection of open letters, *Open brieven uit Japan, Ter Nederlandsche Drukkerij*, i.e., on the Dutch printing press at Deshima.[14] His second stay in Japan was, however, short-lived. He was requested to leave again in 1861 and would never return to the country. In Edo in 1857 Japanese editions were printed of two works by Matthijs Siegenbeek: the second edition of *Grammatica, of Nederduitsche spraakkunst* (1822) and his *Syntaxis of Woordvoeging der Nederduitsche Taal* (1810). The former was a re-print of *Oranda bunten zenpen* ('Dutch grammar. First/Front part', 1842), while the latter had the title *Oranda bunten kōhen: seikuron* ('Dutch grammar. Second (lit. Back) Part. On (Dutch) Phrases').[15] Both were based on earlier prints by Mitsukuri Genpo.

By 1860, there was still a large trade in Dutch books and learning materials for Dutch. However, there was also demand for books written in other Western languages and learning materials for other Western languages. These were often written in Dutch, underlining its rôle as a thuralect. Lists of books imported at Deshima in that year include 64 copies of French-Dutch dictionaries and 100 copies of a French learner published by the Van der Pijl printing house in Dordrecht.[16] The lists also included 50 copies of Lindley Murray's English learner *Engelsche Spraakkunst* (1st ed. Haarlem 1816); '50 Peel Leerboek der Engelsche taal in 2 deeltjes', a learner, possibly published by the Van der Pijl

---

12 Ueno collection number 645. This has the seal of the *Bansho shirabesho* and the *Kaiseijo*. The place where this book was printed is not given.

13 WUL 文庫 08 C0471.

14 Ueno collection number 3635.

15 Leiden University Library shelfmark: LUB 1371 C 18: 1 (*Grammatica/Oranda bunpen zenpen*) and LUB 1371 C 18: 2 (*Syntaxis: Oranda bunten kōhen*). There is also an edition of Siegenbeek's *Syntaxis of Woordvoeging* printed in Japan in 1843/4 (*Tenpō* 天保 14) in Leiden University Library. It has the shelfmark LUB SINOL Gulik E 170.

16 This is listed as *Leerwyze der fransche taal*, although Van der Pijl's book is called *Leerboek der fransche taal*.

printing house; twenty copies each of Dutch-English and English-Dutch dictionaries by Willem Holtrop (given as Haltrop) (first ed., Dordrecht, 1789) and even four Latin-Dutch dictionaries (Itazawa 1959: 664–683). This surge in book imports was possible for by now more than one Dutch ship a year was arriving at Deshima.

3.3 *Official Actions*

Japanese officials attempted to control the import and circulation of Dutch books, but in some sense their actions were too little, too late. Towards the end of the Tenpō era (1830–44), laws were enacted to control commercial publishing, including translations, more strictly (Clements 2015: 149). A few years before Perry's arrival, in 1850, the *bakufu* had ordered that all Dutch books had to be registered with the city commissioners. In 1856, the *Bansho shirabesho* ('Office for the Investigation of Barbarian Books') was founded in Edo (Clements 2015: 193). It was not only an office but also an educational institution for the study of the West, including its languages and sciences. It assumed the translation responsibilities of the *Bansho wage goyō* ('Office for the Translation of Barbarian Books'), with the *rangakusha* Mitsukuri Genpo and Sugita Seikei, Genpaku's grandson, being appointed as its first principal professors (Verwayen 1998: 338).[17] Initially, the *Bansho shirabesho* focussed on Dutch materials, primarily relating to military matters. Mitsukuri Genpo and fellow *rangakusha* such as Oda Matazō (1804–70) were ordered to translate Dutch books (*ransho* 蘭書). One new source of Dutch translation was the newspaper the *Javasche Courant*. This was translated at the *Bansho shirabesho* into Japanese. This institution represented a concerted effort by the shogunate to concentrate and control translation activity in Edo. These attempts to control translations had mixed results. In the mid- to late-1850s the annual number of translations of works in Dutch and other Western languages rose, reaching a peak in the late-1850s of almost sixty a year, although by 1860 it had dropped back sharply to about half that number (Clements 2015: 147). In due course, however, there would be an increasing number of translations from other Western languages. For example, in 1867 Kanda Takahira's translation of William Ellis's 'Outlines of Social Economy', regarded as Japan's earliest study of western economics, was published.

3.4 *Other Western Languages: English*

3.4.1 The *Bansho shirabesho*

By 1857, English had been introduced at the *Bansho shirabesho*, reflecting the fact that the threat to Japan was seen to come from Anglophone nations, rather

---

17 Verwayen gives the year for the establishment of the *Bansho shirabesho* as 1854.

than the Netherlands. The translation of documents written in English gradually replaced those in Dutch. Given the lack of staff trained in English, those who had studied Dutch were assigned to the translation of English materials. One official Nishi Amane (1829–97) studied English using an English-Dutch dictionary. Already by 1860, English had become the dominant language at the *Bansho shirabesho*. This shift mirrored the dominance of Britain in trade with Japan. By 1868, over 80% of Japan's foreign trade was with Britain (Duke 2009: 26). French and German were introduced at the *Bansho shirabesho*, reflecting their importance, though English remained dominant. As a measure of this, four-fifths of the c. 100 students in the early 1860s were enrolled in the Department of English. The *Bansho* continued to expand and in 1863 its name changed to *Kaiseijo* ('The School of Enlightenment'). Just before the Meiji Restoration, when the overall number of students at the *Kaiseijo* had jumped to 500, 300 students were enrolled in the English department, and another 100 in the French department. This institution would eventually form the basis of Tokyo University. A graduate, Katō Hiroyuki (1836–1916), who became the first president of Tokyo University, was a German specialist (Duke 2009: 19–21).

3.4.2   Japanese Learning English

In this intermediate phase of the shift away from Dutch to other European languages, a knowledge of Dutch was useful to those who wished to learn English. The case of Fukuzawa Yukichi is instructive in this regard. In his autobiography, Fukuzawa (2007: 22) observed that in Nagasaki in the years directly after 1854, European letters were to be seen everywhere, even on the labels of beer bottles and no-one perceived them as strange. An important development in Japan's engagement with the West was the opening of a treaty port at Yokohama. In 1858 Fukuzawa Yukichi came to the port and tried his Dutch on foreigners there, but to no avail. English had quickly established itself as the LWC in Yokohama and so Fukuzawa recognized the need to shift quickly to English.[18] It may well be Fukuzawa to whom the American businessman, Francis Hall (1822–1902), who resided in Yokohama from 1859 to 1866, refers in a diary entry on 17 November 1860. He observed that a Japanese (he refers to him simply as 'the samurai') who knew Dutch and who had learnt English with the help of a Dutch-English dictionary, spoke English quite well (Hall 1992: 276, see fig. 32). Already in 1860 Fukuzawa (2007: 432) published

---

18   English language publications were produced, which were aimed at the foreign community in Yokohama. In 1861 the English cartoonist and columnist for the Illustrated London News Charles Wirgman (1832–91) arrived in Yokohama. In 1862, he established the satirical 'Japan Punch', which continued to be published in English until 1887.

FIGURE 32
Photograph of Fukuzawa
Yukichi (1834–1901), Robillard,
Grande Morskaia
WUL 文庫 08 J0225

an English-Japanese dictionary, (*Zōtei*) *Kaei Tsūgo*), which was a translation of
a Chinese-English dictionary that he had purchased in San Francisco. In 1862
Fukuzawa was the first Japanese to use English materials for the instruction of
English in place of Dutch grammars (Bownas 2005: 231). He would later give
lectures on economics using an English-language textbook—this was Francis
Wayland's 'The Elements of Political Philosophy' (Fukuzawa 2007: 211, 361–
362). Fukuzawa would subsequently establish Keiō University (慶應義塾大学).

Other Japanese, too, were quick to notice that the linguistic sands were
shifting and that they would do well to learn other European languages. One
such Japanese, whom the Dutchman Assendelft de Coningh encountered in
Yokohama, was 'Sakfsabro'. This is Nakayama Sakusaburō (1838?–68), an interpreter from Nagasaki. He had been moved to Yokohama, because he had been
considered 'very clever' (*zeer kunstig*) in English by the Nagasaki Governor

and acted as interpreter for the English consul and the Governor. Sakusaburō admitted that he could translate for them much more quickly after a couple of glasses of gin! (Assendelft de Coningh 1879: II:58–59; 2012: 47–50). In 1861, Francis Hall recorded that Japanese learning English would frequently come to him with an English book and ask him to help them make sense of it (Kornicki 2001: 305). Hall also recorded that in Hakodate, another treaty port, he had met a ship's carpenter who had picked up 'a fair conversational knowledge' of English in two years (Hall 1992: 276). In the new situation one of the Japanese who thrived was Ōkuma Shigenobu (1838–1922). He was born into a samurai family near Nagasaki. He acquired an early knowledge of Dutch and English, which helped him to gain a position in dealing with foreign relations in Nagasaki after 1860 and he subsequently became a leading expert for the national government in financial matters and foreign affairs (De Bary et al. 1958: 680). Among his other achievements were to establish Waseda University and become Prime Minister of Japan.

An important change after 1854 was that Japanese were now allowed to travel abroad. An embassy went to Europe in 1862. Four years later, in 1866, a group of fourteen young Japanese were sponsored by the late Tokugawa regime to study in England (Bownas 2005: 231). One of these was Nakamura Masanao (1832–91). One way in which he put his knowledge of English to good use was to translate Samuel Smiles' famous work 'Self-Help' into Japanese (Duke 2009: 48).

3.4.3   The Rôle of Dutch-Americans

Several Dutch-Americans went to Japan during this period. They could engage both with Japanese who spoke the language of the past, Dutch, and those who spoke one of the languages of the future, English. One elderly Dutch-American, whom Assendelft de Coningh (2012:112) encountered in Japan, was 'Mr. Shobber'. Mr. Shobber had been born in the Netherlands and had lived and worked for thirty years in Amsterdam before moving to America. This explains why he spoke 'good Dutch' (*goed Hollandsch*) (Assendelft de Coningh 1879: II:136). An interpreter who worked for the Americans was Hendrik (Henry) C.J. Heusken (1832–1861). He was born in Amsterdam but his family had migrated to the United States. In 1856 he became the secretary and personal assistant to the first American Consul-General in Japan, Townsend Harris (1803–78). Sadly, in 1861 Heusken was assassinated by a group of anti-foreigner *rōnin*, or masterless samurai (Vos 1963: 378).[19]

---

19   See also Hesselink (1994) and (2018).

Some Westerners who went to Japan after 1854 did so in order to promulgate Christianity. The first Protestant missionaries from the USA and Europe arrived in 1859. However, as Christianity was still officially proscribed, they had to work under the guise of teaching English. The ban was eventually lifted in 1873 in response to pressure from Western powers (Kaiser 1996: 9). In this regard, the case of the Dutchman Guido Verbeck (1830–98), a Dutch Reformed Church missionary, is instructive.

Verbeck had lived in America for several years before arriving in Nagasaki in 1859. In 1864 he was employed by the Nagasaki city government which sponsored an English-language school called the *Eigosho*, at which Verbeck would teach English (Duke 2009: 42–46). He continued to teach English until 1868 (Beukers 2018: 99). Verbeck also secretly led bible classes for young samurai (Griffis 1900: 99–101). Unfortunately, we are not told which language he did this in. One possibility is Dutch, although in a diary entry for 5 June 1862, he notes that one of the Japanese told him he had bought an English bible. Verbeck went to his house and found that it was in fact a small volume of the American Tract Society, so Verbeck gave him an actual bible. Again, the language is not mentioned, but it is likely to have been in English (Griffis 1900: 102). Verbeck's biographer, W.E. Griffis, reports that soon after his arrival in Nagasaki in 1859, Verbeck was glad to hear some Dutch words on the lips of Japanese. For example, he heard what is transcribed as *briki* from the Dutch *blik* ('tin') (a loanword mentioned in Chapter 7) and the names of medicines such as *rauda* from laudanum. He also mentions words of Portuguese or Spanish origin such as *bidoro* for 'glass' (Portuguese *vidro*) and *castira*, a type of sponge cake still eaten in Nagasaki (カステラ *kasutera* < Port. *pão de Castela*) (Griffis 1900: 82). Verbeck clearly had an ear for language and noted, with particular relevance to his own presence in Nagasaki, that in 1862 informers would receive rewards for handing over Christians to the authorities: 500 pieces of silver for a *bateren* (i.e., a 'father' or priest) or 300 for an *iruman* (i.e., a 'brother' from the Portuguese *irmão*) (Griffis 1900: 96).

Before Verbeck arrived in Japan in 1859, Chinese versions of the New Testament and the Bible, translated by Western missionaries in Chinese, were being brought to Japan by Chinese sailors (Griffis 1900: 74). While the ban on Christianity was still in force, Verbeck gave Chinese bibles to 'educated samurai' or wearers of two swords (Griffis 1900: 97). Verbeck worked for several years on a Japanese Bible translation. Further investigation may reveal his source language (Griffis 1900: 301).

3.5 *Dutch as the Language of Diplomacy*
Despite examples such as this, which illustrate that English was gaining ground, as something of a counterpoint Dutch did continue to be the LWC between

European diplomats and Japanese officials for several years after 1854. In 1860, there was the 'Moss case', in which an English trader Michael Moss had shot and wounded a *yakunin* (役人, a government official or constable), while on a hunting expedition. He was interrogated at the English consulate. This was a tortuous process as one of the *yakunin* who had arrested Moss gave testimony in Japanese. This was then translated into Dutch and then from Dutch to English (and one assumes English went through similar machinations on the way back to Japanese) (Hall 1992: 281). Although by this time there were Japanese English interpreters in Yokohama, the American Francis Hall had earlier observed in 1859 that they 'had a very limited knowledge of [English]' (Hall 1992: 70).

After the Americans had concluded the Convention of Kanagawa with Japan, signed on 31 March 1854, other nations quickly followed. The Dutch reached a temporary agreement with the Japanese government on 9 November 1855, which became a formal treaty on 30 January 1856. On 7 February 1856, Russia concluded a treaty with Japan. This was written in Dutch (De Ruyver 2016: 23).

Having concluded treaties with several major Western powers, in some sense with a gun at their collective head, the Japanese were not keen to make new treaties. Belgium began attempts to conclude a treaty with Japan in 1859, although it took seven years before negotiations were successfully concluded. Initial contact on behalf of the Belgians was made by the British representative at Edo, Sir Rutherford Alcock (1809–97). Some if not all of the correspondence between Alcock and Japanese representatives on behalf of the Belgians was in Dutch (De Ruyver 2016: 28–29).[20] Further investigation may reveal whether Alcock himself wrote Dutch or whether he used the offices of a Dutch speaker for this correspondence. By 1865, little progress had been made, but this changed with the arrival of Auguste t'Kint de Roodenbeek (1816–78) in Japan. He was from Antwerp and probably spoke French as a first language but had at least a passive knowledge of Dutch (De Ruyver 2016: 51). He opened negotiations from Yokohama with a letter in French dated 21 December 1865 to the councillors of foreign affairs in Edo. Six days later he received a visit from a Japanese commissioner of foreign affairs at the residence of the Dutch political agent and Consul-General in Japan, Dirk de Graeff van Polsbroek. A Japanese translator interpreted from Dutch to Japanese. This, t'Kint remarked, allowed him to refamiliarize himself with Dutch. When the next day the Governor of Yokohama paid him a visit, he was given the choice of conversing in Dutch or English and chose Dutch (De Ruyver 2016: 50). Negotiations on a

---

20 De Ruyver reproduces a letter dated 19 February 1860 from the Japanese Councillors Wakisaka Yasuori and Andō Nobumasa in good Dutch.

treaty between Belgium and Japan continued to be conducted in Dutch and it was finally concluded on 1 August 1866. The treaty was written in Japanese, French and indeed Dutch, with the Dutch version serving as the original in case of doubt, giving it legal priority (De Ruyver 2016: 68–69). At this time and well into the twentieth century, French had a certain priority in Belgian public life. The priority given to Dutch in this case reflects the fact that it was still the primary LWC between Japanese and Europeans in the diplomatic sphere.

The Dutchman, De Graeff van Polsbroek, had arrived at Deshima from Batavia in 1857. Here, he was employed as the Assistant, 2nd class at the Dutch trading post. He resigned in 1859 to set up his own trading company, moving to Yokohama. In July 1859 he was appointed by the last *opperhoofd*, Donker Curtius, as Vice-Consul at Yokohama. In 1861 he was appointed as Consul, and was one of some 45 Dutchmen in Japan listed in a Dutch/Japanese Almanac for the year.[21] In 1863 De Graeff van Polsbroek was appointed Consul-General and in 1868 Resident Minister of the Netherlands in Japan. He played an important rôle in the opening up of diplomatic relations between Japan and several Western countries. By his own will, he was honourably dismissed from Japan in 1870. He kept a journal which has been published and which provides valuable information about the changes that took place in the late Tokugawa and early Meiji periods (De Graeff van Polsbroek 1987).

Correspondence between the Italian mission to Edo and the Japanese councillors of foreign affairs survives. Some letters from this correspondence were written in Dutch, although others were written in English and Italian.[22] A treaty between Japan and Italy was signed on 25 August 1866. Early negotiations for Denmark to conclude a treaty with Japan were handled by De Graeff van Polsbroek. He corresponded on the matter with Japanese councillors in Dutch (De Ruyver 2016: 72). In 1861 De Graeff van Polsbroek acted as an intermediary for the Kingdom of Siam as it attempted to conclude a treaty with Japan. Initial correspondence between De Graeff van Polsbroek and the Japanese councillors was in Dutch, although the Siamese offer was initially refused (De Ruyver 2016: 95 n. 172).

At the start of our story, back in the seventeenth century, the Dutch often needed to use Portuguese in order to communicate with Japanese. In an interesting, but not unexpected, reversal, the Portuguese in charge of his country's

---

21   In the *Nederlandsche en Japansche Almanak voor het Jaar 1861*, De Graeff van Polsbroek is listed on 1 January 1861 as *Waarnemend Vice-Consul (der Nederlanden)* (Deputy Vice-Consul). There were 25 Dutch at Deshima, 10 at Aku no Ura near Nagasaki, and 10 at Kanagawa (Yokohama).

22   For example, a letter from the Japanese councillors to the Italian mission dated 25 July 1866 was in Dutch (De Ruyver 2016: 70).

negotiations, José Rodrigues Coelho do Amaral (1808–73), wrote a letter to the Japanese councillors from Kanagawa on 11 August 1866 in Portuguese with a Dutch translation. He received a letter in Dutch from the Japanese councillors dated 26 August (De Ruyver 2016: 73).

Early correspondence between the Japanese and the American Consul-General Townsend Harris was in Dutch.[23] As noted above, the Dutch-American Hendrik Heusken worked for Harris, in some sense acting as a linguistic bridge between the Japanese and Americans. Heusken also provided translation services to the Prussian delegation in Japan in 1860–61 before his untimely death (Hesselink 1994: 332). The Prussian envoy Guido von Rehfues (1818–94) arrived in Yokohama in mid-August 1863 with a Prussian-Japanese treaty ratified by the King of Prussia. We have a letter from Von Rehfues to the Japanese councillors in German dated 15 August 1863 and a letter dated 19 February 1864 from the councillors to the Prussian consul Maximilian von Brandt (1835–1920) in Dutch (De Ruyver 2016: 42).

4 1868 Onwards

So, in the period between the arrival of Perry in 1853/4 and the Meiji Restoration in 1868, two linguistic forces (*taalkrachten* to re-work a Dutch word) were at work. On the one hand, other European languages were gaining ground, while on the other hand, Dutch continued to play an important role in Japan, above all in the diplomatic and intellectual spheres. However, winds of change were blowing through Japan, which altered not only the political and social landscape, but also the linguistic landscape of the country. Eight years earlier, in 1860, the Dutch trading post at Deshima, which had been functioning for over two hundred years, was closed and replaced by a vice-consulate at Nagasaki (De Groot 2005: 2). The Japanese realized that there were more powerful nations in the world, such as America, Britain, Germany and France, with which they needed to engage, and this was also true of their languages. Dutch did continue to be used, but to an ever-decreasing degree, for its heyday had now passed.

Boxer (1950: 64) observes that Dutch continued to be the official language for the transaction of foreign affairs until the third year of the Meiji era (1870).

---

23 Two examples serve to illustrate this. Harris received a letter in Dutch from the Japanese councillor in charge of foreign affairs Hotta Masayoshi (1810–64) dated 14 April 1858. De Ruyver reproduces a letter dated 1 May 1861 to Townsend Harris from the Japanese Councillors Kuze Hirochika and Andō Nobumasa in Dutch (De Ruyver 2016: 33, 48).

The close association between the Dutch language and Western medicine continued for a period after 1853, in part driven by the close association between the two in the Japanese mind that had lasted some two hundred years. In 1870, however, the Japanese government concluded that it should follow the German medical model instead of the Dutch one and a request was submitted to the German government for medical specialists. They arrived in July 1871. Clearly news of this shift did not reach everybody's ears in Japan straightaway. As late as 1879 Seki Gōsai (1844–1907), having passed his medical examinations, decided to go to Edo, by now called Tokyo, to study the Dutch language and *rangaku*. However, he was thwarted in his ambition, for by now the sun was setting on *rangaku* (Nakamura 2005: 167–168).

4.1   *Further Dutch Arrive in Japan*

Even in the final chapter of this story, Dutch continued to come to Japan. One, Koenraad Gratama (1831–88), arrived in Japan in 1866. In 1867, the Japanese government required him to move to Edo to set up a school for physics and chemistry there. In 1869, he moved again, to Osaka, where he set up the *Seimikyoku* school of chemistry (Beukers 2018: 98). Another Dutchman who was an important figure in the introduction of modern pharmacy to Japan was A.J.C. Geerts (1843–83). He arrived in Japan in 1869, just after the beginning of the Meiji era. He worked as a chemist and teacher of various scientific subjects at the school attached to Nagasaki hospital. The school continued to function until 1874 (Beukers 2018: 98, 101). He gave instruction in Dutch which was translated into Japanese. Geerts remained in Japan and is a good example of how even for a Dutchman it became necessary to communicate in languages other than Dutch. He became the head of a new government scientific laboratory in Kyoto. Along with a fellow Dutchman, Alexander Langgaard (1847–1917), he wrote a new version of the *Pharmacopoea Neerlandica* (The Hague, 1871) in German (Beukers 2018: 104). He addressed the Asiatic Society several times in English on a range of scientific subjects.[24] In a meeting of the Society in 1877 the publication was announced of a book that Geerts had written in French, *Les Produits de la Nature Japonaise et Chinoise, partie inorganique et minéralogique* (Beukers 2018: 113). He would have learnt French from early on in his education in the Netherlands. He also translated out of Japanese into French and German underlining his credentials as a linguist as well as a scientist. Two weeks before his untimely death in 1883 he was awarded with the Order of the Rising Sun (Beukers 2018: 117). Geerts had collected over three hundred Japanese

---

24   Opinions of the native English-speakers about Geerts's own English were not so positive.

books, which were brought to the Netherlands and catalogued by Serrurier (1887). Some of these were Japanese translations of Dutch works, for example, *Ihan teikō* ('Concise Model of [Western] Medicine') by Udagawa Genshin, which drew on several Dutch medical sources. Geerts also owned a copy of Ōba Sessai's *Yaku Oranda bungo* ('Dutch Grammar in Translation') (Serrurier 1887: 21, 61).

In 1872, the Japanese government invited the hydraulic engineer C.J. van Doorn along with the military engineer I.A. Lindo to study many rivers in Japan with the aim of making them navigable (Toussaint 2000). Several other Dutch accompanied them including another hydraulic engineer Johannis de Rijke (1842–1913). He designed a new harbour for Osaka, which is now one of the most important in Japan (Toussaint 2000: 29). He corresponded in Japan with another Dutch engineer, George Escher. They of course corresponded in Dutch. One linguistic insight we gain is that De Rijke referred to Japanese officials with whom he had to deal as 'Jaapjes'—little Japanese—clearly a disparaging term. One difference between the conditions for the Dutch now compared to those that pertained prior to 1854 was that they could bring family members with them to Japan. De Rijke brought his wife, Johanna Hassoldt, and his children with him to Japan (Toussaint 2000: 30). She died of cholera in 1881 and in 1885 De Rijke married another Dutch woman, Maria Heck. He continued to have contact with Dutch engineers, but by 1890, they had completed their work and left Japan, leaving De Rijke as the only Dutch engineer in Japan (Toussaint 2000: 31). He would leave the country at the turn of the century. Finally, De Rijke passed on his knowledge of hydraulic engineering to Japanese students (Toussaint 2000: 32).

4.2 Belgians in Japan

As well as Dutch, there were also Belgians in Meiji Japan. In the period 1876 to 1900, however, they never numbered more than about 30 and we currently do not know which language they spoke (Sakurai 2016: 222). With the advent of the Meiji regime, Japan needed a new constitution. The Belgian constitution formed an important source for those who helped to shape the framework for the Japanese constitution, in part because Belgium was a relatively new country, as in some sense Japan was in the Meiji Restoration. However, it was sources in French, the language which had priority in Belgian political life, rather than Dutch, to which the Japanese turned. Two Japanese who wrote on the subject were Inoue Kowashi (1844–95), an administrator in the Department of Justice and Sufu Kōhei (1850/1–1921). Inoue translated the Belgian constitution using a French work, Edouard Laferrière's *Les Constitutions d'Europe et d'Amérique*

(Paris, 1869) as his main source. Soon after the Meiji Restoration, Sufu became a student of French with the translator, Mitsukuri Rinshō (1846–97), a member of a famous family of *rangakusha*. He produced a detailed outline of Belgium, its legal system and constitution, based on French sources (Vanoverbeke 2016: 162–163).

4.3   *Dutch Books in Japan: Signs of Decline*

A small but important step away from Dutch came in 1872. Dutch-Japanese dictionaries had typically not included European technical vocabulary or Japanese equivalents. By contrast, English-Chinese dictionaries compiled in the nineteenth century had included technical vocabulary. In Tokyo in 1872, (*Yōgo*) *On'yakusen* was published by Murata Fumio (1836–91). This included technical vocabulary drawn from Chinese sources in Japanese editions, which one assumes, in turn drew on English-Chinese dictionaries. By now there was no attempt to produce Dutch-Japanese technical dictionaries and so the European source language for translating technical vocabulary into Japanese in this case became English rather than Dutch (Kaiser 1996: 25).

In 1878, a list of books in the library of the Asiatic Society of Japan was made. Most of the books in the library were in English, with a few French and German books (Transactions 1877–78). The library had only one book by a Dutch author, Isaac Titsingh. It was listed as 'Illustrations of Japan'. This is probably a copy of the English edition of the book published in London in 1822. So, it seems there was little interest in Dutch amongst Anglophones in early Meiji Japan.

The Professor of Chinese and Japanese at Leiden University, J.J. Hoffmann, mentioned above, worked on a Japanese grammar, which appeared in 1868 as *Japansche spraakleer*, but simultaneously in English as 'A Japanese Grammar'. The ministry also commissioned a Japanese-Dutch dictionary, which Hoffmann would work on. For several reasons, it was not until 1881 that the first instalments of this lexicon saw the light of day. In the meantime, Dutch had lost its pre-eminence in Japan and at one point there was talk of simply replacing it with an English-Japanese dictionary. In the end both Dutch-Japanese and English-Japanese instalments were printed, but this episode illustrates how quickly Dutch had lost its near-monopoly as an LWC in Japan (Kuiper 2015: 387–390).

After 1868, books in Dutch were still printed in Japan, but their number was dwindling. A block re-print of the 1822 edition of Siegenbeek's *Grammatica: of, Nederduitsche spraakkunst* was made in Tokyo in 1875. The naval engineer Pieter Gerard van Schermbeek spent several years in Japan. In Tokyo in 1886, he published his Dutch translation of the Japanese fairy tale *Shitakiri suzume* with the title *De musch met de geknipte tong* ('The Sparrow with the Cut Tongue')

FIGURE 33 *De musch met de geknipte tong* ('The Sparrow with the Cut Tongue'), Tokyo, 1886
NDL

as a *chirimen-bon* (縮緬本, the pages of the book were of crêpe-paper, which made it attractive) (see fig. 33). His name was rendered as *Fansukerunbēki* (フアンスケルンベーキ) on the title page. No further books were published in the Dutch language in Japan in the nineteenth century. This beautifully-illustrated book, in which Japanese and Dutch sit side-by-side on the first double-page, was perhaps a fitting conclusion to almost three centuries of contact. Two years later, a quadrilingual dictionary of physics was published in Japan. Tellingly, it included terms in Japanese, English, French and German, but not in Dutch (Montgomery 2000: 222).[25]

---

25 The dictionary 'Vocabulary of physical terms in the four languages, English, Japanese, French and German' was compiled by Yamakawa Kenjirō.

5   Conclusion

This chapter has identified three phases in the nineteenth century in the shift away from the use of Dutch in Japan. The first phase was framed by the arrival of ships from two Anglophone countries, Great Britain and the USA. Between 1808, the year of the *Phaeton* incident, and 1854, when Commodore Perry compelled the Japanese to sign the Convention of Kanagawa, the fortunes of Dutch were somewhat mixed. On the one hand, there was an increase in the number of Japanese learning Dutch and in the volume of translations from Dutch, as Japanese recognized the need to acquire Western knowledge. On the other hand, there were official measures to control the import and translation of Dutch books. Furthermore, as a consequence of the *Phaeton* incident and other incursions in Japanese waters, there were official moves to promote the learning of other European languages, above all English and Russian, as fears of a possible foreign invasion grew. Thus, for the first time in more than one hundred years, Dutch faced competition in Japan from other vernacular European languages.

The second phase in the shift away from Dutch covered the period 1854 to 1868, when the Meiji Restoration brought an end to the Tokugawa regime. During this intermediate phase, other European languages, above all English, rapidly gained ground. Nevertheless, Dutch still had a rôle to play in Japan. First, it was the language through which Japanese such as Fukuzawa Yukichi learnt other European languages. In this regard I have coined the term *thuralect*. Second, it played an important rôle in diplomatic negotiations between Japan and European countries, serving as an LWC, with a native Dutch speaker such as Dirk de Graeff van Polsbroek acting as a linguistic intermediary. Third, the fact that it still functioned as an L2 in the sphere of learning meant that there was demand for Dutch books re-printed in Japan.

The final phase was ushered in by the Meiji Restoration. Here, although Dutch did continue to be used, the overall picture is one of decline. English continued to gain ground and German and French also established themselves as important languages in Meiji Japan. This is most clearly symbolized by the dictionary of physics published in 1888 which alongside Japanese included these three languages, but not Dutch.

It is worth briefly reflecting on why the shift away from Dutch was so rapid. One reason is that for most users, Dutch was not their native language. Furthermore, there were few native speakers to maintain its use and certainly after the closure of the trading post at Deshima in 1860 little sense of an indigenous or native speaker language community to sustain it. The Dutch government attempted to maintain the rôle of Dutch as a *lingua franca* in Japan, but its efforts met with little success.

One sphere or social domain in which languages persist outside the area with which they are most closely associated is religion. In migrant communities, the 'heritage' language often continues to be used in the religious domain long after its members have shifted to the language of the recipient culture in other domains (Pauwels 2016: 137–139; Joby 2015: 131). The case of Dutch in Japan is slightly different, as for most users in Japan it was never an L1. Looking at things from another perspective, if it had been associated with religion, it might have persisted for longer than it did. However, it was precisely because the Dutch agreed not to proselytize or practise their religion openly that the Japanese authorities allowed them to remain in the country. So, when the shift away from Dutch really got underway after 1854, there was no religious community, Japanese or Dutch, to sustain it.[26]

Another possible reason for the rapid shift away from Dutch, in particular after 1868, was its association with the old Tokugawa regime. Just as the old regime was replaced by a new one, so in the sphere of language, Dutch was quickly replaced by other European languages. Meiji (明治) means literally 'bright' or 'enlightened reign'. It may be going too far to suggest that, in some Japanese minds at least, the other European languages were associated with the enlightenment heralded by the Meiji Restoration, while Dutch was associated with the 'dark' feudal period of Tokugawa Japan, but, I would argue, the possibility is there.

On a practical level, the shift to other European languages was made easier by the closeness of Dutch to some of these languages, above all English and German. This allowed more forward-thinking Japanese such as Fukuzawa Yukichi to make the shift to English in a couple of years. For students of medicine and chemistry, the shift to German would not have been so dramatic. If they had learnt the names of chemical elements in Dutch, they would have been relieved to see how many of the names looked similar to or even the same as the names in German.

Finally, of course, politics and commerce played a rôle in this shift. The Japanese quickly realized that the Anglophone, Francophone and German-speaking countries were more powerful and commercially important than the

---

26   On the link between religion and the continued use of a language, see also Ó Tuathaigh (2015: 19–23).

Netherlands. In the prologue I wrote that the Dutch language crashed onto the shores of Japan in 1600. To continue the maritime metaphor, in the wake of the Meiji Restoration it gradually sank beneath the waves as other Western languages overwhelmed it. It did not do so, however, without trace, for it left an indelible mark on the language, culture and society of Japan. More will be said on this in the epilogue.

Epilogue

In April 1600 when the survivors of the shipwrecked *Liefde* crawled onto the shores of Japan with their language, it almost goes without saying that they can have had no idea of the effect it would have on the Japanese language, or indeed on Japanese society and culture. This book has told the story of what did happen when Dutch came into contact with varieties of Japanese and other languages in Japan in the three centuries after their arrival. This epilogue attempts to do three things: first, to frame this story by analysing the various roles that the Dutch language played in Japan; second, to offer future research opportunities arising from this study; and finally to return to the central research question posed in the prologue.

1   The Roles Dutch Played as a Contact Language in Japan

In the first instance, Dutch was a trading language. In the early years of contact with Japan, it faced competition from Portuguese. However, after the expulsion of Portuguese native speakers in 1639, Dutch was gradually able to establish itself as the primary language with which VOC employees did business with Japanese merchants. It was also the language in which the Dutch recorded their trading activities in the *dagregister*, which has been an invaluable source for this book. The Dutch in the *dagregister* and other commercial documents was often laced with words from Japanese, but also words from Malay, Sinitic varieties and other Asian languages. Its lexicon therefore differed somewhat from that of other varieties of Dutch and so it could be understood as an *emporiolect*, and perhaps even a *thalassolect*, a language of the seas, in South and East Asia.

Over time, Japanese scholars and leaders of Japanese society such as *daimyō* realized that the Dutch had something to offer them, first in the field of anatomy and medicine and thereafter in fields such as astronomy, botany, chemistry, geography and physics. They were able to do this as a result of the scientific revolution that was well underway in Europe and which continued throughout the Dutch period in Japan. This swept away knowledge received from ancient authors and replaced it with knowledge based on observation and experiment. Copernicus turned the dogma of a geocentric planetary system on its head. In anatomy, Vesalius opened up the human body and in so doing was able to challenge the knowledge derived from ancient authors such as Galen. The investigation of the skies and the natural world was assisted by advances in optical technology, which owed much to men in the Dutch Republic such as Hans Lippershey, Antonie van Leeuwenhoek and Christiaan Huygens. In the eighteenth century, the Leiden professor Herman Boerhaave revolutionized clinical methodology. He also influenced Carl Linnaeus, whose binomial nomenclature brought order to the previously unsystematic approach to naming plants. This was quickly adopted by 'apostles' such as Carl Peter Thunberg, who in time would apply it to Japanese plants. The second half of the century saw the emergence of a new science, chemistry, and the discovery of new chemical elements and the invention of new processes. It was these new ways of seeing, ordering and processing the world that Dutch mediated to Japan. Furthermore, taking my lead from Foucault, I have suggested that *rangaku* emerged from the nomination of the new objects, ideas and processes introduced via Dutch.

In the Dutch Republic, there was a well-developed printing culture, which allowed for the rapid reproduction and circulation of information about these new discoveries and inventions. Much of it was initially produced in other European languages but reached Japan in Dutch translations. It was perhaps serendipitous that Dutch, and not, for example, English or French, was the language in which much of this scientific progress was mediated to the Japanese. There can be little doubt that the high degree of 'morphosemantic transparency' in Dutch terminology facilitated the development of the new Japanese technolects that emerged during the nineteenth century in medicine, physics and chemistry. Many of the loan translations coined by Japanese translators such as Shizuki Tadao and Udagawa Yōan are still in use today. Some have in turn been adopted by Mandarin Chinese and Korean.

As many of the Japanese with whom the Dutch came into contact were from the ruling classes, Dutch became a language of the elite in Japan, an H-language, language of prestige or *acrolect*. Ozeki San'ei from peasant stock, whom we met in Chapter 6, is one exception to this as are the Nagasaki *compradors*, who, according to Cornelis Assendelft de Coningh, spoke Dutch. However, they are relatively few in number. The interpreters and translators were mainly samurai, albeit often from the lower echelons of this caste. Avid supporters of *rangaku* such as the *ranpeki-daimyō* Matsūra Seizan and Shimazu Shigehide were among the most powerful and influential men in Tokugawa Japan. Many of the lexical and grammatical changes that these and other men from the Japanese elite introduced into Japanese through contact with Dutch would eventually be adopted by all users of the language. In sociolinguistic terms, to borrow from Labov (2006: 203), we can talk of 'changes from above' which were then adopted over time by others lower down the social order. This is not necessarily the whole story. Some loanwords, such as those adopted by the Nagasaki dialect, were probably first borrowed by merchants or other Japanese who came into contact with the Dutch.

For most of the time, the native speakers of Dutch were confined to their trading posts in Western Kyushu. In this regard we can talk of Dutch as a topolect, or more specifically as I have suggested a *nesolect*, an island language, either of Hirado and Deshima, or more broadly of Kyushu. The number of Dutch in Japan using this nesolect was always very small, never more than about twenty. If one compares this with the population in late Tokugawa Japan of about 26 million, then one may wonder in the first instance how Dutch was able to exert such an influence on the Japanese lexis. Part of the answer to this question is to be found in the role of Dutch as a *metalect*. However, as discussed in Chapters 3 and 7, it was also the sense of the exotic that Dutch conjured up, the sense of the 'other' written in a 'strange' script that ran sideways rather than vertically. Here, one might describe it as an *allolect*, the language of the other, or otherness.[1] It was this that attracted artists such as Shiba Kōkan to the language, alongside Western perspective, which offered another new way of viewing the world. *Rangakusha*, too, wrote in Dutch, but also signed their names in *rōmaji* and even adopted Dutch names. It is perhaps going too far to say that they 'became Dutch' but by using the Dutch language in this way, they in some sense attempted to inhabit the world from which *rangaku* emerged.

In the final chapter of this story, when Japanese shifted their L2 or L3 from Dutch to other European languages, for several decades Dutch functioned as a *thuralect*, acting as the door or gateway to these other languages. The fact that two of these languages, English and German, were also West Germanic languages, may well have speeded up the process of language shift, as the learners of these 'new' languages, recognized, perhaps to their relief, familiar lexical items and syntactic patterns in these linguistic cousins of Dutch. In this final stage, Dutch became a language of diplomacy, a *lingua franca* for Japanese and Europeans and Americans.

Dutch was also a *linguifer* or *ferolect*, bringing other European languages to Japan. One of these was Latin. In some cases, as in the Virgilian couplet translated by Shizuki Tadao, the Latin stood apart from the Dutch text. In other cases, such as books on botany, Latin and Dutch were interwoven. Some of the loanwords analysed in Chapter 7, such as the names of chemical elements, were often Latin formulations, modified to a greater or lesser extent in Dutch, before being transported to Japan. Dutch also brought French with it in the form of bilingual dictionaries. Halma's famous bilingual dictionary formed the basis of two important Dutch-Japanese lexicons, which would challenge

---

1 This term has been used by Michael J. Shapiro.

existing paradigms in Japanese lexicography. As the nineteenth century progressed, French would gain increasing importance in Japan in its own right and eventually eclipse its erstwhile *linguifer*.

Dutch opened doors, but occasionally closed them. In Chapter 2, it was suggested that it acted as a *cryptolect* among the Nagasaki interpreters, the preserve of a few, chosen individuals, standing in the Japanese tradition of *hiden* (秘伝, 'secret transmission'). In social groups and discursive spaces, it could be used to include, but also exclude, either as a social marker, or as a linguistic barrier to those who did not know Dutch. Finally, one role that Dutch did not assume in Japan was that of a *hierolect*, a language of religion. In contrast to Catholic Spain and Portugal, the Dutch kept their Calvinist faith to themselves, an approach in some sense symbolized by the sealing of bibles in barrels when Dutch ships arrived in Nagasaki Bay. This allowed them to remain in Japan after the expulsion of the Portuguese and to be the only European country to trade with Japan for more than two hundred years.

In summary, Dutch took on many different roles, or assumed many faces, in Tokugawa Japan. What is perhaps most striking is that it performed several roles in Japan that it did not perform in Europe. For example, in nineteenth-century Europe, Dutch rarely if ever, enjoyed the status of a diplomatic language. Here, we might return to Bakhtin's notion of *разноречие* or the heteroglossia of Dutch, or view it as a polyergic language, fulfilling many different functions in Japan.

2   Further Research Opportunities

Although this book has covered much ground in relation to Dutch as a contact language in Japan, there remain areas which provide further research opportunities. Here, brief mention is made of four such opportunities. First, further work could usefully be done on analysing code switching into Dutch in Japanese texts. Saitō (1967), to which frequent reference was made in Chapter 7, cites many Japanese texts in which Dutch words were inserted. These texts would provide a useful starting point for an analysis of switching into Dutch by Japanese authors. Code switching is often the first step towards loanword integration and therefore such a study might allow us to understand better the process by which Japanese adopted certain loanwords. Second, while this book has made extensive use of Japanese secondary sources, there remain sources which have probably not been fully exploited. One example of this is the five-volume work on *rangaku* by Sugimoto Tsutomu (1976–82). In part, this is a result of a desire on the part of the present author to focus on the

Dutch language, although it was of course functioning in a contact situation with other languages. Third, while this book has focussed on Dutch in Japan, it has also analysed other European languages including Portuguese, Latin and French. Further work could usefully be done on analysing how these languages functioned in Japan and the outcomes of contact between them and other languages. Finally, the methodology used in this book whereby the lifecycle of Dutch in Japan has been analysed by language process could be applied to other cases of language contact involving Dutch or indeed other languages in a historical context. In the case of Dutch, it would be interesting to analyse the processes that resulted from contact in socio-semiotic contexts that it shared with other languages in East Asia. For example, in seventeenth-century Taiwan Dutch had intensive contact with Formosan languages, Sinitic varieties and other European languages, such as Spanish. In the Indonesian archipelago, it came into contact with Malay and other Austronesian languages, as well as Arabic and Portuguese. It might then be instructive to compare the language processes in these various contact situations.

3 Concluding Remarks

Finally, we can return to the question posed in the prologue: 'what happened when Dutch came into contact with other languages in Tokugawa Japan?' and reflect on the extent to which this has been answered. What this book has illustrated is that as a result of this contact, many thousands of Japanese learnt Dutch, in the late Tokugawa period many of them in schools established for the study of Dutch and *rangaku*. The knowledge of Dutch was operationalized in numerous ways in Japan, some of which took it far away from the community of native speakers in western Kyushu. Apart from *rangaku*, it was used in visual art, in correspondence between Dutch and Japanese, in toponymy and in the adoption of Dutch personal names. It faced competition, first from Portuguese and later from English, French, German and Russian. Throughout the Tokugawa period, it rubbed shoulders with literary Sinitic, which competed with it, but which also provided scholars with the 'habitus' with which to interpret and translate Dutch texts. Users of Dutch often switched to other languages, above all Japanese, to bridge the gap between cultures. But it was the translation of over 1,000 books from Dutch to Japanese, which was the most profound consequence of this contact. Within linguistics, we can place this aspect of our story within the framework for language contact proposed by Thomason and Kaufman (1988: 73–76), and state that the results of this contact, i.e., non-essential lexical borrowing and slight structural borrowing, accord with level 2 on their scale. Furthermore, several of the morphemes loaned by Dutch continue to be productive today. However, the consequences of this contact went far beyond the linguistic. The reading and translating of Dutch texts resulted in changes (from above) to Japanese social, intellectual and cultural life. These, it could be argued, made Japan more receptive than other nations in East Asia to Western modernity, which smashed the chains of *sakoku* Japan in 1854.

As a coda to this discussion, one question on which scholars in Dutch Studies sometimes reflect is why Dutch did not become a world language in the manner of, say, English or Portuguese, given that the Dutch traded with so many parts of the world in the Age of European Expansion. The answer to this question is complex. However, although Dutch did not become a world language, contact between Dutch and other languages has resulted in the emergence of many contact-induced words in these other languages as well as in Dutch (Van der Sijs 2010). In the case of Japanese, while it probably adopted around 300 *gairaigo* from Dutch, other lexical contact phenomena such as hybrid words and loan translations make the total number of contact-induced words much higher, and this is before we begin to analyse dialectal contact-induced words. But again, while important this is by no means the whole story. What this book has attempted to do is to tell this story using an interdisciplinary approach, which one could perhaps describe as heteroglossic, to appeal to Bakhtin one final time. In some chapters, such as 5 and 7, matters internal to language such as phonology, morphology and syntax were in the foreground, while in other chapters, such as 3 and 6, priority was given to matters external to language such as the social, cultural and political context in which Dutch functioned. This approach, it is to be hoped, has taken us some way towards answering the question of what happened when Dutch came into contact with Japanese and other languages in Japan between 1600 and 1900.

Bibliography

Manuscripts

Leiden, Universiteitsbibliotheek (LUB)

BPL 3651. Jan Cock Blomhoff, *Aantekeningen op de Reize Na-en-Van Jedo*, Cock Blomhoff's official report of the 1818 *hofreis*.

D H 213. *Verklaringh op verscheyden Vragen 't Japance Rijk concernerende door den Edele Heer Philips Luijcasz, Directeur-Generaal wegens den nederlanschen Stand in India voorgestelt ende door den Edele President François Caron beantwoord* ('Explanation on various questions concerning the Japanese Empire proposed by the noble Mr. Philips Luijcasz. Director-General arising from the Dutch position in the East Indies and answered by the noble president François Caron').

London, British Library (BL)

Add. MS 9393 fols. 2r–3v. English translation of a letter from Isaac Titsingh to Kutsuki Masatsuna dated 4 June 1807.

Sloane MS. 2921, Travelogue of Engelbert Kaempfer.

Sloane MS. 3060, Engelbert Kaempfer: History of Japan.

The Hague, Nationaal Archief (NA)

1.04.02, nr. 1092, fols. 340–344. Journal kept by Pieter Muijser and Isaacq Bogaert on the *hofreis* (*Journael vande Reijse*) from Hirado (*Firando*) to Edo (17 October 1625 to 29 January 1626).

1.04.02, nr. 1095, fols. 449–509. Journal kept by Pieter Muijser and Pieter Nuyts for their *hofreis*, which departed from Hirado on 15 August 1627.

1.04.02, nr. 1134 (*Vierde boek* (*fourth book*) 1641), fols. 467–469. List of books and other documents despatched from Japan to Taiwan when the VOC trading post at Hirado was closed; fol. 471v request to Batavia in 1641 for book on the planets for Inoue Masashige.

1.04.21–1A1. The trade permit (*handelspas*) that the Dutch obtained in 1609.

1.04.21, nrs. 53–249. The Factory Journals for Hirado and Deshima (1633–1833).

1.04.21, nr. 250–259. 'Secret journals' kept by Dutch at Deshima.

1.04.21, nr. 270. Journal kept by Pieter Muijser, October 1628.

1.04.21, nr. 271–274. *Dagregister* kept by Willem Jansz. Amersfoort between 1631 and 1633.

1.04.21, nrs. 276–349. VOC letters written in Dutch to factories in Japan.

1.04.21, nrs. 482–591. VOC letters written in Dutch from the factories in Japan to the Governor-General in Batavia, other Dutch factories in South and East Asia and the Japanese authorities.

1.04.21, nr. 609. Two letters from 1748 translated from Chinese into Dutch via Malay.

1.04.21, nr. 614. Document for the import of cloves signed by the Nagasaki interpreters (1784).

1.04.21, nrs. 1613–1624. Deshima *dagregisters* for 1843 to 1860 (a few years are missing).

1.04.21, nrs. 1703–1706 for the *Apart Nieuws* reports for 1850, 1852, 1853 and 1854.

Editions of Primary Sources and Printed Primary and Secondary Sources

Adams, James (2003). *Bilingualism and the Latin Language*. Cambridge: CUP.

Adams, James and Simon Swain (2002). 'Introduction', in J. Adams, M. Janse and S. Swain, ed., *Bilingualism in Ancient Society: Language Contact and the Written Text*. Oxford: OUP, pp. 1–20.

Adams, George (1766). *A Treatise Describing and Explaining the Construction and Use of New Celestial and Terrestrial Globes*. London: George Adams, Fleet St.

Adams, George (1770/1). *Gronden der starrenkunde* ['Principles of astronomy'], trans. Jacob Ploos. Amsterdam.

AIKAWA Tadaomi *et al.* (2007). *Rangaku no furontia: Shizuki Tadao no sekai* ['The Frontier of Dutch Studies: the World of Shizuki Tadao']. Nagasaki: Nagasaki bunkensha.

AKIZUKI Takako (1989). 'Japanese Manuscript Sources on 19th Century Russia in HUL', *Acta Slavica Iaponica* 7, pp. 149–153.

AOKI Toshiyuki (1998). *Zaison rangaku no kenkyū* ['Research into Dutch Studies in the Countryside']. Kyoto: Shibunkaku Shuppan.

ARAKAWA Sōbei (1977). *Gairaigo jiten dai 2 ban* ['Gairaigo dictionary 2nd ed.']. Tokyo: Kadokawa Shoten.

Bailey, Don C. (1962). *A Glossary of Japanese Neologisms*. Tucson: The University of Arizona Press.

Barnhart, Michael A. (1995). *Japan and the world since 1868*. London: Edward Arnold.

Batchelor, John (1905). *An Ainu-English-Japanese Dictionary*, 2nd ed. Tokyo: The Methodist Publishing House.

Baumgarten, Nicole and Demet Özçetin (2008). 'Linguistic variation through language contact in translation', in Peter Siemund and Noemi Kintana, ed., *Language Contact and Contact Languages*. Amsterdam: John Benjamins, pp. 293–316.

Beasley, William G. (1973). *The Meiji Restoration*. London: OUP.

Bernard, Henri (1940). 'Traductions Chinoises D'Ouvrages Européens au Japon Durant la Période de Fermeture (1614–1853)', *Monumenta Nipponica* 3(1), pp. 40–60.

Bersma, René P. (2002). *Titia. The first western woman in Japan.* Leiden: Hotei.

Beukers, Harm (1991). *Red-hair Medicine: Dutch-Japanese Medical Relations.* Amsterdam: Rodopi.

Beukers, Harm (2000). 'De Leidse Chirurgijn Gerard Dicten en de Hollandologie in Japan' ['The Leiden Surgeon Gerard Dicten and Dutch Studies in Japan'], *Historische Vereniging Oud Leiden, Jaarboekje 2000,* pp. 107–120.

Beukers, Harm (2018). 'A.J.C. Geerts (1843–1883): een Nederlands apotheker in Japan' ['A.J.C. Geerts (1843–1883): a Dutch pharmacist in Japan'], *Vergezichten Nederlands-Japanse Vereniging Lustrumboek.* Leiden: Ginkgo, pp. 94–118.

Blaeu, Joan (1648). *Nova totius terrarum orbis tabula* ['New Map of the Lands of the Entire World']. Amsterdam.

Blaeu, Willem Jansz. (1608). *Het Licht der Zeevaert* ['The Light of Navigation']. Amsterdam: Ghedruckt bij Willem Janszoon (Blaeu).

Blaeu, Willem Jansz. (1666). *Tweevoudigh onderwiis van de hemelsche en aerdsche globen* ['Two-fold instruction on the heavenly and earthly globes'] [1st ed. 1634]. Amsterdam: ter druckerye van Joan Blaeu.

Blomhoff, Jan Cock (2000a). *De hofreis naar de shōgun van Japan: Naar een persoonlijk verslag van Jan Cock Blomhoff* ['The court journey to the shogun of Japan: According to a personal account by Jan Cock Blomhoff'], Matthi Forrer, ed. Leiden: Hotei Publishing.

Blomhoff, Jan Cock (2000b). *The court journey to the shōgun of Japan: From a private account by Jan Cock Blomhoff,* Rudolf Effert, ed. Leiden: Hotei Publishing.

Blussé, Leonard (J.L.) (1986). 'Butterfly or Mantis', in L. Blussé, ed., *Strange Company: Chinese Settlers, Mestizo Women and the Dutch in VOC Batavia.* Dordrecht: Foris, pp. 179–253.

Blussé, Leonard (2000). 'Pieter Nuyts (1598–1655). Een Middelburger gegijzeld in Japan', ['Pieter Nuyts (1598–1655). A Middelburger imprisoned in Japan'], *Zeeuws Tijdschrijft* 2000(3), pp. 15–17.

Blussé, Leonard (2003). 'Bull in a China Shop: Pieter Nuyts in China and Japan (1627–1636)', in L. Blussé, ed., *Around and About Formosa. Essays in honor of Professor Ts'ao Yung-ho.* Taipei: Ts'ao Yung-ho Foundation for Culture and Education, pp. 95–110.

Blussé, Leonard (2003a). 'The Grand Inquisitor Inoue Chikugo no Kami Masashige: Spin Doctor of the Tokugawa Bakufu', *Bulletin of Portuguese Japanese Studies* 7, pp. 23–43.

Blussé, Leonard *et al.* (eds.) (1992). *The Deshima diaries, Marginalia, 1700–1740.* Tokyo: Japan-Netherlands Institute.

Blussé, Leonard *et al.* (eds.) (2000). *Bridging the Divide: 400 years The Netherlands-Japan.* Leiden: Hotei Publishing.

Blussé, Leonard and Willem G.J. Remmelink (eds.) (2004). *The Deshima diaries, Marginalia, 1740–1800*. Tokyo: Japan-Netherlands Institute.

Bodart Bailey, Beatrice M. (1988). 'Kaempfer Restor'd', *Monumenta Nipponica* 43(1), pp. 1–33.

Booij, Geert (1995). *The Phonology of Dutch*. Oxford: Clarendon Press.

Boomgaard, Peter (ed.) (2013). *Empire and Science in the Making: Dutch Colonial Scholarship in Comparative Global Perspective, 1760–1830*. Basingstoke: Palgrave Macmillan.

Boot, Wim (2008). 'Shizuki Tadao's *Sakoku-ron*', in Wim Boot and Willem Remmelink, ed., *The Patriarch of Dutch Learning Shizuki Tadao (1760–1806)*. Tokyo: The Japan-Netherlands Institute, pp. 88–106.

Boot, Wim (2011). 'The Words of a Mad Doctor by Sugita Genpaku', *The Netherlands-Japan Review* 2(4), pp. 48–61.

Boot, Wim (2013). 'The Transfer of Learning: The Import of Chinese and Dutch Books in Togukawa Japan', *Itinerario* XXXVII(3), pp. 189–206.

Boot, Wim (2014). 'Edo-jidai no hokorubeki kyōiku to gakumon' ['Education and Research in the Edo Period, on which Japan may pride itself'], *HITO, KENKŌ, MIRAI* 4, pp. 20–28. Originally given as a lecture 'De institutionalisering van de wetenschapsbeoefening in Japan in de vorm van een aantal grote en prestigieuze "rijksonderzoeksinstituten".' ['The institutionalization of the practice of science in Japan in the form of a number of large and prestigious "national research institutes"'].

Boot, Wim and Willem Remmelink (eds.) (2008). *The Patriarch of Dutch Learning Shizuki Tadao (1760–1806)*. Tokyo: The Japan-Netherlands Institute.

Bourdieu, Pierre (1972). 'Esquisse d'une théorie de la pratique, précédé de trois études d'ethnologie kabyle'. Geneva: Librairie Droz.

Bownas, Geoffrey (2005). *Japanese Journeys: Writings and Recollections*. Folkestone: Global Oriental.

Boxer, Charles R. (1935). *A True Description of the Mighty Kingdoms of Japan & Siam by Caron & Schouten* [Reprint 1971]. London: The Argonaut Press.

Boxer, Charles R. (1950). *Jan Compagnie in Japan, 1600–1850; An essay on the cultural, artistic and scientific influence exercised by the Hollanders in Japan from the seventeenth to the nineteenth centuries* [2nd ed. 1968]. The Hague: Nijhoff.

Boxer, Charles R. (1951). *The Christian Century in Japan 1549–1650*. London: Cambridge University Press.

Boxer, Charles R. (1988). *The Dutch seaborne empire 1600–1800* [Repr.]. London: Pelican Books.

Boxer, Charles R. (1988). *Dutch Merchants and Mariners in Asia 1602–1795* [Repr.]. London: Variorum Reprints.

Braasem, W.A. (1953). 'Indonesische klanken in oud-vaderlandse mond' ['Indonesian sounds as spoken by Dutch people in old times'], *De Nieuwe Taalgids* 46, pp. 104–108.

Brown, Yu-Ying (1976). 'The Von Siebold Collection from Tokugawa Japan', *The British Library Journal* 2(1), pp. 38–55.

Brugmans, Sebaldus Justinus *et al.* (1807). *Bataafsche Apotheek* ['Batavian Phaemaco-poeia']. Amsterdam: Johannes Allart.

Bruijn, Iris (2009). *Ship's Surgeons of the Dutch East India Company: Commerce and the Progress of Medicine in the Eighteenth Century.* Leiden: Leiden University Press.

Bruijn, Jacobus (J.R.) *et al.* (ed.) (1979). *Dutch-Asiatic Shipping in the 17th and 18th centuries. Vol. II. Outward-Bound voyages from the Netherlands to Asia and the Cape (1595–1794).* The Hague: Martinus Nijhoff.

Buijs, Johannes (1800). *Natuurkundig Schoolboek* ['Schoolbook of Physics'], 1st ed. Leiden: D. du Mortier en zoon.

Buijs, Johannes (1811). *Volks-natuurkunde* ['Popular physics'], 1st ed. Amsterdam: Cornelis de Vries.

Burke, Peter (2004). *Languages and Communities in Early Modern Europe.* Cambridge: CUP.

Burke, Peter (2005). *Towards a Social History of Early Modern Dutch.* Amsterdam: AUP.

Burke, Peter (2007). 'Cultures of translation in early modern Europe', in P. Burke and R. Po-Chia Hsia, ed., *Cultural Translation in Early Modern Europe.* Cambridge: CUP, pp. 7–38.

Burke, Peter (2014). 'Diglossia in Early Modern Europe', in V. Rjéoutski, G. Argent and D. Offord, ed., *European Francophonie: The Social, Political and Cultural History of an International Prestige Language.* Bern: Peter Lang, pp. 33–50.

Burke-Gaffney, Brian (2009). *Nagasaki: The British Experience, 1854–1945.* Folkestone: Global Oriental.

Buys, Egbert (1769–1778). *Nieuw en volkomen woordenboek van konsten en weetenschappen* [...] ['New and complete dictionary of the arts and sciences']. Amsterdam.

Caron, François (1661). *Rechte beschryvinge van het machtigh koninghrijck van Iappan* ['True Description of the Mighty Kingdom of Japan']. The Hague: Johan Tongerloo.

Cats, Jacob (1632). *Spiegel van den Ouden ende Nieuwen Tijdt* ['Mirror of the Old and New Time'], *1st ed.* The Hague: Isaac Burchoorn.

Chatterjee, Shantonu Abe, and Tinde van Andel (2019). 'Lost Grains and Forgotten Vegetables from Japan: the Seikei Zusetsu Agricultural Catalog (1793–1804)', *Economic Botany* 73(3), pp. 375–389.

Chiu, Hsin-Hui (2008). *The Colonial 'civilizing Process' in Dutch Formosa: 1624–1662.* Leiden: Brill.

Chomel, Noël (1709). *Dictionnaire oeconomique* ['The Family Dictionary']. Paris: Le Conte.

Chomel, Noël (1778–93). *Algemeen huishoudelijk-, natuur-, zedekundig- en konstwoordenboek* [...] ['General dictionary for the home, natural world, ethics and technical terms'], trans. J.A. de Chalmot, 7 vols. Leiden: Johannes Le Mair.

Clark, Timothy (ed.) (2017). *Hokusai: Beyond the Great Wave*. London: Thames & Hudson.

Clements, Rebekah (2015). *A Cultural History of Translation in Early Modern Japan*. Cambridge: CUP.

Cleyer, Andreas (1985). *Tagebuch des Kontors zu Nagasaki auf der Insel Deshima 20. Oktober 1682–5. November 1683*, E.S. Kraft, ed. Bonn: Förderverein "Bonner Zeitschrift für Japanologie".

Clulow, Adam (2010). 'From Global Entrepôt to Early Modern Domain: Hirado, 1609–1641', *Monumenta Nipponica* 65(1), pp. 1–35.

Clulow, Adam (2012). 'The Pirate and the Warlord', *Journal of Early Modern History* 16.6, pp. 523–542.

Clulow, Adam (2013). 'Commemorating Failure: The Four Hundredth Anniversary of England's Trading Outpost in Japan', *Monumenta Nipponica* 68(2), pp. 207–231.

Clulow, Adam (2014). *The Company and the Shogun: The Dutch Encounter with Tokugawa Japan*. New York: Columbia University Press.

Cobbing, Andrew (1998). *The Japanese Discovery of Victorian Britain: Early Travel Encounters in the Far West*. Richmond, Surrey: Japan Library.

Cocks, Richard (1978). *Diary Kept by the Head of the English Factory in Japan, Diary of Richard Cocks, 1615–1622*, 3 vols. Tokyo: Tōkyō Daigaku Shiryō Hensanjo.

Collins, James T. (1998). *Malay, World Language: A Short History*. Kuala Lumpur: Dewan Bahasa dan Pustaka.

Commelin, Isaac (ed.) (1969). *Begin ende Voortgangh van de Vereenighde Nederlantsche Geoctroyeerde Oost-Indische Compagnie*. ['Beginning and Continuation of the United Dutch Chartered East India Company'], 4 vols. Amsterdam: Facsimile Uitgaven Nederland.

Consbruch, Georg Wilhelm (1817). *Handboek der Algemeene Ziektekunde* ['Manual of General Pathology'], trans. F. van der Breggen. Amsterdam: L. van Es.

Cook, Harold J. (2007). *Matters of Exchange: Commerce, Medicine, and Science in the Dutch Golden Age*. New Haven: Yale University Press.

Coolhaas, Willem Ph. (1960–1964). *Generale missiven van gouverneurs generaal en raden aan Heren XVII der Verenigde Oostindische Compagnie* ['General missives from the Governors-General and Councils to the Lords XVII of the United East India Company']. The Hague: Martinus Nijhoff.

Cornelle, Louis (1783). *Beknopte en klaare leerwyze der Fransche taale* ['Concise and clear learner for the French language']. Rotterdam: Dirk Vis.

Corr, William (1995). *Adams the Pilot: The Life and Times of Captain William Adams*. London: Routledge Curzon.

Cortazzi, Sir Hugh (1983). *Isles of Gold, Antique Maps of Japan.* New York: Weatherhill.

Coulmas, Florian (1989). *Language Adaptation.* New York: CUP.

Covens, Johannes and Cornelis Mortier (1730). *Nieuwe Atlas* ['New Atlas']. Amsterdam: Covens and Mortier.

Cullen, Louis M. (2006). *A history of Japan: 1582–1941; internal and external worlds.* Cambridge: CUP.

Dalton-Puffer, Christiane (1996). *The French Influence on Middle English Morphology.* New York: Mouton de Gruyter.

De Bary, William T. *et al.* (1958). *Sources of Japanese Tradition.* New York: Columbia University Press.

De Bary, William T. *et al.* (2001). *Sources of Japanese Tradition, 2nd ed., I, From Earliest Times to 1600.* New York: Columbia University Press.

De Bary, William T. *et al.* (2005). *Sources of Japanese Tradition, 2nd ed., II, 1600 to 2000.* New York: Columbia University Press.

De Bary, William T. (2013). *The great civilized conversation: education for a world community.* New York: Columbia University Press.

Defoe, Daniel (1720). *Het leven en de wonderbaare gevallen van Robinson Crusoe.* Amsterdam: Jansoons van Waesberge.

De Fourcroy, Antoine-François (1801–2). *Système des Connaissances Chimiques et de leurs applications aux phénomènes de la nature et de l'art.* Paris: Baudouin.

De Gorter, Johannes (1744). *Gezuiverde Geneeskonst* ['Purified Medicine']. Amsterdam.

De Graeff van Polsbroek, Dirk (1987). *Journaal van Jonkheer Dirk de Graeff van Polsbroek, 1857–1870: belevenissen van een Nederlands diplomaat in het negentiende eeuwse Japan* ['Journal of the nobleman Dirk de Graeff van Polsbroek, 1857–1870: experiences of a Dutch diplomat in nineteenth-century Japan'], H.J. Moeshart, ed. Assen: Van Gorcum.

De Groot, Henk (2000). 'Shizuki Tadao, pionier in de Japanse linguïstiek' ['Shizuki Tadao, pioneer in Japanese linguistics'], in L. Blussé *et al.*, ed., *Bewogen Betrekkingen.* Hilversum: Teleac/NOT, pp. 119–120.

De Groot, Henk (2004). 'The great Dutch-Japanese dictionaries in early nineteenth-century Japan', *Voortgang, jaarboek voor de neerlandistiek* 22, pp. 161–176.

De Groot, Henk (2005). *The Study of the Dutch Language in Japan During its Period of National Isolation (ca. 1641–1868).* (Ph.D. thesis). Christchurch, New Zealand.

De Groot, Henk (2010). 'Engelbert Kaempfer, Imamura Gen'emon and Arai Hakuseki, an Early Exchange of Knowledge between Japan and the Netherlands', in Siegfried Huigen, Jan L. de Jong, and Elmer Kolfin, ed., *The Dutch Trading Companies as Knowledge Networks.* Leiden: Brill, pp. 201–209.

De Groot, Henk (2016). 'Dutch as the Language of Science and Technology in Japan: The *Bangosen* Lexical Works', *Histoire Epistémologie Langage* 38/1, pp. 63–82.

De Lairesse, Gerard (1707). *Het Groot Schilderboek* ['The Great Painter's Book']. Amsterdam: Willem de Coup.

De Lange, William (1998). *A History of Japanese Journalism, Japan's Press Club as the Last Obstacle to a Mature Press*. London: Japan Library.

De Lange, William (2006). *Pars Japonica. The First Dutch Expedition to Reach the Shores of Japan*. Warren, Conn.: Floating World Editions.

De Marolles, Michel (1655). *Tableaux du Temple des Muses tirez du Cabinet de feu Mr. Favereau....* Paris: Nicolas L'Anglois.

De Ruyver, Dirk (2016). 'The First Treaty Between Belgium and Japan (1866)', in W.F. vande Walle, ed., *Japan & Belgium: An Itinerary of Mutual Inspiration*. Tielt: Lannoo, pp. 21–112.

De Vooys, Cornelis G.N. (1970). *Geschiedenis van de Nederlandse taal* ['History of the Dutch Language']. Groningen: Wolters-Noordhoff.

De Vries, P. (2002). 'Het Leven van Dirck Gerritsz Pomp alias Dirck China' ['The Life of Dirck Gerritsz Pomp alias Dirck China'], in K.W.J.M. Bossaers, ed., *Dirck Gerritsz Pomp alias Dirck China*. Enkhuizen: Vereniging Oud Enkhuizen, pp. 7–24.

Diaries Kept by the Heads of the Dutch Factory in Japan: *Dagregisters Gehouden bij de Opperhoofden van de Nederlandsche Factorij in Japan* (*Diaries*) (1974–). Tokyo: Tōkyō Daigaku Shiryō Hensanjo.

Dictionarium Latino Lvsitanicvm, ac Iaponicvm ['Latin, Portuguese and Japanese dictionary']. (1595). Amakusa: Collegio Iaponico Societatis Iesv.

Dodoens, Rembert (1554). *Cruydt-boeck* ['Herbal']. Antwerp: Jan van der Loe.

Doeff, Hendrick (1833). *Herinneringen uit Japan* ['Recollections from Japan']. Haarlem: De erven François Bohn.

Donaldson, Bruce (1983). *Dutch: A Linguistic History of Holland and Belgium*. Leiden: Martinus Nijhoff.

Donker Curtius, Janus Henricus (1857). *Proeve eener Japansche spraakkunst* ['Model of Japanese grammar']. Leiden: A.W. Sythoff.

Duff, John Wight and Arnold Mackay Duff (trans. and ed.) (1934). *Minor Latin Poets*. London: Heinemann.

Duke, Benjamin (2009). *The history of modern Japanese education: constructing the national school system, 1872–1890*. Piscataway, N.J.: Rutgers University Press.

Du Rieu, Willem (1875). *Album studiosorum Academiae Lugduno Batavae MDLXXV–MDCCCLXXV: accedunt nomina curatorum et professorum per eadem secula*. The Hague: Martinus Nijhoff.

Earns, Fumiko (1993). *Language Adaptation: European language influence on Japanese syntax*. Ann Arbor, Mich.: UMI.

Earns, Fumiko (1996). 'Dutch Influence on the Japanese Language at the Syntactic Level', *Asian Culture* 24(1), pp. 64–71.

Effert, Rudolf (2008). *Royal Cabinets and Auxiliary Branches: Origins of the National Museum of Ethnology*. Leiden: CNWS Publications.

Effert, Rudolf (2012). 'The Dūfu Haruma. An Explosive Dictionary', in A. Beerens and M. Teeuwen, ed., *Uncharted Waters: Intellectual Life in the Edo Period: Essays in Honour of W.J. Boot*. Leiden: Brill, pp. 197–220.

Elison, George (1973). *Deus Destroyed: The Image of Christianity in Early Modern Japan*. Cambridge, Mass.: Harvard University Press.

Errington, Joseph (2008). *Linguistics in a Colonial World: A Story of Language, Meaning, and Power*. Oxford: Blackwell Publishing.

Even-Zohar, Itamar (1990). 'The Position of Translated Literature within the Literary Polysystem', *Poetics Today* 11(1), pp. 45–51.

Eylenbosch, Joseph M. (1940). 'Foreign Survivals in the Japanese Language', *Monumenta Nipponica* 3(2), pp. 579–589.

Farrington, Anthony (1991). *The English Factory in Japan 1613–1623*, 2 vols. London: The British Library.

Feenstra Kuiper, Jan (1921). *Japan en de buitenwereld in de achttiende eeuw* ['Japan and the outside world in the eighteenth century']. The Hague: Nijhoff.

Ferguson, Charles A. (1982). 'Religious Factors in Language Spread', in R.L. Cooper, ed., *Language Spread Studies in Diffusion and Social Change*. Bloomington, Ind.: Indiana University Press, pp. 95–106.

Foucault, Michel (1994). *The Order of Things: An Archaeology of the Human Sciences* (ET). New York: Vintage Books.

Frellesvig, Bjarke (2010). *A History of the Japanese Language*. Cambridge: CUP.

French, Calvin L. (1974). *Shiba Kōkan: Artist, Innovator, and Pioneer in the Westernization of Japan*. New York: Weatherhill.

Frijhoff, Willem (2010). *Meertaligheid in de Gouden Eeuw: Een Verkenning* ['Multilingualism in the Dutch Golden Age: An Exploration']. Amsterdam: KNAW.

FUKUOKA Maki (2012). *The Premise of Fidelity: Science, Visuality, and Representing the Real in Nineteenth-Century Japan*. Stanford: Stanford University Press.

FUKUZAWA Yukichi (1934). *Fukuō jiden* ['The memoirs of old man Fukuzawa']. Tokyo: Jiji Shinpōsha.

FUKUZAWA Yukichi (2007). *The Autobiography of Fukuzawa Yukichi*, trans. Eiichi Kiyooka. New York: Columbia University Press.

Gaastra, Femme (1991). *De geschiedenis van de VOC* ['The History of the VOC']. Zutphen: Walburg Pers.

Gaastra, Femme (2003). *The Dutch East India Company: Expansion and Decline* (ET). Zutphen: Walburg Pers.

Gardner-Chloros, Penelope (2009). *Code-Switching*. Cambridge: CUP.

Goodman, Grant K. (2000). *Japan and the Dutch 1600–1853*. Richmond, U.K.: Curzon.

Goodman, Grant K. (2013). *Japan: The Dutch Experience*. London: Bloomsbury Academic.

Greenblatt, Stephen (2011). *The Swerve: How the World Became Modern*. New York: W.W. Norton.

Griffis, William E. (1900). *Verbeck of Japan. A Citizen of No Country: A Life Story of Foundation Work Inaugurated by Guido Fridolin Verbeck*. New York: Fleming H. Revell.

Groeneboer, Kees (1998). *Gateway to the West: The Dutch Language in Colonial Indonesia: 1600–1950: A History of Language Policy*. Amsterdam: AUP.

Grotius, Hugo (1609). *Mare Liberum* ['The Free Sea']. Leiden: Elzevir.

Gunn, Geoffrey (2018). *World Trade Systems of the East and West: Nagasaki and the Asian Bullion Trade Networks*. Leiden: Brill.

Hageman, H.H. (1838). *Enchiridion Medicum: handleiding tot de geneeskundige praktijk* ['*Enchiridion Medicum*: manual for medical practice']. Amsterdam: Santbergen.

Hakvoord, Barend (1727). *Oprecht Onderwijs der Letter-konst* ['True Instruction in Grammar']. Amsterdam.

Hall, Francis (1992). *Japan through American eyes: the journal of Francis Hall, Kanagawa and Yokohama, 1859–1866*, Fred G. Notehelfer, ed. Princeton: Princeton University Press.

Halma, François (1708). *Woordenboek der Nederduitsche en Fransche Taalen* ['Dictionary of the Dutch and French Languages']. Amsterdam: F. Halma.

HARADA Hiroji (2000). 'De Tolkenfamilie Motoki' ['The Motoki Family of Interpreters'], in L. Blussé *et al.*, ed., *Bewogen Betrekkingen*. Hilversum: Teleac/NOT, pp. 122–124.

HARADA Tomohiko (1964). *Nagasaki: Rekishi no tabi e no shōtai* ['Nagasaki: An invitation to a journey into history']. Tokyo: Chūō kōron-sha.

Harting, Pieter (1865). *Anno 2065 Een Blik in de Toekomst* ['The Year 2065: A Look in the Future']. Utrecht: Greven.

Haugen, Einar (1953). *The Norwegian Language in America: A Study in Bilingual Behavior. Vol. 1: The Bilingual Community; Vol. II: The American Dialects of Norwegian*. Bloomington: Indiana University Press.

Heister, Lorenz/Laurens (1741). *Heelkundige Onderwijzingen* ['Lessons in Surgery'], trans. Hendrik Ulhoorn. Amsterdam: Jansson van Waesberghe.

Hemmes, Jolien C. (ed.) (2017). *Brieven uit Deshima: met het manuscript van het verslag over de reis naar Japan van Jan Cock Blomhoff en Titia Bergsma met hun zoontje en hun verblijf daar samen, tegen de regels van de Sakoku* [...] ['Letters from Deshima: with the manuscript of the account of the journey to Japan by Jan Cock Blomhoff and Titia Bergsma with their little son and their stay there together, in contravention of the rules of Sakoku']. Zierikzee: Vivi Techni.

Henry, William (1799). *An Epitome of Chemistry*, 1st ed. London: J. Johnson.

Henshall, Kenneth (2012). *A History of Japan: From Stone Age to Superpower*, 3rd ed. London: Palgrave Macmillan.

Hermans, Theo (1985). 'Introduction—Translation Studies and a New Paradigm', in Theo Hermans, ed., *The Manipulation of Literature—Studies in Literary Translation*. London: Palgrave, pp. 7–15.

Hermans, Theo (2007). *The Conference of the Tongues*. Manchester: St. Jerome Publishing.

Hesselink, Reinier (1994). 'The Assassination of Henry Heusken', *Monumenta Nipponica* 49(3), pp. 331–351.

Hesselink, Reinier (1995). 'A Dutch New Year at the Shirandō Academy 1 January 1795', *Monumenta Nipponica* 50(2), pp. 189–234.

Hesselink, Reinier (2001). (Review). 'Grant K. Goodman, *Japan and the Dutch 1600–1853* (Richmond, Surrey: Curzon Press, 2000)', *Journal of Asian History* 35(2), pp. 206–208.

Hesselink, Reinier (2002). *Prisoners from Nambu: reality and make-believe in seventeenth-century Japanese diplomacy*. Honolulu, Hawai'i: University of Hawai'i Press.

Hesselink, Reinier (2005). 'A New Guide to an Old Source', *Monumenta Nipponica* 60(4), pp. 513–523.

Hesselink, Reinier (2016). *The Dream of Christian Nagasaki: World Trade and the Clash of Cultures, 1560–1640*. Jefferson, N.C.: McFarland & Company, Inc., Publishers.

Hesselink, Reinier (2018). 'Heusken, Henry (1832–61)', in *The Encyclopedia of Diplomacy* Vol. II. Chichester: Wiley Blackwell.

Het Leven van Bonaparte (1801). ['The Life of Bonaparte'] trans. from the French by Johannes van der Linden. Amsterdam: Johannes Allart. (French author unidentified).

Heylen, Ann (2001). 'Dutch Language Policy and Early Formosan Literacy (1624–1662)' in Ku Wei-ying, ed., *Missionary Approaches and Linguistics in Mainland China and Taiwan*. Leuven: Leuven University Press, pp. 199–252.

HIRAMATSU Kanji (1999). *Nagasaki yūgakusha jiten* ['Dictionary of scholar-visitors to Nagasaki']. Hiroshima: Keisuisha.

Hoffman, Charlotte (1991). *Introduction to Bilingualism*. New York: Longman.

Hoffmann, Johann J. (1882). 'Verzameling van Japansche boekwerken door Mr. J.H. Donker Curtius, Nederlandsch Commissaris voor Japan, op zijne reis naar Yedo in 1858 voor het rijk ingekocht' ['Collection of Japanese Books purchased for the state by Mr. J.H. Donker Curtius, the Dutch Commissioner to Japan, on his journey to Edo in 1858'], *Bijdragen tot de Taal-, Land- en Volkenkunde* 30, pp. 27–39, 91–93.

Hoffmann, Johann J. and Lindor Serrurier (1882). *Verzameling van Japansche boekwer-ken, door J.H. Donker Curtius op zijne reis naar Yedo in 1858 voor het rijk ingekocht* ['Collection of Japanese Books purchased for the state by J.H. Donker Curtius on his journey to Edo in 1858']. The Hague: s.n.

Holmstedt, Robert D. (2006). 'Issues in the linguistic analysis of a dead language, with particular reference to ancient Hebrew', *Journal of Hebrew Scriptures* 6(11), pp. 1–21.

Hoogstraten, David (1704). *Nieuw woordenboek der Nederlandsche en Latijnsche taal* ['New Dictionary of the Dutch and Latin Language'], 1st ed. Amsterdam: Hendrik Boom.

Horiuchi Annick (2003). 'L'apprentissage du hollandais au Japon au début du XIXe siècle'. Paper read at *1er Congrès Réseau Asie/1st Congress Réseau Asie-Asia Network 24–25 sept. 2003*. Paris, France.

Hübner, Johann (1722). *Kort begryp der oude en nieuwe geographie* ['Short Sketch of Old and New Geography']. Amsterdam: Nicolaas ten Hoorn.

Hübner, Johann (1769). *Algemeene Geographie, of Beschryving des Geheelen Aardryks* ['General Geography or Description of the Whole Earth'], trans. W.A. Bachiene and E.W. Cramerus. 6 parts. Amsterdam: Pieter Meijer.

Hufeland, Christoph Wilhelm (1836). *Enchiridion Medicum: oder Anleitung zur medizinischen Praxis*. Berlin: Jonas.

Huyssen van Kattendyke, W.J.C. (1860). *Uittreksel uit het dagboek van W.J.C. Ridder Huyssen van Kattendyke, kapitein-luit. ter zee, gedurende zijn verblijf in Japan in 1857, 1858, en 1859* ['Extract from the journal of W.J.C. Ridder Huyssen van Kattendyke, Commander, during his stay in Japan in 1857, 1858 and 1859']. The Hague: W.P. van Stockum. http://babel.hathitrust.org/cgi/pt?id=nyp.33433082441936;view=1up;seq=15. Accessed 15 February 2020.

Ianello, Tiziana (2012). *Shōgun, kōmōjin e rangakusha: Le Compagnie delle Indie e l'apertura del Giappone alla tecnologia occidentale nei secoli XVII–XVIII*. Padua: Libreria Universitaria.

IJzerman, J.W. (1915). *Dirck Gerritsz. Pomp Alias Dirck Gerritsz China: De Eerste Nederlander die China en Japan Bezocht (1544–1604)* ['Dirck Gerritsz. Pomp Alias Dirck Gerritsz China: The First Dutchman who visited China and Japan (1544–1604)']. The Hague: Martinus Nijhoff.

IRIE Ichirō (1987). *Nagasaki hakurai kotoba* ['Nagasaki Loanwords']. Nagasaki: Nagasaki Literature Company.

Irwin, Mark (2011). *Loanwords in Japanese*. Amsterdam: John Benjamins.

ISHIGURO Yoshimi (1963). *Nippongo no sanpo* ['A stroll through the Japanese Language']. Tokyo: Kadokawa shoten.

ISHIWATA Toshio (1985). *Nihongo no naka no gaikokugo* ['Foreign words in Japanese']. Tokyo: Iwanami Shoten.

ISHIWATA Toshio (2001). *Gairaigo no sōgōteki kenkyū* ['A general study of loanwords (in Japanese)']. Tokyo: Tōkyōdō Shuppan.

ISOMURA Shūsaku (1929). *Kanagawa ken kōjō kyōkai zasshi* ['Kanawaga Prefecture Factory Association Journal'], 11–10.

Israel, Jonathan (2011). *Democratic Enlightenment: Philosophy, Revolution, and Human Rights 1750–1790*. Oxford: OUP.

ITAZAWA Takeo (1933). *Rangaku no hattatsu* ['Development of Dutch Studies']. Tokyo: Iwanami Shoten.

ITAZAWA Takeo (1959). *Nichi-ran bunka kōshōshi no kenkyū* ['Study on the History of Japanese-Dutch Cultural Relations']. Tokyo: Yoshikawa Kōbunkan.

IWAO Seiichi (1959). 'An Early Dutchman in Japan', *Japan Quarterly* VI, pp. 308–315.

IWAO Seiichi (1961). 'A Dutch Doctor in Old Japan', *Japan Quarterly* VIII, pp. 170–178.

IWAO Seiichi (1976–79). *Oranda fūsetsugaki shūsei* ['Collected Dutch Books of Rumours'], 2 vols. Tokyo: The Japan-Netherlands Institute.

IWASAKI Shōichi (2018). 'Passives' in HASEGAWA Yoko, ed., *The Cambridge Handbook of Japanese Linguistics*. Cambridge: CUP, pp. 530–556.

Jackson, Terrence (2009). *Socialized Intellect: The Cultural Network of Rangaku in Late Tokugawa Japan*. (Ph.D. thesis), Indiana University.

Jackson, Terrence (2016). *Network of Knowledge: Western Science and the Tokugawa Information Revolution*. Honolulu: University of Hawai'i Press.

Jacobs, Els M. (1983). *The Redhaired in Japan: Dutch Influence on Japanese Cartography (1640–1853)*. Leiden University, M.A. thesis.

Jacques, Benjamin and Samuel Hannot (1699). *Dictionarium Latino-Belgicum*. Rotterdam: Pieter van der Slaart.

Jaillot, Alexis Hubert (1692). *Nouvelle Introduction a la Geographie pour l'usage de Monseigneur le Dauphin*. Paris: H. Jaillot.

Jannetta, Ann (2007). *The Vaccinators: Smallpox, Medical Knowledge, and the 'Opening' of Japan*. Stanford, California: Stanford University Press.

Jannetta, Ann (2009). (Review). *The Patriarch of Dutch Learning Shizuki Tadao (1760–1806)*. Volume 9 of *Journal of the Japan-Netherlands Institute*, W.J. Boot, ed., *Monumenta Nipponica* 64(1), pp. 177–180.

János, Hanák (2012). 'Christovão Ferreira két arca', in *Közel, s Távol II*. Budapest: Eötvös Collegium, pp. 271–280.

Jansen, Marius (1992). *China in the Tokugawa World*. Cambridge, Mass.: Harvard University Press.

Joby, Christopher (2014). *The Multilingualism of Constantijn Huygens (1596–1687)*. Amsterdam: AUP.

Joby, Christopher (2015). *The Dutch Language in Britain (1550–1702)*. Leiden: Brill.

Joby, Christopher (2016). 'Recording the History of Dutch in Japan', *Dutch Crossing* 40(3), pp. 219–238.

Joby, Christopher (2017). 'Dutch in Eighteenth-Century Japan', *Dutch Crossing*. Published online 7 October 2017. https://doi.org/10.1080/03096564.2017.1383643.

Joby, Christopher (2018). 'Dutch in Seventeenth-Century Japan: A Social History', *Dutch Crossing* 42(2), pp. 175–196.

Joby, Christopher (2019a). 'The Reception of Ancient Latin and Greek Authors in Japan (1550–c. 1850)', *International Journal of the Classical Tradition* 26(3), pp. 270–294.

Joby, Christopher (2019b). 'The Dutch language in seventeenth-century Taiwan, Japan and Maluku: a case-study in language spread', *Nanying History, Society and Culture V: Early Tainan Region*, Tainan: International Center of Tainan Area Humanities and Social Science Research, pp. 105–134.

Jonston, Johannes (1660). *Naeukeurige beschrijving van de natuur der vier-voetige dieren*, ['A precise description of the nature of quadruped animals'], trans. M. Grausius. Amsterdam: Schipper.

Jörg, Christiaan J.A. (2007). 'Japan and the West Export Porcelain and Lacquerware', in SHIRAHARA Yukiko, ed., *Japan Envisions the West: 16th–19th century Japanese art from Kobe City Museum*. Seattle, Wash.: University of Washington Press, pp. 165–94.

Kaempfer, Engelbert (1712). *Amœnitatum Exoticarum politico-physico-medicarum fasiculi v* ['Five fascicles of Exotic Political-Physical-Medical Delights']. Lemgo: Henricus Wilhelmus.

Kaempfer, Engelbert (1727). *The History of Japan: giving an account of the antient and present state and government of that empire*, trans. John Caspar Scheuchzer, 2 vols. London: Printed for the translator.

Kaempfer, Engelbert (1729). *De Beschrijving van Japan. behelsende een verhaal van den ouden en tegenwoordigen staat en regeering van dat ryk*. The Hague: P. Gosse en J. Neaulme.

Kaempfer, Engelbert (2001–). *Werke: kritische Ausgabe in Einzelbänden*, D. Haberland *et al.*, ed. Munich: Iudicium.

Kaiser, Stefan (1996). 'Translations of Christian Terminology into Japanese, 16–19th Centuries: Problems and Solutions', in John Breen and Mark Williams, ed., *Japan and Christianity: Impacts and Responses*. Basingstoke: Palgrave Macmillan, pp. 8–29.

Kaiser, Stefan *et al.* (2001). *Japanese: A Comprehensive Grammar*. London: Routledge.

Kaiser, Stefan *et al.* (2013). *Japanese: A Comprehensive Grammar*, 2nd ed. London: Routledge.

Kampen, N.G. (1816–17). *De Aarde Beschouwd in Haren Natuurlijken Toestand en Verdeeling* ['The Earth viewed in its Natural State and Division']. Haarlem: s.n.

KATAGIRI Kazuo (1985). *Oranda tsūji no kenkyū* ['A Study of the Dutch Interpreters']. Tokyo: Yoshikawa Kōbunkan.

KATSUMORI Noriko (2007). 'The Influence of Ransho on Western-style Painting', in SHIRAHARA Yukiko, ed., *Japan Envisions the West: 16th–19th century Japanese art from Kobe City Museum*. Seattle, Wash.: University of Washington Press, pp. 99–118.

KATSURAGAWA Hoshū (1978). *Kratkie vesti o skitanijach v severnych vodach = Chokusa monrjaku*. Vladimir Konstantinov, ed. Moscow: Nauka.

KAWAMOTO Yumiko (1998). 'On "The Glossary of English and Japanese Words" by Ranald MacDonald. Phonological approach to determine the dialectal words', *Historical English Studies in Japan* 30, pp. 151–168.

KAWASHIMA Junji (1992). 'Kawaguchi Ryōan-cho Orandago-chō kara', *Koga-shi ishikaihō* (24), pp. 1–9.

Keene, Donald (1969). *The Japanese Discovery of Europe, 1720–1830*. Stanford, Calif.: Stanford University Press.

Keene, Donald (2006). *Frog in the Well: Portraits of Japan by Watanabe Kazan 1793–1841*. New York: Columbia University Press.

Keill, John (1725). *Introductiones ad veram Physicam et veram Astronomiam* ['Introduction to the True Physics and Astronomy']. Leiden: J. and H. Verbeek.

Keill, John (1741). *Inleidinge tot de waare natuur- en sterrekunde* ['Introduction to the True Physics and Astronomy'], trans. Johan Lulofs, 1st ed. Leiden: J. and H. Verbeek.

Kennedy, Malcolm (1963). *A Short History of Japan*. London: Weidenfeld and Nicolson.

Kerlen, Henri (1996). *Catalogue of Meiji Japanese Books And Maps in Public Collections in the Netherlands*. Amsterdam: J.C. Gieben.

KINSUI Satoshi (1997). 'The influence of translation on the historical development of the Japanese passive construction', *Journal of Pragmatics* 28(6), pp. 759–779.

KISHIMOTO Hideki (2018), 'Negation' in HASEGAWA Yoko, ed., *The Cambridge Handbook of Japanese Linguistics*. Cambridge: CUP, pp. 300–331.

Kloeter, Henning (2005). *Written Taiwanese*. Wiesbaden: Harrassowitz Verlag.

Kobe City Museum = Kōbe shiritsu hakubutsukan (1998). *Nichi-Ran kōryū no kakehashi. Exhibition 'Bridge between Japan and the Netherlands: Through the Eyes of the "Oranda-Tsūji" or the Japanese Interpreters for the Dutch'*. Kobe: Kobe City Museum.

KOGA Jūjirō (1966). *Nagasaki yōgakushi* ['Nagasaki Chronicle of Western Studies'], 1. Nagasaki: Nagasaki Bunkensha.

KOGA Jūjirō (2000). *The Collected Words of Foreign Origin ... The best book to trace the etymology of Japanese originated in Portuguese, Dutch, Latin, or Chinese*. Nagasaki: Nagasaki Konin University Comparative Culture Research Institute.

Koller, Werner (2000). 'Übersetzungen ins Deutsche und ihre Bedeutung für die deutsche Sprachgeschichte', in W. Besch *et al.*, ed., *Sprachgeschichte: Ein Handbuch zur Geschichte der deutschen Sprache und ihrer Erforschung*. Berlin: Mouton de Gruyter, pp. 112–129.

Koolen, Ben (2011). *VOC & Onderwijs: Een inventarisatie* ['VOC and Education: An Inventarisation']. Assen: Boekwinkeltjes.

Kornicki, Peter (2001). *The Book in Japan: A Cultural History from the Beginnings to the Nineteenth Century*. Honolulu: University of Hawai'i Press.

Kornicki, Peter (2018). *Language, scripts and Chinese texts in East Asia*. Oxford: OUP.

Kouwenhoven, Arlette (2000). *Siebold and Japan: His life and work*. Leiden: Hotei.

Krieger, Carel C. (1940). *The Infiltration of European Civilization in Japan during the 18th Century*. Leiden: Brill.

Kuiper, Pieter Nicolaas (Koos) (1993). 'Dutch loan-words and loan-translations in modern Chinese: an example of successful sinification by way of Japan', in L. Haft, ed.,

Words from the West, Western texts in Chinese literary context, Essays to honor Erik Zürcher on his sixty-fifth birthday. Leiden: CNWS Publications, pp. 116–144.

Kuiper, Pieter Nicolaas (Koos). (2015). *The Early Dutch Sinologists: A Study of their Training in Holland China and their Functions in the Netherlands Indies (1854–1900)*, 2dln. (Ph.D. thesis). Leiden University.

Kulmus, Johann Adam (1722). *Anatomische Tabellen* ['Anatomical Tables']. Danzig: Von Beughern.

Kulmus, Johann Adam (1734). *Ontleedkundige Tafelen* ['Anatomical Tables'], trans. Gerard Dicten. Amsterdam: Janssoons van Waesberge.

Labov, William (1982). 'Building on Empirical Foundations', in W.P. Lehmann and Y. Malkiel, ed., *Perspectives on Historical Linguistics*. Amsterdam: Benjamins, pp. 17–92.

Labov, William (2006). *The social stratification of English in New York City*, 2nd ed. Cambridge: CUP.

Labrune, Laurence (2012). *The Phonology of Japanese*. Oxford: OUP.

Lach, Donald F. (1965). *Asia in the Making of Europe, vol. I, The Century of Discovery, Book Two*. Chicago: The University of Chicago Press.

Lach, Donald F. (1977). *Asia in the Making of Europe, vol. II, A Century of Wonder. Book Three*. Chicago: The University of Chicago Press.

Laferrière, Edouard (1869). *Les Constitutions d'Europe et d'Amérique*. Paris: Cotillon.

Laver, Michael S. (2011). *The Sakoku Edicts and the Politics of Tokugawa Hegemony*. Amherst, N.Y.: Cambria Press.

Lavoisier, Antoine (1789). *Traité élémentaire de chimie*. Paris: Cuchet.

Le Page, R.B. and Andrée Tabouret-Keller (1985). *Acts of identity: Creole-based approaches to language and ethnicity*. Cambridge: CUP.

Lequin, Frank (1990). *The Private Correspondence of Isaac Titsingh*, 2 vols. (vol. 1 1785–1811; vol. 2 1779–1812). Amsterdam: J.C. Gieben.

Lequin, Frank (1992). *The Private Correspondence of Kutsuki Masatsuna and Isaac Titsingh (1785–1807)*. Amsterdam: J.C. Gieben.

Lequin, Frank (2002). *Isaac Titsingh (1745–1812): een passie voor Japan leven en werk van de grondlegger van de Europese Japanologie* ['Isaac Titsingh (1745–1812): a passion for Japan life and work of the founder of European Japanology']. Alphen aan den Rijn: Canaletto/ Repro-Holland.

Lequin, Frank (2003). *A la Recherche du Cabinet Titsingh: its history, contents and dispersal: catalogue raisonné of the collection of the founder of European Japanology*. Alphen aan den Rijn: Canaletto/Repro-Holland.

Lequin, Frank (2005). *Isaac Titsingh Private Correspondence (1783–1812) as the reflection of an enlightened 'voyageur philosophique'*. Unpublished paper.

Lequin, Frank (ed.) (2009). *De Particuliere Correspondentie van Isaac Titsingh (1783–1812)* ['The Private Correspondence of Isaac Titsingh (1783–1812)'], 2 vols. *Titsingh Studies* 4.1–2. Alphen aan den Rijn: Canaletto/Repro-Holland.

Lequin, Frank (2011). *Isaac Titsingh: Opperhoofd van Japan: Drie Geschriften als Filosoof, Diplomaat & Koopman* ['Isaac Titsingh: Opperhoofd in Japan: Three Pieces of Writing as Philosopher, Diplomat and Merchant']. Alphen aan den Rijn: Canaletto/Repro-Holland.

Lequin, Frank (2013). *Varia Titsinghiana: addenda & corrigenda*. Leiden: Titsingh Instituut.

Lim, Lisa and Umberto Ansaldo (2015). *Languages in Contact*. Cambridge: CUP.

Liss, Robert (2009). 'Frontier Tales: Tokugawa Japan in Translation' in Simon Schaffer, ed., *The brokered world: go-betweens and global intelligence, 1770–1820*. Sagamore Beach, Calif.: Science History Publications, pp. 1–47.

List of foreign books collected under the Shogunate regime = Lijst van boeken in buitenlandse talen verzameld door het Shogunaat (1957). Tokyo: Institute for the study of the Netherlands books (Ueno catalogue).

Loh, Joseph F. (2013). *Worlds Collide-Art, Cartography, and Japanese Nanban World Map Screens*. (Ph.D. thesis). Columbia University, New York.

Lohanda, Mona, *et al.* (2018). *VOC Glossary Indonesia*. Published Version 1.0 on February, 6th 2018.

Loonen, P.L.M. (2000). 'The Influence of the Huguenots on the Teaching of French in the Dutch Republic during the 17th Century', in Jan de Clercq *et al.*, *Grammaire et enseignement du français*. Leuven: Peeters, pp. 317–333.

Loveday, Leo J. (1996). *Language contact in Japan: A sociolinguistic history*. Oxford: OUP.

Luyken, Jan and Kaspar (1694). *Spiegel van het menselyk bedryf* ['Mirror of Trades'], 1st ed. Amsterdam: Nicolaus Visscher.

Macé, Mieko (2016). 'Le Hollandais et une Nouvelle Approche Scientifique ou les *Rangaku* (les Etudes Hollandaises) et les Médecins Traducteurs Japonais au XIXᵉ S.', *Histoire Epistémologie Langage* 38/1, pp. 83–102.

MacDonald, Ranald (1923). *The Narrative of his Early Life [...] 1824–1894*. William S. Lewis and MURAKAMI Naojiro, ed. Spokane, Washington: Inland-American Publishing.

MAKINO Seiichi and TSUTSUI Michio (2009). *A Dictionary of Basic Japanese Grammar*. Tokyo: The Japan Times.

Marcon, Federico (2015). *The knowledge of nature and the nature of knowledge in early modern Japan*. Chicago: University of Chicago Press.

Marin, Pierre/Pieter (1752). *Nieuwe Fransche en Nederduitsche spraakwyze [...]* ['New French and Dutch Learner']. Amsterdam.

Martin, Samuel (1975). *A Reference Grammar of Japanese*. London: Yale University Press.

Martinet, Johannes (1777–79). *Katechismus der Natuur* ['Catechism of Nature']. Amsterdam: Johannes Allart.

Massarella, Derek (1990). *A World Elsewhere: Europe's Encounter with Japan in the Sixteenth and Seventeenth Centuries*. New Haven: Yale UP.

MATSUDA Kiyoshi (1998). *Yōgaku no shoshiteki kenkyū* ['The bibliographical research on Western learning']. Kyoto: Rinsen shoten.

MATSUDA Kiyoshi (2000). 'Robinson Crusoe op de Japanse eilanden' ['Robinson Crusoe on the Japanese Islands'], in L. Blussé *et al.*, ed., *Bewogen Betrekkingen*. Hilversum: Teleac/NOT, p. 127.

MATSUDA Kiyoshi (2001). 'The Reception and Spread of Dodonaeus' Cruydt-boek in Japan', in W.F. Vande Walle, ed., *Dodonaeus in Japan: Translation and the Scientific Mind in the Tokugawa Period*. Leuven: Leuven University Press, pp. 192–220.

MATSUDA Kiyoshi (2006). *A List of the Dutch titles identified from the Yōsho Mokoukru (Catalogue of Western Books) of the Saga Nabeshima clan*. Kyoto: Kyoto University.

MATSUKATA Fuyuko (2007). *Oranda fūsetsugaki to kinsei nihon* ['The Dutch Book of Rumours in early modern Japan']. Tokyo: Tokyo Daigaku Shuppankai.

MATSUKATA Fuyuko (2011). 'King Willem II's 1844 Letter to the Shogun "Recommendation to Open the Country"', trans. Adam Clulow. *Monumenta Nipponica* 66/1, pp. 99–122.

MATSUKATA Fuyuko (ed.) (2012). *Betsudan fūsetsugaki ga kataru 19-seiki: hon'yaku to kenkyū: The Dutch Special news reports to Japan: a depiction of the 19th century*. Tokyo: Tokyo Daigaku Shuppankai.

MATSUKI Akitomo (2006). *Baba sadayoshi-yaku 'tonkahiketsu' shahon ichi roku-shu no shoshigakuteki kentō* ['A bibliographical study on sixteen extant manuscripts of "Tonka Hiketsu" translated by Baba Sadayoshi']. *Nihon Ishigaku Zasshi* 52(4), pp. 561–600.

MATSUMOTO Norihisa (2000). *Rangaku-kan zuroku* ['Illustrated Book of the Rangaku House']. Takeo City: Takeo Toshokan.

MATSUMOTO Yoshiko (2018). 'Clausal Noun Modification', in HASEGAWA Yoko, ed., *The Cambridge Handbook of Japanese Linguistics*. Cambridge: CUP, pp. 463–484.

MATSUO Bashō (2004). *Bashō's Haiku, Selected Poems of Matsuo Bashō*, trans. David Landis Barnhill. Albany, N.Y.: State University of New York Press.

Matsūra Western books catalogue. Hirado: Matsūra Historical Museum.

McMaster, John (1992). *Sabotaging the shogun: Western diplomats open Japan, 1859–69*. New York: Vantage Press.

McOmie, William (2006). *The Opening of Japan 1853–1855: a comparative study of the American, British, Dutch and Russian naval expeditions to compel the Tokugawa Shogunate to conclude treaties and open ports to their ships*. Folkestone: Global Oriental.

Meier-Lemgo, Karl (1965). *Die Briefe Engelbert Kaempfers. Abhandlungen der Mathematisch-Naturwissenschaftlichen Klasse Jahrgang* 1965 (6). Wiesbaden. s.n.

Meijer, Lodewijk (1805). *Woordenschat, bevattende in drie deelen, de verklaring der basterdwoorden, kunstwoorden en verouderde woorden* ['Lexicon, comprising in three parts, the explanation of bastard words, technical terms and obsolete words'], 12th ed. Dordrecht: Blussé.

Meijer, Pieter (1763–). *Algemeene oefenschoole van konsten en weetenschappen* ['General practice school of arts and sciences']. Amsterdam: P. Meijer.

Meilink-Roelofsz, M.A.P. (1962). *Asian Trade and European Influence: In the Indonesian Archipelago between 1500 and about 1630.* The Hague: Martinus Nijhoff.

Meilink-Roelofsz, M.A.P. (1976). *De VOC in Azië* ['The VOC in Asia']. Bussum: Fibula.

Merklein, Johann Jacob (1663). *Ost-Indianische Reise, welche er im Jahr 1644 löblich angenommen und im Jahr 1653 glücklich vollendet.* Nuremberg: Michael and Joh. Friedrich Endters.

Mervart, David (2015). 'The Republic of Letters Comes to Nagasaki: Record of a Translator's Struggle', *Transcultural Studies* 2015.2, pp. 8–35.

Miao-Ling M. Tjoa (1990). 'Sakoku: The Full Range of Tokugawa Foreign Relations?' in Erika de Poorter, ed., *As the Twig is Bent ... Essays in Honour of Frits Vos.* Amsterdam: J.C. Gieben, pp. 209–236.

Michel, Wolfgang (1985). 'Japan in Caspar Schmalkaldens Reisebuch' ['Japan in Caspar Schmalkalden's Travel Journal'], *Dokufutsu Bungaku Kenkyū* 35, pp. 41–84.

Michel, Wolfgang (1986). 'Ein frühes deutsch-japanisches Glossar aus dem 17. Jahrhundert' ['An Early 17th Century German-Japanese Glossary'], *Kairos* 24, pp. 1–26.

Michel, Wolfgang (1989). 'Willem ten Rhijne und die japanische Medizin (I)', *Dokufutsu Bungaku Kenkyū* 39, pp. 75–125.

Michel, Wolfgang (1993a). 'Engelbert Kaempfers Beschäftigung mit der japanischen Sprache' ['Engelbert Kaempfer's involvement with the Japanese language'], in Detlef Haberland, ed., *Engelbert Kaempfer: Werk und Wirkung.* Stuttgart: Franz Steiner, pp. 194–221.

Michel, Wolfgang (1993b). 'Engelbert Kaempfer und die Medizin in Japan', in Detlef Haberland, ed., *Engelbert Kaempfer: Werk und Wirkung.* Stuttgart: Franz Steiner, pp. 248–293.

Michel, Wolfgang (1995). 'Hans Jurian Hancke, Mukai Genshō und Zacharias Wagener— Aspekte einer "lehrreichen" Begegnung im 17. Jahrhundert' ['Hans Juriaen Hancke, Zacharias Wagener and Mukai Gensho—Aspects of a 17th Century Cross-Cultural Encounter'], *Bulletin of the Graduate School of Social and Cultural Studies, Kyushu University* 1995(1), pp. 109–114.

Michel, Wolfgang (1996). 'Hans Jurian Hancke—ein Breslauer in Japan' ['Hans Juriaen Hancke—a Citizen of Breslau in Japan'], *Dokufutsu Bungaku Kenkyū* 46, pp. 59–88.

Michel, Wolfgang (1999). *Von Leipzig nach Japan. Der Chirurg und Handelsmann Caspar Schamberger (1623–1706)* ['From Leipzig to Japan. The Surgeon and Merchant Caspar Schamberger (1623–1706)']. Munich: Iudicium.

Michel, Wolfgang (2001). 'On the Reception of Western Medicine in Seventeenth Century Japan', in YOSHIDA Tadashi and FUKASE Yasuaki, ed., *Higashi to nishi no iryôbunka* ['Medicine and Culture in East and West']. Kyoto: Shibunkaku Shuppan, pp. 426–412/3–17.

Michel, Wolfgang (2005). 'Western Medicine and Pharmaceutics in 17th Century Japan', *Proceedings of the Tenth International Conference on the History of Science in East Asia*. Shanghai: Shanghai Jiao Tong University Press, pp. 173–181.

Michel, Wolfgang (2007). 'Ōe Shuntō, Physician of the Nakatsu Clan', *Nakatsu Municipal Museum for History and Folklore, Medical Archive Series No. 6*. Nakatsu, pp. 58–77 [in Japanese].

Michel, Wolfgang (2010a). 'Johann Caspar Scheuchzer (1702–1729) und die Herausgabe der History of Japan' ['Johann Caspar Scheuchzer (1702–1729) and the Publication of the History of Japan'], *Asiatische Studien Études Asiatiques* LXIV 1, pp. 101–137.

Michel, Wolfgang (2010b). 'On early red-head-style external medicine and the Confucian physician Mukai Genshô', *Nihon Ishigaku Zasshi—Journal of the Japanese Society for Medical History* 53(3), pp. 367–385 [in Japanese].

Michel, Wolfgang (2010c). 'Medizin, Heilmittel und Pflanzenkunde im euro-japanischen Kulturaustausch des 17. Jahrhunderts' ['Medicine, remedies and botany in the European-Japanese Cultural Exchange of the 17th century'], *Hōrin— Vergleichende Studien zur japanischen Kultur* 16, pp. 19–34.

Michel, Wolfgang (2011). 'Glimpses of medicine in early Japanese-German intercourse', in International Medical Society of Japan (IMSJ), ed., *'The Dawn of Modern Japanese Medicine and Pharmaceuticals', The 150th Anniversary Edition of Japan-German Exchange*. Tokyo: International Medical Society of Japan (IMSJ), pp. 72–94.

Michel, Wolfgang (2012). 'Geographical names on early modern Western maps of Japan', in Jason C. Hubbard, ed., *Japoniae Insulae: The Mapping of Japan*. Houten: Hes & De Graaf, pp. 106–125.

Michel, Wolfgang et al. (2014). *Nihon o ugokasu! Takeo Nabeshima-ka yōgaku shiryō* ['Move Japan! Takeo Nabeshima Western Studies Materials']. Takeo City: Takeo Nabeshima.

Michel, Wolfgang (2015). 'On the emancipation of materia medica studies (honzōgaku) in early modern Japan', Tao Zhang et al., ed., *Proceedings of the 5th International Symposium on History of Indigenous Knowledge*. s.l.: s.n., pp. 93–106.

Michel, Wolfgang (2018). *Genten taiyaku Basutārudo jisho* ['Original text, parallel translation. Bastard dictionary']. Nakatsu: Nakatsu-shi Rekishi Minzoku Shiryōkan.

Michel, Wolfgang and SUGITATSU Yoshikazu (2003). 'Ôtaguro Gentan no Oranda-geka menkyojô to sono haikei nitsuite' ['The Surgical Licence of Ôtaguro Gentan and its Background'], *Journal of the Japan Society of Medical History* 49(3), pp. 455–477.

Miller, Roy A. (1967). *The Japanese Language*. London: The University of Chicago Press.

MISHIMA Saiichi (2004). *The History of Ophthalmology in Japan*. Oostende: J.P. Wayenborgh Press.

MITSUKURI, K. (1877). 'The early study of Dutch in Japan', *Transactions of the Asiatic Society of Japan* 5(1), pp. 207–216.

MIYASITA Saburō (1975). 'A bibliography of the Dutch medical books translated into Japanese', *Archives Internationales d'Histoire des Sciences* 25, pp. 8–72.

MOCHIZUKI Mia (2009). 'Deciphering the Dutch in Deshima', in Ben Kaplan *et al.*, ed., *Boundaries and their Meanings in the History of the Netherlands*. Leiden: Brill, pp. 63–94.

Moeshart, Herman (2001). *Arts en koopman in Japan 1859–1874: een selectie uit de fotoalbums van de gebroeders Bauduin* ['Doctor and merchant in Japan 1859–1874: a selection from the photo albums of the brothers Bauduin']. Amsterdam: De Bataafsche Leeuw.

Montgomery, Scott L. (2000). *Science in Translation: Movements of Knowledge Through Cultures and Time*. London: University of Chicago Press.

Moonen, Arnold (1706). *Nederduitsche spraekkunst, ten dienste van in- en uitheemschen* [...] ['Dutch grammar, for natives and foreigners']. Amsterdam: Adriaan Wor.

MORISHIMA Chūryō and ŌTSUKI Gentaku (1972). *Kōmō zatsuwa: Ransetsu benwaku*, SUGIMOTO Tsutomu, ed. Tokyo: Yasaka shobō.

Morris, James Harry (2018). 'Anti-Kirishitan Surveillance in Early Modern Japan', *Surveillance & Society* 16(4), pp. 410–431.

Morris-Suzuki, Tessa (1994). *The Technological Transformation of Japan: From the Seventeenth to the Twenty-first Century*. Cambridge: CUP.

Mulder, W.Z. (1985). *Hollanders in Hirado, 1597–1641*. Haarlem: Fibula-Van Dishoeck.

MURAKAMI Naojirō and MURAKAWA Kengo (eds.) (1900). *Letters Written by the English Residents in Japan, 1611–1623 With Other Documents on the English Trading Settlement in Japan in the Seventeenth Century*. Tokyo: The Sankōsha.

MURATA T. (1999). 'Koan Ogata's obtainment of Dutch scientific books', *Kagakushi Kenkyū*, Summer 38(210), pp. 65–70.

Myers-Scotton, Carol (1993). *Social Motivations for Codeswitching: Evidence from Africa*. Oxford: Clarendon Press.

Nagasaki Shiritsu Hakubutsukan (2000). *Hizō Kapitan no Edo korekushon: Orandajin no Nihon shumi: Nichi-Ran kōryū 400-shūnen kinen = A very unique collection of historical significance: the Kapitan (the Dutch Chief) collection from the Edo period: the Dutch fascination with Japan*. Nagasaki: Nagasaki Shiritsu Hakubutsukan.

NAGAZUMI Yōko (1993). 'Foreign Intelligence and its Interpreters', in Detlef Haberland, ed., *Engelbert Kaempfer: Werk und Wirkung*. Stuttgart: Franz Steiner, pp. 30–38.

NAGAZUMI Yōko (1998). *18-seiki no ransho chūmon to sono rufu* ['Orders placed for Dutch books in the 1800s and their dissemination']. s.n., s.l.

NAJITA Tetsuo (1991). 'History and Nature in Eighteenth-Century Tokugawa Thought', in J.W. Hall, ed., *The Cambridge History of Japan IV: Early Modern Japan*. Cambridge: CUP, pp. 596–659.

Nakamura, Ellen Gardner (2005). *Practical Pursuits: Takano Choei, Takahashi Keisaku, and Western Medicine in Nineteenth-Century Japan*. Cambridge, Mass.: Harvard University Asia Center.

NARA Kannosuke *et al.* (1965). *Kinsei no yōga: Akita Ranga* ['Modern Western Painting: Akita Ranga']. Tokyo: Meiji Shobō.

NARUSAWA Katsushi (2007a). 'The Art Scene in and around Nagasaki', in SHIRAHARA Yukiko, ed., *Japan Envisions the West: 16th–19th century Japanese art from Kobe City Museum*. Seattle, Wash.: University of Washington Press, pp. 75–98.

NARUSAWA Katsushi (2007b). 'Two Streams of Namban Painting', in SHIRAHARA Yukiko, ed., *Japan Envisions the West: 16th–19th century Japanese art from Kobe City Museum*. Seattle, Wash.: University of Washington Press, pp. 57–74.

Nederlandsche en Japansche Almanak voor het Jaar 1861 ['Dutch and Japanese Almanac for the year 1861']. Deshima. Ter Nederlandsche drukkery. (Kerlen 1120).

Nihon Daijiten Kankōkai (1972–76). *Nihon kokugo daijiten dai 1-han* ['Large Japanese dictionary. First Edition']. Tokyo: Shōgakkan.

Nishikawa-Van Eester, Masako (2017). 'Rangaku, "Dutch Studies" and Oranda-tsuji "Dutch Translators"—from the perspective of English Education in Japan', *Nisshō gakuen sōritsu 100 shūnenkinen ronbun Heisei*, II 29, pp. 227–269.

NUMATA Jirō *et al.* (1976). *Yōgaku (jō)* ['Western Studies (Part I)']. Tokyo: Iwanami shoten.

NUMATA Jirō (1992). *Western Learning: A Short History of the Study of Western Science in Early Modern Japan*. Tokyo: The Japan-Netherlands Institute.

Nyland, Petrus (1670). *Der Nederlandtse Herbarius of Kruydt-boeck* ['The Dutch herbal']. Amsterdam: Marcus Doornick.

ŌBA Osamu (2012). *Books and Boats: Sino-Japanese Relations in the Seventeenth and Eighteenth Centuries*, trans. Joshua A. Fogel. (reprint). Portland, Maine: Merwin Asia.

OGATA Tomio (1971). *Rangaku to Nihon Bunka* ['Dutch Studies and Japanese Culture']. Tokyo: Tokyo Daigaku Shuppankai.

OGATA Tomio and the Nichiren Gakkai (eds.) (1980). *Edo Bakufu kyūzō ransho sōgō mokuroku / List of Dutch Books Collected by the Tokugawa Shogunate*. Tokyo: The Japan-Netherlands Institute.

OKA, Yasumasa (2007). 'Hollandisme in Japanese Craftwork', in *Japan Envisions the West: 16th–19th century Japanese art from Kobe City Museum*. Seattle, Wash.: University of Washington Press, pp. 135–163.

Omar, Asmah (1975). *Essays on Malaysian Linguistics*. Kuala Lumpur.

ORII Yoshimi (2015). 'The Dispersion of Jesuit Books Printed in Japan: Trends in Bibliographical Research and in Intellectual History', *Journal of Jesuit Studies* 2(2), pp. 189–207.

Osterkamp, Sven (2009). 'Selected materials on Korean from the Siebold Archive in Bochum—Preceded by Some General Remarks Regarding Siebold's Study of Korean', *BJOAF* 33, pp. 187–216.

ŌTORI Ranzaburō (1964). 'The Acceptance of Western Medicine in Japan', *Monumenta Nipponica* 19(3/4), pp. 254–274.

ŌTSUKA Mitsunobu and KITA Takashi (1999). *Esopo no haburasu. Honbun to sōsakuin* ['Aesop's Fables: Main text and general index']. Osaka: Seibundō Shuppan.

ŌTSUKI Gentaku (1978). *Seihin Taigo* ['Encounters with Western guests']. Tokyo: Nichiran gakkai.

Ó Tuathaigh, Gearóid (2015). *I mBéal an Bháis: the Great Famine & the language shift in nineteenth-century Ireland*. Hamden, Conn.: Quinnipiac University Press.

Overmeer Fisscher, Johannes F. van (1833). *Bijdrage tot de kennis van het Japansche rijk* ['Contribution to the knowledge of the Japanese Nation']. Amsterdam: Müller and Co.

Paré, Ambroise (1592). *De Chirurgie* ['Surgery']. Dordrecht: Jan Canin.

Pauwels, Anna (2016). *Language Maintenance and Shift*. Cambridge: CUP.

Pel, C.M.H. (1852). *Handleiding tot de Kennis der Versterkingskunst* ['Guide to the Knowledge of Fortification']. Den Bosch, s.n.

Plutschow, Herbert (2006). *A Reader in Edo Period Travel*. Folkestone: Global Oriental.

Pomian, Krzysztof (1990). *Collectors and Curiosities: Paris and Venice, 1500–1800*, trans. Elizabeth Wiles-Porter. Cambridge: Polity Press.

Pompe van Meerdervoort, Jhr J.L.C. (1867–68). *Vijf jaren in Japan (1857–1863). Bijdragen tot de kennis van het Japansche Keizerrijk en zijne bevolking* ['Five Years in Japan (1857–1863). Contributions to the knowledge of the Japanese Empire and its people']. 2 vols. Leiden: Van den Heuvell & Van Santen.

Pompe van Meerdervoort, Jhr J.L.C. (1970). *Doctor on Desima. Selected chapters from Jhr. J.L.C. Pompe van Meerdervoort's Vijf jaren in Japan [Five years in Japan] 1857–1863*. transl. and annotated by Elizabeth P. Wittermans and John Z. Bowers. Tokyo: Sophia University.

Ravina, Mark (2017). *To Stand with the Nations of the World: Japan's Meiji Restoration in World History*. Oxford: OUP.

Reglement op de Exercitien en Manoeuvres der infanterie ['Code for infantry drills and manoeuvres']. Breda, 1855, re-print Nagasaki, 1857 (Ser. 536, Kerlen 1316).

Remmelin, Johannes (1634). *Pinax Microcosmographicus* ['Microcosmic Diagrams']. Amsterdam.

Remmelin, Johannes (1667). *Ontleding des menschelyke lichaems* ['Anatomy of the human body']. Amsterdam: Justus Danckersz.

Renard, Louis (1745). *Atlas van zeevaart en koophandel door de geheele weereldt* ['Atlas of Navigation and Trade through the whole World']. Amsterdam: Reinier and Iosua Ottens.

Richerand, Anthelme (1821). *Nieuwe Grondbeginselen der Natuurkunde van den Mensch* ['New First Principles of Human Physiology']. Amsterdam: C.G. Sulpke.

Roberts, Laurance P. (1976). *A Dictionary of Japanese Artists: Painting, Sculpture, Ceramics, Prints, Lacquer.* New York: Weatherhill.

Rodrigues, João (1604). *Arte da Lingoa de Iapam.* Nagasaki: Collegio de Iapão da Companhia de Iesu.

Roessingh, Marius P.H. (1964). *Inventaris van de archieven van de Nederlandse Factorij in Japan te Hirado [1609–1641] en te Deshima, [1641–1860], 1609–1860* ['Inventory of the archives of the Dutch factory in Japan at Hirado (1609–1641) and at Deshima, (1641–1860), 1609–1860']. The Hague: Algemeen Rijksarchief.

Romaine, Suzanne (1995). *Bilingualism*, 2nd ed. Oxford: Blackwell.

Romaine, Suzanne (2000). *Language in Society: An Introduction to Sociolinguistics*, 2nd ed. Oxford: OUP.

Rubinger, Richard (1982). *Private Academies of the Tokugawa Period.* Princeton: Princeton University Press.

Sansom, George B. (1973). *The Western World and Japan: A Study in the Interaction of European and Asiatic Cultures.* New York: Vintage Books.

SAITŌ Makoto (1985). *Nihon ni okeru Orandago Kenkyū no Rekishi* ['The History of Research on the Dutch Language in Japan']. Tokyo: Daigakusyorin.

SAITŌ Shizuka (1935). 'The Dutch Influence on Japanese', *Studies in Loan-Words* III, 1, pp. 7–28. s.l.

SAITŌ Shizuka (1967). *Nihongo ni oyoboshita Oranda-go no eikyo* ['The Influence of Dutch on Japanese']. Sendai: Tōhoku gakuin daigaku sōritsu hachijū shūnen kinen tosho shuppan iinkai.

SAKAGAMI Shizuka (2000). *Garaigo: The Semantics of Western Loanwords in Japanese.* (Ph.D. dissertation). Columbia University.

SAKURAI Ryōju (2016). 'A Quantitative Analysis of the Belgian Population in Japan from 1876 to 1938', in W.F. vande Walle, ed., *Japan & Belgium: An Itinerary of Mutual Inspiration.* Tielt: Lannoo, pp. 215–227.

Satow, Ernest (1900). *The Voyage of Captain John Saris to Japan, 1613.* London: Hakluyt Society.

Satow, Ernest (1921). *A Diplomat in Japan.* Philadelphia: Lippincott.

Savenije, Henny (2003). *Het journaal van Hendrick Hamel: De verbazingwekkende lotgevallen van Hendrick Hamel en andere schipbreukelingen van het VOC-schip de Sperwer in Korea (1653–1666)* ['The journal of Hendrick Hamel: The Amazing Adventures of Hendrick Hamel and other castaways from the VOC ship the Sperwer in Korea (1653–1666)']. Rotterdam: Ad Donker.

Schenck, Petrus (1700). *Atlas contractus sive Mapparum Geographicarum Sansoniarum auctarum et correctarum Nova Congeries*. Amsterdam.

Schendl, Herbert (2012). 'Multilingualism, code-switching, and language contact in historical Sociolinguistics', in J.M. Hernandez-Campoy and J.C. Conde-Silvestre, ed., *The Handbook of Historical Sociolinguistics*. Oxford: Blackwell, pp. 520–533.

Schmalkalden, Caspar (1983). *Die wundersamen Reisen des Caspar Schmalkalden nach West- und Ostindien 1642–1652*. Leipzig: Veb F.A. Brockhaus Verlag.

Schodt, Frederik (2013). *Native American in the Land of the Shogun*. Berkeley, Calif.: Stone Bridge Press.

Scholten, Jack (1990). '"De Jonker" en "De Blaauwe Ruiter": Rangaku en Nederlandse Literatuur', in Erika de Poorter, ed., *As the Twig is Bent … Essays in Honour of Frits Vos*. Amsterdam: J.C. Gieben, pp. 189–208.

Screech, Timon (1996). *The Western Scientific Gaze and Popular Imagery in Later Edo Japan: The Lens with the Heart*. Cambridge: CUP.

Screech, Timon (2000). *The Shogun's Painted Culture: Fear and Creativity in the Japanese States 1760–1829*. London: Reaktion Books.

Screech, Timon (2001). 'The Visual Legacy of Dodonaeus in Botanical and Human Categorisation', in W.F. Vande Walle, ed., *Dodonaeus in Japan: Translation and the Scientific Mind in the Tokugawa Period*. Leuven: Leuven University Press, pp. 219–240.

Screech, Timon (2005). *Japan Extolled and Decried: Carl Peter Thunberg and the Shogun's Realm, 1775–1796*. London: Routledge Curzon.

Screech, Timon (2006). *Secret Memoirs of the Shoguns: Isaac Titsingh and Japan, 1779–1822*. London: Routledge.

Screech, Timon (2012). *Obtaining Images: Production and Display in Edo Japan*. London: Reaktion Books.

Seeley, Christopher (2000). *A History of Writing in Japan*. Honolulu: University of Hawai'i Press.

Serrurier, Lindor (1887). *Catalogue des Livres Japonais de feu M. le docteur A.J.C. Geerts*. Leiden: Brill.

Serrurier, Lindor (1896). *Bibliothèque Japonaise: catalogue raisonné des livres et des manuscrits Japonais enrégistrés à la bibliothèque de l'Université de Leyde*. Leiden: Brill.

Sewel, Willem/William (1708). *Nederduytsche Spraakkonst* ['Dutch grammar']. Amsterdam: Assuerus Lansvelt.

Shapinsky, Peter. D. (2006). 'Polyvocal Portolans Nautical Charts and Hybrid Maritime Cultures In Early Modern East Asia', *Early Modern Japan*, pp. 4–26.

Shapinsky, Peter D. (2014). *Lords of the Sea, Pirates, Violence, and Commerce in Late Medieval Japan*. Ann Arbor, Mich.: University of Michigan.

SHIBA Kōkan (1927). *Seiyū nikki* ['Diary of a Western Journey']. Tokyo: Nihon koten zenshū kankōkai.

SHIBATANI Masayoshi (1990). *The Languages of Japan*. Cambridge: CUP.

SHIMADA Ryūto (2006). *The Intra-Asian Trade in Japanese Copper by the Dutch East India Company during the Eighteenth Century*. Leiden: Brill.

SHIMOJI Michinori (2018). 'Dialects', in HASEGAWA Yoko, ed., *The Cambridge Handbook of Japanese Linguistics*. Cambridge: CUP, pp. 87–113.

SHIRAHARA Yukiko (ed.) (2007). *Japan Envisions the West: 16th–19th century Japanese art from Kobe City Museum*. Seattle, Wash.: University of Washington Press.

SHIRAHATA Yōzaburō (2001). 'The Development of Japanese Botanical Interest and Dodonaeus' Role: From Pharmacopoeia to Botany and Horticulture', in W.F. Vande Walle, ed., *Dodonaeus in Japan: Translation and the Scientific Mind in the Tokugawa Period*. Leuven: Leuven University Press, pp. 263–280.

SHIRŌKA Keiji (2011). 'Der erste auslandische Deutschlehrer im sich modernisierenden Japan: Jakob Kaderli (1827–1874)', *Jinbun ronshū: Shizuokadaigaku jinbungakubu shakai gakka-gengo bunka gakka kenkyū hōkoku* 62(2), pp. 105–126.

Siderer, Yona (2017). 'Udagawa Youan's translation of light and heat reactions in his book Kouso Seimika', *Foundations of Chemistry* 19(3), pp. 223–240.

Siegenbeek, Matthijs (1810). *Syntaxis of Woordvoeging der Nederduitsche Taal*. Leiden: D. du Mortier en Zoon.

Siegenbeek, Matthijs (1822). *Grammatica of Nederduitsche Spraakkunst* ['Dutch Grammar'] 2nd ed. [1st ed. 1814] Leiden: D. du Mortier en Zoon.

Sims, Richard (1998). *French Policy Towards the Bakufu and Meiji Japan 1854–95*. Richmond, Surrey, U.K.: Japan Library.

Söderblom Saarela, Mårten. (2017). 'Mandarin over Manchu: Court-Sponsored Qing Lexicography and Its Subversion in Korea and Japan', *Harvard Journal of Asiatic Studies* 77(2), pp. 363–406.

Sohn, Ho-Min (1999). *The Korean Language*. Cambridge: CUP.

SONODA Kōji (1975). *A Descriptive Study of English Influence on Modern Japanese*. (Ph.D. dissertation). New York University.

Stegeman, Jelle (2014). *Handbuch Niederländisch: Sprache und Sprachkultur von den Anfängen bis 1800*. Darmstadt: WBG.

Steiner, Erich (2008). 'Empirical studies of translations as a mode of language contact: "Explicitness" of lexicogrammatical encoding as a relevant dimension', in Peter Siemund and Noemi Kintana, ed., *Language Contact and Contact Languages*. Amsterdam: John Benjamins, pp. 316–345.

Steininger, Brian (2017). *Chinese Literary Forms in Heian Japan: Poetics and Practice*. Cambridge, Mass.: Harvard University Press.

Stellingwerff, J. (1981). 'Reconstructie van Deshima?' ['Reconstruction of Deshima?'], *Japan en de Lage Landen; Driemaandelijks Cultureel-Historisch Tijdschrift* 1–4, pp. 52–57.

Stevin, Simon (1594). *De Sterctenbouwing* ['The construction of fortifications']. Leiden: Francoys van Ravelenghien.

Struys, J.J. (1676). *Drie aanmerkelijke en seer rampspoedige Reysen, door Italien, Griekenlandt, Lijflandt, Moscovien*. Amsterdam: Jacob van Meurs.

Subrahmanyam, Sanjay (2012). *The Portuguese Empire in Asia, 1500–1700: A Political and Economic History*, 2nd ed. Chichester: Wiley-Blackwell.

SUGIMOTO Masayoshi and David L. Swain (1989). *Science and Culture in Traditional Japan*. Tokyo: Tuttle.

SUGIMOTO Tsutomu (1976–1982). *Edo jidai Rangogaku no seiritsu to sono tenkai* ['Dutch Linguistics in the Edo period, its Formation, Growth and Development'], 5 vols. Tokyo: Waseda Daigaku Shuppanbu.

SUGIMOTO Tsutomu (1979). *Rangogaku to sono shūhen*. Tokyo: Ōfūsha.

SUGIMOTO Tsutomu (1980). 'Seiō shiika honyaku, sōsaku no ranshō', *Kokubungaku kaishaku to kanshō* XXXXV 8, pp. 172–179 & 9, pp. 156–171.

SUGIMOTO Tsutomu (1983). *Nihon honyaku-go-shi no kenkyū* ['A Study of the History of Translation in Japan']. Tokyo: Yasaka Shobō.

SUGIMOTO Tsutomu (1989). *Seiyōjin no Nihongo hakken. Gaigokujin no Nihongo kenkyūshi 1549–1868* ['The Discovery of the Japanese Language by Western People: A historical survey of learning and study of Japanese 1549–1868']. Tokyo: Sōtakusha.

SUGIMOTO Tsutomu (1990). *Nagasaki-tsūji Monogatari* ['The Story of the Nagasaki-tsūji']. Tokyo: Sōtakusha.

SUGIMOTO Tsutomu (2013). *The Dutch Impact on Modern Japanese Language*. s.l. Yasakashobo.

SUGITA Genpaku (1969). *Dawn of Western science in Japan. Rangaku kotohajime*, trans. MATSUMOTO Ryōzō and OGATA Tomio. Tokyo: Hokuseido Press.

SUGITANI Akira (2014). *Nabeshima Naomasu (1814–1871)*. 3rd ed. Saga City: Museum of Saga Castle.

Swain, Simon (2002). 'Bilingualism in Cicero? The Evidence of Code-Switching', in J. Adams, M. Janse and S. Swain, ed., *Bilingualism in Ancient Society: Language Contact and the Written Text*. Oxford: OUP, pp. 128–167.

Sweerts, Emanuel (1612). *Florilegium* ['Anthology']. Frankfurt-am-Main: Anthoni Kemptener.

TAIDA Ichiro (2017). 'The earliest history of European language education in Japan: focusing on Latin education by Jesuit missionaries', *Classical Receptions Journal* 9(4), pp. 566–586.

TAIDA Ichiro (2018). 'History and Reception of Greek and Latin Studies in Japan', in Almut-Barbara Renger and Xin Fan, ed., *Receptions of Greek and Roman Antiquity in East Asia*. Leiden: Brill, pp. 73–90.

TAKEUCHI Melinda (2004). 'Introduction', in M. TAKEUCHI, ed., *The Artist as Professional in Japan*. Stanford: Stanford University Press, pp. 1–16.

TANAKA Sadao (2017). *Recherches sur l'Etude du Français au Japon chez Murakami Eishun*. Internet Resource, National Institute of Information, Tokyo.

Tanaka-van Daalen, Isabel (2000). 'Dutch Words and Expressions in Japanese', in Leonard Blussé *et al.*, ed., *Bridging the Divide: 400 Years The Netherlands-Japan*. Leiden: Hotei Publishing, p. 129.

Terwiel, Barend J. (1993). 'Kaempfer's Journal from Batavia to Japan and the Writing of "Heutiges Japan"', in Detlef Haberland, ed., *Engelbert Kaempfer: Werk und Wirkung*. Stuttgart: Franz Steiner, pp. 394–409.

Thomason, Sarah Grey and Terrence Kaufman (1988). *Language Contact, Creolization, and Genetic Linguistics*. s.l. Berkeley Univ. of California Press.

Thomason, Sarah Grey (2017). 'Extracts from "Contact languages I: Pidgins and Creoles"', in Joseph T. Farquharson and Bettina Migge, ed., *Pidgins and Creoles: Critical Concepts in Linguistics*, I. London: Routledge, pp. 62–93.

Thompson, Edward M. (ed.) (1883). *Diary of Richard Cocks, cape-merchant in the English factory in Japan, 1615–1622: with correspondence*. London: Hakluyt Society.

Thunberg, Carl Peter (1784). *Flora Japonica*. Leipzig: I.G. Mullerianus.

Thunberg, Carl Peter (1792). 'Observationes in linguam japonicam', *Nova Acta Regiae Societaties Scientiarium Upsaliensis* 2/5, pp. 258–273.

Titsingh, Isaac (1820). *Mémoires et anecdotes sur la dynastie régnante des djogouns* ['Memoirs and anecdotes on the ruling dynasty of shoguns']. Paris: Nepveu.

Titsingh, Isaac (1822). *Illustrations of Japan*, trans. Frederic Shoberl. London: R. Ackermann.

Toby, Ron (2019). *Engaging the Other: 'Japan' and Its Alter-Egos, 1550–1850*. Leiden: Brill.

TOKUGAWA Munemasa (1979). *Nihon no hōgen chizu* ['Maps of Japanese dialects']. Tokyo: Chūō kōronsha.

TORII Yumiko (2000). '"Dutch Studies": Interpreters, Language, Geography, and World History,' in Leonard Blussé *et al.*, ed., *Bridging the Divide: 400 Years The Netherlands-Japan*. Leiden: Hotei, pp. 117–118.

Toussaint, Bert (2000). 'Johannes de Rijcke (1842–1913). Japanse verering voor Colijnsplaatse watergod', *Zeeuws Tijdschrift* 2000/3, pp. 28–32.

TOYODA Minoru (1969). *Nihon Eigaku-shi no kenkyū* ['Study of Japanese-English History']. Tokyo: Senjō Shobō.

Traganou, Jilly (2004). *The Tōkaidō Road: Traveling and Representation in Edo and Meiji Japan*. London: Routledge Curzon.

Transactions of the Asiatic Society of Japan (1877–78), vol. 6(1), pp. 207–216.

TSUKAHARA Akira (2007a). 'The Early Copperplate Prints of Shiba Kōkan and Aōdō Denzen', in SHIRAHARA Yukiko, ed., *Japan Envisions the West: 16th–19th century Japanese art from Kobe City Museum*. Seattle, Wash.: University of Washington Press, pp. 119–134.

TSUKAHARA Akira (2007b). 'The Opening of Japan and Its Visual Culture', in SHIRAHARA Yukiko, ed., *Japan Envisions the West: 16th–19th century Japanese art from Kobe City Museum*. Seattle, Wash.: University of Washington Press, pp. 195–215.

TSUKAHARA Tōgo (2000a). 'The Westernization of Chemistry from Different Angles: An Examination of Three Manuscripts by Contemporaries of Yoan Udagawa and His Seimi Kaiso'. *Historia Scientarium* 9(3), pp. 191–214.

TSUKAHARA Tōgo (2000b). 'Udagawa Yōan, de grondlegger van de scheikunde in Japan', in L. Blussé *et al.*, ed., *Bewogen Betrekkingen*. Hilversum: Teleac/NOT, pp. 96–97.

Tuckey, James Kingston (1819). *Aardrijkskunde voor zeevaart en koophandel* ['Geography for seafaring and trade']. Rotterdam; Immerzeel.

Turnbull, Stephen (1996). 'Acculturation among the *Kakure Kirishitan*: Some Conclusions from the Tenchi Hajimari no Koto', in John Breen and Mark Williams, ed., *Japan and Christianity: Impacts and Responses*. Basingstoke: Palgrave Macmillan, pp. 63–74.

Twine, Nanette (1991). *Language and the Modern State: The Reform of Written Japanese*. London: Routledge.

UDAGAWA Yōan *et al.* (1975). *Seimi Kaiso* ['Principles of Chemistry']. Tokyo: Kodansha.

UENO Kagetomi (1980). *Eigo-goi no kenkyū* ['Study of English vocabulary']. Tokyo: Kenkyūsha shuppan.

UMEGAKI Minoru (1963). *Nihon gairaigo no kenkyū* ['Study of Japanese gairaigo/loan words']. Tokyo: Kenkyūsha shuppan.

UNNO Kazutaka (1994). 'Cartography in Japan', in J.B. Harley and D. Woodward, ed., *The History of Cartography*. Chicago: University of Chicago Press, II, ii, pp. 346–478.

Van Assendelft de Coningh, Cornelis Th. (1856). *Mijn Verblijf in Japan* ['My Stay in Japan']. Amsterdam: Gebroeders Kraay.

Van Assendelft de Coningh, Cornelis Th. (1856b). *Drie Maanden op Decima* ['Three Months on Deshima']. s.l., s.n.

Van Assendelft de Coningh, Cornelis Th. (1879). *Ontmoetingen ter zee en te land, 2 delen* ['Encounters at Sea and on Land, 2 parts']. Haarlem: De Graaff.

Van Assendelft de Coningh, Cornelis Th. (2012). *A Pioneer in Yokohama: A Dutchman's Adventures in the New Treaty Port: From Ontmoetingen ter Zee en te Land*, ed. and trans. Martha Chaiklin. Cambridge: Hackett Publishing.

Van Dam, Pieter (1929). *Beschrijvinge van de Oostindische Compagnie, Eerste boek, deel II* ['Description of the East India Company, First Book, Part II']. The Hague: Martinus Nijhoff.

Van der Eb-Brongersma, Titia (2017). *De Hollandsche Begraafplaats in Nagasaki: Een cultuurhistorisch erfgoed* ['The Dutch Cemetery in Nagasaki: A Cultural-historical legacy'], 2nd ed. Oegstgeest: Hans Meijeraan.

Van der Horst, Joop (2008). *Geschiedenis van de Nederlandse syntaxis* ['History of Dutch syntax'], Part 1. Leuven: Leuven University Press.

Van der Pijl, Roelof (1819). *A Practical Grammar of the Dutch Language*. Rotterdam: Arbon & Krap.

Van der Sijs, Nicoline (1996). *Leenwoordenboek* ['Loanword dictionary']. The Hague: SDU Uitgevers.

Van der Sijs, Nicoline (2004). *Taal als mensenwerk: het ontstaan van het ABN* ['Language as Man-made: the emergence of ABN—"General Civilized Dutch"']. The Hague: SDU Uitgevers.

Van der Sijs, Nicoline (2006). *Calendarium van de Nederlandse Taal: De geschiedenis van het Nederlands in jaartallen* ['Calendar of the Dutch language: the history of Dutch by year']. The Hague: SDU Uitgevers.

Van der Sijs, Nicoline (2010). *Nederlandse woorden wereldwijd* ['Dutch words worldwide']. The Hague: SDU Uitgevers.

Van der Wal, Marijke and Cor van Bree (1992). *Geschiedenis van het Nederlands* ['History of Dutch']. Utrecht: Spectrum.

Vande Walle, Willy F. (ed.) (2001). *Dodonaeus in Japan: Translation and the Scientific Mind in the Tokugawa Period*. Leuven: Leuven University Press.

Vande Walle, Willy F. (2001a). 'Introduction', in W.F. Vande Walle, ed., *Dodonaeus in Japan: Translation and the Scientific Mind in the Tokugawa Period*. Leuven: Leuven University Press, pp. 9–32.

Vande Walle, Willy F. (2001b). 'Linguistics and Translation in Pre-Modern Japan and China: A Comparison', in W.F. Vande Walle, ed., *Dodonaeus in Japan: Translation and the Scientific Mind in the Tokugawa Period*. Leuven: Leuven University Press, pp. 123–147.

Vande Walle, Willy F. (ed.) (2016). *Japan & Belgium: An Itinerary of Mutual Inspiration*. Tielt: Lannoo.

Van der Velde, Paul (1993). 'Die Achse, um die sich alles dreht. Imamura Genemon Eisei (1671–1736). Dolmetscher und ebenbürtiger "Diener" Kaempfers', in Detlef Haberland, ed., *Engelbert Kaempfer. Werk und Wirkung*. Stuttgart: Franz Steiner Verlag, pp. 174–193.

Van der Velde, Paul (1995). 'The Interpreter Interpreted: Kaempfer's Japanese Collaborator Imamura Genemon Eisei', in B.M. Bodart-Bailey, ed., *The Furthest Goal: Engelbert Kaempfer's Encounter with Tokugawa Japan*. Folkestone: Japan Library, pp. 44–58.

Van der Velde, Paul (2000). 'Janis Reijnhout (1816–1870). Goessenaar vrijt zich een grafsteen', *Zeeuws Tijdschrift* 2000/3, pp. 26–27.

Van der Velde, Paul (2000a). 'Het Japanse Dagboek van een Fliplander', *Zeeuws Tijdschrift* 2000/3, pp. 18–23.

Van der Velde, Paul (2000b). '"Vadertje Ginnemon". De tolk Imamura Gen'emon', *Zeeuws Tijdschrift* 2000/3, pp. 24–25.

Van der Velde, Paul (2000c). '"Vadertje Ginnemon". De tolk Imamura Gen'emon', in L. Blussé *et al.*, ed., *Bewogen Betrekkingen*. Hilversum: Teleac/NOT, pp. 130–133.

Van Gulik, Thomas M. and NIMURA Yuji (2005). 'Surgical History: The Global View: Dutch Surgery in Japan', *World Journal of Surgery* 29, pp. 10–17.

Van Gulik, Willem R. *et al.* (1986). *In the Wake of the Liefde: Cultural Relations between the Netherlands and Japan, since 1600.* Amsterdam: De Bataafsche Leeuw.

Van Gulik, Willem R. (2000). *Een Verre Hofreis: Nederlanders op Weg naar de Shôgun van Japan* ['A Distant Court Journey: Dutchmen on the way to the Shogun of Japan']. Amsterdam: Stichting Koninklijk Paleis Amsterdam.

Van Hier tot Tokio: 400 jaar handel met Japan ['From here to Tokyo: 400 years' trade with Japan']. (2009). Karijn Delen *et al.*, ed.. The Hague: De Verdieping van Nederland.

Van Linschoten, Jan Huyghen (1596). *Itinerario; voyage ofte schipvaert*. Amsterdam: Cornelis Claesz.

Van Linschoten, Jan Huyghen (1979). *Een Zestiende-Eeuwse Hollander in het Verre Oosten en het Hoge Noorden: Leven, werken, reizen en avonturen van Jan Huyghen van Linschoten (1563–1611)* ['A sixteenth-century Hollander in the Far East and the Far North: Life, work, travel and adventures of Jan Huyghen van Linschoten (1563–1611)'], A. van der More, ed. The Hague: Martinus Nijhoff.

Van Oostendorp, Marc and Nicoline van der Sijs (2018). *'Een mooie mengelmoes': Meertaligheid in de Gouden Eeuw* ['"A right mishmash": Multilingualism in the Dutch Golden Age']. Amsterdam: AUP.

Van Opstall, Margaretha E. (1972). *De reis van de vloot van Pieter Willemsz. Verhoeff naar Azië, 1607–1612* ['The journey of the fleet of Pieter Willemsz. Verhoeff to Asia, 1607–1612'], 2 vols. The Hague: Martinus Nijhoff.

Van Opstall, Margaretha E. *et al.* (1983). *Vier Eeuwen Nederland Japan: Kunst-Wetenschap-Taal-Handel* ['Four Centuries Netherlands Japan: Art-Science-Language-Trade']. Lochem: Uitgeversmaatschappij de Tijdstroom, BV.

Vanoverbeke, Dimitri (2016). 'Japan and the Belgian Constitution: The Influence of a new small Nation State on Meiji Japan', in W.F. vande Walle, ed., *Japan & Belgium: An Itinerary of Mutual Inspiration*. Tielt: Lannoo, pp. 159–169.

Van Rossum, Matthias (2014a). 'Lost in translation? Maritime identity and identification in Asia under the VOC', *Journal for Maritime Research* 16(2), pp. 139–152.

Van Rossum, Matthias (2014b). *Werkers van de wereld: globalisering, arbeid en interculturele ontmoetingen tussen Aziatische en Europese zeelieden in dienst van de VOC, 1600–1800* ['Workers of the world: globalisation, work and intercultural encounters between Asian and European sailors in the service of the VOC, 1600–1800']. Hilversum: Verloren.

Van Schermbeek, Pieter Gerard (1886). *De musch met de geknipte tong* ['The Sparrow with the Cut Tongue']. Tokyo: Kōbunsha.

Van Sterkenberg, Pieter *et al.* (1994). *Kodansha's Nederlands-Japans woordenboek (Kōdansha Oranda-go jiten)*. Tokyo: Kodansha.

Van Wijk, Judith (2007). *The Acquisition of the Dutch Plural*. Utrecht: LOT.

Vekeman, Herman and Andreas Ecke (1992). *Geschichte der niederländischen Sprache*. Bern: Peter Lang.

Vermeulen, Ton *et al.* (eds.) (1986–). *The Deshima dagregisters*, 13 vols. Leiden: Leiden Centre for the History of European Expansion.

Verwayen, Frans B. (1996). *Early Reception of Western Legal Thought in Japan, 1841–1868*. (Ph.D. thesis). Leiden: Leiden University.

Verwayen, Frans B. (1998). 'Tokugawa Translations of Dutch Legal Texts', *Monumenta Nipponica* 53(3), pp. 335–358.

Viallé, Cynthia and Frederik Cryns (2018). 'Jacques Specx in Hirado (1609–1621): laverend tussen handel en kaapvaart' ['Jacques Specx in Hirado (1609–1621): navigating between trade and privateering'], *Vergezichten Nederlands-Japanse Vereniging Lustrumboek*. Leiden: Ginkgo, pp. 10–35.

Vocabulario da Lingoa de Iapam com a declaração em Portugues. (1603). Nagasaki: Collegio de Iapam da Companhia de Iesus.

Volker, T. (1971). *Porcelain and the Dutch East India Company: As Recorded in the Dagh-registers of Batavia Castle, those of Hirado and Deshima and other Contemporary Papers 1602–1682*. Leiden: Brill.

Von Krusenstern, Adam J. (1813). *Voyage round the world in the years 1803, 1804, 1805 & 1806, ... under the command of Captain A.J. von Krusenstern of the Imperial Navy*, trans. Richard Belgrave Hoppner. London: John Murray.

Von Plenck, Joseph Jacob (1803). *Grondbeginselen der Scheikunde of oversicht over alle de vakken der scheikunde* ['First Principles of Chemistry, or overview of all the disciplines within chemistry'], trans. J.S. Swaan. Amsterdam: J.B. Elwe, J.L. Werlingshoff.

Von Siebold, Philipp Franz (1897). *Nippon*, 2nd ed. Leipzig: Leo Woerl.

Von Siebold, Philipp Franz (1973). *Manners and Customs of the Japanese in the Nineteenth Century*, T. Barrow, ed. Rutland, Vermont: Charles E. Tuttle.

Von St. Clara (a Sancta Clara), Father Abraham (1719). *Iets voor Allen* ['Something for everyone'], trans. Isaac le Long. Amsterdam: Joannes Pauli.

Vos, Frits (1963). 'Dutch Influences on the Japanese Language', *Lingua* 12, pp. 341–388.

Vos, Frits (1971). 'Forgotten Foibles: Love and the Dutch at Dejima, 1641–1854', in *Festschrift fuer Horst Hammitzsch zu seinem 60. Geburtstag*, Lydia Bruell and Ulrich Kemper, eds. Harassowitz: Wiesbaden, pp. 614–633.

Vos, Frits (1976). 'Nawoord: Hollanders als curiosa', in J. van Tooren, ed., *Senryū—De waterwilgen: Vierhonderdnegentig Senryū-gedichten*. Amsterdam: Meulenhoff.

Vos, Frits (1978a). 'De Japanse Taal' ['The Japanese Language'], *De Gids* 140, nos. 4/5, pp. 261–268.

Vos, Frits (1978b). 'Onze voorouders in Japan: Handel, wetenschap en liefde' ['Our forefathers in Japan: Trade, science and love'], *De Gids* 4/5, pp. 215–266.

Vos, Frits (1980). *Van Keurslijfjes en Keesjes, Bosschieters en Lijfschutten: Onze Voorouders in Japan en Korea en het begin der Japanse en Koreaanse studiën in Nederland*. Leiden: Universitaire Pers.

Vos, Frits (1989). 'Mihatenu Yume-An Unfinished Dream: Japanese Studies Until 1940', in *Leiden Oriental Connections 1850–1940*. W. Otterspeer, ed., Vol. 5. Leiden: Brill, pp. 354–377.

Vos, Frits (2000a). 'The Influence of Dutch Grammar on Japanese Language Research', in Sylvain Auroux *et al.*, ed., *History of the Language Sciences*. Berlin: De Gruyter, pp. 102–104.

Vos, Frits (2000b). 'Latent Dutch in Modern Korean', in *Cahiers d'études coréennes* 7. Paris: Centre d'Etudes Coréennes du Collège de France, pp. 295–320.

Vos, Frits (2014). 'Dutch Influences on the Japanese Language', *East Asian History* 29, pp. 153–180 (re-publication).

Vos, Ken *et al.* (1989). *Oranda: de Nederlanden in Japan (1600–1868)* ['Oranda: the Netherlands in Japan (1600–1868)']. Brussels: Generale Bank.

WAKABAYASHI, Bob Tadashi (1986). *Anti-Foreignism and Western Learning in Early-Modern Japan: The New Theses of 1825*. Cambridge: Harvard University Press.

Wardhaugh, Ronald, (1987). *Languages in Competition*. Oxford: Blackwell.

Weber, T. (2004). 'Hans Wolfgang Braun von Ulm—deutscher Pionier in Japan 1639/40', *Scripsimus* 13, pp. 25–43.

Weijnen, Antonius (1968). *Zeventiende-eeuwse Taal, 5de druk* ['Seventeenth-Century Language. 5th edition']. Zutphen: W.J. Thieme.

Weiland, Pieter (1812). *Handwoordenboek voor de Spelling der Hollandsche Taal* ['Concise Dictionary for the Spelling of the Dutch language'] 1st ed. The Hague: Johannes Allart.

Weiland, Pieter (1846). *Nederduitsche Spraakkunst* ['Dutch grammar'] [1st ed. 1805]. Dordrecht: Blussé en Van Braam.

Weinmann, Johann Wilhelm (1735). *Phytanthoza Iconographia* (1st ed.). Regensburg.

Wells, David (2004). *Russian views of Japan, 1792–1913: an anthology of travel writing*. New York: Routledge.

Werger-Klein, K. Elke (1993). 'Engelbert Kaempfer. Botanist at the VOC', in Detlef Haberland, ed., *Engelbert Kaempfer: Werk und Wirkung*. Stuttgart: Franz Steiner, pp. 39–60.

Wieder, F.C. (ed.) (1923–25). *De Reis van Mahu en De Cordes door de Straat van Magalhâes naar Zuid-Amerika en Japan, 1598–1600. Scheepsjournaal, rapporten, brieven, zeilaanwijzingen, kaarten, enz.* 3de Deel. The Hague: De Linschoten-Vereeniging.

Wiersema, John H. and B. León (2013). *World Economic Plants: A Standard Reference,* 2nd ed. London: CRC Press.

Willemyns, Roland (2013). *Dutch: Biography of a Language.* Oxford: OUP.

Willemyns, Roland and Nicoline van der Sijs (2009). *Het Verhaal van het Nederlands: Een geschiedenis van twaalf eeuwen* ['The Story of Dutch: A history of twelve centuries']. Amsterdam: Bert Bakker.

Willman, Olof Eriksson (1667). *Een kort Beskriffningh På een Reesa till Ostindien och förbeskreffne Japan Then een Swänsk Mann och SkepsCapiteen Oloff Erichsson Willman benembdh giordt hafwer.* Visingsborg: Johann Kankel.

Willman, Olof Eriksson (2013). *The journal of Olof Eriksson Willman: from his voyage to the Dutch East Indies and Japan, 1648–1654,* trans. and ed. C. Blomberg. Leiden: Global Oriental.

Winford, Donald (2003). *An Introduction to Contact Linguistics.* Oxford: Blackwell.

Winkel, Margarita (1999), 'Academic traditions, urban dynamics and colonial threat: The rise of ethnography in early modern Japan', in Jan van Bremen and SHIMIZU Akitoshi, ed., *Anthropology and Colonialism in Asia: Comparative and Historical Colonialism.* London: Routledge, pp. 40–64.

Winkel, Margarita (2004). *Discovering Different Dimensions: Explorations of culture and history in early modern Japan.* (Ph.D. thesis). Leiden University.

Wispelwey, Berend (2004). *Japanese biographical index = Japanischer biographischer Index.* Munich: K.G. Saur.

Woyt, Johann Jacob (1700). *Gazophylacium medico-physicum,* 1st ed. Leipzig: Lanck.

Wu, Jiang (2015). *Leaving for the Rising Sun: Chinese Zen master Yinyuan and the authenticity crisis in early modern East Asia.* Oxford: OUP.

YAMASHITA Kazumasa (1998). *Japanese Maps of the Edo Period.* Tokyo: Kashiwashobo Publishing.

YONEMOTO Marcia (2003). *Mapping Early Modern Japan: Space, Place, and Culture in the Tokugawa Period (1603–1868).* Berkeley: University of California Press.

YOSHIOKA Akiyoshi (1965). *Considérations sur la "Nouvelle méthode" de Pieter Marin: rédaction d'un dictionnaire français-hollandais-japonais à Nagasaki. Furansu bungaku ronshū,* Vol. 1(0), pp. 25–56.

YOSHIZAWA Norio and ISHIWATA Toshio (1979). *Gairaigo no gogen* ['Etymology Of Loanwords']. Tokyo: Kadokawa Shoten.

Index of Japanese Primary Sources by Title

Key: 'Kerlen' and 'Ser.' (= 'Serrurier') refer to the catalogues by these editors. See bibliography. 'WUL' refers to the call number in Waseda University Library. Online scans of these works are available at the website, https://www.wul.waseda.ac.jp/kotenseki/search.php. 'ID' refers to the ID number in the database of the National Institute of Japanese Literature (NIJL) https://www.nijl.ac.jp/. Where information is available, the names of the author of the source text, the translator and editor are given.

Index of Non-Japanese and Non-Chinese Names

Index of Japanese and Chinese Names

Index of Subjects and Places

Printed in the United States
By Bookmasters